C000069404

1 MONTH OF
FREE
READING

at
www.ForgottenBooks.com

By purchasing this book you are eligible for one month membership to ForgottenBooks.com, giving you unlimited access to our entire collection of over 1,000,000 titles via our web site and mobile apps.

To claim your free month visit:
www.forgottenbooks.com/free119874

* Offer Is valid for 45 days from date of purchase. Terms and conditions apply.

ISBN 978-0-484-83661-6
PIBN 10119874

This book is a reproduction of an important historical work. Forgotten Books uses
state-of-the-art technology to digitally reconstruct the work, preserving the original format
whilst repairing imperfections present in the aged copy. In rare cases, an imperfection in
the original, such as a blemish or missing page, may be replicated in our edition. We do,
however, repair the vast majority of imperfections successfully; any imperfections that
remain are intentionally left to preserve the state of such historical works.

Forgotten Books is a registered trademark of FB &c Ltd.
Copyright © 2018 FB &c Ltd.
FB &c Ltd, Dalton House, 60 Windsor Avenue, London, SW19 2RR.
Company number 08720141. Registered in England and Wales.

For support please visit www.forgottenbooks.com

BIOGRAPHICAL REVIEW

OF

Calhoun County, Michigan

CONTAINING

HISTORICAL, BIOGRAPHICAL, *and* GENEALOGICAL
SKETCHES *of*

MANY OF THE PROMINENT CITIZENS OF TO-DAY
AND ALSO OF THE PAST

'"Biography is the only true history."—EMERSON

ILLUSTRATED

CHICAGO
HOBART & MATHER
1904

Charles Austin

for only four years, passing away January 14, 1842. The children were: Henry; Charles; George; William; James, who died in New Orleans while on his way home from the Mexican war; Elizabeth, who was the wife of David Smith; Mary, and Marcia, the wife of Andrew Helmer. All are now deceased with the exception of William and Marcia, both residents of Calhoun county.

William Andrus began his education in Binghamton, New York, and afterward attended the district school near his home on Goguac prairie for a short time, after which he remained at home until seventeen years of age, when he took up his abode in what was then the village of Battle Creek. Here he obtained employment and he also attended a private school for a year. In 1845 he accepted a position in a drug store owned by Allen T. Havens, who died in 1852, when Mr. Andrus purchased the stock and succeeded his former employer. This was the first and largest drug store of the town and was located at No. 6 Main street, and the ground at that point is still in possession of the subject, although the original store building has long since been demolished. He continued the business successfully and in 1867 built the Andrus block, at Nos. 6 and 8 Main street—one of the first three-story, substantial brick structures of the city. There he conducted his drug store until 1872, when he sold out to Grandine & Hinman, after which he became an important factor in manufacturing circles of the city. He was instrumental in establishing a number of enterprises of value to Battle Creek and which also returned a splendid income to the stockholders. He organized the Battle Creek

Machinery Company, now known as the American Steam Pump Company, and remained its president from the beginning until he disposed of his interest. He was connected with it for fourteen or fifteen years and saw the business well established on a paying basis. In the meantime he assisted in re-organizing the Advance Thresher Company and during the second year of its existence acted as its president, during which time his successful and capable control resulted in making the enterprise a profitable one. In the '90s he sold his interest in that company, since which time he has given his attention to his personal investments, looking after his own estate and also supervising other estates, which have been placed in his care by reason of his well known reliability, business capacity and trustworthiness.

Many lines of progress and business activity have been benefited by the co-operation of Mr. Andrus. He has advanced the attractive appearance of the city by erecting many residences and numerous business blocks, but has now sold most of these. The site of the new postoffice of Battle Creek is that which was occupied by his residence from 1860 to 1903. He was one of the organizers and one of the first directors of the First National Bank, now known as The National Bank, and he has in various ways encouraged and stimulated business enterprise, leading to the formation of new companies engaged in manufacturing interests here.

On the 2d of June, 1852, Mr. Andrus was united in marriage to Miss Francis L. McCamly, a daughter of Samuel W. and Janet McCamly, but she died June 26, 1854, leaving one child. On the 27th of January, 1858, Mr. Andrus wedded Miss

Nellie Grandine, a daughter of Edgar and Harriet Grandine, of Waterford, New York. Her death occurred in December, 1876, at Atlanta, Georgia, where they had gone for the benefit of her health. Like her husband, she belonged to the Episcopal church, and was active in its work, while her many estimable characteristics won her the respect and love of those with whom she was associated. For many years Mr. Andrus served as one of the vestrymen of the church, but in 1902 refused a re-election, anticipating an absence from the city. He was chairman of the building committee at the time of the erection of the present house of worship and took general charge of the work. He contributed most liberally to the cause and has ever been generous in his gifts to the church and charitable work. He belongs to Battle Creek lodge, No. 12, F. & A. M., of which he is a past master; Battle Creek Chapter, No. 19, R. A. M.; Zabud Council, No. 9. R. & S. M., of which he was thrice illustrious master; and Battle Creek Commandery, No. 33, K. T., of which he was the first eminent commander. His political support has always been given to the Democracy and yet he has never been an aspirant for office. For many years he has been numbered among the most prominent and progressive citizens of Battle Creek. He may well be termed one of the founders of the city, for he has been the promoter of many of its leading enterprises, and the growth and development of a community depend upon its commercial and industrial expansion. He has earned for himself an enviable reputation as a careful man of business, and in his dealings is known for his prompt and honorable methods, which have won him the deserved and unbounded confidence of his fellowmen.

HON. JOHN C. PATTERSON.

We herewith publish a portrait of Hon. John C. Patterson, of Marshall, who has long been known as an influential citizen, and one of the most prominent and successful lawyers of the state. Standing as he does at the head of the Calhoun county bar, no history of our county would be complete without a sketch of his life. Not only in current affairs has his influence been felt, but his achievements have been crystalized into the institutions, statutes, jurisprudence and progress of our state. And yet, though so pre-eminently entitled to a place in our local history, no sketch of his life has ever been published.

The subject of our sketch was born in the pioneer log cabin of his parents, David and Harriet (Waite) Patterson, in the township of Eckford, Calhoun county, Michigan, March 27th, 1838. His parents were natives of the state of New York, who located in this county in 1835. He traces his paternal lineage through New Hampshire and North Ireland, to the family of William Patterson of Argyleshire, Scotland, the founder of the Bank of England. His ancestry on the maternal side runs back through the Waites and Greenes of Eastern New York, Rhode Island and Connecticut, to a prominent Welsh-English family of the seventeenth century. Three of his paternal ancestors served in the Continental army during the Revolutionary war. Of these, his great-great-grandfather, Alexander Patterson, while under General Stark's command, fought and was wounded at the Battle of Bunker Hill; and his great-grandfather, Joseph Patterson, while under General Washington's command, was wounded at the battle of White Plains. His maternal

John de Huse—as the name was then spelled —who in 1066, A. D., received the grant of a manor in Berkshire, England, and from him in unbroken line the lineage of John Howys was traced. The family settled in Norfolk county, England, in 1457, during the reign of Henry VI, from which time Besthorpe was the family seat for seven generations. Thorpe is an old English word for town and "bes" in a corruption of "best," and the latter word was chosen because of the extreme fertility of the land. Thomas Howes, in the seventh generation from John Howys, with his wife Mary Burr emigrated to America and settled in that part of Yarmouth, which is now Dennis, on Cape Cod, in 1637. From this couple the line of descent is traced down through Jeremiah Howes, who was born during the passage of Thomas Howes and his wife to America. Then came three who bore the name of Prince, two Samuels, and George E., of this review.

Samuel Alfred Howes, the father of our subject, was born in Putnam county, New York and there reached adult age. He was married there to Miss Raymond and soon afterward removed to western New York, settling on a farm which he made his home until 1855, when he went to Minnesota, but about 1860 returned to the Empire State and located near his old home in western New York, where he lived retired until his death in 1883. His wife was a member of the Presbyterian church.

To the public school system of his native state George E. Howes is indebted for the educational privileges he enjoyed in his early youth. He afterward pursued his studies in Canandaigua academy, an institution of high character and of more than local reputation in the east. His early years were

3

passed in school and in assisting his father in the labors of the farm so that manhood found him well equipped, both physically and mentally, for a struggle with the world. The great west, then as now, presented strong attractions to the ambitious, energetic young men of the older states, and upon reaching his majority Mr. Howes determined to try his fortune in the Mississippi valley. Removing to Minnesota, then a territory, in 1856, he pre-empted a claim and began farming operations, which he continued for four years, but loss of crops through hailstones and grasshoppers for two successive years, led to his resolution to return to the east in 1860, and the following year he engaged in the wholesale fruit and produce business in Philedalphia, Pennsylvania, where he remained for fourteen years, meeting with gratifying success in his undertaking. On account of impaired health he then sought a change of climate and investigation as to the business opportunities of Calhoun county, Michigan, decided him in favor of Battle Creek as a permanent place of residence.

Since 1875 Mr. Howes has made his home in this city and has become widely known on account of his extensive operations in handling domestic and foreign fruits and kindred products, for which he has unusual facilities, both for storage and shipment. He has splendid warerooms, some with refrigerator equipments, and he handles annually large amounts of fruit produced in this state and also much which he imports. His sales have now reached very profitable proportions and his trade relations have made him widely known beyond the boundaries of Michigan. He is a man of resourceful business ability and his efforts have not been confined to one line but have extended to many enterprises of a varying character, wherein his capability and indefatigable industry have been demonstrated. He deals extensively in coal, having a very liberal patronage from the manufacturers as well as from private citizens. What he has done for the city along lines of industrial and commercial advancement cannot be adequately told in words, but in this age when the history of a community is largely the record of those who are active in trade circles, the life record of Mr. Howes forms an important chapter in the annals of Battle Creek. He is the president of the Electric Light Company and from its organization, until a recent date, was one of the directors of the National Bank. He was also one of the organizers of the Consumers' Ice & Coal Company, which was incorporated in January, 1902, and during the first year he was chairman of the board of directors, while he is now treasurer and general manager. On the 1st of March, 1903, the two ice companies of Battle Creek were consolidated, the new corporation being known as the Consolidated Ice Company, and of this Mr. Howes is the present chairman. Many other enterprises of the city have profited by his financial assistance, his wise counsel and active co-operation and he is to-day one of the substantial business men of the city.

In 1861 Mr. Howes was united in marriage to Miss Eliza J. Pendry, of Albion, New York, a lady of marked social and intellectual attainments and broad culture. She was one of the two Michigan members of the Ladies' Board of Managers of the World's Columbian Exposition, held in Chicago in 1893, and has long been a leader in social circles here. They now have three living children: Samuel Alfred, who is associated with his father in business, married Mary Crooker. They have five children: Althea, Raymond, Margaret, Harrison and Alfred; Harriet is now the wife of Captain Thomas C. Morgan, of Battle Creek, and has two children, Sidney Howes Morgan and Elizabeth Morgan; George Howes married Bessie Weeks and is now with the Equitable Life Insurance Company in New York City.

Mr. Howes has for many years been an active and consistent member of the Indepedent Congregational church. In politics he has been a Republican since the formation of the party, casting his first vote for president in support of Abraham Lincoln. He was elected alderman from the fourth ward of Battle Creek in 1880 and resigned that position to accept the office of mayor, to which he was elected in 1881. In 1884 he was appointed a member of the board of public works for three years and in 1887 was re-appointed for a term of five years, while in 1891 he was elected president of the board. In 1900 he was a delegate from Michigan to the Republican national convention, which re-nominated Major McKinley for the presidency and chose Theodore Roosevelt for vice president. He is prominent in the councils of the party, his judgment and advice being frequently sought and highly valued, and he might easily attain to high position in political circles if he had aspirations in that direction. A notable social institution of Battle Creek is the Athelstan club, of which Mr. Howes was the first president, serving two terms, and which is composed mainly of business men of this city. Its resident membership reached the constitutional limit of two hundred and a long list of applicants for its first vacancy gives evidence of the high esteem in which it is held. Mr. Howes has been largely instrumental in making the club what is is to-day. In person he is of medium height, erect and of spare figure and his strong, clear-cut features are indicative of the firm, well poised character of the man. He is always courteous and genial, and as one who has known him intimately for years said of him: "Under all circumstances he is a gentleman." His strict integrity and admirable business qualifications, together with his pleasant, social characteristics, make him a leading and popular figure in this locality.

AUGUSTUS J. GALE.

Progress has always centered in the towns and cities and civilization has been advanced, not by the individual, but by the concerted efforts of many, directed by the mind of one who possesses keen sagacity and appreciative understanding of possibilities and an adaptability that enables him to utilize the means at hand and to combine forces so as to produce new possibilities. It is along such lines that all business activity has been secured and it has been through the direction of the labors of others that Augustus J. Gale has built up business enterprises that have been of marked benefit to the community in which they are located, as well as a source of wealth and profit to himself. He is a prominent capitalist of Albion, Michigan, where for many years he was the leading representative of manufacturing interests. He has now largely retired from the manufacturing world, giving his supervision merely to his invested inter-

ests, but as long as Albion stands it will be a monument to the enterprise, business capacity and keen discernment of Mr. Gale.

A native of Vermont, Augustus J. Gale was born in Barry, January 21, 1834, his parents being George and Harriet (Stone) Gale. The father was born and reared in the Green Mountain state and there married Miss Stone, who was a native of the same locality. While in Vermont he engaged in the manufacture of fanning mills and was also connected with the iron industry, but in 1836 disposed of his interests in New England and came to Michigan, settling in Moscow, Hillsdale county, where he established the first furnace west of Detroit or Monroe. He then carried on the foundry business until 1854 and developed a very extensive plant for that time. He engaged in the manufacture of plows, harrows and drags and also did machinist work, having brought the first iron lathe with him from Vermont. In 1854 he disposed of his interest in this business and went to California, where he was engaged in mining for two years. While there he purchased one of the giant trees of that land. The tree was one hundred and three feet in circumference and the bark was removed to a height of one hundred and sixteen feet. This was shipped in numbered sections to New York city, there being over five hundred cords of the bark, which was properly set up and put on exhibition in the first crystal palace ever built in the eastern metropolis. It was on exhibition there for a year and was then sent to the crystal palace in London, where it was destroyed by fire when the palace was burned in 1863. When he made the shipment from California to the east he also went to New York city and spent much of his time there in superintending the enterprise, although he ever regarded Albion as his home. Here he purchased an interest in the hardware business of A. P. Gardner; and since that time some of his family have been continually connected with the enterprise. He had managed his store for two years, when the building in which his stock was located collapsed because of an excavation that had been made on one side of it for the building of another store. Mr. Gale then sold his stock to his son, who now carries on the business in the same location. He afterward lived retired until his death, which occurred in 1871, while his wife passed away only fourteen days later. They left eight living children, while one had departed this life. The family are Universalists in religious faith and Mr. Gale was a staunch Whig in politics in his early manhood, while later he became an earnest Republican. He served as a member of the city council for many years and exercised his official prerogatives in support of measures that proved of marked value to the city, and yet he never aspired to office, prefering that his efforts should be directed into business channels.

Augustus J. Gale acquired his education in the schools of Moscow, Michigan, and there learned the foundry and machinist's trade with his father. He embarked in business with his brother under the firm name of Gale Brothers at Jonesville, Michigan, and they conducted a general iron manufacturing enterprise, making a specialty of agricultural implements. Later Mr. Gale purchased his brother's interest and continued alone in business until 1866, when he disposed of his plant in Jonesville and removed to Albion. Here he purchased the plant and business of Lane & Porter, then a small enterprise situated in the center of the city. In connection with this industry he established a hardware store and became a member of the firm of Charles Gale & Company, a relation that was maintained for five or six years. The business was then incorporated under the name of the Gale Manufacturing Company, and from the beginning Mr. Gale of this review was the manager of the plant. At about the time of the incorporation the business was removed from the original site to the west side, where extensive buildings were erected and thoroughly equipped with the latest improved machinery needed in their line. When twelve or fifteen years had passed there it was again found that their facilities were entirely inadequate to meet the growing demands of the trade and a new site was sought and the present plant of the Gale Manufacturing Company was built. This covers several acres, and the plant now has a capacity exceeding any in the United States for the manufacture of agricultural implements. Various kinds of farming machinery are constructed, and the capacity is such as will permit of the employment of five hundred men. When the company was incorporated the capital stock was one hundred and seventy-five thousand dollars, but as the business grew this was increased until there is now a paid up capital of five hundred thousand dollars. Mr. Gale was actively connected with the development of this great industry as general manager and director until 1887, when he disposed of his interest, at which time his brothers also sold their interest. Their product has been exhibited in the Centennial Exposition at Philadelphia in 1876, and there medals were received upon plows and rakes. They also exhibited at the World's Fair at Pairs in 1878, where they received a grand gold medal on the field trial and also a reward and the highest medal in the buildings, obtaining two different awards. Augustus J. Gale had charge of the exhibit in Paris, and while there made sales to Brazil and other foreign countries. He also placed on exhibition the manufactured product of the company at various state fairs and exhibitions and has received many other medals.

A man of resourceful business ability, his success may be attributed in part, at least, to his ready recognition of opportunities, his understanding of the public needs and his ability to meet these. Whatever he has undertaken in his business career has been carried forward to successful completion along lines of activity that command the highest respect and confidence of the public. His methods have ever borne the closest investigation and scrutiny, and while splendid success has attended his labors, he owes his prosperity to traits of character that all might envy. In addition to the splendid iron industries which he built up he was engaged in the manufacture of buggies for a number of years and became one of the founders of what is now known as the Albion Buggy Company, of which he is still a director and the president. No enterprise of importance in Albion has ever been instituted and put in successful operation without the assistance of Mr. Gale. He was one of the first to take stock in the Albion Malleable Iron Works, and it was due to him and his brother that this enterprise became one of the business interests of Albion instead of another city. He is now a director of the Electric Light plant, the State Bank, the National Bank and is also interested in the Prouty Company. He also owned the Albion Gas plant from 1898

until 1902 and many other enterprises of the city have profited by his co-operation and his sound business judgment. In fact, to give a detailed account of his life work would be to give an extended history of the business development and industrial and commercial achievements of Albion.

Mr. Gale has always regarded it as a duty, as well as a privelege, to support enterprises that would benefit his adopted city, and has taken pleasure in its advancement and upbuilding. In politics he has ever been a Republican and served as mayor of the city in 1878, giving a strong business administration. He has been a member of the city council for eleven years and during that time has exercised his official prerogatives for the welfare of Albion along many lines of substantial improvement. In 1901 he circulated the petition for paving and secured more than the needed number of names. His work is now evident in the finely paved streets of the city. He has cared nothing for office save as it has given him greater opportunity to benefit the city. Fraternally he is a prominent Mason, belonging to Murat lodge, F. & A. M.; Albion Chapter, R. A. M.; Albion Council, R. & S. M.; Marshall Commandery, K. T., and Saladin Temple of the Mystic Shrine of Grand Rapids. He was one of the incorporators of the Leisure Hour club, one of the finest clubs to be found in a town of this size in the entire country.

Mr. Gale was united in marriage in 1857 to Miss Anna Moreley, of Sodus Point, New York. They have four children: Clara, the wife of Frank Nowlin, of Albion; Mabel, the wife of Herbert Mann, of this city; Georgia, the widow of Charles McClellan, who was professor of Albion College, and Albert A., who is now in Seattle, Washington, being musical director in the State University there. Mrs. Gale is a member of the Episcopal church and Mr. Gale has served as one of its vestrymen for forty-five years. In analyzing his history to find the secret of his success it is evident that Mr. Gale has always done with his full power whatever his hand has found to do. He has not looked to the opportunities of the future, but to the possibilities of the present and has exemplified in his life the truth of two of the old axioms that "There is no excellence without labor" and that "Honesty is the best policy." While he has achieved wealth it has ever been gained along business lines that command respect and admiration and without invidious distinction he might well be called the foremost citizen of Albion.

SUMNER ORLANDO BUSH.

If Battle Creek could be characterized by a single term, the most-fitting one would probably be a "productive center." Few cities in the Union of equal size send so much to the markets of the world as does Battle Creek. Its great industrial and manufacturing interests have gained a world wide reputation, and at the head of these concerns stand men of excellent business ability and keen discernment, with power to plan and to execute. Sumner O. Bush is a worthy representative of this class and is now the vice president and general manager of the Advance Thresher Company.

A native of Jackson county, Michigan, he was born May 7, 1847, and is a son of Frederick E. and Cynthia M. (Willard) Bush. The father was one of the early farmers of Jackson county, to which place he removed from Portage Falls, New York. He had been married there to Miss Willard and in Jackson county he carried on general farming for a number of years, or until his removal to his farm in LeRoy, Michigan, in 1853. After some years he retired from active life and both he and his wife spent their last days in the home of their son, Sumner. They held membership with the Congregational church, and his political support was given to the Republican party.

In the country schools Sumner O. Bush began his education, which was continued to Olivet College, from which he was graduated in the class of 1870, winning the degree of Bachelor of Science. During his collegiate course he also taught in the college and later spent one term as teacher in LeRoy township. He was then elected superintendent of schools in the township, serving for several years. After his marriage, which occurred in 1877, he conducted his father's farm for several years and also bought stock, wool and apples, doing a successful shipping business. Ere he left the farm he became financially interested in the Advance Thresher Company and he was elected a member of its board of directors March 1, 1888. The same year he removed to Battle Creek to assume active connection with the company and at that time was elected its vice president. Owing to the absence of Mr. Wright, of Alma, Michigan, its president, the active duties of that office devolved upon Mr. Bush to a large degree. He manifested marked capability in the control of its affairs and in the enlargement of its scope and business. When he became connected with the Advance Thresher Company the plant was comparatively small, occupying only one or two of the buildings now used and giving employment to about one hundred people. From time to time other buildings have been added as the demands have increased, until now this is one of the largest threshing machine plants of the entire country, sending out an annual product valued at more than three million dollars. The plant has been increased until it now covers forty acres, and is situated on the lines of both the Grand Trunk and Michigan Central railroads, thus having excellent shipping facilities. Employment is furnished to about eight hundred men and from one hundred to one hundred and fifty traveling salesmen are all the time on the road. Branch houses have been located in all of the principal cereal growing states of the Union. In the control of this extensive business, Mr. Bush has displayed marked executive force, keen discernment and sagacity and power to plan and to perform. February 16, 1889, he was elected the general manager and he stands today prominent among those who have been the real builders and promoters of the city of Battle Creek.

Into other fields of labor he has extended his efforts with like gratifying results. He is the vice president of the Peerless Portland Cement Company, of Union City, Michigan, the vice president of the Silexoid Portland Cement Company, of Chicago, the vice chairman of the Norka Food Company, limited, of Battle Creek, also of the Battle Creek Creamery Company and an equal partner of the Howes & Bush Company, large wholesale fruit and cold storage dealers. He is the vice chairman of the Consumers' Coal Company and of the Consolidated Ice Company and at a former date was prominently identified with the Consumers' Ice and Coal Company.

On the 26th of September, 1877, occurred the marriage of Mr. Bush and Miss Vernellie Daley, of LeRoy township, Calhoun county, a daughter of Elijah and Mary (Shean) Daley. Unto them have been born three children: Vernon E., Charles S. and Bertha V. The sons are graduates of the University of Michigan and each has taken post-graduate work and they are now connected with the Advance Thresher Company. The daughter is a graduate of the high school of Battle Creek and is a member of the class of 1904 in the Mount Vernon Seminary of Washington, D. C. The family home is at No. 182 Maple street and is the center of many a brilliant social function.

Mr. Bush is a member of the board of directors of the Athelstan club and in his political views is a Republican. He was president of the board of public works of Battle Creek for five years, during which time the work on the sewer system was begun. He served as a presidential elector for Michigan in 1896, casting his ballot for William McKinley. He has frequently been a delegate to the state convention, but has never been an aspirant for office, doing his best public service as a private citizen. He still owns the old homestead farm of three hundred and sixty acres in LeRoy township, where he raises both stock and grain, giving his personal supervision to the operation of the farm, which is to him a source of recreation and pleasure. His achievements in the business world may almost be termed marvelous, and yet if one examines into the life record to find the secret of his advancement it will be seen that he has built his prosperity upon the sure foundation of unfaltering energy, strong purpose and close adherence to the ethics of business life. He is broad in his views and liberal in his judgments, strong in his convictions and earnest in support of his opinions. His is a stalwart character and his life record will bear the closest scrutiny without suffering criticism. Such men leave lasting impress for good and the story of their lives cannot fail to exert a beneficial influence on the youth of succeeding generations.

SIMEON S. FRENCH, M. D.

Many accord to the medical profession the position of greatest usefulness in the world and certainly there falls to the lot of no man broader opportunities for doing good than devolves upon the Christian physician, who carries hope, cheer and comfort into the sick room when alleviating human suffering. To this important calling Simeon Starkweather French has devoted his energies throughout his entire business career and certainly the world is better for his having lived. He has now reached the age of eighty-seven years, but is still engaged in practice. Old age does not necessarily suggest want of occupation or helplessness, nor is it a synonym for weakness or inactivity. There is an old age that is a benediction to all that come in contact with it; that gives out of its rich stores of learning and experience; and grows stronger intellectualy and spiritualy as the years pass by. Such is the life of Dr. French, an encouragement to his associates and an example well worthy of emulation to the young.

The Doctor was born in Otisco, Onondaga county, New oYrk, August 23, 1816,

and was a son of Luther French and a grandson of Ebenezer French. The latter was one of the heroes of the Revolutionary war. Hardly had the news of the battle of Bunker Hill been sent abroad over the colonies when he enlitsed and did valiant service in the cause of independence. He was wounded at the famous crossing of the Delaware, but he remained with the army until it won its glorious victory and lived to enjoy peace and prosperity under Republican rule until he attained the advanced age of eighty-seven years. Dr. Luther French, the father, was a member of the medical fraternity and served his country in a professional capacity in the War of 1812. In 1811 he married Lucy Park, and while he died at the comparatively early age of thirty-nine years, she reached the venerable age of eighty-three.

Dr. French, of this review, was only five years old at the time of his father's demise and when he was still quite young it became necessary that he should earn his own living. His education was acquired entirely through his own unaided efforts and whatever prosperity he has enjoyed has come to him as the reward of his earnest labors. When eighteen years of age he began teaching and thus obtained the funds necessary to continue his own education, which was pursued in Onondaga Academy. Determining to make the practice of medicine his life work, he entered the Geneva Medical College, at Geneva, New York, where he was graduated with the class of 1842. He then opened an office in Onondaga, but in 1847 sought a location in the west and established his home in Battle Creek, where he has since remained. He has ever been a close and earnest student of his profession, keeping in touch with the

SIMEON S. FRENCH, M. D.

progress made by the medical fraternity, and his skill in the administration of remedial agencies and in surgical work soon gained for him a reputation as one of the most skilled members of the profession in this part of the state. He was especially capable in his surgical work and performed many delicate and difficult operations both in his private practice and when in the army, some of which found mention in the Surgical History of the Rebellion.

His patriotic spirit and his desire to aid his fellow men as well as his country led him to join the army in the first years of the Civil war. He became assistant surgeon of the Sixth Michigan Infantry and in 1862 was made surgeon of the Twentieth Michigan Regiment. Being attached to the Ninth Army Corps he was on active duty in eleven states and was present at five of the most sanguinary engagements of the long conflict. He was constantly on the operating staff, always at the front, and a portion of the time acted as brigade or division medical director. For three years he ministered to the sick and wounded soldiers, often using his skill in behalf of those who wore the gray as well as those who wore the blue. His own health failed and he was obliged to resign and return home.

On the 18th of July, 1842, Dr. French married Miss Ruth A. Cox, a sister of Dr. Edward Cox, then one of the leading physicians of Michigan. They became the parents of two children: Maria Theresa, who died in February, 1887; and Edward, who completed the law course in the State University, with the class of 1872, and is now engaged in the practice of his chosen profession. The wife and mother died in October, 1885, and on the 28th of February,

1887, the Doctor was again married, his second union being with Mrs. Libbie Jackson, by whom he has a daughter, Theresa, born August 28, 1889.

While Dr. French has made the practice of medicine his life work, his activities have also touched along many other lines of progress, bearing upon the welfare of the communities with which he has been connected. While serving as superintendent of the schools of Onondaga county, New York, in 1843, he organized what is supposed to have been the first Indian school in the state, that was supported by public money, and thus was the pioneer in instituting a work which has since been continued to the marked benefit of the Red race. He continued to act as superintendent of schools in the Empire state for five years and since coming to Battle Creek has done efficient service in behalf of education as a member of the school board of this city. It was through his efforts in 1847 that the different districts here were united under one system and the first union of the schools of the state was formed. This fact alone would entitle Dr. French to distinctive mention in the history of Michigan and yet along many other lines he has contributed to the general good. He served as mayor of Battle Creek for two terms, was alderman for one term and supervisor for four years. In 1848 he joined the Independent Order of Odd Fellows and has long been recognized as one of its most honored members in the state. He served as grand patriarch in the state and grand representative to the National Grand lodge. He belongs to the Independent Congregational church of Battle Creek, through which avenue he has promoted the moral development of the city, and has for many years been honored as one

of the founders of the Republican party in
Michigan. In early life he voted with the
Whig party and when the issues of the times
caused a new party to spring into existence
he had the honor of reading the resolutions
which gave to the new party its name of
Republican. The first meeting held for the
purpose of establishing a new party convened at Battle Creek and the published account was signed by Dr. French and several
other gentlemen. The resolutions then
adopted were approved at a second meeting
and ordered printed. They breathed a spirit
of patriotism and loyalty which has ever
been one of the salient features of the Republican party. Then came the historic
meeting "under the oaks" at Jackson, Michigan, on the anniversary of the Declaration
of Independence and when the name Republican was proposed by Orlando Moffatt,
it was heartily endorsed by Dr. French, who
was most active and influential in the
various meetings which gave rise to the
great political organization that has shaped
the destiny of the nation, through many
years.

Equally prominent and honored is Dr.
French in the ranks of the medical fraternity. He belongs to various medical societies and was elected president of the
State Medical Society. He has contributed
to the medical literature of the world many
valuable papers which have added to the
sum total of knowledge for the good of the
race, and in his private practice he has
shown a most kindly and benevolent spirit.
Numberless are the homes which have
benefited by his timely assistance in hours
of illness when he knew that no remuneration would be received for his services, but
he responded quickly to all such calls, rewarded by the consciousness of duty well

performed. His influence has been so widely
felt along many lines, his assistance so valuable in political, professional, social and
moral circles that an enumeration of the men
of Michigan whose lives have been an honor
to the state which has honored them would
be incomplete were there failure to make
prominent reference to Dr. S. S. French.

HON. FRANK M. FOOTE, M. D.

Success which comes from capability,
and the honor which is accorded in recognition of true worth, are to-day enjoyed by
Hon. Frank M. Foote, a leading physician
of Marshall and the mayor of the city. He
was born in Carmel township, Eaton county, Michigan, January 28, 1861. His father, Albon Foote, was a native of Battle
Creek, born in 1837, the grandfather, Andrew M. Foote, having located there during
the days of its villagehood. He removed
from Cayuga county, New York, and after
a decade spent in the county seat of Calhoun
county went to Eaton county, where he took
up land. Later he returned to Battle Creek
and for about twenty years was the superintendent of the Wallace Woolen Mills. His
last years, however, were spent in quiet retirement on his own farm in Eaton county.
In the Empire state he wedded Amanda
Phillips, who was a worthy Christian woman, belonging to the Methodist church. She
died in 1876 and he in 1878. Albon Foote
was educated in Battle Creek and after attaining his majority began farming on his
own account, following that pursuit
throughout his entire life. He has held
different township offices and gives an earnest support to the Republican party, yet has

never been a politician in the sense of office seeking. He wedded Henrietta Campbell, who was born at Bellevue, Eaton county, in 1837, a daughter of Samuel Campbell. She died in 1864, when her son Frank was about three years of age, and the father has since wedded Sarah Southwick.

The Doctor began his education in the district schools and continued his studies in the high school of Battle Creek. He afterward engaged in teaching in Eaton county, and then, desiring to become a member of the medical profession, began studying in the University of Michigan at Ann Arbor in the fall of 1880. After pursuing a three-years' course in the medical department he was graduated with the class of 1884, but this did not end his studies, as he has since taken special work in Ophthalmology and Otology under Professor Frothingham, while his private reading and investigation have been continually carried on, largely promoting his efficiency in the line of his chosen calling. For a time he was also acting resident physician of the University of Michigan hospital. After his graduation he located at Ceresco, Michigan, where he built up a good practice and remained for three and a half years. Then seeking a broader field with less country work he removed to Marshall in 1888, and here gained prestige as a leading physician of the city. He belongs to the State Medical Society and he gives the greater part of his time and attention to his practice, save that he has various financial interests in different factories that have led to the industrial development of Marshall and of Battle Creek.

The Doctor is medical examiner for a number of old line life insurance companies and also the Maccabees lodge at this place and at Ceresco. He has always cast his ballot for the Democracy, save when he first voted. He was elected constable in Eaton county before he was of age, but did not qualify. He was for five years health officer of Marshall and did much toward establishing sanitary and health conditions along more modern lines. In April, 1902, he was elected mayor, during which time the city voted to issue bonds for paving. His was a progressive administration, and as an official and also as an individual he made every effort to increase the business of the city through the establishment of factories, with the result that at the present time there are fifty per cent. more people employed in factories here than when he entered office. It was also during his term that the electric railroad was built between Jackson and Battle Creek. That he received the indorsement of the public was shown by the fact that when again nominated in 1903 he received the largest plurality ever given any man in Marshall for mayor. The paving has been completed during his present term. He has also succeeded in settling a long standing law suit against the city by Lampson & Crowley, of Bay City, the city winning in the case to the extent of over four thousand dollars. He has succeeded in putting his administration upon a business basis, which appeals to all practical, fair minded citizens, and his course has won him encomiums from all classes. In Democratic circles he has been very prominent and has frequently served as a delegate to different conventions.

The home life of Dr. Foote has been very pleasant. He was happily married on the 16th of November, 1886, to Miss Cora E. Tefft, of Ceresco, Michigan, a daughter of Corydon A. Tefft. They have two children: Grace E. and Pearl C. Mrs. Foote belongs to the Methodist Episcopal church and he contributes to its support. His career has been one of activity, full of incidents and results. In every sphere of life in which he has been called upon to move, he has made an indelible impression and by his excellent public service and upright life he has honored the city in which he has been honored with official preferment.

Dr. ... ...

... ...

... ...

HON. NELSON ELDRED.

Everywhere in our land are found men who have worked their own way from humble beginnings to leadership in the commerce, the great productive industries, the management of financial affairs, and in controlling the veins and arteries of the traffic and exchanges of this country. It is one of the glories of our nation that it is so. It should be the strongest incentive and encouragement to the youth of this country that it is so. Prominent among the self-made men of Michigan was the subject of this review—a man honored, respected and esteemed wherever known, and most of all where he is best known. At the time of his death he was president of the City Bank of Battle Creek and the oldest bank president in years of continuous service in this part of the state.

Nelson Eldred was born in Laurens, Otsego county, New York, January 9, 1822, a son of Caleb and Phoebe (Brownell) Eldred, both of whom were natives of Pownal, Vermont, the former born in 1781 and the latter in 1783. The paternal grandfather, Daniel Eldred, spent his entire life there and was widely and favorably known in that part of the Green Mountain state.

In 1802 Caleb Eldred and Phoebe Brownell were married and the following year they removed to Laurens, New York, where the father cleared and developed about five hundred acres of land. He built one of the first brick residences in that locality—a large fine home, for which he burned the brick on his own farm. He also operated a gist-mill and saw-mill and in an early day conducted a distillery, in addition to the management of his extensive agricultural interests. In public affairs, as well as in business circles, he was prominent and was called to represent his district in the State Legislature. In 1830 he made a prospecting tour over the country and at Jackson, Michigan, was taken ill. The town then contained but two houses and those were built of logs. With some of the members of the family he removed to this state in 1831, making the journey with a team and crossing the river at Detroit on the ice. They continued on their way to St. Joseph county and up to Prairie Round, traveling much of the time through the snow, and finally reached Kalamazoo, which then contained but one house. Thinking that Comstock would be the county seat Caleb Eldred built a little cabin there and spent the winter in it. In the summer of 1832 he built the first grist and saw mill in Kalamazoo county, and during that summer the other members of the family came to Kalamazoo county. Not a marsh or stream was then bridged between Ann Arbor and Comstock. The land came into market in June, 1831, the land office being established at White Pigeon. The father and a son had sought a location and found a beautiful little prairie. On one occasion, several being present, they were discussing the selection of a name for it. Finally Daniel B. Eldred, a brother of our subject, said: "This caps the climax of all we have seen and I propose we call it Climax," and the name thus adopted has since been retained. The father entered three quarters of a section of land for himself, and his sons also secured other tracts. After two years spent at Comstock he sold his mills and removed to Climax, where he made his home until his death.

Caleb Eldred was one of the prominent pioneers of this part of the state and took a very active part in the work of early development and progress. He was a member of the Territorial Legislature not long after his arrival and was also a member of the first State Legislature, serving at the time when Stephen A. Mason, the first State Governor, was inaugurated. He was in the Legislature in 1837-8, when, the railroad having been built as far as Ypsilanti, the Legislature was invited to take a ride on its first cars. While territorial government still existed he was also selected circuit judge of Kalamazoo county. In early life he gave his political support to the Democracy, but afterward became a stanch Republican. Throughout his business career he continued to carry on farming on an extensive scale. Always a member of the Baptist church he aided in organizing a congregation of that denomination in Climax. He and Elder Merrill were the first to suggest the idea of founding Kalamazoo College. He remembered that Elder Merrill, an educated man from the east, whose family lived at Pontiac, Michigan, had conceived the idea of building a college in this state and had ridden over the country to awaken the interest of others. Caleb Eldred approved of the project and

joined him in the work. They finally secured a charter from the Legislature to found an institute which they decided to locate at Kalamazoo, and eventually secured funds wherewith they established the school, it being originally a Baptist college. Caleb Eldred was for many years chairman of the board of trustees. In 1843 it was reorganized under its present name. Thus Mr. Eldred had much to do with the early educational facilities of the state as well as with its political, business and moral development. He died in 1876, his wife had passed away in 1853. They were the parents of ten children who reached mature years, while two are still living.

Nelson Eldred, coming to Michigan when but ten years old and living in a pioneer district, had but meager school privileges. The father hired a private tutor for his children one winter. In the fall of 1837 he went to Kalamazoo, where he attended the institute which his father had aided in founding, remaining there as a pupil for four years, or until 1841. He afterward worked on the farm at Climax and engaged in farming there on his own account for many years. Up to the time of his death he owned the tract of land on which he began an independent business career and the buildings which he erected in 1849 are still standing. Considerable of the land was entered by his father from the government and a part of it has never been out of the possession of the family, Willard H. Eldred now has the patent deeds signed by President Andrew Jackson in 1833. Mr. Eldred's old homestead comprises two hundred and forty acres, all highly improved, and not far away he owned another tract of eighty acres. Upon his farm he continued to reside until 1866, when he

took up his abode in Battle Creek. The
previous year he had purchased the hardware store of Brooks & Barber and, engaging in its management, he took up his
abode at No. 211 Maple street, having
bought the property in the spring of 1866.
He continued successfully in the hardware
business as a member of the firm of Eldred
& Peters until 1871, when he sold out to
his partners. In 1871, associated with
Richmond and R. P. Kingman, Mr. Eldred established the City Bank. He
became a member of its first board of directors and of its seven members was the
last survivor. He has continuously served
as a director and from 1875 he was its
president, being, at his demise, the oldest
bank president in this part of the state.
The success of this institution, which is regarded as one of the most reliable financial
concerns of southern Michigan, was largely attributable to his efforts, his recognition of business opportunities and to his
sound judgment, which was rarely, if ever,
at fault in the control of financial affairs.
Almost from the beginning the bank enjoyed a large patronage and since the first
two or three years has paid good dividends.
The City Bank is capitalized for fifty thousand dollars and has a surplus of sixty-five
thousand dollars, and a profit and loss account of eleven thousand dollars.

Not alone to the banking business did
Mr. Eldred confine his attention and labors. He was a director in the Battle Creek
Gas Company from the time of its organization in 1871 until a few years ago when
the company sold out to the new organization. They built the gas works here and
increased the plant and its capacity in order to meet the growing demand of the
city. Mr. Eldred was also financially interested in other corporations and his wise

counsel prevailed in business management
with the result that success was thereby
won. He also owned a farm of two hundred acres of valuable land adjoining the
city, of which he sold forty acres and
which has been added to the city under the
name of the Highland Park addition. This
is situated near Goguac lake.

On the 15th of November, 1848, Mr.
Eldred married Miss Sarah Holden, a
daughter of John Holden. She was born
in Arlington, Bennington county, Vermont, and her parents came to Michigan in
1838. She was educated in Vermont and
in 1845 joined her parents in South Climax. She died April 11, 1900, at the age
of seventy-four years, and he September 9,
1903, at the age of eighty-one years and
eight months. On the 15th of November,
1898, at their beautiful home at No. 211
Maple street, they had celebrated their
golden wedding amid pleasing festivities
and the congratulations of many friends.
Through long years they traveled life's
journey together, sharing with each other
its joys and sorrows, adversity and prosperity. Mrs. Eldred was a member of the
Episcopal church, while Mr. Eldred attended and supported the Baptist church.
Two children were born to them: Willard
H., who was graduated in the Battle Creek
high school in 1871, at the age of sixteen
years, is now engaged in the wholesale sad-
dlery and hardware business in Battle
Creek and is the vice president of the City
Bank. He married Jessie M. Green and
they have two daughters: Helena, who is
now in Vassar College; and Morna Marie,
at home. The other child of Mr. and Mrs.
Nelson Eldred died in infancy.

Mr. Eldred always gave his political support to the Democratic party and while
never an aspirant for office he served as

supervisor at Climax and in Battle Creek was a member of the school board and also served as mayor, during which time many improvements in the city were instituted. He was always willing to devote his wealth and his energies to any feasible plan or undertaking that would increase the prosperity of the city and add to the comfort of its inhabitants. His life was a success. He accumulated a large fortune through the employment of only such means as will bear the closest scrutiny. To such men as he, is the development of the west due. His actions were ever such as to distinctively entitle him to a place in this publicaton, and as one of the honored pioneers of the vicinity, who witnessed almost the entire development and growth of this section of the state he is also deserving of mention.

WARREN FRANKLIN ROBERTS, M. D.

Dr. Warren Franklin Roberts, a well known and capable representative of the medical fraternity in Marshall, was born at Pinckney, Livingston county, Michigan, June 27, 1862, a son of Dr. Eliphalet L. and Betsey Ann (Schurt) Roberts. The father practiced his profession for a number of years in Pinckney and afterward removed to Ypsilanti, whence he went to Detroit and later to St. Johns and to Farmington, Oakland county, Michigan. In 1873 he came to Marshall, where he built up a large practice, spending his remaining days here. His professional cares made such heavy demands on his time and energies that his health was undermined and he died at the comparatively early age of fifty-four years, leaving be-

hind him, however, a record of great usefulness, his memory being cherished by many who knew him. His wife survived him but a few years. In the family were four children: Emerson, who died in infancy; W. F., of this review; Melvin, who died at the age of eighteen years, and Etta Josephine, the wife of L. H. Crampton, of Marshall.

In his boyhood Dr. Roberts, of this review, attended school in Farmington and later in Marshall. He manifested considerable interest and ability along artistic lines and when not more than fifteen years of age would go about the country making sketches of stock. He made arrangements to study with E. H. Dewey, who was a leading live-stock artist, connected with various stock journals. When but seven years of age Mr. Roberts made, with an ordinary pencil, pictures of animals, which are still in existence and are most life-like. When he was at the depot ready to start for Mr. Dewey's studio, his father went to the station and told him not to go, as he had other views for him, intending to have him study for portrait work. Later, however, the father determined upon a medical profession for his son, who began his studies under the father's direction, and when but twenty years of age matriculated in Hahnemann Medical College, of Chicago, in which he was graduated with the class of 1884. He began practice in connection with his father in 1885 and afterward went to Cassopolis, where he remained for three and a half years. After his father's death he returned to Marshall and has since engaged in the practice of his profesion with marked success.

Dr. W. F. Roberts was married in this city in 1895 to Miss Minnie L. Parkis, a daughter of George W. Parkis, and the hospitality of the best homes of Marshall is cordially extended them. He was reared in the Republican faith, but is now independent in politics. He cares not for office, preferring to devote his attention to his professional duties, which are continually increasing in extent and importance. He is quick to adopt the new methods which have for their object the promotion of efficient service in the profession and in coping with the intricate problems of disease, he has displayed marked ability and keen discrimination.

PETER HOFFMASTER.

By the death of this honorable and upright citizen the community sustained an irreparable loss, and is deprived of the presence of one whom it had come to look upon as a guardian, benefactor and friend. Death often removes from our midst those whom we can ill afford to spare, and thereby we lose a really great citizen. Such a one was Mr. Hoffmaster, whose whole career, both business and social, served as a model to the young and as an inspiration to the aged. He shed a brightness around everything with which he came in contact. By his usefulness and general benevolence he created a memory whose perpetuation does not depend upon brick or stone but upon the freewill offering of a grateful and enlightened people. No citizen did more for Battle Creek than Mr. Hoffmaster. His connection with the city's business interests, substantial development, and moral growth was largely instrumental in placing Battle Creek in the proud position which it to-day occupies.

Peter Hoffmaster was born in Poland township, Mahoning county, Ohio, on the 28th of October, 1837, and was a son of Gottlieb and Susannah (Eholtz) Hoffmaster. The grandfather, George Frederick Hoffmaster, a native of Germany, brought his family to the new world in 1817. Gottlieb Hoffmaster, a native of Fellbach, Wurtemberg, Germany, was born on the 3d of April, 1809, and in 1817 came to America, taking up his abode in Lancaster county, Pennsylvania. In 1823 he became a resident of Mahoning county, Ohio, and after attaining his majority was married there in 1832 to Susannah Eholtz. For twenty-two years they resided in Mahoning county and then came to Michigan in 1854, settling at Hopkins, Allegan county, where Mrs. Hoffmaster passed away on the 17th of June, 1878. Her husband, long surviving her, departed this life in Allegan county on the 21st of March, 1903.

Peter Hoffmaster, who was the third in a family of seven children, was reared upon the home farm and acquired a fair common-school education. He was ever fond of reading and thus continually broadened his knowledge. He never looked upon the world from a narrow or contracted standpoint, but was ever a gentleman of strong humanitarian principles, of wide sympathy and upright life. He continued to assist his father in the operation of the home farm until after he had attained his majority, when feeling that he no longer wished to follow the plow he went to Wayland, Michigan, where he secured employment in a hotel as a laborer. He was faithful to his work and his ability soon gained him promotion. For about two years he was connected with that hotel and then accepted a clerkship in a dry-goods store at Kalamazoo in 1859 and acted as an employee in the establishment for nine years, when in connection with the senior partner he established a new store in Kalamazoo.

PETER HOFFMASTER

In this enterprise he prospered, continuing his connection with mercantile interests there until 1872, when he came to Battle Creek. Here in company with Charles Austin he established the first exclusive dry-goods house in the city. The business, however, was begun on a small scale in a room at No. 19 West Main street. The capital was limited and the stock was therefore small, but the business grew and the line of goods carried was increased to meet the growing demands of the trade. It soon became necessary to secure one-half of the room at No. 21 and still later this entire room was rented, and thus was established the first double store in Battle Creek. Gradually the business increased both in extent and importance until the amount of trade reached a large figure. As both Mr. Hoffmaster and Mr. Austin had sons whom they wished to have enter the business world they decided to sever their partnership relations and each engage in business alone. Mr. Hoffmaster then purchased Mr. Austin's interest and took his sons into the mercantile house of which he was the proprietor. Wishing them to have a thorough business training he did not at once admit them to a partnership, but took them in as clerks that they might become thoroughly familiar with the trade in its various departments. He made their promotion depend upon capability and merit. In 1880 Rillie F. Hoffmaster entered the store, and in 1883 William M. also became active in the conduct of the business. As the years passed the scope of the enterprise was broadened, various departments being added; and as it became necessary to have more commodious quarters additional space was occupied, this becoming the first large department house in the city. Standing at the head of the business throughout the years

of its existence until his death, Mr. Hoffmaster was a leading spirit in its control, and the business policy which he inaugurated was always maintained. His course was such as to bear the closest investigation and the name of Hoffmaster became a synonym for honesty in trade transactions. The business was carried on along progressive lines. In addition to his store he was identified with other enterprises, becoming treasurer of the Home Savings and Loan Association, a director of the Merchants' Savings Bank, a trustee in the Kalamazoo College, and a director and vice president of the Wequetonsing Resort Association of Traverse Bay, where he spent the heated months in his beautiful summer home. On the 14th of August, 1865, Mr. Hoffmaster married Miss Helen McGown, of Orangeville, Barry county, Michigan. She was born, however, in Battle Creek, a daughter of Edward and Elsie (Deuel) McGown. Her father, a millwright, arrived in Michigan in 1833 and located at Verona. Returning to the Empire state he was there married on the 19th of July, 1837, and brought his bride to the new home which he has established in the west, and was actively identified with the early development of this city and county. Mrs. Hoffmaster is a most estimable lady and, still surviving her husband, makes her home in Battle Creek amid many warm friends who entertain for her the highest regard. The home relations of the family were ideal and Mr. Hoffmaster was a most devoted husband and father, counting no personal sacrifice on his part too great if it would enhance the happiness or promote the welfare of his wife and children.

A man of medium height and slender build, he stood very erect and his shoulders were square and broad. He had dark brown hair and very dark eyes and the expression of his face was always genial and kindly, indicating his disposition. His health, however, was hardly commensurate with his great energy, which was always making strenuous demands upon his strength. In business he attained a most gratifying and creditable success, founding an establishment of great importance to the city as well as to himself, but he was never so occupied with the cares of business that he 'could not find time and opportunity to aid his fellowmen or promote the welfare of the city. He was a man of generous impulses and high ideals and was most zealous and earnest in his advocacy of all that he believed would prove of benefit to his fellow men along material, social, intellectual and moral lines. He passed away December 31, 1901, and was laid to rest in Mountain Home cemetery at Kalamazoo, but his memory is still enshrined in the hearts of all who knew him and his influence remains as a blessed benediction to his family and friends. For many years he held membership in the Baptist church, served as one of its trustees and deacons, contributed generously to its support and did everything in his power to promote its welfare. Always temperate in his habits he never used tobacco or liquor in any form. Intensely interested in young men, his kindly advice and counsel proved most helpful to his own sons and to many outside of the immediate family circle. He was an enthusiastic supporter of the Young Men's Christian Association, and became a charter member of the organization in Kalamazoo. After coming to Battle Creek he aided in the organization of the Young Men's Christian Association, and was untiring in his work to promote the good of the order and to extend its beneficient influence. Perhaps no better estimate of his life and character can be given than to quote from one of his pastors who said, "His understanding of human nature, and his quick intuition in grasping a present situation, amounted almost to a genius. These elements, coupled with his cherry nature and strict integrity, enabled him to begin alone in the world of affairs, and, with only such financial resources as his own brain and hands could supply, became one of the leading merchants of southern Michigan. His ability as a business man was so clearly recognized that in circles outside of his own line of trade his wisdom was desired, and positions of responsibility and trust in bank, building and loan, and like corporations were freely opened to him.

"In his Christian life he was no less active and no less broad. He was untiring in his devotion to his home church. None had a keener eye in looking after its temporal 'well-being, and none was more truly in sympathy with all spiritual progress. Yet he was too large a man to live within such narrow confines. The work of the entire denomination, and, in fact, of the whole Christian world, was dear to him. In the midst of his active life he always found time to give attention to the affairs of the Master's growing kingdom. No appeal for any of our denominational enterprises ever failed to find in his nature a generous and hearty response. The work of Christian education lay close to his heart as his efficient and faithful service as trustee of Kalamazoo college has proved, and with no less earnestness did he give of his money, his time and his ability, in helping to direct the work of the state convention. He always lived under the conviction that material blessings were most fittingly used when a generous portion was converted into spiritual wealth by investing it in the saving of the souls of men.

"But with all his breadth of activities, he was not forgetful of the individual. In his home life, and among those who lived nearest to him, he was known to be one of the most tender-hearted and sympathetic of men. The writer has reason to know that many shall rise up and call him blessed because of the kindly ministries he has performed when no public eye was near to observe and praise. Want has many times been relieved and sorrow lightened by his quiet thoughtfulness."

CHARLES MERRITT.

When death ends a life record it is customary to review the career thus closed and pass judgment upon the work accomplished and the character developed. In reviewing the history of Charles Merritt, we see naught that was dishonorable and much that is worthy of the highest praise and of the closest emulation. He was ever a champion of liberty, and opponent of oppression, an advocate of right, a contestant against injustice and the wrong, he was the soul of honor and the embodiment of truth and possessed a nature that looked upon the world from a broad humanitarian standpoint. In many ways he was really ahead of his age, having a much clearer insight into the future and its possibilities and into the results of existing conditions than the great majority of men. From almost the earliest period in the development of Battle Creek down to the time of his death in 1893 he was a resident of this city, and

business, public and moral interests felt the benefit of his activity and keen foresight.

In Saratoga county, New York, on the 14th of October, 1820, Charles Merritt was born, a son of Joseph and Phoebe (Hart) Merritt. His father was also born at the old homestead there, his natal day being June 19, 1792. There he was reared and married and there his nine children were born. He carried on farming on an extensive scale, but partly on account of his health and also influenced by his desire to secure more land for his sons—seven in number—he came to Battle Creek in 1835, accompanied by his family, save his son William, who had previously come as agent for his father and purchased one section of land, located within the present limits of Battle Creek, comprising property between East avenue and Fremont street. The first dwelling of the family was built where the Merritt home still stands, at the corner of Maple street and Orchard Place. At one time a part of the old house was removed to a more distant part of the farm and was torn down in 1900 to make room for more modern improvements.

Joseph Merritt continued to live at the old home and engaged in farming until his death, which occurred October 24, 1863, while his wife, who was born December 17, 1791, survived him until November 2, 1870. After coming to Michigan, however, Mr. Merritt practically lived retired, but took an active interest in the great questions of the day, especially those relating to slavery. His home became a meeting place for prominent anti-slavery workers, frequently entertaining such men as William Lloyd Garrison, Wendell Phillips, Parker Pillsbury and Henry C. Wright, while Lucy Stone and Sojourner Truth were also frequent visitors in the Merritt household. While Mr. Merritt never took the platform in defense of the abolition of slavery, he nevertheless exerted a strong, though quiet, influence in that direction. Through many generations the Merritts were members of the Society of Friends, and Joseph Merritt, with his brothers Abram and Isaac and his brother-in-law, Jonathan Hart, located and sustained a Friends' meeting-house on the site now occupied by St. Phillip's Catholic church, in Battle Creek. Thus they became active factors in the early moral development of the city and Joseph Merritt left his impress for good along many lines of progress and improvement in pioneer times.

It was on the 18th of August, 1813, that Joseph Merritt was united in marriage to Miss Phoebe Hart, a native of Connecticut, in which state she was reared. While they were living in their first home in Battle Creek—then on the farm—Colonel Stewart, expecting that Verona would be the town site, built the house now occupied by Mrs. Charles Merritt. After the town was deserted the dwelling was purchased by Charles Merritt and with the oxen used for breaking prairie it was removed during the winter season to its present site and remodeled, while later other improvements were added, making it a modern and attractive home. Unto Joseph Merritt and his wife were born the following children: Jane, who became the wife of Thomas Chandler, of Adrian, Michigan; William, who for many years was a resident of Battle Creek, and died in 1902; Jonathan H., who died here in 1837; Daniel, who died in 1839; Charles, of this review; Richard B., who was long a resident of this city, but is now deceased; George, who is now living in In-

dianapolis, Indiana; Phoebe H., the deceased wife of Frank Stickney, and Joseph J., who died in California.

Charles Merritt was a youth of fifteen at the time of the removal of the family to Michigan. He had received good educational privleges in the east and here he attended a private Friends' school, conducted by John Mott. Later he went to the home of his uncle, George Barrett, at Spring Valley, Ohio, where he became familiar with the wollen manufacturing business, and later, in connection with his brother, engaged in business on his own account along that line, under the firm name of Merritt Brothers. Their enterprise prospered and their patronage grew, but feeling that his duty was in Battle Creek, Charles Merritt returned to this city to care for his parents, who were now well advanced in years, and assumed the management of the estate. However, he retained his interest in the wollen mills until about 1865, and in the meantime the plant was removed to Indianapolis. On again locating in Battle Creek he relieved his father of the care and responsibility connected with the management of the estate. Joseph Merritt made extensive purchases of land, including a tract at Homer, on which was a mill, and also property at Bellevue, in addition to the large investments in realty in this locality. His property here was known as Oak Openings. Charles Merritt became one of the pioneer fruit growers of this part of the state and carried on the business extensively, demonstrating the possibilities of the state in this direction, so that his labors proved of marked value to his fellow men, as Michigan has become one of the greatest fruit-producing states in the Union, deriving a large part of its wealth from this source. Mr. Merritt made a specialty of the cultivation of strawberries and peaches, having large beds and extensive orchards, so that his sales reached a large figure annually. He also made a great success with the Lawton blackberries, and his opinions on fruit culture were largely received as authority. He wrote many valuable articles for leading horticultural journals of the country, and only recently one of his early articles, on "Strawberry Culture," which appeared in the New York Agriculturist, was reprinted in a horticultural journal.

Mr. Merritt continued in that line of business until the expansion of the city brought his land into the city market, and the old orchards and gardens were subdivided and platted, being placed upon the market as Merritt's First, Second, Third and Fourth additions to Battle Creek. He then gave his attention to the handling of his real estate. Orchard Place, a beautiful new residence street, extends through the old orchard. During the financial panic of 1872 Mr. Merritt suffered heavy losses, but with marked energy, ability and perseverance he set to work to retrieve his lost possessions and succeeded in winning back a large portion. In all business transactions he was the soul of honor and integrity, and those who knew aught of his methods never called them in question in the slightest degree. He would much rather have defrauded himself than injure another in a business deal.

On the 9th of June, 1857, Charles Merritt married Elizabeth Margaret Chandler, a daughter of William G. and Sarah (Taylor) Chandler. She was born in Lancaster county, Pennsylvania, was educated at Kennett Square, Chester county and lived there and in Philadelphia, where her marriage occurred. Her father spent the days of his boyhood and youth in Philadelphia, and after attaining his majority married Miss Taylor, a resident of Chester county, Pennsylvania. Unto Mr. and Mrs. Merritt were born four children, who are yet living: Mrs. Minnie C. Fay, of Indianapolis, Indiana; Charles Wendell, of Denver, Colorado; Maude E., who is the wife of Professor Joseph H. Drake, a member of the faculty of the University of Michigan, at Ann Arbor, and William Guest, of Detroit. Mr. Merritt died on the 7th of April, 1893, and since that time Mrs. Merritt has supervised the property interests of the estate, showing marked ability in coping with the business world. She conducts the sale of the lots in the Third and Fourth additions to the city with splendid success, and retains her residence at the old home, where her entire married life has been passed.

In the interests touching the welfare of Battle Creek, Mr. Merritt was active and the city benefitted by his labors. While a stanch Republican, he always refused to accept office, yet kept well informed on the issues of the day. As a legacy to Battle Creek he left the record of public-spirited citizenship, to his friends the memory of fidelity and entertaining companionship, and to his family he bequeathed not only a good estate, but also the priceless heritage of an untarnished name and the remembrance of ideal devotion as a husband and father. A prominent friend said of him, in writing to Mrs. Merritt soon after her husband's death: "While the loss is a severe one to you and the children and a sad one for his friends, there are many comforting things connected with his passing away. First, we feel the separation is one for a brief period; then we feel it is well with him. He had a broad, kindly nature, a loving and generous disposition. He was gentle and in addition to this he was thoughtful and he not only thought good things, but what is better, did them. Your children will be better for having had such a father, you for having had such a husband, others for such friendship. He was so entirely frank and honest that one only needed to meet him to realize he knew a good man."

HON. RICHMOND KINGMAN.

Men of marked ability, forceful character and upright purpose leave their impress upon the world written in such indelible characters that time is powerless to obliterate their memory, or sweep it from the minds of men. The force of their example spurs others to emulation and what they have accomplished is an inspiration to those who come after them, while their sterling virtues live on forever in the hearts of those who have known and loved them and is cherished in the annals of the community in which they lived and labored as faithful citizens.

Richmond Kingman became a leading capitalist of Battle Creek and was for many years prominently identified with its financial interests, being connected as a stockholder and as an officer with the banking business.

He was a native of Cummington, Massachusetts, and a son of Levi and Theodocia (Packard) Kingman. The Kingman family were early residents of New England and the first representatives of the name in this country settled at Bridgeport, Massachusetts. The father of our subject was one of the well known business men of Cummington where he conducted a store and also a hotel. Later, however, he retired from commercial life and took up his abode upon his farm. Conspicuous as a leader of his time and of his town he exerted a strong influence in public affairs and he lived to the ripe old age of ninety years, retaining all of his faculties to the last, save his eyesight. In various public offices he served and was ever loyal to the trust reposed in him.

Richmond Kingman, the eldest of his family, was reared and educated in Cummington, attending the old academy of that town, thus enjoying better educational advantages than were afforded to the majority of youths of that day. Before reaching his twenty-first year he engaged in merchandising and in that enterprise prospered. Later he became a traveling salesman and represented a number of prominent manufacturing concerns of Massachusetts. He was one of the early traveling men upon the road and only visited large jobbers in the big cities. He traveled for over a quarter of a century, becoming prominent in his chosen field of labor, and through his business ability accumulated a fortune. While in Cummington Mr. Kingman was elected to represent his district in both the Legislature and the State Senate and the careful consideration which he gave to each measure which came up for settlement, and his earnest championship of various issues caused him to leave a lasting impression upon the legislative house of the state. He was also interested in a proposed extension of the Boston & Albany Railroad and thus he gained a wide acquaintance with business men throughout the state that caused him to be a valued acquisition to the membership of both the House and Senate. He maintained his home at Cummington until his removal to Battle Creek and in the former place was married.

Mr. Kingman was joined in wedlock to Miss Caroline Brown, a daughter of Corydon and Juliet (Loomis) Brown, of Worthington, Massachusetts. Her father was born and reared in Worthington, and there lived until his death, devoting his energies to farming throughout his business career. He was ever a highly respected citizen and an active and prominent member of the Presbyterian church. His wife was born in Southampton. Massachusetts, and she was a daughter of Artimus Loomis, whose wife was a representative of the Bascom family so prominent in literary circles of the Old Bay state. Gershon Brown, the grandfather of Mrs. Kingman, was one of the heroes of the Revolutionary war, serving throughout the struggle for independence and after the close of hostilities he returned to his native town to enjoy the fruits of peace. He, too, represented one of the early colonial families.

In the spring of 1880 Mr. and Mrs. Kingman removed from New England to Battle Creek, Michigan. Prior to this time, associated with Nelson Eldred, he had founded the City Bank here and had become one of the well known and leading financiers of this section of the state. Upon the organization of the bank he became its first president, but later resigned because of his frequent absence from the city and Mr. Eldred, who was a prominent resident here, was elected in his stead. However, he continued to be one of the largest stockholders of the institution and was identified therewith up to the time of his demise. He had also been prominently interested in the First National Bank of this city and was one of its directors. He was well known as a capitalist, his influence being not only felt in financial circles, but also in other walks of life. He was the owner of large tracts of land in Dakota and had business interests in New York and other places. A man of resourceful business ability and broad capacity for business, he formed his plans readily, carried them forward to successful completion and was seldom, if ever, at fault in matters of business judgment. Having made his way through the world by dint of his own efforts he always had a kindly sympathy for those whom he found starting in life as he had started. He interested himself in advancing men who were struggling to obtain a foothold in the business world and many a man who is now enjoying a successful career owes to Mr. Kingman a debt of gratitude for assistance received from him in early life. It was Mr. Kingman who obtained for Marshal Field, the multi-millionaire of Chicago. his first position in Pittsfield, Massachusetts. Through his influence and aid he obtained many positions for deserving young men and thus laid the foundation for their future prosperity.

Unto Mr. and Mrs. Kingman were born three children: Howard R., of this city; Richmond, who has charge of the Dakota interests of the family estate; and Emily T., who is now the wife of Robert Taft, of Columbus, Ohio, a cousin of Ex-Attorney General Taft, who is secretary of war. Mr. Kingman provided a splendid home for his family. He purchased an extensive tract of land on Main street, east, and built thereon a beautiful brick residence, commodious and of modern style of architect-ure. It was adorned with all that wealth could secure and refined taste suggest, and stands in the midst of beautiful grounds. Mr. Kingman died here January 28, 1895, and his widow still occupies this place. They held membership in the Independent Congregational church, to which they were most liberal contributors, and Mrs. Kingman yet maintains her interest in the church work. He was a man of exemplary habits, strictly temperate and in all relations was a refined, courteous gentleman. During his active business career his well directed efforts brought him a handsome pecuniary reward and an upright honorable life gained him the warm regard of an extensive circle of friends, but while the life of one of Battle Creek's most enterprising and public spirited citizens has ended, his memory remains as an inspiration to those with whom he was associated. These closing words fittingly express his merit:

"Life's work well done,
Life's race well run,
Life's crown well won."

HON. FRANK M. RATHBUN.

Hon. Frank M. Rathbun, now deceased, was for many years a prominent, influential and honored resident of Battle Creek. His history is closely interwoven with the business development, the political life and the moral advancement of this city, and so honorable and upright was his life that he enjoyed in marked degree the unlimited confidence and good will of those with whom he was associated. His life record, too, is most commendable on account of the excellent

success which he won in the control of legitimate business interests; and no history of Battle Creek would be complete without the record of his career.

Mr. Rathbun was a native of the Empire state, his birth having occurred in Laurens, Otsego county, New York, on the 20th of November, 1844. His parents lived upon a farm and there he spent his boyhood days, early becoming familiar with the duties and labors that fall to the lot of the agriculturist. In the common schools he acquired his literary education and at the age of twenty-one years he went to Poughkeepsie, New York, where he pursued a full course in Eastman's Business College, from which he was graduated. Mr. Rathbun next returned home, but was not satisfied with the life of the farm, and as Henry Potter, his cousin, had located in Battle Creek and had reported favorably concerning this place, Mr. Rathbun resolved to establish his home here and seek a fortune in the new and growing city of the west. He was first employed in a lumber yard of the firm of Potter & Gilman, working as a common laborer there for about six months. William H. Mason was also employed in that yard, and, later, the two young men concluded to purchase the business, which they did, becoming proprietors in 1867. Their yard was then located on the corner where the Presbyterian church now stands and they continued in business there until about 1883, when they removed to South Jefferson street. In the meantime they admitted James Green to a partnership and he retained his connection with the business until his death. Mr. Rathbun embarked in business here on his own account with a capital of about five hundred dollars, and borrowed the remainder of the money necessary to purchase the lumber yard, paying

Franks M Rathbun

for it ten per cent. interest. Diligence, close appplication, and keen business foresight proved the salient features in his career and made him a prosperous representative of trade circles in his adopted city. At the time of the establishment of the business of the Advance Threshing Machine Company he endorsed the movement, and though many fought against it he became a stockholder in the new concern to the extent of ten thousand dollars in order to help push the business. Mr. Rathbun became a member of the first board of directors and remained such up to the time of his death. It was not long before it demonstrated the soundness of his judgment in this regard, for the enterprise soon became a profitable one and is now one of the leading industries in Battle Creek. He was also a director in the Citizens' Electric Light Company, and was interested in various other business concerns.

On the 10th of November, 1870, in Battle Creek, occurred the marriage of Mr. Frank M. Rathbun and Miss Mary Hughes, a daughter of William and Emma (Prindle) Hughes, both of whom were natives of Elmira, New York, where they were reared and married. Coming to Michigan about 1837, they settled in Battle Creek when it was a hamlet mostly composed of log cabins. They journeyed by canal to Buffalo, N. Y., thence by Lake Erie to Detroit and drove across the country to their destination. Mr. Hughes lived for a time in this city, afterward in Marshall and still later in Kalamazoo. His wife passed away in the last named place when forty-two years of age, and he died in Battle Creek at the advanced age of seventy-six years, passing away about 1882. By the marriage of Mr. and Mrs. Rathbun four children

were born: Luella, who was born in 1873, is now the wife of George H. Williams, of Battle Creek, by whom she has one child, Maxine; Stephen J., born in 1876, married Julia Henning Frazer, and is now engaged in the lumber business in Battle Creek, having continued the business which was formerly owned and operated by his father and is now conducted under the corporate name of The Rathbun & Krafts Lumber Company. He has two children: David Henning and Mary Louise; Frank Jay, born February 17, 1882, is now a student in the law department of the University of Michigan. Earl Henry, born June 29, 1886, the youngest of the family, is in the high school.

In his political views Mr. Rathbun was a Democrat and believed firmly in the principles of that party. For several years he served as alderman and was also supervisor of Battle Creek. He was likewise elected mayor of the city and his administration gave uniform satisfaction because it was businesslike and advanced the welfare and permanent improvement of the municipality. He was filling the position of alderman at the time of his demise. In the Independent Congregational church Mr. Rathbun held membership and was serving as one of its trustees at the time of his death. Socially he was connected with the Knights of Pythias fraternity, with the Independent Order of United Workmen, and with Athelstan club, of which he was one of the founders. On the 29th of December, 1893, he left his home in good health and entered the store of Ranger & Farley. He made his way toward the office beside which was the unguarded opening of the freight elevator. Not realizing his danger in the darkness he stepped into this opening, and besides sustaining a broken limb was injured internally.

While conscious but a few hours, he survived two days, dying at eleven o'clock on the night of December 31, just as the old year was passing out. Mr. Rathbun was very popular in Battle Creek, his social nature and affable disposition winning him many friends, between whom the ties of comradeship and good will were strengthened as the years passed by. His honor in business, his fidelity in public office, and his devotion to his friends were qualities which greatly endeared him to his fellow men and made his example one well worthy of emulation. When the news of his demise was received, the pre-arranged festivities of New Year's day in Battle Creek were all postponed and his death was the occasion for deepest mourning throughout the city. His friends were so numerous that hardly a household felt that it had not sustained a personal bereavement. So closely had he been associated with the business and public life of Battle Creek, and so faithful was he in friendship that his name came to be held in high honor while he lived and his untimely death was regarded with a sorrow which was at once general and sincere.

JAMES HALLADAY.

Back to an early epoch in the history of the colonization of this country can the ancestry of the Halladay family be traced. Its founder in America was a native of Scotland who came here in colonial days. He settled in Connecticut and there, Calvin Halladay, the father of our subject, was born. Removing afterwards to the Empire state, he became the owner of a farm there. Since 1839 the family name has figured on the pages of Michigan's history, for at that date, James Halladay accompanied by his brother William T. Halladay, and wife and Abram and Jane Fiero, a brother and sister of Mrs. James Halladay came to this state, from Ontario, New York. They journeyed by canal to Buffalo, thence by steamer to Detroit and at the latter place hired two teams and an ox team wherewith to complete the journey, their destination being Jackson, where lived Austin Dutton Halladay, a brother of our subject, who had moved there some time previous. Both had visited this locality, having come here in 1837, at which tme James Halladay had purchased one hundred and sixty acres of land in what is is now Bedford township, Calhoun county, about a mile from the present city of Battle Creek, which was then but a small hamlet. and was known by the name of Waupakisco, an Indian meaning "'Fighting River." They spent the winter in the village and during that time James erected a log cabin upon his farm into which he brought his wife and children in the spring of 1840. The cabin had no floor, as no lumber was sawed in this locality, two years passing before any sawmills were established. There were no improvements upon his land except the girdling of five acres. In connection with the cultivation of the soil and general farm work Mr. Halladay established a brick yard, and was the second person to engage in this line of business in Calhoun county. The brick made by him was used in the construction of the first of the Noble block, now occupied by the City Bank. and also in the Brown & Merrill shops, where were manufactured many of the early threshing machines used in this section of the country. After living on his farm for a time he purchased the house and lot where the "Moon" office is now located. He then removed to the town and began the hotel business, conducting what was known as the McCamly House, with which business he had become familiar during hs boyhood, for his father, Calvin Halladay, had owned and conducted a hotel on the pike extending from Canandaigua to Geneva, New York, situated about three miles west of the latter place. The farm which his father had owned in the Empire state, James Halladay traded for a section of land adjoining his own in Bedford township and on his removal to the village of Battle Creek about 1842, he divided his land among his seven children, giving to each eighty acres and reserving one eighty acre tract for himself. This was not located, however, on the section mentioned. The children cast lots for their different farms, and thus possessing good realty were enabled to make a start in life. Both Mr. and Mrs. Calvin Halladay spent their last days in Battle Creek, the former dying at the age of about eighty-six or eighty-seven years, while his wife, who had borne the name of Esther Fisher, passed away soon afterwards.

James Halladay continued to carry on the hotel business for a few years and then traded that property for a farm in Battle Creek township, which he cultivated for several years. Subsequently, however, he returned to the city, where he lived a retired life until called to the home beyond. In his political affiliations he was first a Whig and later a Republican, but he never sought nor desired office. His death occurred when he had reached the age of seventy-three years. His wife bore the maiden name of Mary A. Fiero and she too, has

long since passed away. In the family of this worthy couple were ten children, of which six reached years of maturity: William T.; James C.; Austin S.; Mary Jane, who is the widow of John Stall and lives upon a farm in Bedford township; John F.; and Esther Ann, the wife of Carl A. Hodges, who is connected with the Halladay Inn. They have one daughter, Alice.

WILLIAM THOMPSON HALLADAY.

William Thompson Halladay was a native son of the Empire state, and when a young man came to Michigan with his parents James and Mary Ann (Fiero) Halladay. He was married in Bedford township, Calhoun county, to Miss Rebecca Ann Sweeney, and for a time worked in the brick yard for his father. Subsequently he became proprietor of the Battle Creek House and later owned and conducted a hotel near the former site of the Michigan Central depot. Later he took possession of the Crane House, now the Commercial House, which he conducted prosperously until after the Civil war. At that time the hotel business became dull and he lost considerable. He next began clerking for J. F. Halladay, his brother and later was employed by another brother, A. S. Halladay. He then began business for himself, conducting a grocery store on West Main street, and was thus engaged until failing health caused him to retire from business cares. He was a musician of more than ordinary ability and for many years was a member of the "Halladay Orchestra," which was a noted one in Southern Michigan. He played both violin and the double bass viol. His death occurred May 26, 1902. In the family were ten children, six of whom are now living. Mott S.; Martha, deceased; Mary Ann (Mrs. C. R. Dye); Harvey, deceased; Fred J.; William E.; Claude B.; Thompson Harold, Minerva and George, last two are deceased. The mother died June 13th, 1899, interred in Oak Hill cemetery, where also Mr. Halladay was laid to rest.

AUSTIN S. HALLADAY.

Austin S. Halladay belongs to a family who from pioneer times down to the present has been prominent in Calhoun county, its various representatives taking an active part in promoting the material upbuilding and substantial progress of this section of the state. Mr. Halladay was for many years connected with mercantile interests in Battle Creek, but is now living retired at his home in this city. His birth occurred about three miles west of Geneva in Ontario county, New York, July 9, 1833, a son of James and Mary Ann (Fiero) Halladay. He first opened his eyes to the light of day in a hotel, conducted by his father, which was situated on a farm bordering the pike extending from Geneva to Canandaigua.

Austin Sylvester Halladay spent his early youth upon the home farm and also worked in the brick yard, belonging to his father, until he was twenty-three years of age. He was first married on the 29th of July, 1856, in Bedford township, the lady of his choce being Miss Catherine Halladay, a daughter of Austin Dutton Halladay, his uncle. The young couple began

their domestic life in Battle Creek and for three years Mr. Halladay was employed as a clerk in the grocery store of Isaac C. Mott. In 1859 he began working for Samuel W. McCrea, in whose grocery store he remained as a salesman for four years. At the end of that time the store was destroyed by fire and Mr. Halladay then joined his former employer in a partnership, which was continued for two years. At the end of that time Mr. Halladay sold out and purchased an interest in the business of Mavor Guernsey, with whom he continued for four years. He then again sold his interest to his partner, while he purchased another stock, and as he needed assistance both financially and for the conduct of the business, he admitted his brother John to a partnership. This relation was continued for fourteen years, during which time they both lost and made money. At length on severing their business connection, John Halladay took the wholesale part of the store while Austin S. Halladay continued as proprietor of the retail department, but after about three years sold out and rented the building which is located at No. 22 South Jefferson avenue. He then went upon the road as a traveling salesman for his brother, representing the wholesale grocery house and for fifteen years followed that pursuit. He is now practically living retired, but has financial interests, having invested three thousand dollars in the Malt-Too Company, while he owns a two story brick business block at No. 22 South Jefferson avenue, which he bought immediately after its erection. He also owns a flat building on Cass and Van Buren streets and his property interests return to him a good income.

Unto Mr. and Mrs. Halladay have been

born two daughters. Marian Estelle became the wife of Edward Monroe and died in Battle Creek. Amanda Edith became the wife of Dr. R. Speer, a dentist of Battle Creek and her death occurred in this city. After the loss of his first wife Mr. Halladay wedded Mrs. Esther L. Wood, nee Blakeslee, the wedding occurring in Battle Creek, December 23, 1901. She was born in Jackson, Michigan, and there obtained a good common school education. She first gave her hand in marriage to John C. Wood, of Jackson, by whom she had two sons, William, who died at the age of fourteen years; and Albert, who was married to Maude Roberts in Battle Creek, August 17, 1899.

Mr. Halladay has always been a stanch Republican since casting his first presidential ballot for Fremont in 1856. For two terms he was alderman from the second ward and during his incumbency in the office, the pavement on South Jefferson avenue was laid, while the original building of the fire department was also constructed. He was chairman of the committee on the fire department and was an honorary member of the department. Fraternally he is connected with Battle Creek Lodge, No. 12, F. & A. M., of which he has been worthy master and has also acted as a representative to the Grand lodge. When he was elected worthy master the lodge had an indebtedness of three hundred dollars, which was a very heavy load for it to carry and Mr. Halladay at once set to work to remove this obligation. He planned an excursion which was so successfully carried out that the indebtedness was not only cleared off but a balance of two hundred dollars was left in the treasury. Mr. Halladay has also taken the degrees of the chapter in which he has filled all the chairs ex-

cept that of high priest. He likewise belongs to Zabud Council, No. 9, R & S. M., in which he has filled all of the chairs as he has also done in the Battle Creek commandery. He belongs to the Mystic Shrine in Grand Rapids and is a most prominent Mason, exemplifying in his life the beneficent spirit of the fraternity The career of Austin S. Halladay should serve as an inspiration and encouragement to others. He started out in life on his own account with only five dollars. Three of this he gave to the preacher who performed the wedding ceremony, while the other two dollars he invested in dishes. He then went to housekeeping with his brother, and through industry and economy he has gradually added to his possessions until he is now in very comfortable circumstances. Widely and favorably known in Calhoun county he certainly deserves representation in this volume and it is with pleasure that we present to our readers his life record.

JOHN F. HALLADAY.

John F. Halladay was born in Battle Creek, Michigan, and was reared on the home farm, working in the fields and in his father's brick yard. He acquired a good common-school education and after his marriage embarked in the retail grocery business, which he conducted until 1882. In that year he closed out his store and turned his attention to the oil business in conection with the Standard Oil Company with which he was associated until his death. In 1885 he engaged in the wholesale grocery business at No. 41 East Main street and was thus actively and prominently associated with mercantile interests in this city until his death in 1895. He occupied a leading and enviable position in business circles and was a man whom to know was to respect and honor. He gave his political support to the Republican party and was a prominent member of the Knights of Pythias fraternity, becoming a charter member of the lodge on its organization here and later serving as its representative to the grand lodge. His wife bore the maiden name of Caroline M. Squier and her demise occurred in 1896. They were the parents of two children, Frank E. and Blanche, now Mrs. Hilliard Lyle, who now resides in Detroit.

JAMES C. HALLADAY.

James C. Halladay was born in Ontario county, New York, Feb. 27, 1831, and was eight years of age, when his parents came to Michigan. He acquired a good common school education, and was reared upon the old homestead, assisting his father in the manufacture of brick and the cultivation of the soil. In Bedford township, on the 24th of November, 1852, he wedded Miss Martha Sweeney, a sister of the wife of his elder brother, and a daughter of John Sweeney, who owned a farm in Bedford township, and who afterwards became the owner of a hotel in Williams, Michigan, which he conducted for a year. When Mr. Halladay left the old homestead at the age of twenty-three, he worked in the hotel at Williams for his father-in-law. He was afterwards employed in the grocery store owned by the firm of Watts & Twitchell.

there remaining for about four years, when he was employed by another firm for a few years and later engaged in the hotel business with his father. In 1861 he removed to Hillsdale, Michigan, where he engaged in the hat and fur business on his own account, continuing in that city for four years. On the expiration of that period, however, he returned to Battle Creek, where he was engaged in the grocery business for more than a quarter of a century, being one of the well known and prominent merchants of this city. He next became a traveling salesman for his brother John F. Halladay, and thus represented the house for two or three years, when he was appointed chief of police by Mayor Green, acting in that capacity for one year. Subsequently, he was night captain for six years on the police force and next clerked in the Halladay grocery house for a year or more. In 1900 Mr. Halladay was called upon to mourn the loss of his wife, who died on the 12th of December of that year. They were the parents of four children, of whom one died in infancy. The others are Melvin E., who is living in Battle Creek; Ida, who became the wife of Edwin Bartlett, and after his death married L. C. Cooley, while her own demise occurred in Kalamazoo, Mich.; and Fermor L., who married Addie St. John and died in Battle Creek.

FRANK E. HALLADAY.

In this enlightened age, when men of energy, industry, and merit, are rapidly pushing their way to the front, those who, by their own individual efforts have won favor and fortune may properly claim recognition. Mr. Halladay is a worthy representative of this class. He is now the manager of the firm of J. F. Halladay & Son, wholesale grocers of Battle Creek. It is true that he entered upon a business already established and yet he began therein as a clerk and as any other employee would have done, mastered the business in its various departments and gained promotion as he displayed ability and energy. Since becoming manager he has enlarged the business until it is now one of the extensive and profitable mercantile interests of the city.

Frank E. Halladay was born in Battle Creek. June 16, 1865, and spent the days of his boyhood and youth here in the usual manner of lads of that period and in the public schools acquired his education, while his business training was received under the direction of his father. When the wholesale house was established he entered the store as an employee and after mastering the business was admitted to a partnership. The enterprise has grown to be three times the original size and six men are now employed in the store, while others are in the service of the house in different capacities. A large and carefully selected line of goods is carried and the business methods instituted by the founder of the house have always been maintained and have won for the company a most creditable position in commercial circles. Frank E. Halladay is also a stockholder in other companies, being a member of the firm of Hodges & Halladay, proprietors of the Halladay Inn; treasurer of the Calhoun County Telephone Company; and treasurer of the Malt-Too Food Company, limited, which is capitalized at three million dollars and has a large factory, furnishing employment to many

people. He is also administrator of the Halladay estate.

In 1887 in Battle Creek Mr. Halladay was united in marriage to Miss Jennie Hunsiker, of Bellevue, Eaton county, Michigan, where she was born and reared, her parents being Henry A. and Elizabeth (Avery) Hunsiker. This marriage has been blessed with three children: Clare, Robin and John F.

Frank E. Halladay has followed in the political footsteps of his father and is a stanch Republican, believing firmly in the principles of the party and their adaptabilty to the best good of the state and nation. He has served for four years as a member of the board of aldermen, during which time he was chairman of both the park and finance committees, and during his incumbency the park system was established and greatly improved, pavements were laid, water works were extended and cement walks were constructed throughout the city. In matters pertaining to the general good Mr. Halladay has always been progressive, putting forth every effort in his power to advance the welfare and upbuilding of this communty. At the same time he has so conducted his business affairs that they have returned to him an excellent financial reward and he is to-day numbered among the prosperous citizens and wide-awake merchants of Battle Creek.

CLAUDE B. HALLADAY.

Claude B. Halladay, who is a stockholder in various corporations in Battle Creek and occupies the responsible position of head bookkeeper with the Advance Threshing Company, was born in this city March 6, 1867, his parents being William Thompson and Rebecca Ann (Sweeney) Halladay. He continued his education in the public schools until three months prior to the time of his graduation in the high school. He then took up a course in the commercial department of the high school and was graduated with the class of 1884. Mr. Halladay entered upon his business career in the postoffice as assistant mailing clerk, remaining there for a year and a half. He was afterward bookkeeper with the firm of Halladay & Lewis, contractors, with whom he continued for thirteen years. On the 1st of March, 1899, he entered the employ of the Advance Threshing Machine Company as assistant bookkeeper, filling that position until the 1st of March, 1903, when he was promoted to his present position. He is one of the stockholders in the company, and also holds stock in the Union Steam Pump Company, the Hygienic Food Company, the National Cereal Company and the Advance Pump and Compressor Company.

On the 16th of March, 1887, was celebrated the marriage of Mr. Halladay and Miss Minnie E. Jenkins, a native of Battle Creek and a daughter of George B. and Frances (Rogers)) Jenkins. Two children have graced this union, Bernice and Norma, both born in Battle Creek. The parents are well known people of this city, where they occupy an enviable position in social circles. Mr. Halladay voted for Benjamin Harrison in 1888 and has since been a Republican, but refused to become a candidate for alderman and in fact has never sought nor desired public office. He attends the Independent Congregational church, contributing to its support and is a member of Battle Creek lodge, No. 35, K. P., in which he was keeper of records and seals. In the city where he now makes his home he has always resided and the fact that many of his stanchest friends are those who have known him from boyhood is an indication that his has been a career worthy of public regard.

HON. HARMON BRADLEY.

The life record of Hon. Harmon Bradley covered almost eighty-five years and the story of his career is that of an honorable man, who was active in business, loyal in citizenship and faithful in friendship. As the day with its morning of hope and promise, its noontide of activity and its evening of completed and successful effort ending in the grateful rest and quiet of the night, so was the life of this upright man. For more than six decades he remained a resident of Michigan, and while he won success through capably conducted business affairs, he was always mindful of his duty to his fellow men and of his obligation to his Maker.

Harmon Bradley was born in Fairfax county, Vermont, November 30, 1817. His parents died when he was still young and from an early age he was dependent upon his own resources. His youth was spent upon a farm in the east where he worked in order to provide for his own support. His educational privileges were therefore limited, but through experience and observation he gained good practical knowledge. On leaving the Green Mountain state he went to Niagara county, New York, accompanying

HARMON BRADLEY

his parents on their removal there during his very early boyhood. Living in the Empire state until 1835, he then determined to try his fortune in the west, hoping that he might have better opportunities in this great and rapidly developing section of the country. He made his way by steamer from Buffalo to Detroit and thence across the country on foot to Calhoun county, Michigan, settling first in Marengo township. There he worked by the month as a farm hand for a time until his labors brought to him capital sufficient to enable him to engage in farming on his own account. He was first married in the town of Marengo, the lady of his choice being Miss Mary Palmer, whom he wedded in 1839. Subsequently he removed to Charleston township, Kalamazoo county, Michigan, establishing his home near Climax, where he continued to reside until 1861. He then again came to Calhoun county, taking up his abode upon a farm in Bedford township, where he became the owner of a fertile and valuable tract of land of three hundred acres. Throughout the remainder of his business career he carried on agricultural pursuits. In the early years he worked in the fields from morning until night and his untiring industry, close application and honorable business methods formed the basis of his success. As he prospered he found it possible to enjoy more leisure and to surround his family with many of the comforts and some of the luxuries of life. His early residence in Michigan was a period fraught with many hardships, trials and difficulties, owing to the pioneer conditions of the state and to his own limited finances.

As the years passed eight children were added to the Bradley household, born of the first union, but two of these died in childhood. George became an attorney, but on account of failing health returned to his home and died under the parental roof; Randall, who became a soldier of the Civil war, died in a hospital in Washington, D. C., and was buried in that city; Charles resides upon the old homestead in Bedford township; Morris H. resides upon a farm near Bellevue, Michigan; Alice J. died at the age of eighteen years; Albert L., who was a graduate of the Kalamazoo College and married Jennie Gaugh, became a minister of the Congregational church and on account of his health went, in 1898, to California, where he died on the 21st of July of that year. Mrs. Harmon Bradley passed away, being called to her final home in 1870. In 1871, in Barry county, Michigan, he again married, his second union being with Miss Frances Kenyon of that county. She was born, however, upon a farm in Monroe county, New York, and with her parents came to Michigan in 1854, the family home being established in Barry county. She acquired a good education in her girlhood days, and afterward engaged in teaching for a number of years in Barry county.

For some time after his second marriage Mr. Bradley continued to reside upon his farm and then in 1884 purchased a lot and erected a pleasant residence in Battle Creek. Removing to his new home, he lived retired from further business cares up to the time of his death. He richly merited the rest which came to him, for through long years he had labored indefatigably, and all that he possessed came as the reward of his earnest toil and sound judgment in business matters.

Mr. Bradley gave his political support to the Whig party in early life, casting his first presidential ballot for William Henry Harrison, and upon the dissolution of that party joined the ranks of the new Republican organization and continued to follow its banners until his demise. He voted for every governor of Michigan from the time of the admission of the state into the Union until 1902. Called to public office by his fellow townsmen who recognized his worth and ability, he served as supervisor for a number of years, and in 1879-80, he represented his district in the State Legislature. He was a public spirited citizen, placing the general good before partisanship, and the welfare of his constituents before self aggrandizement. Perhaps the dominant element in his character was his deep religious faith. On the 1st of January, 1842, he was baptized, becoming a member of the Baptist church and from that time until his death he was one of its loyal adherents and earnest workers. He did everything in his power to promote the growth and extend the influence of the church and contributed generously to its support. For many years he served as one of its deacons, and when, in the evening of life he was unable longer to perform the work of the office, he was elected deacon emeritus for life. He was a most enthusiastic and conscientious follower of the teachings of his denomination, made many sacrifices in behalf of the church, and reared his children in the nurture and admonition of the Lord. In his relations with his fellow men he was always honorable and trustworthy and to his family he left not only a comfortable competence but the priceless heritage of an untarnished name. He departed this life March 30, 1902, in the eighty-fifth year of his age, respected and honored by all who knew him, for his long, useful and upright career.

THOMPSON HAROLD HALLADAY.

Thompson Harold Halladay who for a number of years was engaged in the mercantile business of Battle Creek was born in this city, in what is now the Commercial House, on Jackson street, October 16, 1868. His parents were William Thompson and Rebecca Ann (Sweeney) Halladay and the paternal grandparents were James and Mary Ann (Fiero) Halladay.

Mr. Halladay, the youngest child of the family, attended the public schools of Battle Creek, and at the age of eighteen began to learn the molder's trade in the foundry of Bird & Baker, following that pursuit for twelve years. In 1897 he removed to Little Rock, Arkansas, and there served as car clerk for the Iron Mountain Railroad, continuing in that capacity until 1900, when he returned to Battle Creek. Here he established his grocery store on West Main street where he built up a good business. He continued in this line until the 10th of July, 1903, when he sold out and is now in the shipping department of the Battle Creek Paper Box Co., limited.

On the 26th of August, 1890, he was united in marriage to Miss Myra U. Woods, who was born on a farm in Leroy township, Calhoun county, Michigan, and a daughter of Erastus and Ursula (Preston) Woods. She attended the public schools and remained upon the farm until eighteen years of age. Mr. and Mrs. Halladay are members of the Episcopal church and his political allegiance is given to the Republican party. He is a prominent Mason, belonging to Battle Creek lodge, No. 12, F. and A. M., Battle Creek Chapter, No. 19, R. A. M. and to Zabud Council, R. and S. M. He acted as Scribe in the chapter for two years. He and his wife are members of Bryant lodge. No. 153, of the Order of the Eastern Star, being the first to join after its formation. Mrs. Halladay has served as secretary for three years and conductress for two years. Mr. Halladay also belongs to the Independent Order of Foresters and is regarded as a valued representative of these fraternal bodies. He is yet a young man and has attained creditable success. Their home is at No. 108 Bennett street.

RANSOM W. HOWE.

Ransom Wellington Howe is a contractor and builder of Battle Creek, residing at No. 824 Maple street. A native of the Empire state, his birthplace was in the town of Lester, Livingston county and his natal day was April 13, 1840. His parents were Ira and Sallie (Smith) Howe and the father was a grandson of General Howe of the British army. He died when his son, our subject, was about twelve years of age. In the family were nine children, of whom Ransom was the eighth. All reached years of maturity and Mr. Howe, of this review, now has in his possession a photographic group of the entire family. When he was sixteen years of age he came with his mother and brother Frank to Michigan. Already one brother, Alonzo, had come to Michigan, living in Battle Creek, while another brother, Daniel, also older than our subject, came to this city about two years after the arrival of the mother. Both Alonzo and Daniel Howe were carpenters and removed to Howard City, Michigan, where they died and left families. Buell

Howe, another brother, is a tinner who is married and with his family lives in Rochester, New York. Ira Howe, who was cashier in the First National Bank of Rochester, made his home in that city for a quarter of a century. He was an expert accountant and all of the brothers are good mathematicians. He became so proficient that he could add three columns of figures at a time. His death finally occurred in Rochester, where he left a wife and children to survive him. Simeon Howe, another member of the family, was engaged in silver and gold plating and died in the town of York, Livingston county, New York, leaving two children. Alonzo Howe, of this family was a member of the New York state militia and attained the rank of major. He also served as sheriff of Livingston county for several years. Three of the brothers, Volney, Frank and Buell were soldiers of the Civil war and the first named is now living in Lansing, Michigan.

Ransom W. Howe was about fifteen years of age when, in January, 1856, he came to Battle Creek, making the trip by steamer from Buffalo to Detroit and thence to his destination over the Michigan Central Railroad, which was then using wooden or strap iron rails. Here he supplemented his early educational privileges by one term of study in the high school. He then began to learn the carpenter's trade, receiving fifty dollars and his board the first year and one hundred and fifty dollars the second year, while the third he received a journeyman's wages. He was employed at building for about six years, but at the time of the Civil war he wished to enter the army, enlisting three times, but each time he was rejected. He first enlisted in Company C, First Michigan Infantry, the second time in Company

C of the Twentieth Regiment and the third time he went to Kalamazoo and attempted to become a member of Merrill's Horse brigade. His brother Frank was a member of Company C of the Twentieth Michigan and was encamped at Jackson, this state, and was dispatched orderly for General Wilcox, and, while on duty was hit with a piece of shell at Weldon road in Virginia. He was then taken to the field hospital where his leg was amputated, having been struck on the knee.

After six years of journeyman work Mr. Howe of this review began contracting, and the first house which he erected is still standing. He built this for James Conklin, Jr., one mile west of the Post farm and also built the barn on that place. He hewed the timber and as there was no mill in which he could get his boards planed he planed all the siding himself and matched and dressed all the lumber. About 1870 he erected the Orson Holcomb house at a cost of four thousand dollars and assisted in building several of the early factories of Battle Creek. He was connected with the building of the Nichols & Shepard factory from the beginning until its completion and also with schoolhouse No. 1. To him was awarded the contract of the building of the Battle Creek paper mill, which was afterward destroyed by fire, and many other important buildings of the city were erected by him.

On the 20th of November, 1860, in Battle Creek when twenty years of age, Mr. Howe was united in marriage to Miss A. Jenkins, a daughter of Lyman J. Jenkins. Three children were born to them: Alice, the wife of Newton Squires, who resides upon a farm in Monroe county, Michigan, and has five children: Lyman William, a

carpenter in the employ of the Interior Finishing Company, living with his father; and Carrie W., who died at the age of seventeen years when a member of the senior class in the high school. Her death occurred in March, 1898, and Mrs. Howe passed away January 9, 1902.

In his political views Mr. Howe is a Republican and his first presidential vote was cast for Lincoln in 1864. He has always refused to become a candidate for office, but is interested in the success of his party and in the progress of his city, state, and nation along all lines of general improvement. When he first came to Michigan he purchased three lots upon which his residence now stands. As a contractor and builder he has been actively identified with the improvement and substantial growth of this city, his labors being of material benefit to Battle Creek and at the same time bringing to him a good financial reward.

THOMAS E. BROWNING.

Thomas E. Browning, who is engaged in dealing in coal, wood and feed in Battle Creek, was born in County Galloway, Ireland, July 18, 1847, a son of Michael and Katherine (McLoughlin) Browning. The father became a groceryman of Liverpool, England, in which city his death occurred. The mother then returned with her son and daughter to Ireland and afterward came to America, leaving Thomas E. Browning on the Emerald Isle. In July, 1860, however, he crossed the Atlantic by himself and made his way to Battle Creek. The voyage was made in the steamer Connaught, which was eleven days reaching the American port. The mother, however, had crossed on a sailing vessel that had been nine weeks in making the trip. Mr. Browning joined his mother who had sent him the money for his passage and who was then working in the Noble family of Battle Creek, with whom she remained until her death in 1870.

Thomas E. Browning, on reaching this city, went to live with L. D. Dibble and here had some opportunity for attending school. After a year and a half he began working as a farm hand at five dollars per month and was thus employed until after he had attained his majority. Saving a portion of his wages he purchased the lot where his residence now stands, a small house being on the place at that time. He occupied that until after his marriage which occurred November 29, 1877, the lady of his choice being Miss Jennie McEgan. The wedding was celebrated in St. Phillip's church by Father Brogger. The lady was born in Cleveland, Ohio, a daughter of John and Jane (McCormick) McEgan, and by her marriage has become the mother of three sons: Frank E., who was born October 30, 1878, and is now his father's partner; Thomas, a plumber, working as a journeyman in Battle Creek; and J. William, born April 27, 1888.

Ere his marriage Mr. Browning entered the employ of the Peninsular Railroad Company, now the Grand Trunk Company, with which he was connected for twenty-five and a half years. He started in as fireman and later became engineer, while subsequently he was a boiler maker in the shops. That he was most faithful to his work is indicated by his long service. During one year of that time he was also on the police force, acting as one of the first uniformed police of Battle Creek. In June,

1897, he left the railway service and finally purchased the feed store which he now owns and is successfully conducting. He is also a stockholder in the Battle Creek Feed Company and in the Battle Creek Medicine Company. He owns a nice residence, also the property adjoining and likewise residence property on Wabash avenue. His career proves that the only true success in life is that which is accomplished by personal effort and consecutive industries and it also proves that the road to success is open to all young men who have the courage to tread its pathway. He cast his first presidential vote for Seymour and on one occasion was the Democratic nominee for alderman from the first ward. He knew that he could not be elected because of the great Republican strength here, but allowed his name to be used for the sake of the party. He was reared in the Catholic church and was confirmed in Marshall and has since been identified with that organization.

JOSEPH MOUNT BROKAW.

As the architect of his own fortunes Joseph M. Brokaw builded wisely and well, and his efforts, too, were of material benefit to his city. As a real estate operator he contributed largely to the improvement of certain districts of Battle Creek and while promoting individual prosperity also advanced the general welfare and promoted public improvement. He was practical in all that he did, far-sighted and enterprising and his quick recognition of opportunity enabled him to use time and means to the best advantage. A man of strong purpose, upright in intent and honorable in contact, his name came to be honored while he lived, and his death was the occasion of deep and sincere sorrow among his large circle of friends.

Mr. Brokaw was born in Ovid, Seneca county, New York, October 9, 1834, a son of Tunis and Almira Brokaw, who in 1838 removed to Ypsilanti, Michigan, where the father died soon after. The son acquired a common school education and at the age of fifteen years went to Detroit in order to start out in life on his own account as a machinist's apprentice. When he had completed his trade he worked there as a journeyman for three years, and afterwards went south to New Orleans, Louisiana. He had a brother in that city who died there of yellow fever prior to the Civil war. His other brother, Austin Brokaw, was a very prominent and well-to-do merchant of Angola, Indiana, but he, too, has passed away. The mother, early left a widow, made her home with her son Joseph for more than twenty years and died in Grand Rapids, Michigan. From her son she received the most loving care and filial devotion, and thus he repaid her for the attention and love she bestowed upon him in his early youth.

In his effort to profit by remunerative employment Mr. Browkaw remained in the south for some time and was promoted to the position of master mechanic of what was then the shops of the Jackson & Illinois Railroad Company. After the outbreak of the Civil war he was arrested and taken from the office, being charged with being an Abolitionist. This charge was preferred by some older men in the office, over whose heads he had been promoted because of his superior ability, and who were, in consequence, jealous of his power. In order to get out of the city he let it be known that he was going to St. Louis on business for the company. In the meantime, in June, 1858, he had been married to Miss Mary Dowling, and with his wife, and the escort of three hundred men who had worked under him in the shops and acted as a body guard, protecting him from an angry mob, he made his way to the steamer, which was the last vessel to make the trip up the river until after the close of the war.

Mr. Brokaw returned to his boyhood home at Ypsilanti, Michigan, but he did not wish to be triumphed over by the men who had caused him to leave the south, so he determined to go once more to the Crescent City. He sailed from New York to Havana and thence to New Orleans, arriving there just prior to the capture of Vicksburg and Port Hudson. There were but two vessels insured against the "Alabama," and on one of these he took passage, accompanied by his wife. They remained in New Orleans for about nine months and then again went to Ypsilanti, Michigan, where they spent two years, removing thence to Hudson, where they remained for eighteen years. Mr. Brokaw was engaged in the grocery and produce business, and prospered in his undertakings. After a short residence in Grand Rapids and Owosso, Michigan, he removed to Battle Creek, September 18, 1883, and purchased an uncompleted residence on West Fountain street, now known as the Austin place. This he finished and later sold, removing to East Main street, where he erected a dwelling. He also began to build a business block there and later put up several business houses, in addition to his fine home, two other dwellings and a large three flat building. At the time he purchased property on East Main street there were practically no buildings in that locality, but his keen sagacity prompted him to make what proved a very fortunate and profitable investment. His labors and the improvements which he there established have made that one of the desirable residence districts of the city.

Mr. Brokaw also became active in other fields of enterprise and activity. In 1884 he began dealing in dry-picked poultry, which he shipped by the carload to New York and Chicago markets, following this until 1888, when he established a coal and wood business which he conducted with success until 1900, when he sold out in order to devote his entire time and attention to his real estate operations. The improvements which he made in the section of the city where he had placed his investments added greatly to the value as well as attractive appearance of that district, and at the same time brought to him the merited financial return for his labor.

Unto Mr. and Mrs. Brokaw were born twelve children, of whom six died in childhood. Those who reached mature years were Almira, wife of Dr. J. J. Lawless, of Jacksonville, Colorado, by whom she has two children, Fred and Carrol; Austin, who resides in St. Louis, Missouri; Josephine, at home with her mother; Joseph M., who spent eight years as a student at Sandwich, Ontario, one year at Monroe, Michigan, and two years at Baltimore, Maryland, where he was graduated in June, 1898, and then came to Battle Creek. On the 27th of November, 1898, he was ordained to the priesthood, being now pastor of a Catholic church at Reese, Michigan; Charles, who is engaged in the laundry bus-

iness in Battle Creek, and who married Selina M. Dowling, of Pontiac, Michigan, by whom he has had three children, Clair, Pauline and Charles; and Leo, at home.

During the later years of his life Mr. Brokaw was a Democrat and in 1884 was elected alderman, but after a short time he resigned because of his impaired hearing. He was always a supporter of the Catholic church and in his later years became one of its communicants, doing everything in his power to sustain it and promote its influence. One of the strongest and most commendable elements in his life was his deep interest in young men and their welfare and in this connection he labored most earnestly to develop the best and strongest in the young men with whom he came in contact. He gave them his sympathy, encouragement and counsel and oftentimes his material assistance. Many a man now successful in the business world, acknowledges his indebtedness to Mr. Brokaw for aid rendered and counsel given. He seemed to readily comprehend the nature of young men and had it in his power to bring out the best there was in them. His heart was full of sympathy and his life was guided by broad humanitarian principles.

Mr. Brokaw passed away in August, 1902, and the funeral services were held in St. Phillip's church where gathered one of the largest and most representative congregations seen in the parish in many years. The solemn requiem mass was sung by his son, Rev. J. M. Brokaw, assisted by Fathers Sadlier and Fisher, and the remains were interred in Mount Olive cemetery. In the Sacred Heart church, at Hudson, Michigan, there is a memorial window to his memory. For five years prior to his demise he was a great sufferer, but would never give up and only five days was he confined to his bed, so strongly was he upheld by his will and determination. He bore his illness with Christian fortitude and resignation and when the end came had the loving ministrations of his family and the consolation of the last sacraments of the mother church. The influence of such a man, however, does not end as he passes from this life, but lives in the lives of his friends and is strongly felt in the community where he dwelt. He lived to good purpose, actuated by honorable motives and kindly deeds. While a practical business man, he was also a Christian and had the spirit of the Master who came to do good on earth. He ministered to the needy, assisted those to whom he felt his efforts would prove beneficial, was loyal in friendship and the ties of home and thus shed around him much of the sunshine of life.

JOHN CLIFT.

One of the venerable and respected citizens of Albion was John Clift, who passed away January 20, 1904. He had reached the ninetieth milestone on life's journey and during six decades of his long and useful career was a resident of Albion, having arrived in this city in 1844. He was born in Birmingham, England, April 2, 1813, and there resided until about eighteen years of age, during which time he served an apprenticeship to the shoemaker's trade. He then crossed the Atlantic to Canada and after a short period spent in the Dominion, removed to Auburn, New York, where he was engaged in business as a shoe merchant.

On his arrival in Michigan he located at Ann Arbor, where he remained for a year and not being pleased with the city he resumed his westward journey, traveling as far as Albion. He was more favorably impressed with this town and made a location, beginning his business career here as a shoemaker on the bench. Later, however, he established a shoe store and afterward became proprietor of a grocery store, continuing in the latter line of merchandising until 1865, when soon after the close of the Civil war he retired from trade and enjoyed a well merited rest until called to the home beyond. He owned and dealt in real estate and through his business interests became well-to-do. He made judicious purchases and sales of property and was the owner of a two-story business block and good residence in Albion.

On the 30th of April, 1854, Mr. Clift was united in marriage to Miss Sarah A. Gregory, of Albion, a daughter of Noah and Lucinda (Hackett) Gregory. The father was born in Connecticut and when a young man went to Batavia, New York, where he was married. He afterward removed to St. Catherine, Canada, and there engaged in business as a mason. It was there that Mrs. Clift was born. Her father secured the contract to build the center building of Albion College, and in consequence of this removed to this city in 1840. He continued to make it his home until his death, which occurred in 1844, being survived by a wife and seven children. His widow survived him for more than twenty years, passing away in 1865. Mrs. Clift was educated in Albion and remained with her mother until the time of her marriage. She had two children: Ida May, who died in 1871, at the age of sixteen years; and Annette, the wife of H. M.

JOHN CLIFT

Brown, a grocer of Albion, by whom she has three children—Mildred, born January 1, 1892; Stanley, deceased; and Catherine, who died when only two weeks old, soon after the death of her mother, which occurred May 2, 1900.

Mr. Clift gave his support to the Republican party for a long period, but afterward became an advocate of the Prohibition party, with which he affiliated during his later years. Both he and his wife were prominent and influential members of the Methodist Episcopal church, to which she still belongs. He took a very active part in the work of the church in its many departments and served as class leader for a long period, while for twenty years he was church steward. Because of the infirmities of old age he was not able in his last years to attend church regularly and this he considered his greatest trial. He took great pleasure in always being at his place in the house of worship and he govererned his life by the tenets and teachings of the church, thus living so as to command the unqualified respect of his fellow men. Whatever tended to uplift humanity elicited his interest and in as far as possible he co-operated in all movements in his community for the public good. At the time of his demise he was perhaps the oldest gentleman residing in Albion and his mind bore the impress of the early historic annals of this part of the state. He watched its entire growth and development, and while active in business affairs and also in advancing material improvement of this part of the county, he labored most earnestly for the moral growth of his community. He was a man of strong and honorable purpose, whose integrity was above question and whose life was at all times guided by principles which developed a character of great strength and lofty ideals. He realized fully that the only thing that is of actual value in the world is character—that it is this by which man is judged and through long years he made it the aim and purpose of his life to conform his actions to the rules of conduct of Him who gave to the world the two precepts "To love the Lord, thy God, with all thy heart, and thy neighbor as thyself."

HON. HENRY CLAY HALL.

Colonel Henry Clay Hall is entitled to distinction and to representation in this volume for many reasons. He is a veteran of the Civil war, has been honored with the highest office in the gift of the people of the city and has been representative of this district in the State Legislature. He has also been very prominent in industrial circles and in business life and, moreover, he is one of the native sons of Battle Creek. Upon memory's wall for him hang many pictures of the early days when this now thriving and populous commercial and industrial center was but a village, giving little promise of its present prosperity and marvelous development.

Colorel Hall was born in Battle Creek on the 7th of January, 1834, and is a son of Moses and Mary (Westover) Hall. His paternal grandfather, who also bore the name of Moses Hall, was born in Needham, Massachusetts, March 29, 1759, and, removing to Vermont, became a resident of Sudbury, that state. Subsequently he came to Michigan and spent his last days in Battle Creek, where he died on the 17th of December, 1842. The father of our subject was born in Sudbury, Vermont, September 16, 1797, and was there reared and married. On the 20th of March, 1820, he wedded Miss Mary West-over and they began their domestic life in the Green Mountain state, where they lived for thirteen years. They then came to Battle Creek in a company composed of several families. The journey westward was made by team and they settled on the site of the present city. Mr. and Mrs. Hall brought with them their four children. The father of our subject was a farmer by occupation and, purchasing land of the government, and in other ways adding to his property, became the owner of considerable real estate. It was a timber region at the time of his arrival, in which the Indians had burned out the underbrush. All was wild and unimproved and far separated from the comforts of the older east, the pioneers had to endure many hardships and trials in their new home. As the years passed other children were added to the family until there were nine sons and daughters in the household. Two died in infancy. Edward Hastings, the eldest, who was a farmer of Emmett township, Calhoun county, served for two years in the Civil war and died at his old home in April, 1903, leaving six children. Eliza is the wife of Porter Rawson, of Victor, New York, and has three children. Ellen M. is the wife of Frederick Stebbins, who is living on a farm near Denver, Colorado, and one of her sons is agent for the tourist cars running between Boston and San Francisco. Arunah died in Battle Creek at the age of fifteen years. Cornelia I., who became the wife of Lorin Chadwick, died in October, 1902, leaving one son, Moses, who resides in Battle Creek. Henry C. is the next of the family. Charles T., the

youngest, married Mary McCartney and resides in Battle Creek. He was also a soldier of the Civil war. The family certainly proved their loyalty to the Union cause in the dark days of the rebellion for three of the sons went to the south in defense of the stars and stripes. The mother of these children died on the 11th of August, 1838, and the father was afterward again married, his second union being with Miss Achsah Houck, by whom he had one son, Charles T. In his political views the father was in early life a Democrat and was a warm admirer of Cass. He became a strong anti-slavery man and was also equally ardent in the advocacy of temperance principles. When the Republican party was formed to prevent the further extension of slavery he joined its ranks and remained one of its supporters until his death. For sixteen years he served as justice of the peace and his decisions were strictly fair and impartial, winning him high commendation. In the year 1844 he was elected to represent his district in the State Legislature and left the impress of his individuality upon the early laws of Michigan. His religious faith was indicated by his membership in the Presbyterian church and to its teachings and principles he was always alert. He died May 12, 1860, honored and respected by all who knew him and he is yet held in kindly remembrance by pioneer residents of this county.

Henry Clay Hall, the first white child born in Battle Creek, his birth occurring in a log house at the corner of Marshall and Division streets, obtained his education in one of the early log school houses of the locality. It was the first school house of Battle Creek and stood on East

Main street near Monroe. Subsequently he enjoyed more advanced privileges, becoming a student in an academy at Vermontville, Eaton county, Michigan. When nineteen years of age he entered upon his business career by serving an apprenticeship to the trades of a stone mason and brick layer. For the first year's labor he received fifty dollars, for the second year, one hundred dollars, and for the third year one hundred and fifty dollars. During the term of his apprenticeship he fully mastered the work and continuously followed his trade until 1862.

In the meantime Mr. Hall was married, having on the 9th of February, 1854, at Union City, Branch county, Michigan, wedded Miss Julia A. Stiles, who was born in St. Lawrence county, New York, a daughter of Justus and Aurilla (Clark) Stiles. She was only two years of age when brought by her father to Michigan in 1835, the family settling in what is now Emmett, Calhoun county. In order to provide for his family Mr. Hall worked at his trade until 1862, when feeling that his first duty was to his country in her hour of danger he enlisted as a member of Company D, Thirteenth Michigan Volunteer Infantry, going to the front as a private. The regiment went into camp at Douglas and before leaving for the front Mr. Hall was made first lieutenant. He participated in the battles of Stone River, Chickamauga, the siege of that city, the battle of Misionary Ridge and went with Sherman on the celebrated march to the sea. His valor and meritorious conduct on the field of battle won for him promotion. In November, 1862, he became captain of Company K, of the Thirteenth Michigan Infantry. Later he was commissioned lieutenant colonel

and at Savannah, Georgia, after three years service, he was mustered out in January, 1865. A brave and valorous officer he never needlessly exposed his men to danger and yet when duty called he led them into the thickest of the fight. Thus with a most creditable military record he returned to his home.

Again taking up his trade Colonel Hall became identified once more with the building interests of Battle Creek and has long been known as a most successful and capable contractor and builder. After the fire in Chicago he went to that city and for a time was engaged in its reconstruction. The first building of importance which he erected after the war was the shop of the firm of Nichols & Shepard built in 1869 and the main building used to-day is the one which he erected. In 1870 he built the school building No. 1, and took and executed the contract for the Skinner block and a number of other important business blocks in this city. In fact, on many sides are seen evidences of his superior handiwork and in business circles he sustains a most excellent reputaton because of his fidelity to the terms of a contract. He formed a partnership with his brother Charles T. Hall in 1870, and this firm is still in active business. They have built and sold much property. They laid out Hall Brother's addition to Battle Creek on Lake avenue in 1890. He is also a stockholder in the Whip & Leather Company of Battle Creek.

The home of Colonel and Mrs. Hall has been blessed with two children, the elder being Effie, who was born in Battle Creek August 25, 1854, and is now the wife of Edward Sandford, of this city. They have two children, Howell and Halsey. Charles H., the son. born in Battle Creek, March 28, 1856, follows the plasterer's trade and makes his home with his parents.

He is a member of Farragut post, G. A. R. In his political views the Colonel has always been a stalwart Republican since casting his first presidential ballot for John C. Fremont in 1856. His fellow townsmen, recognizing his worth and ability have several times called him to public office. He has served as a member of the board of aldermen for several terms, being first elected to that position in 1874. In 1887 he was chosen mayor of the city and acted as chief executive for three terms, his administration being of marked benefit to Battle Creek because of his practical and progressive ideas and his stanch support of all measures for the public good. Waterworks, now in use, were constructed during his term of office. In 1892 he was appointed a member of the board of public works, reappointed in 1897, and again in 1902. Part of the time he served as president. During this time the paving was first done and sewers constructed. Like his father he has also been honored with election to the State Legislature, being chosen to that office in 1890, during which term he served as chairman of the committee on state buildings. He declined to serve a second term, preferring to labor for the interests of county and state as a private citizen rather than as an official. He proved, however, a wise and able legislator, taking counsel of mature judgment and supporting measures only after careful deliberation. In whatever relation of life we find Colonel Hall whether in the legislative chambers, in public office or in industrial circles, he is always the same honorable and honored gentleman, whose worth well merits the high regard which is universally given him. Prosperity has come to him through business channels and honors have been conferred upon him because of his capability and marked devotion to the general good. Viewed from any standpoint, therefore, his life might be said to be a success. The study of the character of the representative American never fails to prove of much interest and valuable instruction, and the life of Colonel Hall certainly furnishes food for deep and profitable thought.

CHARLES A. BROCEUS.

Charles A. Broceus, the city salesman, representing the wholesale house of J. F. Halladay & Son, of Battle Creek, was born in Buchanan, Michigan, September 10. 1868. His parents. William and Phebe (Blake) Broceus, are residing upon a farm in Buchanan township, Berrien county. The paternal grandfather. Abram Broceus, was a native of Pennsylvania. and removed thence to Akron, Ohio. where he followed the carpenter's trade. He there married Abigail Smith and they removed to Berrien county in the early '40s, the grandfather entering land from the government. He continued to follow his trade in Michigan and built the first railroad bridge across the St. Joseph river at Niles. He walked each Saturday night to his home. returning in the same manner on Sunday night. As he prospered in his undertakings he invested in land, becoming the owner of four hundred and fifty acres. He lived to be about seventy-four years of age and was twice married, becoming the father of ten children, all of whom are living.

William Broceus is now about sixty years of age. He and his wife were both born in Berrien county where they have always lived. He has one hundred acres of fine farming land and is a self-made man, his success being attributable entirely to his own efforts. In politics he is a stalwart Republican and has held several township offices, the duties of which he has faithfully discharged. He belongs to the United Brethren church and is serving as a deacon.

In the usual manner of farmer lads Charles A. Broceus pursued his education and spent his early boyhood days working in the fields through the summer months. Afterward he had more advanced educational privileges. attending the high school at Buchanan until his graduation with the class of 1888. He next began clerking in a grocery store at South Bend, Indiana, with an uncle, remaining there for about a year, and later he removed to Benton Harbor, where he secured a similar position which he filled for four years. In April, 1894, Mr. Broceus took up his abode in Battle Creek and became a salesman in the employ of Allen Raymond, with whom he continued until his employer sold out, and afterward was with his successor until 1896, when he accepted his present position.

On the 3d of June, 1896, Mr. Broceus was married in Battle Creek to Miss Eva M. Squier. a daughter of Daniel and Patience (Simpson) Squier. The lady was born in this city and obtained a good education here. Two children have graced this marriage: William Charles, born April 12, 1899; and Lodema, born August 25, 1902. The parents occupy an enviable place in

the regard of many friends. Mr. Broceus has a genial manner and a social disposition that has rendered him popular in business circles and in private life. Since casting his ballot in 1892 for Benjamin Harrison, he has continuously supported the Republican party. He has taken all of the degrees in the Knights of Pythias fraternity and also has membership relations with the Knights of the Maccabees.

JOSEPH W. BRYCE.

Joseph W. Bryce, whose real estate operations have made him prominent among the energetic and enterprising business men of Battle Creek, was born at Bathgate, Linlithgowshire, Scotland, June 3, 1860. His parents, Peter and Catherine (Cunningham) Bryce, removed to Canada when their son was about seven years of age and located in Ottawa, where the father spent his remaining days, his attention being given to gardening. He died there in 1900. Joseph W. Bryce remained in Ottawa until nineteen years of age and acquired there a common school education. He then came to Battle Creek where he lived with his brother, James C. Bryce, now mechanical superintendent for the Malta-Vita Company. Our subject was for six months employed by the Grand Trunk Railroad Company and then in the shops of Nichols & Shepard, where he remained for a year and a half. He afterward spent a year as an employee in the bridge department of the Chicago & Grand Trunk Railroad Company and later entered the services of the Canadian Pacific Railroad with which he was connected for two years. Another change in his business

. life made him a real estate dealer at Moose-jaw in the Northwest Territory. He was there when the town was laid out and aided in organizing the village and also in instituting its fire department.

Mr. Bryce returned to Battle Creek, and on the 12th of December, 1883, married Miss Carrie M. Wilcox, a native of this city and a daughter of Waterman and Minerva (Lampson) Wilcox. He was then employed in the Bremen Boiler Works for a short time and afterward spent a year in the bridge department of the Grand Trunk Railroad Company. At the expiration of that period he was transferred to the traffic department and became brakeman, serving in that capacity and as conductor until 1894. In that year he turned his attention to the insurance and real estate business and gained a good clientage in this line. Finally, however, he disposed of the insurance department owing to the heavy demands made upon his time and energies by his real estate operations. He has largely engaged in buying and selling land, in negotiating realty transfers for others, and his business has assumed extensive and profitable proportions.

Unto Mr. and Mrs. Bryce has been born one child, Frank, W., whose birth occurred in Battle Creek, February 22, 1885. He is a graduate of the high school and is now employed by the Consumers Ice Company. On coming to the United States Mr. Bryce took out naturalization papers and has always been loyal to the interests of the country. He is independent in politics but in 1894 was the nominee of the Populist party for sheriff. He did not expect election and, in fact, received far more votes than he had anticipated. So-cially he is connected with the Independent Order of Odd Fellows, the Ancient Order of United Workmen and the Modern Woodmen of America and belongs to the International Congress of Michigan. His character and position illustrates most happily for the purpose of this work the fact that if a young man is possessed of the proper attributes of mind and heart he can, unaided, attain a position of prominence in the business world and gain for himself a place among those men who are foremost in shaping the destiny of their localities.

CHARLES F. BOCK.

Charles F. Bock, whose death on the 16th of November, 1903, deprived Battle Creek of one of its most respected and representative citizens, long occupied a prominent position in commercial circles of the city. It was noticeable in his business career that in whatever connection he was found he was always prominent in the enterprise—a leading spirit in its successful management. If his association began simply as a stockholder his well known ability, executive power and sound judgment soon caused him to be placed in a position where these qualities would be called into action. He stood as one of the strong and successful men of Battle Creek and one whose acquaintance in fraternal circles was as broad and comprehensive as in business life.

Mr. Bock was born in Buffalo, New York, December 23, 1836, a son of Frederick C. and Harriet Bock. On the 4th of March, 1854, when seventeen years of age, he began earning his own living, being first employed in the wholesale establishment of Pratt & Company, dealers in hardward in Buffalo. It was his duty to look after and fill the mail orders received by that firm and in two years he had been advanced until he became the head of the department. In 1861 he came to Battle Creek with his family. The city then contained a population of only three thousand. Here he was first employed as a salesman by V. P. Collier, and in 1865 became a partner of John Cooper and J. W. Arnold in a mercantile enterprise conducted under the firm name of Bock, Arnold & Company. They began business in the same building in which Mr. Bock was carrying on his business at the time of his death, and of which he eventually became the owner. In 1869 he purchased the interest of his partners and associated himself in business with Charles Peters, which connection was continued for fourteen years. In 1883 Mr. Bock sold out to Mr. Peters and opened a store at No. 18 West Main street with his son, Frank F. Bock, as a partner, under the firm style of Charles F. Bock & Son. He not only owned the business block which he occupied, but also the adjoining one, both of which were utilized by him in his business. He conducted both a wholesale and retail business and at the time of his death was the most prominent hardware merchant in the city. For almost half a century he was a representative of the hardware trade in Battle Creek and none were more familiar with this line of commercial activity. He was also identified with various other interests of importance here. He was one of the stockholders of the City Bank and aided in organizing the City Electric Light Company, of which he was a director for nine years, or until he resigned in 1901, because of the pressure of other business cares.

Mr. Brock was vice president of the building committee of the Post Theater Company, which erected one of the finest play houses in Central Michigan. In 1858 occurred the marriage of Mr. Bock and Miss Harriet Hagelberger, of Batavia, New York, and unto them were born two children. The son Frank F. was his father's partner in business and is his successor in the conduct of the enterprise, and the daughter, Kate B., is the wife of George G. Tanner, of Indianapolis, Indiana.

In his political views Mr. Bock was always an earnest Republican and twice served as city alderman, during which time he was chairman of the finance committee that conducted the negotiations for the railroad bonds that were issued at that time. He was also chairman of the Republican county committee during the Garfield campaign in 1880, and had the county well organized, conducting a successful campaign.

He was one of the most active factors in advancing the movement for the erection of the soldiers' monument to the memory of the honored dead, whose faithful service for their country entitled them to the gratitude of the Nation. His work was prompted by a patriotic spirit and by a hearty appreciation of all that the soldiers had accomplished, but in the erection of this memorial stone he also built a monument to himself, it being the visible evidence of his energy and devotion to a cause in which he was deeply interested. Many other public enterprises and movements felt the stimulus of his aid and capable management. At the time of his death, in connection with his active supervision of his varied and important interests, Mr. Bock, then at the age of sixty-seven years, was serving as the president of the Athelstan club, the leading social organization of the city. He was also the president of the Oak Hill Cemetery Association and the senior warden of the St. Thomas' Episcopal church. He was likewise prominent in Masonic circles. He had become a member of Battle Creek lodge, No. 12, F. & A. M., of which he served as master and in the chapter he was high priest. He likewise belonged to Zabud Council, R. & S. M., and was eminent commander of Battle Creek Commandery, No. 33, K. T., the organization of this commandery being more largely due to his efforts than to that of any other Sir Knight. With the Aladdin Temple of the Mystic Shrine at Grand Rapids he also had membership relations. In a summary of his life record we noted that one of his strongest characteristics was his power of management. This made him a leader in every undertaking with which he was connected and always insured a successful outcome of the same. It was as manifest in his social as in his business life, and proved a valued element in many movements for the public good. He was always courteous and approachable, and from the beginning of his residence in Battle Creek his fellow townsmen passed favorable judgment upon him, commending his many excellent qualities and finding little to criticise.

He possessed strong domestic tastes and while he accomplished much in the business world and ratified his friendships by kindly sympathy and thoughtful consideration for others, his greatest depth of love was reserved for his family.

CHARLES B. FURNER.

The loyalty of Charles B. Furner in matters of citizenship has oftentimes been tested, and no man in Calhoun county has been more true to his country and her welfare. He was but a boy when he joined the Union army to fight in defense of the old flag, and in days of peace he has been equally true to the nation's starry banner. As sheriff of Calhoun county, he is demonstrating by fidelity and ability in the discharge of his duties that the confidence reposed in him was well placed, and his course is awakening the commendation of all unbiased and law-abiding citizens.

Mr. Furner was born in Phelps, Ontario county, New York, October 9, 1848, a son of Stephen and Martha (Sherburn) Furner. The father was born in England, and when six years of age came to the United States with his parents. He learned the trade of shoemaking in the State of New York, and at Canandaigua he married Miss Sherburn, after which he made his home at Phelps. Subsequently he took up his abode near Penn Yan, Yates county, New York, and spent the greater part of his life in the Empire state, dying at Rushville.

Charles B. Furner began his education in the public schools of the state of his nativity, but when fifteen years of age he put aside every other consideration in order to aid his country. The flame of patriotism burned strong within his breast, and on the 1st of January, 1864, he joined Company C, Forty-fourth New York Infantry, known as Ellsworth's Avengers. He was among the youngest of the soldier boys of the entire army, but he displayed a valor that equalled

CHARLES B. FURNER

that of many a veteran of twice or thrice his years. With the Army of the Potomac he participated in the battles of the Wilderness, Laurel Hill, Five Forks, Hatches Run, Gravel Run and Appomatox, being present at the surrender of General Lee. He was wounded May 12, 1864, at Spottsylvania, and was in the hospital until October 15, 1864, when he was transferred to the One Hundred and Fortieth New York regiment, of Rochester, New York, known as Ryan's Zouaves. At the close of hostilities he was transferred to a veteran regiment, the Fifth New York Fire Zouaves, and sent to Hart's Island, New York, where he was mustered out August 31, 1865.

Returning home with a most creditable military record, Mr. Furner then learned the barber's trade, which he followed for twenty-four years, spending most of that time at Waterloo, New York. There he was married, May 7, 1871, to Miss Elnora Sutherland, and in 1874 he came to Michigan, locating in Battle Creek, where he conducted an extensive barber shop during the greater part of the time until 1892, when he purchased a farm in Bedford township. He then engaged in horticultural pursuits, and was very successful in the product of fruits. He continued in that business until May, 1899, when he was appointed turnkey and deputy sheriff. He then left the farm but still owns the property.

In politics Mr. Furner has always been an unfaltering Republican and while in Battle Creek was elected a member of the city council, serving for two years, during which time the electric light plant was inaugurated. Mr. Furner was chairman of the supplies and expenditures and also of the fire department committees. While in Bedford township he served on the school board and also as jus-

tice of the peace, filling the latter position most acceptably for four years. He was then appointed deputy by Sheriff Williams, and in November, 1902, he was elected sheriff of the county by a majority of nine hundred, leading most of the ticket, indication of the unqualified trust reposed in him by those who know him best. He carried his old Battle Creek ward, which is usually strongly Democratic, by a larger vote than any other candidate. Mr. Furner entered upon the duties of the office January 1, 1903, and his course has fully justified the support which was given him.

Unto Mr. and Mrs. Furner have been born two children, Francis A. and Mattie E. Mr. Furner attends and supports the Methodist Episcopal church, of which his wife and daughter are active members. He belongs to Battle Creek lodge, No. 573, B. P. O. E., the Ancient Order of United Workmen and C. Colgrove post, Grand Army of the Republic, of Marshall. His business career has been characterized by energy, strong determination and straightforward dealing; his military service by valor and patriotism, and his official career by unfaltering allegiance to the trust reposed in him and by ability in the discharge of his duties.

CHARLES WARREN BROWN.

Charles Warren Brown, of Battle Creek, was born in Seneca Falls, New York, December 13, 1850, and was but seven years of age when his parents, Edmund D. and Abigail (Androus) Brown, removed to Michigan, arriving in this state in 1857. At Seneca Falls the father had been foreman of Silsby's Fire Engine Company

6

and on coming to this state he located in Jackson, where he resided until 1862, when he removed to Battle Creek. On coming to this city he entered the works of Nichols & Shepard Company as foreman, remaining in that employ as long as he was in active business life. Mr. and Mrs. Brown were the parents of three children, of whom the subject of this review is the eldest. The others are Harriet and Nelson A. and the sister resides at No. 61 Cherry street.

Charles Warren Brown was a youth of twelve years when the family arrived in Calhoun county. He at once entered the public schools and continued as a high school student until about seventeen years of age, after which he pursued his studies in a commercial college, in which he was graduated. Being thus prepared for the business world he became a bookkeeper and was thus employed by different firms. In 1870 he entered the employ of Nichols & Shepard as bookkeeper and paymaster, or cashier, thus serving for a number of years, after which he took charge of the business of the firm upon the road, superintending their interest in the northwestern, central and southern states. He traveled for several years or until 1887, when he removed to Kansas City, becoming manager of the branch house of Nichols & Shepard at that place. There he remained in charge for ten years, returning in 1897, at which time he accepted the position of superintendent of the Battle Creek interests and in this position has since remained.

On the 16th of May, 1878, in Battle Creek, Mr. Brown was married to Miss Myrtella Champion, who was born in the same house in which she was married at No. 31 Van Buren street, west. Her parents were Henry J. and Adeline (King)

Champion. Her father was born at Bridgeport, Connecticut, and was a son of John Henry and Rebecca (Seward) Champion, the latter a distant relative of William H. Seward, secretary of war under President Lincoln. The family removed from Connecticut to Pennsylvania and thence to Michigan and after a short residence at Marshall came to Battle Creek in 1835. The grandfather of Mrs. Brown purchased land on Van Buren street, adjoining the E. C. Hinman property, and erected the first two story house built in Battle Creek. Champion street was named in his honor. About six months prior to his death he removed to Decatur, Michigan, where he passed away at the age of seventy-six years, his remains being interred in Oakhill cemetery of this city. His wife, who was well known and highly respected in social circles, reached the advanced age of eighty-three years. When Henry J. Champion was about seventeen years of age he went to live with Alonzo Noble, a merchant of Battle Creek and assisted him as a clerk in his store. The association between them continued for many years and later Mr. Champion engaged in the insurance business, while subsequently he became agent for the American Express Company and acted in that capacity for twenty-two years. His last days were passed in Nebraska and in Kansas City, Mo., where he died in 1899 at the age of seventy-eight years. His wife passed away in Chicago while on her way back to Michigan. Unto Mr. and Mrs. Brown were born three children: Myrta May, who was born in Battle Creek, May 30, 1880, and died September 7, 1881, her remains being interred in Oakhill cemetery; Edwin Charles, who was born in this city May 23, 1883, and attended the high school and commercial college, after which he represented the Malta-Vita Company in Mexico, and is now assistant manager of advertising and gold band department of Armour Packing Co., and Clinton Champion, who was born in Battle Creek November 13, 1887, and is now a student in the high school.

Mr. Brown cast his first presidential vote for Grant in 1872 and has exercised his right of franchise in support of the men and measures of the Republican party. He was reared a Presbyterian and his wife was reared in the Baptist church, but both became charter members of the Independent Congregational church. Throughout almost his entire business career Mr. Brown has been connected with Nichols & Shepard. No higher testimonial of his business integrity and capability could be given. Those whom he represents know him to be worthy of their fullest trust and confidence and throughout his business career he has maintained a reputation that is unassailable.

THOMAS J. BARRY.

Thomas J. Barry, the efficient and popular station agent for the Grand Trunk and Michigan Central railroads at Nichols Station, was born in Battle Creek April 28, 1860, and his parents, James and Sarah (Murphy) Barry, are still living in that city. Both were natives of County Cork, Ireland, and ere their marriage came to America, each locating on Long Island, where they became acquainted and were married January 13, 1851. In 1852 they came to Battle Creek, where they have since resided, and the father entered the employ of the Nichols & Shepard Company, being still retained in their service. For many years he was an iron melter. He is now seventy-two years of age and his wife sixty-eight years of age. In their family were eight children, seven of whom were daughters. The eldest, Elizabeth, died at the age of twenty-one years. The others are Mary, who is with her parents; Sue, the wife of James Plunkett, of Battle Creek, by whom she has a daughter, Mary; Margaret, Frances and Kittie, all at home; Anna, died at the age of thirteen years.

In his boyhood Thomas J. Barry attended the public schools and was graduated in the high school of Battle Creek with the Centennial class when sixteen years of age. Immediately afterward he began teaching and followed that profession for three years in the district schools. He then became telegraph operator for the Michigan Central railroad at Ann Arbor and after a year was transferred to Kalamazoo, where he spent about twelve months. He remained at Detroit for a little more than a year and in 1882 located in Battle Creek as operator and ticket agent. In 1883 he came to Nichols, where he has since been the representative of both the Michigan Central and Grand Trunk railroads. He is freight agent, ticket agent, telegraph operator and express agent and is a most capable official and one who has gained favor with the public because of his uniform course, obliging manner and careful attention to the interests of the patrons of the roads.

On the 30th of April, 1899, Mr. Barry was united in marriage at Schoolcraft, Michigan, to Mrs. Emogene Chamberlain, nee Pettengill, with whom he had became acquainted in Lawton, Michigan. She was born there and was a daughter of Horace B. and Harriet (Watkins) Pettengill. Politically Mr. Barry is a Republican, but was reared a Democrat, and was the first member elected from that party as alderman from the Fifth ward. He was re-elected in 1889 and again in 1891. This is the largest ward in the city and his election was a tribute to his personal popularity and the confidence reposed in him by the public, this being a strong Republican ward. In 1896 he severed his allegiance with the Democracy and joined the ranks of the Republican party. While in the council he was chairman of the committee on public lighting for three years and was chairman of the committee on police and buildings for four years. He was chairman of the supplies and expenditures committee for two years and for four years served on the street and bridge committee, during which time South Jefferson street was paved and the sewerage system was inaugurated. It was also during that time that the first steel bridge of Battle Creek was built and the present fire department building was begun. It was through the efforts of Mr. Barry and one other member of the council that W. P. Weeks was elected chief of the fire department. Mr. Barry was reared in the Catholic church and was confirmed therein at the age of twelve years. Since entering the railroad service his advancement has been continuous and he is now one of the most trusted representatives of the two roads with which he is connected.

CARLTON P. GRANDIN.

The history of America is replete with illustrations of the fact that it is only under the pressure of adversity and the stimulus of competition that the best and strongest in men are brought out and developed. Perhaps the history of no people so forcibly impress one with this truth as the annals of our own Republic. The life record of Carlton Pomeroy Grandin is another proof of this fact and in a business career he won success and made for himself a record that makes his an honored name and causes his memory to be enshrined in the hearts of all with whom he was associated. For many years a respected and honored resident of Battle Creek, he was born in Palmyra, New York, July 17, 1840, his parents being Egbert B. and Harriet (Rogers) Grandin. The family name was originally spelled as it is at the present time, although for several decades just prior to our subject's arrival in Battle Creek, its representatives wrote the name Grandine. Later, however, the final vowel was dropped and the original speling resumed. Egbert Grandin, the father of our subject, was for many years an editor, publishing the Wayne County Sentinel. He was also in the office where the first Mormon Bible was printed. His wife was a daughter of Major William Rogers of Williamston, New York.

During his early childhood C. P. Grandin lost his father. He was educated in the common schools and when a young man came to Battle Creek, where he entered the employ of his brother-in-law, William Andrus, a druggist of this city. Manifesting faithfulness, capability and deep interest in the business, he was afterward admitted to partnership under the firm style of Andrus & Grandin, a relation that was maintained for a number of years, when Mr. Andrus sold out to Charles H. Hinman, a brother of Mrs. Grandin. The firm style of Grandin & Hinman was then assumed and for many years the drug store of the firm was recognized as the leading enterprise of this character in Battle Creek. Both gentlemen possessed good business ability and the honorable policy which they inaugurated in the conduct of their establishment brought to them a gratifying and satisfactory patronage. Mr. Grandin continued in the store until his health failed, when he sold his interest to B. F. Hinman and retired to private life. Judicious investments along other lines made him a capitalist and his name was regarded as a safe one on commercial paper.

On the 13th of November, 1867, Mr. Grandin was united in marriage to Miss Mary Hinman, a daughter of Benjamin F. and Olivia (Swallow) Hinman. Her father was born at Castleton, Vermont, and was a son of Truman Hinman, while the mother's birth occurred in Windsor, Vermont. They lived in the Green Mountain state until their marriage and soon afterward became residents of Bellevue, Michigan, casting in their lot with the pioneer settlers there about 1835, when the work of improvement and progress had scarcely begun in that locality. Mr. Hinman engaged in general merchandising and also operated a lime kiln, being associated in the business with his brother, John F. Hinman. In 1847 he came to Battle Creek, where he turned his attention to merchandising, forming a partnership with his brother, Henry T. Hinman. This association was maintained for thirty-three years and the firm of B. F. & H. T. Hinman was one of the most prominent of the city in early days. The father of Mrs. Grandin became well-to-do and prominent here and because of his known reliability and business capacity he was frequently called upon to settle estates and to

superintend public affairs of moment, among other public duties being a member of the building committee when the high school building was erected in 1870. He died in September, 1889. Mrs. Grandin was born in Bellevue, Michigan, and when about six years of age was brought to Battle Creek, where her girlhood days were passed and her education was acquired. Four children graced this union: Nellie Hinman, now the wife of John B. Martin, a leading musician of this city; Mary Louise, Anna H., now the wife of A. Carlton Freeman, and Frank C., who is advertising manager for the Postum Cereal Company and of the Grandin Advertising Agency.

Mr. Grandin voted with the Republican party. His last days were spent in retirement from business cares and he passed away at his beautiful home, No. 37 North avenue, on the 15th of July, 1888. He possessed many sterling traits of character and his high moral sense, his unfaltering integrity and his own sympathy won him unqualified confidence and the highest regard of all. His kindly spirit and genial disposition brought him friends and he had the happy faculty of drawing them closer to him as the years went by.

HENRY ALLEN WHITNEY.

Calhoun county has been, and is, signally favored in the class of men who have had charge of her financial interests. Among the number is Henry Allen Whitney, who, for twelve years, has filled the position of county superintendent of poor. He has resided in Battle Creek since 1863 and his career has ever been such as to warrant the confidence of the business world and of the general public. He was born in Providence, Rhode Island, on the 6th of November, 1832, and is a son of Leonard and Charlotte S. (Allen) Whitney. The paternal grandfather, Nathan Whitney was a resident of West Minister, Massachusetts. He was at one time a very extensive landowner. He was also addressed as Captain Whitney, having obtained his title by service in the state militia. Leonard Whitney, the father of our subject, was born in Worcester county, Massachusetts, about 1808, and his wife was born in 1809, and was living in Providence, Rhode Island, at the time of her marriage. When a young man Mr. Whitney had gone to Providence and was there engaged in the manufacture of woodenware. After his marriage he came with his family to Michigan, settling in Niles in 1836, among its pioneer residents. There he was interested in a chair factory which he conducted for some time. Subsequently he removed to Dowagiac, Michigan, and spent his last days in St. Joseph, this state, where he was engaged in fruit farming. He was everywhere known as Deacon Whitney, having always served as a deacon in the Congregational church in every locality in which he lived. His worth was always recognized and his deep interest in the church and his efforts for its welfare were most marked. He also served as township treasurer in Lincoln township, near St. Joseph, Michigan, filling the position for many years. His death occurred in 1880, but his wife passed away long years before.

Henry A. Whitney of this review was a little lad of only four summers when brought by his parents to Michigan and in the early schools of this state he obtained his education. By the time he reached his majority he began learning the trade of painting and decorating in Battle Creek; and later he had charge of the furniture store owned by Henry Gilbert and others, acting in that capacity for about ten years, a part of the time conducting the business under his own name. While filling that position he was elected alderman from the fourth ward and following that he was city recorder for four years. During this time the water works, the street car and the electric light systems were installed and thus Battle Creek was greatly benefited. For four successive terms Mr. Whitney was elected recorder on the Republican ticket. His father had been an Abolitionist and his sympathies in early life were with that movement. Upon the organization of the Republican party he joined its ranks and at that time he went over Berrien county, Michigan, in the interest of the first Republican paper published in that county. It was known as the "Niles Inquirer" and was owned by Mr. Carlton of Niles. He has never faltered in his allegiance to the principles of the party with which he became identified almost a half century ago, and it has always been upon this ticket that he has been chosen to public office. Following his service in the recorder's office he was elected county superintendent of the poor for three successive terms, covering a period of nine years. The following year the Republicans lost the county through the fusion of the forces of three or four other parties and thus Mr. Whitney was out of office for one term. He was then re-elected recorder for the term of 1898-9 and after three years was again chosen superintendent of the poor, so that now he is serving for the thirteenth year in the office. No more capable official has ever occupied this position and no higher testimonial of his ability could be given than the fact that he has so many years continued in office. For a number of years he has held the office of county agent of the board of corrections and charities and upon him involves the care of all juvenile offenders in the county. It is also a part of his duty to pass judgment upon the homes that seek to adopt children from any of the state institutions. Mr. Whitney was the second man to hold this position under the law.

On the 11th of September, 1860, was celebrated the marriage of Henry A. Whitney and Miss Anna E. Bellows of Climax, Kalamazoo county, Michigan, a daughter of William Edway Bellows, who removed from the vicinity of Bellows Falls, Vermont, in 1836 to Michigan, thus becoming identified with the early interests in this state. He was a cousin of Dr. Bellows, who became prominent in connection with the sanitary commission during the Civil war and who was a representative of a distinguished old New England family. Unto Mr. and Mrs. Whitney have been born five children: Kate W., Harlan K., T. Schuyler, Rose M. and Lavinia V. The parents and all the children hold membership in the Presbyterian church and take a very active and helpful part in its work. He is one of the charter members of Security lodge, A. O. U. W., and for ten years was its financier. He was likewise a charter member of the National Union and its secretary for the past ten years. He has also been local treasurer of the Standard Savings & Loan Association of Detroit for a decade. He is a man of upright charac-

ter, his Christianity being manifested in his daily life and his kindly and humanitarian spirit is indicated in the daily discharge of his duties in connection with the board of trustees. Over the record of his public career and his private life there falls no shadow of wrong or suspicion of evil.

ERNEST C. SAWDY.

Ernest C. Sawdy, who is city treasurer of Marshall and also agent for the Michigan Central Railroad Company at that place, is a native son of the town, born December 27, 1863, his parents being Edwin and Martha (Pratt) Sawdy. The family was founded in America by John Sawdy, who was in Boston, Massachusetts, in 1654. Jabez Sawdy, the grandfather of our subject, was a resident of Erie, Pennsylvania, where he followed the carpenter's trade. His first wife died there and afterward he brought his children to Marshall, Michigan, where he continued in the same line of business, his death occurring here. Edwin Sawdy, born and educated in Erie, Pennsylvania, worked in carpenter and cabinet making shops there until the removal of the family to Michigan. Here, in 1851, he married Martha Pratt, daughter of Jefferson and Polly (Carver) Pratt. She was born in what was then Euclid, Ohio, now a part of Cleveland, and her parents, who were born near Lake Champlain, New York, removed to Ohio in pioneer times. They came to Marshall in 1840, before the days of railroads, and Mr. Pratt purchased a farm in Convis township, where he lived until his retirement from business life. Both he and his wife spent their last days in Marshall.

After their marriage Mr. and Mrs. Edwin Sawdy lived in Erie and then Lockport, Pennsylvania, where he followed his trade. Later he returned to Marshall, Michigan, and here, in 1863, he enlisted in the Fifteenth Michigan Infantry, attached to the Army of the Cumberland. At Chattanooga, Tennessee, he was taken ill with typhoid fever and sent to the hospital at Cincinnati, Ohio, where he died March 11, 1864, leaving a widow and five children: Frank, now of Minneapolis, Minnesota; Judson and Charles, of this city; Ora M., wife of Richard Martin, and Ernest. The mother remained in Marshall, rearing and educating her children, and is yet a resident of the town.

Ernest Sawdy acquired his early education in the public schools of Marshall and then found employment with the Michigan Central railroad as clerk in the office. Gradually by his ability and fidelity to duty he was promoted from one position to another until he was appointed agent in May, 1903. He has now been with the road for twenty years and this is one of the most important passenger and freight stations on the line. He has about half a dozen men under his direction in the freight and ticket offices.

In politics Mr. Sawdy is an active Democrat and an earnest worker for the party. In 1896 he was elected city recorder and was twice re-elected for consecutive terms, during which time the water plant was purchased from a private corporation and became the property of the city. In 1903 he was elected city treasurer by the largest majority ever given any candidate in the city. This was certainly indicative of the fact that his previous service was most commendable and that he has the unqualified confidence and trust of his fellow townsmen.

On the 5th of May, 1888, Mr. Sawdy was united in marriage to Miss Elizabeth O'Leary, of Marshall, a daughter of Timothy O'Leary, and they have four children: Donald, Ernest, Harold and Burns. The parents are members of St. Mary's Catholic church and Mr. Sawdy belongs to the Knights of the Maccabees Tent of this place. He and his family have a pleasant home on South Eagle street, and are widely known in Marshall, being a most efficient and popular representative of the railroad company, as well as a public officer, whose course commends him to the trust and commendation of all with whom he has been brought in contact.

WILLIAM C. KLAWITER.

William C. Klawiter, whose intense and well directed activity has been one of the forceful factors in industrial life in Battle Creek, is a director of the John Brennan Company, of Detroit and Battle Creek, and is acting as superintendent of the branch of the business located in the latter city. He entered upon the active duties of life unaided by influential friends or adventitious circumstances and has been the sole architect of his own fortunes, molding his own character and shaping his own destiny. To-day he occupies a conspicuous position among the successful young business men of his city, and in his business relations and dealings has applied the principles of a private life in which fidelity to duty, trustworthiness and consideration of others have been salient features. Mr. Klawiter has been a resident of Battle Creek since 1883, and is one of Michigan's native sons, his birth having oc-.

William C. Klawiter

curred in Detroit, August 27, 1864. He is the eldest of the three children born of the marriage of William Klawiter and Katherine Hilbert, both of whom were natives of Germany and came to the United States in childhood. The father entered upon his business career as an employee of John Brennan, in his boiler shop in Detroit and continued his business connection with the works after the incorporation of the business under the firm style of John Brennan & Company. In fact his association with the enterprise was only terminated by death, which occurred after thirty-five years relation with the house. He won successive promotions until he reached the position of foreman and afterward that of superintendent. In 1883, when the company established a branch house at Battle Creek, more especially for the manufacture of engines, the Detroit plant being devoted to the construction of boilers. Mr. Klawiter removed with his family to the former city and as superintendent had charge of the plant until his demise. He had the unqualified confidence and good will of those whom he represented and was a most capable man in the position which he occupied. He died October 1, 1892, but his widow is still living and makes her home in Battle Creek.

William C. Klawiter is indebted to the public school system of his native city for the educational privileges he enjoyed. After completing his literary course there he learned the boiler-maker's trade as an apprentice in the shop of John Brennan & Company, remaining at the boiler works in Detroit for a year and then coming to Battle Creek with his parents. Here he completed his apprenticeship and after becoming a journeyman was promoted through successive stages until, upon his father's death in

1892, he was made his successor, becoming superintendent of the extensive establishment in Battle Creek. He has since given his time and attention almost exclusively to the supervision of the plant, having control of the largest boiler works in this section of the state, giving employment to as many as seventy-five men. He has become a stockholder and a director of the John Brennan Company, which owns the works at Battle Creek and at Detroit, the latter being still more extensive than the plant at Battle Creek. Mr. Klawiter has also made investments in other business enterprises, being interested in the Citizens' Electric Company and a stockholder in other corporate concerns of the city. He has thoroughly informed himself concerning the work at which he served an apprenticeship and is splendidly qualified for the important position which he is now filling. Having a practical knowledge of the trade he is thus enabled to superintend and direct the labors of the men employed in the works and thus bring about the best results for the company, in which he is financially interested.

In his political views Mr. Klawiter is an earnest Republican, in hearty sympathy with the principles of the party, but has never been an office seeker. At one time he was a member of Battle Creek lodge, No. 12, F. & A. M., but demitted to Metcalf lodge, No. 419, upon its organization. He also belongs to Battle Creek chapter, R. A. M., and Battle Creek commandery, No. 33, K. T. His beautiful home, at the corner of Lake avenue and Fountain street, is one of the most attractive residences in the city and stands in the midst of a large and well kept lawn. He is widely known in the city which has been his home for more than two decades, and where he is recognized as a prominent young business man of rare capability and enterprise, whose native talent has led him out of humble financial surroundings to large successes.

L. H. LOVE.

L. H. Love, proprietor and editor of the Athens Times, is a native of the State of New York, his birth having occurred in Niagara county, April 11, 1841. When but two years old he was brought to the west by his parents, Lorenzo and Lois Lorain (Hale) Love. The father was born in Bridgewater, New York, and the mother in Royalton, that state. The former was a farmer by occupation and in 1843, four years after his marriage, he removed to Michigan, settling in Calhoun county, near Ceresco, where he was engaged in operating the five-story stone flour mill owned by A. Wallingford. He remained there for nine years and then took up his abode in Newton township, where he purchased a farm and also conducted the mill for Mr. Wallingford for a time. He then bought a farm in South Newton and subsequently a farm west of Burlington, Michigan, which he improved and made his home until 1888, when he retired from active connection with agricultural interests and resided with his children until his death, which occurred near Benton Harbor, Michigan, when he had reached the advanced age of eighty-seven years. While residing in New York he was a captain in the state militia up to the time of his moving to Michigan.

L. H. Love pursued his education in the public schools and remained at home until about eighteen years of age. He then went to Marshall, where he became an apprentice in the office of the Expounder, then conducted by the firm of Mann & Noyes, with whom he continued for two years. He afterward was employed as a compositor on various newspapers until 1867, when he went to Chicago and entered the office of the Chicago Times, remaining there for about twelve years as type-setter and an assistant in the proof-reading room. He was later compositor for a year or more on the Chicago Tribune, the Inter-Ocean and was also employed in job printing offices in that city. On leaving there he came to Athens, where for a short time he was employed in the general store of Mrs. Love's father, but, resuming his chosen vocation he established a job printing office and in March, 1883, began the publication of the Athens Times, which he conducted for about five years, when he sold out to Edward Wisner. He then engaged in the insurance, real estate and collection business and during that period served as deputy sheriff of the county for four years under Alonzo Prentice. In 1897 he purchased the Athens Times and again began the publication of the paper which he had started some years before. He has since remained its editor and proprietor and has made it a strong local journal, devoted to the best interests of the community and to the dissemination of general news. He has developed his paper along modern lines of journalism and has, therefore, met with success in his undertakings.

On the 10th of October, 1867, Mr. Love was united in marriage to Miss Cornelia Underwood, who was born near Abscota, Calhoun county, and was a daughter of Amasa and Jane (Wells) Underwood. Her father was an early settler of Calhoun county, coming to the west from the State of New York, in which his birth occurred.

In his business affairs he prospered, following agricultural pursuits for a number of years, but in his later life engaging in general merchandising in Athens. He died in 1898, when seventy-six years of age, and his widow is still living, making her home with Mr. and Mrs. Love. By the marriage of our subject and his wife one daughter has been born, Lillian Frances, now the wife of V. D. Lee, who was formerly a school teacher, but is now engaged in farming in Athens township. They have two sons, Ray and Joel. For some years prior to her marriage Mrs. Lee was connected with her father in the newspaper business.

In public affairs Mr. Love has manifested a deep and active interest, and as the champion of many measures for the general good has promoted the welfare and upbuilding of his community. He was instrumental in securing the incorporation of the village of Athens and was appointed by the board of supervisors chairman of the registration and election board. He was also chairman of the committee to obtain right of way and subscriptions in securing for Athens a railroad, now the Battle Creek Division of the Michigan Central. He keeps in touch with modern though and progress and in his community exerts an influence that finds manifestation in the substantial improvement of his town and business.

GEORGE BENRITER.

Although George Benriter has resided in Battle Creek for only a limited time, he is a valued addition to the business circles of the city because of his enterprise and progressive spirit. He is now a member of the Smith & Benriter Company, limited,

dealers in books, stationery, office supplies, wall paper, paints and doing a general contracting business in decorating. Mr. Benriter was born in Monroe, Michigan, September 13, 1871, a son of Frank and Mary (Kull) Benriter. He acquired a common-school education in Monroe and when fourteen years of age went to Milwaukee to learn the plumbing business. After a year and a half he had so thoroughly mastered the trade that he went to Saginaw and worked as a journeyman at regular wages, but six months convinced him that this occupation was not entirely congenial and he gave up a position in which he was earning two dollars a day and accepted a clerkship in a retail wall paper and paint store at three dollars per week. In the new work, however, he found the occupation more to his liking. He spent three years in that establishment and after a year and a half was given charge of the wall paper department. While thus engaged he also gained some knowledge of decorating and has since been a student in this field of activity in which he has made rapid progress. In 1892 he went to Detroit, where he had charge of a wall paper store for five months, and then removed to Chicago, from which place he went upon the road as a traveling salesman for the Lartz Wall Paper Company, his territory covering Michigan, northern Indiana and portions of Ohio. July 1, 1903, the Lartz Wall Paper Company discontinued business and Mr. Benriter then became the traveling representative of the Gledhill Wall Paper Company of New York city, his territory being Michigan, northern Indiana and Illinois.

On the 4th of June, 1896, Mr. Benriter was united in marriage at North Branch, Lapeer county, Michigan, to Miss Eva

Hewitt, who was born in Genesee county, Michigan, a daughter of Albert and Mary (Hankins) Hewitt. They now have one son, Harold George, who was born in Grand Rapids in September, 1897.

After his marriage Mr. Benriter removed to Grand Rapids, where he made his home from 1896 until 1902. In the latter year he came to Battle Creek and purchased an interest in the business which is now being conducted under the name of The Smith & Benriter Company, limited. They carry an extensive line of books, stationery, office supplies, wall paper and paints, and since Mr. Benriter's connection with the store, there has been added a decorating department in which employment is furnished to about thirty men. He gives to this his supervision, and his knowledge of the art of decorating has made him one of the leading representatives of the business in this part of the state. He possesses the progressive spirit which has been the dominant factor in the development of the Mississippi Valley, and in his business affairs is energetic, wide-awake and determined, and such qualities are winning him desirable success. His political support is given to the Republican party and his social relations connects him with the Elks and the Knights of Pythias.

NELSON A. BEARDSLEE.

Nelson A. Beardslee, a dealer in boots and shoes in Battle Creek, was born in the township of Newton, Calhoun county, October 1, 1860. His father, Greenville Beardslee, was born in 1798 and when about ten years old was bound out to service until twenty-one, when he was to be taught the carpenter's trade and he aided in that work on the state prison at Auburn, New York, but not liking the service to which he was bound he left his employer and started out for himself when about fifteen years of age. He remained in the vicinity of Auburn or in Cayuga county and there he married Malana Stone. About 1832 he came to Calhoun county, Michigan, being one of its first settlers and his near neighbors were David Aldrich and Giddings Whitmore, all residents of the town of Fredonia. By his first marriage Mr. Beardslee had three children, two of whom are still living, Mrs. Caroline Cameron, of Marshall, Michigan, and Mrs. Elizabeth Lowell, of Des Moines, Iowa. After the death of his first wife Mr. Beardslee married Charlotte Lawton, who was born at Levanna, on Cayuga lake, New York, a daughter of Abner and Hannah Lawton, with whom she came to Michigan when about fourteen years of age, the family locating at Ann Arbor. With her first husband, Elisha Dorrance, she came to Battle Creek in 1845. In 1851 she became the wife of Greenville Beardslee and they had four children, of whom Greenville, Jr., is now a resident of Battle Creek, and Frank Josiah is a carpenter of Waterbury, Connecticut. Lottie became the wife of Charles H. Lawrence, with whom she removed to Hiawatha, Kansas, and died in that state August 16, 1871. Nelson is the youngest. The parents sold their farm in the fall of 1864 and bought the forty acres where the Postum Cereal plant is now located. This was entered from the government by the famous orator and statesman, Fred Douglass. The father died November 12, 1867, and the mother, with her youngest son, Nelson, moved to Hiawatha, Kansas, in 1871, where she remained until 1883, when they returned to Battle Creek and resided at the old homestead until she sold the property about 1893. Her death occurred in Battle Creek October 1, 1897, and she was laid by the side of her husband in Oak Hill cemetery.

Nelson A. Beardslee was but four years of age when the family removed to the forty acre farm. In 1871 he went with his mother to Hiawatha, Kansas, and there grew to manhood, acquiring a good education in the public schools and in the State University, at Lawrence, which he entered at the age of seventeen, there spending three years. He then engaged in teaching school for three years, after which he returned to Battle Creek, in 1883, and began clerking in a grocery store, while later he traveled for the Metal Album Company for two years. Again he was a clerk, this time in a hardware store, for three years, after which he was appointed a letter carrier and served for eight years. Then resigning he entered his present business April 1, 1899, securing a small stock of boots and shoes. He has, however, been forced to continually increase his facilities in order to meet the growing demands of this trade and now has a large stock and a liberal patronage.

On the 1st of May, 1889, Mr. Beardslee wedded Mrs. Edith Hall, nee Butler. They have two children: Dana DeForest, born in Battle Creek May 9, 1890, and Lawrence Llewellyn, born December 30, 1901.

Since casting his first presidential vote for Blaine in 1884, Mr. Beardslee has been a stanch Republican, but never an office seeker. He belongs to the Knights of Pythias fraternity, of which he is past chancellor, and is connected with the Foresters and Knights of the Maccabees. His business interests, however, chiefly claim his attention, and in addition to his mercantile affairs, he is a stockholder in the United States Register Company, manufacturing side-wall registers for furnaces. In 1883 he and his mother platted what was known as Beardslee's addition to Battle Creek and purchased the interests of the other heirs in the property, a part of which he still owns. His business ability is pronounced and he has attained a position of prominence in trade circles in Battle Creek.

GEORGE RILEY BURNHAM.

George R. Burnham, who for many years was an active business man of Battle Creek, was born in Pendleton, Niagara county, New York, June 11, 1834. His grandfather, Jacob O. Burnham, was born near Meriden, Connecticut, where he was reared and then removed to Otsego county, New York, where he married Lucy Bigelow, who lived to be almost one hundred years of age. The parents of our subject were Hiram O. and Caroline (Robinson) Burnham, who in 1842 came to Michigan. The father was a farmer and purchased land near Climax, spending his remaining days in Charleston township, Kalamazoo county, engaged in agricultural pursuits.

George R. Burnham was a lad of seven years when the family came to this state and on the home farm near Climax he was reared, while in the district schools he obtained his education. He was married November 14, 1861, in Charleston township, Kalamazoo county, to Miss Marietta A. Munn, who was born near what is now

Oakfield, Genesee county, New York, December 11, 1838, a daughter of Jesse and Abigail (Kimball) Munn. Her mother was a sister of Heber Kimball, vice president of the Mormon church and the associate and advisor of Brigham Young. Her father was Colonel Charles Farnham Kimball, who won his title in the War of 1812. He was born and reared in Montpelier, Vermont, and there married Anne Spaulding, while later they removed to Victor, New York. Mrs. Burnham's parents were married near Mendon, New York, and in that locality Mr. Munn secured wild land which he cultivated and improved, but later they removed to Genesee county. Mrs. Burnham came to Michigan with her sister, Mrs. D. C. Reed, and in this state met the gentleman to whom she gave her hand in marriage. It was in 1868 that Mr. and Mrs. Burnham came to Battle Creek and for a time he dealt in grain and hogs as a representative of J. M. Ward and later of Mr. Kellogg. Subsequently he began buying wool for the Middlesex Mills, of Lowell, Massachusetts with Mr. Zeno Gould, and for many years their purchases provided a good market for the wool producers of this region.

Unto Mr. and Mrs. Burnham was born one child, Inez Abbie, whose birth occurred September 12, 1862. She is a graduate of the Battle Creek high school and was married October 15, 1884, to George Adams, a grocer of this city. He was born in Whitley county, Indiana, where he was reared to manhood and acquired a good business education. He lived but six weeks after his marriage, passing away December 4, 1884, his remains being interred in Oak Hill cemetery. He was a charter member of Athelstan club and a popular

and prominent young man, highly esteemed in business as well as in social circles. His political support was given to the Democracy and he attended the Independent Congregational church.

Mr. Burnham was a Repulican in his political views and affiliations and was a stanch temperance man. Long a faithful member of the First Methodist Episcopal church, he served as one of its trustees for many years and in early life was a class leader. His death on the 28th of April, 1903, followed by his interment in Oak Hill cemetery, was deeply regretted by many friends, for during the years of his residence in Battle Creek his sterling work, business honor and loyalty in friendship had won him uniform regard.

WILLIAM KIRKPATRICK.

William Kirkpatrick, now deceased, was a resident of Battle Creek township and was among the worthy sons that Ireland has sent to the new world. He never sought the prestige of place or political power, but directed his energies into business channels, wherein his diligence and effort won him creditable success and enabled him to provide a comfortable home for his family, in whose welfare his interest centered. He was born in County Antrim, Ireland, on the 21st of October, 1830, and there spent his boyhood days. He heard favorable reports concerning America and the advantages offered for business success and in 1851, when twenty-one years of age, he severed the ties which bound him to the Green Isle, and crossing the Atlantic, he landed at New York city, where he remained for a time. Later he came to Michigan and here began to work as a farm hand.

In 1857, however, William Kirkpatrick returned to the east and was married on the 13th of March of that year, in Newburg, New York, to Miss Isabella Moore, who was born in County Antrim, Ireland, on the 14th of May, 1828. On the day of their marriage they started westward, their wedding journey being the trip to Battle Creek. He had earned some money and in 1858 purchased the first land which he ever owned, and as his financial resources increased he added to his property from time to time until he owned three hundred and forty acres. The soil, rich and productive, yielded excellent harvests for his care and labor and he made splendid improvements on his farm, including the erection of a commodious and attractive residence and substantial barns and outbuildings. When he took possession of this place the only building upon it was a small log cabin, and in this he made his home until he was able to erect a more modern building. He had to clear the land, which up to this time was entirely unimproved, but soon the tract was placed under the plow and it was not long before his farm became recognized as one of the best improved properties of Battle Creek township.

The home of Mr. and Mrs. Kirkpatrick was blessed with nine children, of whom four died in infancy. The others are Ella, Elizabeth, Louise, William J. and Marie M. All were provided with good educational privileges, each one spending some time in the high school at Battle Creek, of which Ella and Louise are graduates. Both became successful teachers.

Louise, after completing the public school course spent two years in the Uni-

versity of Michigan, and then following a period devoted to educational work, she spent one summer as a student in the University of Chicago. In June, 1899, in company with her sister, Marie M., she made a trip to Europe. They went to Germany, Austria, Italy, Switzerland, Belgium, France and England, visiting many places of modern and historic interest in these various countries, and lastly they went to Ireland, where they looked upon the scenes amid which their father had spent the days of his boyhood and youth and also visited the room in which their mother was born. It was a most enjoyable trip and brought to them the culture and broad knowledge that is only secured through travel. The eldest daughter, Ella, is now the wife of Eugene B. Root, a resident of Los Angeles, California, and they have one child, Helen. Elizabeth has become the wife of Fred W. Barney, of Battle Creek, and they have three children, Oliver, Isabel and Helen. Louise is now a teacher in the high school of Battle Creek. William J., who acquired a good business education, is now engaged in dealing in coal, wood, hay, grain and other commodities in this city. He was married in 1895 at the home of the bride. Miss Jean B. White, of Albany, New York, and they have three children, Mildred, Madalene and Leland. Marie M., who completes the family, is yet residing with her mother.

Mr. Kirkpatrick was a devoted husband and father and a man who possessed many sterling traits of character. He gave his political support to the Democracy, but neither sought nor desired office, although he held at one time the office of justice of the peace and was most loyal in the discharge of his duties. He belonged to the

Presbyterian church for many years, took an active part in its work and at the time of his demise was serving as one of its elders. His death occurred October 6, 1888, and he was laid to rest in Reese cemetery, in Battle Creek township. Thus ended the life record of an honorable man, who through his perseverance and untiring labors won success and who also gained an untarnished name. The concensus of public opinion accorded him a foremost position among the people of his community, because his life was characterized by all that is straightforward and reliable, and when he passed away his death was the occasion of a grief that was at once general and sincere.

ONYX ADAMS.

At an early epoch in the development and improvement of Calhoun county, Onyx Adams located within its borders and was long known as a leading farmer of Battle Creek township. He was born in Milton, Vermont, in 1843. His father, Hector Adams, born in Burlington, Vermont, September 27, 1800, was a son of Benjamin Adams, who died in the Green Mountain state. The latter was a son of Benjamin and Hannah Adams, the former born October 30, 1765. The grandfather of our subject died in Milton, April 11, 1842. On the 10th of October, 1772, he had married Susan Snell, and they were the parents of four sons and six daughters, of whom Hector was the fifth in order of birth. The mother passed away May 4, 1850.

Hector Adams remained with his father until November 13, 1823. He attended the common schools and after attaining the age of eighteen spent six or eight months in the study of Latin. He engaged in teaching, giving instruction in reading, spelling, writing and geography. English grammar was not then taught and geography was little more than a farce. On the 2d of April, 1821, he went to Milton, Vermont, where he began the study of law under the direction of Herman Allen, a talented attorney with whom he also boarded. At the February term of court in 1823, in Grand Isle county, he was admitted to practice and followed the profession at different times in Chittenden, Grayton and Grand Isle with varied success until 1861. In the January term of the supreme court in Grand Isle county, in 1828, he was admitted to practice before the supreme court of that state, and in January, 1831, he was admitted to practice in the chancery courts, while in May, 1835, at Windsor, Vermont, he was admitted to practice in all of the United States courts. He felt himself but poorly qualified for the profession when he first became a member of the bar, but knowledge, experience, study and reading added greatly to his knowledge and he became successful in his chosen calling. On the 13th of November, 1823, Hector Adams wedded Laura Merriam, and in 1843 they removed to Milton, Vermont, living there until October 24, 1861, when they came to Michigan and withdrawing from the bar Mr. Adams lived a retired life. In 1857 he purchased two farms here and the original homestead of the family is still in possession of representatives of the name.

Hector Adams was quite prominent in public affairs and was honored with many offices. In 1823 he became examiner of school teachers and thus served five years; was overseer of the poor three years; town

ONYX ADAMS
(FROM PHOTO TAKEN 1866)

MRS. BESSIE ADAMS

treasurer nine years; on the grand jury two years; postmaster of South Hero, Vermont, for nine years; justice of the peace for a quarter of a century; and first selectman for seven years. He was agent, auditor and treasurer of his town for one year each; trustee of surplus revenue for three years; for five years represented his district in the State Legislature; state's attorney for eight years; master of chancery eleven years; superintendent of schools two years; and many times acted as representative to the conventions of his party. His political allegiance was given to the Republican party after its formation. His activity in public life proved of benefit to the communities with which he was connected for his labors were ever directed toward the public good. For eight years Mr. Adams served as president of the Farmers' Mutual Fire Insurance Company of Calhoun county, and was one of its directors for three years. His death occurred in May, 1875, while he was visiting in Grand Isle, Vermont, and his wife died in Adamsville, Michigan, in 1889, her remains being interred in South Battle Creek. They were the parents of eight children, but only two are now living.

Onyx Adams spent his boyhood and youth in Vermont and when nineteen years of age came to Calhoun county, his sister, Mrs. Sanderson, living in Newton. This was two years before the arrival of his family. He followed farming and also engaged in teaching the district schools. In 1866, in Vermont, when twenty-two years of age, he was married to Bessie Wickware, a native of Colchester, that state, and he brought his bride to Michigan, settling upon the farm where they have since lived with the exception of three years spent upon the Jasper farm, his father having given up general

farming, at which time Onyx Adams took charge of the property. His time, however, was largely given to the development, cultivation and improvement of the farm in Battle Creek township, and his labors made it a valuable property.

Unto Mr. and Mrs. Adams were born seven children, of whom six are living: Nellie, the wife of Clarence Wheeler, was the oldest child. She died November 7, 1898, and is interred in Dubois cemetery at Battle Creek. She had two children, Ray and Lynn, whose home is with Mrs. Bessie Adams, their maternal grandmother. Ray was born at Arvilla, North Dakota, February 2, 1895, and Lynn in Battle Creek, Michigan, September 11, 1896. Rollin W., at home; Milton D., who married Ruth McCallam and resides in Battle Creek; Lillian, the wife of Charles Reid of Battle Creek, and the mother of two children, Russell and Maurice; Shirley, who was a volunteer of the Spanish-American war, and after his return from Santiago had the Cuban fever in Battle Creek. He was married September 16, 1903, at Battle Creek, to Miss Alta Arms; Orwin, and Julia, who is a teacher.

Mr. Adams usually endorsed the principles of the Republican party but voted independently of party ties. He served as clerk of his township and in other minor offices and at the time of his death was the secretary of the Calhoun Farmers' Mutual Fire Insurance Company. He passed away October 27, 1899, and his remains were interred in Dubois cemetery. The entire period of his manhood was passed in this county, and his reputation in business life and in citizenship was most creditable. He was active and energetic in agricultural pursuits, and in his dealings with his fellow men was honorable and reliable.

EDWARD MORRIS BRIGHAM.

While Edward M. Brigham has been a factor in the business life of Michigan, his chief interest and object in life has been scientific re-search and investigation concerning the pre-historic conditions and civilizations of the new world and as an explorer and lecturer his work has become known throughout the country. He has added to the world's scientific knowledge and accordingly is ranked with those whose names are engraven on the pages of history by reason of what they have accomplished in the field of science.

Mr. Brigham was born in Otsego township, Allegan county, Michigan, April 17, 1857, a son of Eben and Sarah (Warrant) Brigham. The father was a native of Shutesbury, Massachusetts, but at the age of two years was brought by his parents to this state. During the early years of his manhood he was a prosperous merchant in Plainwell, but becoming very ill was unable to again engage in labor until two years had passed, when in 1872 he came to Battle Creek and engaged in the sewing machine business, his physicians recommending an outdoor occupation. In more recent years he was a traveling salesman, representing the Kalamazoo Corset Company until his death, which occurred at Kalamazoo in March, 1900, his remains being brought back to Battle Creek for interment. His wife was born in Rochester, New York, and was educated in the Tracy Institute there. She possessed an exquisite sense of the beauty and harmony of nature and took the greatest delight in scientific re-search along natural lines. Botany was to her of especial interest and throughout her life she continued her studies of natural laws and enthused into her children her own interest in the work. She had three children, two of whom reached mature years. Her daughter, Mrs. Carrie B. Packard became particularly proficient in floral and landscape painting. At her death she left two daughters who were then cared for by the grandmother. The surviving son is the subject of this review. For a number of years prior to her death Mrs. Brigham had been planning a new family residence, which was to include a conservatory to furnish material for scientific work, a laboratory and space for the orderly storage of scientific collections. There was also to be a room for the meetings of a scientific society. From her girlhood she was a member of the Baptist church but had the true spirit of Christianity which transcends all denominational lines. She belonged to the Lake Avenue Benevolent Association and her deep interest in her fellowmen was manifest in active co-operation for the good of the race. Her life was attuned to harmony with nature and with all that is true and beautiful and no death in Battle Creek has ever been more deeply regretted.

Edward M. Brigham was about fourteen years of age when his parents came to Battle Creek and here he attended the high school, while later he spent three years in the State University, although his course there was not continuous. He entered upon his business career as a traveling salesman and has always had some business interests. While with the Kalamazoo Corset Company his attention was called to the need of a new clasp for corsets and he began working upon such a device. He has now perfected his invention and taken out patents in this and all other civilized countries; has also perfected machinery for the manufacture of the clasp and has organized a company to place his invention before the public in marketable form.

All through these years, however, Mr. Brigham has continued his scientific studies and re-searches, for his interest centers upon the laws of the natural world as manifest in animate and inanimate creation. In 1879 he went to South America with the Steere Exploring Expedition and spent the three months of vacation in this way, proceeding only to the island of Marajo in the mouth of the Amazon. They began excavations but had to abandon them. In 1881 Mr. Brigham again went to South America as the representative of the Albion and Hillsdale Colleges, the Public School Museum of Battle Creek and the Smithsonian Insitute at Washington, and sent to each a collection which he made while there. In 1884 he fitted out another expedition at his own expense, proceeding to the mouth of the Amazon and going up that stream as far as possible, then across the Andes to the Pacific coast. He also spent considerable time in the West Indies, making marine collections, this expedition being of fourteen months' duration; after which he returned by way of the isthmus. The trip, which he made in 1893, covered six months. He proceeded from New York, crossed the isthmus, continued the journey to Peru, to Lake Titicaca, Bolivia, and other points of historic and scientific interest. The results of his travels and researches have been given to the world not only in valuable collections given to museums but also in lectures which have won him wide renown. He felt that the new world was being neglected and for years, therefore, has devoted himself to explorations in South America with marked persistence, zeal and daring. In the intervals

between his travels he has lectured in various parts of the United States, addressing some of the largest audiences that have assembled in this country. His first lecture, entitled "The Other Half of the Discovery," treated of his explorations and travels over six thousand miles of the southern continent, including the region of the Andes and the Amazon; and was illustrated by pictures made from photographs taken on these expeditions. His second lecture was on the "Untold Treasures of Peru" and is composed of material gleaned from two trips into the country embraced in the empire of the Incas at the time of the discovery of America. He learned of their wonderful industrial life, their temples, castles, palaces, fortresses, citadels, bridges, quarries, monuments, fountains, hanging gardens, agricultural terraces, irrigation and drainage systems, as well as pastoral life, and brings all this vividly before his audiences not only by means of his word painting but also with the aid of the stereopticon. These lectures have attracted the most favorable comment of scientific and learned men as well as of popular audiences, and testimonials have been sent him from many of the most noted educators of the country, showing the value of his research and knowledge which he has given to the world of tribal races which flourished many centuries ago.

On the 29th of April, 1896, Mr. Brigham was married to Cora B. Sutherland, a native of Allegan county, and a daughter of Mortimer W. and Nettie (Potter) Sutherland. They have two children, Corabel, born in Battle Creek, July 22, 1901, and Edward Morris, born March 26, 1903. The parents are members of the Independent Congregational church, and in his political affiliations Mr. Brigham is a Republican, but has never been an active political worker nor office seeker. His genial disposition and social qualities have made him friends wherever he has gone both in this country and among the people of South America, while his scientific labors have won for him admiration and recognition among the most learned men of the continent. Long after he shall have passed away his work and the results of his investigations will remain as a monument to his memory and cause his name to be honored among men.

CARL GARTNER.

Twelve years ago Carl Gartner started out upon an independent business career in Battle Creek with almost no capital and to-day he is the leading baker of the city, conducting a business of large proportions and furnishing employment to more workmen than any other establishment of the kind in the city. Since 1884 he has lived in the county and his record has always been characterized by industry, ambition and capability.

Mr. Gartner was born near Heidelberg, Germany, November 24, 1870, a son of Julius and Elizabeth (Ruebel) Gartner. A small town near Heidelberg had been the home of the family through many generations and there our subject was reared, receiving the ordinary school privileges between the ages of six and fourteen years. He then came to America. He was a young boy to make the voyage alone and start out for himself with no pecuniary assistance and without the aid of influential friends, but he

possessed a courageous spirit and strong determination. He came at once to Battle Creek and soon obtained a position as a farm boy on the Betterly farm. He did not know a word of English at the time of his arrival, but in the two years he spent on the farm he became quite proficient in the use of the language. He then came to the city and served an apprenticeship to the baker's trade, being thus employed until twenty-one years of age, when he began business for himself on a small scale, doing his baking at night and attending to the sales department in the day time. He began with very limited stock, but he possessed energy and ability and soon worked his way upward, gradually increasing his business until its growth seems almost phenomenal. He was first located at No. 93 South Jefferson avenue, where he remained for eight years, when he purchased a lot and built a fine business block at No. 78 South Jefferson ·avenue, a two-story brick building, twenty-five by seventy-eight feet, which he utilizes for his business. He also built a building of similar size facing on Hamblin avenue, which is occupied as a bake shop. It is also a brick structure, is twenty-four by eighty-four feet, is supplied with all the latest improved machinery and patent ovens and is the only bake shop in the town thus completely equipped. In the rear of this he has a barn which furnishes shelter for his teams. He gives employment to seventeen men, which is more than double the number in the service of any other baker in the city, and his payroll amounts to over two hundred dollars per week. He also handles flour in wholesale quantities, supplying many of the stores and bakeries of the city, in addition to what he uses. He has made as many as thirty-four hundred loaves of bread in a single day, besides pies, cakes and other bakery goods in proportion. Thus it will be seen that his business has grown until it has reached mammoth proportions and has become one of the leading manufacturing enterprises of the city. His business ability is clearly demonstrated in the success of the business. In addition to his buildings he also owns other real estate in the city. Although he started in business with no capital October 31, 1891, he has met with a high degree of prosperity and is now at the head in his line in this section of the state.

Mr. Gartner is a member of the German Workingmen's Society and of the Lodge of Eagles. He was married on the 25th of November, 1891, to Miss Emma Rother, of Louisville, Kentucky, and in addition to their residence in this city they have a beautiful summer home at Gull lake, on Franklin beach. They are members of the German Evangelical church, and have a wide acquaintance and many friends in both places.

GEORGE M. EVARTS.

George Martin Evarts has resided in the vicinity of Battle Creek since 1851. Thus more than half a century has come and gone since his arrival and throughout this long period he has been an interested witness of the development and progress of the city, sharing in the work of improvement and indorsing all measures for the public good. As a pioneer resident, whose life has been active, useful and honorable, he well deserves mention in this volume. He was born at Middlebury, Vermont, July 4, 1821. His paternal grandfather, Gilbert

Evarts, was a soldier of the War of 1812 and spent much of his life in Connecticut, but his last days were passed in the home of his son, Martin Evarts. The latter, the father of our subject, was born at Salisbury, Connecticut, and when a young man removed to the Green Mountain state, where he carried on farming. Well fitted for leadership, he became a prominent and influential resident of the community and held the office of magistrate. He was a member of the Congregational church, well devoted to its work and faithful in his allegiance to its teachings. He wedded Mrs. Electra (Nobles) Foot.

In the public schools George Martin Evarts acquired his education and upon his father's farm became familiar with the labors and duties which fall to the lot of the agriculturist. On starting out in life for himself he came to Emmett township, Calhoun county, Michigan, where he purchased a farm, and as his financial resources increased he added to that property. Later, however, he sold his first land and bought other farms. In fact, he was continually engaged in buying and selling farms and his name was frequently found on the abstracts, either as the owner of property or the holder of a mortgage. By his judicious investments in real estate he gained a splendid competence. He was an excellent judge of land and manifested keen discrimination in his purchases which seldom failed to net him a good profit. He continued as an active farmer until 1886, when he sold his home property in Bedford township and purchased a residence at the corner of East Main and Mary streets, in Battle Creek. Here he has a beautiful location and a large lawn, eight by nine rods. There are many fruit and shade trees upon the place and the home is pleasing in appearance, constituting one of the attractive residences of this portion of the city. Mr. Evarts has also owned other city property. He is now living retired, his former business activity having brought to him a very desirable capital that enables him to rest from further labor.

The lady by whose side he has now traveled life's journey for many years was in her maidenhood Miss Eliza A. Sessions, of Middlebury, Vermont, a daughter of Daniel and Esther (Champlin) Sessions. Her father was a farmer and also engaged in the operation of a lumber mill. Her grandfather, Paul Champlin, was one of nature's noblemen, his life being ever upright and honorable, his character strong and steadfast. He was one of the most prominent residents of Middlebury and a man whom to know was to respect and honor. It was in Middlebury that Mrs. Evarts was reared and educated. She has been to her husband a faithful companion and helpmate on the journey of life, and because of her kindly spirit, broad sympathy and many excellent traits of character she has won the love and respect of many friends, and the world is better for her having lived.

In his political affiliations in early life Mr. Evarts was a Whig and upon the organization of the new Republican party he became one of its first supporters. He has held different township offices, but has never been an aspirant for political preferment, desiring rather to give his time and attention to his business affairs. He has seen Battle Creek grow from a town of twenty-seven hundred to a city of many thousand and has been deeply interested in the progress, development and substantial improvement of Calhoun county. He and his wife have been for many years attendants and supporters of the Independent Congregational church. Through an active business career he has so conducted his affairs that he has not only won success but also a good name.

FREDERICK E. PERRY.

Frederick Edwin Perry, now deceased, was for some years a well known agriculturist of Calhoun county, making his home in Battle Creek township and the qualities of an upright manhood were his and endeared him to those with whom he came in contact. He was born in Orleans county, New York, on the 24th of February, 1813, and his life's record covered seventy-eight years, his death occurring on the 24th of April, 1891.

On first coming to Michigan Mr. Perry purchased a tract of land and then returned to New York, where he remained for two years. On the expiration of that period he again came to this state, where he continued to reside until his demise. The journey from Detroit to this place was made partly on foot and partly with an ox team. All was wild and unimproved here, pioneer conditions existing on all sides and Mr. Perry cast his lot with the early settlers who were re-claiming the land for the purposes of civilization. He had a farm of one hundred and twenty acres, for which he paid eight dollars per acre. The new place was uncultivated save a tract of ten acres which had been cleared and on which stood a log house. As the years passed he developed an excellent farm until the well cultivated fields yielded golden harvests in return for the care and labor bestowed upon them. Mr. Perry also replaced his pioneer buildings by those of modern construction and ultimately his farm was known as one of the best improved in the locality because of his attractive residence and substantial outbuildings. He speculated quite largely in real estate and at different times was the owner of extensive tracts of land.

In New York, Frederick E. Perry was united in marriage to Miss Emily Treadway, who was born on the 15th of October, 1818, and who died on the 23d of June, 1845. Their children were Elbert, Harriet, Eugene and Helen M. Of this number Eugene is now living retired at Goguac lake, Battle Creek. For his second wife Mr. Perry chose Miss Clamana Stevens, who was born on the 4th of October, 1816, and who died on the 22d of April, 1877. The children of this marriage were Emily C., who died in childhood; Helen A., who is now Mrs. Dickerson and makes her home in Florida; George S., who resides on the home farm; Mrs. Caroline Pugsley, who resides at Eaton Rapids, Michigan; and Robert, deceased. In his political views Mr. Perry was a Republican and in antebellum days was a stanch advocate of Abolition principles. In the Baptist church he was a prominent and influential member and did all in his power to promote its growth and extend its influence.

George S. Perry, who now occupies the home farm and is a practical and progressive agriculturalist of Battle Creek township, was born in this township on the 1st of July, 1849, and was reared under the parental roof in the usual manner of the farmer lads of the period. He began his education in the district schools and attended through the winter months while in the summer seasons he worked in the fields and meadows. Throughout his entire life he has carried on general farming and has met with success in his undertakings. He is widely known as a capable and enterprising agriculturalist of the community and the fine appearance of his property indicates his careful supervision.

When twenty-five years of age Mr. Perry was united in marriage to Miss Luella M. Johnson, a native of Vermont, who died in 1878 and was buried in Williston, Vermont. On the 20th of October, 1880, Mr. Perry wedded Alice E. Thompson, who was born in Ontario county, New York, and when a child came to Calhoun county with her parents, Archibald R. and Laura (Piper) Thompson. They have had eight children: Luella, who became the wife of William Rosier, died leaving one child, Glenn, who resides with his grandfather on the home farm. The others are Ada, George A., Edwin M., Winifred, Lora, Harry and one that died in infancy. Mrs. Perry was a member of the Methodist Episcopal church. In his political views Mr. Perry is independent, supporting the men whom he thinks best qualified for office and the measures which he believes will contribute most largely to the general good.

CHARLES N. FELLOWS.

Charles N. Fellows, who is a well known representative of an honored pioneer family of Calhoun county and for many years an active and enterprising farmer here, was born in Elba, Genesee county, New York, November 22, 1838. His father, Asa Fellows, was born in Franklin county, Massachusetts, June 11,

1802, and was a son of Solomon Fellows, one of the patriot soldiers of the Revolutionary war. In early life Asa Fellows learned the trade of a woolen manufacturer and followed it until after his marriage, which occurred in Riga, Monroe county, New York, November 8, 1830, Miss Lucy Baldwin Morse becoming his wife. She was born November 26, 1808. The young people began their domestic life upon a farm in the Empire state and there lived until 1846, when they drove to Buffalo, whence they took passage on a lake vessel bound for Detroit and from the latter place they drove across the country to Calhoun county, Michigan, settling upon a farm of one hundred and eighty acres on section 27, Bedford township. Later he sold forty acres and of the remainder only forty acres had been broken. By the cultivation of the fields and the erection of substantial buildings Mr. Fellows developed a fine property and his farm became very productive. Later he sold there and bought eighty acres on section 15, Bedford township, where Mr. Charles N. Fellows is now living.

Unto Asa and Lucy Fellows were born four children, of whom one died in early life. Lura A., born December 15, 1834, is now the widow of Garrett Vedder and resides at No. 516 West Main street, in Battle Creek; Charles N. was the second, Emma F., born August 21, 1841, is the widow of William Haug. The father died March 12, 1890, and the mother's death occurred September 29, 1862. They were members of the Presbyterian church and he was a Republican and earlier a strong Abolitionist, voting that ticket when there were only two or three in the neighborhood that held similar views.

Charles N. Fellows attended the district

schools, spending a year or two in a log school house, and later he began farming, which occupation he has since followed on the old family homestead with the exception of the year 1890, when he went to Tennessee, where he conducted a sawmill in connection with agricultural pursuits.

On the 3d of March, 1864, Mr. Fellows wedded Charlotte A. Acheson, who was born August 22, 1839, in Ontario county, New York, a daughter of Alexander and Jane (Harrison) Acheson. Her father was born in 1801 and was married December 22, 1824. Both he and his wife were natives of County Roscommon, Ireland, and he came to America when nineteen years of age. By trade he was a blacksmith, but at the age of thirty he began preaching the gospel as a member of the Methodist Episcopal church, and later became connected with the Methodist Protestant church. He was engaged in preaching in Leroy township, Calhoun county, when he contracted a fever and died March 1, 1866. It was in 1854 that he brought his family to this state and here Mrs. Fellows was reared. Two children grace this marriage: Jessie Benton, born June 14, 1866, and Frank C., born December 7, 1877, and now in the employ of the Michigan Central railroad at Detroit. Our subject and his wife are both representatives of old and respected pioneer families of Michigan.

DEWITT C. ADDINGTON, M. D.

In a successful career as a member of the medical profession, Dr. Dewitt C. Addington gained recognition as one of the most able representatives of his profession, win-

DEWITT C. ADDINGTON, M. D.

ning the respect of his brethren of the fraternity, and the confidence of the public. In the evening of life, he put aside the arduous duties of the calling to spend his remaining days in retirement and in the superintendence of his invested interests, and thus he lived, until called to his final rest December 2, 1903.

A native of Aurora, Erie county, New York, he was born December 12, 1828, his parents being Hawxhurst and Hulda M. (Abbott) Addington. The father was born in Long Island and was a son of Hosea Addington. At the place of his nativity he was reared, and at an early day removed to Erie county, New York, where he became a prominent and influential citizen, and an extensive landowner, but later in life lost some of his property in Buffalo, in land speculations. He passed away in Erie county as did his wife, who was born in Bennington, Vermont, and was a daughter of Seth Abbott, a representative of an early New England family. The Doctor pursued his education in the schools of Erie county and in an academy at Buffalo. When about eighteen years of age he began teaching, which profession he followed for four terms. He also became the successor of the township superintendent of schools. Later Dr. Addington entered the office of Drs. Nott and Prindle, the leading physicians of Erie county, who directed his reading for three years. He attended a course of lectures at the Buffalo Medical College, and his father having a very extensive and practical knowledge of indigenous plants and their uses, desired his son to enter the office of Dr. Blakely, who was a leading botanical physician. Dr. Addington remained with that gentleman for three years, practicing a portion of the time. He spent six or seven years in the preparation of his profession,

and was thus splendidly qualified for the important duties which devolve upon the physician when he entered upon his chosen life's work. For four years he practiced in his native county, and for two years at McKean, Erie county, Pennsylvania, where he met with good success. The opportunities of the growing west, however, attracted him, and in October, 1857, he arrived in Battle Creek.

The city was then a mere hamlet, but Dr. Addington opened his office and soon gained a large and lucrative business. He made his home here continuously from that time, although he had spent four winters in California on account of the severity of the climate here. Through nearly half a century he labored among the people of this city and vicinity, in the alleviation of human suffering and the place which he occupied in the hearts of many as the loved family physician cannot adequately be expressed in words, but is manifested by the expressions of gratitude, friendship and good will which are heard on all sides when Dr. Addington is mentioned. He gained a very large patronage and not until he decided to retire from practice did his business cease growing. He always kept in touch with the progress of the times, read broadly and carried his investigations far and wide into the realms of medical science. After coming to the west he continued his studies and was a graduate of the Bennett Medical College of Chicago of the class of 1877. While in that institution he became a member of the Eclectic Medical Society. The Doctor was also quite extensively engaged in dealing in real estate, handling both city and country property, and owned valuable realty here.

Dr. Addington's first marriage was to Miss Bryan, a daughter of Judge Russell Bryan, of Eagle, New York, and unto them was born one son, Spencer Howard, who died when young at Erie, Pennsylvania; and two daughters, Helen M., now the wife of Frederick Russell, of Kansas City, Missouri; and Aylett Amanda, the wife of Frank Wagner, of Battle Creek. They have one son, John A. In 1880 Dr. Addington wedded Miss Maria Antoinette Davidson, of Battle Creek, a daughter of William Davidson, who came to this city from Cherry Valley, Otsego county, New York. For many years Dr. Addington's office was at the corner of Main and McCamly streets where the Post block now stands. In politics he was independent as he was also in religious views. There was no man who had a stricter regard for right, justice and truth than had Dr. Addington. He was liberal in his support of good causes, generous in his contributions to benevolent objects and most kindly and charitable to the poor. He was a man of wide experience and broad mind, who had many friends all over the state, being one who was clearly entitled to be classed as one of nature's noblemen—a man whose strong individuality was the strength of integrity, virtue and deep human sympathy.

MARY CLARK, M. D.

For nearly fifty years Dr. Mary Clark has engaged in the practice of medicine and has undoubtedly practiced longer than any other physician of Central Michigan. She was born in Dansville, Livingston Co., N. Y., a daughter of Ashville R. and Laura (Williams) Grover. The family were early pioneers of New York and the father followed farming in the Empire state until 1844, when he removed to Barry county, Michi-

gan, where he purchased a large tract of new land. He had a log house in the midst of the green woods and there lived for a number of years before he could get material for the erection of a larger dwelling. He cleared his land and developed a fine farm, upon which he and his wife spent their remaining days. They were members of the Methodist Episcopal church and their home was always open for the reception of the early ministers who visited the neighborhood.

Amid such scenes Dr. Clark spent her early girlhood days and at the age of ten came to Battle Creek, at which time there was but a single store in the place, and it stood in the middle of the road. She lived at the home of Reuben Pew, who was then the leading man of the place and who regarded Miss Grover as his child. She obtained a good education here and by her own reading and study has continually broadened her knowledge until her mental attainments have reached a scholarly nature. After her school days were over, and when she was about sixteen years of age, she became possessed of a strong desire to practice medicine, and began reading with Dr. Brown, a leading physician of Michigan, then residing at Albion, and who at different times was president of the State Medical Association. For about twelve years she continued her studies with him, but possessing natural gifts for the profession, she began practice when twenty-three years of age and met with marked success from the beginning. She first located in Albion, where she soon gained a lucrative patronage. Later she was called to Kalamazoo to treat a banker and built up a most successful practice there, not only winning desirable financial returns for her labor, but also gaining a splendid reputation for success in the cure of chronic diseases to which she has ever given special attention.

Dr. Clark was called to Burlington, Iowa, to treat Mrs. Grimes, wife of Senator Grimes. Mrs. Grimes had traveled in Europe for four years and had been treated by the most celebrated physicians without success. Mrs. Clark, in three and one-half hours located the trouble, and cured her by magnetic hand massage. While at Burlington she treated over four hundred people, and could not get away until she had nervous prostration, caused from overwork, and for sixteen weeks was laid up, but cured herself without the use of medicines. A number of leading citizens of that place persuaded her to open an office there and again she soon demonstrated her ability to cope with the intricate problems of disease. But the climate did not agree with her and she returned to Battle Creek, where most of her active business life has been passed. Through a quarter of a century she has now devoted her attention to home practice and many remarkable cures are credited to her skill and superior ability. She does not adhere in her practice to any particular school of medicine but with the comprehensive knowledge of the science, she uses the methods which she thinks will prove most helpful in each specific case and her labors have been fraught with blessings to others. Her knowledge of medicine is supplemented by a strong and magnetic personality and what may well be termed a God-given insight into the needs of suffering humanity. Great changes have occurred since Dr. Clark entered upon practice nearly fifty years ago. At that time it required great courage to face the popular opinion against the woman physician, but she gradually overcame all opposition and to-day is one of the most popular and honored as well as successful women physicians of this portion of the state. She continually endeavored to broaden her knowledge and thus render her efforts more effective. To this end she attended lectures in both Chicago and Cincinnati and her fame has gone abroad throughout the United States. She has been called to Washington for the treatment of United States Senators, and several would not be there now except for her wonderful ability to cure; and her services have also been sought in wealthy homes in Hartford, Connecticut; and Minneapolis, Minnesota. In all of these cities she effected remarkable cures, having frequently been solicited to take charge of a case after other physicians had failed. She seems never at fault in the diagnosis of a case and when she recognizes the fact that the patient is beyond help, frankly admits it, but in the large majority of instances her labors have proven most beneficial in coping with diseases and restoring to man his most priceless heritage—heatlh.

George Ward, of Chicago, at three different times has rented an office for her opposite the Palmer House in Chicago and guaranteed her six thousand dollars and all expenses for six months if she would come there, but she loves Battle Creek too well to leave. She has so many dear friends here and prefers to remain in the city that has been so many years her home and where she has met with such marked success.

The Doctor was married in 1851, becoming the wife of Erastus Clark, of Battle Creek, who was a partner of her foster father engaged in the hotel business. He was a leading and popular hotel proprietor until his health failed him. Having gone security for a man who failed to meet his indebtedness Mr. Clark was called upon to stand the amount and his loss effected his mind. For over twenty years thereafter Dr. Clark took care of her husband, his business interests, and her own practice. He died in 1885 leaving one son Edwin Everett Clark, who is now an architect and builder of Battle Creek and who was for some years a druggist of this city. For many years the Doctor has held membership in the Episcopal church, but the demands made upon her time for professional service renders it impossible for her to engage actively in church work at the present time. Having long since gained public favor by reason of her acknowledged skill, her womanly qualities, and her kindly spirit. Dr. Clark has for many years occupied a most enviable and creditable position in the ranks of the medical fraternity of Michigan.

GEORGE G. CUMMINGS.

George G. Cummings, a retired farmer now living in Battle Creek, has resided in Calhoun county since 1872. His parents were Asher T. and Permelia (Willett) Cummings and in the family home in Onondaga township, Onondaga county, New York, his birth occurred on the 15th of June, 1828. His father was a native of Connecticut and a representative of an old New England family. Oliver Cummings, the paternal grandfather of our subject, became one of the pioneer settlers of Onondaga county, New York, locating within its borders when the work of improvement had scarcely been begun there. Through-out his remaining days he lived in that locality. Asher T. Cummings was an extensive farmer of Onondaga county and an influential and leading man in his locality.

He wedded Permelia Willett, whose family also came from Connecticut, the father being William Willett. Mr. Cummings spent his active life in the Empire state, but after the death of his wife came to Michigan to live with his son George and here passed away in 1876.

In taking up the personal history of our subject we present to our readers the life record of one widely and favorably known in Calhoun county. He was the eldest son in a family of four children and obtained a good common school education, remaining upon the homestead farm until he had attained his majority. In November, 1848, he wedded Miss Jeannette Wood, of Onondaga county, New York, and then engaged in farming in the Empire state until his removal to Michigan in 1860. He first purchased a farm in Charleston township, Kalamazoo county, comprising one hundred and fifty acres for which he paid fifty-five dollars per acre. Five or six years later he sold that property for ninety dollars per acre and then bought two hundred and eighty acres of land in Convis township, Calhoun county, where he was extensively engaged in farming, his well tilled fields returning to him golden harvests. His wife died in 1876, leaving three children: William, now of Lansing, Michigan, married Miss Harriet Huggett. They have one son, Fred; Charles, at Battle Creek, who married Miss Augusta Jandell. They are the parents of five children: Grace, Louise, Le Verne, Belva, and Harold; and Frank, of Lafayette, Indiana. Later Mr. Cummings wedded Mrs. Jane Kane, of Battle Creek township, and unto them was born a daughter Georgia, who is now the wife of Edgar Van Valin of Battle Creek. The second wife, however, died when the daughter was a small child.

Mr. Cummings continued to reside upon his farm until 1900, although he retired from its active management many years before. He then removed to this city and has since occupied a beautiful home at No. 33 Merritt street, which he had previously purchased and which later he gave to his daughter. Indolence and idleness, however, are utterly foreign to his nature and for the sake of having something to occupy his time he has to some extent engaged in housepainting. His political support has long been given to the Democracy. In religious faith he is a Baptist, but does not belong to the church. His life has been quietly and uneventfully passed, yet his history is well worthy of consideration for it shows that in the every-day walks of life one may find abundant scope for the exercise of energy and business capacity. As an agriculturist Mr. Cummings has lived and labored and to-day as the reward of his diligence and earnest purpose is the possessor of a handsome competence which supplies him with all the necessaries and many of the comforts of life.

ALFRED LATTA.

Alfred Latta, now deceased, was actively associated with the work of development and improvement in Battle Creek for many years. As a real estate dealer he would buy land, improve it by the erection of substantial buildings and then sell. In this way he added to the upbuilding of the city as well as to his individual success and his operations were guided by such reliable business methods that he won the unqualified confidence of the public.

Mr. Latta was born in Lewiston, New York, April 6, 1821, a son of John and Milly (Smith) Latta. The father was an extensive property owner who had land near Lewiston and a large tannery and other business interests. During the War of 1812 his tannery and other buildings were destroyed by fire, but after the close of hostilities he rebuilt and continued to make his home in Lewiston until called to his final rest. His son Alfred was there reared and acquired a good academic education. He was one of twins in a family of ten children, eight sons, not one of whom was ever intoxicated or formed any bad habits. His twin brother Albert now lives on Grand Prairie near Kalamazoo, Michigan. Alfred Latta wished to attend college and prepare for the bar, but as his father needed his assistance in business he put aside his cherished plan and worked in connection with the management of his father's interests. When twenty-one years of age he went to Wisconsin, where he took up land from the government but after a year and a half returned to New York at the request of his father to look after his interests. A well informed man, he taught school in both New York and Wisconsin.

It was on the 6th of April, 1848, in Parma, New York, that Alfred Latta was married to Miss Martha E. Hill, who was born at Livonia Center, Livingston county, a daughter of Rufus and Sarah W. (Brown) Hill, who removed to Lewiston, New York, during the early girlhood of their daughter. When she was eleven years of age she had attended school where Mr. Latta was a teacher. She received a good education, partly under private instruction and three times she had her trunk packed preparatory to going to college, when failing health forced her to forego this plan. Mr. and Mrs. Latta remained in Lewiston for four years and then started westward with the intention of going to Minneapolis, but stopping at Kalamazoo. Mr. Latta there invested in property and began dealing in real estate. In 1865 he purchased a farm of six hundred acres in Pennfield township, east of Battle Creek, and this he divided into lots and afterward sold. Removing then to the city he began real estate operations here, buying, improving and afterward selling property until he became one of the most active factors in the substantial upbuilding of the city. His business was conducted along progressive lines and brought him gratifying success.

Unto Mr. and Mrs. Latta were born five children: Sarah P., the wife of Eli S. Glover, of Pullman, Washington, by whom she has four children—Grace, Edith, Arthur L. and Sheldon L.; Frank Hill, who is now postmaster at Battle Creek; Mary L., the wife of A. R. McIntyre, who was assistant superintendent of the Grand Trunk Railroad for years and lives in Battle Creek; Alice M., the wife of Clarence J. Paul, an attorney of Minneapolis, by whom she has two daughters, Florence and Leila; and Homer A., a stockholder and director of the Union Steam Pump Co., who married Lulu Perry and resides at No. 202 North avenue.

Mr. Latta passed away January 13, 1887, and Battle Creek thus lost one of its valued and honored citizens. In politics he was a Whig in early life and voted for Henry Clay. In 1856 he became a Republican, supporting Fremont, and remained an advocate of that party until his death. He was a stanch advocate of educational advancement and was really ahead of his times in this way. When he advocated manual training he was called visionary but could he have seen the schools of the country to-day he would find that in every city his idea is now embodied in the curriculum. After his marriage he became a member of the Congregational church, his wife having been reared in that faith. He was a kind and indulgent husband and father, and the filial love and care which he bestowed upon his father, even to the sacrifice of his own interests, foreshadowed the consideration which he ever gave to his wife and children. He was a man of five feet, nine inches in height, weighing from one hundred and ninety to one hundred and ninety-five pounds, was of fair complexion, with light hair and blue eyes. His expression was genial and kindly and yet he was not without that strength of character which is the basis of all forceful manhood. In his business affairs he prospered and took great delight in providing the comforts of life for his family. He might well have been called one of nature's noblemen, for his life was actuated by high principles and free from all that was degrading, and his memory remains as a blessed possession to his family and friends.

SAMUEL J. TITUS.

Through fifty years, the firm name of Titus & Hicks has figured in the business history of Battle Creek, and while the senior members have passed away, the sons have taken up the work of the fathers, and have carried it on, enlarging the scope of the business in order to keep pace with the progressive spirit of the times. The firm of Titus & Hicks to-day owns and controls the Star Flouring Mills, an industry of importance, having a large output.

Samuel J. Titus, whose name introduces this review, and who is the senior proprietor of the present firm, was born on the 16th of January, 1846, in the family home at No. 115 Maple street, in this city, his parents being Richard F. and Frances (Walling) Titus. The father was born at New Rochelle, New York, on the 20th of October, 1800, and his parents were Samuel and Sarah (Pearsall) Titus. The paternal grandfather of our subject was a miller at New Rochelle and in his youth Richard F. Titus became familiar with the business, working in his father's mill. Afterward, however, he went to sea and followed that life for many years, working his way upward with great rapidity, until at the early age of eighteen years he was serving as captain of a vessel. He sailed in the West Indies and South American trades until, abandoning the sea, he came to Battle Creek in 1843. The following year he was married in Cleveland, Ohio, and at once brought his bride to this city. For a time he was engaged in merchandising in partnership with Jonathan Hart, and later, was engaged in the lard and oil business with Henry Cantine. In 1853, however, he purchased the interest in the mill of Chester Buckley, and in the control of this enterprise was associated with Ellery Hicks, who had previously become part owner of the mill. Thus the firm of Titus & Hicks was formed and the name has since been maintained. Mr. Hicks, however, died soon afterward and was succeeded by his son, William, who is the partner of Samuel J.

Titus, of this review. Richard F. Titus died in 1868, and our subject then succeeded to his place in the business, so that the firm name of Titus & Hicks has been retained for a half century. Mr. Titus was a birthright member of the Society of Friends and was loyal to its teachings and the principles which it inculcated among its representatives. In ante-bellum days he was a stanch advocate of the cause of abolition and his influence was ever given for the benefit of freedom, peace and right. In his family were two sons, and the younger, Richard Titus, died at the age of three years.

In taking up the personal history of Samuel J. Titus we present to our readers the life record of one who is widely and favorably known in Battle Creek. He completed the high school course in this city and afterward spent a year in the Commercial College here. On putting aside his text books to enter upon his business career he became bookkeeper for V. P. Collier, a hardware merchant of Battle Creek, and subsequently acted in the same capacity for the Upton & Brown Threshing Machine Company. In 1867 he entered the mill and has since been active in its control and operation. He and his partner have worked together in entire harmony and established an industry of importance to the city, which is a source of desirable revenue to them as well. In 1874 they tore down the old mill and erected the present structure, increasing the capacity from twenty-five to one hundred and twenty-five barrels of flour per day. The old Burr system was still retained, but in 1885 was replaced by a modern roller process and the capacity of the mill was increased to two hundred barrels. It is operated by water power and the output is of such excellent quality that the product finds a ready and profitable sale upon the market.

Mr. Titus has for many years been a member of the State Millers' Association and was at one time its vice president, while for several years he has been one of its directors. He is well known among the representatives of his chosen line of business in Michigan and has ever kept abreast with modern methods and improvements. For seven or eight years he has been treasurer of the Michigan Millers' Mutual Fire Insurance Company, which is now established on a strong financial basis with a cash surplus of over a quarter of a million dollars and cash assets amounting to over one million three hundred thousand dollars, while it paid in compensation of losses in 1903 the sum of two hundred and twenty-seven thousand dollars. This is one of the strongest and most reliable mutual companies of the state. Mr. Titus has also been a director of the National Bank of Battle Creek since 1894, and in his business career he has steadily advanced until he now occupies a foremost position among the representative men of worth and prominence in this city.

On the 21st of November, 1871, Mr. Titus was united in marriage to Miss Kate F. Hill, of East Aurora, New York, and unto them have been born three children, June who is now the wife of William H. Skinner, of Battle Creek; Frances H., and Richard H. Mr. Titus now has a beautiful home at No. 115 Maple street. It is the house in which he was born, but has been greatly remodeled and improved, being transformed into a modern residence with all the equipments and accessories known to the modern dwelling of the twentieth century.

Since age gave to Mr. Titus the right of franchise he has supported the men and measures of the Republican party, casting his first presidential vote for Grant in 1868. While he keeps well informed on the questions and issues of the day, he has never been a politician in the sense of office seeking. He attends the Episcopal church, although not a member, and is serving as one of its vestrymen. Socially he is connected with the Benevolent and Protective Order of Elks; and aided in the organization of the Ancient Order of United Workmen, of which he is a charter member. He also belongs to and is a director of the Athelstan club. The fact that many of the warmest friends of Mr. Titus are numbered among those who have known him from boyhood is an indication of an upright and honorable career. He has labored continuously along lines of business activity, bringing a good return; and the favorable judgment which the world passed upon him at the outset of his career has in no degree been set aside or modified, but, in fact, has been strengthened as the years have passed.

WALTER S. KEET.

As a citizen of public spirit and progressive, as a business man, capable, enterprising and determined, Mr. Keet has left the impress of his individuality upon the public life of Battle Creek, and to-day is one of its leading and valued citizens. He is the sole proprietor of a very extensive undertaking establishment, in fact, one of the largest of southern Michigan, and, at the present writing, he is actively associated with the edu-

W. S. Kurl—

cational work of the city as a member of the school board.

Mr. Keet was born in Waterloo, New York, October 16, 1857, a son of George and Maria (Bedle) Keeta. The father was born in Richmond, a part of London, England, October 10, 1810, and there learned the trade of a carpenter and millwright. He was also married there to Miss Bedle, whose birth occurred in the same city, and in 1835 he brought his family to the United States, locating in Waterloo, New York, where he carried on business for a few years. His death occurred July 14, 1889, and his wife passed away in 1859, when her son Walter was but a year old. In public affairs Mr. Keet had become prominent and influential in Waterloo, and served as assessor of his township. Both he and his wife held membership in the Episcopal church.

Walter S. Keet, the youngest of thirteen children, obtained his education in the public schools of his native city and after putting aside his text books, learned the trade of carpenter and millwright with his father. In December, 1878, he came to Battle Creek and began working at his trade in the employ of Nichols & Shepard, with whom he continued for seven years, when he entered upon an independent business career as a carpenter and builder. He followed that pursuit until 1890, when he joined the firm of Baker & Caldwell, undertakers of Battle Creek, with whom he remained for four years. He next purchased a stock of furniture and undertaking goods of J. H. Mykins on West Main street, where he successfully engaged in business for two years. After the dissolution of the firm of Baker & Caldwell he joined the former gentleman in the partnership under the firm style of Baker

8

& Keet, the new enterprise being established on the 1st of March, 1897. They continued in the furniture and undertaking business until the spring of 1903, when they closed out the furniture business in order to devote their entire time to the undertaking department, the business of which had grown to extensive proportions, in fact, the trade had increased until their business ranked first in this section of the state, its proportions being such that it became necessary that exclusive attention should be devoted to this line. The partnership was maintained until June 17, 1903, when Mr. Keet purchased Mr. Baker's interest and has since been alone. January 1, 1904, he opened very extensive and modern undertaking parlors at No. 80 East Main street, occupying the building erected for the Baptist parsonage by Charles Willard in memory of his sister, Laura Harris Willard. He is a member of the State Association of Funeral Directors and Embalmers and has served as its treasurer for one year.

On the 28th of September, 1881, Mr. Keet wedded Miss Angie L. Davis, a daughter of Gilbert and Susannah L. (Blanchard) Davis. With his family Mr. Davis removed from Lockport, New York, to this city at an early day, and as a stone mason was connected with the construction of many of the early buildings of this city. In matters of citizenship Mr. Davis was prominent, helpful and loyal. His devotion to his country was manifested at the time of the Civil war, when he joined the Union army for three years, becoming a member of the First Michigan Sharp Shooters, which command was among the first to go to the front. Both he and his wife are now deceased and Mrs. Keet is the only surviving member of the family.

Mr. and Mrs. Keet now have one child, Marjorie. The parents are prominent in social circles and are devoted members of the Maple street Methodist Episcopal church, in which Mr. Keet is serving on the board of trustees.

Fraternally Mr. Keet is prominent, belonging to Battle Creek lodge, No. 29, I. O. O. F., the Knights of the Maccabees, the Modern Woodmen of America, Battle Creek lodge, No. 12, F. & A. M., and is a charter member of Battle Creek lodge, No. 35, K. P., of which he is past chancellor and has been a representative to the Grand lodge.

In politics Mr. Keet has always been an active Republican, but the honors and emoluments of office have had no attraction for him. He has taken a special interest in the public school system and in September, 1897, was elected a member of the school board and has since acted in that capacity. During his first term school building No. 5 was rebuilt. He has taken an active stand in favor of needed improvements, and because of his progressiveness in this line was re-elected in 1900 for a second term of three years and in 1903 was again re-elected. During this term school building No. 2 has been enlarged by the addition of twelve rooms, making a sixteen room building; and school building No. 10 has been erected containing ten rooms. Altogether ninety-seven teachers are employed in Battle Creek and Mr. Keet believes in paying such wages that the best services can be secured. He is a gentleman of intelligence, capability and sagacity and his name is closely associated with the substantial development of Battle Creek, and his valuable counsel and his activities along useful lines have made him a representative man of the city. Noting the salient features in his career, the reader cannot but render him respect and admiration and those who have been actively associated with him give him their warm regard, confidence and friendship.

TERRY E. HOWELL.

To Terry E. Howell has been vouchsafed a period of rest after years of activity in the business world. He was born near Laingsburg, Shiawassee county, Michigan, October 11, 1845, and is a son of Ezra and Mary (Parshall) Howell. The father was a native of New York, and his father was Dr. Howell, who came to Michigan in the early '30s and for a time lived in the vicinity of Pontiac. Ezra Howell became a farmer and owned and operated land in Shiawassee county. When his son Terry was but seven years of age his parents removed to Palmyra, New York, but three years later returned to Michigan, locating in Battle Creek. It was in that city that our subject was reared and educated and when twenty years of age he began teaching school. Subsequently he accepted a clerkship in a general store in his native town and later he again engaged in teaching through the winter term. Afterward he became a brakeman on a passenger train on the Michigan Central Railroad and was thus employed for a number of years, after which he became a baggage man and was also station baggage master at Laingsburg for several years. On the expiration of that period he removed to the west, becoming connected with the Chicago, Burlington & Quincy Railroad as a representative of the north division running between Chicago and Minneapolis. While thus engaged he made his home in the city of Minneapolis. In 1900 Mr. Howell retired from the railway service and came to Battle Creek, where he built a residence at No. 89 North Union street. After about a year he bought a lot at No. 441 Lake avenue and, in 1902, erected his present home.

In 1873, in Eaton county near Charlotte, Michigan, Mr. Howell was united in marriage to Miss Esther D. Bowen, a daughter of Melintus and Hannah (Leach) Bowen. One son has been born of this marriage, Herbert R., who is now a dentist. He was graduated in the high school at LaCrosse, Wisconsin, afterward studied in Minneapolis for three years and then became a student in the Northwestern Dental College of Chicago, in which he was graduated in the spring of 1902. He is now engaged in practice in Memphis, Tennessee. Both Mr. and Mrs. Howell are members of the Methodist Episcopal church at LaCrosse, Wisconsin, and his political support is usually given to the Republican party, but at times he has voted for Democratic candidates, never considering himself bound by party ties. Soon after attaining his majority he was made a Mason in the lodge at Laingsburg and he now holds membership in Battle Creek lodge, No. 12, F. & A. M. While in the railroad service he was always a trusted employee, careful and conscientious in the performance of his duty and as the years passed he saved from his earnings a sum which is now sufficient to enable him to live retired in the enjoyment of an attractive home and surrounded by many of the comforts of life.

LEVI PITMAN.

Levi Pitman, who during his latter years was a retired farmer, lived at No. 850 Maple street in Battle Creek, claimed New Jersey as the state of his nativity, his birth having occurred in Burlington county on the 22d of December, 1819. He traveled life's journey for eighty-four years, and there are in his life's history many chapters that are of interest, showing his strong force of character, his sterling purpose and the upright principles which have actuated his career. His parents were Aaron and Matilda (Furman) Pitman, also natives of New Jersey as were probably the grandparents. In the family were ten children, seven of whom reached mature years, our subject being the seventh in order of birth. Four of the number lived to be more than eighty years of age and the eldest brother reached the advanced age of eighty-nine years. One sister, Mrs. Elizabeth Watson, is now over eighty-seven years of age. She is the wife of James V. Watson, formerly president of the Consolidated National Bank of New York City and her home is now in Philadelphia, Pennsylvania. A younger sister, Mrs. Rebecca Taylor, has passed the age of four score years and she, too, lives in Philadelphia. The father of this family died in New Jersey in 1854 at the age of seventy-three years and the mother afterward went to live in Bucks county, Pennsylvania, dying in Taylorville in her eighty-first year. The remains of both were interred in Mansfield, New Jersey. The religious faith of the family was that of the Society of Friends and the picture of the old Friends' meeting-house near the old family homestead in the far east is now in possession of the family. This church was erected in 1812.

Levi Pitman was reared upon his father's farm. When about ten years of age he was kicked by a horse just over the right eye and after that he did not attend school to any great extent. When fifteen years of age he began working in his brother's blacksmith shop, where he was employed for five years. He then worked for a brother on a truck farm until 1854 when he went to Morrow county, Ohio, where he spent ten months.

In 1862 Mr. Pitman married Miss Emma Webb, of New Jersey, who lived for about a year. It was about the time of her death that Mr. Pitman became a member of the Pennsylvania Reserves, serving for eight weeks or during the time when Lee threatened Philadelphia and the north. He was attached to Company A of the Forty-fourth Regiment under Captain Simpson and Colonel Woodworth and though in the state militia was under United States military regulations. In April, 1864, he came to Michigan and purchased forty acres of land in Bedford township, Calhoun county. He then returned to the east and on the 12th of October, 1864, was joined in wedlock to Miss Rachel a sister of his first wife, and a daughter of Mathias and Ann (Hodgson) Webb. She was born near Manchester, England, and was seventeen years of age when her people came to America.

After their marriage Mr. and Mrs. Pitman started for his new home in Michigan, traveling over the Pennsylvania Central Railroad to Cleveland, Ohio, thence by boat to Detroit and on to Battle Creek over the Michigan Central Railroad. They resided upon the farm until 1888 and then removed to the present home where Mr. Pitman carried on gardening until within the last four years. His second wife died March 12, 1902, and was buried in Oakhill cemetery. By this union there were four children: Florence M., became the wife of John Lalonde of Butte, Montana, and they have three children; J. Webb, Rachel

M. and Florence I. Mary H. is the wife of John Codling, a painter by trade who is now engaged in setting up engines in the works of Nichols & Shepard. They have one son Verree, who was born in Battle Creek September 25, 1899; Emma W. is the wife of James H. Tagg, assistant foreman with the Advance Thresher Company of Battle Creek and they have a son Clifford, born April 3, 1890. Matilda, the youngest member of the Pitman family, remained at home with her father till his death, which occurred November 10th, 1903. He is interred beside his wife in Oak-hill cemetery.

In early life Levi Pitman voted with the Whig party, his first presidential ballot supporting Zachary Taylor. He voted for Fremont in 1856, for Lincoln in 1860 and has since been a stalwart Republican. He served as treasurer of the school board in Bedford township, but was never active as an office holder. Reared in the Society of Friends he always adhered to that faith and was connected with the church of that denomination in Battle Creek. The teachings of that religious organization permeated his entire life and shaped his career, making him an honorable man who in the evening of his days could look back over the past without regret and forward to the future without fear.

FRANK E. McNary.

Frank E. McNary, who is filling the position of county clerk in Calhoun county, was born in Leroy township, this county, September 24, 1855, a son of Henry and Caroline F. (Crosier) McNary. The family, of Scotch lineage, was established in America by the great-grandfather of our subject, who settled in the Empire state. John McNary, the grandfather, was a millwright who lived in Oneida county, New York, and afterward in the western portion of the state. He died at the age of forty-two years, his death resulting from an injury received while following his chosen pursuit. Henry McNary was born in Oneida county, June 16, 1808, and after his father's death, lived with an uncle in Connecticut until sixteen years of age, when he removed to western New York, where he remained until he attained his majority. Soon after he purchased a farm in Ohio, but following a brief residence in that state came to Michigan in 1835 and entered land from the government. As there was no railroad in this district he walked from Detroit to Calhoun county. After making selection of what he considered a favorable site he walked to the land office to enter his claim. Subsequently, he returned to New York and after a short time brought his mother to the west. He then built a house upon his land and began the work of improvement and cultivation. When he had made preparations for a home of his own he went to Ohio, where he was married to Miss Caroline Crosier on the 8th of November, 1838. Her parents, Andrew and Catherine Crosier, removed from Massachusetts to the Buckeye state, making the journey in a wagon when their daughter, Mrs. McNary, was but six weeks old. Their first home was in Cuyahoga county, near Cleveland. Mrs. McNary, who was born in Massachusetts, October 21, 1816, spent her girlhood days on the old homestead in Ohio, and in early womanhood engaged in teaching school. After her marriage, she accompanied her husband to Michigan. The railroad had by that time been built as far as Ann Arbor, but as they reached Detroit the only train for Ann Arbor was just leaving the station and they were forced to remain there for twenty-four hours. Mr. McNary became one of the successful farmers of Calhoun county, his years of active labor resulting in bringing to him a very desirable competence. He was also one of the early stockholders of the First National Bank of Battle Creek under its original charter. In his political views he was a Republican and served as treasurer and justice of the peace, although he preferred to leave office holding to others in order to devote his energies to his business pursuits. He died October 15, 1899, and his wife passed away in March, 1886. They were the parents of two sons who reached mature years, the brother of our subject being George M. McNary, who was a member of Company H, of Merrill's Horse during the Civil war and died while in the army on the 15th of January, 1865.

Frank E. McNary obtained his early education in the public schools near his home and afterward attended the high school of Battle Creek He assisted his father in the work of the farm in early boyhood and later assumed the management of the home place. About 1880 he began the raising of registered Holstein cattle and was the owner of a large herd. In fact, he was the first to introduce that grade of cattle into the county and for a number of years did a successful business in the breeding of Holsteins. On disposing of his interest here he took a carload to Tacoma, Washington, being twelve days upon the road and thus introduced Holsteins into that territory. He realized an excellent profit from this sale and later he followed general farming with like success. He is to-day the owner of valuable farming property, including the old homestead comprising two hundred and forty acres. Mr. McNary was married to Miss Cora Scott, of Leroy township, who died leaving two children: George E., born March 11, 1881; and Theron, born February 23, 1884. For his second wife Mr. McNary chose Miss Nannie Fuller, of Athens township, Calhoun county, a daughter of Zelora and Jane Fuller. This marriage was celebrated on the 1th of February, 1886, and has been blessed with two children, but Gladys died in infancy. Ray, born February 24, 1892, is still with his parents. Both Mr. and Mrs. McNary are members of the Methodist Episcopal church at West Leroy, in which he has served as steward for a number of years and was also superintendent of the Sunday-school until his removal to Marshall. He belongs to Prairie lodge, No. 288, I. O. O. F., at Climax. Michigan, and to Climax lodge, No. 59, F. and A. M. He is also a member of the Knights of the Macabees and the Modern Woodmen of America. In his political views he is a stanch Republican and in 1892 was elected supervisor, filling the position for four years. He was also a member of the county committee for two terms and in the work of the board has been active and helpful. In 1902 he was nominated and elected to the position of county clerk, assuming the duties of the office on the 1st of January, 1903. In his official service he is methodical, systematic and thoroughly reliable. During his long residence in the county. he has become widely known and

his history is familiar to his fellow townsmen, who, recognizing his worth and ability, felt that he would prove a most capable incumbent in office.

JOHN J. WALBRIDGE.

John J. Walbridge, now deceased, was for many years a resident of Battle Creek and his steadfast nature. honorable principles and fidelity to every trust reposed in him made him a man well worthy of the uniform regard which was given him. He was born in Gaines, Orleans county, New York, May 4, 1826, his parents being John J. and Caroline M. (Collins) Walbridge. The father was born in Bennington, Vermont. in 1798, and as a young man removed to Gaines, New York, where he followed merchandising and spent the remainder of his days, passing away May 31, 1841. His wife was born in Ellington, Tolland county, Connecticut. April .10, 1802, and with her father, Thomas Collins, and his family removed to Gaines, where on the 1st of February, 1825, she gave her hand in marriage to John J. Walbridge. She died November 4, 1888, at Battle Creek in the faith of the Presbyterian church, of which she had long been a devoted member. Politically Mr. Walbridge was very prominent and served as a member of the State Legislature while William H. Seward was governor of New York.

John J. Walbridge, having attended the common schools and gained a knowledge of the preliminary branches of learning, pursued an academic course and was thus well qualified for a business career. He entered life as a salesman in a drygoods store at

Gaines and later was employed in a similar capacity in Rochester. He was a cousin of Mrs. Daniel Powers of the latter city. After his marriage Mr. Walbridge was connected with a store at Lockport, New York, and prior to 1860 came to Michigan, settling at Lowell, where he owned and conducted a large grocery store. In 1865 he removed to Battle Creek, where he was again engaged in merchandising for a short time. Later he became one of the early commercial travelers, representing a Detroit firm and later a Chicago house. He made extensive trips and held prominent positions in his line, continuing in that department of business actively until his retirement.

On the 16th of April, 1850, in Gaines, New York, Mr. Walbridge wedded Miss Martha M. Moss, who was born in Morganville, Genesee county, New York, October 5, 1831, a daughter of Samuel and Mercy (Sherman) Moss. Her father was born in Watertown, Connecticut, November 12. 1778, and was of English lineage. John Moss having emigrated from England to New Haven, Connecticut, in 1670, thus becoming the founder of the family in America. For his second wife Samuel Moss wedded Mercy Sherman, at Bethany, Genesee county, New York. He had removed to the west with his family at an early day and became one of the large land owners and prominent citizens of this section of the Empire state. In politics he was a Whig and was a most devoted member of the Presbyterian church, in which he served as deacon for forty years. He died in Gaines at the age of sixty-one years and his wife passed away in Battle Creek, May 20, 1876, at the age of seventy-four years. Mrs. Walbridge was educated in Albion Seminary, in the academy at Gaines and in

Mount Holyoke Seminary at LeRoy, New York is a lady of superior culture and refinement. By her marriage she became the mother of two children: Fred J., born in Gaines, New York, July 4, 1851, has for thirty-two years been in the office of Nichols & Shepard, of Battle Creek, and is now the vice president of the Johnson Machine & Foundry Company. He married Louise MacKinnie, of Battle Creek, and they have four children: Howard, Harold, Helen and Fred, Jr. The other son, Harry C. Walbridge, was born September 8, 1853, at Lockport, New York, and is now living in Chicago. He married Celia Smolik and has two children: Marjorie and Robert M. The latter has lived with Mrs. Walbridge, his grandmother, since three years of age. She is a member of the Presbyterian church and an estimable lady whose circle of friends is extensive. Mr. Walbridge passed away April 28, 1889, his death being deeply regretted by all who knew him. He was an approachable gentleman, according to all the courtesy of an interview, was kind, genial and charitable in his opinions of others and his social nature made him popular with those with whom he was associated in neither business or social relations.

MONTFORD F. GARFIELD.

Montford F. Garfield, who is serving as turnkey and deputy sheriff at Marshall, Michigan, was born in Washington couny, New York, April 24, 1846, his parents being Benjamin Franklin and Eliza (Bennett) Garfield. The father was born in Essex county, New York, where he spent his boyhood days. He was educated for the minisry and for many years was a clergyman of the Baptist church, acting as pastor of that denomination at Saratoga, Waterford, and Port Edwards, New York, for many years. He spent a short time in the west, but soon returned to the Empire state, spending his last days in Saratoga. His wife, however, died in Battle Creek, Michigan.

Montford F. Garfield is indebted to the public schools of Washington and Saratoga counties, New York, for the early educational privileges he enjoyed. He afterward pursued his studies in Middletown, New York, and in the Port Edwards Collegiate Institute, and when a young man he came to Battle Creek, Michigan, in 1869. Here he secured employment with Upton, Brown & Company, a pioneer threshing machine company with whom he continued for seven and a half years. He then turned his attention to the hotel business and for a long period was the popular proprietor of the Williams House, then the leading hotel of Battle Creek. He continued in the business until 1894, when he sold his interest and removed to Saginaw, Michigan, where he again conducted a hotel, being proprietor of the Everett House for some time. He afterward returned to Battle Creek, but subsequently went to Auburn, N. Y., where he was manager of a hotel for three years. On the 1st of January, 1900, he came to Marshall, Michigan, with Sheriff Williams to accept the office of deputy sheriff and turnkey, and he has faithfully and efficiently performed the duties devolving upon him since that time. His early political support was given to the Democracy, but in later years he has been an active Republican.

For a number of years Mr. Garfield was a prominent member of the Masonic fraternity and he long held membership in Athelstan club of Battle Creek. He was likewise one of the incorporators of the Battle Creek Driving Park and Field Sports Association, of which he acted as secretary and director for a number of years. Always deeply interested in fine horses, he did much to promote a love for them in Calhoun county and his efforts resulted in bringing many fine specimens of the noble steed to this part of the state.

Mr. Garfield married Mrs. Leocade White, of Pennsylvania, and they make their home in Marshall, where they are now well known.

LA FAYETTE SILLIMAN.

LaFayette Silliman, one of the prosperous agriculturists of Calhoun county, living in Albion, and widely and favorably known in that city, was born in Fairfield county, Connecticut, October 26, 1823. His parents were Peter and Mary Silliman, and the father, about 1834, removed with his family from Connecticut to Monroe county, New York, establishing his home in Pennfield township. He afterward took up his abode in Clarkson, in the same county, and LaFayette Silliman, who was eleven years of age at the time the family left the Charter Oak state, was reared in the Empire state, acquiring his early education in the district schools of Monroe county and afterward attending the Pennfield and Clarkson academies. He was thus well qualified by liberal educational privileges for the practical and responsible duties of life. When twenty-two years of age he began operating a farm which he conducted for two years, and later was for several years engaged in the agricultural implement business at Brockport, New

LAFAYETTE SILLIMAN

MRS. LAFAYETTE SILLIMAN

York under the firm style of Silliman, Bowman & Company, conducting that enterprise for three years during the Civil war period.

It was in 1869 that Mr. Silliman arrived in Calhoun county, Michigan. He chose Albion township as the place of his residence, and purchased one hundred and seventy-five acres of land, lying just west of the village, but now the greater part of this is within the corporation limits of the town. He erected upon his place all the buildings that are now seen there. These are substantial and are ever kept in a state of good repair. He also planted the trees and made other modern improvements, which add to the attractive appearance and value of his place. His entire life has been devoted to agricultural pursuits and because of his continued energy, unfaltering industry and unabating perseverance, he has gained a place among the substantial residents of this part of the state, possessing a handsome competence that now enables him to enjoy many of the privileges, the comforts and the luxuries of life, which were denied him in earlier years.

Mr. Silliman was united in marriage to Miss Caroline Porter, a native of New York, a daughter of Samuel M. and Maria Porter. Her father belonged to an old and distinguished family of Connecticut. Mrs. Silliman is a very charming woman, an ideal wife and mother and a faithful friend, and in Albion and Calhoun county she is very popular. Unto Mr. and Mrs. Silliman have been born six children. Caroline Frances, the eldest, is the wife of Charles F. King, who resides upon her father's farm, which he is now operating. They have five children: Herbert C., who is a resident of Los Angeles, California. He is married and has one child, Herbert LaFayette, who is a dentist. Floss Caroline, the second child of

Mr. and Mrs. King, is the wife of Lewis C. Rauch, a resident of Detroit, and they have one son, Charles Herbert. Fadge H. is now a student in Albion College. Zella resides with her sister in Detroit. Georgia is attending school in Albion; Charles Herbert, the eldest son of Mr. and Mrs. Silliman, married Blanche Brazelton, and they are now traveling in Europe. C. H. Silliman is connected with the banking interests in New York city; Irving P. married Ada Morrell. He is proprietor of a ranch in California and is also identified with irrigation interests of that state; Minnie became the wife of William G. Gulick and died in Florida, leaving one son, Horace; Hattie died in infancy; George, the youngest of the Silliman family, was a very promising young man, but died at the age of eighteen years.

LaFayette Silliman gives his political allegiance to the Democracy. He has been a member of the common council of Albion for four years, representing the fourth ward. He has ever been public spirited and progressive in citizenship, contributing to any measure that he believes will promote the material, intellectual and moral welfare of his community. Both he and his wife are popular and highly esteemed residents of Albion. During the past three years they have spent the winter seasons in California and prior to that passed several winter seasons in Florida.

EUGENE R. COLE.

A noticeable fact in the commercial history of the world is that a large majority of young men are at the head of extensive and important industrial and commercial interests and in the control of business enterprises of magnitude, they display wonderful sagacity, splendid managerial ability and unfaltering energy. Of such a class Eugene R. Cole is a representative. He is now the secretary and general manager of the Record Printing & Box Company of Battle Creek, one of the leading industries of this manufacturing center. He was born near Rochester, New York, December 29, 1873, and is a son of Richard D. and Frances E. (Jones) Cole. The father was born in Irondequoit township, Monroe county, New York, his father Mason Cole having been one of the pioneers of that portion of the state. The family originally removed from Pennsylvania to Monroe county and there Mason Cole carried on the occupation of farming. After arriving at years of maturity Richard D. Cole became a commission merchant and was a man of prominence not only in business cricles, but also in molding public opinion and in shaping the public policy. He took an active part in Democratic circles and three times was a member of the general assembly of New York, leaving the impress of his individuality upon the legislation enacted during his years of connection with the house. He married Miss Frances E. Jones, who was born and reared in Irondequoit, a daughter of David Jones who was also a farmer of that locality. They became the parents of four children, of whom the subject of this review is the youngest. Mrs. Cole is now the wife of Henry F. Bechman, who lived for a time in Chicago and then came to Battle Creek with his family in the fall of 1893. He is now superintendent of the Duplex Printing Company and also chairman of the Record Box & Printing Company. Unto him and

his wife has been born a son, Francis E.

When eight years of age Eugene R. Cole accompanied his mother to Chicago, Illinois, where he attended the public schools, pursuing the high school course. He then came with his family to Battle Creek in the fall of 1893 and for three years thereafter was associated with the Duplex Printing Press Company. Having become connected with the military interests he was a member of Company D, Second Michigan National Guard and on the breaking out of the Spanish-American war he offered his services to his country, enlisting as a member of Company D, Thirty-second Michigan Volunteer Infantry. He went to the front as a corporal, but soon afterward was promoted to the rank of sergeant. The men proceeded direct to Tampa, Florida, and were held there and at various camps in the south until the close of the war.

After receiving an honorable discharge Eugene R. Cole returned to Battle Creek and became connected with journalistic interests. He purchased the "Sunday Record," which was then a small paper and the plant and paper were both in a dilapidated condition. For two years he remained its editor and publisher and his success in the enterprise was uniform and rapid from the beginning. He made the Record one of the leading Sunday papers of central Michigan and more than doubled its circulation during his connection therewith. Having grown to large proportions the business was incorporated in 1901 as The Record Publishing Company, Mr. Cole being chairman and editor from that time to the present. At the time of the orgarization the company also embarked upon a general line of commercial printing.

This branch of the business has also grown with gratifying rapidity until it has become an extensive and profitable department of the business. In January, 1902, the company was re-organized and incorporated as The Record Printing & Box Company, with a capital stock of one hundred and twenty-five thousand dollars. Mr. Cole becoming its secretary and general manager. The company owns a splendidly equipped plant, the building having been erected especially for the purpose by Frank Turner who is the treasurer of the company. It is supplied with the most modern equipments for doing all classes of printing and also has a large plant for the manufacture of food cartons. The building is furnished with electric light and the presses are operated by electric power. Employment is furnished to about one hundred and fifty people and since the completion of the plant the machinery department has been in operation twenty-two hours a day. This is one of the largest box manufacturing plants of Battle Creek and much of the success of the enterprise is attributable to Mr. Cole, who has developed the business in a few years from a small and unsuccessful Sunday paper to is present prosperous proportions. It is now recognized as one of the leading industries of the city. He gives his attention exclusively to the business, keeps in touch with it in all of its departments and in every detail, and his practical supervision has certainly been one of the strongest elements in its growth. In 1899 he established the publication "Dogdom," which is now known to all dog fanciers through the English speaking countries. He is its editor and owner, being himself a lover of fine dogs. He has brought the publication to a point where it is recognized as authority on the subject. It has a large circulation which is constantly increasing.

On the 11th of June, 1902, Mr. Cole was united in marriage to Miss Blanche P. Cummings, of Battle Creek, a daughter of A. Cummings, who was one of the early founders of this city. They are members of the Independent Congregational church and Mr. Cole belongs to the Battle Creek lodge, No. 35, K. P., also to the Benevolent Protective Order of Elks, being a charter member of Lodge No. 573. Also to the Independent Order of Foresters and the Knights of the Maccabees. He likewise belongs to Athelstan club, of which he was treasurer for two years. In business affairs he is energetic, prompt and notably reliable, never making an engagement that he does not fulfill or incurring an obligation which he does not meet. He is a man of much force of character and strong individuality; and his pleasant, social manner has won him a host of warm friends.

WALTER S. POWERS.

Walter S. Powers is actively connected with a profession which has important bearing upon the progress and stable prosperity of any section or community, and one which has long been considered as conserving the public welfare by furthering the ends of justice and maintaining individual rights. His reputation as a lawyer has been won through, earnest, honest labor, and his standing at the bar is a merited tribute to his ability. He has a very large practice and his careful preparation of cases is supplemented by a power of argument and a forceful presentation of his points in the courtroom, so that he never fails to impress court or jury, and seldom fails to gain the verdict desired. He is now actively engaged in practice, with offices in the Powers block in Battle creek and a pleasant residence at No. 132·North Avenue.

His birth occurred upon a farm in Genesee county, New York, on the 14th of January, 1849, his parents being John R. and Hannah (Johnson) Powers. The father, John Richard Powers, was born in Bedford township, Cayuga county, New York, about twenty-five miles from the city of Auburn on the 28th of November, 1818, and was a son of John and Eunice (Squires) Powers, the former a native of Vermont and the latter of the Green Mountain state. John Powers always followed farming and at an early day became an agriculturist of New York. His wife lived in Rochester, that state, when there were only three houses in the now populous city. John Powers, coming to Michigan on a visit, died soon afterward in Barry county at the home of his son, John Richard Powers. One son, William Powers, served as a soldier in the War of 1812.

John Richard Powers was but eight years of age when his parents removed from Cayuga to Genesee county, New York, and there he made his home until coming to Michigan. He had but limited educational privileges, pursuing his studies for a short time in the district schools, but largely educating himself in the chimney corner by the light of the .fire. By reading and study in this manner he broadened his knowledge until he was capable of teaching and for several terms followed that profession in the Empire state, but his father's failing health

making it necessary that he should take up the farm work, he returned home, remaining there until 1850, when he came to Michigan, accompanied by his wife and three children. The trip was made in the fall of 1849, proceeding by rail to Buffalo, thence to Detroit by way of the lake and from Detroit to Battle Creek by rail, after which he drove to his destination in Barry county. He purchased one hundred and twenty acres of land in that county on which was a rude shanty. He had only one hundred dollars, but with this· he made a partial payment, going in debt for the remainder. In the little primitive home in this place he established his family. When he had brought his wife and children with him to Michigan he had only ten dollars left. He made arrangements to buy a cow for sixteen dollars, giving the ten dollars in payment and then arranging to split rails for fifty cents per hundred in order to pay off the remaining six dollars. In order to provide a better shelter for his wife and children he built a cabin of sided logs, but it required two years to accomplish this task, for it was necessary that he should work at other labors in order to gain ready money to meet the family expenses. The shingles for his house he made by hand. As the years passed his land became more productive and he continued to reside in Barry county until about twenty years ago, when he removed to Bedford, Michigan, trading his first farm for land upon which Urbandale is now built. Later he sold this property to his youngest son with the exception of a tract of twenty acres. Before leaving Barry county he purchased his present farm of sixty acres in Bedford township.

John Richard Powers was united in marriage to Miss Hannah Johnson, a native of Genesee county, New York, where the wedding was celebrated. Later Genesee county was divided and their home became a part of the land set off for Wyoming county, New York. Unto Mr. and Mrs. Powers were born eight children, four sons and four daughters. Lydia Ann is a teacher in the public schools of Battle Creek; James M. is a practicing attorney of Battle Creek and a member of the firm of J. M. Powers & J. L. Powers. He is married and has three children: LaVerne, an attorney of Marshall, Michigan; Harry and Leslie. The third member of the family is Walter S. Powers; Agnes is the wife of John Wing, a resident of Bedford township, and has two children, Glenn and Lynn; Herbert A. is a physician of this city; Eunice is the wife of Walter Stringham, of Battle Creek, and has three children: Gladys, Earl and Lolie. Daniel J. is a farmer of Bedford township; and Lida, who lives with her father. Throughout his entire life the father of this family followed agricultural pursuits. He is a self-made man who started out with no capital, but by industry and perseverance he has steadily worked his way upward until he has acquired a comfortable competence.

Walter S. Powers, whose name introduces this review, spent his boyhood days on the home farm in Barry county, being very young when brought by his parents to this state. He pursued his early education in the public schools and while yet a boy at home formed the determination to one day become a lawyer. When twenty-two years of age he began teaching, being first employed in the country schools in Newago county. He had gone north to work in the pine woods in the winter months and thus found opportunity to be-

gin his professional work as a teacher in northern Michigan. Subsequently he taught successfully in Barry county and afterward went to New London, Ohio, where he was employed as a teacher in the village school. While there he took up the study of law under the direction of his cousin Rollin Powers, a successful attorney and after acquiring considerable knowledge of the principles of jurisprudence was admitted to the bar. Wishing, however, to become more proficient in the profession which he had determined to make his life work he entered the law department of the University of Michigan, in which he was graduated in the class of 1877.

Mr. Powers began the practice of law in Bellevue, Eaton county, Michigan, but remained there for only a few months. His brother, James, who had entered the junior class in the law department of the State University when our subject became a senior had now graduated and, going to Bellevue, became his brother's successor, while Walter S. Powers removed to Nashville, Barry county. In his practice there he was very successful, having a large and distinctively representative clientage, which embraced connection with all departments of the science of jurisprudence. In 1899 he removed from Nashville to Battle Creek and has since practiced in this city. He has a large clientage and his business connects him with much of the important litigation tried in the courts of this district. Walter S. Powers purchased the block in which his office is located and which is called the Powers block. While he has a large law practice making heavy demands upon his time he has also become interested in other enterprises of the city.

He owns stock in various companies here and is the secretary of the Grape Sugar Cereal Company.

While residing in Bellevue, Michigan, Mr. Powers was married in Battle Creek on the 24th of May, 1877. He has two children: Blanche, who is a graduate of the high school of Nashville and also of the Detroit Conservatory of Music, has been a successful teacher of music in the public schools of Charlotte and is now connected with the public schools of Battle Creek. Aubra, born in Nashville, November 3, 1888, is yet at home.

In his political affiliations Mr. Powers is a Democrat and has taken an active interest in the work of his party. He was once the Democratic nominee for prosecuting attorney, but did not expect election because of the large Republican majority in Barry county. For four years he served as justice of the peace, was president of the village of Nashville for two years and also president of the school board and while in Nashville he was appointed postmaster by President Cleveland. He became a member of the Masonic lodge at New London, Ohio, and filled some of its offices. While in Nashville he transferred his membership to the lodge there and is now associated with the craft in Battle Creek. He is a charter member of the Independent Order of Foresters of Nashville and has transferred his membership from the Knights of Pythias lodge in that place to this city. He is both a stockholder and treasurer in the Battle Creek Business University, with which he has been connected since its organization and there he lectures to the students on commercial law at various times. His legal learning, his analytical mind and the readiness with which he grasps the points in an argument all combine to make him one of the capable attorneys at the Calhoun county bar and he enjoys the respect and confidence of his professional brethren, as well as of the general public.

ABRAM BRAMBLE.

In the year 1857 Abram Bramble became a resident of Battle Creek, then a small town of less than three thousand inhabitants. Here he began carpentering and contracting and with the industrial interests of the city was long and actively connected. Now he is living retired, his labors having brought to him the competence that supplies him with the necessities and comforts of life. He was born in the town of Orwell, Rutland county, Vermont, November 5, 1824, a son of John and Elizabeth A. (Humphrey) Bramble. The father a shoemaker by trade, left the Green Mountain state and removed to Detroit when our subject was but two years old, and after following shoemaking there for a time he went to Plymouth county, settling about three miles northeast of Ypsilanti, where he entered land from the government. There his wife died and his death occurred when his son Abram was but four years of age. The boy and a younger sister were then taken back to Victor, New York, and he lived with his uncle, Abram Humphrey, until he was twenty years of age, acquiring a good education in the common schools. At the age of sixteen he began learning the carpenter's trade and during the first year of his apprenticeship received his board and thirty-five dollars while the second year he was given forty and the third year fifty dollars and board. He afterward continued with his employer for a year as a journeyman and then came to the west.

In Steuben county, at Thompson Mills, in the township of Jackson, Indiana, Mr. Bramble began contracting and during the four years there spent, built a house on a farm belonging to Governor Luce near the Indiana line. Returning to Victor he followed his trade for a year and then began building freight houses and water tanks for the New York Central Railroad Company. A year later he resumed building operations in Victor, where he spent four years.

During that time Mr. Bramble was married, November 3, 1852, to Mary E. Snedeker, who was born in Farmington, Ontario county, New York, October 22, 1832, a daughter of Peter and Jane A. (Johnson) Snedeker. She had taught school one year and was expecting to go to Lima, New York, and complete her education when she met Mr. Bramble and they were married. They had been reared within four miles of each other, but had never become acquainted until after attaining their majority. Locating in Carleton, New York, Mr. Bramble there worked at his trade for three years and in 1857 came to Battle Creek, where he began contracting. For a number of years he was closely associated with the building interests of this city and evidences of his handiwork are still seen in some of the substantial buildings here. He was ever conscientious in his work and the number and importance of the contracts awarded him made him one of the well-to-do citizens, now enabling him to live retired.

Unto Mr. and Mrs. Bramble were born four children: Charles Elmore, born in Victor, New York, October 17, 1853, was attending the public schools of Battle Creek, when during the Civil war, at the age of nine years he left home without his parents' consent and made his way to Chattanooga, proceeding thence to the mouth of the White river where he enlisted on the gunboat Tyler as a cabin boy. His people did not hear from him from June until the following Christmas eve. He spent two years on the Tyler and then after returning home he worked his way to Montreal and from there to London, being gone on this trip three years. In London he went to the American consul and applied for aid to get home. His request was granted but instead of returning to this country he boarded an English vessel and went to Russia, sailing between the two countries, until after an absence of three years he again came to the United States. On reaching New York he wrote to his people asking for funds to bring him to. Michigan. This the father sent and in Battle Creek he then worked for a time for Nichols & Shepard. He next went west among the Sioux Indians and after learning their language became a government interpreter and scout. In the latter capacity he had many exciting adventures and narorw escapes. He was with the troops of General Miles and came very nearly being with General Custer's forces at the time of the massacre. For about ten years he remained in the west, during which time he made several visits to his parents. About six months before his death he was again in Battle Creek and was in poor health when he returned. He died and was buried in Glasgow, Montana, his death being the result of an accident which he sustained when a sailor. He fell from the rigging of the vessel one day and never fully recovered, the fall causing intestinal trouble. Peter S. Bramble, the second son of our subject, was born in Carleton, New York, November 20, 1855, and is a painter and decorator. He married Emma Dale, lives with his father, and has one child, Albert J. The third son, John J., died in infancy. Victor Hugo, born in Battle Creek, September 27, 1869, married Lina Merrill and is general state agent for the Advance thresher. He has two children, Helen and David Merrill.

In 1848 Abram Bramble cast his first vote, supporting Zachary Taylor and since the organization of the Republican party became one of its stanch advocates. In the Fremont campaign he and his wife went to Albion, New York, to hear Henry Ward Beecher. He is now a Prohibitionist and belongs to the Presbyterian church, while his wife holds membership in the Independent Congregational church. Since 1851 he has been a Mason, having been raised in the lodge at Victor, New York. His life has been in conformity with the teachings of the craft and his straightforward business dealings, his public-spirited citizenship and the sterling traits of his manhood have made him a citizen whom to know is to respect.

HON. MARVIN FERGUSON.

Hon. Marvin Ferguson, a leading and practical farmer of Marshall and formerly a member of the State Legislature, was born near Penn Yan, Yates County, New York, March 7, 1843, a son of Walter S. and Miranda (McAlpine) Ferguson. The family was founded in America by the great-grandfather of our subject who emigrated

from Scotland when this country was still numbered among the colonial possessions of Great Britain. He took up land in Vermont and it was there that Peter Ferguson, the grandfather, was born and reared. He enlisted in the War of 1812, but was only in the service for a brief period. He spent his early years in Orange county, New York, and then became a pioneer settler of Ontario county, that state, establishing his home in the midst of the green forest. Walter S. Ferguson was born in Ontario county, in 1809, and when a young man went to Yates county, where he married Miss McAlpine, whose birth occurred at Hudson, New York, and who was a daughter of Andrew and Thankful (Crego) McAlpine, who were also of early Scotch ancestry. After his marriage Mr. Ferguson engaged in merchandising for a number of years and later became an extensive farmer. He was prominent in public affairs, served as postmaster of his town and filled other local offices. There he died in 1887, but his widow is still living at the advanced age of eighty-two years. He was a Universalist in religious faith and Mrs. Ferguson is a member of the Baptist church.

In the public schools of his native county Marvin Ferguson began his education and afterward attended the academy at Penn Yan. In his youth he worked at home with his father and also served as clerk in a store in Geneva, New York. In his early manhood he became deeply interested in political affairs and was active in the work of the Democratic party but never sought office as a reward for his allegiance to those principles. While still living in the east he married Miss Anna Ellerington, of Penn Yan, a daughter of Harold Ellerington, the wedding taking place, October 13, 1875.

MARVIN FERGUSON

Mr. Ferguson afterward engaged in farming and remained in the east until 1883, when he came to Marshall, Michigan, and purchased a beautiful home at No. 745 E. Mansion street, together with a fine farm of one hundred and seventy acres, most of which is within the city limits. He was successfully engaged in the dairy business for many years, becoming the largest milk dealer of the city, but he retired from that business in 1902 and has since devoted his energies to general agricultural pursuits. His place is characterized by the utmost neatness and his systematic work and progressive methods have made him one of the representative and prominent farmers of the county. He has also been interested in industrial concerns of Marshall and is now connected with the Page Buggy Company, of which he was one of the original stockholders. He has been a director from its organization to the present time and is now the vice president. This is an extensive enterprise, owning a large and well equipped plant and giving employment to about ninety skilled workmen. It has become one of the most profitable manufacturing industries of the city and is of vast importance to the trade interests of Marshall as well as to the owners, yielding a splendid dividend upon the investment. The product is shipped to all parts of the United States and to some of the foreign markets as well. Mr. Ferguson was also connected with the Marshall Wagon and Windmill Company, during its existence.

His deep interest in the political situation of the country and the issues of the day continued for some time after his arrival in Marshall. In 1887 he was elected alderman of his city from the first ward and held the office for two years. In 1896

he was nominated and elected a member of the State Legislature and served on a number of important committees during the session. In 1892 he was again elected in a Republican district and as the legislature was Republican he was not made chairman of any committees, but served on a number of important ones, including the committees on State Affairs and Public Lands. He was especially interested in the bill Providing a new school building for the Industrial Home for girls, at Adrian. He introduced the measure and after much labor secured its passage, and the modern building, now at Adrian, therefore stands as a monument to his efforts. He was always an active and conscientious supporter of every bill in which he strongly believed, and he labored ever for the welfare of the entire state. In 1896 he was nominated and elected mayor of Marshall and gave the city a progressive, practical and businesslike administration which resulted in the inauguration of needed reforms and improvements. He is not in sympathy with his party on the Free-Silver question and is therefore not active in politics at the present time. He attends and supports the Presbyterian church, of which he is a trustee, and is also a member of the board of trustees of the Dulcema Home for Aged and Indigent Women. He has been a member and secretary of the board since its formation and was a member of the building committee that erected a beautiful home at a cost of twenty thousand dollars, whereby shelter and comfort is given to needy women.

Mr. and Mrs. Ferguson have become the parents of five children: Mary, Walter S., Susan M., Harold M. and Alden, and the family is prominent in the community, the members of the household occupying an enviable position in social circles. The life record of Mr. Ferguson chronicles untiring activity and a career that has been useful and straightforward. He has never faltered in his allegiance to his honest views and neither fear nor favor can deter him from following the course which he believes to be right.

JAMES H. HALBERT.

There has never been a resident of Calhoun county held in higher regard by friends and neighbors or who have been more worthy of the public trust and confidence than James Henry Halbert. His life was upright and honorable and was characterized by so many sterling traits of character that his name was almost a synonym for honesty and integrity in the affairs of life. His birth occurred in Genesee county, New York, on the 10th of September, 1831, and his parents were James and Aletha (Stanard) Halbert. The father died when the son was only a year old and thus the boy did not enjoy many of the privileges and opportunities which most lads of the period enjoy. His birth occurred upon a farm and he received only a common school education. In 1846 when he was fifteen years of age the family came to Calhoun county, Michigan, settling in Bedford township. Four children accompanied the mother, namely: Thomas, who died in Battle Creek; Jasper, who is now deceased; William, who has also passed away and who is represented on another page of this work; Mrs. Alice Henika, a resident of Battle Creek; and James. After a short residence in Bedford township the mother with her two children Alice

and James removed to the city of Battle Creek and established their home at the corner of West Van Buren and Washington streets, where Mr. James H. Halbert resided for many years. A small house stood there at the time and in it the mother of our subject located with her son and daughter.

James Henry Halbert entered upon his business career in 1852 by becoming a station agent for the Michigan Central Railroad Company, at what was then Calumet, but is now Kensington, Illinois, a suburb of the city of Chicago. For two years Mr. Halbert filled that position in a most capable and faithful manner and at the end of that time handed in his resignation to the company. So loath were his employers to lose his services that they offered a home to his mother and sister free of rent if he would remain, but he felt that his mother needed his services and as she did not care to leave Michigan he returned once more to Battle Creek. Here he soon became identified with industrial and civic developments of the city. For several years he engaged in business as a contractor and builder and later became interested in the manufacture of sash, doors, and blinds, also building material. In this enterprise he prospered carrying on the work for twenty-one years. As time passed he increased his facilities in order to meet the growing demand of the trade and became the possessor of a large and important industry that figured prominently in the manufacturing circles of the city. In 1870 he formed a partnership with Andrew Knight under the firm name of Halbert & Knight for the purpose of manufacturing sash, doors and blinds and for some time the business relations between them were continued. Mr. Halbert was a man of unquestioned integrity in trade circles and also possessed strong sagacity, unfaltering diligence and the ready adaptability with which he overcame all difficulties and obstacles in his path and steadily worked his way upward to success. In the year 1890, however, he was stricken with disease and for ten years thereafter was an invalid, his death occurring on the 11th of September, 1900. In his political views Mr. Halbert was a stalwart Republican, firm in his faith in the party. In 1863 he was marshal of Battle Creek under Mayor Chester Buckley and in 1878 he was treasurer of this city. In 1873-4 he served as one of its aldermen and he ever exercised his official prerogatives in support of general progress, reform and improvement. For ten years he was a member of the school board and the interests of education found in him a warm friend who believed in raising high the standard of the schools, believing our free school system to be one of the bulwarks of the nation. During his incumbency on the board the question of prayer in the schools came up for settlement and although not a member of any church Mr. Halbert believed in its beneficial influence and voted in its favor. The question was finally decided as he wished after much discussion. At the time when he was taken ill he was serving as president of the school board, but because of his health he was forced to resign. He was deeply devoted to the cause of education, gave much of his time and influence toward furthering the work along that line. It seemed that every improvement with which he became allied for the benefit of the public made marked progress through his assistance and Battle Creek often acknowledged its indebtedness to him for effective labors in her behalf. Mr. Halbert

was never a politician in the sense of office seeking although he was frequently called to public service. It was a case of the office seeking the man. When public duties were given him he discharged them with conscientious ability, but he felt that he could do as good service for the public when not in office. Several times he was urged to become a candidate for mayor but always declined to do so. No man ever more thoroughly believed in America, her institutions and their final triumph than he. He was loyal to the interests of the United States and when the country was passing through the dark days of the rebellion and many were overwelmed with despair his faith in the final triumph of the right never faltered. Few watched with keener interest than Mr. Halbert the grand achievements made in science, literature and art. He was especially interested in the stupendous feats of engineering which marked the pathway of America's wonderful advancement. He was also a deep and earnest student of history and was familiar with the events of the past which find place on the pages of our annals as well as with more modern progress. Few had a wider or more profound knowledge of history than he and his familiarity with this subject was not confined alone to the history of our country but embraced that of other nations. He held the highest admiration for the genius of Napoleon. During the ten years of his illness he read extensively and found great pleasure in watching the world's advancement. Although shut out from active participation in what was going on he was yet in touch with the universal advancement in a mental way.

On the 19th of July, 1866, was celebrated the marriage of James H. Halbert and Miss Helen Fordham, a native of Battle Creek, and a daughter of Joel and Abigail (Pierce) Fordham, who were natives of Genesee county, New York. Coming to the west about 1835, they settled in Calhoun county, Michigan, first stopping where the Phelps sanatorium is now located, but as soon as possible Mr. Fordham secured a home of his own into which he moved his family. He was a carpenter by trade and the last years of his life were spent in work along that line in the shops of the Nichols & Shepard Thresher Company. Unto Mr. and Mrs. Halbert were born two children: Adeline Sophia, the wife of Emil H. Wicks, now resides with her mother. She has one son, Alton Halbert. Arthur James, their only son, died in 1882 at the age of ten years. In 1902 Mrs. Halbert erected a fine block on Washington avenue on a lot adjoining her own pleasant home and at the same time Mrs. Wicks erected the adjoining block.

Mr. Halbert's religious views could probably be summed up in the two words "live uprightly." He certainly followed this motto and over the record of his public career and his private life there falls no shadow of wrong or suspicion of evil. He was a man of very generous and kindly spirit, but though he gave much in charity he always did it in the spirit of Him who admonished us not to let the left hand know what the right hand doeth. It mattered not who was in need he was always ready to assist and he realized that the truest happiness comes from making others happy. When called to his final rest he was laid by the side of his son in Oakhill cemetery where also sleep his mother and two brothers. Mr. Halbert was certainly a self-made man, for all that he possessed was acquired through hard work and honorable dealing. He realized the value of industry and unabating energy in the active affairs of life and it was along these lines that he won his prosperity. To his employees he was always just and considerate and in all his business relations he was honorable and straightforward. His many excellent traits won for him the love of all who knew him and he left to his family not only a comfortable competence but also the priceless heritage of an untarnished name. He was a man, too, who enjoyed the pleasures of life and loved all manly games and sports. He was an enthusiastic hunter and felt great delight when tramping through the woods with his gun. He also had a particular fondness for nature in all her various moods and aspects and always found

"A pleasure in the pathless woods
A rapture on the lonely shore."

In early days he became known to his friends as "Jimmie" Halbert. This name clung to him through life and became a term indicative of endearment and companionship. When he was called from this world to the home beyond his death was widely and deeply mourned and his memory is still enshrined in the hearts of those who know him.

SAMUEL W. McCREA.

For long years Samuel Winthrope McCrea was a prominent and enterprising business man of Battle Creek and a citizen whose honorable life and upright career gained for him a leading position in the ranks of the representative men of this section of Michigan. He was born at Balston, Saratoga county, New York, on the 18th of April, 1819, a son of the Rev. John and Mary (Dunham) McCrea. The family was of Scotch ancestry, but in early colonial times the first of the name crossed the Atlantic from the land of the heather and established a home in the new world. Jane McCrea, of Revolutionary fame, was a great-great-aunt of the subject of this review. Leaving the east Rev. John McCrea removed to Dover, Ohio, and became a pioneer minister of that state. For some years he devoted his life to this holy calling and afterward retiring from the ministry he located in Westfield, Ohio, where he rested from further labor. His wife died during their residence in Dover. She was a daughter of Captain Dunham, who was lost at sea, and later her mother became the wife of Mr. Davis, a prominent physician of Balston, New York. Judge McCrea, a distinguished lawyer and jurist of Saratoga, New York, was an uncle of our subject.

After the death of his mother Samuel McCrea went to live with his grandmother, Mrs. Dr. Davis, and was partially educated in Poughkeepsie, New York. Later he became a student at Oberlin College, of Oberlin, Ohio, and subsequently continued his studies in Bissell's Academy for some time. He afterward engaged in teaching penmanship and bookkeeping, for commercial schools were not known at that period. When a young man, he engaged in merchandising at Seville, Medina county, Ohio, where he also acted as postmaster for one term. He built up a successful business, but wishing a more extended field he disposed of his interests there and came to Battle Creek, Michigan, in the year 1848. At that time the Michigan Central Railroad had been completed only as far as New Buffalo, but the embryo city gave promise of further development and Mr. McCrea believed that it would prove an excellent field of labor. Accordingly he established a grocery store located on what is now Main street. During the greater part of his mercantile life he was connected with the grocery trade and developed his original enterprise into a wholesale business. For many years he continued to be a leading grocer of Battle Creek. During this time he was also engaged in the dry-goods business for a number of years and in both branches of his commercial interests he met with success. Intricate business situations he seemed to comprehend at a glance and his judgment was rarely if ever at fault in regard to commercial interests. He possessed keen sagacity, unremitting diligence and unfaltering perseverance and upon these elements as a foundation he reared the superstructure of his success. He also owned a block on Main street which is still in possession of the family. He gave his entire attention to his mercantile interests and met with most gratifying success in his work.

On the 7th of August, 1847, Mr. McCrea was united in marriage to Miss Frances M. Porter, of Medina county, Ohio. The lady is a daughter of Arba and Atlanta (Beecher) Porter. Her father was a resident of Connecticut and a representative of an old time New England family, while the mother was a cousin of Dr. Lyman Beecher. Mr. Porter was a soldier of the War of 1812 and spent his last years at Twinsburg, Ohio. His wife lived to the extreme old age of ninety-five years and won distinction as a lady of superior intelligence and of marked literary talent. Her father Burr Beecher was a soldier of the Revolutionary war and was with Washington's army during the memorable winter at Valley Forge. Thus it is that Mrs. McCrea and her descendants are eligible to membership with the Daughters of the American Revolution. Mrs. McCrea was born in Prospect, New Haven county, Connecticut, and at an early day accompanied her parents on their removal to Portage county, Ohio, where her father engaged in farming. She pursued her education in Bissell's Academy and in the Western Reserve College at Hudson, Ohio. By her marriage she became the mother of three children: John W., who is now a well known florist of Battle Creek; Ida; and Harry F., a druggist of Denver, Colorado. It is a fact worthy of note that for forty-seven years from the time of her marriage there was not a death in the family, or a funeral in the house in which she resided, the first death being that of Mr. McCera on the 13th of March, 1892. For many years both Mr. and Mrs. McCrea held membership in the Episcopal church and for a long period he served as one of its vestrymen. He occupied a prominent position in the business circles of the city and was always a welcome addition to social circles. A dignified and highly educated gentleman whose life was broadened by travel, he commanded the respect and confidence of all. The people of Battle Creek are to be congratulated upon a character of such splendor of development, such refinement, purity of purpose and such devotion to the highest and best interests of the state as were exhibited in the private and public life of Samuel Winthrope McCrea. No one was ever more respected in this city and no one ever more fully enjoyed the confidence of the people or better deserved such respect and confidence. Mrs. McCrea still resides in the home which was erected by her husband many years ago, but with her daughter spends the winter months in the south, the winter of 1892-3 having been passed in Cuba.

BERTHIER D. WHITFORD.

Berthier D. Whitford, one of the oldest native sons of southern Michigan, was born in Comstock, Kalamazoo county, on the 18th of March, 1834. His father, Joseph Whitford, was born near Garrettsville, Otsego county, New York, December 25, 1807, and married Rhoda Harrington, who was born in the same locality on the 20th of October, 1806. Her father was Francis Harrington while the paternal grandfather of our subject was Robert Whitford, one of the early settlers of Otsego county, where he owned and developed a farm. After the marriage of Mr. and Mrs. Joseph Whitford they came to Michigan, accompanied by his father's family. This was in the fall of 1833 and he established his home in Comstock, when there were very few settlers throughout this portion of the state. He secured a farm of one hundred and twenty acres at Charleston, purchasing the land from the government and later added to it a tract of forty acres. The farm which he there developed has since been in possession of the family and is now the property of Berthier D. Whitford.

Upon his arrival the father built a log house, in which the family lived in true pioneer style. He continued to cultivate and improve his farm, making his home thereon until his death. For many years he served as township clerk and always took a prominent and helpful part in township affairs. He and his wife were among the first members of the Baptist church in Charleston and they left the impress of their individuality for good upon the public life. He died August 10, 1888, and his wife passed away in September, 1895. They left six children: Arabella, now deceased; Helen, the deceased wife of Eli Moore; Berthier D.; Wilbur S., of Augusta, Michigan; Theodore, of Ypsilanti, this state; and Mariette, the wife of R. Wilson, of Battle Creek.

Berthier D. Whitford obtained his education in a primitive log schoolhouse with puncheon floor and slab seats. Through the summer months he performed the usual duties alloted to the farmer lad and after attaining his majority he continued upon the old homestead. He married Miss Alice LaBar, a daughter of Alanson and Esther (Teeter) LaBar, of Augusta, Michigan, the wedding taking place July 1, 1865. Her father was a son of John LaBar, who married a Miss Graham of Tompkins county, New York. At a very early day he came to the west, settling in Bedford township, Calhoun county, where he purchased a farm, and later his death occurred in Augusta, this state. His son Alanson was born and reared in Tompkins county and was united in marriage to Esther Teeter, a daughter of Peter Teeter of that county, who served his country as a soldier in the Revolutionary war. Mrs. Whitford was born in Tompkins county and in 1831 her

parents removed westward to Charleston, Michigan. Later they returned to New York, but again came to Michigan and Mr. LaBar engaged in the shoe business in Battle Creek, being for some time a merchant of this city. Afterward he went to Augusta, where he conducted a shoe store for thirty years and was one of the honored and leading business men of that place. Through several terms he served as postmaster there. Later he retired to private life and established his home in Galesburg, Michigan, where he died in 1893, while his wife passed away two years later.

At the time of his marriage Mr. Whitford took his bride to a farm which he owned in Ross township, Kalamazoo county, and later for a number of years was employed by the Michigan Central Railroad Company, his home being at Gibson, Illinois, near Chicago. Subsequently he represented the railroad company at Augusta, Michigan. He then purchased a good tract of land of one hundred and twenty acres near Charleston, this state, and for twenty-two years carried on general farming there, meeting with very gratifying success in his undertakings. It continued to be his place of abode until 1898, when he removed to Battle Creek, where he has since lived retired. He yet owns the old homestead, however, and derives from it a good income.

Unto Mr. and Mrs. Whitford was born one son, Walter F., whose birth occurred in 1866 and who was educated at Galesburg. He afterward learned the machinists' trade and is now an expert machinist connected with the Advance Thresher Company of this city. The parents hold membership in the Methodist Episcopal church and Mr. Whitford votes with the

Democracy, believing firmly in the principles of the party. He owns a good home at No. 57 Bartlett street, where he and his wife are now living and his active labor in former years was the source of the prosperity which he is now enjoying.

CARL FRANZ BEACH.

The activity and energy which has led to the commercial life of Battle Creek finds exemplification in the life of Carl F. Beach, a dealer in carpets and all kinds of floor coverings, also in ladies' suits and ready-made clothing. He is the chairman and manager of the LaGripper Wrench Company, limited. He was born in Battle Creek township, Calhoun county, March 20, 1866, a son of Erasmus Darwin and Ovieda (Strong) Beach. The father was a farmer by occupation and the son spent his boyhood days upon the farm, acquiring his education in the country schools, also in a high school and a business college, being graduated from the latter at the age of seventeen years. He entered upon his business career as a clerk in a dry-goods store, where he remained for two years and when a young man of nineteen started in business on his own account as a partner of Hiram Strong, his uncle, in the conduct of a grocery house in Jackson, Michigan. He was thus engaged for more than a year and next went upon the road as a traveling salesman for the Noyes Wagon Company of Kalamazoo, whom he represented for three years, being very successful in that undertaking. When he started upon the road he was but a mere boy. Going to Mr. Stone, the manager, he asked for the position. Mr. Stone asked him what remuneration he wanted and the reply came, 'All I can earn." It was not long before the company recognized his ability to earn a good salary. Later he accepted a position as a clerk in the dry-goods store of E. Trump, of Battle Creek, with whom he remained until 1896, when he established his present business at No. 37 Main street, west. Here he carried a large and well selected line of carpets, floor coverings, ladies' suits, and ready-made goods; and because of his well selected stock and earnest desire to please his patrons he has secured a gratifying trade. He has always displayed considerable inventive genius, this being manifested when he was but a boy. He was still in his minority when he invented an adjustable buggy spring. In 1899 he began experimenting with a wrench, which he calls the LaGripper wrench and which he patented the same year. He then organized a company and began its manufacture in April, 1902. As the result of his inventive ability he has also produced the safety screw driver and has applied for a patent on this device.

Mr. Beach now owns the old homestead, comprising two hundred and twenty acres in Battle Creek township, and also a nearby farm of eighty acres. These he manages personally, devoting them to dairying and stock raising; making a specialty of high grade Durham cattle and Berkshire swine. He not only keeps the largest herd of cattle but is the largest milk producer in this section of the county. He is also interested in city real estate, and at present owns a fine flat building on Fountain street and also one on Alwood street, both of which were erected by him.

Mr. Beach was married in Battle Creek, October 18, 1888, the lady of his choice

CARL F. BEACH

being Miss May Clark, of Battle Creek, who was born in Bloomington, Illinois. They have one son, Harold Clark. Mr. Beach has ever been a stalwart Republican, voting for the party since he cast his first ballot for Harrison in 1888. Socially he is connected with the Knights of Pythias and also with the Dramatic Order of the Knights of Korassan. He was one of the first members of the Athelstan club, having been a member about eighteen years. His advancement in business life is attributed to his own efforts and his career has been creditable and also attended with gratifying success.

WILLIAM HENRY FONDA.

William Henry Fonda has been a factor in the improvement, development and expansion of Battle Creek, especially along the lines of his real estate operations. He was born in Poughkeepsie, New York, August 29, 1834, and is a son of Cornelius and Esther (Moe) Fonda. The father was born at Kinderhook, Columbia county, New York, in 1809, and was a son of Cornelius and Mary (Davis) Fonda. The grandfather of our subject was a native of Germany and was one of the earliest settlers of eastern New York in the vicinity of the Hudson river. Unto him and his wife were born seven children. The oldest, Colonel William C. Fonda, was a native of Columbia county, New York, and in 1835, came to Michigan, casting in his lot with the early settlers of Calhoun county. He settled upon a farm in Pennfield township, which constituted a part of the farm now owned by the heir of Henry Foss. From the government he entered about five hundred

acres of land, which was entirely unimproved, and with characteristic energy he began to clear and develop his property. Joining the state militia, he served for some years in its ranks and won the title of colonel. He was pre-eminently a military man, tall and erect and without a knowledge of fear. He married Laura Avery and when they came to the west there were three children in their family, while after their arrival three more were added to the household. Colonel Fonda was a man of marked influence and enterprise in his day and was also a most progressive agriculturalist, becoming the owner of one of the finest farms in his part of the county. He took an active and helpful part in the early development of this section of the state and his name certainly deserves to be inscribed high on the roll of honored pioneers. The other members of the family of Cornelius Fonda, senior, were John, who now lives in Cahoonzie, New York; Cornelius, deceased; Mrs. Margaret Whitlock; Isaac; Harriet and Edwin.

Cornelius Fonda, the father of him whose name introduces this review, spent the days of his boyhood and youth in the state of his nativity and then he, too, became a pioneer resident of Michigan, arriving in Calhoun county in the spring of 1838. He made the journey up the Hudson river by steamer, across the country by the Erie canal to Buffalo, thence by boat to Detroit and from there by wagon to his destination, twenty-three days being required to make the trip. He was accompanied by his wife and three sons and the journey across Michigan was made with a double ox team. In New York he had married Miss Esther Moe, who was born in Pleasant Valley, Dutchess county, that state, in 1814. Arriving in Calhoun county they settled upon the property where the Independent Congregational church now stands and at the Verona mills Mr. Fonda secured slabs with which he erected a small slab shanty, this being the first home of the family. Soon afterward, however, he built a house across the road. He was a blacksmith by trade and opened a smithy where the Trump block now stands. It was entirely unroofed, save that there was a covering over the bellows. Cornelius Fonda made the iron work for the first thresher built by Nichols & Shepard and in his later years he presented the firm with the hammer with which he did that work and to-day the implement is to be seen in their office. For many years he followed the blacksmith's trade and became the first foreman in the blacksmithing department in the Nichols & Shepard shops. He was an expert mechanic and proved a most capable and trusted employee of the house, but about 1850 he retired from active connection with blacksmithing and removed to his farm east of the city. He had there one hundred and five acres of land now comprised within what is now known as the Fonda addition to Battle Creek. On that property he spent his remaining days, devoting his energies to the supervision of his agricultural interests. He was a great lover of horses and owned some of the finest running stock to be found in the county. He took great pleasure in testing their ability and he once trained a horse to run without a rider and it made such splendid records that it passed everything on the race track. Mr. Fonda died in 1897, having survived his wife for about three years and his remains were interred by her side in Oak Hill cemetery. Mrs. Fonda was a

member of the Methodist church and a most estimable lady. Mr. Fonda cast his first presidential ballot in support of the Republican party. Through an active business career he gained an enviable reputation for reliability that made his name an honored one in trade circles. Unto him and his wife were born four sons: Isaac, who died in infancy; John, who passed away in 1895; William H., of this review; and Gilbert, who died in Poughkeepsie. New York, in 1848. The second son, John, was a foundryman who for some time conducted a foundry. He learned the trade in Poughkeepsie, New York, and afterward began work in the shops of the Nichols & Shepard Thresher Company, serving as head molder for several years. On leaving that employ he built a foundry on Hamblin avenue which he also conducted for a number of years. He wedded Mary Jones, who is now deceased. They had three sons, Edward and Frank, who are residents of this city, and George who died in Battle Creek in November, 1903.

William Henry Fonda was reared to the occupation of farming and early became familiar with the duties and labors that fall to the lot of the agriculturalist. He was educated in the public schools and after putting aside his text books assumed the management of his father's farm which he operated while the father and brother worked in the shops of Nichols & Shepard in the city. He continued to occupy the homestead until 1861, when his father purchased what is now the Clifton Hotel and then Mr. Fonda, senior, in connection with his son William Henry conducted the business for a year and a half. It was purchased at the price of twenty-seven hundred dollars, and eighteen months later was sold for seventy-five hundred dollars. After leaving the hotel William H. Fonda became deputy postmaster and filled that position in a most creditable manner for nine years under five different postmasters. In 1873 he became private secretary to President Dibble of the old Peninsular Railway Company, now the Grand Trunk, and continued with him for five years. Since that time Mr. Fonda has served as ticket agent for the Grand Trunk Railroad, and was also cashier of the freight department and ticket agent for the Michigan Central Railroad.

In 1865 was celebrated the marriage of Mr. Fonda and Miss Mary E. Caldwell, of Williamsport, Pennsylvania, and unto them has been born one child, Helen M., who is now the wife of Edson D. Clarage, manager of the Crucible Steel Company of America at Cleveland, Ohio. They also have a daughter, Eleanor.

Mr. Fonda gives his political support to the Republican party and his wife is identified with the Presbyterian church. They are both people of sterling worth and the hospitality of many of the best homes of the county is graciously and freely accorded them. Mr. Fonda served as city assessor of Battle Creek for three years, but has never been active in search for office, preferring to devote his time and energies to business affairs. He is now a stockholder of the Agricultural Company and gives considerable attention to the supervision of his realty interests. In 1892 he platted the Fonda addition, which is one of the most desirable additions to the city. With the growth of Battle Creek there came a demand for further property within its border and the old family homestead was subdivided and is now upon the mar-

ket. Already much of this has been sold, but Mr. Fonda still retains valuable property holdings, both in the city and country. No history of the pioneer families of Calhoun county would be complete without mention of our subject who for sixty-five years has been a witness of the growth and development of this locality. He has seen the forests cut down and the wild lands transformed into beautiful homes and farms, while in their midst cities and villages have sprung up, having all the advantages of the older east. In the work of progress and improvement he has taken a just pride in what has been accomplished and by reason of his success in business and his unblemished character he may well be called one of the leading citizens of Battle Creek.

FRANK PALMER.

Frank Palmer, now widely and favorably known in the business circles of Battle Creek, has attained to his present enviable position through a steady rise. His worth and capability winning ready recognition, he found in each promotion opportunity for further development and for the acquisition of broader knowledge concerning business methods. To-day he is an extensive dealer in and repairer of automobiles, bicycles and sporting goods and his enterprise, capable management and industry are the potent factors in the development of a business which has already brought to him gratifying success.

He was born in Convis township, Calhoun county, December 9, 1868, a son of Seneca and Catherine (Wood) Palmer, who are now living retired in Bellevue. The father was born near Syracuse, New York, May 4, 1833, a son of Seneca and Abigail (Guthrie) Palmer, who removed to Genoa, Ohio, when he was still a boy and there he was reared to manhood and married. His wife was born near Tiffin, Ohio, and was the daughter of Garrett Wood. Mr. Palmer was a soldier in a New York regiment for four years during the Civil war and the year following the close of hostilities he came to Michigan, settling in Calhoun county near the Eaton county line, where he spent his active life.

On the home farm Frank Palmer became familiar with the duties of the agriculturist and after attending the common schools he became a student in Olivet College, where he pursued the English course. When twenty-one years of age he went upon the road selling books and was thus successfully engaged for about a year. He next entered the Gage bindery, where he remained for eight years and then he again became a traveling salesman—the representative of the Royal Cycle Works of Marshall, Michigan. While thus engaged he gained an intimate knowledge of the bicycle business which he has put to practical use in the conduct of his own enterprise. He continued with that house until the business was closed out, but it was while he was still in their employ that he established his present business, in connection with Charles Jones and William Swindeman. In 1900 he purcased Mr. Jones's interests and in 1901 became sole proprietor. In September, 1902, he began dealing in automobiles and has developed this department of his business until it is perhaps the most important section of his successful enterprise. His place of business extends from Nos. 40 to 50, inclusive, on

North Jefferson street, where he has a fine salesroom and also space for automobile storage. He conducts an extensive repair shop for expert work on automobiles and his place of business is the largest in the state outside of Detroit or Grand Rapids. He was one of the first to handle automobiles in Battle Creek, giving his special attention to that branch of his business and is thoroughly posted concerning the trade. As the horseless carriage has grown in popular favor his sales have constantly increased, and throughout this section of the state there are many machines upon the road which have been introduced to the public through his establishment. He also deals in bicycles and sporting goods and does expert repair work along these lines. His business methods commend him to the patronage of the public, and his energy, diligence and honorable dealing have been the strong elements in his success.

On the 1st of January, 1891, Mr. Palmer was married in Marshall, Michigan, to Miss Etta Mathews, who was born near Kenton, New York, a daughter of George and Emma Mathews, who provided her with good educational privileges. She came to Battle Creek to live with an uncle, and attend the Seventh Day Adventist College. While here she became acquainted with Mr. Palmer and to him gave her hand in marriage. They have one son, Fred. who was born in Battle Creek, August 26, 1892. Their home is pleasantly located at No. 369 Lake avenue and its hospitality is greatly enjoyed by their many friends. Mr. Palmer is independent in his political views and socially is connected with the Knights of Pythias and the Benevolent Protective Order of Elks. He is a young man, alert and enterprising and also possessing the laudable ambition without which there is little accomplished in the business world. He has become a well known promoter of commercial activity in Battle Creek and stands as a representative of that class of American citizens who find in necessity, competition and intricate business conditions the spur of ambition and the stimulus of effort that leads to large successes.

LYCURGUS McCOY.

Rev. Lycurgus McCoy, the chaplain of the Battle Creek Sanitarium and also one of its directors and managers, was born in Washington township, near Greensburg, Decatur county, Indiana, April 30, 1835, a son of Barton S. and Eunice (Lawson) McCoy. In the maternal line especially he is descended from an illustrious family that has furnished many notable members, both in this country and in England. They have been gifted and talented men widely known throughout their respective countries, and the superiority of their mental powers, combined with loyalty in citizenship and chivalrous defense of what they have believed to be right, has justly gained for them leadership.

While the members of the McCoy family have, perhaps been less widely known, they have been none the less worthy of the respect and trust of their fellow men. The paternal ancestry of our subject can be traced back to William and Jean McCoy, who were born amid the highlands of Scotland, and in 1774 came to America with their five children, settling in Washington county in the Wyoming valley of Pennsylvania. Subsequently they removed to

Bourbon county, Kentucky, where the parents died. Their son, Daniel McCoy, who was born in Scotland, went with the family to Kentucky, where he spent his remaining days. He was married in this country to Christina Sutherland and followed farming in the Blue Grass state. He was the father of ten children and the youngest, twins, were born April 10, 1802. One of these was Barton S. McCoy, who at the age of twenty-one years removed from Kentucky to Decatur county, Indiana, and there on the 14th of April, 1831, married Eleanor Hamilton, who died April 25, 1832. For his second wife he chose Eunice Lawson.

Her parents, John and Betsey Lawson, were born in Ireland, of Scotch ancestry, the former in 1786 and the latter in 1788. Her maiden name was Betsey Stewart. About 1792 he came to the United States, settling in Indiana county, Pennsylvania, whence they removed to Decatur county, Indiana, in 1832. The father was a well-to-do farmer and hotel keeper. He died in 1854 and his wife passed away in 1863. They left ten children of whom Mrs. McCoy, the eldest, was born in Pennsylvania, July 14, 1810. John Lawson was a son of William Lawson, who came to Pennsylvania in 1792. Through many previous generations the family had lived in Scotland and in England, tracing their ancestry back to the time of King Henry III of England, during whose reign John Lawson was Lord Fawlesgrave, of County York, England. From this time on the name occurs frequently on the pages of English history. One of the name was Lord High Admiral of the English Navy, in the time of Cromwell. Dr. John Lawson was president of the Royal College of Physicians in London, in 1694, and in 1718 Sir Wilfred

Lawson was elected a fellow of the Royal Society of London. Several members of the family have been prominent in the literary world as authors and professors. John Lawson was surveyor general for the British government in North Carolina, in 1700, and lost his life at the hands of the Indians. Thomas Lawson was surveyor general of the United States and died about the time of the breaking out of the Civil war. Sir Wilfred Lawson, baronet, of Brasenthwait manor, Cumberlandshire, England, was a member of the royal commission to this country at the time of the Centennial Exposition in Philadelphia. He was also a member of the English Parliament, also the acknowledged leader of the temperance movement in England and a man of great excellence of character as well as prominence in public life. John L. Lawson, Esquire, of Philadelphia, Pennsylvania, was a Republican elector from that state in 1888, and thus through many centuries members of the family have been leaders in those walks of life demanding high intellectuality.

It was on the 24th of April, 1834, that Eunice Lawson gave her hand in marriage to Barton S. McCoy, and unto them were born three children, all yet living, Lycurgus McCoy being the eldest. His sister, Mary E., is now the widow of William S. Skinner, of Chicago; and Franklin N., is residing in Kansas City, Kansas. With his family Barton S. McCoy removed from Indiana to Keokuk county, Iowa, in 1850, and there died in 1857, at the age of fifty-five years. The mother had passed away April 30, 1842. He was an elder of the Christian church throughout the periods of his married life and a man of deep religious convictions. In the early days he was a

Whig and a strong anti-slavery man, voting for the anti-slavery candidates, and when John C. Fremont became the candidate of the Republican party—formed to prevent the further extension of slavery —Mr. McCoy gave to him his political support. He did much to aid fugitive negroes who had escaped from bondage and were on their way to freedom in the north. One of the early pioneers of Iowa, he took an active part in the development of that state and was a man of considerable influence in social and political circles.

Lycurgus McCoy received his mental training in the schools of Decatur county, Indiana, having no opportunity to attend school after the removal of the family to Iowa, which occurred when he was fifteen years of age. During the winter following his seventeenth birthday he taught school and for a number of years followed that profession. In early manhood he married Miss Sarah A. Lawson, a daughter of Hugh Lawson, of Keokuk county, Iowa, the wedding taking place December 27, 1855. He then engaged in farming and teaching for a number of years, settling on raw prairie land which he transformed into a fine farm, although during the process he had to undergo many of the hardships and trials incident to pioneer life. Unto this union were born four children, of whom three are living: Eunice E., born on the 1st of March, 1857, was married December 5, 1877, to A. C. Sheridan, and they resided at Centerville, Iowa, until August, 1903, when they removed to Buffalo, N. Y. They have two children Kate K. and McCoy. For twenty years Mr. Sheridan has been agent for the Chicago, Rock Island & Pacific Railroad there and is now chief clerk in the office of the division superintendent of the Delaware, Lackawanna & Western Railroad at Buffalo, N. Y.; Harriet L., the second child, was born December 16, 1861, and died July 31, 1863. Barton Sherman, born December 16, 1864, was married November 20, 1893, to Carrie E. Fox, and their two children are Marguerite E., born August 18, 1894; and Sarah Eloise, born December 16, 1897, Barton S. McCoy is now employed as manager of the Battle Creek Breakfast Food Company of Quincy, Illinois, and his wife is telegraph operator of the Postal Cable Company, of Battle Creek. Henry Clay McCoy, born May 31, 1868, is a steam fitter of this city and the youngest of the family.

In 1862 Lycurgus McCoy enlisted in the Union army as a member of Company F, Thirty-third Iowa Volunteer Infantry and on its organization he was elected second lieutenant. This was in August, 1862. While the regiment was on guard duty at McDowell College Military prison in St. Louis, where some eight hundred rebel prisoners were incarcerated, Lieutenant McCoy received a wound in the left ankle through the accidental discharge of an Enfield rifle, which crippled him for life and necessitated his resignation from the service, in March, 1863. This was a great disappointment to him as he had enlisted a number of the men of the company and expected to remain with them, and without doubt would have been captain of his company in a very few months by the regular line of promotion. For three months he was confined in the hospital in a very precarious condition, his life hanging in the balance, but ultimately he recovered and returned to his home the latter part of January.

In the autumn of the same year Mr. McCoy was elected treasurer of Keokuk county, entering upon the duties of the office January 1, 1864, at Sigourney. He was afterward re-elected for a second term of two years. During the latter term he engaged in the real estate business, entering into partnership with S. A. James. The firm did an extensive loan and real estate business and also compiled a complete set of abstracts of titles for that county. They continued in business until 1877 when they sold out and Mr. McCoy began preaching the gospel under the auspices of the Iowa conference of the Seventh Day Adventists. In 1879 he received a call from Dr. J. H. Kellogg, of the Battle Creek Sanitarium, to take the position of business manager and chaplain, which position he filled for two years, the length of time agreed upon. He then returned to his home in Sigourney, Iowa, in June, 1881, and again entered the church service as an evangelist under the direction of the Iowa Seventh Day Adventists Conference, continuing the work for seven years. In the meantime he was elected president of the Iowa conference. In the spring of 1888 he received a unanimous call from the Battle Creek Sanitarium to return and accept the position of secretary and chaplain. This he accepted and has since made his home in Battle Creek, being still prominently identified with the sanitarium. He is now one of its directors and also one of its managers. This is the largest sanitarium in the world, having accommodations for between eight hundred and one thousand patients. The entire possessions of the institution are estimated to be worth one million dollars. From the main institution some sixty branches have arisen and from the parent stem they receive assistance in the way of physicians and nurses. Mr. McCoy's services are confined entirely to the sanitarium. Before the fire there were fiften hundred people who had religious· instruction here and it is expected that the number will soon exceed that.

Mr. McCoy was one of the organizers and the first president of the Calhoun County Telephone Company, and under the re-organization he was retained as one of the directors and the vice president. His only object in the formation of this company was to cheapen the rates of telephone service, and his work resulted in cutting the rates in two and in keeping them at that price. From the time he was old enough to vote he was an ardent Freesoiler and also a strong temperance man. He cast his first vote for John C. Fremont and has since been identified with the Republican party. While in Sigourney, Iowa, during his service as county treasurer he was elected mayor of the city and while in the latter office the Chicago, Rock Island & Pacific Railroad, the first railroad in that city, was constructed. He has been a member of the city council of Battle Creek from the third ward for four years, and during this time the system of street paving was instituted and Mr. McCoy is proud of the fact that the city's rapid and substantial development has taken place during this period. He has not been an active politician, but believes that every citizen should cast his influence on the side of good government. When urged to accept office under the city and county government, however, he has always refused to do so. In 1897 he made an extended trip over Europe, visiting many parts of Great Britian and also the points of modern and

historic interest in continental Europe, going as far south as Naples and as far east as Vienna. He takes a broad view of the world, is a student of its history and possibilities and his humanitarian principles have brought him into close and helpful contact with his fellow men. His record has been in harmony with that of a distinguished and honorable ancestry.

DAVID WEST MURREY.

There is no name in Calhoun county which carries with it more of integrity, of uprightness, of earnest citizenship, or calls forth more universal expressions of regard, than that of David West Murrey, now the oldest living male settler of Lee township. Whatever of virtue in the character of Mr. Murrey, whatever of quality in his living, has been directly fou :ded upon traits inherited from an ancestry rich in the virtues of patriotism, loyalty, steadfastness and principle, which has stood the test of a mighty trial.

The first American emigrant being an Irishman, while the mother was of Holland birth. Two sons, Peter and George, were born of this union and were both in young manhood at the time of the struggle for American independence. Before hostilities had actually begun Peter and George were engaged one day in threshing grain with a flail in the barn, when they fell into a heated discussion as to the situation of the colonies in regard to the mother country. Peter was stanch in his support of the colonies, while George espoused the Royalist cause, and so excited did the two become that they forgot work

DAVID W. MURREY

MRS. CHARITY C. MURREY

and brotherhood and fell to fighting. When war finally broke out Peter enlisted with the Continental army, while George accepted a colonelcy with the British army. In an engagement Peter was taken prisoner and sent to Prison Isle, near Quebec. where he was confined for nearly three years, undergoing hardships and deprivations that would have made a less brave heart fail. George Murrey made him three different visits and was much affected by the hardships which were a part of the life of his brother. He offered to secure his release and a commission in the British army if he would desert the American cause. In the midst of his suffering and probable death Peter Murrey replied, "Rather than to desert the cause I believe to be right I would die and let my bones be bleached by the St. Lawrence river." The cause triumphed and Peter Murrey lived to see the victors going peaceably back to their labors, in store, shop and field. He was exchanged in time and after the close of the war quietly resumed his farming duties in his native town, there dying full of years and honors. While still in service he had offered his services as guard at the time of the battle of Plattsburg. With the spirit of self reliance, energy and ambition that had distinguished his early career he became prominent in public affairs in his own community and gave liberally of time and money toward all public enterprises. His wife died early in life, leaving a son, David W., who was but six months old.

David W. Murrey, who was born in Granville, Washington Co., N. Y., was placed in the home of a Mr. Blossom, of Rutland, Vt., making his home with him until he had atained his majority. He then

gave his attention to farming in the summers, while in the winters he was engaged as a cloth dresser. Later in life he located at Adams, Jefferson county, New York, where he remained until 1822, removing then to Pawlet, Vermont. After a year's residence in that location he brought his family to Washington county, New York, afterward locating in Sardinia township, Erie county. He purchased a farm in that locality of the Holland Purchase Company upon which he remained until 1843, in that year taking up his journey westward until he arrived in Michigan, making his home in the village of Marengo until the following spring, when he removed to Lee township. Purchasing a farm of forty acres, he remained in this location until his death. Politically he was a Democrat and religiously both himself and wife were identified with the Baptist church, being strong in the faith and works of that denomination. He and his wife both sleep in the cemetery at Partello, in Lee township. His wife, formerly Lucy Hanks, was a native of Rutland county, Vermont, her birth having occurred at Pawlet, where their marriage had taken place. She was a daughter of Arunah Hanks, who was a farmer, blacksmith and goldsmith, a man of much mechanical genius. To Mr. and Mrs. Murrey were born ten children, of whom eight attained maturity and four are now living: David West, the personal subject of this review, born at Adams, Jefferson county, New York, July 31, 1818; Lucy, who married Justin Carey, of Clarence township, this county; Lucius B., of Bailey, Muskegon county, Michigan, and Laura, who married George Belcher, of Partello, also this county.

10

Up to the time he was fourteen years old Mr. Murrey remained a member of his father's household, receiving a rather limited education in the meantime. At the age of fourteen years he was employed as tow boy on the Erie canal and later as boatswain. The temptations which beset a boy at that age and in such employment are such as to imperil his young manhood, but though Mr. Murrey remained in that occupation for several years, with more or less constant association with many rough characters, he retained all those qualities which distinguished his ancestry. He was never engaged in brawls, which were so frequent in those days and that location; never indulged in smoking, drinking or chewing tobacco, holding himself aloof from all evil associations. At the age of seventeen years he was taken ill, and did not work again until the following year. He then joined his parent in Erie county and worked out by the day until attaining his majority. From the time he was twenty-one years old he worked for one man for three years at $11 per month, losing but three and a half days in the entire time. At the end of that period he took up one hundred acres of land in Sardinia township, Erie county, New York, and with a brother cleared up ten acres. He then joined his father and family and came to Michigan, leaving New York July 20, 1843, making the trip across Lake Erie by boat, by wagon to Ypsilanti, where they remained until the fall of the year, pursuing their journey then to the village of Marengo. In the following spring he purchased forty acres in Lee township, erecting a log house for their shelter, their entire capital being then but three cents in

money and provisions for two weeks. Undaunted by the prospect they made maple sugar, which they sold in Marengo, tiding them over until a crop could be raised. A little land was immediately cleared, the trees chopped down, the brush burned and among the stumps their first crop of potatoes and corn was planted. This was the beginning of their life in Michigan. During the years that have intervened Mr. Murrey has done much toward the material development of the country, clearing many acres of land and making many improvements. He has at times owned a large amount of land, but having recently disposed of the greater part, he now owns but seventy-nine acres, upon which he is living a retired life.

The marriage of Mr. Murrey occurred in Erie county, New York, September 22, 1842, and united him with Miss Charity C. Young, a native of Schoharie county, that state. She was born January 20, 1820, and died August 29, 1889, leaving the following children: Voleray D., now deceased and buried in Pottersville, Michigan; Amanda A., who married M. C. Thomas and has one child, Arhut Thomas, their home being with Mr. Murrey; Parthena, now deceased, who married Henry J. Gibson; Alvarado, deceased, and Eldorado, who lives in Charlotte, Michigan. Mrs. Murrey was a woman of exceptional character, a sweet and lovely nature, and with her death was lost from the home that which made it fair. She is gone, but not forgotten in the home circle.

In addition to his agricultural pursuits in the county, Mr. Murrey has been identified with the commercial enterprises of his community. In 1873 he opened a store at

Partello, handling general merchandise, conducting the interests of the same until 1881, when his other business so engrossed his attention that he disposed of his stock. He was largely instrumental in establishing the postoffice at Partello and acted as its postmaster from 1871 to 1881. In 1880 he was one of the prime movers in establishing a cheese factory, which was operated for two years, and in 1887 he purchased a half interest in the factory and from that time on he and his son have devoted it to apple drying purposes. Politically Mr. Murrey is a stanch Democrat, and for many years has been active in political movements in his community. Perhaps no other man in the community has served in more capacities and more continuously than Mr. Murrey. For thirty-two years he has acted as notary public, township clerk for over ten years, supervisor for four years; township treasurer for five years, during which time he saved the township many hundreds of dollars by faithful attention to the duties of office and also acted as highway commissioner, drain commissioner and school director for many years. He was once elected justice of the peace, but would not qualify. In religion he is a firm believer in the faith of the Christian church, but there being no church of that denomination in the community he is not identified with any religious body, though uniformly liberal and generous in his support of all religious or philanthropic measures. What Mr. Murrey has accomplished for this community cannot be measured in words, the fruits of his living will go on beyond the borders of the present and blossom again, bringing into the lives of those yet to come the beauty and richness of an unselfish, pioneer life, strong in the elements upon which a statehood is always founded.

JAMES COVELL HALL.

James Covell Hall, in whose life record there is much that is worthy of emulation and whose memory is dear to the hearts of a large circle of friends who knew and honored him during his active life, was born in Genesee county, New York, February 3, 1834, a son of Henry Augustus and Rebecca (Brown) Hall. Entering the common schools of his native county, he pursued his studies and at the age of thirteen went to Iowa with a neighbor's family with whom he remained for a time. Subsequently he removed to Cairo, Illinois, where he entered a naval school. He had been a student for two years when the Civil war broke out. Prompted by a spirit of patriotism, he enlisted in the navy and served in the Mississippi squadron under Commodores Foote, and Foster. He entered the army as a seaman and was promoted until at the close of the war he was acting ensign. He took part in all of the naval engagements on the Mississippi river and was wounded five times. The shot which struck his left forearm proved the most disastrous and caused him trouble throughout his remaining days. He always carried the rebel lead, the bullet having lodged in the bone. This wound was sustained at Fort Pillow. In March, 1866, Mr. Hall was honorably discharged and retired from the army with a most creditable military record.

He then returned to his boyhood's home in Batavia, New York, and on the 16th of

April, 1866, he was united in marriage, in Buffalo, to Miss Kate Underhill, who was born in Batavia, a daughter of Alfred and Margaret Underhill, worthy pioneer settlers of Genesee county. They were natives of Connecticut and at an early period in the development of western New York removed to the Empire State. After their marriage Mr. and Mrs. Hall came to Michigan, settling in Hastings, where they remained for a year and a half, coming thence to Battle Creek. Mr. Hall followed the carpenter's trade for a time in this city, but on account of the wound in his left arm was forced to abandon that occupation and became a traveling salesman. remaining upon the road until about two years prior to his death. which resulted from the injuries he sustained in the war. He passed away March 15. 1895. He was a member of Farragut post. G. A. R., and one of its first commanders. He also belonged to the Ancient Order of United Workmen and both the post and the lodge attended the funeral in a body and laid him to rest in Oak Hill cemetery.

Unto Mr. and Mrs. Hall were born two children: Mildred O., who is now principal of School No. 3 in Battle Creek; and Mattie May. the wife of Charles Curry of this city, by whom she has one son, James Howard. For some years the family resided at 136 Kalamazoo street and Mr. Hall then purchased the adjoining lot and erected a fine residence. in which he spent his remaining days and in which his widow and elder daughter now reside. He voted with the Republican party and had firm faith in its principles, doing everything in his power to promote its growth and success. His genial manner and cordial disposition made him popular with a large circle of friends and wherever he went he gained the warm esteem of those with whom he was brought in contact.

EDWARD ARNOLD.

Capability is the secret of the success which has attended Edward Arnold in his business career. Without the aid of influential friends or of wealth he has steadily worked his way upward and to-day occupies the responsible position of lost freight agent for the Grand Trunk Railroad at Battle Creek. His connection with this road dates from 1880 and no higher testimonial of fidelity and excellence of service could be given.

Mr. Arnold was born at Kingston, Ontario, August 26, 1865. a son of George and Mary (White) Arnold. The father was born at Oxford, England. Through many generations the family has been connected with Magdalene College at that place, the oldest college in the country, and one of the oldest in Europe. Professor Henry Arnold. recently deceased, was one of the faculty and George Arnold was reared and educated in that famous institution of learning in Oxford. When a young man he served through the Crimean war and soon after crossed the Atlantic to Ontario, where he had charge of the military service in the Dominion of Canada, occupying that position for nearly forty years or until the time of his death which occurred in 1879, when he was sixty years of age. For many years he was connected with the government service and held the rank of colonel. He wedded Mary White, of Montreal, who was of Irish lineage. They held membership in the Episcopal church and enjoyed the high regard of all who knew them. Our subject is the youngest of a family of seven children. all of whom grew to mature years: William, who was a rancher died in Ft. Qu Appelle; George, of Detroit, Michigan; Charles, holds a government position in Montreal; Mrs. Nellie Hutchinson, of Rochester, New York; Mrs. A. H. Walters, the wife of Professor Walters, who occupies the chair of mathematics in Morin College of Quebec; Isabelle, who died at Kingston, Ontario, in 1902, and Edward.

Edward Arnold was educated in Kingston. Ontario, attending the public schools and a business college. He then entered upon his business career as a telegraph operator and station agent, with the Grand Trunk Railroad Company at Montreal. He was promoted to various stations on the Grand Trunk line, as agent, and subsequently was sent to the general offices in Chicago in 1885. There he remained until 1890, when he came to Battle Creek to accept his present position as lost freight agent of the Grand Trunk Railroad Company. He handles all the freight claims for this corporation in the western division which comprises the line from Port Huron to Chicago and all of its branches. This is one of the more important positions in the service of the company. He adjudicates claims amounting to many thousands of dollars every week and his responsible position has been earned through his own able and excellent business methods and marked fitness for the duties that devolve upon him. He travels many thousands of miles every month, in fact, much of the time is spent upon the road. His rise in railroad service has come in acknowledgement of his personal qualifications and unfaltering fidelity

to the trust reposed in him and to the important tasks which form a large part of the work of the office. He has become quite extensively interested in real estate in Battle Creek, having made judicious investments in property here from time to time.

Mr. Arnold is a popular member of the Athelstan club and one of its oldest representatives. He also belongs to the Masonic fraternity. having been raised in Cornwall lodge, No. 125, F. & A. M. Aside from his business duties his attention is most largely given to the study of ornithology and he has personally made one of the finest collections of birds and eggs to be found in the entire country. having twelve thousand birds' eggs, a collection of which many a college might covet. and it would prove a valuable addition to the exhibits in many a public museum. He has written a large number of interesting and instructive articles upon birds and ornithology for the leading magazines and his own private collection secured throughout this country and Canada has been visited by collectors from all parts of the United States. He has also donated type specimens to the National Museum at Washington. At the present time Mr. Arnold is collecting data for the history of birds of Michigan, which when completed will be a valuable standard work far in advance of anything previously published. He has made ten different trips to the barren lands of this country and has traveled thousands of miles in canoes and in buck-boards in order to secure rare specimens of game-birds and their eggs, which cannot be obtained otherwise. His entire leisure time for the past fifteen years has been devoted to this work and his collection from a financial, as well as a scientific standard, is extremely valuable. In earlier years Mr. Arnold was very fond of hunting, but although he now spends much time in the woods he never kills birds excepting for the purpose of study. In this age of specialization when the individual usually directs his efforts solely along one line it is seldom that we meet a successful business man who is at the same time a devoted scientist simply from the love of the work. Mr. Arnold, however, has, through reading, investigation and research become a man of broad scholarly attainments and his efforts have added to the scientific knowledge of the world. He is president of the Audubon Society for the State of Michigan and an old member of the American Ornithologists's Union.

LUKE E. SMITH.

One of the progressive farmers of Calhoun county now residing on section 10, Battle Creek township, was born in Seneca county, New York, on the 22d of January, 1845. He comes of Holland ancestry, the family having been established in America, however, at an early period in the development of the new world. His parents were Josiah and Margaret (Eckerson) Smith, both of whom were natives of Rockland county, New York. The father of our subject entered upon his business career without capital, but though he was a poor man at the beginning, he ultimately became a prosperous citizen. In early life he learned the trade of a stone and brick mason and, taking up his abode in the town of Junius, Seneca county, he there became actively identified with building interests, erecting many cobble-stone and brick residences, also business blocks, churches and schools.

In 1864 he left New York for Michigan and settled upon the farm in Calhoun county now owned and occupied by his son Charles M. Smith on section 3, Battle Creek township. The trip westward made overland with a team driven by the sons, Luke and Charles, both being under age, and occupied three weeks, reaching their destination on the day before Lincoln was elected to the presidency for a second time, Mr. Smith and part of the family remaining in New York until after election to vote. Although Mr. Smith took up his abode upon a farm he continued to work at his trade to some extent in this county and erected a cobble-stone schoolhouse and also a residence in Pennfield township, the latter requiring one hundred days in its construction. He was the only man who could lay cobble stones in this part of the state. His farm comprised one hundred and twenty acres of land, for which he paid sixty-five dollars per acre. As the years passed modern improvements were placed upon it and it is now a very valuable property. Mr. Smith gave his political support to the Democracy, but he had neither time nor inclination for public office, feeling that he had done his full duty as a citizen by supporting the measures which he believed would contribute most largely to the general good. He left to his family not only a comfortable competence but also an untarnished name and an example well worthy of emulation. His life was characterized by untiring industry. He realized that there is no royal road to wealth and as the result of his perseverance, close application and diligence he gained a valuable property. Unto him and his wife were born seven children, of whom five are now living: John S. and Theodore, residents of Ottawa county, Michigan, John S. at the time of the Civil war was living in Wisconsin and joined the Union army as a soldier from that state; Luke E., whose name introduces this review; Charles M., who is represented elsewhere in this work, and Emma, the wife of William Coaman, whose father was one of the first settlers of Barry county, Michigan, where William and Emma Coaman still reside.

Luke E. Smith spent the first fifteen years of his life in his parents' home and during that time acquired a fair English education by attendance at the public schools. He then went to Wisconsin to live with his brother John, remaining in that state for a year. On the expiration of that period, however, he returned home and began working as a farm hand by the month. In the fall of 1864 he accompanied his parents on their removal to Michigan. Here he continued to work by the month, thus being employed by an uncle of the lady who later became his wife. He received twenty dollars per month during the winter seasons and twenty-six dollars during the summer.

In 1868 Mr. L. E. Smith and his wife went to Columbia, Wisconsin, where his brother, John S., resided, and entered into partnership with him in mercantile and milling business, and was there until 1870, when he returned to Michigan on account of poor health. In 1871 he and his brother Charles M. bought eighty acres of land, which he now owns, having bought his brother's share.

On Christmas eve of 1866, when twenty-two years of age, Luke E. Smith was united in marriage to Miss Cornelia M. Reese. The family name had formerly been spelled without the last "e." Her parents were Albert and Beatta (Sheppard) Reese and the former was born in Massachusetts in 1814,

while the latter's birth occurred in Palermo, Oswego county, New York, on the 23d of June, 1826. Albert Reese came to Calhoun county, Michigan, in 1836 with his parents Andrew and Electa (Burgett) Reese, the family home being established on section 3, Battle Creek township, where the father secured two hundred acres of wild wooded land which he entered from the government. This he at once cleared and placed under cultivation, being assisted in the work by his sons. The journey westward had been made in the slow primitive manner of the times. They traveled overland with an ox team, camping at night along the way. At that early period in the development of southern Michigan all produce had to be taken to market at Detroit and from the latter place they hauled other provision back to their home. It required about a week to make the long trip. The family endured all the hardships and trials of pioneer life. The greater part of the land in this locality was still in possession of the government and was therefore wild and unimproved. Often through the forests there was nothing but an old Indian trail, roads not yet being made, while the streams were unbridged and the entire country undeveloped. The Reese family bore an important part in the work of early improvement here. Andrew Reese and his wife continued to reside in this county until their life's labors were ended in death, when they were laid to rest in the Reese cemetery. Albert Reese, the father of Mrs. Smith, lived with his parents until about three months after his marriage, when, having completed for himself a little home upon a small tract of land given him by his father, he removed with his bride to that place. As the years passed he became a well-to-do farmer and was also held in the highest esteem because his life was upright and honorable and because in all his trade transactions he was straightforward. On the 4th of March, 1846, he was united in marriage to Miss Beatta Sheppard, a daughter of Albert and Nancy (Mosher) Sheppard, both of whom were natives of New York. Her parents came with their family to Calhoun county, Michigan, in 1836, arriving on the 29th of August, in Battle Creek township. Both Mr. and Mrs. Sheppard spent their remaining days here. Mrs. Albert Reese accompanied her parents on their westward emigration to Assyria township, Barry county, and by her marriage she became the mother of ten children: Cornelia, who is now the wife of our subject; Merritt, deceased; Clara, who is the wife of John V. Wood, a resident of Battle Creek township; Andrew, who resides in Grand Rapids, Michigan; Edward, who is living in the State of Washington; Abigail, the wife of William Cotton, a resident of Battle Creek township; Frederick, who is living in the city of Battle Creek; Marian, the wife of Byron Tinney, of Chicago; and Belle, the wife of Joseph Mix, who resides in Ashville, Michigan; Jennie, a nurse, lives in the city of Battle Creek.

The home of Mr. and Mrs. Smith has been blessed with three children. Wellington, who resides in Battle Creek, married Miss Carrie Mapes and they have two children, Arthur and Gladys; Agnes L. married Edward Wilbur, by whom she had a daughter Hazel, and after the death of her first husband she became the wife of William Van Wagner, a resident of Battle Creek; and Victor S. married Zada Van Wagner and they reside in Battle Creek township.

Mr. Smith of this review is the owner of one hundred and seven acres of fine farming land and has placed upon it all of the improvements there seen. He has a fine dwelling, substantial barns and other outbuildings necessary for the shelter of grain and stock. His fields are richly cultivated and annually return to him golden harvests and the neat and thrifty appearance of the place indicates his careful supervision. He has never been active as a politician and, in fact, is independent in his political affiliations. In 1887, however, he was elected township treasurer on the Prohibition ticket. His worth as a man and citizen are widely acknowledged and he belongs to that class known as self-made men because they have triumphed over obstacles and depending upon their own resources have worked their way upward to prosperity.

ZENO GOULD.

Zeno Gould was a resident of Battle Creek for nearly forty years, and during the first twenty years of that period was one of the representative men in the industrial and municipal affairs of that city. Through his own efforts and natural ability he became a successful business man, whose sound judgment and sterling worth commanded the highest respect of the community in which he passed the most fruitful years of his life.

Mr. Gould was born at Sand Lake, New York, March 20, 1818, and back to a very early epoch in the colonization of the new world his ancestral history can be traced. Zaccheus oGld, the progenitor of the family in America, was a native of England, and from Hempstead, in Herfordshire, emigrated to the new world, settling

ZENO GOULD

in Topsfield, Massachusetts, in 1638. Zeno Gould was a direct descendant in the seventh generation of Zaccheus Gould. Representatives of the name, through successive genrations, have figured prominently in public life, and the family records, as well as the Massachusetts Bay records, prove the parent stock in this country to have been of importance in colonial affairs; also to have been of stanch integrity and liberal in their religious views; the history saying that they rebelled against the strict church discipline and were "arrested for harboring Quakers." At the time of the Revolutionary war the family was well represented in the patriot army and did its full share toward winning the nation's independence. His maternal ancestors were equally prominent and distinguished, and among the number was William L. Marcy, a noted statesman and diplomat, who was an uncle of Mr. Gould.

Zeno Gould was a son of Ophir and Rhoda (Marcy) Gould, in whose family were thirteen children. His brother, William Gould, became a resident of Calhoun county in 1869, and died on his farm near Battle Creek, Michigan, March 18, 1902, at the age of eighty-eight years, leaving a widow, with whom he had lived sixty-five years. He passed away a few months before the death of the subject of this review, who died October 12th, 1902, and who was the last of the older generation. Zeno Gould's mother died when he was but two years of age, a fact which he never ceased to regret even in his old age, believing, as he did, that in losing his mother, he lost many chances of education and advancement, as well as the tender care and counsel which only a mother can give. His boyhood and youth were passed with relatives near his birth place. In 1834, when sixteen years old, he determined to "seek his own fortune," and went alone to Genesee county, New York. Thus early, he began to acquire those lessons in self reliance and industry; and laid the foundation of a character, developed and strengthened in later years, which enabled him to leave a name linked to honor and success. He continued to reside in Genesee county until he came to Michigan in 1854. He was married in Alabama, New York, in 1839, ot Miss Clarissa Baker, a daughter of Nathan Baker, who was born at Saratoga, New York, while her mother, who bore the maiden name of Mahala Shattuck, was born at Mason, New Hampshire. While living in Alabama, Mr. and Mrs. Gould became the parents of four daughters, Mary E., Emma G., Carrie A. and Annie.

Mr. Gould and family arrived in Battle Creek in February, 1854, where they passed a few weeks with Nathan Baker, Mrs. Gould's father, but later settled in Schoolcraft, Michigan. They remained there until December, 1859, when they removed to Albion in order to give their children better educational advantages. Of the children of Mr. and Mrs. Gould, Mary E. was married in Albion, Michigan, in 1861 to Dr. Thomas H. Briggs, of Schoolcraft, Michigan, and now resides in Battle Creek; Emma G., now of Atchison, Kansas, was married in 1867, in Battle Creek, to Lewis M. Briggs, also of Schoolcraft, and in 1869 Carrie A., now of Hiawatha, Kansas, became the wife of Henry C. Baker, of Battle Creek, in which city their marriage was celebrated.

In Battle Creek, November 15, 1894, occurred the death of Mrs. Gould, and

March 12th, 1898, Miss Annie Gould, the youngest daughter, passed away.

Mr. Gould and his family remained in Albion until 1863, when they came to Battle Creek. Here Mr. Gould made a permanent home. He served the city well in various municipal capacities, being widely known as a stanch Republican, unfaltering in the performance of his duties and in his allegiance to the cause which he espoused. His business interests were of an important character and contributed to the prosperity of the city, as well as to his individual success. During his active business life he had an extensive acquaintance with the farmers of the community and was deeply interested in the agricultural welfare of the country, taking great delight in the advances made in methods of farm work, in the improvement of machinery, and in every progressive effort that was of benefit to the agricultural class.

Mr. Gould possessed a logical mind, formed his own opinions and knew how to defend them. He was a discriminating reader, well posted on all the important questions of the day, and especially interested in finance, politics and religion. Personally, he was conservative in business, radical in politics, and held liberal religious views. Nearly twenty years prior to his death, he retired from active outside interests, still conducting his private business with sound judgment and ability.

His career was characterized by unfaltering integrity in all trade transactions and his word was known to be as good as his bond. To the last, his business ability and his keen insight into all matters requiring clear and sound judgment, never faltered. One of his life long friends said of him: "Nature gave him manhood, mental capacity and superb moral strength. His instinctive reserve hindered him from pushing into places to which his real merit commended him, and such were the conditions around him that the public failed to avail itself of the tithe of his civic value."

ARTHUR B. WILLIAMS.

Success is a criterion of ability, especially in professional circles where advancement must depend upon individual merit, and therefore the large and lucrative practice which Arthur B. Williams enjoys, is indicative of his superior qualifications as a lawyer. He is widely recognized as one of the prominent attorneys of Battle Creek, where he has been in practice continually since 1894. He was born at Ashland, Ohio, January 27, 1872, a son of Andrew M. and Almira E. (Stealy) Williams. The father was also born in Ashland and came of an old Pennsylvania family of Scotch-Irish ancestry on the paternal, and of Pennsylvania German on the maternal side. He was reared and educated in Ohio, and followed farming at his native place until about 1877, when he removed to Charlotte, Michigan, where he again entered upon agricultural pursuits. He has taken an active part in local political affairs as a supporter of the Democratic party and has served in several township offices. His wife, who also survives, is likewise a native of Ashland. They are now living retired at Charlotte, Michigan.

A. B. Williams, the eldest of their three children, who reached mature years, was a student in the country schools until fourteen years of age, when he entered Olivet College, there pursuing a regular preparatory and collegiate course until his graduation in 1892, with the degree of bachelor of letters. He was a member of and took an active part in the Adelphic Society, of which he was the president. During his collegiate course he also began reading law under the direction of Hon. Frank A. Dean. Later he studied with the firm of Huggett & Smith, of Charlotte, and subsequently was in the office of George W. Radford of Detroit. Upon examination at Detroit, Michigan, he was admitted to the bar in 1893. In the early part of 1894 he came to Battle Creek, where in a short time he secured a liberal patronage, that has constantly grown in volume and importance. He first engaged in general practice, but as his skill and ability have become more generally recognized he has given more of his time to corporation and commercial law. He has likewise gained a splendid reputation as a trial lawyer, and is very successful in his work before judge and jury. He is a pleasing and impressive speaker and it is worthy of note that Mr. Williams, as counsel, or as attorney, has been connected with a number of cases of great importance. He is a man of marked eloquence and ability, a deep and earnest student and has one of the best and most extensive law libraries of Battle Creek.

Mr. Williams is also prominently identified in a business way with many enterprises of importance here. He is the secretary of the Hygienic Food Company, manufacturers of Mapl-Flak. He is also identified with other corporate interests of the city, but has always avoided the directorship, not desiring to interfere with his professional labors, which he regards of the first importance in his life work. His devotion to his clients' interests is proverbial, and the recognition of this fact, combined with his broad and comprehensive knowledge of law has gained for him an enviable clientage.

January 1, 1904, Mr. Williams formed a partnership for the practice of the law, with Ira A. Beck, who came from the city of Chicago for this purpose. The style of the firm is Williams & Beck.

On the 12th of January, 1897, Mr. Williams was married to Miss Sue M. Wilson, of Charlotte, a daughter of Mr. and Mrs. John T. Wilson. Her father was well known in financial circles of that place, where he made his home for many years prior to his death which occurred only a few years ago. While in Charlotte Mr. Williams became a member of the Masonic fraternity and afterward demitted to Battle Creek lodge, No. 12, F. & A. M. He has also been active in Battle Creek lodge, K. of P., and is identified with the Independent Order of Foresters, in which he has served as chief ranger of the local court. He has also attended the high court of the state and in 1902 was delegated from this jurisdiction to the supreme court, which met at Los Angeles, California. He likewise belongs to the Benevolent Protective Order of Elks and also to the Athelstan club, of which he is president. While he served as vice president, its elegant and commodious club rooms were opened and fitted up in the Post building.

Mr. Williams has always paid allegiance to the Democratic party and in 1901 was nominated for the office of mayor of the city of Battle Creek. That city being a Republican stronghold he was not elected, but ran largely ahead of his ticket.

With keen intellectuality and analytical mind, and devotion to the details of practice as well as to the important points of a case,

Mr. Williams has gained distinction as a
lawyer of ability whose knowledge of the
science of jurisprudence is comprehensive
and exact; and whose application of his
knowledge to the points at issue is correct
and convincing.

LEVANT COLE.

Since 1888 Levant Cole has engaged in
business as a florist of Battle Creek and his
success has been large and well merited. He
was born in Batavia, New York, September
30, 1852, and on the paternal line comes
of Scotch ancestry. The grandfather removed from Vermont to western New York
in the beginning of the nineteenth century
and became one of the pioneer settlers of
that locality. He purchased wild land at
Batavia, forming a part of what was known
as the "Holland Purchase" and became an
extensive land holder and farmer, while in
the work of early improvement and development there, he took an active and helpful
part. When the country again became engaged in hostilities with England he joined
the American army for the protection of
our national interests. His son, Walter Cole,
the father of our subject, was born in
Batavia, New York, and after arriving at
years of maturity he married Miss
Sophronia Blanchard, a descendant of the
prominent Trall family, well known in
western New York, Dr. Trall having become
prominent in connection with the conduct of
a sanitarium and watercure establishment.
After his marriage Walter Cole engaged in
farming and the raising of fine stock of high
grades. At length he sold his farm and
stock to "Lucky" Baldwin, of southern Cali-

fornia and at a latter date the Cole family
removed to southern California, where Walter Cole is now a prominent ranchman. He
was long recognized as a leading figure in
Republican and official circles in Genesee
county, New York, and exerted a wide influence in behalf of the principles which he
supported.

In the common schools of Batavia,
Levant Cole began his education, which was
continued in the high school there, and at
the age of sixteen years took a course in
Eastman's Business College, of Poughkeepsie, New York. He then became connected
with the florist's business, as an employee of
the firm of Storrs & Harrison, of Painesville, Ohio, while later he was with James
Vick, of Rochester, New York, then one of
the most noted florists and seedsmen of the
country. There he had charge of the pro-
pagating department, a most responsible position, which he held until 1882, when he
removed to St. Joseph, Missouri, where he
was again engaged in the same line of business, but his health failing him in that climate, he removed to Battle Creek about
1888 and here formed a partnership with
John W. McCrea, under the firm name of
McCrea & Cole. Mr. Cole had charge of the
building of the first greenhouse, at No. 87
Wendell street. It was at first a small plant
but was enlarged to meet the growing demands of the trade. On April 10, 1900,
Mr. Cole purchased his partner's interest
and has since conducted the business alone,
having now the largest greenhouse in the
city. It is splendidly equipped for the conduct of the business and Mr. Cole's long
connection with this line of activity has
given him a thorough understanding of the
best methods of growing flowers and plants.
He sells largely to the local trade and also

to surrounding towns in Michigan, making a specialty of roses, cut flowers and plants. To this work he gives his undivided attention, with the result that his efforts have been crowned with success and he has long since advanced far beyond the humble position in which he started out in life, being now accounted one of the men of affluence in the city.

Mr. Cole was united in marriage to Miss Ada Merry, of Geneva, New York. They have four children: Margery, Walter B., Fannie and Howard. The family attend the Methodist Episcopal church, of which Mrs. Cole is a member, and to its support he contributes. His persistency of purpose, his thorough understanding of the best methods of flower culture and his continuous connection with the business in which as a young tradesman he embarked are probably the strongest characteristics of his successful business career.

HIRAM STAPLES.

Hiram Staples, whose activity in business circles has made him one of the leading and successful men of Battle Creek, was born in Temple, Franklin county, Maine, in March, 1841, a son of Alvah and Lydia C. (Burbank) Staples. The father, also a native of Franklin county, was a son of George Staples, who removed from England to the new world and secured a tract of land in Franklin county, Maine, where he developed a good home at an early day. Alvah Staples, possessing natural mechanical ability, conducted a blacksmith's shop on his farm and did much work in that line when all labor was performed by hand. For many years he continued his residence in the Pine Tree state, but after his children had neared years of maturity he removed to East Douglas, Worcester county, Massachusetts, in order to give them opportunities to obtain work in the manufactories of that place. He also was identified with business interests there, making a specialty of the manufacture of edge tools. Subsequently, he removed to New Hampshire and his death occurred in Nashua, in that state, where his wife also passed away.

Hiram Staples was one of a family of thirteen children and his early education was acquired in Massachusetts while later he continued his studies in New Hampshire. He had the opportunity of attending school about three months a year, but managed to acquire a good practical education and as the years have passed, he has continually broadened his knowledge through experience, reading and observation. On putting aside his text books he learned the trade of an edge tool maker. Indeed, he had begun work in this line during the months of vacation, when twelve years of age, and when his school life had ended he worked regularly at this pursuit. When seventeen years of age he had fully mastered the business and was in the forging department. There he continually advanced until, when twenty years of age, he was considered one of the most expert workmen in that department, there being nothing connected with the business which he could not do. Often in those days when prices paid for labor was much lower than at the present time, he could earn from three to three and a half dollars per day on piece work. On leaving Massachusetts he removed to Philadelphia, where he continued the work as an edge tool maker until a short time prior to the Civil war, when he returned to East Douglas and obtained a good position with the Douglas Ax Company.

When President Lincoln issued his first call for troops to serve for three years, however, Mr. Staples put aside all business and personal considerations and offered his services to the government, enlisting in Company A, Twenty-fifth Massachusetts Volunteer Infantry. This company occupied a post of honor, being stationed at the right of the regiment and also of the brigade, the division and the army corps. The first service of the regiment was in the Burnside expedition. With his comrades Mr. Staples was present at the bombardment of Roanoke Island and participated in the two days' fight on the seventh and eighth of February, 1862. He was also present at the engagement at New Berne, North Carolina, on the 14th of March, 1862, when the Union troops re-captured the guns that had been taken from them at Bull Run. He took part in the battle of Kingston, North Carolina, on the 14th of December; at Whitehall on the 16th; and at Goldsboro, on the 18th; and aided in the burning of a bridge near Kingston on the 16th of March, 1863. He was also at the battle of Deep Gully on the 13th of March; at Gunswamp on the 22d of May, where an effort was made by the rebel forces to surround the Union troops. It was at that place that Mr. Staples was promoted from the ranks to a position in the signal corps of the United States army, his duty being to carry dispatches for which purpose he was furnished with the fastest horses that could be secured. He carried dispatches and also aided in showing the signal lights which conveyed to other parts of the army important knowledge of military positions. At various places Mr. Staples was stationed,

doing important service in behalf of his country until the close of the term of his enlistment. After his discharge he was delayed from returning home for some time because of a quarantine on account of yellow fever, and while detained by quarantine and waiting patiently at New Berne, N. C., for his papers, his discharge papers were captured, with other mail, by the rebels at Dismal Swamp canal. The southern men were discovered and on being surprised they threw the mail into the fire, and much of it was burned. Mr. Staples's discharge papers were saved, but somewhat burned and shriveled up, but being on parchment, saved them from total destruction. He highly prizes them on that account, and also as a memento of his army experience.

After reaching Massachusetts Mr. Staples resumed his old position in the Douglas Ax factory, with which he was connected for some time. He afterward removed to New Albany, Indiana, where he entered the services of the Western Ax & Edge Tool Company and when that business was suspended he entered the plow works of B. F. Avery & Company, of Louisville, Ky., occupying a splendid position. However, he met with a terrible accident through falling into hot steel, whereby his arm was almost burned off. Because of this he was obliged to give up future work at his trade. In the meantime, Mr. Staples had been reading and studying, and, as the result of his investigation and his deep thought, combined with mechanical skill, he brought out a number of inventions, secured his first patent on the 27th of July, 1869. This was an improved composition for concrete sidewalks and roofing. He had secured this patent while still working at his trade and while recovering from his injury and not yet able to work, parties from the American Edge Tool Company came to him with an offer for him to superintend the placing of the machinery in a plant for the manufacture of edge tools at Battle Creek. He accepted the position and arrived in this city in 1870, retaining his connection with the house during its existence in Battle Creek. Mr. Staples has since made his home in this city and for more than a quarter of a century gave his attention to his sidewalk patent. He made a large number of walks in Battle Creek; in fact, built the first ever constructed in Calhoun county. Employment was furnished to many men, and his enterprise was of importance in the industrial circles of the city and at the same time returned to him a very gratifying income. When many years had passed in this way, he finally sold out to Fay B. Green, who still conducts the business. In the meantime Mr. Staples has taken out a number of other patents upon inventions, some of which have come into general use.

In 1872 was celebrated the marriage of Mr. Staples and Louisa Ann (Byers) Huff, the widow of George Huff, and they occupy a beautiful home in Battle Creek. Soon after coming to this city Mr. Staples purchased property on South Jefferson street, which he has improved, developed it into a splendid residence. He also has several houses which he rents, and other property in this city and is justly regarded as one of the substantial business men of Calhoun county. One of the noticeable features about his home are the beautiful elm trees in front of his house, which were planted by himself. There are no finer specimens of this tree to be found in this city and Mr. Staples has every reason to be proud of them. Socially he is connected with Farragut post, G. A. R., and while residing in Massachusetts, belonged to Solomon's Temple lodge, at Uxbridge,

of the Masonic fraternity. He stands to-day as one of the leading and representative men of Battle Creek and has attained this position in the face of difficulties that would have discouraged many a man of less resolute spirit. His strong integrity and honesty of purpose has led him to use only the most worthy and unquestionable means to secure success in any undertaking, and as a citizen is as true and loyal to his country and her welfare as when he followed the starry banner upon the southern battlefields.

JAMES L. WHITCOMB.

From 1860 up to the time of his death which occurred on the 27th of May, 1899, James L. Whitcomb was regarded as one of the most prominent and influential men of Battle Creek. He was born at Bolton, Chittenden county, Vermont, June 10, 1819, a son of Robert and Mary Ann (McCoy) Whitcomb. The father was a farmer and a man of standing in his day. Upon the old home farm the son was reared and in the district schools he began his education which was continued in Jericho Academy. He afterward engaged in agricultural pursuits up to the time of his marriage which occurred on the 1st of May, 1850, the lady of his choice being Miss Mary A. Smilie, a daughter of the Hon. Nathan and Esther (Green) Smilie, of Cambridge, Vermont, in which place Mrs. Whitcomb was reared and educated, completing an academic course there. Her father was a native of Haverhill, Massachusetts, and as a young man removed to Cambridge, Vermont, where he became an extensive farmer. There he wedded a daughter of

Jonathan Green, a representative of an old New England family. One of the distinguished and eminent citizens of his portion of the state, Mr. Smilie served for sixteen consecutive years as a member of the Vermont Legislature and in 1846 was the Democratic nominee for governor, failing of election by only a few votes. He was also prominently identified with the banking and other financial interests of his vicinity and was not only active in business affairs, but became very influential in public life, his ability well fitting him for leadership in molding public thought and action. Mr. and Mrs. Whitcomb resided upon the farm which Mr. Whitcomb owned at Underhill until 1869, when they removed to Battle Creek.

Here Mr. Whitcomb became at once identified with business affairs and soon gained a leading and influential position in commercial circles. He was engaged in the sale of agricultural implements and splendid success attended his efforts. He became the owner of the Whitcomb block at the corner of Main and Jefferson streets, the most prominent corner in the city and in addition was the owner of two fine farms. While in Vermont he had been one of the most extensive landowners and agriculturists of his locality. After remaining some years in Battle Creek he retired from commercial life, devoting his attention to the supervision of his farming interests and the superintendency of his investments. Having prospered, he had made purchases of land and also placed his money in other business interests which made him one of the capitalists of the city.

Unto Mr. and Mrs. Whitcomb were born two children: Louise S., who was educated in Boston; and Florence E., who was a graduate of the literary department of the University of Michigan and is now the wife of John H. Welch of Nicholasville, Kentucky. Mr. Whitcomb and his family have traveled extensively through Europe, visiting many scenes of historic as well as of modern interest and gaining that knowledge which only travel can bring, while one's views of life are equally broadened by a recognition of the possibilities of all nations and the dominant traits of character manifested by each race. Mr. Whitcomb attended and supported the Episcopal church and his political allegiance was given to the Democracy, of which he was a strong and earnest advocate. He was not, however, an aspirant for office and never would consent to serve in official positions, save that he acted as selectman while in Vermont and held the office of mayor in Battle Creek. Like all who walk through life on a higher plane than the great majority of his fellows, his companionship was select, rather than large; but the many who looked up to and respected him, realized as fully as did the few who were nearer him, that a true man had passed away.

JOHN POWELL.

John Powell, deceased, one of Marshall's honored citizens, and one whose memory is cherished by all who knew him, was born on a farm in Fredonia township, Calhoun county, Michigan, October 7, 1843. His preliminary education was received in the common schools of the county, after which he attended the high school of Marshall and Olivet College, completing his studies at Ypsilanti. With an energy of

JOHN POWELL

purpose which characterized his entire life, he had set about the task of acquiring a substantial foundation for the structure which he hoped to rear in later years, and had never swerved from his ambition until it had been fulfilled. Upon leaving the school room he became a teacher in the common schools of the state, meeting with a success which bespoke an unusual ability in the pedagogical line. For a time he served efficiently as a school inspector. Not content with the more or less circumscribed life of a teacher, Mr. Powell subsequently became interested in the lumber and · grain business, with headquarters at Ceresco, this county. In 1889 he removed to Marshall and continued in the grain business, becoming widely known throughout the county as a dealer, his straightforward way of doing business making him many friends among the business men of the community.

Mr. Powell became a popular man among all classes and as a citizen who never shirked any public duty he was chosen to represent the people in 1900 for the mayoralty, serving one year, when he was re-elected. He gave to the discharge of duties involved by his acceptance of office, that earnest, thoughtful attention and thoroughness which had made him a successful business man, and impressed the people with the idea of the principles upon which his life work was founded. At the time of his death he was a member of the electric light and water commission. Another public office which he had filled to the entire satisfaction of all concerned was superintendent of the poor of Marshall.

Mr. Powell was married October 20, 1897, to Miss Mabel Sterling, who was formerly a teacher in the public schools, of Marshall, an intelligent and well educated lady, with many social gifts and accomplishments. With her two children, Margaret, born August 7, 1898, and Robert Carlton, born January 9, 1901, she survives her husband and makes her home at No. 502 West State street, the residence purchased and furnished with the evidences of the thought and care which Mr. Powell lavished upon his family. He had acquired considerable property as the result of his years of effort, owning two farms in Fredonia township, also two in Newton township, as well as nearly a complete interest in the old Powell homestead. Until his marriage Mr. Powell had always attended the Baptist church, which was that to which his parents had belonged, but his wife being a member of the Presbyterian church, he became a regular attendant and gave his support to that denomination. His death occurred February 15, 1903, and from the Presbyterian church, where the religious services were held and largely attended, the beautiful floral offerings bespeaking the affection in which he was held, he was borne to his last resting place in Oakridge cemetery. In fraternal circles Mr. Powell was an honorary member of the Maccabee lodge, at Marshall, and politically was a Democrat. He was a most devoted husband and father, loyal to his home and his own fireside and finding his greatest pleasure among its comforts and in the bosom of his family.

Mr. Powell was a popular man among the higher classes, the business men admired the masterly ability which characterized his success in the commercial world, his unimpeachable character stood for high principles, which left their impress upon the community. and the devotion to his home life instinctively appealed to all who revere the highest and holiest of relations. The moral and mental purpose of his life will live beyond the brief sixty years which compassed his existence, and still influence and uplift his fellowmen.

JAMES W. BLANCK.

James Willis Blanck, of Emmett township, was born in Venango county, Pennsylvania, May 14, 1853, a son of Samuel W. and Lydia (Morris) Blanck. The father was a native of New York City, while the paternal grandfather was born in Holland. When fourteen years of age Samuel Blanck became a sailor on the ocean and when sixteen years of age was a sea captain. He became a partner of his father and they owned and operated a number of vessels engaged in trade with the West Indies, but one of their ships was captured by pirates and this so crippled them financially that they left the sea and went to Pennsylvania, having then but one thousand dollars. They spent the first night under a tree, but soon a log cabin was built on a farm of two huntred and four acres, which they purchased for a dollar and a quarter per acre. It was in Pennsylvania that Samuel Blanck reared his family. Eleven children were born unto him, of whom one died in infancy, one at the age of six and one at the age of twelve years. Jacob T. was the eldest. The others were Thomas Jefferson, Julia Ann, the widow of James D. Potter. now living with her mother in Battle Creek; Aaron E., also of Battle Creek; George, Mary, James W., Lydia, Lettie and Ella.

Samuel Blanck cleared and improved his farm in Pennsylvania and was the first man to discover oil there. He afterward sold his land for two hundred thousand dollars and went to Canandaigua, New York, where he purchased two large farms within the corporation limits of the town, but there he lost two-thirds of his money through speculation. While he was ill he also lost a valuable herd of merino sheep. Then selling his property at a sacrifice he went down. the Mississippi river for the benefit of his health, which he partially regained, after which he became a resident of Dexter, Michigan. There he formed a partnership in the produce business, in which he continued until his removal to Battle Creek in 1865. He bought some city property and a farm of one hundred and forty acres and, turning his attention to the lumber business, conducted a yard for four years. On the expiration of that period he took up his abode upon his farm, which he made his home until his death. which occurred March 29. 1879, when he was sixty-six years of age. He belonged to the Methodist Episcopal church and was a Republican in his political views.

In the district schools and in the city schools of Battle Creek James W. Blanck pursued his education, after which he entered the threshing machine factory of Brown and Upton and was also employed in a hoe factory. After working on the old Peninsular railroad. now the Grand Trunk line, he took charge of his father's farm, on a part of which he has since remained, and his enterprise and diligence have been the secret of his very desirable success.

On the 13th of November, 1878, Mr. Blanck was united in marriage to Miss Inez S. Ethridge, a native of Emmett township and a daughter of Joseph and Ann (Dickinson) Ethridge. Her father was born in New York and his father, Samuel Ethridge, was one of the early senators of Michigan. The mother of Mrs. Blanck was Julia Ann Dickinson, who was born in Phelps, Ontario county, New York, January 20, 1823, a daughter of Dexter and Mary (Wooden) Dickinson. She was a great-granddaughter of Gilbert and Julia Ann Aldrich. The former was taken prisoner by the Indians at the time of the Revolutionary war, but killed the red man who acted as his guard and managed to return home. He died, however, during the infancy of Mrs. Waters. Her maternal grandfather, John Wooden, was born in Newburg, Orange county, New York, in 1796, and was one of the earliest settlers of the town of Phelps, Ontario county, New York. He married Julia Ann Aldrich. Her grandfather Dickinson was killed by a stick of timber falling upon him when he was assissting in the raising of the Presbyterian church at Oaks Corners, in the town of Phelps, New York. The parents of Mrs. Waters, Dexter and Mary (Wooden) Dickinson, were both natives of Phelps, Ontario county, and after their marriage they removed to Monroe county, that state. In 1832 Dexter Dickinson brought his family to Michigan, his daughter, Mrs. Waters being then ten years of age. They made the trip by steamer to Detroit and the party found that on landing they still had the motion of the boat. There were no sidewalks in the little town of Detroit, but the ground seemed to them very uneven as they walked from the landing to a boarding house, which was kept by a Mrs. McMelon. They spent the first night in Michigan at that boarding house and in the morning Mr. Dickinson hired a man and his team to take him and his family to a

town called Mankin, in Wayne county, about twenty miles from Detroit. They remained there for a year, during which time the youngest brother was born, making the sixth child of the household. Mr. Dickinson, who was a blacksmith by trade, there engaged in the manufacture of axes. When the baby was six months old he started with his family for Calhoun county to make his home in the midst of the green woods. His household goods were loaded into a lumber wagon. His possessions consisted of a yoke of oxen, a wagon, a few chickens, a cow and a little pet dog. They were upon the road at that time for a week, their path being marked by blazed trees through the woods and, as they journeyed on it seemed that they were hardly out of one mud hole until they plunged into another. They spent one night at a log tavern conducted by a Mr. Gardner, two miles from their destination and on the morning of the 6th of April, 1833, they came to where their home was to be, the father having purchased forty acres of land in what is now Emmett township. He unloaded the wagon in the midst of the forests and the family ate their first breakfast there, using the bottom boards of the wagon for a table. Mr. Dickinson then took his ax and cut down small trees which he could lift and laid three sides of a shanty. He selected two large oak trees which grew near enough together to form the frame work of a door and across the spaces between he hung a quilt. Places were cut in the trees with his ax and a chisel so that he could place one end of a pole in the aperture, and thus the trees were laid one above the other as children make cob houses. The boys and girls of the household then gathered dry leaves and piled them up in the back end of the shanty upon the ground.

These were covered with blankets and this served for a bed. That night the father built a large fire outside of the quilt door and placed his gun within reach, and then they all laid down to rest, with the hungry wolves howling about them. The father did not sleep much, but the children felt safe and slept as soundly as in their former home, having perfect confidence and faith in their parents as protectors. Mrs. Waters says that the children were more afraid of the Indians than they were of the wolves. The year of 1833 was the hardest the pioneer family experienced. The father would take his yoke of oxen and go to the neighbor's farm and assist in the breaking of the land and in return the neighbors would come to the Dickinson farm and aid him in such work, so that in the first season he had four or five acres of land plowed, and planted this to potatoes and corn. His wife had saved seeds for a garden the year before and also some peach and plum seeds and these were planted and the garden soon yielded its vegetables. As they had no stove or any other device for baking the father built a stone oven, there being a quarry upon his land. He made a solid foundation of stone four feet wide and six feet long and built up the sides to a height of three feet. He spread clay all over the foundation to make it smooth, then arched it over, leaving a place for the door, which was hewed out of an oak log. An armful of fine split wood was then kindled in the smooth bottom of the oven, and it required an hour to heat it. Later the pans of bread and pies were set in. The first year the family had no white bread, living entirely on "johnny cake," while Indian pudding and milk served for the evening meal. That fall they enjoyed the luxury of potatoes, which they had

raised from seed brought with them. Frequently the father would take his gun and kill a deer, and a dish of venison was greatly enjoyed by the family. Mrs. Waters said that they would have been entirely happy had it not been for the bears, wolves and Indians, which frightened herself and children of the household. When they were left alone, as they had to be at times, they were always instructed to stay in the house and keep the doors shut. On one occasion her brother had to go to the spring for water, and he found there a great gray wolf, which snarled and snapped at him as he shut the door in its face. Their father told them they need not be afraid of the Indians coming after dark, as the red men never traveled at night. It was late in the fall of the first year that the pioneer family was installed in their log house, and glad they were to have their stone hearth and chimney, for the nights were getting cold, it being the last of October. Up to this time if the family enjoyed the luxury of sitting by the fire it had to be outside of the shanty. Although they had only boards enough to lay half the floor in the little cabin, they had a roof to keep out the storms, for Mr. Dickinson had made the shingles, and the family felt much safer in their new home. About this time, however, he and his wife had occasion to go to Marshall. They started early in the morning taking the baby, Dexter, with them, but they did not reach their destination until two o'clock owing to the bad condition of the roads and the slow travel of the oxen. They left Mrs. Waters at home to keep house for her brothers John and Cotton and her little sister Elizabeth, four years old. She was instructed to keep the house door shut after the sun went down lest they might be molested by the wolves, and also to keep a good fire. She prepared their supper of bread and milk and rocked the little sister to sleep, after which she sat down on the foot of the cradle, with the two boys close by. All at once they heard talking outside and they knew the Indians were there. At length the door opened and an Indian head was thrust in. He took a look and then stepped back. Again they heard the talking and a second time the door opened and in walked two Indians, their knives and tomahawks glistening in the firelight. The larger one began talking with Mrs. Waters in his native tongue, but she only shook her head, so frightened was she that she could not speak a word, for she and her brothers supposed that the Indians had come to kill them. She, however, says that she felt that she must continue to rock the cradle and keep the little sister asleep, because the child was so afraid of the Indians that she might scream herself to death if she awakened and saw them there. The red men sat down and warmed themselves before the fire and after a time one got up and produced a large bundle, from which he took a great piece of bear meat. Then the lump seemed to go out of Mrs. Waters's throat, for she realized that they were not to be killed, as the Indians seemed to want to appease their hunger instead. They cut off great slices of meat, and by signs and a few words managed to make known that they wanted a kettle in which to cook it. They also indicated in a similar manner that they wanted water and potatoes, and when these were furnished one of the boys raised the trap door in the floor and got out a large pan of milk. The Indians hung the kettle over the fire half full of meat and water and then put in the potatoes without washing or pealing them. Then they sat down on the hearth to wait for the meal to be cooked. All at once the children heard the father call out to the oxen. The boys jumped up and ran to meet the parents, leaving Mrs. Waters with the Indians. In relating the incident she, too, would, undoubtedly have run had she dared to leave the little sister. Such were some of the pioneer experiences which came to the early settlers. The home, however, was a happy one and as time advanced Mr. Dickinson added to his farm until it comprised one hundred and sixty acres, on which he and his wife spent their remaining days. He died in 1855, just when he had gotten his farm in condition to enjoy the comforts which it would bring him, and his wife passed away in 1874. Mrs. Waters is the only one left of her father's family. By her first marriage she became the mother of three children: Dexter, of Quincy, Michigan; John, deceased, and Mrs. Blanck.

After the death of her first husband Mrs. Ethridge became the wife of Levi Waters, who died on the 31st of December, 1902, in the eighty-first year of his age. He, too, was a native of the Empire state, born in the town of Florence, Oneida county. Their only child, a son, died in infancy. Mrs. Waters now makes her home with our subject. The home of Mr. and Mrs. Blanck has been blessed with three children: Alta Dell, who attended the Normal Business College and is now a stenographer of Battle Creek; Josephine, a graduate of the same school and now the wife of A. C. Wisner, of Battle Creek, by whom she has a daughter, Maxine, and Aaron James, at home, a student in the Normal Business College.

When Mr. Blanck took charge of his present farm his father was ill and the entire management fell upon him. He paid off fifteen hundred dollars indebtedness upon the place and upon his father's death the estate was divided and he purchased the interest of the other heirs in forty acres of land, which he has since devoted to market gardening, selling his products to both the wholesale and retail trade and doing an excellent business. He votes with the Republican party, but has neither time nor inclination for public office, preferring to devote his energies to his business interests, which are now capably conducted and are bringing him a substantial return for his labor. In all his dealings he is strictly fair, and has gained public confidence and the good will of those whom he meets in trade and in social relations.

GEORGE R. PEET.

George R. Peet, one of the leading farmers of Battle Creek township, Calhoun county, has had the honor of serving as township supervisor for nine consecutive years. He was born December 2, 1848, on the farm which he now occupies, his parents being Frederick and Mary A. (Norton) Peet. The father was a native of Connecticut, born in 1812, and in that state he resided until 1844, when he emigrated westward, establishing his home in Calhoun county, Michigan. He settled upon the farm now owned by our subject, securing ninety acres of unbroken land, which he at once began to clear and improve, developing it into a very fertile tract. He had added to this from time to time as his financial resources permitted until at his death he was the owner of one hundred and eighty acres, constituting a very valuable and productive farm. His political support was given to

the Whig party in early life and upon its dissolution he joined the ranks of the new Republican party, following its manners continuously until his demise. For several years he served as township clerk in Battle Creek township. In early manhood he wedded Miss Mary A. Norton, who was born in New York, and they became the parents of five children: Ova, who died at the age of thirty-one years; George R., whose name introduces this record; Emma, the wife of John Knight, a prominent resident of Battle Creek; Henry, deceased, and Fred, who makes his home in Chicago, Illinois. The father died in the year 1879, and the mother, surviving him for a number of years, passed away in 1894 at the age of seventy-three, and was laid to rest by his side in Oakhill cemetery, at Battle Creek. She was a member of the Congregational church.

In the district schools near his home George R. Peet acquired his early education, which was supplemented by study in the schools of Battle Creek and the State Agricultural College at Lansing. He put aside his text books at the age of seventeen years and went to Chicago, where he was engaged in the tea business until 1879, but upon the death of his father returned to the home farm to care for his mother and assume the management of the property, which he has since conducted. He is a progressive agriculturalist, following modern methods in his farm work.

November 1st, in 1883, George R. Peet was united in marriage to Miss Debbie Stites, a native of Hillsdale county, Michigan, and their marriage has been blessed with four children: Irving, who resides in Minneapolis, Minnesota; Edna, Lawrence and Dorothy.

In 1889 Mr. Peet was elected, on the Republican ticket, as treasurer of Battle Creek township and acceptably filled that position for four years. At the end of that time he was out of office for a year and was then elected supervisor of his township, in which capacity he has served continuously ever since, receiving a very large and flattering majority at the last election. In 1901 he was chairman of the board. In office he has ever exercised his official prerogatives for the general good and for public progress, and his efforts have received the indorsement of his fellow men, as shown by his re-election. Several times he has been a delegate to the county Republican conventions and was a delegate to the state convention in the year in which Governor Bliss was nominated. He stands high in the esteem of his fellow citizens and has gained many friends during the years of his residence in this county.

ALANSON ORLANDO ABBEY.

For many years a respected resident of Battle Creek, Alanson O. Abbey, although now deceased, lives in the memory of his friends as one whose life commended him to the confidence and good will of all. He was born in Otsego county, New York, on the 1st of August, 1822, his parents being James and Mary (Head) Abbey. The grandfather, a native of England, emigrated to the new world and established his home in Connecticut, where his son James was born. The latter became a pioneer farmer of Otsego county, New York. He was married to Miss Treat, who died, leaving four children, and later he wedded Mary Head, by whom he had eight children, the youngest being the subject of this review. In 1845 James

Abbey left the east and came to Oakland county, Michigan, living with his son until the time of his death, which occurred in 1849, when he had attained the advanced age of eighty-five years.

Alanson O. Abbey was educated in the common schools of Otsego county, New York, and from the time of his mother's death, which occurred when he was about twelve years of age, he depended upon his own resources. He was reared by a Quaker family, for whom he had great love and respect. After attaining his majority he engaged in farming, and, desiring a companion and helpmate for the journey of life, he chose Miss Harriet Jane McNamara, of Wheatfield, New York, a daughter of Thomas and Phoebe J. (Flyn) McNamara. She, too, had lost her mother when about eight days old and was reared by Mr. and Mrs. Albert Huggett, of Monroe county, New York. Mr. and Mrs. Abbey were married December 2, 1852, and the first farm which they ever owned was located in Rush township, Monroe county, New York, where they resided for three years. They then came to Calhoun county, Michigan, and Mr. Abbey purchased a farm in Pennfield township. This was a new tract of land, wild and unimproved, and with characteristic energy he continued its cultivation for three years. Later he engaged in farming in Leroy township, and was one of the pioneer threshers of the county, following that business extensively for thirteen years. He owned one of the first steam threshers ever used in this locality. Failing health, however, caused him to leave the farm, and, removing to Battle Creek, he remained a resident of this city for thirty years, having in the meantime acquired a comfortable competence which enabled him to live retired in the enjoyment of the fruits of his former toil.

Unto Mr. and Mrs. Abbey were born seven children: Alice, the wife of William Perry; Emma, the wife of Marion Baxter; Mary Isadore, the wife of Charles Scott; Albert J., Frank S., Martin C., who is foreman for the American Steam Pump Company, and Hattie. All of the children are yet residents of Battle Creek.

Politically Mr. Abbey was a Republican, but the honors and emoluments of office had no attraction for him, although as a retiring citizen he was public-spirited and progressive and loyal to the welfare of his community. He deserved much credit for what he accomplished in life, for starting out empty handed he worked his way steadily upward, overcoming all difficulties and obstacles in his path and advancing until he had reached the plane of affluence. He died December 27, 1895, respected by all who knew him, and his remains are interred in Oakhill cemetery. His widow now has a beautiful home at No. 183 Fremont street, where she is surrounded by all the comforts of life. She is an honored guest in the homes of her children and is passing her declining days in an ideal manner, having the loving devotion of sons, daughters and grandchildren, as well as the kindly regard of many friends.

ALBINIUS F. BOEHME.

In the enterprising and growing city of Battle Creek there are many inhabitants of foreign birth who, attracted by more progressive institutions, broader educational facilities and the superior advantages of making a living, have come here with their families and means intending to found a home in a new country. These valuable additions to the native population have by their industry, economy and honorable methods, become essential factors in the growth of the city. Of such a class Albinius Franciscus Boehme was a representative. He came from Germany and here, by his patriotic and exemplary life, won for himself an honored name, and gained many friends who entertained for him the highest regard and who felt the deepest regret when he was called from this life.

Moreover, he developed his own character in harmony with nature and her laws, and with constantly growing appreciation for her beauties he lived a life that brought him "near to nature's heart."

Mr. Boehme was born in the city of Altenburg, in the duchy of Sachsen-Altenburg, Germany, February 6, 1824, a son of August and Selima (Lueder) Boehme. His father, Meister Boehme, was hofrchlosser (court locksmith), and superintendent of the locksmith work of the ancient Altenburg schloss (castle). He died when his son Albinius F. was twelve years of age. The latter was educated in the common schools and it was his wish to continue in order to become a proficient professional florist.

But for financial reasons he was required by his guardians to learn the locksmith trade and continue the work carried on by his father. This proved so distasteful to him that he only followed it until he reached his majority, when, in accordance with the laws of the country, he was required to enter the army and serve four years.

However, it was destined that his wish to become a florist was to be realized later

ALBINIUS F. BOEHME

MRS. ALBINIUS F. BOEHME

in life and in a foreign land. From his early childhood he was filled with the spirit of personal liberty, which characterized the early Germans, and a love of freedom, and when, in 1848, the people uprose against the tyranny of the nobility, he took an active part in the struggle.

When it was found that their cause was lost he determined to forsake the fatherland and seek in America the benefits of a government of the people and for the people. He accordingly crossed the Atlantic in 1849, and on the eve of his departure from Germany was married to Miss Johannah Huster by a civil marriage rite, the religious ceremony taking place in Philadelphia, to which city they proceeded immediately after landing in New York. Mrs. Boehme was born in the village of Roda, Sachsen-Altenburg, Germany, December 7, 1823, a daughter of Carl and Fredericka (Durkhardt) Huster the former a custom shoemaker. She was educated in the schools of that place and resided there until her marriage. She then, with brave heart and filled with confidence and trust in the future, bade adieu to home, kindred and dear friends to take up the responsibilities of wifehood and motherhood, in all of which she was most faithful, in the strange land that was to be her home.

Mr. and Mrs. Boehme removed to Westchester, Pennsylvania, where they resided until 1854, when they came to Michigan. Mr. Boehme took up his residence in Bedford township, Calhoun county, and in the fall of 1855 removed to Battle Creek, where he built the house which continued to be his home until the end of his life.

There was no native son of America more loyal and devoted to its interests than was Mr. Boehme, and in October, 1861,

he gave proof of his loyalty by enlisting as a member of Company D, Thirteenth Michigan Infantry. After two years' service, he re-enlisted, continuing with that command until the close of the war. He was in fifteen severe engagements, including the battles of Stone River, Shiloh, Chickamauga, the siege of Corinth, the siege and battle of Chattanooga, the march through Georgia to the sea under General Sherman, and the battles of Savannah, Bentonville and Misisonary Ridge. He participated in the Grand Review in Washington, D. C., the greatest military pageant ever seen in the western hemisphere. And he was honorably discharged at Louisville, Kentucky, in August, 1865. His was a most creditable military record, during which he never faltered in his allegiance to the cause he espoused, but was always found as a faithful defender of the Union. While her husband was serving in the army, Mrs. Boehme was doing all in her power to help the cause and alleviate the suffering occasioned by the awful ravages of war, besides bearing alone the responsibility of rearing her children and caring for the home during the four years' absence of the father.

After the close of the war Mr. Boehme turned his attention to wood carving. His artistic nature and natural talent for drawing enabled him to make his own designs, and he displayed marked ability and skill in the work, which also was of great beauty.

In 1872, however, he embarked upon the pursuit which it had been his earnest desire to follow—the cultivation of flowers. He began with one greenhouse, eighteen by fifty feet, built on the lot where his residence stood. He was assisted in this enterprise by his wife, and they were the first to engage in the florist business to any extent in Calhoun county, practically being the pioneers in that line and laying the foundation for the proportions to which the florist business has attained at the present time. Together they made this their life work, and received the encouragement and support of the most cultured people. As their patronage increased other houses were added from time to time. Two for miscellaneous stock, one to be devoted to the cultivation of palms and tropical plants and one to roses and carnations, the last one being built in 1882. Mr. Boehme was a successful propagator and grower, and in his collection were many specimens whose cultivation required the most painstaking and patient care. It was his pride to offer for sale only such plants and flowers as were of the first quality. He was for many years a member of the Society of American Florists and took much interest in their conventions, which he occasionally attended in the larger cities. In the arrangement and making up of cut flowers Mrs. Boehme's exquisite and artistic taste was unsurpassed. Because of their inherent love of flowers they strove to cultivate in others a similar appreciation, and to foster a love of their beauty that all might enjoy benefits of their uplifting and refining influence, knowing that it is a step which leads from "Nature up to Nature's God."

Mr. and Mrs. Boehme were exceedingly fond of young people, especially children, and Mrs. Boehme by her original and interesting manner of talking to them about flowers won their regard and esteem in a marked degree.

Unto Mr. and Mrs. Boehme were born three children: Charles Augustus, whose life record follows on another page; Cecilia, who was born in Westchester, Pennsylvania, in 1852, and was a student in the Battle Creek high school, and Louise, who was born in Battle Creek in 1856. She was married December 15, 1875, to Mr. F. C. Butze, of Toledo, Ohio, and died in St. Louis, Missouri, in 1888.

Mr. and Mrs. Boehme were reared in the Lutheran church, but in Battle Creek were identified with the Episcopal church, of which their two daughters became communicants. They accepted for themselves, however, the broad religion of nature, which is constantly showing forth the handiwork and great law of the Maker. Mr. Boehme was an extensive reader of the best literature and kept well informed on the leading topics of the day. He was, moreover, a man of strict integrity, sterling worth and high moral standing. His industry was untiring and only ended with his life. He never gave up his allegiance to the fatherland by becoming a naturalized American citizen, but by taking up arms in defense of his adopted country he became entitled to all of the privileges of citizenship.

Mr. Boehme died June 10, 1900, and his wife survived him only until the 8th of November, 1901, when she was laid by his side in Oak Hill cemetery.

When the Ladies' Library Association, now the Woman's Club, was organized in 1863, she became a charter member. She was always interested in works of philanthropy and charity and was one of the organizers of the German Ladies' Benevolent Society, acting as its president continuously until it was disbanded. She was a steadfast child of nature, with unbounded trust in God and the utmost confidence in humanity, and she ever sought and found good in everything. Her life's work among her flowers was ever her joy and delight, and she often was heard to say, "God gave them to me because I love them so." She constantly used the flowers to express her sympathy with those in sorrow and suffering from illness, and sent them to strangers as well as friends. It always gave her great pleasure to see others happy and on all joyful occasions flowers were her favorite means of expressing her gladness. These and many other kindly deeds made up her beautiful and well lived life and together with her interesting and attractive personality. her sunshiny disposition and kindly spirit, made her a general favorite throughout the community in which she lived, and caused her to be much beloved by every one.

To Mr. and Mrs. Boehme their home was the aim and end of all their efforts, and all of its sacred relations were cherished with a fondness that shed around them an influence that was like the sunshine. bringing joy, growth and hapiness.

Their memory is dear to many who knew them and needs not perpetuation through marble monument or tablet of bronze. for it is enshrined in the hearts of all those whom they numbered as their friends.

GEORGE S. WOOLSEY.

In the pioneer days of Calhoun county's development the Woolsey family was established within its borders, and from that time to the present its representatives have taken an active and helpful part in matters pertaining to the general progress. They have been the champions of many measures for the public good and none have been more helpful in public work than has George S. Woolsey. He has also won a foremost place in the ranks of the leading agriculturists of the county. and as the result of judicious investments is now one of the prosperous citizens of southern Michigan.

Mr. Woolsey is a native son of Marshall township, born February 29, 1840, his parents being Daniel and Julanna (Shaver) Woolsey. The family is of English lineage and the great-grandfather of our subject was one of the heroes of the Revolutionary war. who laid down his life on liberty's altar, being killed while in battle. Richard Woolsey, the grandfather of our subject. and his brother, were soon afterward bound out and did not again meet. The former became a Baptist minister and was pastor of the church at Pepacton, Delaware county, New York. for forty-two years. There Daniel Woolsey was born March 5, 1808. and there he was reared to manhood. Times were hard and money scarce and when still but a boy he had to work out in order to earn his own living. He utilized every opportunity for securing an education and was eventually enabled to teach. With the money thus secured he made his way to Marshall, Michigan, and purchased two hundred and forty acres of land. Prior to this time he was married in Delaware county, New York, to Miss Julanna Shaver, who was born in Colchester township, near Pepacton, January 15, 1810. They had removed to Seneca county, New York, accompanied by Mr. Woolsey's father, who died there. In 1836 Daniel Woolsey again came to Calhoun county, accompanied by his wife and two children, one of whom was four years of age, the other a babe. They drove the entire distance and located on section 8, Marshall township, where Mr. Woolsey built a log house. There he cleared his farm of one hundred and sixty acres, placed it under a high state of cultivation, erected a fine home and made substantial and modern improvements. Mr. Woolsey became a successful agriculturist, and the farm which he owned has never been out of the possession of the family, being now owned by our subject and his brother, and has never had a mortgage upon it. Daniel Woolsey was one of the leading and early members of the Baptist church in Calhoun county, and when the church of that denomination was organized in Battle Creek he became one of its active workers, and from the beginning served as a deacon, the last few years serving as deacon emeritus. His political allegiance was given to the Whig party until its dissolution, when he joined the ranks of the new Republican party, being a strong anti-slavery man. He was honored with a number of local offices, and for eight consecutive years served as supervisor of his township. He cast his first Republican vote for John C. Fremont. He died June 27, 1887, and his wife on the 2d of September, 1862. She was a daughter of Henry Shaver, of an old Pennsylvania Dutch family.

George S. Woolsey was the fourth in order of birth in a family of six children who grew to adult age. He was a student in the district schools between the ages of six and fourteen years and then went to the Olivet Institute, intending to prepare for a professional career, but his eyesight failing him, he was obliged to abandon his studies and for four years thereafter was not allowed to use his eyes for any reading.

When twenty years of age he began teaching, which profession he followed for three years, and in the vacation periods he worked on the home farm. He then assumed entire management of the old homestead, which he operated for four years.

About this time, on the 1st of January, 1867, he married Miss Martha A. Lamphier, of this county, a daughter of Marcus and Susan (Lines) Lamphier, who came to Michigan from Genesee county, New York, during the early girlhood of the daughter. The father was one of the early farmers of Jackson county and was also one of the men who went to Pike's Peak at the time of the discovery of gold there. His death occurred in the Colorado gold fields.

After his first marriage Mr. Woolsey continued the management of the home farm until 1871, when he purchased a tract of land on the Marshall avenue road, a mile north of the city. There he has one hundred and eighty-five acres. He made all of the improvements on that property, erected a fine modern home and built two large barns, one of which is ninety feet long and forty-six feet high to the eaves. The work of development has been carried on there until the farm is unsurpassed by any in the county. Mr. Woolsey also owns one hundred and twenty acres of the old homestead and has other valuable property interests which return him a good income and indicate his sound business judgment in investment. Mr. Woolsey remained upon his farm until his return to the city in April, 1901, and since that time he has lived on West State street.

Unto Mr. Woolsey by his first marriage were born six children who grew to mature years: Marcus D., who is now running the home farm, was married to Elida Brown, and they have one child, George R.; Edgar L., died at the age of twenty-two years; Mary, became the wife of John Southworth and died January 12, 1903, leaving a daughter, Martha; Mabel, is the wife of Howard Pratt, of the Marshall "Statesman"; Charles R., a farmer, with the brother on the home farm, and Edna, at home, complete the family. Mrs. Woolsey died February 15, 1890, at the age of forty-three years, her birth having occurred February 8, 1847. Mr. Woolsey afterward married Mrs. Phoebe Dunham, of Marshall, October 7, 1890, a daughter of Caleb Hanchett, one of the pioneers of this locality. She was born in Marengo township and was the widow of Henry E. Dunham.

In politics Mr. Woolsey is a stanch Republican and has held many official positions, to which he has been called by his fellow townsmen, who recognize his worth and ability. Soon after attaining his majority he was township school inspector and held that office for many years, or until the law was changed. During the most of the time he was also on the township board, and has been justice of the peace, assessor and supervisor. He was township treasurer and township clerk for two terms each, also supervisor for two terms. During this time the court house proposition was brought up and the supervisors voted for its construction. In 1882 Mr. Woolsey resigned as supervisor, having been elected county treasurer, and assumed the duties of the latter position January 1, 1883. When in that office he paid off the last of the bonds issued to erect the court house. He was re-elected in 1884 and held the office until December 31, 1886, an efficient and honored incumbent. During his service the legislature had changed the entire system of taxing and tax

sales and he had to work out a method to meet the new requirements. After much study he got up a form for the blank books to be used in the office, and entirely without his solicitation the Ihling & Eberhart Company, of Kalamazoo, began the making of these, and the form is still used in the state generally. In 1896 Mr. Woolsey was nominated for senator on the Silver-Republican ticket and carried his own county by three hundred, while in Kalamazoo county his opponent received enough votes so that there was a majority of less than one hundred and fifty against Mr. Woolsey. Again he was nominated in 1898.

In 1880 Mr. Woolsey was one of the committee of three to draft the articles of association of the Citizens' Mutual Fire Insurance Company, of Calhoun county, and went to Lansing to get the plan accepted by the commissioner of insurance. At the first annual meeting of the company he was elected secretary and has served either in that office or as director almost continuously since. This has proved a very successful insurance enterprise and has been of great benefit to many of its members. He is a member of the Calhoun County Agricultural Society, and for many years was its secretary. Mr. Woolsey has been a member of the Baptist church since his boyhood days, joining in 1856. Soon after attaining his majority he was elected deacon, his special care being the younger members of the congregation, and he has served continuously since, being now senior deacon. He was for twenty years a member of the board of church trustees and has been superintendent of the Sunday-school. He was likewise a member of the building committee when the new church was built, and in every possible way has advanced the interests of the congregation. To estimate the life work of Mr. Woolsey would be to determine his usefulness in connection with many lines of activity, business, political and church interests having all been promoted through his labors, profiting by his sound judgment and benefitting by his championship. He has justly earned the distinction of being called one of the most representative men and honored citizens of Marshall.

CHARLES H. ROSE.

One of the younger representatives of business life in Marshall is Charles H. Rose, who for one year has been proprietor of a grocery store here. He was born in Flint, Michigan, December 17, 1874, a son of Charles H. and Mary A. (Miner) Rose, both of whom were natives of New York, and when young people came with their respective parents to Michigan, being married in Flint. The father was a millwright and mill builder and erected many of the flouring and lumber mills over the state in an early day. He also became the owner of a farm and of real estate in Flint, and held various local offices, being active in the ranks of the Democratic party. His death occurred March 8, 1902, and his widow is still living.

Charles H. Rose began his education in the public schools of Flint, also attended the high school there, and was afterward graduated in the high school of Girard, Michigan. with the class of 1893. He then learned the miller's trade at Coldwater, Michigan, serving an apprenticeship of three years and after fully mastering the business worked as a journeyman for some time, being employed in leading flouring mills in North Adams, Jackson and Marshall, Michigan, coming here in 1900, where he was employed in the Stevens's mill for one year and then in the Rice Creek mills, where he remained until 1903. When his labors and economy had brought him some capital he determined to engage in business on his own account, and opened a grocery store at the corner of South Marshall avenue and Monroe street, in Marshall, where he has since been located. He has enjoyed a good trade from the start and his patronage is constantly increasing. Today he is one of the leading young merchants of the city and his prosperity is well merited, as it has come as the legitimate outcome of his own labors.

On the 10th of February, 1898. Mr. Rose was united in marriage to Miss Gertrude Nutten, of Hillsdale county, Michigan. and they have two children, Glen LeRoy and Lawrence. Mr. Rose and his wife are members of the Methodist Episcopal church and while at North Adams he served at chorister and as secretary of the Epworth League. He has been very active and helpful in church work.

GLOVER J. ASHLEY.

For the past seven years Glover J. Ashley has served as assessor of Battle Creek and has long been in public service, discharging his duties with promptness and fidelity that has made him a most capable official. He was born in Erie, Pennsylvania, May 17, 1847, a son of Joseph and Minerva (Ashley) Ashley. His paternal grandfather, James Ashley, was an early resident of Chautauqua county, New York. where he followed farming until his death. It was in that county that the father of our subject was born on the 31st of July, 1801. He spent his early days in the new country and there he married Minerva Ashley, a daughter of Jadutham Ashley, who was likewise a pioneer of Chautauqua county. Devoting his energies to farming, he remained in that locality until after the birth of his older children, when he went with his family to Erie county, Pennsylvania, where he continued farming until 1856. At that time he became a resident of Ashtabula county, Ohio, and his last days were spent in Battle Creek, Michigan, having come to this state in 1876. His wife, however, passed away in Ashtabula county, Ohio, in 1863. They were both members of the Methodist Episcopal church. Mr. Ashley gave his political allegiance to the Whig party in early life, while later'he became a Republican.

In the public schools of Ashtabula county Glover J. Ashley pursued his studies, and completed them in a good school at Kingsville. He continued upon the home farm during his minority and after his marriage he took charge of the place for his father, carrying on its cultivation until 1876. He then located in Emmett township, Calhoun county, Michigan, where he engaged in farming for a year, when he purchased a tract of land in Convis, which was his place of residence until 1882. In that year he removed to Burlington township, where he resided until 1893, when he sold his farm property and came to Battle Creek. In Burlington township he had held the office of supervisor for three years and had taken an active part in local politics as a supporter of the Republican party. He was also one of the first members of the Citizens' Mutual Fire Insurance Company, and four years after its organization was elected its presi-dent, thus serving for five years, during which time the membership of the company was largely increased. At the annual election following his removal to Battle Creek he declined to serve longer in that office. Here he turned his attention to the real estate and insurance business, handling property both for himself and others and negotiating many important realty transfers. He built up a nice business and secured a large patronage, but in the spring of 1900 abandoned this on account of his official duties. He still does conveyancing, however, and other notary work. He was one of the organizers of the Hibbard Food Company, which was incorporated in February, 1902, with a capital stock of five hundred thousand dollars. Mr. Ashley was then chosen president and still serves in that position. The factory is located at Augusta, where the plant is equipped with excellent facilities and where it turns out a manufactured article known as Coco Cream Flake. It has already been largely introduced to the market and has met with a favorable reception by the public.

In 1895 Mr. Ashley was appointed assessor of Battle Creek and the following year was again chosen for the office. In 1900 he was elected under the change of charter for a term of two years and in 1902 he was elected for a full term of three years. He has filled the office of chairman of the board, this devolving upon the senior member. The valuations of the city have largely increased, for in 1895, when he became assessor, the amount was four million nine hundred and sixty-six thousand six hundred and ninety dollars, while in 1903 it had reached the sum of fifteen million two hundred thousand. The amount of work in the office has correspondingly increased and in systematizing this and in controlling the affairs of the position Mr. Ashley has manifested excellent business ability. In politics he has always been an earnest advocate of Republican principles and has attended many conventions of the party.

On the 27th of February, 1867, occurred the marriage of Mr. Ashley and Miss Harriet Risdon, of Ashtabula county, Ohio, a daughter of Elial Risdon, one of the early farmers and ship builders of the western reserve. Mr. and Mrs. Ashley have four children: Frank C., Lula I., the wife of Murray French; Fred R., and Edith M., the wife of Sumner Byce. All are residents of Battle Creek. They have a comfortable home at No. 28 Michigan avenue, which they have occupied for ten years. Mr. Ashley now belongs to Battle Creek lodge, No. 12, F. and A. M., coming here on demit from Union City lodge, in which he was raised. Over the record of his business career and his official service there falls no shadow of wrong or suspicion of evil. He has always been loyal to the trust reposed in him and his capability and fidelity are acknowledged by all who know aught of his official life.

CHARLES A. BOEHME.

There has, perhaps, been no death in Battle Creek that has occasioned more profound and sincere sorrow than that of Charles A. Boehme. The passing of the aged, when life's work has been well done, is somewhat like the passing of one season, that having accomplished its mission, is succeeded by another, but the death of the young comes as an awful shock, leaving behind a feeling of deepest desolation.

This was especially true when Charles Augustus Boehme passed away. Not alone was he endowed with splendid mental attributes and rare business qualifications, but possessed those sterling personal characteristics which bind man to man in ties which naught can sever. He added to the accomplishments of a college course a winning manner, a kindly, generous and sympathetic spirit, a love of humor and a genuine devotion to high purposes and ideals.

His birth occurred in Westchester, Pennsylvania, in 1850, and he was provided with excellent educational privileges, of which he made the best possible use, possessing a brilliant mind. He completed the high school course in Battle Creek when but thirteen years of age, and afterward matriculated in the University of Michigan, pursuing courses in the literary and scientific departments. Subsequently he entered the pharmaceutical and medical departments and was graduated with high honors. He was chosen president of the pharmacy class of 1870, and was popular and prominent among his associates in the University. Subsequently he pursued postgraduate work in the same institution. In addition to his scientific knowledge and attainments, he was very proficient in languages and translated into English for publication various scientific articles from foreign periodicals. For two years following his graduation he was at the head of the pharmaceutical department of the drug store of Grandin & Hinman, of Battle Creek, and later became associated with Park, Davis & Company, of Detroit, prominent manufacturing pharmacists. The confinement of the laboratory, however, proved detrimental to his health and

CHARLES A. BOEHME

he accepted a position as traveling salesman with Merrill & Company, of Cincinnati, a large wholesale drug house. Because of his frail constitution, however, he contracted typhoid fever and lived but two days after his return home, his death occurring on the 14th of September, 1874. His loss was a great blow to his parents, sisters and many friends, for he had become endeared to them by his genial, social qualities, as well as by reason of his kind heart and cultivated mind. He had a sensitive and spiritual nature, and was a kind and affectionate son and brother and a warm and large-hearted friend. During his residence in Detroit he was an attendant on the services of Grace church and was a member of the Young Men's Association of that parish. In his religious views, however, he was liberal and progressive, his ideas being in accordance with the teachings of nature. He usually attended the Episcopal church and his mind was unbiased by any particular creed.

Mr. Boehme was always a student and possessed many scholarly attainments. He attained prominence in his special line of work and was a versatile writer on scientific subjects. His mind was analytical, his reasoning logical and his presentation of a subject cogent and forceful, and yet unlike many who devote much time to scientific investigation, he was fitted to adorn any social function and was always the life of any gathering. There was naught of the recluse about him. He found the greatest pleasure in the companionship of his friends, and his ready appreciation, his repartee and thought, at times bright and sparkling, at others deeply earnest, made him a favorite with young and old. His entire life went to prove that real pleasure

12

is not frivolity, but is based upon the development of the best in one's nature—the expansion of the mind and soul.

JOSEPH H. CUNNINGHAM.

Joseph Henry Cunningham, one of the respected and well known residents of Battle Creek, was born in Whitehall, New York, December 26, 1863, and is a son of James and Susan (Mullin) Cunningham. The father was born in Glasgow, Scotland, and on the Isle of Man was united in marriage to Miss Mullin, with whom he then crossed the Atlantic to the United States, making the voyage about 1842. They located at Whitehall, New York, and afterward removed to Troy, New York, and thence to Cayuga county, in the Empire state, where the father engaged in farming for a number of years. In 1873 the family came to Michigan, settling in Kalamazoo county, where James Cunningham devoted his energies to agricultural pursuits until his death, which occurred in 1897. The mother had passed away the year previously.

In the family were six children, of whom four are living, Joseph Henry Cunningham being the youngest. He obtained his education in the public schools of Galesburg, Michigan, and was engaged in farm work with his father until he attained his majority, early becoming familiar with all the duties and labors incident to the cultivation of the fields and the care of stock. He and his sister remained at home and took care of the parents in their declining years, conducting the farm until after their demise.

Mr. Cunningham then wedded Miss Anna Rose Rogers, of Bedford township,

Calhoun county, the wedding being celebrated December 26, 1900. The lady is a daughter of Erastus B. Rogers. At the time of their marriage Mr. and Mrs. Cunningham returned to Battle Creek, where he was instrumental in the organization of the Battle Creek Oil and Varnish Company, which was incorporated with a capital stock of one hundred and fifty thousand dollars. In this he is still interested and the company is now one of the successful manufacturing concerns of the city. He next became the promoter of the Battle Creek Food Company, which was incorporated with a capital stock of five thousand dollars, and in this Mr. Cunningham is extensively interested. The company has erected a new plant near the Grand Trunk railroad shops and is doing an extensive business, the trade having reached mammoth proportions. The buildings are well equipped with every facility needed to carry on the work and a large market has been found for the product. Mr. Cunningham has also promoted the American Fruit Juice Company, limited, of Battle Creek, with a factory at Mattawan, Michigan. This company also has a capital stock of five hundred thousand dollars and its business is the manufacturing of grape and other unfermented fruit juices, and is in a very prosperous condition. He is one of the board of managers, and his sound business judgment and wise counsel have proven important factors in its successful control. Mr. Cunningham has raised all the money needed to carry on these various enterprises and when it is taken into consideration that he devoted all of his earlier years to the care of his parents and has almost at once sprung into prominence as a successful promoter of several financial concerns in Battle Creek, his ability is easily recognized. Well may he be termed one of the captains of industry. He has an extensive acquaintance among the men of southern Michigan and has the entire confidence of all with whom he has come in contact, for his upright character and devotion to sterling principles have gained for him the good will and trust of all with whom he has been associated.

Fraternally Mr. Cunningham is connected with Richland lodge, F. and A. M., of Richland, Michigan, and both he and his wife are members of the Order of the Eastern Star. In politics he is a Republican, exercising his right of franchise in support of the men and measures of the party, yet never consenting to become a candidate for office, as he prefers to devote his undivided attention to his business affairs. While he is yet a young man he has already advanced to a prominent position in manufacturing and commercial circles, and Battle Creek recognizes him as a valued addition to its business ranks. With keen discernment he recognizes the opportunities of the moment and the possibilities of the future and, utilizing these, he is rapidly gaining the goal of prosperity.

ALBERT H. GEDDES.

Albert H. Geddes, one of the oldest and best known blacksmiths of Battle Creek, has been in this city for more than half a century, locating here in the fall of 1851. He came here to learn the blacksmith's trade and throughout his entire life has followed the pursuit, which he mastered in his early manhood. He was born in the township of Cambridge, in Lenawee county, Michigan, November 21, 1836, and is a son of Paul and Anstris (Pierce) Geddes. The father was born September 14, 1805, in Northumberland county, Pennsylvania, and was a son of Samuel Geddes, who was descended from James Geddes, a native of Scotland, from which country he had been driven by religious persecution to the north of Ireland, whence he afterward came to America. He established his home not far from what is now Lewisburg, Northumberland county, Pennsylvania, and became a member of the community of safety during the Revolutionary war. He assisted in various ways in achieving independence for the colonists during that long struggle. The grandfather of our subject was a farmer by occupation and also learned and followed the trade of house building. About 1833 he came to Michigan with his family, settled in Lenawee county, near the birthplace of our subject. He was one of the first residents of that part of the state and from the government entered a large tract of land, which he cleared and developed into a good farm, making his home thereon throughout his remaining days. In fact, he aided in laying broad and deep the foundation for the present prosperity and development of the county and his name is enrolled among the honored pioneers of this state. He was a man of considerable prominence, leaving the impress of his individuality upon public thought and action. He served as justice of the peace and, being a man of excellent judgment, fair in his opinions, he settled many more cases through conciliation than by trial.

Paul Geddes, the father of our subject, removed with his parents to western New York, where he was reared and educated, and there he married Miss Pierce, who was born in Tyringham, Massachusetts, whence she removed to western New York in company with her father, John Pierce. He belonged to an old New England family and his birth occurred in Rhode Island. In 1833 Paul Geddes came with his family to Michigan, settling in Cambridge township, Lenawee county, where he entered land from the government. He removed to the vicinity of Climax, Kalamazoo county in 1846, and later came to Battle Creek, where he lived for many years. Several times he served as city recorder and was also city treasurer. He died here on the 10th of February, 1880, and his wife passed away in November, 1882. They were the parents of six children, who reached adult age, Albert H. being the fifth in order of birth.

In the district schools Albert H. Geddes obtained his early education, but by reading and observation has greatly added to his knowledge. At the age of fifteen years he entered upon an apprenticeship to the blacksmith's trade with the firm of Seymour & Son, who were among the earliest carriage makers of this city. He served for four years and received thirty, forty, fifty and seventy-five dollars per year, respectively, in addition to his board. On the completion of his term he was employed as a journeyman for a number of years and through a long period was in the service of Adams & Smith, successors to Seymour & Son. He was the foreman of their blacksmith department up to the time when he established business on his own account. He opened his shop at No. 20 West Jackson street, where he does an extensive business in general blacksmithing and carriage repairing. That he has a liberal patronage is indicated by the fact that he now employs six men, and his business is proving of profit to him. His life has been one of untiring industry, in which his perseverence and fair dealing have also been salient features in bringing him merited success.

In Battle Creek, on the 25th of September, 1861, Mr. Geddes was united in marriage to Harriet M. Thiers, who was born in Tompkins county, New York, a daughter of Henry Thiers, one of the early residents of Battle Creek township. They now have four children: Kate H., who is the wife of John H. Staley, of this city; James, who is with the firm of L. D. Brockett & Sons, of Battle Creek; Paul W., who is an employee of the Advance Thresher Company, and Norman N., who is a fireman on the Grand Trunk railroad. Mr. Geddes has a pleasant home at No. 255 Calhoun street and has made many excellent improvements there. He has taken quite an active part in public affairs and his influence has been of no restricted order. He served as alderman, representing the Fourth ward, and was a member of the school board for six years, during which time new buildings were erected and the schools were largely developed along progressive lines. Mr. Geddes has always been found on the side of improvement. In 1888 he was nominated by the Republican party for the office of register of deeds in Calhoun county and received a handsome majority. He filled that office successfully and faithfully and in 1890 was re-elected, acting in that capacity for four years. He then retired from the position as he entered it—with the confidence and respect of the entire community. He has since given his attention to his business affairs, in which he is now meeting with signal success.

Fraternally he is connected with the Ancient Order of United Workmen, in which he has filled all of the chairs, acting for a number of years as receiver. His life has ever been characterized by enterprise and diligence and these are the qualities which never fail to win financial reward.

HOWARD LINCOLN ACKLEY.

Carlyle has said that biography is the most interesting as well as the most profitable study of mankind. There are few lives that do not furnish their lessons, and the record of Mr. Ackley is rich in those traits of character which command respect and are well worthy of emulation. He did not rise to a position in political, military or business circles that has commanded the attention of the world, but in his home community he so lived that all men honored and respected him and he left the impress of his individuality for good upon Battle Creek and her people. He was born in Convis township, Calhoun county, September 16, 1863, his parents being George W. and Frances (Mudge) Ackley. The father was born on the old home farm in the same county near the Ackley lake, a body of water named in honor of the family, for the grandfather was a pioneer settler there. Throughout his entire business career George Ackley has carried on agricultural pursuits and still makes his home in Convis township.

In the public schools Howard L. Ackley began his education, which was continued in Olivet College. Later he read law with the firm of Rollin & Morse, one of the leading law firms of Detroit, but because of failing eyesight, prior to the time for examination, he had to abandon his hope of entering professional life. Returning to his native county, he then learned the blacksmith's trade and conducted a shop in Tekonsha, where he met with success, combining mechanical skill with good business ability. He was a man highly respected by all, and his strong force of character and upright principles won him the regard of those with whom he came in contact. In 1897 he removed to Batavia, Branch county, where he again opened a blacksmith shop, conducting the business there until his death.

On the 20th of March, 1888, Mr. Ackley was united in marriage to Miss Jennie L. Sackett, of Bellevue, Eaton county, Michigan, a daughter of George S. and Rachel (Hetchler) Sackett. Her father was born in Massachusetts and is descended in direct line from King Henry and also from Ethan Allen, the famous Revolutionary commander of the Green Mountain boys. The grandfather, Nodiah Sackett, of Massachusetts, established large flouring mills in that state. George Seymour Sackett, whose middle name was given him because he was descended from the Seymour family, came to Michigan as a young man and located near Mount Clemens, where he engaged in teaching. A large number of the representatives of the family became successful teachers and were noted for strong intellectuality, while other members were identified with agricultural interests. George S. Sackett was joined in wedlock to Miss Hetchler, who was born in Pennsylvania and is of German lineage. Establishing his home in McKean county he there spent his active life as a farmer and later lived retired in Bellevue, where his last days were passed. His widow afterward departed this life in Barry county, Michigan. Their daughter, Jennie, spent her girlhood days in Massachusetts and enjoyed the advantages of the excellent public school system of that state. Later she went to Bellevue, Michigan, where she successfully engaged in teaching until her marriage. Unto Mr. and Mrs. Ackley were born four children: Rexford H., Robert S., Grace, Lucile and Kathleen M. Mr. and Mrs. Ackley were members of the Methodist Episcopal church, and while residing in Tekonsha he took an active and helpful part in church work, acting as usher for more than two years and contributing in large measure to the growth of the organization. He carried his Christianity into the everyday walks of life, living in harmony with his professions. Socially he was connected with the Knights of the Maccabees and was trustee of his lodge for two years. In politics he was a Democrat, and while deeply interested in the success of his party, he was never an aspirant for office, although he served as marshal of his village. His deepest interest centered in his family and he found his greatest enjoyment at his own fireside. He was devoted to the welfare of his wife and children and considered no personal sacrifice on his part too great if it would enhance their happiness. He passed away August 20, 1898, but his memory is enshrined in the hearts of those who knew him, and is especially dear to his family, who always found in him a devoted, considerate and kind husband and father.

CAPTAIN JAMES E. BEVIER.

Captain James E. Bevier, who is serving as a captain on the Battle Creek police force, was born in Livingston county, New York, June 6, 1848, a son of Nathaniel and Anna F. (Ferguson) Bevier. When he was six years of age the parents removed to Michigan and for a year resided in Hermonia, after which Mr. Bevier purchased a farm in Bedford township. He died, however, before removing to the place, but his widow and her nine children afterward took up their abode there. They were left in straightened financial circumstances and found it necessary not only to provide for their own support but to meet some indebtedness.

Captain Bevier was the youngest of the family. He acquired a limited education, and at the age of sixteen years enlisted for service in the Civil war as a member of Company H, Merrill's Horse, which became known as part of the Second Missouri Cavalry. Mr. Merrill was a captain in the regular army, but after organizing the regiment was made colonel. Our subject was first under fire at the battle of Big Blue in Missouri and participated in a number of skirmishes with bushwhackers. He remained in the service for about a year and then returned home, spending several years upon the farm. When about twenty years of age he went to Missouri to visit a brother and while there looked upon the old battle grounds on which he had met the rebel forces. When twelve months had passed he returned to Michigan and then remained at home until about twenty-eight years of age. In 1877 he went to California, spending three years on the Pacific coast, being for two years of that time in the street car service in Sacramento. On again coming to Michigan in December, 1880, he turned his attention to the painting business, which he followed for a few years in Bedford township, after which he became a painter in the employ of the Advance Thresher Company, with which he was connected for four and one-half years. Subsequently he followed painting as a contractor for one season and

then became a member of Company No. 1 of the fire department, acting as pipe man in that service for five years. Mr. Bevier assisted in survey work in and about the city streets of Battle Creek and for three months was engaged in the preliminary survey of the traction line to Gull Lake and Kalamazoo. In 1898 he was elected constable for the second ward, but soon after was made patrolman on the police force and never served as constable. He acted for two years as patrolman and was then promoted to the captaincy in which position he has since discharged his duties with admirable fidelity and promptness.

On the 15th of September, 1897, in Battle Creek, the Captain wedded Mrs. Eva Mills. Fraternally he was connected with Bedford lodge, F. & A. M., and filled most of its chairs. He has since transferred his membership to Battle Creek lodge No. 12, F. & A. M., and also took the degrees of Battle Creek Chapter, No. 19, R. A. M., and Beaumanoir Commandery, K. T., being a valued representative of the craft. In politics he has been an earnest Republican since casting his first presidential vote for General Grant in 1872.

HARLAN P. POTTER.

Harlan P. Potter owns and operates one hundred and twelve acres of land in Battle Creek township, whereon he has lived since 1873. He has developed this into a fine farm with modern buildings, splendid equipments and is to-day regarded as one of the most enterprising and progressive agriculturists of his locality. He was born in Marion, Wayne county, New York, on the

1st of November, 1838, and is a son of Thomas and Rowena (Hill) Potter. The family is of English lineage and the ancestry can be traced back for about four hundred years of direct ancestry since coming to America. At an early period in the development of this country, representatives of the name established homes in the new world. Both of the parents of our subject were natives of the Empire state, whence they removed to Indiana.

Under the parental roof Harlan P. Potter spent the days of his boyhood and youth in the usual manner of farmer lads, his father being an agriculturist. During the summer months he worked in the fields and the sun shone down on many a tract which he plowed and planted. He pursued his education in the schools of Marion, New York, and in early manhood learned the trades of painter and carpenter and joiner, serving an apprenticeship in both lines. He possessed good mechanical ability and through this means has been able to keep everything about his place in excellent condition. His life has been one of untiring industry. He continued to follow his trades in New York until 1857, when he came to Shiawassee county, Michigan, where he was employed one season, when he returned to New York and was there on October 25, 1860. In 1864 he went to Titusville, Pennsylvania, where he followed his trade in the oil region. In 1865 he went to Toledo, Ohio, and was there till 1867, when he moved to Adrian, Michigan, and that fall to Battle Creek, where he has been with the exception of a period spent in Missouri. His work in the city was vigorously prosecuted and his untiring energy brought to him creditable success. With the money he acquired he at length purchased the farm

which he now owns and which came into his possession in 1873. In that year he took up his abode thereon and it has now been his home for three decades. Great changes have occurred on the place since he took possession. He has placed the fields under a very high state of cultivation and has made excellent improvements in the way of erecting fine buildings. He built a very attractive, commodious and modern residence in 1893, it being one of the best country homes in Battle Creek township and it stands as a monument to the enterprise and thrift of the owner. In his farm work he uses the latest improved machinery and at all times is progressive. In connection with the cultivation of the cereals and fruits best adapted to the soil and climate he is also engaged in stock-raising and thereby adds materially to his income.

In 1860 Mr. Potter was united in marriage to Miss Harriet A. Howell, a native of Palmyra, New York. For forty-three years she traveled life's journey by his side, sharing with him the joys and sorrows, the adversity and prosperity which checker the careers of all. She indeed proved to him a faithful companion and helpmate and in her home was a devoted and loving wife and mother and on the 19th of March, 1903, she was called to her final rest. As she had endeared herself to many friends her death was deeply mourned throughout the community as well as in her immediate household. She left a daughter, Carrie Marie, who is now the wife of J. B. Mapes, a resident of Battle Creek township, by whom she has six living children: Clella Hattie, Eva May, Albert Arland, Vern, Carl and Grace.

In his political views Mr. Potter is independent, voting for the men whom he

thinks best qualified for office and supporting
measures which he believes will contribute
most largely to the general good. He is a
very prominent and active member of the
Grange and ranks high in its circles. He has
steadily advanced in the order until he has
become a member of the state and national
Granges, taking the highest degree in the
organization. Mr. Potter deserves great
credit for what he has accomplished in life,
for in early manhood he started out upon
his own account empty handed. He mastered the two trades mentioned and by his
close application and excellent workmanship he managed to acquire the capital
which he invested in his farm. As the
architect of his own fortunes he has builded
wisely and well and his life history proves
what can be accomplished through energy
and determination coupled with honorable
business methods.

HIRAM M. ALLEN.

Hiram M. Allen, who since 1877 has
resided in Battle Creek, is now living a retired life and stands to-day as a splendid
representative of the class of men that the
world calls self-made. He was prominently identified with business interests in
New England and afterward in this county, and although he is now a capitalist,
he was left a penniless boy when five years
of age, and, almost from that time to the
present, has depended entirely upon his
own labors for whatever he has possessed
and enjoyed. His is an honorable record
of a conscientious man, who by his upright
life has won uniform confidence. He has

now reached four score years, and although the snows of several winters have
whitened his hair he has the vigor of a
much younger man and in spirit and interest seems yet in his prime. His career
clearly illustrates the possibilities that are
open in this country to earnest, persevering young men, who have the courage of
their convictions and are determined to be
the architects of their own fortunes.

Hiram M. Allen was born at East
Windsor, near Hartford, Connecticut,
April 20, 1823. His paternal great-great-
grandfather settled in that locality at a
very early period in its development and
there made his home until his death. The
great-grandfather also lived there upon
the same farm, and it was there that the
grandfather, Solomon Allen, was born and
reared. He served during the latter part
of the Revolutionary war as a lieutenant,
joining the army when but a boy. The
father of our subject was Solomon Allen,
Jr. He, too, was born and reared on the
old family homestead and always continued farming there. He became a leading and influential man of his township.
He married Miss Rhuma Pease, a daughter of Simeon Pease, who owned the place,
at Enfield, Connecticut, where Washington afterward remained for a time. He,
too, was one of the soldiers of the Revolutionary war and commanded a Connecticut regiment with the rank of Colonel. Later in life he became a farmer. Mrs. Allen
was a most devoted and loving wife and
mother, doing everything in her power for
the benefit of her children, who were three
in number: Samantha, the eldest, reached
years of maturity, married Mr. Bartlett
and is now deceased; the second is the sub-

HIRAM M. ALLEN

MRS. HIRAM M. ALLEN

ject of this review; Martha A., the youngest, is the wife of George Nye of Hartford. Connecticut.

In the district schools in what is now Melrose, Connecticut, Hiram M. Allen obtained his early education. His tuition, however, had to be paid for. He lost his father when only five years of age and after that time had to care for himself and as soon as possible contributed to the support of his mother. He first worked as a farm boy and later was employed in the Broad Brook Woolen Factory. There he engaged in the draying and transfer business. Becoming the owner of a farm, he cultivated it and in connection with that work kept teams used for the transfer business of the Broad Brook Woolen Factory. This he found lucrative and in that way he gained his start. For some years he also engaged in buying and packing tobacco at Broad Brook, and in Hartford conducted a store where he sold the tobacco to the wholesale trade. In that business he continued throughout his residence in the east and became one of the leading tobacco merchants of that section of the country. Keen and clear headed, always busy and always careful and conservative in financial matters, moving slowly and surely in every transaction, he had few superiors in the steady progress which invariably reaches its objective point. He handled tobacco on a very extensive scale, making large annual sales until he became one of the best known tobacco dealers of Hartford, Connecticut, his trade reaching mammoth proportions. He was also an extensive producer of tobacco himself, annually raising from two to seven tons. Another field of activity claimed his attention. He became a large dealer in horses and owned

some very fine stock. In this way he was widely known and annually added to his income.

On removing to the west Mr. Allen first settled at Newton, Calhoun county, where he purchased a farm, but soon took up his abode in Battle Creek. While cultivating his land he also continued in the tobacco business, buying in the east and selling here. He established a tobacco store in Battle Creek and soon gained for it a large patronage. As he saw opportunity he also invested in various farms in this portion of the state and his purchases and sales have yielded him a very good financial return. He has also been interested in residence property in the city, purchasing improved property and also buying vacant lots upon which he has built good dwellings. He is now practically living retired although he gives his personal supervision to his invested interests. He was, however, at one time, a large real estate dealer here, handling his own property. He also early became interested in the Battle Creek Electric Light Company and was one of the stockholders in the Art Album Company and acted as its director for a number of years. Many business enterprises have profited by his financial aid, his wise counsel and his keen foresight. He has been interested in southern property to quite an extent, at one time owning fourteen hundred and forty acres in Virginia only forty-five miles from the city of Washington, D. C.

Before leaving the east Mr. Allen was united in marriage to Miss Lucy A. Terry, of Enfield, Connecticut, and they became the parents of four children: Asaph T., who is living in Battle Creek, is now conducting a cold storage business, having a plant of his own on Locust street; Mary E. is the wife of Dwight Beasley, a farmer of Ellington, Connecticut; Edwin A. is now practically living retired in Battle Creek, save for the supervision which he gives to his property interests; and Charles H. makes his home in this city. On the 8th of February, 1877, Mr. Allen was united in marriage to Mrs. Mary A. Stebbins, of Battle Creek, who was born in Eagle, Wyoming county, New York, a daughter of Vertot D. Beach, who came to Michigan when Mrs. Allen was a young lady. By her first marriage she had two children: Fred D. Stebbins, now lives in Denver where he went for his health. He was but eighteen years of age when he entered the hardware store of C. F. Bock & Son in Battle Creek, and he was with him for thirteen years, but because of his health he went upon the road as a traveling salesman for the Dowagiac Stove Company. Before her marriage, his wife, Christina Bleasdale, was for four years employed as bookkeeper by Mr. Bock. Will T. Stebbins, of Battle Creek, was educated in the city schools here and later pursued a scientific course in the University of Michigan, giving especial attention to electrical engineering, graduating with the degree of Bachelor of Science and Electrical Engineering. He is now connected with the Duplex Printing Company of this city.

In his political views in early life Mr. Allen was a Whig and upon the dissolution of that party joined the ranks of the new Republican party and has since continued to follow its banners. While in East Windsor, Connecticut, he was selectman of his township for several years and he also held other local offices. In Battle Creek he has been active in politics, but not as an aspirant for official preferment. In East Windsor, Connecticut, he was made a Mason and afterward demitted to Marshall Lodge, F. and A. M. His life has been a very busy and useful one. He practically did the work of several men and now at the age of eighty years still possesses a strong physique and his mental faculties are unimpaired. Old age is not necessarily a synonym of weakness and need not suggest inactivity as a matter of course. There is an old age which grows stronger and better as the years pass and such has been the career of Mr. Allen. His life record, too, should serve as a source of inspiration to the young. When but a mere boy he started out to fight life's battle, and steadily pursuing his way undeterred by the obstacles and difficulties in his path he has achieved prosperity, of which he perhaps did not dream a few decades ago. Steady application, careful study of business methods and plans to be followed, close attention to details, combined with untiring energy directed by a superior mind—these are the traits of character which have brought him success and made him one of the foremost men of Battle Creek.

RILLIE F. HOFFMASTER.

Rillie F. Hoffmaster is the treasurer of P. Hoffmaster Sons Company, limited, of Battle Creek, and his active connection with commercial interests of this city has ever sustained the enviable reputation which has always been associated with the family name in this city. His industry and well directed activity has made him an important factor in community affairs. A son of Peter and

Amelia (Blodgett) Hoffmaster, he was born in Kalamazoo, Michigan, on the 31st of August, 1862, and accompanied his parents on their removal to Battle Creek ten years later. He is a twin brother of William M. Hoffmaster and throughout much of their business career as in their boyhood days they have been closely associated. They were students in the city schools and afterward entered business college here, subsequent to which time they entered their father's store. Rillie F. Hoffmaster became a clerk in the establishment in 1880 and continued there until the father's death on the 31st of December, 1901, having in the meantime largely mastered business principles and the methods of conducting extensive commercial enterprises at the present stage of the world's business development. The brothers, as executors of the estate, continued in the management of the store, and, on the 1st of February, 1903, the business was incorporated under the present style of the P. Hoffmaster Sons Company, limited. It was capitalized for seventy-five thousand dollars and W. M. Hoffmaster was chosen chairman, R. F. Hoffmaster treasurer, and Helen M. Hoffmaster secretary. This is now the oldest dry-goods establishment of the city and a leading enterprise, the extent and volume of the business being such that it demands a stock occupying three store rooms and basement in the Opera House block. Along modern and progressive lines the business is conducted, under the capable supervison of the brothers who are continually enlarging the scope of the enterprise. Rillie F. Hoffmaster has operated to a considerable extent in real estate and has thus added materially to his income. In 1899 he built the Hoffmaster block located at No. 85-87 West Main street—a fine two

story brick structure. In 1903 he built the new Hoffmaster block at No. 79-81-83 West Main street, a splendid three story business and office building, and both of these he still owns. He has for some time been a director in the Merchants' Savings Bank and in business circles is widely known as a man of sound judgment, laudable ambition and untiring endeavor.

Rillie F. Hoffmaster was married on the 6th of January, 1892, to Miss Helene Schoonmaker, of Savanah, New York, a daughter of DePuy and Bianca (Stiles) Schoonmaker, who were descended from early Dutch ancestors. Unto them have been born three children, but the eldest, Peter Hoffmaster, died in 1896. Louise and Florence are still with their parents in their home at No. 219 East Main street. Mrs. Hoffmaster is a member of the Presbyterian church and contributes generously to its support. He belongs to the Knights of Pythias fraternity, is a charter member of the Elks lodge of Battle Creek and also belongs to the Athelstan club. He and his brother have made their life work an integral factor in the commercial development of Battle Creek and from boyhood days down to the present have occupied an enviable position in public regard as representatives of the enterprising spirit which dominates the west.

JAMES M. PEEBLES, A. M., M. D., Ph. D.

Indelibly engraved on the pages of history is the name of Dr. James Martin Peebles. Man's worth in the world is determined by his usefulness, by what he has accomplished for his fellowmen—and he is certainly deserving of the greatest honor and regard whose efforts have been of the greatest benefit to his fellow men. Judged by this standard Dr. James M. Peebles may well be accounted not only one of the most eminent and distinguished citizens of Battle Creek but also of America, for throughout his professional career, covering many decades his efforts have been of a most helpful nature. Not alone as a practitioner of medicine and surgery has he become widely known, but also as a teacher, an author and a scientist, disseminating knowledge along various lines that has had an immeasurable effect in the world. His deep research and investigation have rendered more effective the labors of his profession and have also touched upon many lines of scientific study, relating to man's mission in the world and the best use to which he may put his powers. No enumeration of the men of distinction in Michigan would be complete were there failure to make specific mention of him whose name initiates this review.

The Doctor was born in Whitingham, Windham county, Vermont, March 23, 1822, a son of James and Nancy (Brown) Peebles. The family ancestry may be traced back to the ancient town of Peebles in Peebleshire, Scotland, where at a very early date in the history of Anglo-Saxon civilization, representatives of the name received titles rendering them eligible to membership in the national parliament. In 1718 some of the family crossed the water to New England and under the Rev. Mr. Abercombie established a settlement at Phelham, Massachusetts. James Peebles, the father of the doctor, was born in Whitingham, Vermont, and followed the occupation of farming. He served as a captain in the southern division of the Ver-

mont militia for a number of years and also held various township offices, while by his fellow townsmen he was held in the highest regard. He married Nancy Brown, who was born and reared in Windham county, where she had been engaged in teaching school prior to her marriage. Her father was a well known farmer and stock dealer of Whitingham.

After attending the common school of his native town Dr. Peebles continued his studies in a select school at Binghampton, New York, and later pursued a course in Oxford Academy, of the same state. When twenty years of age he entered the Universalist ministry, and for several years preached with ability and success in the churches of that denomination in Oswego and Elmira, New York, and in other cities. Deciding to leave the ministry and make the practice of medicine his life work, he entered the University of Medicine and Surgery at Philadelphia, Pennsylvania, where he completed a full course of study and was graduated with the class of 1876, with the degree of M. D. In 1877 he received from the same institution the degree of Master of Arts, while in 1882 the Medical University of Chicago conferred upon him the degree of Doctor of Philosophy. After his graduation Dr. Peebles began the practice of medicine in Philadelphia and also, at the same time, conducted a practice at his place of residence, Hammonton, New Jersey, while for some time he had charge of a medical ward in the city hospital of Philadelphia. After practicing there for some time, during which he had been very successful in the treatment of chronic diseases, he removed to San Antonio, Texas, and opened the first sanitarium of that locality, conducting it for some time. He enjoyed a large patronage there and during his residence in San Antonio he was called to the chair of physiology, psychology and ontology in the Eclectric Medical College at Cincinnati, Ohio. He retained his position as professor in that college for a number of years and gained the reputation of being a profound thinker, a fluent speaker and a teacher of more than ordinary ability.

Disposing of his interests in San Antonio and severing his connection with the college, he removed to San Diego, California, where he purchased property and opened what was known as the Health-Home Sanitarium, the place being splendidly equipped and furnished for the purpose used. Not caring to be situated on the very border of the country, however, Dr. Peebles disposed of his interests there and in 1896 came to Battle Creek, opening a medical institute which he still conducts and of which he is the president, while several other physicians assist him in the care of the patients. This institution has also proved a successful undertaking for Dr. Peebles' reputation is a broad one and his skill is constantly sought by those in need of medical treatment.

The Doctor's efforts, however, have never been confined entirely to the treatment of diseases for his research has compassed many lines and his labors have been of a varied nature. At one time he established and published a monthly called the "Temple of Health," which secured a large circulation. His prominence in public affairs led to his selection for various positions of trust and responsibility. In 1868 he was appointed a member of the Northwest Congressional Indian Peace Commission, and in this work he was associated with Generals Sheridan, Sherman and Harney, Colonel S. F. Tappan and other prominent men. They were stationed at Cheyenne and there received the complaints of dissatisfied Indians. In 1869 Dr. Peebles was appointed by General Grant to the position of United States consul at Trebizonde, on the Black sea, in Turkey, Asia, where he served for two years and then resigned. On the return trip he stopped in Rome, there spending the winter. In 1886 he represented the United States arbitration league at the International Peace Commission of Europe, held in Berlin, and was a delegate to the Universal Peace Union which met at Buffalo during the Pan-American Exposition.

Dr. Peebles has also been prominently connected with various fraternal organizations, having for their object the amelioration of the conditions of his fellow men. In early manhood he was raised to the degree of a Master Mason and also became a member of the chapter, council and commandery at Elmira, New York. He joined the Independent Order of Odd Fellows, and became an active worker later with the Sons of Temperance. He was instrumental in the organization of the Independent Order of Good Templars, and on his third journey around the world he established at Cape Town, Cape Colony, five lodges of Good Templars, to which he delivered several lectures, the dean of Cape Town presiding. His membership embraced connection with various societies for research and for the dissemination of knowledge. He is a member of the Anthropological Society of London, to which he made several reports while in Asiatic Turkey; the Psychological Association of London, to which he has contributed papers, and is the vice-president of the London Pyscho-Therapeutic Society. He is also a member of the Academy of Arts and Sciences of Naples; a member of the International Climatic Association; the American Institute of Christian Philosophy; the Victoria Institute and Philosophical Society; a peer of the Royal Society of London; and other organizations of prominence embracing in their membership some of the most distinguished scholars of the world. That Dr. Peebles is entitled to membership in these at once indicates his mental standing.

The Doctor is a communicant of the Episcopal church and yet is a pronounced believer in spiritualism in its broader and religious sense. In matters of hygiene he is a vegetarian, believing that life can be greatly prolonged by avoiding the consumption of animal flesh and obeying the hygienic laws of nature. He took an active part in the anti-slavery movement when it required great personal and moral courage to stand firm in its support, and he occupied the lecture platform with Garret Smith, Henry C. Wright and Sojourner Truth, who was a resident of Battle Creek; and was with William Lloyd Garrison at the time of his great speech in Syracuse, New York. With these distinguished disciples of liberty and with others hardly less prominent, the Doctor was intimately associated and he has lived to enjoy the benificent influence of the cause for which they labored. He also lectured frequently on the subject of Woman's suffrage, on temperance and on all living issues and reforms which have claimed the attention of the people since 1840.

Four times the Doctor has circumnavigated the globe, completing the last trip after he was eighty years of age, and at present he is considering a call from Cal-cutta, India, to make a lecturing tour of that country, which he will probably do. He has spent much time in the Pacific islands and in Egypt, India and Ceylon, and is a financial contributor to and an official of the Museus school for the education of Buddist girls, located at Cinnamon Gardens, Colombo, Ceylon. His thought, study and investigation seems to have touched upon every subject bearing upon the physical, mental and moral development of the people, not only of his own race, but of the world. He has issued many pamphlets on scientific and psychical subjects. He is also the author of a large volume of six hundred pages entitled, "Three Journeys. Around the World," published in Boston in 1897; "The Seers of the Ages," a volume of five hundred pages, published in 1860, which has already passed through nine editions, the tenth being now in press, while it has also been translated and was published in Calcutta in the Bengalese language. He is the author of "Immortality and Our Future Homes," three hundred and fifty pages, published in 1880, and now in the eighth edition; "How to Live a Century and Grow Old Gracefully," in 1881, several editions, one of twenty thousand volumes; "Death Defeated or How to Keep Young," 1900, three editions; "Compulsory Vaccination a Menace to Health and Personal Liberty," 1900, a volume of five hundred pages. He also edited a symposium entitled "The Christ Question Settled," to which he largely contributed, together with Rabbi I. M. Wise, Robert G. Ingersol, Professor J. R. Buchanan, and others. He has published, recently, a volume entitled, "Who Are These Spiritualists," gathering the names of the most distinguished and brainiest men in the world which have believed in the psychic phenomena. The book is a large volume and soon a second edition was required.

On the 23d of May, 1852, Dr. Peebles married Miss Mary M. Conkey, a daughter of Mr. and Mrs. Thomas H. Conkey, of Canton, New York. Prior to her marriage she was a successful teacher in the Clinton Liberal Institute of Clinton, New York. Of recent years he has made his home in Battle Creek, but the boundaries of the state and of the nation are too limited for the capabilities of such a man. His work along any line wherein he has labored for the benefit of the physical, the mental or the moral nature of man, would alone entitle him to distinction as a man of world-wide fame; and among the thinking men of civilized lands he is recognized as a kindred spirit, whose labors have added to the sum total of knowledge and reform.

PAUL SMITH FOX, M. D.

The persistency of purpose which Dr. Paul Smith Fox displayed while acquiring his education, indicates the elemental strength of his character and gave promise of a successful future, and his career since leaving school has been in harmony with the promises of his youth and early manhood. He is now a successful practicing physician of Athens, having a large patronage.

The Doctor was born in Park township, St. Joseph county, Michigan, July 14, 1860, a son of George W. and Lydia (Smith) Fox. He spent his boyhood days on the home farm and began his education in the district schools, while later he spent three years as a student in the high school at Three Rivers, this state. He then engaged in teaching for a number of successive terms after which he attended the Ann Arbor high school, in which he was graduated with the class of 1882. He then followed teaching until becoming a student in the medical department of the University of Michigan in 1883, therein pursuing his studies at intervals until his graduation with the class of 1888. When not in college he was engaged in teaching in order to defray the expense of his professional course. For two years of that time he was principal of the high school of Athens.

In August, 1888, Dr. Fox opened his office in Athens, where he has remained continuously since, engaged in the general practice of medicine but also making a specialty of the treatment of diseases of the eye, ear, nose and throat. He is most careful in diagnosing a case and applies with accuracy his knowledge of the medical sciences to the needs of his patients. For ten years he has served as health officer of either the village or township and sometimes of both, and is now filling that position in the township.

In October, 1888, was celebrated the marriage of Dr. Fox and Miss Della M. Childs, who was born in his native county, and they now have two sons, James Childs Fox and Edmund Burke Fox.

The Doctor and his wife are members of the First Reformed church of Athens, and fraternally he is connected with Athens lodge, F. & A. M. His political allegiance is given to the Democracy and he has served for two terms as a trustee of the board of education. He now owns and occupies a fine home, supplied with all the comforts of life, and acquired through his earnest toil. The favorable judgment which the world passed upon him at the outset of his professional career, has been in no degree modified or set aside, but on the contrary has been strengthened as the years have gone by.

THOMAS H. BRIGGS, M. D.

Although Dr. Thomas H. Briggs has passed away, he is yet held in loving memory by many who knew him. He won the gratitude of the public because of his skill in his profession, and his kindly spirit and many excellent traits of heart and mind, endeared him to all who were at all familiar with his upright career. The world is better for his having lived and his life history contains many lessons that are worthy of emulation.

The Doctor was born in Belvidere, Illinois, February 2, 1840. The ancestral history can be traced back to the time of the first settlers of Yates county, New York, by the Society of Friends. Among the colonists who removed from North Kingston, Rhode Islands, to Yates county were John and Peleg Briggs. They were relatives and located at Milo Center. John Briggs wedded Elizabeth Bailey, of Rhode Island, and their eldest child, John Briggs, Jr., married Ardery Place in Rhode Island. They, however, located at The Friends' Place in the town of Milo, Yates county, New York. He was clerk of the Society for many years and died about 1825, when seventy years of age. He had two children: Thomas P., and Mary. The latter, it is related, was living in the home of Bene-

dict Robinson, when on one occasion, she spun a hundred knots of woolen yarn in a single day. This was woven into cloth and put on exhibition at the first Agricultural fair in Ontario county, New York, where it received a premium. She became the wife of Ezekiel Blue and they removed to Calhoun county, Michigan, locating near Marshall where they spent their remaining days and where their descendants still reside. Thomas P. Briggs married Hannah, a daughter of James Moore, and their eldest son of Dr. Joseph Briggs, the father of our subject. The grandfather's home was on a farm in Fredonia township, not far south of Marshall. Their son, Joseph Briggs, was born in 1813 and was reared at the old home in New York, where he was educated, and after studying under preceptors he completed his medical education at LaGrange, Indiana. In the meantime his family removed to Marshall, Michigan, and later he located in Schoolcraft, where he practiced his profession until his death, which was caused by a runaway accident in 1854. He was married in 1839 in Yates county, New York, to Emaline A. Crook, who was born in Rutland, Vermont, in 1817, a daughter of Samuel and Susan (Davis) Crook. She was reared and educated, however, in Yates county and is a woman of superior mental ability and of charming individuality. She is still living in Schoolcraft, and has for many years been a member of the Methodist Episcopal church. In the family were three children; Thomas H., Lewis M. and Annette.

Dr. Thomas H. Briggs was but fourteen years of age at the time of his father's death. He acquired a good education, attending Albion College and afterward the University at Ann Arbor, where he was

THOMAS H. BRIGGS, M. D.

pursuing a course in medicine when the Civil war broke out. He enlisted in Company G, Eleventh Regiment of Michigan Volunteers and was made first lieutenant, while on the 14th of November, 1862, he was promoted to captain. He took part in fifteen hard fought battles and his promotion came soon after the battle of Stone River in recognition of his bravery and loyalty. He sustained a number of wounds, for he always led the men into the thickest of the fight. In the fall of 1863 he entered the hospital service on account of wounds received at Chickamauga, and later, resigned his commission. While in that service, however, he took up the study of his profession in Nashville and was there graduated in 1864, with the degree of Doctor of Medicine.

The Doctor had been married in Albion, Michigan, November 7, 1861, just after his enlistment. He wedded Mary E. Gould, a daughter of Zeno and Clarissa (Baker) Gould, and she remained with her parents while he went to the front.

After his return from the army, Dr. Briggs began practicing medicine in Albion, Michigan, and in June, 1866, removed to Belvidere, Illinois, his native town. He was there but a little less than a year and built up a good practice, but his father-in-law urged his return to Michigan. Accordingly he located in the village of Mattawan, Van Buren county, where he resided until 1882, when he came to Battle Creek, and here he soon won a large and lucrative practice. In public affairs he was also prominent, and served as a member of the school board of Van Buren county. After coming to Battle Creek he was pension examiner and also served as health officer, as coroner and as chairman of the Republican executive, committee. He was a

member of the County Medical Society, the State Medical Society, the American Medical Association and the National Association of Railway Surgeons. In 1894 he received the honorary degree of Doctor of Medicine from the University of Michigan.

Unto the Doctor and his wife were born three children: Blanche, born in Albion, is a graduate of the high school of Battle Creek with the class of 1884. She taught school in this city for two years, and then entered the University of Michigan, in which she was graduated in 1890, with the degree of Bachelor of Letters. She married A. Lincoln Knisely, also a graduate of the State University, winning the degree of Master of Arts, in 1891. He is now state chemist of the Agricultural College of Oregon, at Corvallis. They have two children: Margaret Gould, born in Ithica, New York, and Malcolm Briggs, born in Battle Creek. Clare Briggs, the second of the family, was born in Mattawan, Michigan, and graduated in the Battle Creek high school in 1888. In 1894 she was graduated in the University of Michigan, on the completion of a four years' course, with the degree of Bachelor of Science, in chemistry. She then taught in the public schools, \ as supervisor of drawing for four years. Ima Gould Briggs, born in Mattawan, was graduated in the high school in Battle Creek in 1893, entered the University of Michigan in the same year and was graduated in 1897 with the degree of Bachelor of Philosophy. The Doctor and Mrs. Briggs ever favored the higher education of women and gave to their daughters splendid advantages.

The Doctor was a valued member of the Masonic fraternity, in which he attained the Knight Templar degree; and he was

13

also, at one time, commander of Farragut post, G. A. R. He was a man five feet ten inches in height and of rather heavy build. He had brown hair and blue eyes and showed a genial disposition. Like his wife, he belonged to the Independent Congregational church. He died April 7, 1899, and Battle Creek mourned one of its honored citizens. In the exercise of his professional duties he had ample opportunity to show forth the charitable side of his nature. He was very generous, giving freely of his means for public improvement and was ever quick to respond to the call of the sick and suffering, many times giving his service when he knew there was no hope of pecuniary reward. It was this that made him so beloved among his fellowmen, and which developed in him a character that was most commendable. He was one of nature's noblemen and in his life record, his family may ever feel a just pride. His widow, still living in Battle Creek, is a most estimable and cultured lady and has been a member of the board of education of the city.

SAMUEL F. DOBBINS.

One of the most substantial industries of this county is the Marshall Furnace Company, whose interests are ably managed by the proprietor, Samuel F. Dobbins, a man of marked business and executive ability, a progressive and enterprising spirit, and one whose efforts have given a strong impetus to the commercial life of the city. A native son of the state, he was born in Plymouth, Wayne county, November 4, 1856, the son of Charles M. and Lucy A.

(Smith) Dobbins, and was reared to a practical manhood upon a farm in his native county. His first knowledge of books was obtained in the public school in the vicinity of his home, after which, at the age of eighteen, he went to Buffalo and completed a commercial course in the Bryant & Stratton Business College. Returning to Michigan, he located in this city, since which time he has been identified with the commercial, social and municipal life of the community, making his influence widely felt.

Upon his settlement in Marshall, Mr. Dobbins accepted a position with his cousin, James L. Dobbins, who was engaged in the furnace business, in addition to his duties as a bookkeeper acting as traveling salesman. He remained in this connection for the ensuing five years, adding to his native ability the practical training which laid the foundation for his success in an independent venture. At the expiration of that period he entered into partnership with E. H. Grant and established the business which has since grown to its present remunerative proportions. In 1889 Mr. Dobbins purchased the interest of his partner and has since conducted the business alone. For several years they purchased their castings of Mr. Bullard, a well known business man of this city. In 1890, however, Mr. Dobbins began the manufacture of his own supplies. The factory of Mr. Bullard was at first leased in the interest of the younger firm, but within the period of five years the present property was purchased and fitted for the successful conducting of a constantly increasing trade. Since the purchase in 1895 Mr. Dobbins has increased the size of the building from one story to three, in addition to which he has also put up a two story office building and warehouse. Upon the establishment of the manufactory he employed a force of ten men, while at the present time a corps of ninety is required to supply the demand for this manufacture, which finds a market in Ohio, Indiana and Michigan, while a smaller number is sent to the southern states and to Wisconsin. Upon the establishment and successful conducting of such enterprises depends to a large extent the material advancement of a city's prosperity, and Mr. Dobbins is justly entitled to much credit for his efforts along this line.

The marriage of Mr. Dobbins occurred in Owosso, Michigan, February 14, 1883, and united him with Miss Marie L. Mitchell, who was born in New York City, the daughter of William and Hester (Rogers) Mitchell. Their union has been blessed with three children, of whom the eldest, Dale Mitchell was born in Marshall, June 9, 1884, and after his graduation from the high school of this city he entered Kenyon College, at Gambier, Ohio, from which institution he will graduate with the class of 1906. Charles W., the second son, was born in Marshall, August 2, 1886, and will graduate from the high school with the class of 1904. Samuel Fremont, Jr., was also born in Marshall, April 26, 1888, and will graduate with the class of 1906.

A Republican in politics, Mr. Dobbins supports the principles endorsed in the platform of his party, and though never desirous of official recognition he has still participated largely in the affairs of the community, at the urgent solicitation of those who recognize his fitness for public office. For two terms he represented the citizens of his ward in the city council, being on the committee that had charge of the water

works system, and for one term discharged the duties of mayor, and while in office established the electric light commission, and appointed the members of the first board. As a member of the committee for putting in water works and electric lights he was largely instrumental in securing these desirable improvements for the city. In addition to his other interests he has always been identified with the educational development of Marshall, being at present in office as school director, which position he has maintained for the past seven years, the erection of the new high school building in 1901 being due to the efforts of Mr. Dobbins and a few others. Mr. Dobbins has been interested in the First National Bank of Marshall, and a director of it for four years. He is also well known in fraternal circles, being a member of St. Albans lodge No. 20, F. & A. M., in which he has served as master for three terms; Lafayette chapter No. 4, where he has served as high priest for four years; and in the Marshall commandery has passed most of the chairs, being eminent commander for two years. He is also identified with Moslem Temple of the Mystic Shrine of Detroit.

Mr. Dobbins is one of those men whose talents have not been confined to the accomplishment of one idea. Well equipped for the battle of life with education, energy and ambition, he early felt his ability to cope with the adversities which are a part of a business career, and though he has adhered with exceptional perseverance to his first occupation, his success still shows the broadening influences which have found their way into a busy and active life. The citizens of Marshall are justly proud to claim him as a representative of their interests, and point with equal pride to the industry which he has made a part of the city's advancement.

GEORGE T. BULLEN.

George T. Bullen stands to-day as one of the leading merchants of Albion. His native talent has led him out of humble circumstances to success, through the opportunity that is the pride of our American life. Nor is his success to be measured by material standards alone. He has developed that higher type of character that makes for ethical ideals in business and in society, and in both his commercial and private life he has applied principles that command respect and admiration.

For twenty years Mr. Bullen has resided in Albion, and is a native son of Michigan, his birth having occurred at Parma, Jackson county, June 14, 1867. His parents, George and Mary Ann (Height) Bullen, were natives of England, living in Broughton, Huntingtonshire, and soon after their marriage they came to the United States. After a short period spent in Ohio. they removed to Parma, Michigan. where the father carried on business as a farmer, stockman and butcher. He was drowned during the infancy of his son George, leaving a widow and six children. The mother died. in 1891.

In the public schools of Parma, George T. Bullen acquired his education, and in the summer vacations was variously employed. When sixteen years of age he came to Albion and entered the service of McGinniss & Company in 1883. The following year he secured a similar position

with E. M. Slayton & Company, with whom he remained for two years; and subsequently he spent three and a half years with G. F. Bundy. After two months spent with E. F. Mills & Company, Mr. Mills sold out to M. D. Galloway, a commercial traveler, and Mr. Bullen continued with the new firm as manager for two years, during the absence of Mr. Galloway. On the expiration of that period he formed a partnership with C. S. Tucker under the firm style of Bullen & Tucker, and they purchased the drygoods business of W. B. Crane. That partnership continued for two years, and Mr. Bullen then sold out, February 19, 1894. On the 31st of March, of the same year, he opened a small store in the Eslow Block. where he remained for two years, when the growth of his business necessitated larger quarters and he moved across the street to the Dalrymple block. and enlarged his store by adding a stock of cloaks and carpets. The business has grown continuously and substantially, and after four years spent at the second site he purchased the S. M. Tuttle block, where for forty years or more a drug store had been conducted. Improving and remodeling the building, he made it into a three story and basement building, and increased his line of goods. Needing still more room, in 1903. he purchased the Brockway block at the corner of Erie and Superior streets, which he has remodeled into a large and thoroughly modern establishment. It is forty-six feet front, by one hundred and fifteen deep. and is three stories in height with basement. It is thoroughly equipped with modern accessories, is stocked with a large and carefully selected line of dry-goods, carpets, cloaks, suits and ladies' furnishing goods, and is as fine a store as can be found in southern Michigan, outside of Detroit. The volume of his trade has justified the expenditure which he has from time to time made in improvements, which in turn, have brought to him a still greater patronage.

In Albion, Michigan, August 27, 1890, Mr. Bullen was united in marriage to Miss Ella Young, a daughter of John and Katherine Young, early residents of Albion. Three sons have been born unto them: Donald D., Ralph R. and George E. The family residence is the old Irwin homestead, at No. 303 Irwin avenue and its free-hearted hospitality is commensurate to that which is so freely accorded them in the best homes of the city. Both Mr. and Mrs. Bullen are members of the Methodist Episcopal church, of which Mr. Bullen is one of the trustees. He has taken high degrees in Masonry, belonging to Murat lodge, No. 21, F. and A. M.; Albion Chapter, R. A. M., and Marshall Commandery, K. T. He also belongs to Albion lodge, No. 57, K. P., of which he is a past chancellor, and he has been representative to the Grand lodge. He has for a number of years been a director and also vice-president of the Leisure Hour Club, and in 1902 was its president. In politics he is an earnest Republican, but has never aspired to office, preferring to give his attention to his business affairs. In his business career every step has been carefully and judiciously made. He has watched for opportunities and has judged possibilities from every standpoint, and while thus making no false steps, he has at the same time followed progressive ideas that have resulted in the development of an establishment which will bear comparison with any

similar business in this part of the state. He has also been influential in community affairs and as a merchant, citizen and private individual has made a record which is worthy of commendation and approval.

HON. WILLIAM A. LANE, M. D.

Worldly goods and an influential position have been won by this gentleman, who is a native-born citizen of Calhoun county. Dr. William A. Lane was born in the township of Convis, March 1, 1845, and practically all his life has been spent here. His parents, James and Sarah Lane, who came from England in 1835, constituted one of the first three families which settled in that township. They were devoted Christians and were each endowed by nature with those attributes of mind and character which, broadened by education, made them useful and valuable members of society.

William, the youngest of the five children, spent his boyhood days on the farm, receiving his early education in the district school, afterwards attending Vermontville Academy and Olivet College. He then entered the University of Michigan, where he pursued a full course in medicine, and in 1867 received his degree as doctor of medicine at Philadelphia, and in later years spent several months visiting the leading hospitals and medical colleges of Europe. For thirty years he practiced his chosen profession at Homer, and was an active participant in every important public and social movement in that community.

Dr. Lane has been eminently successful, not only in his professional career, but in any and all public matters with which he has been identified. He is one of the best known men in the county.

Notwithstanding Dr. Lane is a Democrat, he has four times been elected president of that Republican stronghold, the village of Homer, and is the first member of that party who has been called in nearly fifty years to the position which he now holds. He was elected judge of probate of Calhoun county in 1896 by a plurality of 281. He was re-elected in 1900 by the increased plurality of 654, notwithstanding the fact that the Republican presidential electors carried the county by a plurality of 763.

In all the varied work coming under his jurisdiction in the office he holds he has shown discretion, ability and a high moral purpose, which makes the right man indispensable in a position of such importance, and in all he has presided as a fearless, impartial judge, and one whose record is an honor to the county.

In religion, Judge Lane is a Presbyterian, fraternally he is a member of several lodges of high order; he is a Mason, a Knight Templar, an Odd Fellow, a Knight of the Maccabees and a Workman.

His family consists of a wife and two daughters, Mrs. Dwight W. Knickerbocker of Marshall, and Miss Mabel I. Lane, with her parents of that city.

ULYSSES S. MOORE.

Since 1877 Ulysses S. Moore had made his home in Battle Creek and during thirty-six years he maintained an enviable reputation as an honorable business man and one whose worth of character entitled him to uniform respect and consideration. A native of New York, his birth occurred in Belfast, Allegany county, October 10, 1839. His father was born in Massachusetts and belonged to an early New England family, while the mother's birth occurred in the Green Mountain state. The trade of the father was a shoemaker and he followed that pursuit in Belfast, when the business of manufacturing shoes by hand was a very important industry; and his patronage was so great that he employed seven or eight workmen. He afterward removed to Fairmount, Martin county, Minnesota, where both he and his wife passed away when eighty-one years of age.

Ulysses S. Moore, the eldest of their thirteen children, was indebted to the public school system of his native city for the educational privileges he enjoyed in his youth. On putting aside his text books he learned the shoemaker's trade at Rushford, Allegheny county, New York, but prior to that time was employed as a boy on the Erie Canal, being thus engaged for five seasons before he mastered his trade. When still living in Rushford, Mr. Moore was united in marriage on the 3d of July, 1866, to Miss Maria L. Cole, who was there born, October 15, 1844, a daughter of Nathan and Aldulia (Farwell) Cole, the former a veterinary surgeon and butcher.

In the spring of 1867 Mr. and Mrs. Moore removed westward to Fairmount, Minnesota, in which locality he secured one hundred and sixty acres of land, spending one season there. He then came to Battle Creek, where he resumed work at his trade in the employ of L. L. Livingston with whom he was connected for seven years. He then established a shop of his own on Main street, where for some years he did an extensive business, furnishing work to three or four men and prospering in his undertakings. When factory made shoes came into general use he retired from the manufacture of shoes but conducted his repair shop. In the meantime he purchased a fine property on East Van Buren street and there built a good home. In more recent years he was engaged in the manufacture of domestic wines and developed his business from a small beginning to one of large proportions, selling his product for family use. His wines obtained a splendid reputation for purity and quality and were recommended by the leading physicians. Mrs. Moore belongs to the Methodist Episcopal church and Mr. Moore attended its services and contributed to its support. He was quite prominent in Masonic circles, belonging to Battle Creek Lodge, No. 12, F. and A. M. and Battle Creek Chapter, R. A. M. and Battle Creek Council, R. and S. M. He was true to the teachings and tenets of the craft and in his life exemplified its helpful and beneficent spirit. Whatever success he achieved was attributable to his own labors, business foresight and capable management. He possessed a comfortable competence as the reward of his labors and his life history proves the force of activity, energy and straightforward dealing in industrial and commercial circles. During his residence in Battle Creek he witnessed many changes as the city advanced to a prominent place as a business center of the west, and in all public measures pertaining to general improvement and substantial upbuilding he manifested an active interest and took a helpful part.

He died November 12, 1903, and is buried in the White cemetery, Rushford, New York, where he had gone on a business trip.

HOWARD H. BATDORFF.

Howard Halsey Batdorff, who is filling the position of justice of the peace in Battle Creek and who was formerly affiliated with business interests in this city as a carpenter and builder, claims Ohio as the state of his nativity, his birth having occurred there in Fulton county, on the 30th of May, 1870. His parents were Austin and Lydia (Halsey) Batdorff, who in 1882 came to Michigan with their family and for a time resided in Eaton county, not far from Charlotte. After five years the father sold that property and entered the ministry of the United Brethren church. He has since resided in various places, to which he has been sent by the conference, but since 1901 has made his home in Bedford township, Calhoun county, where he purchased one hundred and fifty acres of land, constituting a very desirable farm. He has now retired from active ministerial work, although he is deeply interested in his church and its progress.

Howard Halsey Batdorff accompanied his parents to Michigan and when about sixteen years of age became a student in the high school of Charlotte, where he completed three years' work. He engaged in clerking in a grocery store nights and mornings and on Saturday in order to help pay his expenses while in school. Later he received a teacher's certificate but never followed the profession. When nineteen years of age he put aside his text books and began learning the carpenter's trade. He had previously worked at barn building and during his apprenticeship he received for the first year his board, while during the second year he was paid fifty cents per day. After his marriage he established his home in Battle Creek, where he has since followed carpentering, and during the last three years has been foreman for John Tait, a well known contractor of this city. He is thoroughly familiar with the builder's art and his broad experience and capability have gained for him the important position which he is now filling. About 1898 he began reading law as he had opportunity and he has accumulated a good law library which is of marked assistance to him in carrying on his official duties. On the 26th of March, 1890, Mr. Batdorff was married in Battle Creek to Miss Dora E. Harrison, who was born and reared in Athens township, Calhoun county, a daughter of Jeremiah and Cordelia (Clark) Harrison, her father, a distant relative of the two presidents of that name. Mr. Batdorff is also related to the same family by marriage on the maternal line.

Mr. and Mrs. Batdorff have a good home in this city and he also owns stock in the Flour & Cereal Company. His political support is given to the Republican party and his first ballot was cast for Benjamin Harrison in 1892. In the spring of 1903 he was elected justice of the peace and assumed the duties of the office on the 4th of July of the same year. That was on Saturday and on Monday he found a man standing at the foot of his stairs waiting for him, wishing to bring suit for larceny.

Thus his official service began early and has been continued since. He has tried many cases yet none have ever been appealed, his decisions being strictly fair and impartial. His fraternal relations are with the Carpenter's Union, with the Tribe of Ben Hur and the Knights of the Maccabees, also the Independent Order of Odd Fellows.

JOHN L. RAMSDELL, M. D.

Dr. John L. Ramsdell, engaged in the practice of medicine and surgery at Albion, has attained high standing as a representative of the profession because of his excellent qualifications and his devotion to the duties which devolve upon him in this connection. He was born in Butler township, Branch county, Michigan, October 12, 1851. His parents, Vincent S. and Elvira (Taggart) Ramsdell, were natives of Wayne county, New York, where they were reared and married. About 1845 they came to Michigan, and for two years resided in Alpine township, Kent county, after which they removed to Branch county, where the father purchased one hundred acres of wild land that he cleared and improved. Thereon he built his home and afterward purchased another fifty acre tract, on which he spent his remaining days. His death occurred in February, 1899, and his remains were interred in Gerard cemetery. In the family were five children: Henry M. wedded Clara Farwell and died on the old family homestead; William F., now a retired farmer of Coldwater, Michigan, married Frances Hamilton, who died leaving a son Hugh, and after her demise he wedded Miss Emma Chivers, by

JOHN L. RAMSDELL, M. D.

whom he had a son Ray; John L. is the third of the family; Blanche is the wife of Thomas Sinclair and resides in California; Minnie is the wife of William Lott, of Geneva, Ashtabula county, Ohio, and they have one son, Ralph. The mother and brother of our subject died within six hours of each other in March, 1894. The former was buried in Gerard cemetery and the latter in the Butler township cemetery.

In his boyhood days Dr. Ramsdell remained upon the home farm and his early education was acquired in the district schools. Subsequently he attended the high school at Quincy, Branch county, Michigan, and when twenty years of age he began teaching, following that profession through five winter terms, while in the summer seasons he carried on agricultural pursuits. Having determined, however, to make the practice of medicine his life work, he took a step in this direction, when, in 1877, he went to Marshall, Michigan, where he worked in a drug store and also began the study of medicine under the direction of Dr. Richard Wood. In 1879 he matriculated in the medical department of the University of Michigan at Ann Arbor, and was graduated in 1881. He entered upon the active work of his profession in Tekonsha, where he built up a large and lucrative business, there continuing until 1897, when he established his home in Albion, where he has since been located. His practice in the latter city has grown to profitable proportions and he is accorded high rank in the profession by his brethren of the medical fraternity. The Doctor has taken three post-graduate courses in the Chicago Polyclinic and in 1903 took a post-graduate course at the State University of Michigan in Ann Arbor. In 1901 he became a stockholder in the Prouty Manufacturing Company, in order to aid in the establishment of the business upon a firm basis.

On the 23d of December, 1881, in Gerard, Michigan, Dr. Ramsdell wedded Miss Mary Ronan, who was born in Clarendon, Calhoun county, a daughter of Thomas and Mary Ronan. Prior to her marriage she was a successful teacher. Two children have been born of this union: Nella Blanche, born in Tekonsha, October 27, 1882, is a graduate of the high school of her native town and also of Albion, and will complete the literary course in Albion College with the class of 1904. She completed the conservatory course in 1903. Donald Ronan, born December 26, 1886, is a member of the class of 1904 in the Albion high school.

Dr. Ramsdell is an earnest Republican, but has never been an aspirant for office. He belongs to the Presbyterian church, of which his wife and children are also members and he is affiliated with Washington lodge. No. 27, F. and A. M., of Tekonsha; Albion Chapter, R. A. M., at Albion; and the Order of the Eastern Star, to which his wife likewise belongs. He, too, has membership relations with the Knights of Pythias and the Maccabees and in the line of his profession is connected with the Calhoun County Medical Society, the Michigan State Medical Society, and the American Medical Association. That he is regarded as a foremost representative of his calling is indicated by the fact that he has been called upon to prepare and read papers before these different professional organizations and during one year he served as president of the county society. He has continually broadened his knowledge and promoted his efficiency through reading and investigation and few men of this locality are better qualified for the arduous duties in connection with the practice of medicine and surgery.

HARVEY RANDALL.

Going back into English history over eight hundred years, it is found that when William the Conqueror invaded England, there came with him one John Randall, who, like the renowned Norman, was by choice a warrior and an invader. The name of John Randall appears in the noted Doomsday-book as one of the favored followers of the Conqueror, who received his share of the Saxon territory upon its division. While the name of Randall often appears in the official court records of England, the family can not be said to have attained any very high stations under kingly rule. There was an occasional Randall coat-of-arms, which the generations past considered evidence of prominence, but all such insignia has faded from sight and the descendants of John Randall are mostly found in the United States to-day.

So far as known the first Randall to sail from England was William Randall, who left his native country for America in 1635, leaving the port of London April 24th for Providence, Rhode Island. William Randall was born about 1609 and died October 13, 1693. He had nine children, the last of whom, Isaac Randall, lived to be 101 years of age. From the family of William Randall, the Puritan, have descended a numerous progeny, whose living representatives may be found in nearly every state in the Union.

Harvey Randall: It has been wisely said that the greatest fortune that can fall to an individual is to have been born of wise and good parents. This was the especial good fortune of the subject of this sketch. His father, John Randall, born in Bridgewater, Oneida county, New York, was a man of sterling qualities, of English descent, and could trace his ancestry back through nearly eight centuries. He was a Whig in politics, a Baptist in religion, and inclined to puritanism in the discipline of his family.

The mother, Lucinda (Granger) Randall, came of good stock and was possessed of a hopeful, generous disposition. She was born at Sheffield, Conn., October 29, 1793, four years after the adoption of the Constitution of the United States, and died September 22, 1884, at the advanced age of nearly 91 years. Such was the consistent, Christian life of the father and mother that everyone of their children early embraced religion, and were active in church work and Christian benevolences. They were charter members of the First Baptist church of Burlington, organized September 24, 1845. John Randall died in 1855. His wife, Lucinda, joined the Baptist church in Tekonsha in 1860, and continued a faithful member until her death. The family consisted of five children, viz: John G., who died in 1844; Charles G., who died in 1895; Sarah Ann, who died in 1888; Francis W., who died in 1887; Harvey, who died January 22, 1897.

John Randall established his home, after marriage, at Sweden, Monroe county, New York, where the subject of this sketch was born, June 10, 1819. It was here that he received such educational advantages as could be found in the district schools of that early day. The curriculum of studies consisted of Webster's spelling book, Dayboll's arithmetic, Kirkham's grammar, and a text book in geography, besides penmanship, which was taught by the school-master from original copies made with a quill pen.

The school house was of a very primitive order, seated with benches, and without a blackboard or apparatus of any kind, and yet with such meager advantages Mr. Randall was enabled to gain sufficient knowledge to perform all of his duties as an officer and citizen with credit to himself.

Partaking of the emigration excitement of the "40's," he came to Michigan in 1842, six months before his parents. The parents followed and located land on section 19, one and a half miles east of the present village of Burlington. Near the close of the year, December 28, 1842, he was married to Rhoda M. Howard, a daughter of Alanson and Pricilla Howard, residents of Tekonsha township.

After marriage the real, stern work of life began. With no equipment but two strong hands, a brave heart, and a courageous spirit, loyally and earnestly supported by his dear wife, he set about establishing a home in the Michigan wilderness. Those early days of trial, against obstacles that would appall a young man of to-day, were filled with vicissitudes that would fill a volume with interesting reminiscences. Their children were: John Wesley; Alinda M. (Randall) Nichols, wife of Dr. D. J. Nichols, of West Plains, Missouri; Arah H., deceased; Arthur G., ex-commissioner of schools of Calhoun county, died 1904;

Alice A. (Randall) Main, now living on the old homestead; Harvey N. A second marriage was made by Mr. Randall July 26, 1888, to Mrs. Charlotte E. Wilson, of Tekonsha, who was born in Cayuga county, New York, August 15, 1832, but reared in Ohio. This marriage was a happy one, and abruptly terminated by death after nearly nine years of martial felicity.

The homestead is located on section 29, Tekonsha, and has never changed titles since purchased by Mr. Randall in 1849. It consists of one hundred and twenty acres of land, easy of tillage and highly productive.

When first located the land was covered with heavy timber, which was felled by the owner's ax and heaped into great log piles by the aid of an ox team. Farming at that time was crude, and the tools used were such as could be made at home, with ax and saw. Wheat was sown on the virgin soil and dragged in with a bushy tree of moderate size. All the products of the farm were marketed at Marshall, a distance of nearly sixteen miles.

Upon the homestead this God fearing, industrious and thrifty couple, raised their family of six children, giving all of them educational advantages not dreamed of by themselves when young. Mr. Randall was a carpenter by trade and constructed all of the buildings upon his farm, together with the barns and houses of nearly the entire neighborhood. The Baptist church in the village of Tekonsha was designed and built by him in 1870. Conscious of his worth and ability, his fellow townsmen elected him to various offices from justice of the peace to supervisor.

During the Civil war he served as enrolling officer and at one time assisted in organizing and drilling a regiment of troops, preparatory to their going south. In 1867 he was elected to the State Legislature, serving one term, representing his constituency to their entire satisfaction. His greatest efforts were in the interest of the Christian religion. He was converted while a youth and identified himself with the regular Baptist church, of which he was a consistent member for nearly sixty years. During all of this long period he never shirked a duty, whether it came in the way of benevolence or Christian activity.

In his family he was firm, yet kind, dignified, yet sympathetic. His affection for his children was deep and tender, and there was no sacrifice too great for those he loved. In all that goes to make up a strong and unfaltering manhood, worthy of the highest respect of his fellow citizens, he was every inch a man.

Mrs. Randall was born in the township of Sweeden, Monroe county, New York, August 2, 1821. Her parents were of English descent and noted for their intense piety. It was from these pious parents that Mrs. Randall received her deeply religious nature, which so distinguished her in after life. Her educational advantages were very meager, being such as was afforded by the district schools of the day. In her youth she was distinguished for her cheerful, buoyant and trustful disposition, which afterwards ripened into a character rich in all the Christian graces.

In 1842, together with her parents and six brothers and sisters, she came to Michigan. Her death occurred April 1, 1887, at her home in Tekonsha, in a startling and unexpected manner. She was in her usual health, and retired at night with her husband, who awoke in the morning to find her dead at his side, with no evidence of the slightest struggle. Her sudden departure was deeply mourned, not only by her large circle of friends and relatives, but by the entire community.

She was converted in a series of meetings held in the First Baptist church at Ogden, New York, in 1841. Hers was a glorious conversion, in which the marvelous power of the Divine Spirit filled her soul with the throbbings of the life immortal, flooding her heart with the brightness of the peace of God, which passeth understanding. After coming to Michigan, she united with the Baptist church of Burlington, subsequently with the Baptist church of Tekonsha, of which she was a faithful member until her death.

The story of her Christian life could best be written by an angel's hand. She had a motherly heart large enough to enfold all of the stricken ones of earth, and a sympathy as deep as ever dwelt in a human soul. Her love for her husband and children could be likened to nothing less than the love of Christ to fallen men. Were there burdens to bear? She bore them. Were there sacrifices to make? She made them. Were there deeds of charity and love to perform? She performed them. Were there hearts to comfort? She comforted them. Rest was nothing; ease was nothing; toil was nothing, so that she might minister to those she loved and lighten their burdens.

Such a life, though spent in apparent obscurity, "far from the crowd's ignoble strife," is beautiful as sunlight and sweeter than the dews of heaven. Sweet is the thought, sweeter the hope, that death to her was but the dawn of life immortal and that her pure spirit, freed from its tenement, found its true home in the paradise of God.

Thus ends the chapter of these two heroic lives. The story of king and peasant is simply told—they lived, they labored, they died. The highest eulogy that can be pronounced upon either is—they were true to the laws of their higher being, they lived blameless before God and men and, dying. left a rich legacy of golden deeds performed in love and hope.

HARVEY N. RANDALL.

Harvey N. Randall was born on the old Randall farm west of the village of Tekonsha, in the township of that name, Calhoun county, Michigan. September 7, 1859, and was a son of Harvey and Rhoda M. (Howard) Randall, the father's sketch appearing upon another page of this work. He received his scholastic education in the district schools of this county, and also attended the graded schools of Tekonsha, acquiring a practical education. At the age of twenty years, with the independence characteristic of the sons of the middle west, he began life for himself. He first engaged in the buying and selling of produce at Tekonsha, in which enterprise he met with gratifying success. In time he added a grocery and crockery department to his establishment, conducting the same for fourteen years, when he also added a hardware department to the business. This latter he found profitable for several years. carrying the three lines of stock until the spring of 1903, when he closed out the grocery department and now conducts

only the hardware and crockery with the produce business. This business alone invoices between seven and eight thousand dollars. This is one of the reliable and substantial enterprises of Tekonsha, and Mr. Randall is one of its most enterprising and successful business men.

Mr. Randall was married in 1886, to Miss Adell Warboys, who was born in the state of New York, and to them have been born three children: Howard, Danna and Wesley. Mrs. Randall is a member of the Baptist church. In his political preferment Mr. Randall is a Republican. He has held various offices, among them being that of treasurer of the village. while at present he is acting as trustee and a member of the school board. Mr. Randall owns considerable property in this locality, having erected in 1898 a handsome dwelling house, one of the finest in the village, and he also owns a farm of one hundred and thirty acres of valuable land located just west of the village as well as considerable other village property, among which is his store building. He is one of the most enterprising citizens of Tekonsha, taking a keen interest in all movements that affect the welfare of the community, and exerting the force of a well balanced and practical mind in behalf of good government and general advancement. He has the entire esteem and respect of those with whom he has been associated in a business, political or social way for so many years.

JOHN WESLEY RANDALL.

The name which appears above is a familiar one in the business circles of Tekonsha, for he has been connected with the commercial life of the village for thirty-five years, being active in its development since the time when two stores situated upon the corners formed by cross roads, marked the site of a possible town. Mr. Randall was born upon the old Randall farm west of Tekonsha, December 3, 1843, a son of Harvey and Rhoda M. (Howard) Randall, the father's sketch appearing upon another page of this work. He received his education in the common schools in the vicinity of his home, after which he attended a commercial college at Albion, Michigan. Returning to the farm he remained for a short time, after which he engaged as a clerk in the general mercantile establishment of W. C. Aiken, of Tekonsha. This position was retained for four years, after which he engaged in business for himself, for fifteen years thereafter conducting a general store in the village. He then opened and conducted a boot and shoe store, disposing of his interests in this business in 1903, since which time he has been assisting his brother Harvey N., in the hardware business.

The marriage of Mr. Randall occurred in February, 1869, and united him with Miss Carrie E. Eisman, a native of Monroe, Monroe county, Michigan, and of this union were born four children, three of whom are now living, namely: Luella W., a teacher of music, having received her instruction at Albion College; Daisy, who died at the age of fifteen months; Bessie, who married Earl Fox and resides in Tekonsha township, and John Wesley, Jr., who makes his home with his parents. Politically Mr. Randall is a Republican and has served as a member of the council of Tekonsha. He is a member of the Baptist church and for many years has officiated as trustee, and fraternally affiliates with the Ancient Order of United Workmen.

EARLE W. RANDALL.

Earle W. Randall is a young man of marked business enterprise and executive force, and his connection with the milling business has resulted in the successful continuance of the enterprise which was conducted by his father. The name of Randall has long been associated with the milling interests in Tekonsha, and it has ever been a synonym for business energy and integrity.

Earle W. Randall was born in Tekonsha, November 23, 1876, and is a son of Arah Howard and Ada A. (Tucker) Randall. The father, also a native of Calhoun county, was born April 9, 1848, being the third child of Harvey and Rhoda (Howard) Randall, pioneers in this part of southern Michigan, and long and favorably known here. He was reared upon a farm and acquired a good education, which was completed by graduation from Hillsdale College, in the class of 1873. He was married in Tekonsha, June 24th, of that year, to Miss Ada A. Tucker, and was for a time principal of the schools there, being the first to hold that position after the erection of the brick school house. Not long after his marriage, Mr. Randall embarked in merchandising with his brother, J. W. Randall, and later engaged in farming in Branch and Calhoun counties, Michigan, following which he engaged in teaching school. In 1883 he purchased the Calhoun Mills at Homer, conducting them until 1889, when he sold out and joined with his brother, Arthur G., in the purchase of the Tekonsha Mills. This enterprise had been established in the early thirties to meet the demands of a pioneer community, and about 1835 the water power had been developed.

In 1850 the main portion of the present gristmill was built—a three story structure, thirty-six by fifty feet, with basement. Changes were made from time to time in the early milling system as the necessities of the case demanded, but the old stone process was not discarded until the mill became the property of the Randall Brothers, who at once made it a roller process mill, with a capacity of seventy-five barrels of flour per day. In 1899 the plant was again remodeled and the capacity increased to one hundred barrels per day.

On the 29th of June, 1900, Arah H. Randall went over to the mill at about six o'clock in the morning to start the machinery. An hour later his son went to the mill. He found that the machinery was not in operation, and began a search for his father, whom he found drowned in the flume, with a broken collarbone. His death was the occasion of profound sorrow throughout the community, for he was an enterprising citizen as well as a progressive business man and a devoted husband and father. No man in town had a larger circle of acquaintances; and few, if any, had more friends. A man of sterling business integrity and very genial, he was beloved by all with whom he came in contact. He was generous, faithful and strong. Always a stanch Republican, he served as township clerk for several years and was supervisor of Tekonsha township for a long period. He also served as supervisor while living at Albion, and after he removed to Homer, he was several times elected to the same position. He was a member of the school board of Tekonsha at the time of his death. About 1889 he was the Republican nominee for the State Legislature, and lacked but a few votes of election in a district strongly Democratic, a fact which stood in incontrovertible evidence of the favorable regard entertained for him by his fellow townsmen and the confidence which they had in his ability. He belonged to the Masonic fraternity at Homer, and was an exemplary follower of the craft, and was also a member of the A..O. U. W. In his family were five children of whom two died in infancy. Ray A., born June 6, 1874, is a graduate of the Michigan State Normal School, and also of the University of Michigan, and is now superintendent of the schools of Plymouth, Indiana. He was married in Dexter, Michigan, to Miss Edith Waite, and they have a daughter, Eleanor; Daisy died in infancy; Earle is the next of the family; Edna M., born February 12, 1883, in Homer, is a graduate of the graded school of Tekonsha, and the wife of Joseph E. Eldridge, of Tekonsha; Eleanor died at the age of eighteen months.

Earle W. Randall was well qualified for his business career by liberal educational advantages. He is a graduate of the graded schools of Homer, Michigan, and of the business college at Ypsilanti. He began work in his father's mill when fifteen years of age and after his return from college he once more entered the mill, gaining a practical knowledge of the business. In 1897 his father gave him an eighth interest in the business and soon afterward he purchased a similar interest which had been given to his older brother. At his father's death he inherited a larger interest and the management of the mill devolved upon him. The business is now carried on under the name of the A. H. Randall Mill Company. He was very young to assume the responsibility of managing the property at his father's death, but his practical training, sound common sense and good judgment stood him in stead of years, and he has made for himself an enviable place in industrial circles of the village and of Calhoun county.

Earl W. Randall was married in Tekonsha, April 18, 1900, to Miss Kittie M. Batt, who was born in that place, a granddaughter of Samuel Batt, who at one time, in the '60s, was owner of the Tekonsha Mills. Mr. Randall's maternal grandfather, Thomas W. Tucker, was also owner of the enterprise at another time, so that the property is in possession of the descendants of two of the early proprietors. Mrs. Randall is a daughter of L. M. and Phebe (Allen) Batt, and by her marriage has one son, Tom R., born in Tekonsha, May 13, 1901.

Mr. Randall is a Republican, and in 1899 was elected a member of the village council and was re-elected in 1901, but resigned in 1902. He served on the committee on streets and sidewalks and was chairman of several committees. In 1898 he was made a Mason and for one year served as senior deacon. His wife is a member of the Eastern Star and is serving as an officer in her chapter. They are prominent and popular young people of the village and their circle of friends is very extensive.

CHARLES M. ADAMS.

Charles M. Adams was born in Greene, Chenango county, N. Y., November 12th, 1841, a son of Elijah and Betsey Adams. He is descended from the distinguished Adams family of Massachusetts so many of whose members have been men of national character. The father was engaged in the milling business. Both he and his wife were members of the Baptist church, in which he served as a deacon, taking an active part in church work. He held the office, and discharged the duties of supervisor in his township, with credit to himself, and profit to his constituency, but was never active in politics, save in the performance of the duty which devolves upon every American citizen to support the measures and principles which he believes will best enhance the nation's welfare. Charles M. Adams began his education in the common schools of his native state, which was afterwards continued in a private school. Later he engaged in the milling business with his father, and subsequently carried on a similar enterprise of his own. He came to Michigan in 1865, locating in Homer, where a liberal patronage was extended him. In 1883, his health failing him, he sold out his business and took up his residence in Battle Creek, where his attention was called to Christian Science. He received such help through the study of its text book, "Science and Health with Key to the Scriptures," by Mary Baker G. Eddy, its discoverer and founder, that he decided to devote his life to the work of carrying this healing gospel—"Glad tidings of great joy"—to suffering humanity. He was admitted, with his wife, to membership with "The First Church of Christ, Scientist," in Boston, Mass., December 29, 1894. He is a normal-course graduate of "The Massachusetts Metaphysical college," located in Boston, receiving the degree of C. S. B. and certificate as teacher in 1901. As a result of his labors "First Church of Christ, Scientist," of Battle Creek, Mich., was organized in 1898. Previous to this there had been a Christian Science Society, but it

CHARLES M. ADAMS

MRS. CHARLES M. ADAMS

was not organized as a church under state law. When Mr. Adams undertook the work of formation there were but two persons, beside himself and wife, who were regular attendants at the services, but others were soon added to the number. For the first year and a half Mr. Adams bore all the expenses of the hall, and incidentals as well, but by the end of the next year and a half the society paid all the expenses. The year following the organization under the state law, the church paid the readers a small salary. Although the amount was limited, it indicated a feeling of appreciation for the services rendered. Mr. Adams and his wife were the first readers of the church, serving in that capacity for nearly nine years. There are now about fifty members, and a much larger attendance. The work, however, can not be measured by numbers, for there is no measurement for the good accomplished. For eighteen years Mr. Adams has devoted his time to "healing the sick," and "binding up the broken hearted" in obedience to the command of the Master. Many are living to-day in health and happiness who would not be, but for the revelation of Christian Science. As a teacher and practitioner of this Science, his time is fully occupied, and he can not but feel a just gratitude in that he has been the agent in accomplishing so much good.

Mr. Adams was united in marriage to Miss Narcissa Fitch of Greene, N. Y. Three children were born to them: Ethan C., of Battle Creek, and Elizabeth C. who is now Mrs. Charles J. Wells, also of Battle Creek, and Miss Mina M., who is a teacher in the public schools. Mrs. Adams taught the first Christian Science Sunday School class in Battle Creek, and is now the superintendent of a flourishing school. She has

14

been a great helpmeet to her husband in his work, and both have been strong factors in the moral development of this city, in recent years. This brief biography can be closed in no more fitting manner than by giving to Mary Baker G. Eddy, the discoverer and founder of Christian Science—that noble, Godlike woman—the tribute so justly earned, and to recommend to all who may scan this brief record, the study of her renowned book, "Science and Health with Key to the Scriptures."

RICHARD SMITH MILLER.

Richard Smith Miller was well known in industrial circles of Battle Creek for thirty years, and as a mason bore an excellent reputation as a skilled artisan, gaining a proficiency in the line of his chosen pursuit that made his services in constant demand. He was always reliable and trustworthy and yet it was not his business record alone that made him widely and favorably known in this city; his character and upright manhood gaining him the regard, confidence and good will of all, so that his memory is yet cherished by those with whom he was associated in the active walks of life.

Mr. Miller was born in Sullivan county, New York, September 6, 1815, upon his father's farm. His parents were James and Sarah (Brown) Miller, and he remained upon the old homestead until sixteen years of age when he began learning the tailor's trade, which he followed until he attained his majority. The close confinement, however, proved detrimental to his health and abandoning that pursuit he learned the mason's trade, which he continued to follow until the year of his death.

While living in the east Mr. Miller was married on the 8th of January, 1844, at Monticello, New York, to Miss Lucinda J. Montanye, a daughter of Benjamin and Theodosia (Clark) Montanye, who were of an old and prominent French family. Abraham Montanye, the grandfather of Benjamin Montanye, came to America from France, where he represented an influential and distinguished ancestry. He settled in New York prior to the Revolutionary war and thus became the founder of the family in the new world. Benjamin Montanye, his son, was a Baptist minister and at the time of the Revolutionary war he joined the colonial troops and fought for the independence of the nation. He was assigned the duty of carrying the mail in the army and while thus engaged, carrying a mail pouch that contained a letter for General Washington, his horse was shot from under him and he was captured and taken prisoner. Benjamin Montanye, Jr., the father of Mrs. Miller, was reared at New Vernon, Sullivan county, New York., and made that place his home during his life. He learned the shoemaker's trade in New York city, and afterward had a custom shop at New Vernon. Miss Clark, his wife, was a daughter of Samuel and Deborah (Stewart) Clark, farmers near New Vernon. Mrs. Miller was born in Wortsboro, Sullivan county, New York, about three and a half miles from the birthplace of her husband. After their marriage they lived for about nine years in the Empire state and then came to Battle Creek, Michigan, arriving in April, 1854.

Mr. Miller purchased a home at No. 64 West Van Buren street, at which time here were but few houses west of the river. They occupied that place for a number of years and he then erected a fine brick residence on the adjoining lot, which continued to be their place of abode for a long period. In the meantime he had begun work at his trade, and at times was employed by others and again took and executed contracts for himself, but no matter in which way he worked his labors were always characterized by precision, thoroughness and perfect reliability. He never slighted any task and he thus enjoyed the entire confidence of those by whom he was employed. His name in business circles came to be regarded as a synonym for honesty and furnished an example that is indeed worthy of imitation.

The marriage of Mr. and Mrs. Miller was blessed with four children: Josephine, the wife of John Courtney, of Bay View, Michigan; James Henry, a contractor in cement work at Battle Creek, who married Lizzie Reid and has two children, Garth and Thelma; Emma J., wife of Philetus G. Elwood, of Battle Creek; and Jay J., who married Miss Della Platt and is connected with his brother as a contractor in cement work in Battle Creek.

Mr. Miller regarded it the duty as well as the privilege of every American citizen to give his support to the measures which he believed would best advance the interests of his country, and his study of political questions led him to advocate Republican principles. He kept well informed on the issues of the day and did active work locally for his party. Both he and his wife were members of the Methodist Episcopal church and for many years he served as one of its class leaders, filling that position at the time of his death. He worked earnestly for the church and the extension of its influence, and his life was molded by its teachings, his daily conduct exemplifying his Christian faith. He died June 9, 1884, and his remains were laid to rest in Oak Hill cemetery. Pleasant thoughts remain of him with his friends, for his upright character commanded their respect, his kindly nature their warm regard. For forty years he had been a faithful husband to her who is left behind, and she is therefore blessed with the memory of a most pleasant and congenial married life. Mrs. Miller still resides in Battle Creek. Like her husband she shared in the work of the church and hers is a charitable and benevolent spirit, which has prompted her to many good deeds.

SAMUEL THUNDER.

A careful and methodical farmer, a conscientious citizen and a good neighbor and friend, Samuel Thunder has left behind him a record which will long keep his memory in the hearts of those who knew him best. From the midst of comfort and luxury in the beautiful home which he has built in Marshall about four years previous to his death, he was called to the higher life, April 24, 1903, laying down alike the responsibilities and pleasures of living to render the account which all must give in time. His life had been well and worthily spent, a brief sketch being herewith given among the representative men of the community.

Mr. Thunder was a native of Calhoun county, his birth having occurred in Fredonia township, August 17, 1839. His parents, James and Mary (Lee) Thunder, both natives of England, where they were married, emigrating with their one son, James, at an early date, coming directly to Calhoun county and locating on a farm in Fredonia township. With no capital but energy and ambition the father set to work to obtain a competence for his family, taking up one hundred and twenty acres of government land which he developed and improved, and upon which he lived until his death. Both himself and wife are interred in the Lyon Lake cemetery. Mr. Thunder was one of nine children, and in the straightened circumstances of his parents he was necessarily unable to obtain anything but a limited education. He remained at home until he was twenty years old when he married Diana Lee. He then went to Eckford township and bought sixty-five acres of new land, developing it and making a home for his growing family. He subsequently sold this farm and bought eighty acres, with industry and energy bringing the number up to three hundred and thirty-one acres of well cultivated farm land, before he was called upon to lay down the burdens of life. Through his systematic and careful management he met with the success which is the result of only such effort. Politically he was a Democrat.

Mr. Thunder was entirely a self-made man. Without a dollar that he could call his own when he started out in life, he still was undaunted by the prospect, adding to his inherited tendencies that perseverance which is characteristic of the citizen of the middle west, and in time meeting with the reward for his undivided effort. In disposition he was a quiet, unassuming man, with a kindly courtesy which won and retained for him many friends. He is interred in Lyon-Lake cemetery, Fredonia township.

Seven children were born of the first union of Mr. Thunder, namely: George, H., Emma, Lillie, Nellie, deceased, Rose, Jennie and Minnie. Mrs. Thunder died March 18, 1874, and Mr. Thunder married Adeline Fisk, two children being born of this union, namely: Philip S. and Lewis. The wife died March 3, 1900. Mr. Thunder's third marriage was with Mrs. Florence (Hewitt) Brewer, in December, 1901. Mrs. Thunder, who survives her husband and makes her home in the beautiful and well furnished residence on North Mulberry street, is a native of Marshall and a daughter of Charles and Julia (Merwin) Hewitt. Her parents were both natives of New York state and came to Marshall when their daughter was only a child, the father engaging in farming in Lee township. Mrs. Thunder has one daughter by a former marriage, Mary, who resides with her.

AUSTIN SAMUEL PARKER.

Deeds of valor have been the theme of song and story throughout all the ages, and, while memory remains to the American people, they will hold in grateful recognition the men who fought for the preservation of the Union, in one of the most sanguinary struggles that has ever been recorded in the annals of the world. For more than four years Mr. Parker was one of the "boys in blue" and yet he was no more loyal to his duties of citizenship in times of war than he is in days of peace.

Battle Creek has found him a faithful and capable officer, and at the present writing he is serving as her city treasurer.

Mr. Parker was born in town of Harpersfield, Ashtabula county, Ohio, on the 17th of July, 1842, and is a son of Samuel Merriman Parker. Samuel was a son of Archelaus R. Parker, who, at an early date, moved to Ohio from New York state and lived in Ashtabula county until he had reached an advanced age, his last days were spent in Illinois where his death occurred in his ninety-fourth year. The father of our subject was born in New York state and when a boy removed with his parents to Ohio. He acquired a common school education and followed the occupation of tilling the soil. His death occurred at Saybrook, at the very advanced age of ninety-two years, while his wife died in 1864.

To the common schools of Ohio, Austin S. Parker is indebted for the educational privileges which he received. He was not yet nineteen years of age when the Civil war was inauguarted, but he had noted with interest the progress of events in the south; and he resolved that if an attempt was made to overthrow the Union he would strike a blow in its defense. Hardly had the smoke of Fort Sumter's guns cleared away, when in April, 1861, he offered his services in response to the first call for troops to serve for three months. The company, however, did not organize, and in May he again placed his name on the enrollment list, but again the company failed to organize. In June, however, he became a member of Company B, Twenty-third Ohio Volunteer Infantry for three months. On reaching Columbus, the regiment was informed that it would not be accepted unless the men were willing to enlist for three years. They agreed to this, and the Twenty-third Ohio practically became the first three year's regiment. ' Mr. Parker joined the army as a private and was at Camp Dennison until July, 1861, and with his comrades went to West Virginia and was first under fire at Carnifax Ferry. Later, he participated in many important engagements, including the battles of Princeton, Cloyd Mountain, New Berne and New River Bridge. There they attempted to burn the bridge but failed. Mr. Parker was also in the battles of Salt Pond Mountain and Lexington, Virginia, and the two days' at Lynchburg, after which he returned to West Virginia, where the regiment went into winter quarters for the winter of 1862-3. There he re-enlisted and returned home on a furlough. Again going to the front, the regiment made a second attempt to burn the New River Bridge, and in this were successful. After the winter of 1861 they were at Pack's Ferry and were ordered in Washington. Part of the regiment, however, took part in the second battle of Bull Run, but Mr. Parker was not in that engagement. He was, however, at South Mountain and at Antietam, returning to West Virginia and his regiment became a part of the army of West Virginia. He was afterwards in the engagements at Berryville, Winchester, Cedar Creek and Fisher Hill, and his active connection with the army covered four years and three months. Being asigned to special duty, he was stationed near Winchester, and his regiment was mustered out of service at Cumberland, Maryland. While on detached duty he acted as clerk in the quartermaster's department. In the fall of 1861, he was taken ill and spent that winter in the hospital at Clarksburg and Parkersburg, West Vir-

ginia, but was never wounded or captured and almost constantly was found with his regiment in active service. He made for himself a most creditable military record as a valiant soldier. He had three brothers who were also in the army. Albertus N. whose home is in Saybrook, Ohio, served for about three years, and was also never wounded or captured. Archelaus B., who is living in Allegan county, Michigan, served for the same length of time, and in the same regiment and company as our subject. He was captured, however, at Winchester and was for several months a prisoner at Lynchburg and at Danville. At one time he managed to escape, but was afterwards recaptured. Joel E. was a member of the Seventh Ohio Regiment, as a substitute near the close of the war and now lives in Antigo, Wisconsin.

After being mustered out of the army, Mr. Parker went to Painesville, Ohio, where he pursued a commercial course. He then entered upon his business career as a brakeman on the Lake Shore & Michigan Southern Railroad, being thus employed until 1868. The following year he came to Allegan county, Michigan, and for a time worked at the carpenter's trade with his brother. He then accepted the duties of brakeman with the Chicago & Michigan Lake Shore Railroad and was later promoted to conductor, serving with that company for seven years, during which time he made his home at Grand Junction and at Holland, Michigan. In 1876, however, he left that road and went south for the Missouri Pacific Railroad. It was in 1877 that he came to Battle Creek and for a few months was brakeman on the Grand Trunk Railroad, after which he was promoted to the position of conductor. In

1880 he lost his arm while switching a train at Stillwell, Indiana. As soon as he had sufficiently recovered from his injury, Mr. Parker was made ticket agent at Battle Creek and occupied that position for nineteen years, proving most capable, and becoming popular as a representative of the road. He resigned this position in 1900, having received a government appointment as special agent in the general land office at Ashland, Wisconsin. Later he was transferred to Chamberlain, South Dakota, and in 1902 he returned to Battle Creek.

Very soon after his return from the war Mr. Parker was married in 1865, in Jefferson, Ashtabula county, Ohio, to Miss Stella L. Phillips, who was born in the town of Harpersfield, Ashtabula county, Ohio, a daughter of James B. and Marcia (Lovell) Phillips. At the time of her marriage she was living in Geneva, Ohio. Two children have been born of this union: Charles A., whose birth occurred at Geneva, Ohio, married Mayme Hoyt, and lives in Brooklyn, New York, where he is city passenger agent for the Lehigh Railroad Company. Maude, born in Holland, Michigan, is the wife of Frank W. Irwin and resides in Battle Creek.

The Parker family has always been identified with the Republican party since its organiation and Austin S. Parker of this review cast his first presidential vote for Abraham Lincoln in 1864. In 1893 he was elected mayor of Battle Creek and served for two terms, his administration being businesslike and progressive. During that time fire station No. 1 was built and the old fire station was remodeled into the waterworks and treasurer's office. The first brick pavement of Battle Creek was laid during his term of office and the water works and sewer systems were greatly extended. In December, 1902, Mr. Parker was oppointed city treasurer and is now acting in that capacity, his capability and fidelity being widely acknowledged. Mr. Parker was initiated into Grand River lodge, No. 297, F. and A. M, at Ashtabula, Ohio, becoming a master Mason. He now has membership with Battle Creek lodge No. 12. He also belongs to the Knights of Pythias and Maccabees fraternities and the Benevolent Protective Order of Elks and was at one time a member of the Grand Army of the Republic. Fidelity to duty has perhaps been one of the strongest characteristics in the life record of Mr. Parker, for this has been manifested during his long connection with railroad service, upon the battlefields of the south, and in public office. It is certainly a most commendable trait and one which has gained for him high regard.

WILLIAM J. GARFIELD.

William J. Garfield, who was the secretary of the Battle Creek Food Company from the time of its organization till his death and also deputy state oil inspector, was born at Schroon lake, Essex county, New York, on the 27th of October, 1862. He was a son of Leman J. and Lovisa E. (Magoon) Garfield. It is known that the family is of English ancestry, and was founded in America by Edward Garfield, who was born in 1575. He was a widower at the time he crossed the Atlantic to America and he was accompanied by his son,

Edward, Junior. The latter had a wife and two or three children when they landed in the new world in 1630, establishing their home in Watertown, Massachusetts. The family did not leave that locality, but continued for several generations to live in Watertown and Waltham, in Sudbury, Western and Lincoln, Massachusetts. The great-grandfather of our subject was Elijah Garfield, who was born in. New England and for some time was a resident of Leicester, Vermont, where the grandfather, Leman Garfield, was born. Subsequently the family removed to Essex county, New York, taking up their abode there in March, 1800, when the grandfather was four years of age. His father purchased land in the township of Schroon. Essex county, and made his home thereon until his death. On the old family homestead the grandfather was reared to years of maturity and afterward owned and occupied the homestead until called to his final rest in the year 1880. He was one of the leading and influential men of his township and was frequently called to serve in positions of public trust. He married Miss Salome Terrell, a native of Essex county, who died in the year 1873.

It was also upon the old family homestead that Leman J. Garfield, the father of our subject, was reared to his manhood and he still lives upon the old home farm which has been his place of residence for sixty-seven years, his birth having occurred in 1837. His political support has ever been given the Republican party and he has taken an active interest in its work, doing all in his power to promote its growth and extend its influence. Various public offices have been conferred upon him and in the discharge of his official du-

ties he has ever been prompt and reliable. On the 6th of January, 1857, Leman Garfield was united in marriage to Miss Lovisa E. Magoon, who was born in the northern part of Vermont. Her father, Joseph E. Magoon, removed to Schroon township when she was a little maiden of six or seven years and there she lived until the time of her marriage when she went with her husband to the old family home. They became the parents of four children, of whom the subject of this review was the second in order of birth. They hold membership in the Methodist Episcopal church.

William J. Garfield was educated in the district schools of his native township and at the Port Henry high school where he prepared for college. He then entered the State University at Burlington and was graduated with the class of 1885, at which time the degree of Bachelor of Arts was conferred upon him. Subsequently he engaged in teaching school for four years, being principal of the school in the home locality. He afterward spent a year in the south and in 1889 came to Battle Creek, where he engaged in the real estate and insurance business, carrying on operations along that line until January, 1902. He handled property both for himself and others and was a well known representative of this line of business activity, keeping well informed on realty values. He was one of the organizers and promoters of the Battle Creek Food Company, limited, which was incorporated in 1902, with a capital stock of five hundred thousand dollars. He became a member of its first board of directors and at the first meeting was elected secretary. This company built a well equipped plant and the enterprise is now in successful operation. This plant has a capacity of one car load per day and manufactures Vicereo, a malted and peptonized wheat food.

On the 27th of December, 1888, Mr. Garfield was united in marriage to Miss Phoebe A. Wing, a native of Saratoga Springs, New York, and a daughter of Seth E. and Frances L. Wing. They had two children: Charles M. and Harry W. The parents attended and supported the Grace Temple Institutional church, of which Mrs. Garfield is a member. Mr. Garfield gave his political support to the Republican party and in August, 1899, was appointed deputy state oil inspector by Governor Pingree. He filled the position for two years and was then re-appointed for another term by Governor Bliss, his territory being the fourth district. Socially he was connected with the Knights of the Maccabees, of which he was an early and active member, and also was a charter member of the Fraternal Order of Eagles. January 12, 1904, Mr. Garfield went to New York in the interest of the Food Company and while there was taken ill with what the physician called la grippe. Feeling better January 20th he started for home. On the journey, pleuro-pneumonia developing, he grew rapidly worse and at Detroit was taken from the train to the Wayne Hotel, in a critical condition, and there died January 28, 1904. His remains were interred in Oak Hill cemetery, Battle Creek, under the auspices of the lodges of which he was a member.

In his death Battle Creek lost one of its active, prominent and honorable younger business men. He won for himself a creditable and enviable position in business circles and made a good reputation by reason of his reliability, his promptness and his entire trustworthiness.

ANTONE EGELER.

Antone Egeler, a resident of Marshall, Calhoun county, Michigan, was born December 15, 1839, in Wurtemburg, Germany, a son of Christopher and Johanna Barbara (Schwagler) Egeler. Mr. Egeler brought his wife, a daughter of Jacob Schwagler, and children to America in 1847, the ocean trip consuming fifty-six days, on September 5, of the same year, locating in Detroit, Michigan, where they remained for twenty-two months. From that location they removed to Albion in 1849, a year later purchasing a farm of eighty acres in Fredonia township, Calhoun county, upon which they continued to make their home for two years, thirty acres of the land being under cultivation. They then came to Marshall, where the father worked at his trade which was that of a blacksmith. He died in 1876, his wife having passed away in 1868, and they are both interred in Oakridge cemetery. The father had been a member of the Lutheran church throughout his entire life. To Mr. and Mrs. Egeler were born eleven children, of whom five were brought to America by their parents, one dying during the passage.

Anton Egeler remained at home with his parents until he was twenty-eight years old, receiving a common school education while he assisted his father at his work. In 1855 he began an apprenticeship to learn the trade of iron and brass moulder, and after a period of three years when he had finished his apprenticeship, he worked as a journeyman at Dixon, Illinois, for seven months, going there in the fall of 1857. He returned to Marshall in April, 1858, and there worked as a journeyman continuing until 1865, when he

ANTONE EGELER

spent a few months in Pittsburg, Pennsylvania. Returning to Marshall the same year he was employed until 1884, when he opened a foundry and machine shop of his own and has since continued in business for himself for a period of twenty years. At present his work is mostly in repairs, although at one time he was engaged in the manufacture of plows. He now owns the shop which he has occupied many years, and also owns a good home on Locust street.

December 10, 1868, Mr. Egeler married Mary Louisa Karstaedt, a daughter of Frederick and Louise (Salzfelder) Karstaedt, whose biography appears on another page. To them was born one daughter, Nellie Matilda, her birth occurring March 11, 1869. She lived but a short time beyond the age of ten years, dying December 1, 1879. She had early developed a taste for study and had shown herself a conscientious and painstaking student, securing many prizes in competition. She was also quite talented in music.

Two relics of his native land, Mr. Egeler keeps in his home, one being his German primer, printed in 1843, and the other the family Bible. This ancient book was printed in 1736, and was owned by Mr. Egeler's grandmother, and probably was in the family previous to that. Though quite young when he left Germany he remembers many customs and implements common to the country at that time, one of which is the wooden plow.

Mr. Egeler has become a prominent man in this community, as a Democrat in politics, his first presidential ballot being cast for McClellan, and he has often been called upon to serve in the interests of this party. For fourteen years he has repre-sented the fourth ward as alderman, and has occupied the office of city treasurer for two years. At the present time he is acting as supervisor of the fourth ward, this being his second year. Fraternally he has been a member of the Knights of the Maccabees since 1883, being a charter member of the lodge here, in which he has acted as finance keeper and lieutenant commander. He is also a charter member of the German Benevolent Association and has held all of the offices of that organization. Mr. Egeler is a very extensive reader, and has thus kept himself well informed on the topics of the day, in which he takes the greatest interest. He is a broad minded and public spirited man and gives his most enthusiastic aid toward the promotion of all enterprises calculated to advance the general welfare.

HON. FREDERICK KARSTAEDT, SR.

Hon. Frederick Karstaedt, Sr., deceased, was born September 6, 1817, in New Sparow, in the Grand Duchy of Mecklinburg-Schwerin, now a portion of the German Empire. His father died when he was about one year old. His mother married again, but died the year he was fourteen, leaving him with no near relatives save his stepfather and two half brothers. He soon apprenticed himself to a tailor in his native town and learned that trade. During 1840-2 he traveled over a large part of Germany and Switzerland visiting about two hundred and fifty of the largest cities, stopping in each from one or two days to as many months as he found work to do. He then determined to come to America, and landed in New York January 8, 1843, as completely alone in the world as a young man could well be, for he had never heard one word of news from his kindred after he bade them farewell before sailing for the New World. But after reaching New York, his smiling face and happy disposition enabled him to easily find employment and to make new friends. Among the latter was a Saxony lass about four years younger than himself. Their friendship ripened into love, and on October 25, 1843, the young emigrant and Louisa Salfelder were wedded in New York City. In 1845 the young couple determined to seek their fortune in the west, and on June 11th arrived in Marshall, Michigan. Mr. Karstaedt rented a house on West State street, and there began housekeeping and working at his trade. Two or three years later with his young family he occupied the Deacon Lord house for eighteen months; then moved "down town" to a small building that stood near the present McHugh shoe store. By rigid frugality they had saved a fair portion of his earnings, and tiring of paying rent, Mr. Karstaedt purchased, in 1848, the lot now 117 West State street. In 1855 he moved the old frame building back from the street and erected thereon a brick building afterward occupied by Mayor Bosley as a hardware store. He then added ready made clothing to his business, and in a few years discontinued working at the bench, but continued the retail trade until 1880, when he retired to a farm in Convis township, where he spent the remainder of his life.

Having come among entire strangers, Mr. Karstaedt found it necessary to reside here five years before he could furnish sufficient proof that he had lived in the United States that

long, so it was not until November, 1850, that he secured his final naturalization papers and became a full fledged American citizen. In 1852 he was elected a village trustee, running on the Democratic ticket. He did not take kindly to politics, and although often solicited to accept political preferment, would never allow his name to be so used. However, in 1870, he was nominated very much against his wishes for mayor, was elected and filled the office with credit to himself and the city.

While living in New York Mr. Karstaedt was made a Master Mason, and he was the last survivor of the eight charter members of the first Masonic lodge organized in Marshall, it being Marshall lodge, No. 20, organized in 1846, which was succeeded in 1855 by St. Albans lodge, No. 20. He was also a member of Marshall commandery, No. 17, Knight Templar. Mr. and Mrs. Karstaedt's married life was an unusually pleasant one. They were the parents of fifteen children four of whom died in infancy. Of the eleven who grew to years of maturity, Mrs. Augusta Bauer passed away in 1884. The other children in the order of their births were Mrs. Louisa Gauss, now a resident of Marshall; Mrs. Mary Egeler, wife of Antone Egeler, a sketch of whose life appears in this work; Frederic Karstaedt, Jr., now deceased; Matilda, now the wife of Rudolph Rohr, of Marshall; Sarah, who married Emil Hartel, now resides in Newton township; Charles Karstaedt, of Newark, N. J.; Lizzie, now dead, was the wife of Charles Vogt; Christina, wife of John Reese, of Marshall; Lewis, now a resident of Beloit, Wisconsin; and Frank, of Chattanooga, Tennessee.

Mrs. Karstaedt was born in Staadtelm, Saxony, June 11, 1821. Her family name is

Salfelder. With her parents she came to America in 1840. She died April 23, 1885. Mr. Karstaedt passed away May 15, 1890. The funeral was conducted by St. Albans' lodge, F. & A. M., Marshall commandery, Knight Templar, acting as escort. Mr. and Mrs. Karstaedt are buried in Oakridge cemetery.

THOMAS J. BRADLEY.

Thomas Jefferson Bradley is a native of the State of New York, but has resided in Michigan since 1865, and is now living a retired life in Battle Creek. He was born in Remsen, Oneida county, New York, February 16, 1843, a son of Thomas and Mary Bradley. The mother died in 1859, the father in 1860. The son began his education in the place of his nativity and in 1863 emigrated to Michigan, continuing his studies in Kalamazoo. In 1865 he came to Battle Creek as agent for Mutchler & Robinson, dyers, of Kalamazoo, whom he represented for three years, when he established a dye house of his own on South Jefferson street, conducting it for a number of years. While thus engaged he began the manufacture of overalls and shirts and later manufactured all kinds of men's clothing, carrying on an extensive business until 1889. His trade grew, the business constantly expanded in volume and scope and the financial return which he received made him one of the substantial citizens of Battle Creek as well as a leading representative of manufacturing interests. His success now enables him to live retired in the enjoyment of many of the comforts of life. He gave employment to about thirty hands who were always well paid and most of whom own valuable property in the city at the present time. Thus through the influence of Mr. Bradley and the employment he furnished, the city has been to a large extent improved.

Mr. Bradley has also bought and improved much real estate in the city, and is still the owner of much improved as well as vacant property, to which he gives his attention.

In 1867 Mr. Bradley purchased an attractive lot at the corner of West Division and Cherry streets in one of the best residence portions of the city on which is a large brick house. This fine home is supplied with all the comforts and many of the luxuries of life, and is noted for its gracious hospitality, being presided over by Mrs. Bradley, a most estimable lady, of natural refinement and culture, who has the happy faculty of placing her guests at once at their ease. It was on the 1st of May, 1867, that Mr. Bradley led to the marriage altar Miss Ellen Shaw, a native of England, and a daughter of Joseph Shaw, who was at one time proprietor of a meat market in Battle Creek and afterward lived retired. Four children have been born to Mr. and Mrs. Bradley: James, now deceased; Clarence, of Houston, Texas; Lettie, a music teacher of Battle Creek, and Mary, who is teaching in the public schools here. The daughters reside with their parents.

The family are members of the First Presbyterian church. For twenty years Mr. Bradley has been connected with the Knights of the Maccabees, while his political allegiance has usually been given the Republican party. While not an aspirant for office, he is a public spirited man and it is worthy of mention that he had made and placed in position, the first signs marking streets ever put up in Battle Creek. This was done in 1865. He is a man of retiring disposition, with a circle of friends that is select rather than large. His interest centers in his home and he finds his greatest delight in promoting the happiness and welfare of his family, for whom he has provided a most beautiful place of residence. In business he sustained a high reputation for reliability and enterprise and those who know him well, prize his friendship most highly.

J. THEODORE WATTS.

One of the rising young business men of Battle Creek is J. Theodore Watts, who was born August 30, 1866, in this city in the house where he now lives, his parents being James J. and Emily (Pray) Watts. The father was born at Cherry Valley, Otsego county, New York, in 1833, and was there educated. About 1851 he came to Battle Creek, finding here, however, not a populous city, but a hamlet and its promise of future development was not a very brilliant one. He engaged in the grocery business as a member of the firm of Watts & Twitchell, a connection that was continued for several years with gratifying success. He afterward went to Detroit, where he spent two or three years. In early manhood he married Emily Pray, a sister of Mrs. Theodore Wakelee, in connection with whose sketch the ancestral history of the family appears. The wedding was celebrated in 1855 and unto them were born four children, of whom Mr. Watts of this review is the youngest. His father's death occurred February 22,

1866, before the birth of the son, and the mother died February 27, 1876, when her son was not yet ten years of age.

J. Theodore Watts was reared by his aunt, Mrs. Wakelee, and acquired his education in the grammar and high schools of this city. At the age of seventeen he entered upon his business career, being first employed as a collector by the Battle Creek Gas Light Company. He filled that position for three years and then by reason of his faithfulness and ability was promoted to the position of superintendent in which responsible and important capacity he served for twelve years. On the expiration of that period he resigned. On severing his connection with the Gas Company he became connected with the ice business, in which he was associated with John C. Bayley. After four months Mr. Bayley sold out to Messrs. Lovell & Price, and the latter remained a partner in the business until October, 1901, while Mr. Lovell retained his interest until March 1, 1903. The ice companies of the city were then consolidated and incorporated under the name of the Consolidated Ice Company, limited, of Battle Creek. Mr. Watts continued with the various firms and now has charge of the office of the Consolidated Company, a very responsible position as this company sells all the ice used in the city—a business that involves a large amount of office work. From the foregoing it will be seen that Mr. Watts, throughout his business career, has been connected with only two lines, and that the change made was a voluntary one on his part.

On the 13th of April, 1898, Mr. Watts was united in marriage to Miss Edith Lillian Swift, a daughter of David Swift, who is mentioned elsewhere in this volume. They have one son, David Alden. Mr. and Mrs. Watts attend the Presbyterian church, of which she is a member, and to its support he freely contributes. They are well known in Battle Creek and the hospitality of the leading homes is extended to them.

HIRAM JEROME JOHNSON.

Hiram Jerome Johnson is engaged in the insurance, real estate and loan business in Battle Creek. He was born on a farm in Lenox township, Madison county, New York, September 4, 1841, a son of Amos S. and Harriet (Benedict) Johnson. His mother died during his infancy and his father afterward married again, remaining in the Empire state until his death in his ninety-first year. Our subject obtained a common school education and in 1858 came to this state, remaining for one year with an older brother, Thomas Johnson, in the town of Newton, Calhoun county. He then came to Battle Creek and spent two terms as a student in the city schools. In the spring of 1860 he began clerking in the store of Stone & Hyatt, with whom he remained until the fall of 1861. In the month of August he offered his services to the government, enlisting in Company H of Merrill's Horse, or what became known in the war department as the Second Missouri Regiment. He continued in the service until the 31st of October of the same year and was detailed as cook, but becoming ill was honorably discharged. After that he began to lose his hearing, and at the time of this writing is compelled to use an ear trumpet. After his partial recovery, Mr. Johnson

went to Ceresco, where he was engaged in clerking for a time and in 1862 he became a clerk in the postoffice at Battle Creek, but after a few months was obliged to give up his position because of his growing deafness. He next clerked in a drug store for about a year and was then again appointed a clerk in the postoffice, acting in that capacity until 1865, when he went to Poughkeepsie, New York, where he pursued a course of study in Eastman's Business College. In the fall of 1865 he located in Kalamazoo, Michigan, where he spent one year as a clerk in the employ of A. E. Bartlett and for two months was a clerk in a store at Dowagiac, Michigan, assisting a new firm in the establishment of their business there.

On the expiration of that period he came to Battle Creek and began dealing in confectionery, books and newspapers, having his stock in the corner of the postoffice, where he remained until 1870, when he removed to another store, conducting it until 1878. His deafness then caused him to sell out and in 1879 he became a clerk in the freight office of the Michigan Central Railroad, filling that position acceptably for four years. In 1883 he established a collecting agency and also acted as bookkeeper for different firms. In 1891 he took charge of a book bindery which he managed for a year and in 1892 he opened his insurance office, in which he has built up a fair business. He is also a real estate and loan agent and in this conection is now associated with the business life of Battle Creek.

In 1871, in Rochester, New York, Mr. Johnson was married to Fannie Freeman, who was born in Victor, New York, and was visiting relatives in Michigan when Mr. Johnson became acquainted with her. Her parents were Benjamin F. and Mary

(Boughton) Freeman. She obtained an academic education, received special training in music and for twenty-five years engaged in teaching music in Battle Creek, being one of the most successful representatives of this art here. Unto Mr. and Mrs. Johnson was born one daughter, Franc Caroline, who died in infancy. The wife died March 2, 1898, and on the 27th of March, 1903, Mr. Johnson was again married, his second union being with Mrs. Julia Foote, nee Beckman.

Since casting his first presidential ballot for Lincoln in 1864 Mr. Johnson has been a stalwart Republican. He belongs to Farragut Post, G. A. R., in which he has served as adjutant. As the years have passed and success has attended his efforts, he has made judicious investments of his capital and he now owns two houses and lots located at Nos. 131 and 133 Van Buren street, west, and a residence at No. 46 Glenwood avenue. He is connected financially with several of the leading manufacturing companies of Battle Creek. Thus he derives a good income in addition to that which he secures from his private business interests. His long residence in Battle Creek has made him known to many of its citizens and he has gained the friendly regard of the large majority of those with whom he has been brought in contact.

FRANK HOUGHTALING.

Business conditions of the present age are constantly devolving new business enterprises and the successful man is he who recognizes and uses his opportunity. This Frank Houghtaling has done and although yet a young man, has made for himself a creditable position in the world of trade and manufacture, and is reaping a good harvest for his labor. He is now chairman of the Economy Business Association, limited, with offices on the second floor of the Marjorie block. This company operates the Staines-Houghtaling Advertising Agency, the Business Office Supply Company and the Economy Manufacturing & Supply Company.

,. Mr. Houghtaling was born in Freeland, Saginaw county, Michigan, November 10. 1870, a son of Francis Sylvester and Susan J. (Clark) Houghtaling. He attended the common schools and remained upon the home farm until fourteen years of age, when he came to Battle Creek to attend the Seventh Day Adventist College in which he spent two years, and while there took manual training. Later he engaged in the manufacture of rubber stamps. While he was in college his father, who was an estimator of pine lands, went to Duluth, Minnesota, on business and there Frank Houghtaling joined him after a few months. There he started out to sell books, which he followed with fair success, and later he canvassed the state, selling rubber stamps, gaining experience of great value to him in later years. In 1887 he returned to Battle Creek and for a year did whatever he could find to do, from trimming carpets to farming. Subsequently he was connected with a rubber stamp manufactory for a year, when his health again failed and he went upon the road, selling Parsons' Hand Book for several months. Returning to this city he worked in the office of Mr. White as foreman of one of his departments until he began selling the book entitled "History of the Sioux War," and later the "Johnstown Flood" and other books. He afterward entered upon a business arrangement to train men for the book business in Indiana, and in the fall of 1890 he accepted a position in the book bindery of the "Review and 'Herald," serving until April, 1891. This was followed by his purchase and conduct of a rubber stamp manufactory. He had but little capital but made the venture and later admitted his brother to a partnership. They purchased a small press and began job printing, and after a time Mr. Oxley became a partner. The business grew so rapidly that in the fall they had to move to larger quarters on South Jefferson street, where they had all they could do. They published the Opera House Program, the largest and best ever issued, and were successful in the conduct of their enterprise. Mr. Oxley sold out to another of Mr. Houghtaling's brothers and they purchased more printing material and another press and removed to quarters where they could get power. His brother who had been his partner, returned to work for him and was given the management of the business while Frank Houghtaling began studying in college and also solicited work for the printing establishment. In that year he finished the preparatory course of study. In 1895 he took a company of three men to sell books published by the Seventh Day Adventist Association, but did not have success at that and began again selling stamps, returning after a trip of several months. He next resumed charge of his office, but the succeeding year decided to go out of the business. He spent one summer in Bay City and for a time worked for the Seventh Day Adventist Mission in Chicago.

Again coming to Battle Creek, Mr. Houghtaling sought employment in a printing office, but found no vacancy until at last he offered to work for the Ellis Publish-

ing company at a small salary. He began to solicit for them and soon gained many patrons. After three weeks work, with no knowledge of what his salary was to be, he was promised fifteen per cent and soon demonstrating his ability, was given a good salary. He was with that company through the summer and sold his rubber stamp business to them. His next work was writing advertisements and this led to the establishment of the Staines-Houghtaling Advertising agency, the business of which is constantly growing and has already reached large proportions. They advertise throughout the country for many firms, using the best methods, which after thorough investigation, they are convinced will bring the best returns. In connection with the Advertising Agency is conducted the interests of the Business Office Supply Company, the sales of which are almost phenominal. They handle an exceptional quality of goods, ask reasonable prices and through able management have secured an extensive patronage. The Economy Manufacturing & Supply Company is another branch of this enterprise. It sells incubators and brooders, and like the other departments of the business, the amount of trade has become very large and the department therefore profitable. They have made it their study to understand the business situation of the country and to meet its needs and conditions both in the way of advertising and office supplies and the new and progressive methods which they have followed have led to the expansion of their own business to large and profitable proportions.

On the 10th of June, 1894, at Liberty Center, Iowa, Mr. Houghtaling was married to Miss Cora V. Spencer, a daughter of John W. and Minerva J. (Morrison)

Spencer. They have two children: Griselda M., born in Battle Creek, February 15, 1897; and Theron D., born March 4, 1900. Mr. Houghtaling was reared in the Seventh Day Adventist faith and in his political belief is a Republican, but not an active politician, preferring to devote his time and energies to the development of his business in which he is meeting with signal success.

AARON E. BLANCK.

Aaron E. Blanck, a representative of the building interests of Battle Creek, was born in Allegheny township, Venango county, Pennsylvania, February 9, 1847, a son of Samuel W. and Lydia A. (Morris) Blanck. The father was a farmer and also a carpenter and dealer in lumber and logs. He would cut timber in the Allegheny mountains and float it down the Allegheny to the Ohio river and thence to Cincinnati. In 1865 he removed to Canandaigua, New York, purchasing a tract of land within the corporate limits of the town. Subsequently he sold out there and in 1867 established his home in Dexter, Michigan. In March, 1866, he came to Battle Creek and purchased a farm in Emmett township, two and one-half miles east of the city. Our subject assisted in the farm work in his early youth and also in the lumber woods and in making the runs on the river. He acquired a common school education and when sixteen years of age began working at the carpenter trade, being associated with his father for a year. After the removal of the family to Canandaigua he attended the academy there and subsequent to the removal of the family to Dexter, Michigan, he completed his apprenticeship at the carpenter's trade. After his father purchased a farm in Calhoun county, Aaron E. Blanck continued its operation for two years in connection with his younger brother, George W. He then rented two hundred and fifty acres of land in Bedford township, where he was successfully and extensively engaged in agricultural pursuits for three years. In 1877 he went to Sacramento, California, where he had charge of a ranch of several hundred acres. Subsequently he was employed as a conductor on the street railway in the city of Sacramento. He then returned to Michigan with the intention of again going to California; in fact, he arranged for a position in the Central Pacific shops. In the meantime he was married in Battle Creek, in 1870, to Miss Lucretia Doy, who was born in Hull, England, a daughter of Dr. John and Jane (Dunn) Doy. Mr. Blanck's parents and his wife did not wish him to return to California, and therefore he decided to remain. Entering the Upton-Brown Threshing Machine works he was thus employed for two years, after which he bought the old homestead in Emmett township from the heirs, his father having died in March, 1879. Through the succeeding three years Mr. Blanck cultivated his land and then sold it, returning to Battle Creek, where he began carpentering in the services of the Grand Trunk Railroad Company as a bridge and depot builder. He was with that corporation through two years. He then took charge of the building of the Wakelee block, as superintendent, and later began contracting and building on his own account. He has erected many substantial structures here; was the contractor for the Rupert & Vesey block, and was superintendent of the building of the Stone block. He also had charge of the building of the Malta-Vita plant, and a storage building for the Sanitas Nut Food Company. He has erected many

AARON E. BLANCK

residences and has built a number which he has sold. He put up a building which he sold to the Grape Sugar Cereal Company, and in 1902 he reconstructed the Wheelock Mills, one of the modern structures of this city, for the same company. In 1903 the whole plant was destroyed by fire and Mr. Blanck built the present plant, one of the largest and most substantial factories of the city, together with a large line of other work. Mr. Blanck bought a fine business lot at 37 South Madison street, where he erected his contracting and building plant, which is equipped with the latest machinery. He is also extensively interested in various corporate companies, being a heavy stockholder in the Grape Sugar Cereal Company; was one of the organizers of the Citizens' Electric Company and has been a member of the board from the time of incorporation, in various capacities, as director, vice president and president. He was also one of the organizers and directors of the Whip and Leather Company, whose plant he erected. Mr. Blanck also owns a large amount of residence property as well as other business interests here. He is ever active in the support of any measures that promise benefit to the city. He is also interested in the Advance Steam Pump and Compressor Company. In addition to his contracting, Mr. Blanck makes a specialty of estimating fire losses, as an expert, both for owners and for insurance companies.

Mr. Blanck was made a Mason in Bedford lodge, No. 207, F. & A. M., and he also belongs to the chapter, council and commandery of Battle Creek. He likewise holds membership in Saladin temple of the Mystic Shrine of Grand Rapids. In politics he has always been a Republican since casting his first vote for Grant in 1868. He was formerly active in politics, but not an aspir-
15

ant for office. He has been watchful of all the details of his business and all of the indications pointing toward prosperity; and his keen perception, tireless energy and common sense have been the salient features of his successful career.

SAMUEL FOST CALDWELL.

The name of Samuel Fost Caldwell became actively associated with the business history of Battle Creek and in trade circles he sustained an unassailable reputation, but those who knew him in other walks of life also entertained for him the highest regard. He was a man of high principles, of strong moral worth and of deep sympathy and the sterling traits of his character endeared him to all with whom he came in contact. He was born in Pennsylvania, July 27, 1859, and passed away in this city July 30, 1902, being accidentally killed by a street car. He was deprived of the usual educational advantages which most boys enjoy, never attending school altogether for more than six months. His education was acquired by his own fireside and he became a man of broad general information, reading extensively.

Leaving the east, Mr. Caldwell removed to Schoolcraft, Michigan, when about fifteen years of age, and there remained for some time. He secured employment in a dry goods store and while working in the day time devoted his evening hours to study, beginning with the old first reader. His love of learning caused him to make rapid progress in this direction and while continually adding to his knowledge concerning literature, history and science, he also was laying for himself a foundation for a successful business career through his close application to the duties entrusted to him in mercantile lines. After a time he became connected with a grocery store in which he remained until his removal to Marcellus, Michigan, where he resided for a number of years, conducting the largest grocery house in that place. Seeking a still broader field of labor he removed to Battle Creek two years prior to the strike here and purchased a grocery store on East Main street, just back of the First Methodist Episcopal church. In this enterprise he met with prosperity, securing a large patronage and conducting his store with success until March, 1902, when he sold out and became the promoter of the manufacturers' and retailers' association. He was treasurer of the association and held that position up to the time of his death.

November 7, 1880, Mr. Caldwell was united in marriage to Miss Hannah Boyce, a native of Schoolcraft, and they became the parents of three children: Burtie, who is a bookkeeper for the firm that his father established; Orley and Beulah, both in school.

Mr. Caldwell erected the block at No. 70 East Main street in Battle Creek and also built a substantial structure in Marcellus while located there. A splendid advocate of the cause of temperance, he voted as he believed, giving his allegiance to the Prohibition party. When quite a young man he joined the Methodist Episcopal church and remained one of its faithful adherents until his death. He held many official positions in the First Methodist church of this city, and took a very active part in its work and contributed generously to its support. Socially he was connected with the Odd Fellows and the Maccabees. In his later life he was a prosperous citizen, his financial position being then in great contrast to his condition when as a poor, bare-footed boy he began working in a store to provide for his own support. His success was the direct result of his own labors and came to him as the reward of his honesty and diligence. Since her husband's death Mrs. Caldwell has purchased a fine home at No. 45 Meritt street, where she resides with her children, her mother, Mrs. Ann Boyce, also being a member of the household. Mrs. Caldwell is a devoted member of the Methodist Episcopal church and a lady of innate culture and refinement. The relation between husband and wife was ideal and theirs was a most happy home. The memory of Mr. Caldwell is enshrined in the hearts of all who knew him. He lived a life in harmony with the highest principles of manhood, was reliable in business, loyal in citizenship and most faithful to the duties of friendship and of the home.

CHARLES F. McKENZIE, L. L. B.

Among the younger and leading attorneys of Battle Creek is Charles F. McKenzie, who has practiced here for about four years. A native of Banfield, Michigan, Mr. McKenzie was born September 7, 1874, his parents being John and Carrie E. (Fish) McKenzie. The father was born near Aberdeen, Scotland, and is a representative of the old McKenzie clan of that country. When seven years of age he accompanied his parents on their emigration to Ontario, Canada, the family home being established near London, where he was reared to maturity. In 1865 he removed to Barry county, Michigan, and engaged in farming near Banfield. He there wedded Miss Carrie E. Fish of that county, in which locality her parents had located on their removal westward from New York. She died May 6, 1903, but the father is still living on the old homestead.

To the district schools of this state Charles F. McKenzie is indebted for the early educational privileges he enjoyed. He afterward attended Albion College, where he pursued an elective course preparatory to taking up the study of law. Having spent four years at Albion, he went to Ann Arbor and enrolled as a student in the law department of the University of Michigan in 1896. After studying there for a time he engaged in business in Detroit for one year. He had for some time been a member of Company L, Detroit Light Infantry of the National Guard, when the Spanish-American war was inaugurated. With this company he enlisted and was mustered into the United States services as a member of Company L, Thirty-second Michigan Volunteer Infantry. The command was sent to Tampa, Florida, and was stationed there and at Fernandina, until the close of the war. Upon his return to the north Mr. McKenzie resumed his law studies in Ann Arbor and after two years was graduated with the class of 1900, winning the degree of Bachelor of Law. Immediately after he was admitted to the bar he went to Detroit and remained with a prominent law firm of that city for a time. In the fall of 1900 he came to Battle Creek, where he opened an office and has succeeded in building up a good practice, winning the confidence and esteem of his fellow members of the bar and of the general public. He has been connected with a number of well known cases of importance and is attorney for a number of corporations. He prepares his cases with great fairness, is painstaking and careful in his work, and his knowledge of the law is accurate, exact and comprehensive.

On the 14th of December, 1899, Mr. McKenzie was joined in wedlock to Miss Birdie L. Miles, of Battle Creek, a daughter of Amos S. and Alice A. (Marsh) Miles. They now have a daughter, Pauline Louise. Mr. McKenzie was one of the early members of the Association of Spanish War Veterans, becoming a charter member of the post in this city. He has held the office of chaplain and at the present time is serving as aid-de-camp on the staff of M. Emmett Murell, the commander in chief, which gives him the rank of colonel, his commission bearing date January 2, 1903. Mr. McKenzie met with the national encampment held in New Haven, Connecticut, in September, 1903. He took an active part in the founding of the command in Battle Creek and is helpful in this work and prominent in the organization. A young man of ability, he is winning enviable success in his profession and in private life is gaining that warm personal regard which arises from geniality, kindliness and deference for the opinions of others.

CHARLES A. CALDWELL.

Charles A. Caldwell, street commissioner of Battle Creek, was born in Goshen, Indiana, June 27, 1864. His father, Andrew Caldwell, was a native of Virginia and when a young man emigrated westward, establishing his home in Michigan City about 1831. By trade he was a cooper and manufactured barrels at Michigan City, hauling from across the country to Chicago. He afterward removed to Goshen, Indiana, where he engaged in coopering and also in farming. He likewise had a sawmill and was thus actively identified with industrial and agricultural pursuits. In Goshen he wedded Miss Eleanor Burns, who was born in Pennsylvania and removed to Indiana with her parents. Subsequently Mr. and Mrs. Caldwell went to Anderson county, Kansas, where he is still living at the venerable age of eighty-nine years, but the mother has passed away. Like her husband she was a member of the Adventist church.

To the public school system of this country Mr. Caldwell is indebted for the early educational privileges he enjoyed and later he attended the Battle Creek College and afterward became a student in the Northern Indiana Normal School at Valparaiso. Subsequently he engaged in teaching school for three years in Kansas, after which he turned his attention to merchandising and to the grain business at Lone Elm, Kansas. There he prospered, not only conducting a successful store, but also becoming the owner of a good farm. He was likewise prominent in public affairs there, and served as township clerk. In 1896, however, he disposed of his interests in the Sunflower state and came to Battle Creek, where for a time he was engaged in the real estate business, in teaming and contracting. In connection with his brother and sister he is the owner of the Caldwell addition to the city which his father laid out in 1885, purchasing the land as an in-

vestment. This is well located on the hill and as the city has increased the investment has become a profitable one. Mr. Caldwell also continued in general contracting until 1902.

On the 9th of September, 1892, occurred the marriage of Charles A. Caldwell and Miss Flo Miller of Lone Elm, Kansas, a daughter of Joseph and Maggie (Heller) Miller, who removed to Kansas from Illinois at an early period in the development of the former state and there engaged in farming. In 1901 Mr. Caldwell was called upon to mourn the loss of his wife who died in that year, leaving four children: Don M., Trella Mitt, McKinley and Max.

Mr. Caldwell is an advocate of the Republican party and its principles, and upon its ticket was elected a member of the city council of Battle Creek in 1899. He was appointed on the street, bridge and sidewalk committee and did effective service for the city in that regard. He was afterward re-elected to the same office, but resigned before the expiration of his second term to accept the office of street commissioner, to which he was appointed in April, 1902. During his term a large amount of street work has been done and under his supervision fifty men are now engaged in improving the streets of the city. Mr. Caldwell is a progressive official and is practical as well, his efforts proving of material benefit to Battle Creek. Socially he is identified with the Knights of the Maccabees. On coming to Battle Creek he built a pleasant home at No. 57 Corwin street, where he is now residing. With a recognition of the business opportunities here he is so conducting his affairs that his real estate operations have proven profitable and at the same time his dealings are a benefit in the upbuilding and development of his section of Battle Creek.

JOHN SMYTH.

John Smyth is well known in Marshall as a representative of the building interests of the city and also as the leader of the Social Labor party. He was born in Quebec, Canada, April 24, 1842, and was a son of John and Fanny (Dickson) Smyth. The father was born in Ireland and was of English descent. When a young man he went to Quebec, where he was engaged in general contracting, principaly in the loading of vessels. In that place he married and made his home until his death, which occurred in 1853. His wife, long surviving him, came to Marshall, Michigan, in 1868, with her family and died in this city. Both Mr. and Mrs. Smyth were members of the Episcopal church.

John Smyth acquired his education in the schools of Quebec, but his opportunities were limited because he was only eleven years of age at the time of his father's death, and soon after he found it necessary to earn his own living. Not only did he provide for his own support, but also aided in the support of the family consisting of seven children, two sons and five daughters. His brother, George H., entered the Union army at the time of the Civil war and was killed in battle. In early life John Smyth learned the carpenter's trade, and, following his apprenticeship was employed as a journeyman until after his removal to Marshall. He came to this city with his mother in 1868, and later began contracting and building on his own account. His excellent workmanship and his reliability in trade transactions has secured for him a large and constantly growing patronage and many of the fine residences of the county stand as monuments to his enterprise and handiwork. In recent years he has also engaged in moving buildings and receives all of the contracts for such work, having splendid equipments for accomplishing it. He built a fine home at No. 320 South Kalamazoo avenue and also erected a beautiful residence adjoining, that is now the property of E. H. Ryder.

In earlier years Mr. Smyth was active as a supporter of the Democratic party and upon this ticket he was elected a member of the city council in 1901 from the third ward. While serving in that capacity, the subject of conveying power from the Kalamazoo river to the city water works by electricity, came before the council and was favorably acted upon. Mr. Smyth was a member of the committee on paving, fire and sidewalks. Always a student of the political situation of the country and the issues of the day, he became convinced by reading and research, that the Social party contained the best elements of government that would prove of most benefit to the people. Allying his strength to that of the organization in Marshall he has become the recognized leader of the party here. At this writing he is the president of the society and is putting forth every effort in his power to promote its principles.

On the 29th of September, 1868, Mr. Smyth was married to Miss Anna Bagley, of Quebec, Canada, and unto them have been born four children: Georgia A., the wife of E. H. Rider, who is a student of Ann Arbor; Fannie E.; John R.; and Lillie

B. All have been given good school advantages, Mr. Smyth realizing the importance
of educational training as a preparation for
life's work. He has through his own efforts
accumulated a fair competence and has
gained the respect and good will of his fellow men. He is unfaltering in his support
of any idea which he believes to be right
and is ever true to his honest convictions.

ABRAM HAMILTON.

Abram Hamilton is one of the native
sons of Calhoun county, his birth having
occurred here on the 19th of February,
1838. His parents, John and Mary
(Young) Hamilton, were both natives of
New York, the former born in Cayuga
county and the latter in Albany county.
They were married in the Empire state and
in 1836 started for Michigan, making the
journey by way of the lakes from Buffalo
to Detroit and thence across the country
by wagon. Earlier in the spring two families had located in Bedford township where
the Hamilton family took up their abode.
They were very early pioneers and their
home was located at the southeast corner of
section 6, Bedford township, where the
father secured a claim of eighty acres; the
same amount on section 8, and forty acres
on the southeast quarter of section 5. This
was covered with timber and not a furrow
had been turned or an improvement made
upon his place. He built a log house and
in true pioneer style began life here, continuing to make the place his home until
1850, when he was called to his final rest.
His wife, who long survived him and who
was born in 1804, died on the eighty-

seventh aniversary of her birth. They held
membership in the Congregational church
and Mr. Hamilton gave his political support to the Whig party. This worthy couple were the parents of five children, four
sons and a daughter: William, now deceased; George J.; Abram; Melvina, the
deceased wife of J. N. Gregory; and John
J. The pioneer history of Calhoun county
should certainly contain the names of Mr.
and Mrs. Hamilton, who at an extremely
early period in the development of this locality established their home here and aided
in reclaiming the wild land for the purposes
of civilization. Their remains now rest in
Bedford cemetery.

In the little log cabin home Abram
Hamilton was born and amid frontier
scenes and experiences he was reared. He
can remember when the greater part of this
locality was covered with the native forest
trees, the woodman's ax having not as yet
awakened the echoes as the monarchs of
the forests fell before his sturdy strokes.
For many years Mr. Hamilton worked at
farm labor on the old homestead and in the
winter months attended school until eighteen years of age. Throughout his entire
life he has carried on agricultural pursuits
and all that he possesses has been won
through his own labors. In 1862 the family
purchased the farm upon which he now resides and to-day he and his brother are joint
owners of two hundred and ninety-seven
acres. He helped to clear the land where
his home now stands and has made all of
the improvements upon his property.

In 1865 Mr. Hamilton was united in
marriage to Miss Mary J. Wilson, a daughter of Harvey Wilson, and the following
year they took up their abode upon the farm
which is yet their place of residence. Unto

them have been born the following: John F., the oldest, who works in the Advance Thresher shops; Walter, a resident of Battle Creek, who married Clara Bullis, by whom he has two children, Nellie and Max; William, who wedded Miss Jessie Pickworth, by whom he has one son, Flutell; Arthur, who died when four years of age; Charles, who is living on the old homestead; and Grace, who is the wife of Francis Murphy, of Battle Creek and has one daughter, Josephine.

Mr. Hamilton exercised his right of franchise in support of the men and measures of the Republican party and in 1896 he was elected on its ticket to the office of supervisor of Bedford township. Since that time he has been continually re-elected each year so that his incumbency covers seven consecutive years. This is certainly a most creditable record as it indicates his fidelity to duty and the unqualified trust reposed in him by his fellow townsmen. In 1901 he had the honor of serving as chairman of the county board of supervisors. In his farm work he has prospered. There was very little of his land cleared when he took possession of the old homestead and the present highly improved condition of the place indicates his life of industry while the buildings thereon stand as monuments to his enterprise and progressive spirit.

HENRY RUPERT.

Henry Rupert is the senior member of the firm of Rupert & Morgan, dealers in coal, wood, feed, hay and building material, in Battle Creek. He was born in Cleveland, Ohio, November 18, 1853, and is a son of Daniel and Anna M. Rupert, who were born, reared and married in Switzerland, whence they sailed for the new world in 1852, establishing their home in Cleveland, where their son Henry was born the following year. The father died in that city during the infancy of our subject, and the mother afterward removed with her family to Medina county, Ohio, where Henry Rupert was reared to manhood, acquiring his education in the common schools. When a little more than fifteen years of age he began to earn his own living by working as a farm hand through the summer months, receiving about seven dollars per month in compensation for his services. With the return of the winter season he went again to his home and until spring came once more he attended school. His wages went to the benefit of his mother until he was about eighteen years of age. At that time he entered upon an independent business career, coming to Michigan where he has since made his home. For a time he was located in the city of Lansing, being there employed in a chair factory, but soon he was given an opportunity to run an engine and acted in that capacity for several months. He remained a resident of Lansing from 1871 until 1873, after which he was employed in other places in Michigan until the fall of the latter year, when he came to Battle Creek and secured a situation in a table factory, in which he was employed for a year and a half. On the expiration of that period he returned to Lansing, where he continued until the fall of 1880, working at machine work in a furniture factory. Again coming to Battle Creek he entered the employ of the firm of Mason & Rathbun, having charge of their engine in the planing mill for more than three years. He next formed a partnership with Mr. Hollis and began repairing and manufacturing furniture, conducting the business for about one year. Mr. Rupert then sold out and established a flour and feed store at No. 26 Main street, west, where he carried on business from 1884 until 1898, meeting with very creditable and desirable success. He then disposed of his enterprise and for more than a year rested from further labor. Having previously purchased the building at No. 26 West Main street he came to his present location in May, 1900, and has since conducted a profitable business here as a member of the firm of Rupert & Morgan. The firm now has a large and constantly growing patronage and its annual sales have reached a very gratifying figure. Mr. Rupert is likewise interested in manufacturing concerns of Battle Creek, especially in the line of food products and is now stockholder in the Hygenic Food Company, The Korn Krisp Food Company, and the Tryabita Food Company. He has also invested in real estate and has improved property here, having built several residences and also a business block located at No. 217 West Main street, which is known as the Rupert block and which he still owns.

On the 18th of May, 1876, in Battle Creek, was celebrated the marriage of Mr. Rupert and Miss Alella M. Robbins, who was born in Vermont and is a daughter of Samuel I. and Yidelia Robbins. They had one child, Grace Maude, who was born in Lansing, August 28, 1878, and who died in Battle Creek on the 25th of June, 1890. They now have an adopted daughter, Marguerite Belle, who came to their home when less than two years of age. Both Mr. and Mrs. Rupert are very kind hearted people, whom to know is to respect and honor. They are members of the Independent Con-

gregational church, of which he served as a deacon. In politics he has been independent, voting as he deems best, regardless of party affiliations. His career clearly illustrates the possibilities that are open in this country to earnest, persevering young men who have the courage of their convictions and are determined to be the architects of their own fortunes. When judged by what he has accomplished, his right to a first place among the representative citizens of Battle Creek cannot be questioned.

STEPHEN HEALY WILLIS.

Through long years Stephen Healy Willis was a resident of Calhoun county and was classed with the leading agriculturists of this portion of the state. He had to enter business life handicapped to some extent by physical infirmity, and yet he achieved a success that many a man sound in limb might well envy. He had the force of character, the strong purpose and the laudable ambition that enabled him to win prosperity, and, moreover, his life was characterized by unfatering honesty and by unremitting loyalty to duty so that his name became honored and respected by all who knew him. His life record covered almost eighty-four years and he left behind him a name and memory that are cherished and revered.

Mr. Willis was born on the 5th of January, 1805, in the town of Greene, Chenango county, New York, and was the third child of Matthew and Sarah (Lyon) Willis, both of whom were natives of Connecticut, whence they removed to the Empire state. At an early date Matthew Willis took up his abode in Tompkins county, New York, and

STEPHEN H. WILLIS

MRS. H. M. WILLIS BRYANT

later resided in Clyde, New York. He conducted a tavern in the former county and became quite wealthy, but through going security for a friend, he lost all of his wealth, and with his family was turned out of doors when their youngest child was a babe of about six months. This occurred when Stephen H. Willis was ten years of age. Owing to the impoverished condition of the family he was bound out, and his crippled condition did not win for him the kind treatment that it should have done, and because of ill usage he returned home. At the age of seventeen years he accompanied his parents to Clyde, New York, and remained at home until twenty-four years of age, his labors proving a helpful factor in assisting his father to purchase a farm. He then started out upon an independent business career, securing employment in a glass factory in 1824. Subsequently he was employed on the Erie canal and afterward went to Rochester and later to East Bloomfield, New York.

The spring of 1835 witnessed the arrival of Mr. Willis in Calhoun county. He came to Michigan in company with his future brother-in-law, their destination being Albion, and for a time lived with Judge Olin, for whom he worked. The idea of the unsettled condition of the county may be gained from the fact that there were no houses in Albion, Marshall or Battle Creek townships. The land was wild and unimproved, but Mr. Willis recognized the natural resources of the country, and in the fall of 1835 entered two hundred and eighty acres of land from the government, receiving his parchment title which was signed by President Van Buren, and which is still in possession of his daughter, Mrs. Bryant. It has always been a treasured keepsake in the family, and Mr. Willis exhibited it with pardonable pride for there has never been a scratch of a pen against it. In May, 1838, he returned to East Bloomfield, New York, where he was married to Miss Thankful Case, a native of Rhode Island, and a daughter of Jesse and Tabitha (Hopkins) Case, who removed to Ontario county, New York, during the early girlhood of Mrs. Willis. With his bride Mr. Willis returned to the west and they established their home upon the land which he had entered from the government. Theirs were the usual experiences and hardships of pioneer life. Their means were extremely limited and they frequently found it difficult to raise money enough to pay the postage—then twenty-five cents—upon letters which they returned to their friends in the far off east. Two children were born unto them, but the younger, Jesse C., died at the age of six months and lies buried beside his father and mother in the Riverside cemetery at Albion. The daughter, Hannah M., is therefore the sole representative of the family in Albion.

With public affairs Mr. Willis was closely connected through many years, and his name figures conspicuously and honorably in connection with the history of Albion and this portion of the county. The old town used to be known as The Forks, and it was upon the petition of Mr. Willis and Amos Babcock to the legislature that a charter was obtained for changing the name, these gentlemen bearing the expense. Albion was chosen because it was the name of a town near Mr. Willis's old home in New York. In all matters pertaining to the welfare of the community, Mr. Willis took a very active and helpful part, greatly desiring the progress and substantial upbuilding of this part of the state. He was always an in-

dustrious man and as the result of his industry and prudence he accumulated a valuable property, including the home farm of
four hundred acres. This land was wild
and uncultivated when it came into his possession, but he resolutely set to work to
transform it into a productive tract, and as
the years passed, it yielded to him splendid
crops as a result of his labor and care. He
was one of the workmen employed in the
building of the mills in Battle Creek, and
also those in Tekonsha, and the evidences of
his handiwork are seen in many other enterprises and landmarks in this vicinity. He
was never known to take advantage of his
fellowmen in any trade transaction, but was
ever strictly honorable and trustworthy. His
success came as the result of earnest, indefatigable labor guided by sound business
judgment, and his example should serve to
encourage and inspire others who, having
begun life as he did, empty-handed, have
gained prosperity in the business world. His
life history, if given in detail, would present
a clear and forcible picture of pioneer conditions in Calhoun county.

Mr. and Mrs. Willis traveled life's journey together most happily for many years,
but in 1881 he was called upon to mourn the
loss of his wife, who died at the age of
seventy-nine. It was about seven years later
that he passed away. In the meantime, he
had made his home with his daughter, Mrs.
Hannah M. Bryant, who had cared for him
most faithfully and cheerfully in his declining years, leaving nothing possible undone
that would add to his comfort and happiness
or relieve his suffering. About three years
before his demise he fell and broke his hip,
but although he recovered sufficiently to get
out with the aid of a crutch, he never en-

joyed good health afterward and on the 13th
of October, 1888, passed away at the age of
eighty-three years, nine and a half months.
He knew that death was approaching and
showed his faith in the life beyond, saying
one day, "My case rests with the Almighty,
I trust in Him." He was reared in the faith
of the Presbyterian church, and in early
manhood united with that denomination, but
was greatly interested in the Baptist church
of Albion and contributed most generously
to its support. In addition to the money
which he gave he also donated a window
which bears his name. His Baptist friends,
appreciative of his generosity, surprised him
with a gift on his eightieth birthday of an
easy chair which afforded him much comfort during the last three years of his life.
He had a heart easily touched by a tale of
sorrow or distress, and the poor and needy
ever found in him a warm friend, his helping
hand being often extended to those who
needed assistance on life's uneven pathway.
His political support was given to the Democracy and he never swerved in his allegiance to the cause, but put forth every effort in his power to secure the adoption of
its principles. He lived a life which bore
testimony to an honorable character, sterling
purpose and to upright principles. A local
publication at the time of his death said,
"He was a man of strict integrity, true to
what he believed to be right, energetic and
persevering, doing well whatever he undertook. He was known to everybody as a
good man and we have yet to hear the first
word against his character. He was a great
reader and possessed more than ordinary intelligence. His presence will be greatly
missed, but his good example and wise coun-
sels will not soon be forgotten. Thus has

passed away another of our old settlers and a man whose memory will be cherished by a large circle of friends."

Mrs. Hannah M. Bryant, the only surviving member of the Willis family, was born and reared in Calhoun county, and on the 27th of February, 1867, she gave her hand in marriage to Mr. Squire Calhoun Bryant, who was born November 8, 1838, near Dansville, New York. He spent the days of his boyhood and youth in the Empire state and at the age of twenty years came to Calhoun county, Michigan, where he remained until 1863, when he went to California. There he followed mining for a year, after which he returned to Albion and was connected with various lines of work until his death, which occurred in the year 1870. After his demise his wife resided for six years in Rochester, New York, and in 1878 returned to her father's home and remained with him until his death. She now owns and occupies the farm which he entered from the government seven decades ago. Her father left her four hundred acres of land and to-day she is the owner of more than seven hundred acres of finely developed farm land. She is a woman of excellent business ability, careful in management, of keen discrimination and sound judgment. She has so conducted her business affairs and made her investments that she is to-day one of the prosperous residents of the community. She thoroughly understands farming methods and work, and in the supervision of her property displays an intimate and correct knowledge of the best ways of carrying on agricultural pursuits. She has made many improvements upon her property and in 1899 she erected a farm residence at a cost of five thousand dollars. This is one of the beautiful homes of Calhoun county and it has since been occupied by Mrs. Bryant, who delights to extend its hospitality to her many friends. She not only possesses good business ability but is rich in those social qualities which win one friendship and high regard.

WARREN G. MOREHOUSE.

Among the veterans of the Civil war is numbered Warren G. Morehouse and he is also entitled to mention in this volume because of his long connection with the city and its interests. Hardly had Battle Creek been established on the prairies of the west when Mr. Morehouse located here, his residence dating from 1835. At the time of his arrival the little hamlet contained three log houses, a crude shanty and the frame for a sawmill. He has seen as many as five hundred Indians encamped along about where Main and Jefferson streets have since been laid out. Time and man have wrought many changes of which Mr. Morehouse has been an interested witness and many times a cooperant factor in measures for the general good.

Born in Balston township, Saratoga county, New York, on the 27th of January, 1825, Mr. Morehouse is a son of Bradley and Sally (Morehouse) Morehouse. The parents, though of the same name, were not related. The father was born and reared in Balston township and afterward leased part of his father's land and engaged in farming. His wife was born and reared in Connecticut and was a daughter of Aaron Morehouse, who was a shoemaker, tanner and currier. He and his family and Bradley Morehouse and family came to Michigan in

1835. The maternal grandfather of our subject, was too old to labor then, but he had been a fiddler and he traveled all over the country to play for general trainings and dances. Bradley Morehouse secured five eighty-acre tracts of land where South Battle Creek now stands and built one of the first houses in that part of the township. At the time of the arrival eighteen people occupied a house containing two rooms until the homes for the Morehouse families could be built. The father gave his attention to the cultivation and improvement of a good farm, upon which he lived throughout his remaining days, although his death occurred while he was on a visit in Van Buren county. In politics he was a Democrat and he and his wife were members of the close communion Baptist church. Their children who reached mature years were six in number: Mary, the wife of William Langley; Martha, the wife of Asa Langley; Warren G.; Louise, the wife of Charles Stewart; Joseph, who died in Van Buren county, and Talcott, of Cass county, Michigan.

Warren G. Morehouse attended school in New York until ten years of age and then accompanying his parents on their removal into the wilderness of the west where there were no schools he did not again attend until six years had passed away. He afterwards spent one winter as a student, but in the school of experience has acquired a practical education. He underwent all of the hardships of pioneer life, assisting in the arduous task of developing a farm. Much of the time through six summers he drove from four to six yoke of oxen to a breaking plow. The land was full of grubs and the work was very difficult. He continued at home until he attained his majority and then started out in life with nothing to depend

on save a pair of willing hands and a strong determination to gain success. As a companion and helpmate for life's journey he chose Hannah Henika of Battle Creek, the wedding taking place in 1848. She had come to the west with her parents, Henry and Elizabeth Henika, of New York.

Mr. Morehouse purchased one hundred acres of land south of Battle Creek and built thereon a house and began the development of a farm which he continued to cultivate for three years. He next located in the city where he began working at the carpenter's trade, but as that proved detrimental to his health he began dairying and prospered in the undertaking. He followed the pursuit until 1859, when he was elected constable, serving until after the inauguration of the Civil war. On the 16th of August, 1861, he enlisted in Company I, Merrill's Horse Second Missouri Cavalry. For three years he served in southwestern Missouri and Arkansas and on the 28th of May, 1862, was detailed for service in the quartermaster's department. He was stationed at Springfield and Sedalia, Missouri, at Fayette and Glasgow and all of the time held the rank of sergeant in his company. Subsequently he became forage master and wagon master, having charge of six wagons and in the fall he was made regimental forage master. In June, 1862, he went to St. Louis, Missouri, where he was relieved from special duty that he might join the regiment band, but not being able to blow the horn he reported to his company. Before he had gone into camp, however, he was again ordered to report to the quartermaster and again made forage quartermaster, acting in that capacity and as wagon master until late in the year 1863, when he was made a brigade wagon master. Subsequently he went to Little

Rock, Arkansas, where he became regiment wagon master, looking after the sick horses and mules. Although Mr. Morehouse's service did not call him to the field of battle his work was nevertheless of an important nature and whatever the task assigned him he did his duty uncomplainingly and faithfully. On the 15th of September, 1864, he was mustered out at St. Louis and returned to Battle Creek.

As wages were high Mr. Morehouse went into a shop to work at wagon-making and after learning the trade he carried on a shop of his own for several years. When he had disposed of that he entered the employ of the Advance Thresher Company and also purchased stock of them, but for the past ten years has lived retired at his home at No. 30 Adams street, which he purchased in 1854 and which he has since occupied. The property is now very valuable, owing to the rise in real estate. He has here ninety-four by one hundred and twenty-five feet at the corner of Frelinghuysen and Adams streets.

Unto Mr. and Mrs. Morehouse was born a daughter, who died when he was in the army, and on the 14th of November, 1900, he was called upon to mourn the loss of his wife. On the 2d of January, 1902, he was again married, his second union being with Mrs. Jennie Underhill, of Battle Creek. Socially he is connected with Battle Creek lodge, No. 12, F. & A. M., and also with the chapter and council in Masonry. He belongs to the Independent Order of Odd Fellows, to the encampment in the Patriarchs Militant and is a past commander of Farragut post, G. A. R. He attended many of the encampments of the organization, but in recent years has withdrawn from them. In politics he was a stanch Democrat until

1856, when he joined the ranks of the new Republican party and has since followed its banners. In 1868 he served as city marshal and in matters of citizenship he is as true and loyal to-day as when he followed the old flag upon the battle-fields of the south. The city in which he makes his home has profited by his efforts in its behalf and his endorsement of public measures, and he takes great pride in what has been accomplished here. Few indeed are the residents of Battle Creek who have longer made their homes in this locality and his mind bears the impress of the early historical annals of the state and forms a connecting link between the primitive past and the progressive present.

JOSEPH L. HOOPER.

Joseph Lawrence Hooper, who is serving as prosecuting attorney of Calhoun county with office at Nos. 305-6 Post building, Battle Creek, is a native of Cleveland, Ohio, his birth having occurred there on the 22d of December, 1877. He is a son of Dr. J. R. and Florence R. (Lawrence) Hooper, who removed to Wellsville, Columbiana county, Ohio, when the subject of this review was only four or five years of age. When he was a youth of thirteen the family came to Battle Creek, and the father soon after died, but the mother still survives and is living in this city. Two children were born of this union, of whom the younger is Alfred, a reporter on the "Inquirer" of Battle Creek.

In the public schools of this city Joseph L. Hooper acquired his education and was graduated on the completion of the high school course in 1896, with a class of thirty-six members. He afterward prepared more especially for the duties of a business life by attending the business college of this city, where he pursued a course in stenography and typewriting. His knowledge of those arts he used as a means to enable him to earn a living, while he was preparing for the practice of law in the office of Williams & Lockton. He did their stenographic work while mastering the principles of jurisprudence. For three years he studied there, and then successfully passed the required examination, whereby he was admitted to the bar in October, 1899. His dependence upon his own efforts for an education showed the elemental strength of his character and argued well for a successful future.

In July, 1900, Mr. Hooper entered upon the practice of his chosen calling in Battle Creek, and in the following November was elected circuit court commissioner on the Republican ticket, acting in that capacity for two years. In November, 1902, he was elected Prosecuting Attorney and in September of the same year he entered into partnership with H. P. Stewart and L. H. Sabin under the firm name of Stewart, Sabin & Hooper. He is one of the ablest young members of the Calhoun county bar, having that mental grasp which enables him to readily discover the points in a case. A young man of sound judgment, he manages his cases with masterly skill and tact and is regarded as one of the strong jury advocates in this city. He is a logical reasoner and has a ready command of the English language.

Born and reared in the Republican faith, his mature judgment has sanctioned the platform and policy of the party; and he does everything in his power for its promotion and growth. He has served as a delegate to various conventions and has de-livered many campaign addresses in behalf of Republican principles. Socially he is connected with the Knights of Pythias fraternity, with the Independent Order of Odd Fellows and with the Knights of the Maccabees, and in the last named organization he served as commander in 1902. He is likewise a popular member of the Yonkers and Athelstan clubs and in the city where much of his life has been passed he has many warm friends.

LOREN B. ALEXANDER.

Loren B. Alexander, the proprietor and manager of the Battle Creek Storage & Carting Company, was born in Penn township, Cass county, Michigan, on the 25th of September, 1875, and is a son of George Rollin and Mary (Hinshaw) Alexander. The father was also a native of Penn township born in 1854; the grandfather of our subject, John Alexander, having been an early settler of Cass county. He was born in North Carolina and when a young man emigrated westward, taking up his abode in Cass county where he met and married Miss Sarah Jones. He entered a tract of land in Penn township and although it was covered with timber when it came into the possession of Mr. Alexander he soon cleared and improved it and in course of time gathered abundant harvests as the reward of his labors. Subsequently he engaged in general merchandising in Vandalia, Cass county, where he conducted a successful business for some time and then confined his attention exclusively to the hardware trade. He was one of the prominent and influential men of the township and for some years was president of the bank in Vandalia. His activity touched upon many lines of business and proved a helpful factor in each. In public affairs he was always a loyal and energetic citizen and he rendered capable service to his fellow townsmen in the office of postmaster and supervisor. He was also a very earnest worker in the Christian church, of which he and his wife were long devoted members. Her death occurred in Vandalia and he passed away in Mishawauka, Indiana. George R. Alexander was reared on the old family homestead in Penn township, Cass county, and to the public schools of the locality is indebted for the educational privileges he received. He has been variously engaged along business lines, having for a time been connected with the livery business in Vandalia. While in South Dakota he took up a large tract of land at Watertown and gave considerable attention to its improvement. After returning to Michigan he located at Cassopolis, where he again engaged in the livery business, also conducted an agricultural implement store and at one time he was a traveling salesman for a harvesting machinery house. On the 1st of January, 1889, he came to Battle Creek and was here engaged in the livery and hack business for a number of years. He is now again upon the road as a commercial traveler. In the interest of his varied business concerns and also for pleasure, he has traveled broadly, seeing much of the country, especially in the western portion. In early manhood he wedded Miss Mary Hinshaw, who was also born in Penn township, Cass county, a daughter of Abijah Hinshaw, one of the very prominent and well-to-do citizens of that locality, where he established his home in pioneer times. Unto Mr. and Mrs. George Alexander have

been born three children: Loren B., Ernest J. and Maude, but the last named died at the age of two years.

In the schools of Cass county Loren B. Alexander began his education which was continued in Battle Creek. He pursued his high school course here and also attended business college in this city, after which he entered upon his business career in the employ of Charles J. Austin, of the firm of Austin & Company, dealers in groceries and table supplies. Mr. Alexander remained with them for several years as a most trusted and reliable employee of the house, and at length resigned his position in order to establish a business of his own. In 1898 he embarked in the storage and carting business, establishing a storage warehouse and also engaging in the transfer business. His business has steadily increased until it has needed more commodious quarters and he leased the block at No. 49-51 South Jefferson street, now occupying the entire building for his storage business. His patronage has steadily grown and he now has the leading business in his line in Battle Creek. He started out with only one team, but now has six together with the needed vans and drays. He does a general furniture-packing business, also the forwarding of freight to all parts of the country. Although young in years Mr. Alexander is to-day acknowledged to be one of the successful and enterprising business men of Battle Creek. A new building is being built on South Madison street, which will be four stories high, and Mr. Alexander will occupy the entire building, on which he has a long lease. It will be constructed on modern lines, especially adapted for a storage warehouse.

On the 25th of August, 1898, occurred the marriage of Loren B. Alexander and

Miss Jessie Belle Murray, of this city, a daughter of Mrs. Rosa Murray. They have one child, Marie. They attend and support the Presbyterian church and Mr. Alexander belongs to Metcalf lodge, F. & A. M. and also to the Ancient Order of United Workmen. During business hours his entire attention is confined to the storage and carting business and he certainly well deserves the success which has come to him, for it is the direct result of close application, sound judgment and laudable ambition.

JAMES COURT.

In the history of James Court there is much that should serve to inspire and encourage young men, for his record proves that success is not a matter of genius nor the outcome of fortunate circumstances, but may be gained through strong determination, laudable ambition and earnest labor. Practical industry, wisely and vigorously applied, never fails of success; it carries a man onward and upward, brings out his individual charcter, and acts as a powerful stimulus to the efforts of others. The greatest results of life are usually attained by simple means and the exercise of the ordinary qualities of commonsense and perseverance. The everyday life, with its cares, necessities and duties, affords ample opportunities for acquiring experience of the best kind, and its most beaten paths provide a true worker with abundant scope for effort and for self-improvement. It was along such lines that Mr. Court won a place of prominence in business circles. It is, therefore, with pleas-

ure that we present to our readers his life history, for he well deserves mention among the representative men that in past days or at the present time have been closely connected with the business development of Calhoun county.

James Court was born November 26, 1839, in Berkshire, England, and was the only son of James and Tryphosa (Crutchfield) Court. The father, who was a farmer by occupation, was accidentally killed when his son was but four years of age. The mother afterward married again and James Court, of this review, for a short time attended the local schools, but his education was principally acquired through private study and through the employment of his leisure hours in extensive reading. He thus became a well informed man for he possessed an observing eye and retentive memory. Hearing favorable reports concerning the business opportunities of the new world and desirous of learning something of other countries beside his native land, he determined to emigrate to the United States, and in 1855 crossed the Atlantic, landing at New Orleans, whence he made his way up the Mississippi river to Stillwater, Minnesota. He secured employment in a hotel at Marine Mills, but after about a year came to Marshall, in the fall of 1856. Here he was variously employed for a time and then went to Kalamazoo county, where he was engaged in chopping wood and logging. In that way he acquired three hundred acres of heavily timbered land and later took a contract to clear three hundred and twenty acres for the Michigan Central Railroad Company. Employing twenty-five choppers and thirteen teams, he entered upon the work in an energetic manner and his labor proved to him profitable. In the meantime he purchased a

JAMES COURT

tract of undeveloped land in Kalamazoo county, and subsequently traded that for city realty in Marshall.

It was in the year 1877 that Mr. Court returned to Marshall and began dealing in poultry on a small scale. From this beginning, however, he developed a business of great magnitude, his patronage steadily increasing until he was one of the most extensive poultry dealers in Michigan. He began buying and shipping poultry, butter and eggs and so managed his business that its growth ultimately made him one of the most prosperous residents of this part of the state. Eventually he built a large plant for handling dressed poultry, butter and eggs at Marshall, and he associated with him his son, Frank W., under the firm style of James Court & Son. In April, 1897, Mr. Court purchased a tract of land in Allegan, Michigan, and erected there a large storage and packing house along the line of the Detroit, Toledo & Milwaukee Railroad, opposite the depot. Since that time the firm has continued a successful business there. Mr. Court has also built a splendid plant in Bellevue, Eaton county. These three are exclusively under the control of the home firm and they have also a half interest in the plant at Homer, conducted under the style of Court & Hardy. Employment is thus furnished to a large number of men, who, traveling with teams upon the road, collect the poultry, butter and eggs, taking them to the central plants in the cities mentioned for shipment to the markets. As the years have gone by this business has been developed until it is one of the largest of its kind in Michigan and propably is unsurpassed in extent by none. The father continued in the trade until his death, which occurred March 20, 1902, and since that time the business has

16

been conducted by his sons. Mr. Court made shipments to eastern cities and secured all modern equipments to facilitate the business, keeping thoroughly abreast with the improved methods which are needed there in placing the products which he handled upon the market. It was in 1891 that at Marshall he erected a large poultry house and double refrigerator, thirty-five by one hundred and ten feet and two stories in height. This was, at the time, the largest in the state.

On the 18th of October, 1862, James Court was united in marriage to Miss Salina Williams, of Kalamazoo county, who was born in Oxford, England, and who came to the United States in early girlhood. The family home was adjacent to that of the refrigerating plant and it was ever noted for its gracious and kindly hospitality. Six children were born unto Mr. and Mrs. Court: Frank W.; Kate; Reuben; and James, Jr. The last named, however, died in early manhood and two others died in infancy. The mother passed away March 4, 1902. Both Mr. and Mrs. Court stood very high in the esteem of a large circle of friends and occupied an enviable position in social circles. They were members of the Congregational church but as there was no church organization of that denomination in Marshall they attended the services of the Presbyterian church. Mr. Court also held membership with the Ancient Order of United Workmen. His political allegiance was given to the Republican party and he was a member of the common council of Marshall for two terms, during which time the electric light plant and water works were brought under municipal control. Mr. Court was deservedly popular with all classes—the young and old, rich and poor—and in the transaction of his affairs he maintained the utmost fairness and justice toward all. He possessed in a marked degree the enterprise, sagacity and discrimination necessary for success in business life. He was a thoroughly representative citizen devoted to the promotion of the welfare and progress of his town and county, and though he sought not to figure in any public life he nevertheless exerted a strong influence in behalf of general improvement, truth and justice. In view of the fact that he commenced his business career empty handed, his success was the more remarkable. His record should prove an inspiration to many a young man in starting out as he did a few years ago, with no capital, save intelligence, integrity, determination and perseverance—which after all are the best capital in the world and without which wealth, influence and position amount to nothing.

ELIAS HALL.

. In taking up the personal history of Elias Hall, now living in Battle Creek, we present to our readers the life record of one of Michigan's native sons whose residence in the state covers a long period. He was born in Allegan county, January 26, 1838. His parents, Silas and Susan (Storms) Hall, removed to Grand Rapids, when he was about four years of age and there his father engaged in contracting and building. In his boyhood days Silas Hall had removed from Corydon, New Hampshire, to Lodi, New York, with his parents, Mr. and Mrs. Elias Hall, Sr., who spent their remaining days there. The town in which they located is now called Gowanda. At an early day Silas Hall removed from the Empire

state to Michigan and was married here. In Grand Rapids, Elias Hall was reared, and after leaving school, he was connected with his father in building operations for a number of years. Finally they turned their attention to the furniture business, working in a factory, by the piece.

It was while living in Grand Rapids that Mr. Hall was married on the 30th of June, 1860, to Miss Martha E. Haire, a native of New York and a daughter of William Haire. About two years later Mr. Hall bade adieu to his young wife in order to aid his country in the preservation of the Union, enlisting in 1862 as a member of Company B, Fifth Michigan Cavalry, which was sent to Custer's Brigade. He was mustered in as a private at Detroit on the 17th of August, and was then sent to Virginia, being first under fire at Fairfax. He remained continually with his brigade until the close of the war except when he was ill in the Armory Square hospital for a few months. He had many narrow escapes at times, bullets flying all around him and often dirt was thrown over him by shot and shell, but he was never wounded nor captured and by general order he was mustered out in 1865. In Washington he participated in the Grand Review, the most celebrated military pageant ever seen in the country. He was first promoted to quarter-master sergeant, and later to orderly sergeant, and at the time of General Lee's surrender he was on the skirmish line at Appomattox.

After his return from the army Elias Hall and his father continued in the furniture business for a time and later he established a dealers' furniture store, which he conducted until 1884. He then began soliciting for the life and accident insurance and continued to make his home in Ludington for a time. but subsequently removed to Reed City and later to Grand Rapids, where he lived until December, 1902.

In 1878 Mr. Hall had been called upon to mourn the loss of his wife, who died at Colorado City, Colorado. on the 28th of May of that year. She had gone west in the hope of benefitting her health and her remains were brought back to Michigan and buried in the Fulton Street cemetery in Grand Rapids. There were two children by this marriage. The elder, William S., who received a college education, became a teacher and was superintendent of Gilroy College. Eva died at St. Joseph, Missouri, at the age of seven years. After the death of his first wife Mr. Hall was again married in Grand Rapids on the 6th of October. 1879, his second union being with Miss Jennie E. Shackelton. They are the parents of two children: George Morgan. who is represented elsewhere in this volume; and John DeWitt. who was born in Grand Rapids, February 6, 1891.

Mr. Hall has been a stalwart Republican since casting his first presidential vote for Lincoln in 1860. He is a member of the First Baptist church of Battle Creek. but was reared in the faith of the Methodist church and at one time held membership with that denomination. In 1867 he was made a Mason in Valley City lodge. No. 86. F. & A. M.. at Grand Rapids. He served as senior warden of his lodge in Ludington for two years and frequently served as lecturer to the candidates. He and his first wife were charter members of the Eastern Star lodge at St. Joseph, Missouri, and at all times he has been loyal to the beneficient teachings of the craft, exemplifying its tenets in his life. He likewise has membership relations with the Foresters and the Knights of the Grip and he maintains pleasant relations with his old army comrades through his membership in the Grand Army of the Republic. As a citizen he is as true and loyal to his country as he was when he followed the old flag on southern battle fields and throughout his entire record he has manifested many traits of character that are worthy of emulation.

DANIEL CAINE.

Daniel Caine was for many years a prominent farmer of Calhoun county and well deserves mention among the prominent residents of this community who in the past were loyal to its best interests and largely promoted the general good. Although some years have come and gone since he was called to his final rest his influence remains as a potent factor in the world, especially along temperance lines. He was indefatigable in his efforts to abolish the evil of intoxication and many a man has reason to be thankful to him for his labors in this line.

Daniel Caine was born at Weedsport, Cayuga county, New York, in 1815, a son of William and Susan (Beach) Caine, the former a pioneer settler of Cayuga county. The subject of this review was reared on the "Oak Lands" near Weedsport and became a farmer. In that locality he was united in marriage on the 9th of April, 1849, to Miss Almira Sawyer, a daughter of John W. Sawyer, who was a prominent pioneer resident of Port Byron, New York. He was also a strong temperance man in that early day when the use of intoxicants was much more prevalent than it is at the present time. He always stood for the highest and best in life, lived in accordance with the most upright principles and used his influence for the moral development of his fellow men. He was also a stanch Abolitionist when it required great physical as well as moral courage to champion that cause. He wished to hold abolition and temperance meetings in the church and when the building was refused to him for this purpose he withdrew from the church. The feeling was so strong that the church which he had built, furnishing funds amounting to twenty-five hundred dollars, was left on his hands to pay for. He never wavered, however, in his allegiance to the principles that he believed to be right and although many opposed him, all respected his conscientious fidelity. He served as supervisor of his township and in his office enforced the temperance laws to a degree that caused him to be threatened with bodily harm. Threats to burn his buildings were also made, but were never carried out. At the time of his death he had one of the largest funerals ever held in that section of the country. It was attended by the poor of the entire community for there was hardly a needy one in all that portion of the state who had not received from him kindly assistance and aid in the hour of distress. Reared in a home amid such influences Mrs. Caine became greatly imbued with her father's spirit, determination and unswerving loyalty, and if there were a few more like her the liquor interests would not find such strong support as is now given it, and the world would be the better for it.

After their marriage Mr. and Mrs. Caine began their domestic life upon a farm in Cayuga county, where they lived until 1861, when they came to Battle Creek and purchased a farm of one hundred and thirty acres within the city limits. This is now one of the most valuable tracts of land in the community. On this Mr. Caine continued farming throughout his entire life. In politics he was a strong Republican, giving unfaltering allegiance to the principles in which he believed. He was also a member of the Methodist Episcopal church and his life was in harmony with its teachings.

Unto Mr. and Mrs. Caine were born three children: John W., who is living in Battle Creek and manages the home farm; Robert E., of this city; and James, who is living in Colorado. Mr. Caine passed away November 9, 1893. He had become widely known in Calhoun county and his many sterling traits of character gained for him the warm regard of all with whom he was associated. He prospered in his business, gaining success through honorable efforts and to his family he left a comfortable competence and also an untarnished name. Mrs. Caine still retains her interest in the farm and is a woman whose strength of character lies in her integrity and her unfaltering devotion to principles which she believes to be right. Her work in behalf of her fellow men has been continuous and far-reaching and in this respect she has ever followed the example of her honored father.

GEORGE F. STONE.

George F. Stone, who is now living retired from active life, and who is one of the older residents of Calhoun county, having lived here for thirty-five years, was born in Henrietta, Monroe county, New York, on the 17th of April, 1833. He is a son of Danford and Delia (Olcott) Stone. The father was born and reared in Massachusetts and when a young man removed to New York. He married Delia Olcott, whose father was a soldier of the Revolutionary war and during two years of his service acted as one of General Washington's bodyguards. Subsequently he removed from his old home in Pennsylvania to Oneida county, New York. He dropped dead of apoplexy, near Rome, New York, when eighty-four years of age. This was occasioned by his excitement on hearing that a special pension had been granted all of Washington's bodyguards.

Soon after their marriage Mr. and Mrs. Danford Stone removed to Henrietta, Monroe county, New York. The city of Rochester was then a mere hamlet. In that county the father became a well-to-do farmer and there lived until the 8th of November, 1848, when his life's labors were ended by death. His wife, surviving him for about twenty years, came with her family to Calhoun county and died in Battle Creek in 1868. They were the parents of seven children: Mary, the deceased wife of Dr. E. Darwin Ransom, of Burlington, Iowa; Maria, the deceased wife of Henry Loomis, of Battle Creek; Elizabeth, deceased, who was the first wife of Henry Loomis; Jane, the deceased wife of Dr. Manderville, of Rochester, New York; Lucy, who became the wife of J. H. Cromwell, of this city, and has also passed away; Jeremy H., who was a soldier of the Eighteenth New York Battery and died in Battle Creek in June, 1903, and George F.

The last named acquired his preliminary education in the common schools of Henrietta, New York, then studied in the academy there and afterward became a student in the Genesee and Wyoming Semi-nary, at Alexander, Genesee county, New York. Subsequently, he remained on the home farm and assisted in its cultivation until he attained his majority, when he removed to Saugatuck, Michigan, where he built a lumber mill with a large capacity, the first well equipped mill of that place. While it had but one saw it could cut two thousand feet of lumber per hour. For two years or until the panic of 1857 he conducted that mill. He then spent some time in the west and at the breaking out of the Civil war was in St. Joseph, Missouri. Returning then to Rochester, New York, he enlisted in the Eighteenth New York Battery and was sent to New Orleans, going to the front as a private. The regiment was assigned to the department of the Gulf under General Banks and his successors. He participated in the siege of Port Hudson, lasting forty-seven days, also the siege of Mobile and then embarked at that place to go up the Alabama river. At that time they learned of the assassination of President Lincoln. Proceeding up the river to Mobile, Mr. Stone was there stationed at the time of the close of the war. He participated in every engagement in which his battery took part and was honorably discharged in June, 1865, after a service of three years, in which he had many times displayed marked bravery and at all times had given proof of his loyalty to the starry banner and the cause it represented. He acquired cotton interests in the south and after he obtained his discharge, located at Baton Rouge to supervise his investments in that part of the country.

On the 8th of November, 1867, Mr. Stone was there married to Miss Mary Smith, whose parents were from Pennsylvania, but she was born in Baton Rouge. Unto Mr. and Mrs. Stone were born three children: Tula, now the wife of William N. Dibble, of Battle Creek; Mrs. J. D. Strohm resides with the subject, and Carrie, the wife of James T. Geddes.

After engaging in cotton raising for two years, and dealing in that commodity for a year longer, Mr. Stone came to Battle Creek in 1868, finding here a city of sixty-five hundred population. He turned his attention to farming near Marshall, and conducted agricultural interests for ten years. Later he lived in the town of Marshall and engaged in the raising of fruit for a similar period. He then sold his interests there and removed to Battle Creek, where he established a fruit and confectionery store. He had a good trade and conducted a profitable business until 1898, when on account of failing health he retired, having a competence which supplies him with all the comforts and many of the luxuries of life.

In 1901 Mr. Stone was called upon to mourn the loss of his wife, who died in February of that year, after they had traveled life's journey together for more than a third of a century. Although reared in the Democratic faith and long a supporter of the party, he now usually gives his allegiance to the Republican party. He was made a Mason in Otsego, Allegan county, Michigan, and now holds membership with Battle Creek lodge, No. 12, F. & A. M. He maintains pleasant relations with his old army comrades through his membership in Farragut post, G. A. R.

CHARLES E. FOSTER.

With sixty years behind him, Charles E. Foster is rounding out a well-spent life as a helpful citizen of Leroy township, Calhoun county, Michigan. A native of Lorain county, Ohio, he was born July 25, 1843, the son of John Chipman Foster, the latter born in Antwerp, New York, the representative of a Welsh family. He married Julia Ann Drake, also a native of Antwerp, New York, whose father served in the Revolutionary war. When our subject was but six years old his father brought the family from Lorain county to Defiance county, where he purchased a two hundred acre farm, the little log house in which they made their home being two miles back in the woods, a heavy growth of timber covering the greater part of the land at that time. His death occurred in Newton township, Calhoun county, Michigan, at the age of sixty-two years.

Charles E. Foster was reared to young manhood upon the paternal farm, and when only eighteen years of age he enlisted, against the commands of his father, as a soldier in Company A, Sixty-eighth Ohio Regiment. Shortly after, however, he was taken ill at Toledo and was discharged, re-enlisting in the spring of 1864 in Company A, same regiment, the former commanded by Captain Richards, and the latter by Colonel Scott, afterward promoted to the rank of general. The regiment marched at once to Chattahoochee, the next morning after their arrival taking part in the fight on the Chattahoochee river. In the six weeks' siege that followed this regiment saw active service, on the 22d of July, taking part in the battle at Atlanta, during which seven charges by the enemy were repulsed by the Union lines. The Seventeenth Army Corps was then marched by night to Jonesboro, surprising the enemy just before daylight, capturing the pickets and twenty-five hundred prisoners. Mr. Foster was then transferred to Atlanta with his company, where he served under Sherman, a member of that band which swept its way across the state of Georgia, leaving, for the sake of the stars and stripes, a track of desolation in its wake. From the coast they passed north through the Carolinas, past Beaufort, on the Broad river. During this campaign the company to which Mr. Foster belonged, composed of sixty men, was sent across the river into Georgia to attempt the capture of three thousand Confederates, the expedition being entirely successful and casting considerable honor upon the company and its leader. While under Sherman's command he had conversation with the great general and was added to the many admirers who trace the results of the closing battles of the war to his ability. At the close of the war, Mr. Foster was mustered out of service at Camp Cleveland, Ohio.

In 1867 Mr. Foster was united in marriage with Miss Celestia Drake, whose birth occurred upon the farm where they now make their home, Mr. Foster having purchased the same, seven years after their marriage. Since that time they have lived in the one locality, adding to the original hundred and sixty acres of land ninety-three acres, and in many ways improving the value of the property. To Mr. and Mrs. Foster have been born two children, namely : Minnie, who married Otto Wittenberg of Battle Creek, and her death occurred September 29, 1903. She is interred in East Leroy cemetery. Charles Everett, also a resident of Battle Creek, engaged in the shoe business. He married Caddie Stingham. A brother of Mr. Foster's also served in the Civil war. Though never desiring official recognition, Mr. Foster has given his best efforts toward the maintenance of good government, in political preference supporting the Republican party. At three different

times he has been elected to the office of justice of the peace, serving twice, but declining the third time. He has given his earnest and intelligent support toward the substantial upbuilding of the community which has so long numbered him among its prominent citizens, and he now enjoys to an unusual degree the esteem and confidence of all with whom he has been associated.

Mr. Foster was for a number of years a member of Farragut post, G. A. R., at Battle Creek.

WALTER J. COLMAN.

Walter J. Colman, who stands at the head of his profession in Battle Creek— that of artistic sign painting—was born in Milwaukee, Wisconsin, July 17, 1871, a son of Alfred R. and Anna Colman. The father was born in Lewis, Sussex county, England, and when a boy came alone to the United States. For a time he remained in New York and after being variously employed he turned his attention to taxidermy, and also to artistic painting. In this way he earned enough money to educate himself. Later he entered the Veterinary College, at Toronto, Canada, and when he had completed his studies there located in Jarvis, Canada, where he is still engaged in the practice of his profession, having become very proficient and successful in that line.

In his childhood Walter J. Colman accompanied his parents on their removal to Canada, where he acquired his education in the public schools. In 1889 he came to Battle Creek, where he learned the trade of sign painting under the direction and in the employ of Charles E. Hitchcock. Having natural artistic ability he has made a specialty of fine sign painting and has come to be the recognized leader in this line in the city. After remaining with Mr. Hitchcock for a few years as an employee he was admitted to a partnership in the business, under the firm name of Hitchcock & Colman, and they continued together until 1899, when he purchased his partner's interest and has since conducted a successful business alone. He has given much time and thought to orignal methods of work and designing and has produced work of a new, unique, odd and attractive character, which is also of very high grade. He is now recognized as a most reliable man, doing artistic and satisfactory work, and his trade has increased accordingly. That his work is pleasing is shown by the fact that many have copied it. He gives employment to a number of men and has worked his way steadily upward, his ability enabling him to leave the ranks of the many and stand among the successful few.

EDWARD J. DENNISON.

Edward J. Dennison owes his education as well as his success at the bar entirely to his own efforts; and in a practice where advancement depends upon individual merit and the possession of well developed talent, he has attained an enviable place. He is now practicing in Marshall and his clientage is of a distinctively representative character.

Mr. Dennison was born in this city September 29, 1874, a son of John and Anna (McCaffrey) Dennison. The father was born in County Dublin, Ireland, and when a young man came to America. He learned the blacksmith's trade, at which he worked in Marshall, thus providing for the wants of his family. His widow, who still survives, was born in Calhoun county and is now about forty-nine years of age.

Edward J. Dennison was a mere lad when his father died, and being the eldest of a large family who were left in limited circumstances, found it necessary to earn his own living when very young. At about the age of fourteen years he began working in the grocery store of Richard Butler and after a year spent in that employ entered the machine shops in Marshall, where he became an expert machinist, thoroughly mastering the business in principle and detail. He next went to Chicago and was employed by the Standard Safety Heating Company on Dearborn street for a year, and later was with the Monarch Cycle Company and other firms of that city, being employed there as a machinist until 1896. He then came to Marshall, and entered the office of R. S. Lockton, thus carrying out a long cherished plan to study law and prepare for the bar. One year was thus devoted to study, after which he returned to Chicago in order to work as a machinist and earn money that he might further prosecute his preparation for legal practice. When his exhausted exchequer had been replenished he returned to Marshall and entered the office of Hon. John C. Patterson. In October, 1900, he was admitted to the bar at Lansing upon examination by Wesley Hyde, of Grand Rapids, Professor Floyd Meacham of Ann Arbor, ex-Judge Durrand of Flint and ex-Judge Van Zile, of Detroit. He met the requirements and at once began practice in Marshall, where he has since succeeded in securing a good clientage. He is very careful in the preparation of his cases, is logical in his de-

EDWARD J. DENNISON

ductions, strong in argument and presents his conclusions with clearness and force.

Edward J. Dennison cast his first presidential ballot for William J. Bryan in 1900, and is an earnest advocate of the Democracy. In the same year he was elected justice of the peace ere his admission to the bar. He was reared in the faith of the Catholic church, being confirmed in Marshall at the age of twelve years by Bishop Borgess. Although a young man, he has displayed marked force of character, strong determination and laudable ambition, and has gained a position of prominence that many an older attorney might well envy.

JOHN C. BARBER.

With the arduous task of developing a farm in the wild forests of Michigan, John Carlos Barber became familiar in his youth. Later, he was for years engaged in the livery business, and for a long period was in the public service as deputy sheriff and as sheriff. The years were fraught with labor, and perseverance and energy were required for him to overcome the obstacles in the path to success; but to-day he is in comfortable financial circumstances, and, moreover he has the regard and confidence of his fellow men by reason of an upright life and fidelity to duty. For eight or nine years he has been connected with Nichols & Shepard, as their collector, and he is also a stockholder in a number of paying corporations. His life history illustrates clearly the force and value of energy and resolute will in the active affairs of life.

Mr. Barber was born in Benson, Rutland county, Vermont, March 14, 1834, a son of Edward H. and Abigail (Griswold) Barber. His mother died when he was but three years old and his father afterward wedded Laura Root. In 1839 he removed to Vermontville, Eaton county, Michigan, making the trip from Whitehall to Buffalo by canal, thence by steamer on the lake to Detroit, and on a wagon to Eaton county. There were five children in the family, of whom our subject was the youngest. The father had visited this state in 1836, and had purchased a large tract of land, all covered with dense timber. With the aid of his sons he cleared and developed the farm, and it was upon the old homestead that John C. Barber was reared. He attended the common schools and as age and strength permitted, assisted in the cultivation of the home place. When twenty-two years of age, he began to learn the carpenter's trade, serving a regular apprenticeship and receiving ten dollars per month. After a few years, however, he sold his tools and abandoned building operations.

In the meantime Mr. Barber had wedded Miss Sarah S. Welch, the marriage taking place in Clinton, Michigan, December 29, 1858. She was born in Orleans county, New York, a daughter of David and Olive (Whitmarsh) Welch, who came to Michigan in the fall of 1851, settling in Charlotte, Eaton county, when Mrs. Barber was fourteen years of age. After his marriage Mr. Barber engaged in the livery business in Charlotte, there remaining until 1861, when he removed his stock to Battle Creek, then a town of thirty-five hundred inhabitants. He located on what is now the corner of State and Monroe streets and continued in the business until elected to the office of sheriff. After retiring from that position, he again conducted a livery barn. Subsequently, however, he became connected with the Union School Furniture Company as a stockholder and director, and was in that business until the factory was destroyed by fire in 1892. This proved a great disaster to him, as he lost everything that he had. A strong nature will triumph over adversity, however, and although many others would have been utterly disheartened and discouraged, Mr. Barber, with resolute spirit, set to work to retrieve his lost possessions. That he has succeeded is shown by the fact that he is now financially interested in a number of important corporations. For eight or nine years he has been collector with Nichols & Shepard, and in this connection has done important service for that large corporation. He is a stockholder and director in the Battle Creek Electric Company, and also its vice president. He was one of the organizers of, and is a stockholder in the Sonora Mining Company, at Sonora, Mexico, in what is called the Alamosa district. This company has two hundred and seventy-four acres of rich mineral lands.

Unto Mr. and Mrs. Barber has been born one child, Nellie B., who was born in Charlotte, Michigan, is a graduate of the high school of Battle Creek and is now the wife of Arthur W. Davis, of this city. They have three children: Louise and Helen, students in the high school, and Edward C. All were born in this city.

Mr. Barber has been a stalwart Republican since casting his first presidential vote for John C. Fremont in 1856, and his political record has been most creditable. He served as deputy sheriff at Charlotte under B. W. Warren for four years and after coming to Battle Creek he was deputy sheriff for two terms, serving under Sheriffs Buck and Richfield. In 1876 he was elected

sheriff and took the office the following year. By re-election he served two terms, and then, after an interval of two terms he was again elected, in the fall of 1884, and once more in 1886, so that he has been the incumbent in the office altogether for eight years. Prompt and fearless in the performance of his duty, his course was a menace to all evil-doers and brought a feeling of safety and security to those who abide by the laws. His administration of the office won high encomiums and no more capable official has ever filled the position in Calhoun county. Mr. Barber is also a valued representative of the Masonic fraternity. He became a Mason in Battle Creek lodge, No. 12, F. & A. M., and has also taken the chapter and commandery degrees. He has traveled quite extensively, visiting all parts of the country on business trips and he and his wife visited the World's Columbian Exposition in Chicago, in 1893. His knowledge has thus been constantly broadened and he relates many interesting incidents of his journeys. His friends are legion, for the dominant characteristics in his life have been such as win regard, loyalty in citizenship, integrity in business, fidelity in office and trustworthiness in social relations.

ISAAC AMBERG.

With two exceptions there is no business man of Battle Creek who has so long been connected with commercial or industrial interests of this city as has Isaac Amberg, who became a factor in trade circles here in June, 1852. He still retains an interest in his business, but is practically living retired in the enjoyment of a well earned rest and of wealth that has been justly and honorably gained.

Mr. Amberg was born near the famed river Rhine, Germany, in the kingdom of Bavaria, his natal day being September 12, 1825. His father was an enterprising business man of Germany until his later life, when he crossed the Atlantic to America, establishing his home in Cincinnati, Ohio, where his last days were passed. Isaac Amberg acquired a good practical education in the place of his nativity and there learned the tailor's trade, but never followed it as a life work. In 1844, when a young man of nineteen years, he came to the United States, going to Cincinnati, Ohio, where he had a brother living. There he started out as a peddler in order to support himself while learning the English language. When a few years were thus passed he embarked in a general mercantile business near Cincinnati and his efforts were attended with prosperity. On selling out there in 1852 he removed to Battle Creek, arriving in the month of June. Here he at once engaged in the clothing business in partnership with Hon. Julius Houseman, who was later a member of Congress from Grand Rapids. They opened their first place of business on Main street near Jefferson. The town was then a small village, but they soon secured a patronage commensurate to its size and for two years they continued together in business, at the end of which time Mr. Houseman removed to Grand Rapids, while Mr. Amberg continued alone as owner of the clothing store here. For ten years he conducted the establishment and then sold out. Soon afterward he formed a partnership with Charles Peters, under the firm name of Amberg & Peters, and opened a drug store.

Later his partner sold his interest to John Helmer, at which time the firm became Amberg & Helmer. They continued at the former location and were successful druggists for some time. At length, however, Mr. Amberg disposed of his interests to his partner and then made arrangement for establishing a store of his own, which he located at No. 5 East Main street, where the business has since been carried on. He had not long been established at this place when he admitted W. J. Murphy to a partnership, that gentleman having formerly been a clerk in the employ of Mr. Amberg. This firm has continued under the same name to the present day, although in 1902 Mr. Amberg retired from the active management of the business, being succeeded in this work by his son, Victor Amberg, to whom he had given an interest in the store. This is one of the largest business houses of the city, and both a wholesale and retail trade is carried on. Since starting in business here Mr. Amberg has ever maintained in his various establishments a policy most commendable. There has been nothing in his entire career, that would not bear the closest investigation and scrutiny. The firm purchased and enlarged the building in which the business is now carried on and from the time when he embarked in the drug trade down to his retirement Mr. Amberg ever enjoyed a liberal patronage. He invested in other realty besides his business block and erected several residences in the city, including his own fine home at No. 121 West Van Buren street. Upon this lot he has resided for forty years. He was one of the original stockholders of the Merchants' Savings Bank and is one of its directors.

Mr. Amberg was united in marriage to Miss Hannah Summers, who was also born in Germany. Their wedding took place in Cincinnati, and they became the parents of six children, five of whom are now living, namely: Lewis, a resident of Grand Rapids; Cora, Victor, Isca and Loowina, all of whom are at home. The wife and mother died in 1885. Mr. Amberg and his children still occupy the fine residence which he erected, and there he is surrounded by all the comforts and many of the luxuries of life. His present condition is in marked contrast to his surroundings at the time he came to the new world. He had no money, neither had he a knowledge of the English language, but he possessed courage and determination and he resolved that he would win success, if it could be gained through honorable, persistent effort. To-day he possesses an independent competence. Such is the history of one of Battle Creek's foremost citizens. For more than half a century he has participated in the business life of the city and during this entire period has so conducted all affairs entrusted to him as to merit the confidence and esteem of the entire community, and no word of censure has ever been uttered against his action.

HENRY H. ELLISON.

Henry H. Ellison, one of the oldest and best known residents of Battle Creek, where he has resided continuously since 1871, is a man whose influence has ever been exerted on the side of right, justice, order and improvements. He was born in the town of St. Johnsville, Montgomery county, New York, January 5, 1846. The family originally lived in Vermont, and Henry Ellison, the grandfather of our subject, became a pioneer settler and farmer of Herkimer county, New York. It was in Herkimer township, that county, that George Ellison, the father of our subject, was born and reared. He wedded Jane E. Hildreth, a daughter of Thaddeus Hildreth, and she, too, was born in Herkimer county, while her father was a representative of an old New England family. Both the paternal and maternal grandfathers of our subject became well-to-do agriculturists of the Empire state. After his marriage George Ellison purchased a farm lying partly in Herkimer and partly in Mongomery counties, and prospering in his chosen vocation he became an extensive and wealthy agriculturist. He held the office of supervisor of his township, but never sought or desired political preferment. Having accumulated a handsome competence he spent his last days in honorable retirement from labor in Utica, Oneida county, New York, where he died in 1883, and his widow passed away in the same city in 1900.

They were the parents of two sons and three daughters, who reached adult age.

Henry H. Ellison was the oldest son and second child. He obtained good educational advantages, attending an excellent school in Fairfield, New York, which prepared students for entrance into the best colleges of the country. On putting aside his text books he turned his attention to farming, which he followed until his removal to Michigan in 1871. For a short time he resided in St. Charles, this state, and early in 1871 came to Battle Creek, where he became identified with commercial interests as a representative of the retail lumber trade. He had a large yard on West Main street, between Jefferson and McCamly streets, and remained at that place for a number of years, building up a large and profitable trade.

After four years, however, he sold out, giving his attention to the supervision of his property interests. He had invested quite extensively in real estate and at one time was the owner of fourteen residences in Battle Creek, thirteen of which he erected. He has thus been identified with the growth and improvement of the city, and as a capitalist he has also loaned money. He has superintended his own investments, and of recent years this has been his principal business. His efforts have always been conducted with strict regard to the ethics of commercial life and although now one of the wealthy men of the city his prosperity has been so worthily achieved that naught can be said in criticism of his career. He has ever been honorable and straightforward in his dealings with his fellowmen, never taking advantage of the necessities of others, and his life record should serve as a source of encouragement and inspiration to those who start out with little or no capital, for his own history proves what may be accomplished through determined purpose and consecutive effort.

Mr. Ellison owns a beautiful home on North avenue, one of the best residence streets of the city, and has here lived since his marriage. On the 31st of July, 1872, he wedded Miss Ella M. Averill, of Battle Creek, a daughter of Rev. Justin P. Averill, who was the pastor of the Universalist church and came to Michigan from the east. Mr. and Mrs. Ellison have three children: Justin G., now of New York City; Cornelia J., who is superintendent of music and drawing at Lenox, Massachusetts, and is a graduate of the Battle Creek high school, though her art studies were pursued in Detroit, and Ruth E., who is taking a special course in music and drawing in Ypsilanti, Michigan. Splendid educational opportunities have been given the children, Mr. Ellison believing this to be an excellent foundation upon which to build character. Soon after attaining his majority he was made a Mason in his home town and has always been an exemplary representative of the beneficent teachings of the craft. A strong temperance man, he gave his political support to the Prohibition party, has been its nominee for mayor and is now serving as treasurer of the Prohibition county committee. For more than thirty years he has lived in Battle Creek, where he is widely recognized as a man of the highest financial and business integrity. He has ever regarded his own self respect and the favorable opinion of his friends as much more valuable than wealth or position, and yet he has been accorded both. Undoubtedly his integrity and the sterling traits of character have been among the strongest elements in his prosperous career and he is to-day an honored man of irreproachable life ranking with the capitalists of the city.

ANDREW KNIGHT.

Andrew Knight is one of the oldest representatives of industrial interests in Battle Creek. Since 1869 he has been continuously engaged in the manufacture of sash, doors, blinds and building material, carrying on the business on an extensive scale. His business record is such as any man would be proud to possess. Planning his own advancement, he has accomplished it in spite of many obstacles and with a certainty that could have been attained only through his own efforts. The obstacles and difficulties which he has encountered have never served to discourage him, but on the other hand have seemed to act as an impetus to renewed efforts and thus steadily and continuously advancing he has won the success which is the reward of capability and merit.

Mr. Knight was born in Marshall, Michigan, May 2, 1838. His paternal great-great-great-grandfather, Charles Knight, was a native of England and braving the dangers incident to an ocean voyage at that time, he crossed the Atlantic to Massachusetts in 1724 and took up a tract of land near Worcester. Charles Knight, the great-grandfather, lived and died on that tract. Charles Knight, Jr., the grandfather, was also there reared and made it his home, and in addition to agricultural pursuits, he owned and operated both grist and sawmills. He also served in the Revolutionary war and was a man of considerable prominence in his locality. The father of our subject also bore the name of Charles Knight, and his birth occurred in Worcester, Massachusetts, where he was reared and educated. There he learned the business of manufacturing sash, doors and blinds, and when a young man he removed to Clarence, New York, where he engaged in business for himself. While there he married Miss Angeline Nash, a daughter of Moses Nash, and they continued their residence in Clarence until 1836, when they removed to Marshall, Michigan, then a small hamlet containing but a few business houses. Mr. Knight again engaged in the manufacture of sash and blinds and in the building business, being one of the first regularly equipped builders of the county. There he resided until 1842, when he removed to Clarendon, Calhoun county, where he spent a year and a half. He then came to Battle Creek, in 1843, and here established an enterprise sim-

ilar to those which he had previously conducted, it being located on the ground where the old threshing works of Nichols & Shepard were later built. He continued in the manufacturing business throughout his entire life. After a time, he built a factory of his own, adjoining the Mason & Ward Woolen factory, on what is now Madison street. Thus the name of Knight has been inseparably interwoven with the history of manufacturing in Battle Creek for about six decades, and throughout the entire period this name, as borne by father and by son —our subject—has been a synonym for honorable dealing. Charles Knight was a Whig in his early political views and upon the organization of the new Republican party he became one of its stanch supporters. In his religious faith he was a Presbyterian, both he and his wife holding membership in the church. They were the parents of eleven children who grew to maturity. Andrew Knight being the fourth in order of birth.

Living in Battle Creek in pioneer times, Andrew Knight pursued his education in its early schools. His first teacher was A. D. P. Van Buren and the first school was held in a log building, twelve by twelve feet, with a slab floor and slab benches, while a large fireplace occupied one end of the room. Later he attended a select school and completed his education in the first union school built in this city. Subsequently he went to Chicago, where he entered upon his business career as a clerk in the old store of Christopher Metz, at No. 52 State street, where he remained for a year and a half, beginning in 1857. He next went to New York and sailed from there to Savanah, Georgia, making two such voyages. He next accepted the position of storekeeper on the steamship Ariel and made five voyages, to England, France and Germany, returning thence to New York after meeting with a terrible disaster. On this last voyage the ship almost foundered, the captain was killed, and all of the other officers were disabled. For twenty-eight days they battled with the storm, being driven hither and thither before the winds, but at length reached the harbor of New York, fourteen days overdue. The ship had been given up for lost ten days before. Again Mr. Knight sailed from New York, this time on board the Philadelphia, bound for New Orleans, by way of Havana, Cuba. He was with his brother on the Gulf of Mexico until May 16, 1861. When the Civil war broke out he was watched, because of his being a northern man, and two weeks passed before he could manage to escape. At last, however, he stole away and took passage on the William W. Morrison, from New Orleans to St-Louis. That was the last ship to make the trip up the river. He arrived in St. Louis the second day after the riots there and reached home June 16, 1861.

A year later Mr. Knight enlisted in Company C, Twentieth Michigan Volunteer Infantry. Following the rendezvous at Jackson, Michigan, the regiment was sent to Washington, D. C., arriving just after the battle of Chantilly. It became a part of the First Brigade, Second Division, Ninth Army Corps, under General Burnsides, and participated in thirty-two battles and numerous skirmishes, including the engagements at Fredericksburg, Vicksburg and Jackson, after which the Twentieth Michigan was sent back to eastern Tennessee, and took part in the battles of Loudon Bridge, Campbell Station, Knoxville, Strawberry Plains and in skirmishes which occurred every two or three days for nearly a year. In the spring of 1864 they were sent back to Washington and afterward participated in the battles of the Wilderness, Spottsylvania Courthouse, Nye River and Bethesda Church, and then crossing the James river, arrived at Petersburg May 16, 1864. He fought on the 16th and 17th and at night of the latter day his brother, George C., who was captain of the First Michigan Sharpshooters, was killed. Andrew Knight went into the battle again on the next day, but about ten o'clock in the morning was wounded and had to be removed to the field hospital and later to the Army Square hospital, in Washington, where he remained for a year. He was then sent to Chester, Pennsylvania, and from the hospital there was discharged June 22, 1865. For six years from the time he sustained his wound he was an invalid and endured much suffering. A brave soldier, he was often in the thickest of the fight, facing wounds and perhaps death in defense of the Union.

In 1869 Andrew Knight assumed the management of the old business carried on by his father and brother—the manufacture of sash and doors. He has since continued in this line and has added the manufacture of building material to the other departments. He is now the oldest man in this line of business in the city, and although many enterprises of the kind have been started here he has outlived them all. He now has an extensive plant, at 147-9 West Main street. He began business at his father's old location, but that was burned and he started anew in the Leggett building. There again a disastrous fire occurred, and removed to his present location, where he is now carrying on a very large business, with which he is thoroughly familiar in every department. His personal supervision is given to the various branches and he employs skilled workmen, to whom he is a just and conscientious employeer, and those who serve him know that faithfulness will be rewarded as opportunity offers for promotion. Mr. Knight is also interested in the Battle Creek Whip and Leather Company, but gives his undivided attention to his sash and door business.

On the 24th of December, 1874, Mr. Knight was married to Miss Delia A. Dilley, of Napoleon, Jackson county, Michigan, a daughter of William Dilley, who removed from Akron, New York, to Napoleon. They have two children, Willard A., an attorney, of this city, married Miss Belle Watson, a former resident of Battle Creek, and Lloyd O., who is acting as his father's bookkeeper. He married Miss Mary Courter, of Grand Rapids, a daughter of Professor Courter, an artist. They have one son, Maxwell Lloyd. They occupy a fine home at 52 Van Buren street, which was erected by Mr. Knight in 1876. Both he and his wife are prominent and active members of the Baptist church, and were formerly well-known workers in the Sunday-school. He belongs to Battle Creek lodge, No. 12, F. and A. M., also the Ancient Order of United Workmen and was one of the original members of the first Grand Army post of Battle Creek, while his membership is now with Farragut post. He has earned for himself the reputation of being a careful man of business, and in his dealings is known for his prompt and honorable methods, which have won him the deserved and unbounded confidence of his fellowmen. As a representative of manufacturing interests, as a veteran of the Civil war, as a pioneer settler of the county and as an upright Christian gentleman, he well deserves mention in this volume.

ALONZO NOBLE.

Alonzo Noble was so closely associated with the pioneer development and with the business interests of Battle Creek that his life history forms an integral chapter in its annals, which, if omitted, would leave an incomplete record of the city. He established the second store in the struggling little hamlet, took account of existing conditions and adapted his interests to meet the requirements of the period and yet he was ever alert to the possibilities of the great west and put forth tangible effort for the upbuilding and progress of his adopted state with the result that his labors were most effective in promoting the growth and improvement in Battle Creek and Calhoun county. He was, moreover, a man whom to know was to honor and respect for in all life's relations he was true to upright principles and from his fellow townsmen he received the esteem and friendship which is everywhere accorded genuine worth.

Alonzo Noble was born in Richmond, Chittendon county, Vermont, June 3, 1809, and was a son of Enoch Noble, whose birth occurred in Westfield, Massachusetts on the 5th of March, 1773, two years prior to the beginning of the Revolutionary war and three years before the Declaration of Independence was written. Enoch Noble was reared to manhood in the place of his nativitiy and was there married to Miss Caroline Matilda Smith, who was born in the Old Bay state July 17, 1771. Soon after his marriage he removed to Richmond, Vermont, where he followed the blacksmith's trade and it was in that town that Alonzo Noble was reared to manhood. He acquired a good practical education and as a boy entered a store in capacity of a clerk.

ALONZO NOBLE

MRS. ALONZO NOBLE

a boy entered a store in capacity of a clerk. His fidelity and capabilities won ready recognition and from time to time he was promoted, finding in each transitional stage of his career opportunity for further advancement and the acquirement of broader knowledge concerning business methods. When his industry and economy had brought to him sufficient capital he engaged in business for himself at Milton, Vermont, there remaining until 1836, when he disposed of his store in that place in order to enjoy the opportunities of the great and growing west. Making his way to Michigan he settled at Battle Creek and established a store at the corner of Jefferson avenue and Main street, bringing to the hamlet its second stock of dry goods, a Mr. Coleman having opened a store a few months before. Mr. Noble built a small building in which was placed the first brick chimney in Battle Creek. It was a two story structure and the second floor was used by him and his wife as a residence. They occupied it for twelve years, at the end of which time Mr. Noble, having in the interim gained a very desirable measure of prosperity, erected one of the most modern as well as beautiful residences of the city. In the year 1850 the frame building in which he had begun business was replaced by a substantial three story brick block, which is still standing and is known as the Noble block. He occupied this with a large and well selected line of dry-goods and for many years was proprietor of the leading mercantile establishment of Battle Creek. He made a business record such as any man might be proud to possess for he never incurred an obligation that he did not fulfill or make an engagement that he did not meet. In all of his dealings he was strictly

17

honorable and just and to his business integrity, his unflagging enterprise and unfaltering industry was attributable in large measure the success which crowned his efforts. The passing years brought him a competence that enabled him at a later date to put aside all business cares and live retired in the enjoyment of the comforts of life.

Ere leaving the east Mr. Noble was married on the 1st of October, 1833, to Miss Rhoda Murray, the wedding ceremony being performed at Williston, Vermont, by the Rev. William Arthur, whose son was the late President Arthur. Mrs. Noble was born June 11, 1812, and was a daughter of Calvin and Rhoda (Allen) Murray. Her father was a farmer and died in early manhood in the Green Mountain state. Unto Mr. and Mrs. Noble was born a daughter, Helen E., who became the wife of Dr. A. T. Metcalf, who is mentioned elsewhere in this volume. Both Mr. and Mrs. Noble had a very wide circle of friends in Calhoun county and in public affairs he was prominent and influential. Never remiss in citizenship he gave active and helpful co-operation to many movements which he deemed would prove of benefit to the locality and instituted many measures, which have had direct bearing upon the stable prosperity and upbuilding of the city. During President Buchanan's administration he served as postmaster of the city, having the office in his store. He was also one of the early mayors of Battle Creek and his administration was business-like and progressive. He was elected to that office on the Democratic ticket, for he was a stanch and inflexible adherent of the principles of that party. However, in the discharge of his duties he placed the municipal welfare before partisanship and the substantial improvement of Battle Creek before personal aggrandizement. He regarded a public office as a public trust and made it the aim of his administration to uphold to the best of his ability law and order, to institute reforms and improvements. Socially he was identified with Battle Creek lodge, No. 12, F. and A. M.; Battle Creek chapter, No. 19, R. A. M.; and Battle Creek Commandery, No. 33 K. T. He took a most active interest in the work of the craft, was a charter member of the lodge and of the chapter and in his life exemplified the beneficent teachings of the order, which has for its basic elements mutual kindness, charity and brotherly helpfulness. In his religious views he was a Universalist and had an abiding faith in the ultimate advancement of the race along the lines of intellectual and moral growth. His wife was also a member of the Universalist church, but since her husband's death has become identified with the Episcopal church. It was on the 27th of March, 1874, that Mr. Noble passed away. His residence in the city had covered almost four decades and during that period he witnessed a wonderful transformation in Battle Creek, but no one in all that time manifested a more public spirited interest in the welfare of the city or took a more active and effective part in its upbuilding. In his business career he advanced from humble suroundings to financial successes through the opportunity which is the pride of our American life and in his career the expression "The dignity of labor" found exemplification. He wrought along the lines of greatest good both for himself, his fellow men and his adopted state, and his name should be inscribed upon the keystone of the pioneer arch of Calhoun county.

WILLIAM DOWSETT.

Among the sons of England who are living in Battle Creek is William Dowsett, for many years proprietor of the Iron yards at No. 44 West Jackson street, but now retired from active business. He was born in Hastings, England, March 28, 1845, a son of James and Mary (Buffard) Dowsett. The mother died when he was but six weeks old and the father afterward married again. He was the youngest of nine children and remained at home until ten years of age, when, not agreeing with his step-mother, he ran away to go to sea and shipped as an apprentice on the passenger packet, American Congress. He served for three years on that vessel, which made trips from London to New York, requiring two and sometimes three months to make the entire journey. The vessel carried as many as nine hundred passengers and was a sailing craft or clipper. Mr. Dowsett had many narrow escapes in several severe storms and at times the people were limited to only one quart of water per day for all purposes, because the delay reduced the amount of supplies. At the end of his apprenticeship he could have been appointed fourth mate, but the Civil war in the United States was in progress and he enlisted in the United States navy as an able seaman, probably the youngest able seaman of the service.

Mr. Dowsett went on board the receiving ship North Carolina, and after three weeks was transferred to the Harriet Lane, a revenue cutter that had been transformed into a gunboat. The vessel proceeded from Brooklyn to Philadelphia, taking on the rest of the crew there and then joining the Western Gulf Squadron to assist in the blockade of the coast of Texas. After three months they went to Galveston on official business under a flag of truce, but were ordered to leave within ten minutes, which they did. However, they ran aground on the way out and remained there until midnight, when they were captured by three cottonboats after a bloody hand to hand fight, in which Mr. Dowsett used a cutlass to good effect. As a prisoner of war he was sent to Galveston, where he was held for three months. His commander, Captain Waynewright, and thirty-eight others were killed on that occasion. Mr. Dowsett was paroled and sent to New York, where he went on board the receiving ship and was then granted a furlough, which he spent with an uncle in Albany, New York. After a month he was exchanged and reported to the receiving ship, on which he remained for about two weeks, when he was transferred to the gunboat Kittitina in the Brooklyn navy yard and again sent to blockade the coast of Texas. Afterward the vessel proceeded to Port Royal, having in the meantime captured two blockade runners, on which Mr. Dowsett later received one hundred and fifty dollars prize money. At Port Royal he was transferred to the sloop of war Hartford, which was Admiral Farragut's flagship, and going to New Orleans participated in the capture of that city. Two months were spent in the Crescent city and he was then transferred to the sloop of war Juniata, following which he participated in the fight at Fort Fisher. There he went on shore with a party and attacked a ferry. While in that fight he was shot in the right ankle by a minnie ball, which grazed the bone, causing a wound that will never be healed. For a short time he was incapacitated for duty, but soon again assisted in blockading the coast of Texas, there remaining until the close of the war,

when he was transferred to the sloop Resaca and went to New York. Again he spent his furlough with his uncle in Albany, and at the end of two weeks again reported for duty and was sent to Panama, being stationed there three months. He became ill with yellow fever, and ninety-eight men on that ship died of the disease in seventeen days. Mr. Dowsett and his fellow members of the command were then relieved by another ship and went to San Francisco, under quarantine. After somewhat recovering they were sent to Sitka under orders that the cold might kill the yellow fever germs, and also to take possession of Alaska. The first man they saw there on landing was an Irishman, and the lieutenant put forth the querry: "Where can you go that you will not find an Irishman?" Pat quickly responded: "Sure, Sir, you can go to hell and you will not find one there."

Mr. Dowsett remained in Alaska for nearly four months and then sailed on the ship which transported to San Francisco the Russian Prince and Princess, which had been in charge there. He received an honorable discharge at San Francisco and went to Sacramento, then a small town. He spent a few days in the mines there, but lost his money through card games. He then determined that he would never again gamble and has closely adhered to this resolution. As he had no money to pay for transportation he walked back to San Francisco and there sailed on the Monarch, a packet bound for London. He next made his way to New York and on to Buffalo, where he became a seaman on the Great Lakes, sailing from Buffalo to Chicago and other points.

In Buffalo, in 1868, Mr. Dowsett became acquainted with Miss Elizabeth Irons, a native of Scotland and a daughter of

Charles and Belle (Stewart) Irons. She was about three years old when brought by her parents to America, and in 1871 she removed to Grand Rapids, where on the 3d of May, of that year, she gave her hand in marriage to Mr. Dowsett. He then left the lake service and began to work for her uncle, Robert Stewart, in a tannery, but the panic of 1872 closed that business and, disposing of his interests in Grand Rapids, Mr. Dowsett removed to Albany, New York, where he began working on the state capital as derrick rigger. Soon he was made manager of the rigging department and occupied the position of foreman for fourteen years, having under his supervision from one hundred to one hundred and seventy-five men. During that time he found it possible to accumulate some money. In July, 1884, he came to Battle Creek, intending to go into the oil business, but instead became connected with iron manufacturing, being for one year on Jefferson street. He then removed to his recent place of business at No. 44 West Jackson street, where he continued in business until the fall of 1903, when he sold out. As his financial resources have increased he has invested in real estate, owning property in Battle Creek, in addition to his home.

Unto Mr. and Mrs. Dowsett have been born six children: William James, born in Grand Rapids and now a plumber, of Marshall, Michigan, wedded May Reed and has one child, Dorothy; Frederick Robert, born in Albany, New York, married Josie Martin, by whom he has a son, Robert. They reside in Battle Creek, where he is employed as draughtsman for the Steam Pump Company; George Charles, born in Albany, and now a pressman with the Duplex Printing Company, wedded Mollie Powers, and has one son, William George; Elizabeth Mary, a graduate of the high school, is at home; Edward John, is a plumber of Marshall; Isaiah Alexander, born in Albany, is a student in the high school. Since voting for Lincoln Mr. Dowsett has been a Republican, but not an office seeker. For eighteen years he has been connected with the Ancient Ordr of United Workmen and is a prominent member of Farragut post, No. 32, Grand Army of the Republic, in which he has held the various offices except that of chaplain. He attends nearly all of the Grand Army reunions, and has been connected with the soldiers' relief committee and spends from four to five hundred dollars annually for the relief of soldiers and their widows. Mrs. Dowsett is a member of the Farragut Relief Corps, No. 32, and at present its president. Few men start out in life at an earlier age than did Mr. Dowsett, for since a youth of ten years he has been dependent upon his own exertions, meeting many hardships and difficulties in life, yet overcoming these by persistent purpose and untiring energy. All that he has has come through his own labors and he might well be termed a self-made man.

WILLIAM ROY ALVORD, D. D. S.

A well appointed suite of rooms constitutes the office and the workshop of Dr. Wiliam R. Alvord, who in his profession has attained an enviable position and gained a very gratifying financial return for his labor. He has lived in Battle Creek since 1882 and was born in Clinton, Michigan, in 1871, his father being Dr. A. W. Alvord. His early education was acquired in the schools of his native city and later he continued his studies in Battle Creek. He next entered Olivet College, at Olivet, Michigan, where he pursued a regular three years' literary course. By broad general information the doctor was thus well fitted for life's practical and responsible duties. When his collegiate work was over he began learning the machinist's trade in the shops of the Duplex Printing Press Company, of which his father was one of the officers. He served the regular apprenticeship, working at that trade as a machinist until 1896, in which year he again entered Olivet College, where he spent three years, pursuing special work preparatory to entering upon his professional studies. It was necessary that he make his own way through college, so he spent another year as a machinist in the service of the Advance Thresher Company, of Battle Creek. He then entered the dental department of the University of Michigan, where he pursued a full course of three years, finishing with the class of 1902. He then located in Battle Creek for the practice of his profession, opening an office in the Post building, where he has since secured a good patronage, gaining an enviable reputation, not only with the members of the dental fraternity, but also with the public at large. There are three elements essential to success in the practice of dentistry. First, an accurate and comprehensive knowledge of the science; second, good business ability in order that the financial affairs may be capably conducted, and, third, superior mechanical skill. Dr. Alvord's early mechanical experience gave him much knowledge that has been of benefit to him in the latter department of his work. His office is well equipped with the latest appliances for the successful conduct of dental practice, and his patronage is now large and profitable. He is also interested in commercial life in Battle Creek

and became one of the incorporators, and is now the secretary, of the Union Steel Screen Company.

On the 25th of June, 1902, occurred the marriage of Mr. Alvord and Miss Edith Vosburgh, of Battle Creek, a daughter of A. E. Vosburgh. She is a graduate of Olivet College and for four years was a teacher of latin in the schools of Morris, Illinois. They are members of the choir of the First Presbyterian church, having fine musical talent and ability. The doctor took up the study of vocal music in Olivet and by reason of his skill has since occupied good positions in choirs. He assisted himself materially in this way in making his way through college. While in Ann Arbor he sang in the First Baptist church and for two years occupied a position in the choir in the Episcopal church in Battle Creek. Mrs. Alvord was educated at Olivet and in Chicago, receiving excellent advantages, and today is recognized as one of the finest contralto soloists of this section. Both hold prominent positions in musical circles, and are members of the Musical Guild, which is an outgrowth of the Derthick club, a musical society of high standing in the city. They likewise belong to the Amateur Musical club, of which he is one of the directors. This club has rendered some of the finest oratorios and cantatas, giving two concerts each season. Their home is at No. 24 Elm street and is the center of a cultured society circle, as well as a favorite resort of lovers of music.

JOSEPH G. STEWART.

Joseph G. Stewart, one of the alert and progressive young business men of Battle Creek, has resided in this city for twenty years, and Michigan is the state of his nativity. He was born in Grand Rapids, October 23, 1872, his parents being Robert and Mary A. (Spires) Stewart. The father was born in the highlands of Scotland, and when a young man sought a home in the new world, locating first in Buffalo, New York, where he followed the tanner's trade. He afterward engaged in the same pursuit in Grand Rapids and later came to Battle Creek, where he died May 13, 1902. His wife, a native of Canada, is still living.

Joseph G. Stewart, the eldest son, and third child in a family of four children, acquired the greater part of his education in the public schools of Battle Creek, and later became connected in business with his father, then a leather merchant of this city. From his childhood days he has been more or less familiar with the business, and on attaining his majority was admitted to a partnership, under the firm style of R. Stewart & Son. The firm name has since been retained, with Mr. Stewart of this review as a general manager. He has dealt in leather longer than any other merchant in the same line in the city, and he now handles hides, belting and fertilizers, as well. The firm has offices and warehouses at No. 20 Hamblin avenue. The business had been conducted for twelve years, with growing success, at No. 53 South Jefferson street, but in September, 1903, they moved to their present location. A fact worthy of note in the career of Joseph G. Stewart is that he has never drawn one cent of wages as an employee except for service in connection with the United States government. All the other money which he has earned has been secured as a partner in a business, which, through his enterprise and good management, has now reached exten-

sive and profitable proportions. The firm owns its own building and also residence property in the city.

In 1895 Mr. Stewart became a member of the Michigan National Guard, joining Company D, of the Thirty-second Regiment, and on the breaking out of the war with Spain he enlisted as a member of what became Company D, Thirty-second Regiment of Michigan Volunteers. With his comrades he went to Tampa and to Fernandina, Florida, where the regiment was stationed until hostilities had ceased. He was then honorably discharged and returned to his home and is now a member of C. W. Post Encampment, of the Spanish-American War Veterans. He likewise belongs to Battle Creek lodge, Knights of Pythias, and has attained the Uniform Rank in that order.

NOXON S. IRELAND.

While industry and capable management of business affairs in former years has brought to him sufficient capital to put aside further work, and while nominally living retired, Noxon S. Ireland has always been too busy a man to feel at ease without business interests of some kind to occupy his attention. Indolence and idleness are utterly foreign to his nature and he still continues to engage in the purchase and sale of farm lands, although he has to some extent laid aside the more arduous duties of the real estate operator.

Since 1866 Mr. Ireland has made his home in Battle Creek. He was born in Albany county, New York, in October, 1821, a son of Selah and Catherine (Noxon) Ireland. The father was born in Vermont of an old New England family and married Catherine, the daughter of Pascoe Noxon, of the same locality. Prior to that time he had removed to Albany county, New York, where he owned a farm. He spent the remainder of his life there, and, in addition to agricultural- pursuits, he labored in the ministry of the Methodist Episcopal church for twenty-five years prior to his demise, which occurred on the old homestead. There his wife also passed away.

Noxon S. Ireland attended the schools of the day, his father having to pay his tuition. He worked on the farm in the usual manner of lads of that period, remaining at home until twenty-three years of age, when he started out to make his own way in the world. He was first employed on a boat on the Hudson river for three years and at the end of the first year became a mate. On leaving the river he purchased a farm at Londonville, three and a half miles from Albany, where he successfully engaged in gardening until his removal to Battle Creek in 1866. Here he turned his attention to real estate operations, purchasing property in different parts of the city. This business also proved profitable, his keen sagacity enabling him to make purchases that could be followed by advantageous sales. He handled his own property and at different times owned large amounts of city and country realty. He now owns land in other states as well and has a pleasant home at No. 83 Upton avenue, where he has lived for fifteen years. Although now well advanced in years and with an income sufficient to support him, although partially incapacitated for business because of paralysis, he cannot bear to give up his former active life altogether and still deals in farm property through a novel method of which he is the

originator. He has photographs of the farms and buildings taken and thus càn indicate at a glance the nature of the property which he has on sale. Other real estate operators have since employed the same methods. He has sold and exchanged over one hundred farms in Calhoun, Kalamazoo, Barry and Branch counties, besides farms in Kansas and other states, together with much residence property in Battle Creek. He is probably the oldest active real estate dealer of this section, and is certainly entitled to distinction by reason of having sold more farms than all the other real estate dealers of the city combined. His business qualifications were well adapted to this line of business, and his energy, industry and honorable methods insured his success.

Mr. Ireland married Miss Ellen Van O'Linda, who was born in Newtonville, Albany county, New York, in 1829, a daughter of Martin and Anna Van O'Linda, of Holland ancestry. Her father was born in the same locality, and after starting on his business career followed farming. He married Anna Heermans, of the same place. They were members of the Dutch Reformed church. Unto Mr. and Mrs. Ireland were born seven children, five of whom are living: Alice, who is the wife of Dr. William Roe, a dentist, of Union City, Michigan; Anna Catherine, the widow of Mortimer Smith, of Battle Creek; Charles H., of Battle Creek, who has been a member of the fire department for a number of years, and is now assistant chief.; Elias H., of this city, and Bertha, at home. The parents are members of the Methodist Episcopal church. In his political views he was first a Whig and on the dissolution of the party became a Republican and at the time of the Civil war contributed financially to the support of the

Union arms. Few men are so widely known
in the business circles of Battle Creek and
none more honorably so. His treatment of
his fellow men has ever been just and conscientious, and in his dealings he has never
taken advantage of the necessities of others,
and now in the evening of life he can look
back over the past without regret, fully deserving the veneration and respect so freely
accorded him.

WILLIAM KIDNEY.

A prominent citizen, and one who has
served his country in time of need, is William Kidney, who is now located upon his
farm in section 21. Fredonia township. Calhoun county. Michigan. He was born in
London, Canada, September 15, 1843, a son
of James and Jane (Sutton) Kidney. The
father was a native of Cayuga county, New
York, where his father, Nathan, a native of
Holland, had settled in an early day, and
where his death occurred. James Kidney
received a limited education in his youth,
and in 1835 came to Michigan. While a
resident of Calhoun county he married, at
Marshall, Jane Sutton, a native of England,
who had come to America with her parents
when but fourteen years old. In 1839 he located in London, Canada, where he followed
his trade of window-blind maker and also
engaged in farming. Returning to Marshall
in 1844, he was employed by the Michigan
Central Railroad to shift cars with a horse,
afterward purchasing eighty acres of land
in section 21. But five acres of this land was
under cultivation, and it became his life
work to develop and cultivate his property.

He died in this location September 9. 1884,
and his wife followed him November 20,
1890, both attaining the age of seventy-two
years. They are interred in Lyon Lake
cemetery.

William Kidney, our personal subject,
was an infant of eight months when his parents came to Marshall, and in this city and
district schools of Fredonia township he received his education. When ten years old
his father removed to his farm in Fredonia
township, and at the age of eighteen years
young Kidney responded to the call of President Lincoln in the time of the country's
need, enrolling in Company M, Second
Michigan Cavalry, in 1861, as a private under Capt. F. W. Dickey. During the years
that followed he was in many engagements,
serving under Sheridan, Granger and Sherman. often doing special orderly duties.
Among the engagements in which he participated were the following: Island No. 10,
New Madrid, siege of Corinth. Guntown,
Perryville. Stone River and after the battle
of Murfreesboro he was engaged at Chattanooga. Chickamauga. Missionary Ridge,
Lookout Mountain, Franklin and Mossy
Creek, and January 4. 1864, he re-enlisted
as a veteran in the same company and regiment. At Nashville they were fitted out
with new arms, after which they went to
Alabama with Sherman until he left Atlanta,
when they followed Hood back to the Tennessee river, to Florence, Alabama, and
were also in the skirmish at Franklin. After
the battle they retired to Nashville, where
they remained until December 22, when they
joined Hood's forces and followed what was
left of them back to the Tennessee. They
then went to Waterloo, Alabama, where
they remained in camp until March 22, after
which they marched through Alabama and

WILLIAM KIDNEY

MRS. WILLIAM KIDNEY

Georgia to Macon, the honorable discharge of Mr. Kidney occurring in Jackson, Michigan, August 17, 1865, with the rank of corporal. During the entire service he was wounded but once, and that being a mere flesh wound, he was not incapacitated. Whether in the heat of battle, on lonely picket or weary march, he was courageous, faithful and stout hearted, ready at a moment's warning to obey any command, and cheerfully undergoing any hardships or privations for the sake of the flag that he loved, and was ready to follow even to death if need be.

After his discharge from the service, Mr. Kidney returned to Fredonia township, where he remained until 1867, in that year crossing the plains to Nevada, traveling by mule team nine hundred miles, though in returning, in 1869, he traveled by rail. He was engaged while in the west in quartz mining, returning to Fredonia township January 1, 1869, when he resumed his farming operations, along the lines of which his early training had been. He bought property in section 22, and fitted up a home, marrying December 15, 1870, Eliza M. Fox, a native of Danville, Montour county, Pennsylvania, her birth occurring there September 21, 1849. She came to Michigan with her parents, Daniel M. and Eliza (Lichtenwalner) Fox, in 1854. She was the youngest in a family of nine children born to her parents, both of whom are now deceased, the mother dying July 5, 1874, and the father May 30, 1881. To Mr. and Mrs. Kidney were born two children, of whom Alma married Charles H. Katz, of Fredonia township, and they have three children, namely: Carl, Donald and Leone; Anna E. married Clarence Miller, their home being located just across the road from her parents. They have a daughter, Bernice, born November 30, 1903.

In his political convictions Mr. Kidney is an adherent of the principles advocated in the platform of the Republican party. He has always taken an active interest in the political movements of the community and wields a wide influence, being at various times called upon to discharge the duties of official position. He has served as township treasurer for one year and justice of the peace for two years. Fraternally he is a member of St. Albans lodge, No. 20, F. & A. M., of Marshall, and belongs to C. Colgrove post, No. 166, G. A. R. Mr. Kidney has been a very successful farmer, accumulating two hundred and five acres of valuable farming land, well developed and improved, with modern and substantial buildings. Both Mr. Kidney and his wife stand high in the esteem of the community, enjoying to an unusual degree the confidence and respect of their fellow citizens.

FRED H. LYMAN.

Prominent in business circles and popular in social life, Fred Hamblin Lyman, who is a native son of Battle Creek, well deserves representation in this volume. He was born at the corner of West Main and South McCamly streets on the 29th of October, 1866, his parents being Charles E. and Mary A. (Hamblin) Lyman. In the maternal line he is descended from one of the honored early settlers and upbuilders of this city, his grandfather being Alexander Carlyle Hamblin, who was born December 10, 1817, and it is thought was a native of Canada. In early life he lived in the home of Azariah Walton, at Alexander Bay, Jefferson county, New York, and served that gentleman as a salesman in his mercantile establishment until he was admitted to a partnership in the business. He had no capital, but his capability was recognized by his employer. He later married Mr. Walton's daughter, Sarah A., the wedding taking place on the 22d of June, 1843. Mr. Hamblin continued an active partner in the commercial enterprise for a long period and then sold his interest, after which he removed to Chaumont, Jefferson county, where he engaged in general merchandising and also in conducting a lumber yard. He likewise operated a sawmill, thus manufacturing much of the lumber which he sold, and he ran a canal boat, Gage, which was used in the shipping business. On disposing of his mercantile interests he began to deal in stock and grain and prospered along these various lines of his business activity. In 1858 he became a resident of Battle Creek, and from that time until his death was closely allied with its business interests. He first rented a corner in the store of Manchester & Averill and, buying out Mr. Lean engaged in business, but a year later he removed to what is now the Merchants' Bank block and became the owner of a banking business, formerly conducted by Mr. Briggs. Soon he was well known as an important factor in financial circles of the city, and his banking house was of value to Battle Creek, as well as a source of profit to himself. He likewise invested extensively in real estate here, whereby his income was materially increased and he became a wealthy man. In his political views he was a Democrat and for several terms served as alderman of Battle Creek. In all life's relations he was con-

spicuous for his integrity, for his kindliness and helpful spirit, qualities which endeared him to his many friends and gained for him the high regard of all with whom he came in contact.

It was his daughter, Mary A. Hamblin, who became the mother of our subject. She gave her hand in marriage to Charles E. Lyman, one of the enterprising residents of Battle Creek, now engaged in the real estate, loan and insurance business. He was born at Hinsdale, Berkshire county, Massachusetts, on the 21st of November, 1836, a son of Henry D. and Ruth M. (Bartlett) Lyman. In his native village he was reared to manhood and there attended school, while later he pursued an academic course. When about eighteen or nineteen years of age, however, he put aside his text books and soon after came to Michigan, settling first in Kalamazoo, where he remained for about four years, being employed as a clerk in a book store. About 1865 he came to Battle Creek.

A short time after locating here, Charles E. Lyman was married in this city to Miss Mary A. Hamblin, and, on establishing his home in Calhoun county he became teller and cashier in the bank owned by his father-in-law, A. C. Hamblin. For fifteen years he was connected with that banking institution and in 1880 he directed his efforts into other business channels, purchasing the Harbeck Insurance and Real Estate Agency. Since that time he has operated in realty, insurance and in loans, and is today one of the leading representatives in this line of business in Battle Creek. His name is regarded as a reliable one on commercial paper and at all times he has sustained a most enviable reputation by reason of business methods, which neither seek nor require disguise.

His political support has ever been given to the Republican party, and he took an active part in the campaign of 1856, although not old enough to vote at that time. His father had been the original and only Free Soil man in Hinsdale, Massachusetts, advocating that party when such a course practically meant social ostracism. Eventually he induced two more men to become supporters of the Free Soil ticket and about 1858, upon the new Republican ticket, he was elected to represent his district in the Massachusetts Legislature, where he served for one term. He was also a delegate to the constitutional convention of Massachusetts. As before stated, Charles E. Lyman took an active part in the campaign work in 1856, and says that he has never enjoyed political activity so much since. His first presidential vote was cast for Abraham Lincoln in 1860, and he has never faltered in his allegiance to the party, although he has steadily refused to become a candidate for office, having no aspirations in that direction. He has always preferred to give his attention to his business affairs, in which he has met with signal success. In 1878 he was called upon to mourn the loss of his first wife and in 1880 he was again married, his second union being with Miss Frances H. Kellogg, of Ann Arbor, Michigan.

Fred Hamblin Lyman was the only child born unto his parents and he was only about twelve years of age at the time of his mother's death. He acquired his literary education in the public schools of Battle Creek, and when about seventeen years of age he spent one term in Rork's College, at Sherwood, Michigan. The school was then removed to Lansing, Michigan, where Mr. Lyman also spent one term as a student. He afterward pursued a business course and

then returned to Battle Creek, entering his father's office, where he remained until the death of his maternal grandfather, A. C. Hamblin, having inherited from the latter's estate what is known as the Hamblin addition. Mr. Lyman then established a real estate office of his own and during the three years in which he has owned this property he has succeeded in locating eight factories in the district, together with many residences. He possesses marked business enterprise, keen sagacity and sound judgment. He forms his plans readily and is determined in their execution, and his labors have been attended with a very creditable measure of success. He is now a stock holder in the Cero-Fruto Manufacturing Company, the Malt-Too Flake Food Company, the Battle Creek Brewing Company, limited, the Battle Creek Interior Finish Company, limited, and the Honey Comb Chocolate Chip Company, limited. These five enterprises are located in the Hamblin addition and have been established there since the property came into the hands of Mr. Lyman. Three other factories have also been located there, these being the Battle Creek Lumber Company, the Bordeau Flake Food Company and the J. H. Dailey Boiler factory. When the Hamblin addition came into his possession, there had already been located upon it the plants of the Duplex Printing Press Company, the Homer Steel Fence Company, which has since become the American Food Company, and the Hern's Carriage Company. Mr. Lyman is also a stockholder in various other important manufacturing and industrial interests of Battle Creek, which are not located on the addition which he owns. These include the Battle Creek Health Beverage Company, limited, of which he is the treasurer; the Compensating Pipe Organ

Company, the Dr. Peebles's Medical Company, the National Food Company, limited, and Johnson Machine and Foundry Company, limited, and the Battle Creek Whip and Leather Company, which has a secret process whereby the hide can be taken off in one day and in twenty-four hours converted into leather.

In March, 1897, in Battle Creek, Fred H. Lyman was united in marriage to Miss Bertha May Blashfield, of this city. She was born in Yorkville, Kalamazoo county, Michigan, and was there reared to womanhood and educated. They now have an interesting little son, Charles Fred, born on the 31st of July, 1902. Their home is the scene of cultured society circles and the number of their friends in Battle Creek almost equals the number of their acquaintances. Mr. Lyman is a Republican and cast his first presidential ballot for Benjamin Harrison in 1888. He takes an active and helpful interest in party work and has been a delegate to various state conventions for a number of years. Socially he is connected with the Benevolent Protective Order of Elks and is a charter member of Eyrie lodge, No. 299, Fraternal Order of Eagles. While yet a young man Mr. Lyman is destined to occupy as prominent a position in business circles and in the public regard as did his honored grandfather, Alexander C. Hamblin. Although he inherited much of his property, in its control he has displayed marked business ability and unfaltering enterprise, and in the expansion of industrial concerns here he has manifested a quick recognition of the business situations and of the importance arising therefrom. His career has ever been such as to warrant the trust and confidence of the business world, for he has ever conducted all transactions in the strictest principles of honor and integrity.

JOHN HENRY DE SHON.

John Henry DeShon, a respected citizen of Emmett township, Calhoun county, was born February 25, 1865, upon the farm where he now resides, his parents being John Richard and Blira (Markham) DeShon. The family is of French lineage, and the ancestry is traced back to Captain De-Shon, a native of France, who sailed the seas for many years. He eventually settled in Connecticut and in that state Joseph De-Shon, the grandfather of our subject, was born and reared. After attaining manhood, however, he removed to New York, where he engaged in farming until his death, and in his business career he prospered, so that at the time of his demise he was the possessor of considerable valuable property. His son, John Richard DeShon, was born at the family home on the banks of the Hudson river at Hudson, New York, November 17, 1816. The west with its growing opportunities, however, attracted him and in early manhood he came to the state of Michigan, entering land that is now included within the site of Grand Rapids. Later he came to Battle Creek and was numbered among the pioneer merchants of this locality. He met with gratifying success in his mercantile ventures, but after a time again turned his attention to agricultural pursuits, purchasing a valuable farm in Emmett township, where he continued to make his home until 1886. He then once more established his residence in Battle Creek, where his death occurred on the 18th of March, 1887, the interment being made in Oak Hill cemetery. His wife, who was a daughter of John Markham, was born on the 20th of October, 1826, and on the 20th of July, 1845, gave her hand in marriage to John R. DeShon. She died on the

21st of March, 1903, and she, too, was laid to rest in Oak Hill Cemetery. Mr. DeShon was one of the first settlers of Calhoun county, and possessing a progressive, enterprising spirit he put forth effective efforts for the material advancement of the community in which he made his home. His marriage to Miss Markham was blessed with eleven children: Laura Elizabeth, born March 10, 1847, died June 8, 1857; Susan Annette, the second, was born January 30, 1850; Ida Amelia, born August 29, 1851, was married November 3, 1874, to James W. Gordon; Rubie Louisa, was born April 4, 1854; Persis Celeste, was born September 28, 1856; Myrta Calista, was born October 29, 1858; Hortense, born October 21, 1860, died May 12, 1862; Mary Ellen, born February 14, 1863, died April 11, 1865; John Henry is the next of the family; Elbert, born November 24, 1867, died August 26, 1877; Jerome, born June 16, 1869, died on the 18th of November, 1887.

John Henry DeShon in his boyhood days assisted in the labors of the home farm as age and strength permitted and through the winter months attended the district schools and for two years was a student in the public schools of Battle Creek. When he had arrived at adult age he made his home at Battle Creek for about eight years and then, in 1897, removed to his father's farm, which has since come into his possession and which he now utilizes in general farming and stock raising business. The fields are well cultivated and everything about the place is kept in harmony with modern progressive ideas concerning agriculture in its various departments.

Mr. DeShon was married in August, 1894, to Miss Carrie Amelia Baltz, a native of Jefferson county, New York, and a daughter of August Eugenia (Simmonet) Baltz. Three children have been born unto them, namely: John Richard, Helen and August Baltz. In his political views Mr. DeShon is an adherent of the principles of the Democratic party and elected upon its ticket he has served for two years as treasurer of Emmett township.

GOTTLOB SCHWEITZER.

While "the race is not always to the swift nor the battle to the strong," the invariable law of destiny accords to tireless energy, industry and ability a successful career. The truth of this assertion is abundantly verified in the life of Gottlob Schweitzer, who is yet a young man, but is now a partner in a business enterprise which is returning to the owners a good profit.

Mr. Schweitzer was born in Wurtenberg, Germany, on the 3d of June, 1860, and is a son of Jacob and Katherina Schweitzer. Reared under the parental roof, he acquired his education in the public schools of the fatherland in accordance with the laws of that country. He afterward entered upon an apprenticeship to the dyer's trade and completed the term, becoming an excellent workman, with a thorough understanding of the business in every department. In 1882, hoping that he might find better openings for business in this country, he crossed the Atlantic to the new world and from the Atlantic coast at once proceeded into the interior of the country, locating in Toledo, Ohio, where he met and married Miss Rohweder. They began their domestic life in Toledo, where Mr. Schweitzer continued to work at his trade until his removal to Battle Creek in 1892. He is associated with Mr. Marxen in business under the firm style of Marxen & Schweitzer, and they have built up an excellent trade, having now a very gratifying patronage. Both he and his wife hold membership in the Lutheran church, and he is a highly respected man. His life has been a success and his entire career is illustrative of the fact that certain actions are followed by certain results—that industry and perseverence, guided by sound judgment always win prosperity in the land of the free, where labor is not hampered by caste or class.

WILLIAM MARXEN.

Among those who have come from foreign lands to become prominent in business circles in Battle Creek is William Marxen, who for twelve years has resided in this city and is now the senior partner of the firm of Marxen & Schweitzer, who conduct a dying establishment here. His success in all of his undertakings has been so marked that his methods are of interest to the commercial world, and yet he has won his prosperity by strict adherence to the rules which govern industry, economy and unswerving integrity. His enterprise and progressive spirit have made him a typical American in every sense of the word, and he therefore well deserves mention in this work. What he is to-day he has made himself, for he began in the world with nothing but his own energy and willing hands to aid him, and by constant exertion, associated with good judgment, he has raised himself to the creditable position which he now holds.

Mr. Marxen was born in Schleswig, Holstein, Germany, March 14, 1838, a son of Henry R. and Sophia E. Marxen. He was reared and educated in his native land and learned the trade of a dyer, serving a complete apprenticeship of four years. He afterward traveled throughout the fatherland, working in various dying establishments in order to familiarize himself with different methods employed. When the Franco-Prussia war broke out he served in the German army for ten months. He had previously located as a dyer in Schleswig, and there carried on business for nineteen years.

In 1865 Mr. Marxen was united in marriage to Miss Maria Charlotta Koehn, of Schleswig and they resided there until 1883, when he disposed of his business interests in Germany and crossed the Atlantic to America, settling first in Adrian, Michigan, where he remained for two years. Later he worked at his trade in Philadelphia, Pennsylvania, and afterward in Toledo, Ohio, and subsequently came to Battle Creek, arriving here in 1891. He then opened business on his own account, forming a partnership with his son-in-law, Gottlob J. Schweitzer, under the firm style of Marxen & Schweitzer. They opened business at No. 76 South Jefferson street, where they have built up a large trade, both being practical and experienced dyers. They not only take an active part in the work themselves, but also furnish employment to four people and their establishment stands at the head of this line in this city, their patronage being received from the best class of people. They have equipped their plant with steam power and modern machinery and now have all the necessary facilities for carrying on their work in a first class manner.

In 1903 Mr. Marxen built a beautiful modern home at No. 63 Cleveland street, where he now lives with his wife and daughter. Mrs. Marxen has three children, two of whom were born by her first marriage, while the third is a child of her present marriage. Theodore Rohweder, the eldest, is now proprietor of a steam dye works in Findlay, Ohio. Dora is the wife of Mr. Schweitzer and Sophia is still with her parents. Both Mr. and Mrs. Marxen are members of the Lutheran church and are people of sterling worth, having many friends in this community.

WILLIS C. KNEELAND, M. D.

In no country is such scope furnished for individual enterprise as in America, and it is a matter of pride with us that this is so; but while in all lines of life, advancement depends upon personal effort and merit, it is especially true that progress in the learned professions results only from individual accomplishment, and when one has attained success and prominence, therefore, it is indicative of talent and skill. As a representative of the medical profession Dr. Willis C. Kneeland is well and favorably known. He resides in Battle Creek, where he has made his home since 1899. His birth occurred in Amsterdam, Montgomery county, New York, July 10, 1860, his parents being Orville and Jane Ann (Ruff) Kneeland. His father was a farmer who followed his chosen pursuit near Amsterdam, New York, in which locality he was born and reared There he married Miss Jane Ann Ruff, a daughter of Thomas Jefferson Ruff, also an agriculturist. In 1869 Orville Kneeland sold his property in the Empire state and re-

moved to Bedford township, Calhoun county, where he purchased a tract of land and continued in farming for many years. He spent his last days in Battle Creek, living retired, his former labor having brought to him a comfortable competence. His political allegiance was ever given to the Democracy, although he never aspired to political preferment. His wife is a member of the Methodist Episcopal church. Mr. Kneeland's death occurred September 11, 1903, and he is interred in Oak Hill cemetery.

Dr. Kneeland pursued his literary education in the public schools and is an alumnus of the Battle Creek high school of the class of 1881. Subsequently, he engaged in teaching school for about two years and then entered upon the study of medicine in 1882, as a student in the office, and under the direction of Dr. G. A. Robertson, of Battle Creek. He matriculated in the Hahnemann Medical College of Chicago in 1883, and was graduated in that institution with the class of 1885, winning high honors, including the Halsey Brothers' prize.

Dr. Kneeland located for practice in Kalamo, Eaton county, Michigan, where he remained for two years, and then removed to Denver, Colorado, where he continued to make his home until the 1st of January, 1899. While living in the west he was a member of the Arapahoe County Medical Society. Returning to Michigan in 1899, he located in Battle Creek, where he has since established a successful practice, being recognized as one of the able physicians of the city. His reading has been along lines connected with the various methods of local practice and he employs whatever methods or agencies he believes will aid in the restoration of health. He belongs to the

State Medical Society and he is interested in the Hygiene Food Company of Battle Creek.

Dr. Kneeland was married to Miss Florence Edna Stevenson, of Denver, Colorado, a daughter of William and Elizabeth (Field) Stevenson, both of whom are now deceased. This marriage was celebrated on the 15th of January, 1889, and has been blessed with three children, Elizabeth Stevenson, Gilbert Stevenson and Charles Stevenson Kneeland. Dr. Kneeland belongs to the Modern Woodmen of America and to the Knights of the Maccabees and in fraternal circles is esteemed because of his social nature, his unfaltering courtesy and his deference for the opinions of others. In his chosen calling he has won the respect and confidence of the members of the medical fraternity by reason of his skill, and his strict adherence to the ethics of the profession, and that he has the confidence of the public is indicated by the liberal support which is accorded him.

STEPHEN J. RATHBUN.

One of the younger representatives of business interests in Battle Creek is Stephen J. Rathbun, and his capability and energy does not seem to be limited by his years, for he is controlling one of the most extensive industrial interests in this part of the state. He is secretary of the Rathbun & Kraft Lumber Company, limited, of this city, an enterprise, the volume of business of which has reached extensive proportions. He is also recognized as a leader in political

circles; and being a native son of this city, it is with pleasure that we present to our readers the record of his career.

Mr. Rathbun was born in Battle Creek, September 21, 1876, and is a son of Frank M. and Mary (Hughes) Rathbun. In his youth he acquired a good education and after pursuing the tenth grade studies took a course in Krugg's Business College wherein he was graduated. He then accepted a position as bookkeeper for the Advance Thresher Company, with which he was connected for three years. In 1896, when Company D, of the Second Regiment of the Michigan National Guard was organized, he joined its ranks as a private, and in 1898 when the Spanish-American war was inaugurated he went with this company to the south as a member of the Thirty-second Michigan Volunteer Infantry, but the command was in camp at Island Lake where they mobilized and thence proceeded to Tampa, Florida. While there Mr. Rathbun was promoted to the rank of corporal. The regiment was assigned to General Shafter's command, but did not go to Cuba as its transport was disabled. Instead they were ordered to Fernandina, Florida, and thence to Huntsville, Alabama, after which they returned to Island Lake. The deepest regret and dissatisfaction was felt throughout the entire regiment, because they did not have the opportunity to take part in an active warfare. It was in September, 1898, that Mr. Rathbun was discharged.

On returning to Battle Creek Mr. Rathbun became bookkeeper for the firm of Mason, Rathbun & Company and in January, 1899, in connection with Mr. Kraft, his present partner, he purchased the business of his employers and has since en-

STEPHEN J. RATHBUN

gaged extensively in the manufacture of lumber, in fact, their business is greater than that of any other firm in southern Michigan, their output reaching twelve million feet of lumber last year. In the control of this enterprise Mr. Rathbun manifests splendid ability, keen discrimination and marked energy; and shows that he is imbued with the spirit of the times—that of great activity in industrial and commercial circles. On the 12th of September, 1899, in Battle Creek, occurred the marriage of Mr. Rathbun and Miss Julia Henning Frazer, a daughter of Sidney and Mary (Henning) Frazer. Her mother was a daughter of David Henning who was president of the Battle Creek Gas Company and for some time was known as the "apple king" of Calhoun county." Two children have been born unto our subject and his wife; David Henning, whose birth occurred February 6. 1901 ; and Mary Louise. born on the 8th of September, 1902.

In his political views Mr. Rathbun is a Democrat, prominent in the ranks of his party, his opinions carrying weight in its councils. He has frequently served as a delegate to its conventions, was appointed alderman in the second ward to succeed his partner upon the latter's removal to another portion of the city. Mr. Rathbun was chairman of the board of health while the smallpox was raging here in 1899. and his efforts were of a most practical and valuable character in checking the disease. In the fall of 1902 he was nominated by the Democracy of this district for representation to the legislature, and, though he did not expect election because of the very strong Republican majority in this locality, he made a strong canvass and ran far ahead of the ticket—a fact which indicated his per-

18

sonal popularity, and the confidence and trust reposed in him by his fellow townsmen. He was reared in the Independent Congregational church, but now attends and supports the Episcopal church of which his wife is a member. Socially Mr. Rathbun is very prominent, belonging to Athelstan Club, the Benevolent and Protective Order of Elks, the Knights of Pythias, the Dramatic Order of the Knights of Khorasson, the Knights of the Golden Eagle and the Ancient Order of United Workmen. The true measure of success is determined by what one has accomplished and taken in contradistinction to the old text that "a prophet is not without honor save in his own country," there is particular interest attaching to the career of the subject of this review. since he is a native son of the place where he has passed his active life, and so directed his ability and efforts as to gain recognition as one of the representative citizens of Battle Creek. He stands to-day prominent among the most enterprising and progressive young business men of his native city and one whose influence and efforts in behalf of public good are of no restricted order.

GEORGE B. JENKINS.

George B. Jenkins, a retired merchant of Battle Creek and one of the early settlers of this part of the state, and, in fact, one of the native sons of Calhoun county, was born on a farm in Emmett township, on the 8th of August, 1844, his parents being Lyman G. and Mary (Brower) Jenkins. Both the father and mother were natives of New York and there resided until after their marriage, coming to Michigan in 1836. They took up their abode in Verona, now a part of the city of Battle Creek and the father, who was a millwright and cabinet maker by trade, became interested in the mills of this locality, being actively identified with industrial interests. In 1850 he removed to Waukeshma, Kalamazoo county, where he began the building of a mill, but was taken ill and died there in the year 1851. He left four children, of whom the subject of this review was the second. The others are Lydia, who became the wife of R. W. Howe and died in Verona in January, 1902, leaving two children; Charlotte, who is the wife of Charles Huggett, of Olympia, Washington, by whom she has two children; and Desdelena, who is the wife of Linden Phelps, a resident of Verona, by whom she has two children.

George B. Jenkins was only seven years old at the time of his father's death. He obtained a fair common-school education and lived upon the home farm until eighteen years of age, when he began to learn the cooper's trade. After a few months he was paid by the piece and was able to make good wages. He made his home with his mother and aided her in the support of the family until he was twenty-two years of age, when he was married in Battle Creek, the wedding day being June 2, 1867. The lady of his choice was Miss Frances I. Rogers, of this city, who was born in Huron county, Ohio, a daughter of Dr. Smith and Harriet (Harris) Rogers. Mrs. Jenkins was but a small girl when her people came to Michigan, establishing their home at Waukeshma. There the mother died and the father afterward came to Battle Creek, where he engaged in the practice of his profession, securing a very large patronage which indi-

cated that the public recognized his skill and ability in the line of his chosen calling. Four children have been born unto Mr. and Mrs. Jenkins: Minnie, who is now the wife of Claude Halladay, by whom she has two daughters, Bernice and Norma; Georgia, the wife of Charles H. Dorman, by whom she has two sons, George and Russell; Elma became the wife of Frank Darling, who died leaving two sons, and after his death she married Grant Miller; and Belle, who is the wife of Clayton Spalding.

After his marriage George B. Jenkins established a meat market in Jefferson avenue in Battle Creek and during the greater part of his business career conducted that line of business. He was the first man in this city to combine a meat market and grocery store. Both branches received a liberal patronage and he conducted his trade with signal success through a long period, but eventually he sold out and for eight years resided upon a farm in order that his health might be benefited by the outdoor life. He is now living retired from business cares, making his home at No. 30 Fountain street, east. His political support is given to the Republican party, but he has never been an aspirant for office. Socially he is connected with Battle Creek lodge, No. 12, F. & A. M. In industrial circles he became known, taking stock in the Johnson Foundry and Machine works here and he is now a stockholder in the Mapl-Flake Food Company. Mr. Jenkins may well be termed a self-made man, for everything that he possesses has been acquired through his own efforts as he started out in life empty handed. He has proven the value of industry and perseverance in the active affairs of life and now as the result of his own labors he has a comfortable competence.

GEORGE E. WILSON.

George E. Wilson, who has served continuously as justice of the peace since 1891 and whose present term will continue until 1906, was born in Highgate, Franklin county, Vermont, on the 24th of November, 1829, a son of George and Catherine (Stinehour) Wilson. The paternal grandfather came from England to America in company with two brothers and established his home in New York. It was in the Empire state that the father of our subject was born and thence he removed to Highgate, Vermont, where he engaged in farming and spent the remainder of his life. His wife was born in Highgate and was a daughter of Henry Stinehour, a representative of one of the old New England families of German ancestry. Mr. Wilson was a member of the Baptist church and was one of the highly respected residents of the community in which he made his home. Unto him and his wife were born two children, the daughter being, Sally Delana, who became the wife of Morency Gardner. Both died in Canada, near Highgate.

The only surviving member of the family is Judge Wilson of this review. He pursued his preliminary education in the schools of Highgate and afterward went to Bakersfield, Vermont, where he became a student in an academy. On putting aside his text books he began preparing for the arduous duties of a business career by learning the blacksmith's trade, at which he served a three years' apprenticeship. He afterward went to Highgate Falls, where he conducted a shop of his own, meeting with fair success in his work.

While there Mr. Wilson was married on the 5th of August, 1853, the lady of his choice being Miss Louisa Lauks, but their married life was of short duration for she died in 1855. Soon after he sold his shop in Highgate Falls and removed to Ausable Forks, New York, where he again established a smithy and again he secured a large patronage, which made his business profitable. There he was married to Miss Helen M. Herns, a daughter of Benajam and Melissa Herns. They became the parents of seven children, of whom three are yet living: Bertha, the wife of Dr. J. B. Cronkrite, of New York city; Charles J., who is now a commercial traveler of Chicago, and Catherine, the wife of Harry R. Pearl, of Battle Creek. The wife and mother died in Battle Creek October 8, 1889, and the Judge has since married Mrs. Elzada Graves, a daughter of Cassius Pearl. She was born in New York city but has been a resident of Calhoun county for many years.

Judge Wilson continued to engage in blacksmithing in Ausable Forks, New York, until 1860, when he removed to Brasher Falls, St. Lawrence county, that state, there remaining until 1864, when he became a resident of Battle Creek. Here he opened a shop on South Jefferson street, where he soon built up a good trade and extended the scope of his business by adding a department for the manufacture of wagons and vehicles. He also sold reapers, mowers and other farm implements, securing a good patronage in the various departments of his business. He purchased property at his first location and continued in business there until 1891, when he sold out, since which time he has not been identified with industrial or commercial pursuits. He has, however, been quite prominent in public affairs and the city finds him a most capable and trustworthy official. In 1879 he was elected to represent the second ward in the city council and in 1882 he was re-elected, serving until 1884. During that time the city began to officially discuss the question of waterworks and of instituting a sewerage system, and Mr. Wilson was appointed to visit other cities to investigate the methods employed in those lines and report thereon. This he did, gaining much valuable information, although the work was not begun until after the expiration of his term. In 1891 he was elected justice of the peace by a large majority and has been continuously re-elected since that time, having always run ahead of his ticket, a fact which indicates his personal popularity. his capability in office and the confidence reposed in him by the voting public. He has a large share of the justice business of the city and has never had a decision, which he rendered, reversed by a higher court,—certainly a most creditable showing.

In politics Judge Wilson has always been an ardent Republican, has been a member of the central and executive committees of his party and has frequently been sent as a delegate to the party convention, but he has never allowed his political preferences to influence his official service in the slightest degree. Fraternally he is a member of Battle Creek lodge, No. 12, F. & A. M., of this city, in which he has filled all the offices with the exception of that of master. He also belongs to Battle Creek chapter, No. 19, R. A. M.; Zabud council, No. 9, R. & S. M.; and Battle Creek commandery, No. 33, K. T. For some years he was the president of the People's Mutual Benefit Society, a local insurance company. He built a pleasant home at No. 403 W. Main street and also has other residence property on the same

street. He has resided in Battle Creek for almost forty years and therefore has a wide acquaintance. which his excellent traits of character have won him the regard of young and old, rich and poor.

HON. FRED H. WEBB.

Among Battle Creek's business men, none are more closely identified with the growth and best interests of the city than Hon. Fred H. Webb, who has made his home there through almost half a century—covering the entire period of his existence—a period within which Battle Creek has attained to her present ·proud position as a commercial and industrial center. For many years he has been known for his sterling qualities, his fearless loyalty to his honest convictions, his sturdy opposition to misrule in municipal affairs and his clear-headedness, discretion and tact as a manager and leader. He is now serving for a second term as mayor of his native city and as chief executive of the city he has not only maintained the high standard of his name but has added to his record new luster.

The endorsement which he received from the best element of the city, regardless of party affiliation, at the last election indicates the high position which he holds in the public regard.

Fred H. Webb was born in Battle Creek, May 10, 1854. son of Caleb and Sarah (Green) Webb, who were natives of Oxfordshire, England, where they were reared and married. In June, 1853, they arrived in the United States and at once came to Battle

Creek, where the father served for many years as sexton of Oak Hill cemetery, making his home in this city throughout his remaining days.

The eldest of a family of seven children, Fred H. Webb spent his boyhood and youth under the parental roof and pursued his education in the grammar schools and high school of the city until 1870, when he entered upon his business career as a farm hand, being employed in that way for about two years. In October, 1872, he entered the employ of Nichols & Shepard, with which firm he has since been connected, being now one of their oldest representatives. His fidelity to duty won him promotion and the most pleasant relations have ever existed between Mr. Webb and the firm. He first entered the shops, serving in the wood working department until 1887, when he was promoted to time-keeper, and in April, 1888, he was made paymaster. He has since acted in that responsible position and has charge of the payment of the five hundred and seventy-five employees now connected with the operation of the extensive plant. Unqualified and well merited confidence is reposed in him, and his devotion to the interests of the house is proverbial.

Early in his business career he sought a companion and helpmate for the journey of life and on the 3rd of June, 1874, he wedded Miss Carola V. Babcock, of Battle Creek. In 1899 he built a fine home at No 98 Green street, where he is surrounded by all the comforts he has ably earned. He had previously erected a four-flat building. which he occupied until he took up his abode in his present attractive residence. His social relations connect him with Battle Creek lodge, No. 35, K. of P., of which he is past chancellor and he has also three times

represented the local lodge in the Grand lodge of the state. He is likewise connected with the Uniformed Rank of the order. He is a charter member of Calhoun tent, No. 54, Knights of the Modern Maccabees, is one of its past commanders and belongs to the Ancient Order of United Workmen.

In politics Mr. Webb has always been a stanch Republican and has taken an active part in the councils of the party. For thirty-one years he has been a member of the fire department of the city, joining the organization in October, 1872, when it was a volunteer department. He joined Tempest Hand Engine Company, No. 2, and attended the National Firemen's Tournament, in Chicago, in 1875. On the 8th of March, 1880. he formed a new hook and ladder company of thirty members. known as the Goguac Hook & Ladder Company, which remained as a volunteer company until October, 1881, when the membership was cut down to fifteen and it became a paid company. Mr. Webb remained with it for thirteen years more, acting as its secretary and treasurer most of the time. On February 5. 1894. he was elected assistant chief, in which capacity he served until 1904, at which time he was re-elected and then resigned. He has witnessed great changes in the fire department of the city and has kept pace with these. His record as a fireman is unparalled in Battle Creek and perhaps in the state. He has worked at every important fire in the city through the last three decades with one exception and has had many narrow escapes, but has never been seriously injured though often in places of the greatest danger. Cool and calm in the face of danger, with a mind alert, comprehending a situation almost instantly, he most capably directs the labor of those who work under him and Battle Creek owes to him a debt of gratitude for what he has done during his long connection with the department.

In April, 1893, Mr. Webb was elected alderman from the fifth ward and during that year the No. 1 fire station was erected. He was re-elected in 1895, and again, after an interval of two years, in 1899. In 1896 fire station No. 2 was built and station No. 3 was erected after he became mayor. In 1901 he was again chosen alderman for a term of two years, and in 1902 was elected mayor and then resigned the office of alderman after eight years' service in the city council—a longer period than that of any other incumbent. During his first term as mayor he stood firmly for a strong and clean business administration and for the enforcement of existing laws. In this way he offended certain elements in the city and a determined effort on their part was made to prevent his re-election, but the better element rallied to his support. His course for law, order and justice was vindicated by his re-nomination and re-election in 1903. While his name was on the Republican ticket, people of all political faiths supported him, his vote coming from the best citizens of Battle Creek, and he won the election by a brilliant majority of seven hundred, the largest vote ever cast in the city election being polled that year. In consequence of his prominence in political, fire and business circles, he has a wide acquaintance and a host of warm friends, whose high and sincere regard, recognizing his genuine worth, he fully possesses. While safely conservative, he yet holds many advanced ideas on questions of governmental policy. The soldier on the battle field has displayed no greater loyalty than has Mr.

Webb in his support of American institutions and his condemnation of political intrigue, practiced by whom it may be. There is no doubt that, had he entered into the methods practiced by many politicians he could have obtained almost any office he might have desired, but with him principle is above party, and purity in municipal affairs above personal interest.

THEODORE WAKELEE.

Theodore Wakelee was for many years a prominent resident of Battle Creek, favorably known in business and political circles and popular with a large circle of friends. He was born at Lancaster, near Buffalo, New York, August 28, 1828. His father, Clement Wakelee was, during his early manhood, a pioneer farmer of western New York. The son was reared and educated at Lancaster and remained with his father upon the home farm until he had reached adult age. He then determined to identify his interests with those of the growing west and in 1849 came to Battle Creek. It was then but a little village. For three years or until 1852 he was employed by his brother, Clement Wakelee, as a clerk, the brother owning a dry goods store. In 1852 Theodore Wakelee decided to try his fortune in California, attracted by the discovery of gold in that state. He went by way of the Isthmus of Panama, and on reaching the Pacific coast made his way direct to the mines in the vicinity of Oakland, California. There he remained for three and a half years and was quite successful in his work, obtaining a sufficient amount of gold to enable him to start in business for himself upon his return to Battle Creek. This he did on the 5th of November, 1855, opening a grocery store in company with a Mr. Burrill under the firm name of Burrill & Wakelee at the corner of Jefferson and Main streets. They owned their two store buildings there and as their patronage increased they enlarged their store, carrying on the most extensive grocery business of that day. Mr. Wakelee was a very popular and pleasing man and his genial manner, kindly disposition and obliging ways were instrumental in securing him a large business. In 1866 heavy losses overtook the firm, occasioned by a disastrous fire. The partnership was then dissolved and Mr. Wakelee afterward engaged in business for himself, purchasing the building which stood on the site now occupied by Fisher's store. There he conducted business for ten years and again he prospered, gaining a very desirable competence.

In political circles Mr. Wakelee was equally prominent and influential and was widely recognized as one of the strong Republicans of the city. He had firm faith in the principles of the party and did everything in his power to promote its growth and insure its success. At one time he served as alderman from the second ward.

On the 26th of July, 1855, Theodore Wakelee wedded Adeline Pray, a daughter of William and Adeline (Austin) Pray. Her father was born in Niagara county, New York, and was married there to Miss Austin of the same county. He was a farmer by occupation and on removing from the east he located at Ann Arbor, Michigan, where he spent two years. It was during his residence here that his wife's death occurred. He afterward removed to Climax, Kalamazoo county, Michigan, in 1837. In that locality he became extensively engaged in agricultural pursuits. His death occurred in Cass county. Mrs. Wakelee was but a small child at the time of her parents removal to Michigan and in this state she was educated. She has no children of her own, but has reared her nephew, James T. Watts, and also a niece, Emma Watts, who died in 1876. She has a beautiful home at No. 76 Main street west, which she erected in 1859 and which has since been her place of residence. Both Mr. and Mrs. Wakelee attended and supported church, but were not members. They occupied a high position in public regard and Mrs. Wakelee now has many warm friends in Battle Creek, where she has long resided.

FRANK P. PITTMAN.

Frank P. Pittman, who is proprietor of a hardware store at No. 36 East Main street in Battle Creek, has spent his entire life in Michigan. He was born in Pontiac, Oakland county, November 3, 1852, a son of Charles and Mary (Starkey) Pittman, the former a clothing merchant of Pontiac. The father was born in England in 1811 and when a young man came to America. In New York city he married Mary Starkey, a native of Philadelphia and they afterward removed to Pontiac. There our subject was reared and educated, attending the public schools until he reached the age of sixteen years, when he entered the Detroit Business College and therein pursued a commercial course. After his graduation he accepted a clerkship in a hardware store in Pontiac and was employed by one firm from 1869 to 1880, his long continuance with the house being a proof of his honesty, close application and capability. Because of failing health he went to New Haven, Connecticut, where he entered a hardware store, spending three years in the east. In 1883 he came to Battle Creek and entered into partnership with a Mr. Flower in the store in which Mr. Pittman now carries on business. In 1891 our subject purchased his partner's interest and has since been alone. He has increased the stock and his business has continually grown, amounting to a large figure in 1903.

On the 17th of March, 1880, Mr. Pittman was married in Pontiac, Michigan, to Miss Myra Satterlee, a daughter of George and Jane O. (Flower) Satterlee. They now have three children: Bessie, who was born in New Haven, Connecticut, and is a graduate of the high school of Battle Creek; and Gertrude and Clayton, born in this city. The latter is now pursuing a commercial course. Mr. and Mrs. Pittman are well known in this city and enjoy the hospitality of many homes here. In politics he has always been a Democrat. His father was a Democrat in political faith and named him Franklin Pierce because his birth occurred on the day in which Pierce was elected to the presidency. While in New Haven Mr. Pittman became a member of the Masonic fraternity and has since demitted to Battle Creek lodge, No. 12, F. and A. M. His career has been that of a business man who is active in the control of his mercantile interests and faithful in the discharge of his duties of citizenship.

HON. ABRAHAM T. METCALF, D. D. S.

Dr. Abraham Tolles Metcalf, although born in the Empire state, has been a citizen of Michigan from his youth down to the present time and although the consecutive years of his residence in Battle Creek date only from 1890, he came to the city as early as 1848 and such has been his prominence in his profession and in Masonic circles that he has been known by reputation if not personally to a large majority of the residents of this city for a long period. For fourteen years, however, he has resided continuously here and his personal efforts and his championship of many public measures have resulted to the city's benefit and upbuilding. He has been honored by the highest official preferment within the gift of his fellow townsmen and is regarded by many of the leading men of both the Republican and Democratic parties as one of the best mayors Battle Creek ever had.

Dr. Metcalf is a native of Whitestown, New York, and is a representative of a family that has been conspicuous in New England history from an early period in the seventeenth century. His ancestors were English dissenters who sought a home and religious liberty in the new world. Dr. Metcalf was born February 26, 1831, and his early education was acquired in an academy in his native town. Upon putting aside his text books he entered upon an apprenticeship as a worker in sheet metal. He became identified with the great west in 1848, when with his father's family he came to Battle Creek. He, however, remained for only a few months and then returned to New York in order that he might take up the study of dentistry in Utica. After careful preparation for the profession he began practice and

ABRAHAM T. METCALF, D. D. S.

MRS. ABRAHAM T. METCALF

in his chosen calling attained prominence and prestige, which are only accorded in recognition of superior skill and merit. He continued in the east until 1854, when he visited his father in Battle Creek and at the solicitation of Governor Ransom, who desired his professional council, he went to Kalamazoo, Michigan, and yielding to the entreaty of many prominent citizens there he took up his abode in that city in February, 1855. His patronage almost immediately reached extensive as well as profitable proportions, but close application to business and the hardships of the climate proved detrimental to his health and he was obliged to seek rest and recuperation. Accordingly in 1857 he went south to New Orleans, where he rapidly recovered and then formed a partnership with Dr. A. P. Dostie, a dentist of that city. After General Butler entered the city, Dr. Dostie was made collector of the port. He was afterwards made a member of the constitutional convention, and for his acts in that body was shot down and killed in the streets of the city. Dr. Metcalf spent the summer months in Kalamazoo, but the winter seasons were passed in the south, where he continued in the practice of his profession until the outbreak of the Civil war.

Dr. Metcalf was a close and earnest student of the great problems which aroused the interest of the country prior to the inauguration of hostilities. His sympathy was with the Union cause and he hesitated not to express his ideas upon the question. In the spring of 1861, soon after Louisiana had passed the ordinance of secession, the Doctor was imprisoned for treason against the state, the first arrest made upon this charge in New Orleans. The affidavit solemnly stated that the good doctor had "uttered seditious language against the government, saying that, if he were in Lincoln's place, before a single state should be allowed to go out of the Union he would burn the city of Charleston to the ground and drown the city of New Orleans with the water of the Mississippi; and other incendiary language." He was released from prison on the authority of the attorney general of the state.

In his professional career Dr. Metcalf attained distinguished honor and successes. He was instrumental in organizing the Michigan State Dental Association in 1855, and was the first secretary of that body, and several times its president and later the historian. He secured from the legislature the first appropriation for the dental department of the University of Michigan, a college that now stands second to no other dental college in the world.

He was also mainly instrumental in securing the passage of the law creating a State Board of Examiners in dentistry, and was the first president of the board and a member of the board for several years.

He invented the dental engine and the first device of this kind ever made he placed on the market. He also invented the dentist's annealing lamp, which was invaluable to the profession previous to the introduction of adhesive gold foil. He was also the first to introduce the preparation for filling teeth known as sponge gold, and with his brother invented the tinman's pattern sheet, which is an indispensible guide to workers in sheet metal. In 1872 the degree of Doctor of Dental Surgery was conferred upon him by the New Orleans Dental College, and thus in the city in which he had once suffered imprisonment because of his loyalty to his honest convictions, he was later honored by a leading collegiate institution. At the time of his removal to Battle Creek, in 1890, he retired from the active practice of his profession and has since given his attention to real estate interests and to the management of several valuable estates, his time being thus fully occupied. He has done considerable building here and has thus contributed in large measure to the improvement and material development of Battle Creek. A man of excellent business ability, he manifested in his dental career and since becoming connected with real estate interests marked enterprise, keen foresight and a recognition of possibilities which have been the foundation of a most successful career.

On the 25th of June, 1857, Dr. Metcalf was united in marriage to Miss Helen E. Noble, a daughter of Hon. Alonzo Noble, one of the prominent pioneer settlers of Battle Creek. She was born in Milton township, Vermont, March 27, 1834, and was brought by her parents to this city in 1836. Here she acquired her early education, which was supplemented by a course of study in the Ladies' Seminary at Rochester, New York. Following her father's death she and her husband came to Battle Creek to care for her mother. They had but one child, Alonzo T. Metcalf, who was a very bright boy, but died suddenly of rheumatic fever when but fourteen years of age. Mrs. Metcalf, because of her recognized culture and innate refinement, her tact and kindly spirit, became a leader in social and church circles in Battle Creek. She was very prominent in the society of St. Thomas's Episcopal church and one of the most valued members of that organization. Her life was largely made up of generous deeds, and it was noticeable that she rarely, if ever, spoke ill of others, always putting a most charitable construction on the motives of those with whom she was associated. She was conspicuous in the fidelity with which she discharged the whole round of her social and domestic duties, and while she won the warm friendship of those whom she met in society circles, she also gained the deep gratitude and love of many whom she befriended. Her death occurred in Los Angeles, California, on the 26th of February, 1898, and her remains were brought back to Battle Creek for burial. As a tribute to her worth and beautiful womanly character the various municipal offices of the city were closed on the day of her funeral from two until five o'clock. Her life might well be likened to a flower that unconsciously shed its perfume abroad and brings a cheering influence through its beauty and fragrance.

Dr. Metcalf is also a member of St. Thomas's Episcopal church. For years he was a vestryman of St. John's church, of Kalamazoo, and after his removal to Battle Creek continued to serve as vestryman here and is now the only warden of the St. Thomas church, the senior warden having been recently removed by death. In Masonic circle he is recognized as a leader throughout Michigan. He was made a Master Mason November 26, 1856, in Kalamazoo lodge, No. 22, F. & A. M., and quickly advanced in the organization until in 1861 he was made worshipful master. He was re-elected in 1862, 1863 and again in 1869 and in 1887 he was demitted with others from Kalamazoo lodge for the purpose of reviving Anchor lodge, of Strict Observance, No. 87, and in February, 1888, he was made the first worshipful master under the restored charter. Soon after his removal to Battle Creek a new lodge was formed and named in his honor, A. T. Metcalf lodge, No. 419, and of which lodge he became the first worshipful master. He was chosen junior grand warden of the Grand Lodge of Michigan, in January, 1862, was re-elected in 1863, and was elected right worthy senior grand warden in 1864-5. He was elected deputy grand master in 1865, 1867 and 1868, and became grand master of the state in 1869 and re-elected in 1870. He succeeded to this office at a critical period in the history of the Michigan Grand Lodge. The many strong and determined acts which he performed during his first year to correct the loose habits into which some of the lodges of the state had fallen aroused marked antagonism on the one hand and remarkable appreciation on the other, and his position and attitude were sustained by the Grand Lodge in the face of all efforts to the contrary. In Capitular Masonry he has held several offices, having been elected high priest of Kalamazoo chapter in 1861 and again in 1868. His identification with chivalric Masonry began in 1860, when he was made a Knight Templar in Peninsular Commandery, No. 8, in Kalamazoo. He served as eminent commander in 1868, 1869 and 1882, and in 1892 he was demitted to Battle Creek Commandery, No. 32, K. T., and was elected commander of the latter about the same time. He is an officer of Zabud Council, R. & S. M., of Battle Creek, and he has been an active representative of the Scottish Rite for many years. In 1866 he was elected commander-in-chief of De-Witt Clinton Consistory and was re-elected each succeeding year up to and including 1870. He is now an active member of the Supreme Council of Sovereign Grand Inspectors General for the northern Masonic

jurisdiction of the United States, and for six years was district deputy for Michigan. He has attained an honor accorded few representatives of the craft, that of being a thirty-third degree Mason. He has ever been earnest, zealous and prominent in the Masonic fraternity and has the respect, confidence and friendship of the members of the order throughout the state and abroad.

In political circles Dr. Metcalf has been equally prominent. As a member of the Democratic party he was elected to the board of trustees in Kalamazoo and was chosen president of that village by popular suffrage in 1879, and represented the second district of Kalamazoo county in the State Legislature in 1875-6. After his removal to Battle Creek he was elected mayor of this city in 1897, and many of his friends in both parties consider him one of the best mayors Battle Creek has ever had. His efforts were directed along progressive and practical lines and he ever exercised his official prerogatives to measures which he deemed would prove the greatest good to the greatest number. He made a close and earnest study of conditions existing, of the possibilities for reform and so directed his labors and exerted his influence that tangible results were effected and substantial and desirable improvements made. One of his salient characteristics has ever been his unfaltering support to what he has believed to be right, as indicated by his position when in the midst of enemies at the time of the outbreak of the Civil war. He stands as a high type of our American manhood, known and honored by all, not by reason of conspicuous ancestry or because of financial success, but because of the sterling worth of his own character.

HENRY W. HERNS.

Henry W. Herns, chairman of the Herns Mail Wagon Company, limited, and thus a representative of the industrial interests of Battle Creek, was born in Ausable Forks, Clinton county, New York, September 28, 1845, a son of Benajah and Malissa (Lyon) Herns. The father, a farmer, by occupation, removed to St. Lawrence county, New York, and there leaving his family proceeded to the mines of California, making the journey in 1860 and dying there about 1864. A short time prior to his death the mother and three of their eleven children came to Battle Creek, and since that time Mr. Herns of this review has lived in the city which he has seen develop from a town of five thousand to a city of thirty thousand inhabitants. He acquired a common school education and was nineteen years of age when he arrived in Battle Creek. Here he soon began to learn the blacksmith's trade and from the beginning earned one dollar a day. After completing his apprenticeship he served as a journeyman for a year and then engaged in business on his own account on West Main street, while later he built a shop on West Jackson street. After seven years there spent, he sold his smithy and became engaged in the grocery business, but found that a losing venture. He next organized the Battle Creek Buggy Company, but sold out after two months and in 1887 built his present shop. He then carried on blacksmithing until 1898, when he began the manufacture of mail wagons and in 1901 organized a company with a capital stock of fifty thousand dollars, known as the Herns Mail Wagon Company, limited. The business growing rapidly the stock was soon increased to seventy-five thousand dollars, and to-day, the sale of their mail wagons, adapted to both city and rural carriers, extends throughout the United States. At the time of organization he was elected chairman and also a director and has since remained at the head of the enterprise.

In Battle Creek, on the 25th of November, 1876, Mr. Herns wedded Miss Hattie L. Gaskell, who was born in Niagara county, New York, a daughter of Varney B. and Louise (Lee) Gaskell. Mrs. Herns had come to Battle Creek to attend college and here met the gentleman to whom she gave her hand in marriage. She died in May, 1902, leaving three children: Ethel, who completed the English course and was graduated in the high school; Mabel G., the wife of Edwin Hunt; and Bessie J., the wife of Urbin Moss, of Battle Creek, by whom she has one child, Edwin Alden. Mr. Herns was again married June 1, 1903, to Miss Hester A. Kellogg, a sister of Dr. J. H. Kellogg, of the Sanitarium.

Mr. Herns cast his first presidential vote for General Grant and has since been a stalwart Republican. He served as alderman of the third ward for two years and was chairman of the committee on sanitary affairs and on public grounds and buildings. He also belonged to the water works committee which purchased the Mingus brook and let its waters into the lake. A canal had to be cut to carry the water from the brook to the lake and this was done at a cost of ten thousand dollars. During Mr. Herns connection with the city council, the charter was granted to the Electric Railway Company and considerable trouble was experienced in locating the line of the road. Mr. Herns was reared in the Seventh Day Adventist faith and for twenty-five years has been a chorister of the Tabernacle and other churches in Battle Creek. He has much natural musical talent and taught vocal music for more than thirty terms. He has been employed as chorister in the Adventist, Episcopal and Baptist churches and is a valued representative of the musical interests of the city. He was leader of the choir at the time of the dedication of the first sanitarium and again served at the dedication of the new brick sanitarium which was burned in the fall of 1902. He also organized the first amateur musical club called the Choral Union and was one of the business directors of this club which had an existence covering several years. His deep love for music and his talents in that direction have been one of the strong characteristics of his life and in musical circles of the city he is prominent and popular.

JULIUS S. NEWLAND, M. D.

Dr. Julius Selwin Newland is a physician and surgeon of the Eclectic School practicing in Battle Creek. He was born in Cleveland, Ohio, September 10, 1844, a son of Albert Mann and Martha A. (Williams) Newland. He was but a year and a half old when his parents in 1846 located in Kalamazoo, Michigan, where the father worked at the carpenter's trade for some years. When the son was a youth of nine the family removed to a farm near the village of Plainwell, Allegan county, where the father purchased land and spent about twelve years. At the expiration of that period he took up his abode in Olivet, Michigan, and subsequently purchased a tract of land near that village, whereon he resided until his death in 1897. His wife survived him but a few months.

Dr. Newland obtained a good education, studying at home in the evenings under the direction of his mother, who was a cultured and well educated lady. His opportunities for attending the public schools, however, were limited, but he spent one term at Gull Prairie Seminary when about eighteen years of age. When a youth of sixteen he began teaching and after spending the winter in the seminary he again followed that profession for two winter terms. Desiring, however, to make the practice of medicine his life work, he became a student in the office of Dr. Hawley of Gull Prairie, with whom he remained through the summer, after which he spent two years as a student in Olivet College preparatory to continuing his preparation for the medical profession. His next medical preceptor was Dr. M. B. Beers, of Portland, Michigan, with whom he studied and also began practice, remaining with him for four years.

During that time Dr. Newland was united in marriage to Miss Phebe R. Beers, a daughter of his preceptor, the wedding taking place in July, 1869, but she died a year later, leaving an infant son, Albert Beers Newland, who is now an engineer, living in California.

In 1873 Dr. Newland went to California, practicing in Grass Valley, that state, and later in Carson City, Nevada. Subsequently, he became a practitioner at Los Angeles, California, where he remained until his return to Michigan. He then opened an office in Olivet, where he continued until after the death of his parents or until 1896, when he came to Battle Creek. He lived at first in the western part of the city and then purchased the building in which he now maintains his office and which formerly stood where the Post tavern is now located. It was moved in 1900. In this city he has gained a good practice and the excellent results which have followed his efforts in checking disease and restoring health have gained for him an enviable reputation with the public and in professional circles.

The Doctor has gained hosts of warm friends during his residence in Battle Creek and enjoys the hospitality of many homes here. He has always been a stanch Republican since casting his first presidential vote for Grant in 1868 and he is a valued representative of and loyal adherent to the teachings of the Odd Fellows society. Formerly he was connected with the Masonic fraternity and he belongs to the Knights of the Maccabees and the Knights of Pythias orders.

KARL WILHELM BURBACH.

Karl Wilhelm Burbach, a retired barber of Battle Creek, was born in Gengenbach, County of Zell, now Offenburg, in Baden, Germany, January 17, 1847, a son of Andrew and Monica Burbach. He obtained a good common-school education in the fatherland and at the age of fourteen began to learn the trade of weaving silk ribbons, serving a three years' apprenticeship. He received but fifty cents per week the first year, one dollar the second year and two dollars the third year. He continued to work at his trade, but found that he could make but little in his own country. At the age of twenty years he went into the army and was bugler of the Fourth Infantry of Baden stationed at the Fort of Rathburg. He gave the bugle signal when his regiment made the attack on fort Strassburg and also the bugle call announcing its surrender. He spent six weeks there and was in the service altogether for four years, taking part in many battles. He and an officer carried the news of the surrender of Napoleon at Sedan to Strassburg. Mr. Burbach had many narrow escapes and his clothes were frequently pierced with bullets, but he never sustained a wound nor was he ill during his army experiences. Three medals were awarded him because of his valiant service.

As soon as his time expired Mr. Burbach crossed the Atlantic to America and after nineteen days spent on the ocean steamer landed at New York. He went at once to LaCrosse, Wisconsin, but being unable to secure work there he came to Battle Creek in January, 1872. He had been married on the 2nd of that month in LaCrosse to Miss Theresa Schilling, who was born in Wittenburg, Germany, and she crossed the Atlantic on the same vessel on which her future husband made the voyage. Her parents were Henry and Susanna (King) Schilling.

After locating in Battle Creek Mr. Burbach obtained employment in the soap factory at a salary of one dollar per day. Ten months later he began working for the Michigan Central Railroad Company, driving a team used in hauling wood to load the locomotive, and during two months spent in that way he received one dollar and ten cents per day. As an employe in the threshing machine factory of Brown & Tipton he was given one dollar per day the first year and afterward was paid one dollar and seventy-five cents per day. While in the army he had learned the barber's trade and eventually secured a position in a barber shop at four dollars and fifty cents per week. For four months he worked and supported his wife and child on that amount. After being employed by others for two years he started a shop of his own and from that time on success attended his efforts. For twenty-three years he did business at No. 7 West Main street and enjoyed a very large trade until failing health forced his retirement.

Two children were born unto Mr. and Mrs. Burbach: Otto, born in Battle Creek December 30, 1872, died at the age of nine months; and Kuna, born in this city October 8, 1874, pursued a course in the college at Battle Creek and became a bookkeeper and cashier for Peter Hoffmaster, with whom he remained for five years. He then occupied a responsible position with Nichols & Shepard until he became ill. For the benefit of his health he went to Phoenix, Arizona, and there died April 3, 1902. His widow, who bore the maiden name of Mabel Stewart, is now living in Battle Creek with her father, James Stewart. Kuna Burbach was a member of the Independent Congregational church and a Republican in his political views and was a member of Athelstan club of Battle Creek.

Our subject is also a Republican and is a charter member of the Knights of Pythias lodge and also connected with the Uniform rank. In 1872 he organized the German Band for campaign purposes and

was one of its members for several years. In the improvement of the city he has been active and has taken much pride in what has been accomplished. He was the first man to lay a side walk along Clay street and when he purchased property there the land was all covered with stumps. He now has a very comfortable residence and in addition to this owns three other residences in Battle Creek, which return to him a good rental. Mr. Burbach is certainly a self-made man and though he has met difficulties and obstacles in his path he has overcome these by determined purpose and resolute will, steadily working his way upward and commanding the respect and admiration of his fellow men by reason of his honorable course and unfaltering perseverance.

CHARLES M. SMITH.

Charles M. Smith, who follows general farming and dairying in Battle Creek township, was born in Seneca county, New York, on the 21st of December, 1847. He is a son of Josiah S. Smith, who is represented elsewhere in this work. The public schools of his native state afforded him his early educational privileges and after the removal of the family to Michigan he continued his studies in the public schools of Battle Creek. His entire life has been devoted to agricultural pursuits, for when he attained his majority he determined to make his life work that to which he had been reared and to-day he is the owner of a fine farm of one hundred and twenty acres in Battle Creek township, a mile west of the city limits. His land is well tilled, so that the fields are rich and productive and there are good buildings upon the place. The house is a fine brick residence surrounded by splendid maple and other shade trees, and altogether the farm is a most attractive one in its appearance. The fields yield good harvests and he also keeps high graded cattle for dairy purposes. His enterprise and good business ability are manifested in the fine appearance of his farm and in the success which has attended his efforts since he attained his majority.

Mr. Smith was married December 24, 1874, to Miss Mary A. Coman, a native of Barry county, Michigan, and a daughter of Nelson and Amanda Coman. Mr. and Mrs. Smith attend and support the Baptist church of Battle Creek, of which Mrs. Smith is a member, and are well known in the community where they make their home. Mr. Smith is independent in his political views, casting his ballot for the men whom he thinks best qualified for office, regardless of party affiliations.

AMBROSE M. MINTY.

Ambrose M. Minty is the president of the Merchants' Savings Bank of Battle Creek and also the leading tobacconist of the city. His present high standing in business circles is in marked contrast to his financial condition in his youth. He is a self-made man, who without any extraordinary family or pecuniary advantages at the commencement of

life has battled earnestly and energetically and by indomitable courage and integrity has achieved both character and financial success. By sheer force of will and untiring effort he has worked his way upward and is to-day accounted one of the leading business men of his adopted city.

His life record began in Bath, England, on the 18th of April, 1842, his parents being Ambrose and Mary (Neale) Minty, and for some years the family had lived at Bailbrook Gardens, near Bath, where the father conducted hothouses and greenhouses, furnishing Bath with both vegetables and flowers. In 1852 he came to the new world, making his way direct to Battle Creek, where he remained for a year and a half. He then returned to England and spent his last days at Woodford, a suburb of London.

In the schools of his native country Ambrose M. Minty acquired his early education, and when ten years of age he came to the United States with his uncle, Maurice H. Neale, and Mrs. Michael Neale, who had been to England on a visit. After the return of his parents to England Mr. Minty remained with Mr. and Mrs. Michael Neale, also an aunt and uncle, and continued his education in the Union school in this city. On putting aside his text books he began work on a farm and after several years entered the employ of the firm of Buck & Hoyt, with whom he remained until 1871. In that year he established a cigar business on his own account, entering into partnership with J. F. Jones, under the firm style of Jones & Minty, a relation that was maintained for four years. They started on a small scale, but their business gradually increased and in 1875 Mr. Minty was enabled to purchase his partner's interest. He then removed to East Main street on the bridge.

AMBROSE M. MINTY

From the first he was engaged in the manufacture as well as the sale of cigars and has gradually increased his capacity until his trade, has assumed extensive proportions. He remained in the old building until its collapse on the 30th of May, 1899. Previously he had purchased the land where the Minty block now stands and in 1902 he completed this handsome modern structure, which is a fine brick building on East Main street, extending from Madison to Munroe street. It is sixty-one feet deep and three stories in height and in it he has his salesrooms, while his cigar factory is located in a new block which he has recently erected on Monroe street. This is a three story structure. Mr. Minty personally owns these two fine blocks and obtains therefrom a splendid rental. In what is known as the Minty block is located not only his salesroom on the first floor, but also the central office of the Western Union Telegraph Company, while above are finely equipped suites of rooms used for office purposes. Having built up a large business in the cigar trade, in May, 1902, Mr. Minty organized and incorporated the Minty Cigar Company, limited, which was formed with a capital stock of thirty thousand dollars. Our subject is the chairman of the company, which is engaged in the manufacture of cigars which are sold to the wholesale trade. Employment is furnished to thirty people and Mr. Minty from a small beginning has worked his way upward until he is now at the head of the cigar and tobacco trade in this city. He has also become interested in different business enterprises of Battle Creek and at the present time is president of the Merchants' Savings Bank. He was one of its original stockholders for some years, was a

director, and was vice president for ten years and in January, 1903, was elected to the presidency. This is now one of the strong financial concerns of the city doing a general banking business and having the liberal support of the public. Mr. Minty has also been quite extensively engaged in real estate operations, making judicial investments in property and in addition to his business blocks he owns some good residences here. He also has a fine farm of ninety acres on Goguac prairie, where he spends considerable time as a recreation.

In October, 1876, was celebrated the marriage of Mr. Minty and Miss Isabel Murgettroyd, of Battle Creek. They have one son, Harry M., and their pleasant and attractive home is located at No. 111 Cherry street. Socially Mr. Minty is connected with the Ancient Order of United Workmen and the Athelstan club, and his political support is given to the Republican party. A man of great natural ability, his success in business from the beginning of his residence in Battle Creek has been uniform and rapid, as has been truly remarked. After all that may be done for a man in the way of giving him early opportunities for obtaining the requirements which are sought in the schools and in books, he must essentially formulate and determine and give shape to his own character; and this is what Mr. Minty has done. He has persevered in the pursuit of a persistent purpose and gained the most satisfactory reward. His life is exemplary in all respects. He thoroughly enjoys home life and takes great pleasure in the society of his family and friends. He is always courteous, kindly and affable, and those who know him personally have for him warm regard.

EDWIN S. McMAKIN.

Edwin S. McMakin, one of the leading roofing contractors of Battle Creek, including building paper and roof paints, was born in Scotts, Kalamazoo county, Michigan, May 21, 1866, his parents being Samuel and Sarah (Magee) McMakin. The family is of Scotch ancestry and at an early day the father of our subject located in Kalamazoo county, settling on a farm near Scotts, where he and his wife are still living.

In the public schools near his home Edwin S. McMakin acquired his education and when about eighteen years of age he left home and traveled through the west for nearly two years, working at the carpenter's trade during a portion of that time. Upon his return he carried on farming for five years and later located in the city of Kalamazoo, where he established a roofing business and secured a good patronage. He built up his enterprise until he was enabled to furnish employment to a number of men during the season. On account of the large amount of work in his line in Battle Creek he removed to this city in 1901 and opened an office at No. 105 South Jefferson street, where he also has extensive warehouses. He has since secured a liberal share of the public patronage here, his business having reached proportions that make continuous and heavy demands upon his services. He took the contract for putting the roof on the new addition of the plant of the Advance Thresher Company, including the foundry and large paint shop, also the roof on the Malta-Vita building and on the plant of the Johnson Foundry and Machine Company and the new Michigan Central freight house, together with many other important buildings in the city and surrounding country, including the roofing of the new Olds Automobile factory at Lansing, Michigan, of 132,000 square feet. His business to-day is one of the largest as a roofing contractor in Battle Creek, and his efforts are attended with gratifying prosperity.

Mr. McMakin belongs to the Ancient Order of United Workmen. He is a man of high standing in the community, respected by all. He has never been active in public affairs because of the demands made upon his services in the line of his chosen calling. Few men can gain military or political prominence, because the number of honors to be won therein are limited, but the field of business is limitless and is ever open to the ambitious, determined man, who persevere in his work and conduct it along lines that win uniform confidence and regard. Such a course has Mr. McMakin pursued, and to-day occupies an enviable place in industrial circles in Battle Creek.

ROLDON PIERCE KINGMAN.

Roldon Pierce Kingman, now deceased, was for many years connected with the banking interests of Battle Creek. He belonged to that class of citizens who by upholding the material, intellectual and moral status of a community, accomplished a great deal of good for the city of Battle Creek. His career was ever honorable in business and reliable in all life's relations. He was born at Cummington, Massachusetts, December 19, 1826. The ancestral history can be traced back to Henry Kingman, who was born in Wales in 1592 and emigrated to Weymouth, Massachusetts, in 1632. He died in 1690. John Kingman, his son, had six children, of whom Isaac Kingman was born in 1748 and died in May, 1838. He wedded Mary Packard of Bridgewater, Massachusetts, in 1769, and in the same year removed to Goshen, Massachusetts. Their youngest son, Levi Kingman, was born June 14, 1786, and died February 17, 1877. He was the father of our subject. He married Thedocia, a daughter of Joshua Packard, on the 26th of November, 1817, and the same year removed to Cummington, Massachusetts, where they spent their remaining days. He owned a farm and also owned and conducted the village tavern. He became an Abolitionist when it required great courage to express one's opinions on that subject and his diningroom in the tavern was the meeting place of many of the stanch advocates of freedom. There William Lloyd Garrison, Garrett Smith and other apostles of freedom met and discussed the burning questions of the time. Mr. Kingman voted with the Whig party and was recognized as one of the leading men and revered patriarchs of his community, widely known throughout that locality as Uncle Levi.

In his native town among the Berkshire hills Roldon P. Kingman was reared and spent his early years in gaining the usual common school education, while later he attended the village academy. Entering upon his business career he went upon the road selling notions to the merchants of the little towns in Massachusetts and Vermont. For a number of years he was thus successfully engaged and then went to New York city, where he was employed as a clerk until 1854.

On the 14th of March of that year Mr. Kingman married Melissa Roxanna Packard, of Albany, New York, a daughter of Russell and Lavina (Clark) Packard. Her father was a professor of music in the public schools of Albany and the leader of the choir in the Pearl Street Baptist church of that city. He was born January 9, 1806, at Goshen, Massachusetts, and was descended from Samuel Packard, who came from Weymouth, England, in 1638, landing at Hingham, Massachusetts. Russell Packard acquired a liberal education and because of his musical talent became prominent in musical circles in the east. On the 17th of February, 1829, he wedded Lavinia Clark, who was born at Pittsfield, Massachusetts, July 15, 1810, and it was in that city that Mrs. Kingman's birth occurred on the 12th of March, 1831. She became a musician of considerable note, winning fame both as a pianist and a vocalist and when her father was chorister in the Baptist church of Albany she was also a member of the choir.

After his marriage Mr. Kingman removed to Detroit, Michigan, where he engaged in business for himself until the spring of 1857. He then removed to Cedar Rapids, Iowa, which was then a small town. He conducted a boot and shoe store there until the close of the Civil War, when he disposed of his store and turned his attention to the real estate business, handling property in that city on an extensive scale. During the period of the war he served as internal revenue collector. In his undertakings in Cedar Rapids he prospered and there remained until 1871, when he came to Battle Creek, where in connection with his brother, Richmond Kingman, and one or two other prominent business men of the city organized the City Bank. His brother was at that time one of the wealthiest men of the city. He did not make his home here, however, until 1879, when he was elected cashier, the management of the bank devolving upon him. Later he was chosen vice president and was active in the control of the institution which was incorporated in June, 1871, with a capital stock of fifty thousand dollars. From the beginning it met with success, soon winning the confidence of the public and gaining thereby a liberal patronage. The growth of the institution has been continuous and satisfactory and it is to-day in better condition than ever before. To the enterprise, ability and careful direction of Roldon P. Kingman is largely attributable the success of the City Bank. He continued his connection therewith until his death and watched with interest the growth of the bank from a small beginnig to an institution of large proportions.

Of resourceful business ability, energetic and enterprising Mr. Kingman extended his labors into other fields, becoming one of the inaugurators of the Gas Light Company. He was also its first treasurer and spent much of his time in placing the business on a substantial and paying basis. He never severed his connection with the company, but continued as an active factor in its prosperous control until his demise. He was one of the organizers of the Citizens' Electric Light Company and his wise counsel and aid also proved valuable in its management. Having great confidence in Battle Creek and its future he became interested in real estate to a considerable degree.

Unto Mr. and Mrs. Kingman were born two children: Frank R. and Fannie J., the latter now the wife of Charles W. Sutton, of Hillsboro, North Dakota. On the 17th of December, 1895, Mr. Kingman passed away and on the 3d of August, 1901, his wife was called to her final rest. In politics he was a Republican, stanch and fearless in his advocacy of the principles in which he believed, yet never an aspirant for office. To every enterprise calculated to advance the prosperity of Battle Creek he was a generous contributor and was an important factor in the development of the city, of which he was a most popular citizen. He was emphatically a man of enterprise, indomitable courage, strict integrity and liberal views. He continually broadened his mind through reading, observation and experience. His reading touched on almost all lines of thought and made him a man of scholarly attainments. He found his greatest pleasure in his home and the companionship of his family at his own fireside. Friendship to him was inviolable and all who enjoyed his confidence found in him one who was ever loyal to the duties of comradeship and fellowship.

FRANK R. KINGMAN.

Frank R. Kingman was born in Detroit, January 19, 1855, and was educated in the schools of Cedar Rapids, Iowa. He came to Battle Creek with his parents in 1871 and afterwards engaged in the boot and shoe business in different places for thirteen years. In 1893 he removed to San Diego, California, where he became interested in fruit growing and there he remained for seven years or until the death of his father which necessitated his return to Battle Creek. He is now one of the directors of the City Bank and is actively engaged in its management and in the control of the family interests in Battle Creek.

DUANE C. SALISBURY.

Attracted by the broader opportunities in Battle Creek Duane C. Salisbury came to this city in 1900 and since that time has gained recognition as one of the most capable of the younger representatives of the legal profession. In 1903 he was appointed city attorney, and in the conduct of litigated interests involving the city, he has shown himself most loyal to the welfare of the municipality.

Mr. Salisbury was born in Midland, Midland county, Michigan, November 26, 1875, a son of Abram D. and Helen (Evans) Salisbury. The father was born in Jefferson county, New York, June 17, 1841, and when he was but two years of age his parents removed with their family to Oakland county, Michigan, where they remained for three years, going thence to Genesee county. They established their home at what is now the town of Burton and there Abram D. Salisbury spent the days of his boyhood and youth. After acquiring a good preliminary education, he began preparation for the profession which he decided to make his life work, entering the medical department of the State University of Michigan, where on the com-

pletion of the prescribed course he was graduated, with the class of 1865. Entering at once upon the practice of his profession, he was located at different places until 1871, when he established his home in Midland and opened a drug store in connection with his office. He has since become prominent in his chosen field of labor and is also well known as an enterprising merchant. Broad and varied experience, added to continued reading, has made him most proficient in his work of alleviating human suffering. He is also active in public affairs and has been called upon to fill a number of important offices, including that of mayor of the city, while the district chose him as its representative to the State Legislature. He has always been a stanch Republican.

After completing the course in the common and the high schools of Midland, Duane C. Salisbury entered the high school of Ann Arbor, where he prepared for his college course, and then became a student in the literary department of the University of Michigan, where he pursued an elective course. Subsequently he was enrolled among the law students in the same institution and was graduated in the class of 1897, with the degree of Bachelor of Law. The same year he was admitted to the bar and then located at Milan, Michigan, where he remained for two and a half years, and secured a good clinetage, but wishing to enter a field of labor that would give him greater scope for the exercise of his powers and the development of his ability, he came to Battle Creek in April, 1900, beginning practice alone. He soon won the favorable regard of the bar and of the public at large and has been quite successful as a general practitioner. He continued alone until April, 1901, when he formed a partnership with Mr. North, under the firm name of North & Salisbury.

Mr. Salisbury has been active in Republican circles and during the McKinley campaign of 1900 he delivered many campaign addresses in the county, being acknowledged a speaker of eloquence and power. On the 20th of April, 1903, he was appointed city attorney of Battle Creek and is now efficiently serving in that office.

Socially Mr. Salisbury is connected with the Masonic fraternity; is a member of Milan Lodge, No. 288, K. P.; Battle Creek Lodge, No. 573, B. P. O. E.; the Modern Woodmen Camp, the Knights of the Maccabees; and the American Insurance Union. He married Miss Emogene Knight, of Milan, Michigan, the wedding being celebrated February 11, 1902. She is a daughter of Hiram S. and Caroline Knight and both Mr. and Mrs. Salisbury are members of the Episcopal church. They own and occupy a fine home at No. 293 Lake avenue. Mr. Salisbury is regarded as one of the rising and influential young men of the city, and his strong mentality, his laudable ambition and devotion to his clients interests promises well for the future.

RALPH B. CUMMINGS.

Ralph B. Cummings, a retired farmer of Battle Creek, prominent and well-to-do, was born in Onondaga county, New York, December 15, 1831, his parents being Albert V. and Emily (Brown) Cummings. The father was likewise a native of Onondaga township, the same county, and the paternal grandfather Oliver Cummings, was one of the pioneer settlers there, removing to the Empire state from Vermont. He took up new land and developed a good home for his family, and upon the farm there Albert Cummings grew to manhood. He wedded Miss Emily Brown, a daughter of Ralph Brown, who had removed from Connecticut at an early period in the development of Onondaga county and established his home in Otisco township. When three children had been born to them Albert V. Cummings and his wife came to Michigan locating on Goguac prairie where he purchased one hundred and sixty acres of land and improved a farm, making a good home. Battle Creek was then a small hamlet and the county was but sparsely settled. He continued farming there until his death which occurred in 1861. His wife had passed away several years before, leaving three children, of whom Willis became a member of Company F, Second Michigan Infantry and died in Andersonville prison during the Civil war; Judson, who was a member of Company C. Second Regiment of Michigan Volunteers, died in Savannah, Georgia; and Ralph B.

In the schools of New York and Battle Creek Ralph B. Cummings was educated and upon the home farm he assisted his father in the work of field and meadow. For a number of years prior to his father's death he had the management of the home place and later became the owner of this farm and successfully carried on general agricultural pursuits. While residing thereon he served as clerk of his township for a number of years and afterward was township treasurer for six years. In 1867 he sold his land and came to Battle Creek. In this locality he bought eighty acres of land which he subsequently sold to the Advance Thresher Company and upon it the plant of that company is now located. This transaction proved very profitable and with the proceeds of the sale Mr. Cummings purchased a beautiful home on West Main street, where he has since lived retired, engaged in no active business save the supervision of his property interests. His property is sixty-six feet wide and extends from West Main to Van Buren streets. He also has other real estate interests and from his property derives a good income.

Mr. Cummings has been twice married. He first wedded Mary Haskins, of Byron, Genesee county, New York, who died leaving a son, A. E. Cummings, now of Sault Ste Marie. He married Nettie Hitchnor and has a daughter Blanche. who is now the wife of E. R. Cole. whose sketch is given o.1 another page of this work. For a short time after his first marriage Mr. Cummings lived in Dowagiac, Michigan. where the son was born, but in Battle Creek he was reared and educated and learned the machinist's trade. In February, 1884. Mr. Cummings was united in marriage to Miss Anna L. Gilmore. of Kalamazoo, whose father was an early settler of that county.

Mr. Cummings was nominated for mayor on the Greenback ticket and has also been the nominee of the Democratic party which is in the minority here. He has been content, however, to perform his duties of citizenship in a private capacity and is very actively and helpfully interested in the measures and movements which he believes will contribute to the general good. His career has been a successful one. also active and useful, and through his well directed efforts guided by sound judgment and characterized by unflagging diligence he has won desirable prosperity.

WILLIAM SEAGER COLUMBUS.

William Seager Columbus occupies a position of distinction in the musical circles of Battle Creek. One of Michigan's native sons, he was born in L'Anse on the 25th of January, 1878. His paternal great-grandfather, Isaac Columbus. was one of the pioneer settlers of Toronto, Canada, to which place he emigrated from France. He possessed superior musical talent and marked ability and he constructed the first pipe organ of Toronto, installing it into the leading Catholic church of that city. He then served as organist and held rank as one of the leading musical celebrities of that section of the country. Louis Columbus. the grandfather of our subject, resided in Toronto and was a respected citizen there. He. too, possessed the family musical talent and was a violinist of some note. but did not exercise his power in this direction as a means of livelihood. Louis Columbus, Sr.. the father of our subject. was born in Toronto and there reared and educated. When a young man he went to Calumet, Michigan, where he became manager of a store and also acted as its bookkeeper. Later he engaged in the lumbering business on his own account in that place, being one of the early lumber merchants there. Subsequently he removed to L'Anse, where he became extensively engaged in the lumber trade. which he followed for a number of years, when he retired from that field of labor and became the owner of a large farm near L'Anse, which is now the home of the family. A prominent and influential citizen, he is regarded as a leader in public thought and action there and at one time he received the nomination of the Democratic party for county clerk. He wedded Miss Jeannette Campbell, likewise a native of Canada, the wedding being celebrated in Calumet, Michigan. They had seven children, six of whom are living. After they had completed the high school course in L'Anse, the family removed to Olivet and afterward to Albion that the children might enjoy the superior educational advantages of those institutions.

It will be seen from the ancestral history of William S. Columbus that his love and ability in the line of music is an inherent trait of his character, which cultivation has greatly developed. When he had completed the high school course at L'Anse he entered Olivet College, pursuing literary and musical studies for two years. Later he spent one year in Albion and was graduated in the conservatory there in 1896, having taken a course on the piano and organ and also in voice work, together with the allied studies of harmony and theory. When he had completed his studies he came to Battle Creek and entered professional circles in this city as a teacher of both vocal and instrumental music. He keeps fully abreast with the times, spending the summers in studying under noted private teachers in Chicago. Professor Columbus soon gained a very desirable reputation as one of the best musicians and instructors of the city, and now stands second to none. He has secured a very large class of students and has been the organist in both the Baptist and Episcopal churches, while at the present time he is occupying that position in the First Methodist Episcopal church in Battle Creek. He was also appointed director of the glee club of the Young Men's Christian

Association upon its organization, and is now developing a splendid musical society. He holds membership in the State Musical Teachers' Association and has composed a number of compositions which have been used in his public work, but have never been published.

Professor Columbus is fraternally identified with A. T. Metcalf lodge, F. and A. M., and with the Knights of Pythias lodge, and also the tribe of Ben Hur. He belongs to the First Methodist Episcopal church and in social circles is prominent. Throughout his business career his entire attention has been given to his art and he is now one of the the most prominent representatives in musical circles in this section of the state. His natural ability has been developed and cultivated until he has reached a high standard, and the impress of his individuality is strongly felt in the development of musical taste and culture in his adopted city.

WILLIAM M. HOFFMASTER.

Marvelous advancement has been made in America along all lines touching the general interests of society and the welfare of the nation, but the progress in no line has been greater than in that affecting business conditions. The successful man is he who can foretell the trend of commercial development and shape his efforts accordingly. This Mr. Hoffmaster has done, and although he entered upon a business already established, he has, in enlarging its scope, displayed excellent commercial resource and ability. He is the chairman of the P. Hoffmaster Sons Company, limited, being in this enterprise associated with his twin brother,

WILLIAM M. HOFFMASTER

Rillie F. Hoffmaster. Their establishment is the oldest as well as one of the leading dry goods houses of Battle Creek. He has also been active in other lines of business.

Born in Kalamazoo, Michigan, on the 31st of August, 1862, he is a son of Peter and Amelia (Blodgett) Hoffmaster, whose sketch is given elsewhere. He came with his parents to Battle Creek in 1872, acquired his education in the public schools here and in a business college, where he pursued his studies for a year. Soon after he entered his father's store in the capacity of a clerk and gradually worked his way upward, finding in each promotion opportunity for new development and the acquisition of greater knowledge bearing upon mercantile life. At length he became a partner in the enterprise and upon his father's death, in 1901, he and his brother, Rillie F., assumed the management of the store as executors, thus continuing until the 1st of February, 1903, when the business was incorporated under the style of P. Hoffmaster Sons Company, limited, with a capital stock of seventy-five thousand dollars. Of the company William M. Hoffmaster is chairman, Rillie F. Hoffmaster treasurer and Helen Hoffmaster secretary. The business now occupies three stores in the Opera House block and is a very large and important commercial enterprise of the city. The company carries a full line of dry goods, carpets, cloaks and suits and was the first exclusive dry goods and carpet store in the city.

William M. Hoffmaster was one of the original stockholders of the Machine and Tool Company, manufacturing gasoline engines. He was chosen a member of the first board of directors and still holds that office. He is also interested in the Advance Pump and Compressor Company, and in the Sherman Manufacturing Company, manufacturers of brass goods. He has dealt to a considerable extent in real estate, owning good business property, and a large amount of resident property, having erected a number of dwellings in the city during the past few years.

Mr. Hoffmaster is a member of the Battle Creek lodge, K. of P., and the Benevolent Protective Order of Elks. He is also a member of the Athelstan club. He attends and supports the Presbyterian church, of which his wife is a member. He was married on the 30th of October, 1890, to Miss Mary Elizabeth Deno, a daughter of Anthony Deno, of Bay City, Michigan. Mr. Hoffmaster possesses the social qualities which have endeared him to friends and family and, long a resident of Battle Creek, he has gained the regard of a large majority of those with whom he has come in contact, both socially and commercially.

JAMES PHILLIPS.

James Phillips, a retired farmer, who since 1855 has resided at his present home, at No. 547 Main street, west, in Battle Creek, came to this city in the spring of 1854, and for almost half a century has been a witness of its expansion, growth and substantial progress. He was born in the parish of Clodock, in Herefordshire, England, December 21, 1821, his parents being James and Mary (Powell) Phillips. He was reared upon a farm, obtained a fair common-school education and followed agricultural pursuits until about twenty years of age, when he began clerking for a lumber merchant. He acted as bookkeeper and also measured the standing timber that was cut into logs. For seven years he remained with one firm and then came to America when thirty-one years of age, leaving Liverpool in 1852. For six weeks and four days the vessel was upon the ocean, encountering severe weather, but on the 15th of June at length dropped anchor in the harbor of New York.

Mr. Phillips went to Geneva, Ontario county, New York, where he remained for a year, when he removed to Seneca county and rented a farm near Waterloo. Two years later he came to Battle Creek, and in Michigan purchased and operated land in different counties. He farmed to some extent and also cut timber from his various possessions. He has also bought and sold real estate and has erected a number of houses in Battle Creek. His business operations have been carefully conducted, his purchases judiciously made and his sales have brought to him a good financial return. In 1890 he platted Phillips's first addition to Battle Creek, and in 1898 platted the second addition. Phillips street is named in his honor and through his real estate operations and as a private citizen he has contributed largely to the improvement and expansion of the city, and is to-day one of the strong and influential pioneer residents of Battle Creek.

Mr. Phillips was married in Battle Creek November 26, 1856, to Mrs. Lydia Townsend, who was born in Orange county, New York. She was first married in that state and lived in Batavia. Her death occurred in August, 1863, and Mr. Phillips was again married March 26, 1884, his second union being with Miss Sophia Williams, who was born in Ragland, Monmouthshire, England, a daugh-

ter of John and Ann (Davis) Williams. She came to America in 1883, and by her marriage had two children, both of whom died in infancy. Mr. Phillips has been a Republican since the organization of the party and is deeply interested in its success and welfare. He held the office of highway commissioner in Battle Creek township for fourteen years, was justice of the peace four years and notary public four years. He and his wife attend the Episcopal church. Mr. Phillips has now passed the eighty-first mile-stone on life's journey and is a venerable and honored pioneer of Battle Creek, repected by young and old, rich and poor.

JACOB HARBAUGH.

Calhoun county lost, in the death of Jacob Harbaugh, a man of strong integrity, and a citizen whose efforts were ever lent toward the maintenance of principle. A native of Pennsylvania, he was born March 22, 1824, the son of John and Mary (Crosser) Harbaugh. After the death of his father in Pennsylvania, he came with his mother to Ohio when only six years old, growing to manhood in the Buckeye state. His life was uneventful until the breaking out of the Mexican war, when he enlisted in the cavalry, serving for two years under General Winfield Scott. Upon the closing of the war he returned north, locating in Fort Wayne, Indiana, where he remained but a brief time before taking the overland route to California in 1849. Upon his safe arrival in the west he engaged in mining, and with his energy, pluck and perseverance soon made for himself a place among the successful men of that section. After two years spent in California, he returned to the middle west, coming by way of the Isthmus of Panama, thence to New Orleans, and up the Mississippi river to Cincinnati, Ohio, from which city he journeyed to his old home, where his mother was then living. Shortly after he removed with his mother to Coldwater, Michigan, where he purchased a farm and became interested in agricultural pursuits. For many years he remained in that location, and was recognized as one of the public-spirited and progressive farmers of Branch county. In June, 1882, he removed to Calhoun county, purchasing a farm of two hundred and ninety-two acres in Athens township, adjoining the village of Athens, where he made his home for ten years. He then built a home on Main street, Athens, and located permanently in the village, retiring from the active duties which had so long engrossed his attention. His death occurred in this location June 4, 1899.

The marriage of Mr. Harbaugh occurred in 1852, and united him with Miss Mary Heyden, whose home had been in Coldwater, Branch county, ever since she was two years old, her parents, Albert V. and Lucy (Done) Heyden, being pioneer settlers of the state. The birth of seven children blessed this union, of whom three died in youth and one after marriage. The four who attained maturity are named in order of their birth as follows: Florene, who first married Millard Pierce, by whom she had one son, Millard, and by her marriage with Henry Kelver, had two daughters, one who died in infancy, and Mary, who married R. E. Wood, of Athens, and has one child, Wanna; Delphine, who married Albert Cole, a resident of Athens township, is now the mother of three children, namely: Vivian, Ara and Basil; Ed-

win, resides in Athens township, and by his marriage with Miss Nora Young has four children, namely: Paul, Eva, Nola and Kenneth; and Adelbert, also a resident of Athens township, married Amanda Rappleye and has one child, Renaud. Adelbert married for his second wife, Theodosia Walker, who was born at Alpena, Michigan. Their marriage took place January 12, 1904. Since the death of her husband Mrs. Harbaugh has purchased another home in Athens, where she now lives, renting the property built upon Main street. In religion she is a member of the New Light.

Mr. Harbaugh was a self-made man. Cast upon his own resources at an early age, he began at once to build up those traits in character upon which his citizenship depended; in manhood being known for an integrity which always placed his business dealings above question. His good judgment and practical business ability resulted in an early acquired competence. In political preferment a Democrat, he was chosen at various times to fill school offices in Branch county, and was active in the support of good government.

AUGUSTUS LUSK.

When Augustus Lusk passed away Calhoun county lost one of its pioneer settlers, a man whose identification with this section of the state dated from a very early period in the development and improvement of southern Michigan. Moreover, he had through a long business career displayed the commendable traits of character which not only win success but also gain the respect, confidence and good will of his fellow men.

He was born on the 24th of July, 1809, in the town of Victor, Ontario county, New York. His father, John Lusk, a native of Stockbridge, Massachusetts, accompanied his parents to Victor, New York, in early boyhood, the family becoming pioneer settlers of that locality. After attaining to manhood he became a prominent and influential factor in community affairs and his labors aided in shaping the public policy of his county. In 1812 he enlisted for service in the second war with Great Britain and in 1814 in recognition of gallant conduct and meritorious service on the field of battle he was promoted to the rank of colonel. In the engagement at Black Rock he was taken prisoner and with other of the war captives was sent to Montreal, Canada, where, after three months he was exchanged. On obtaining his release he returned to Victor and resumed the occupation of farming, remaining in that locality until the spring of 1836, when he and his son John came to Calhoun county, Michigan, to purchase land for a new home, desiring to enjoy the advantages which might accrue from a residence upon the frontier. He became the owner of one hundred and sixty acres on section 11, Eckford township, one hundred and sixty acres on section 1 of the same township, and a quarter section in Marengo township. In the last mentioned locality he built his house and then returning to New York he brought his family to the west in the fall of that year, making the journey over the rough roads and through the forests in a wagon, four weeks being consumed in completing the trip. In pioneer style the family established their home in Michigan and with characteristic energy Mr. Lusk began the development and cultivation of his farm. Some time afterward he sold his place in Marengo

township and moved to his property on section 1, Eckford township. At a later day he also disposed of that farm, which he sold to Gregory Hill, and then bought two hundred acres of land near the village of Marengo, living thereon up to the time of his death, which occurred January 10, 1873. The county thereby lost an honored pioneer, who, by his energy, enterprise and capability, was of much assistance in developing the resources of this portion of the state and his name will ever be honored as that of one of the most useful of the early settlers.

Colonel Lusk was married three times. He first wedded Pruella Brooks, the wedding taking place in Victor, New York, October 10, 1808. Six children were born of this marriage, of whom Augustus was the eldest. The mother passed away in Victor on the 13th of March, 1823, and on the 6th of July of that year Colonel Lusk was married in Victor to Mrs. Dinah Brooks, the widow of Zera Brooks, of that place. They became the parents of five children, two daughters and three sons and the second wife died May 21, 1856. On the 1st of November, 1856, Colonel Lusk at Royalton, Ohio, was married to Mrs. Caroline Lusk, the widow of his brother, Ira. Her death occurred September 21, 1883.

When Augustus Lusk came with his father's family to Calhoun county this section of the country was in a very wild and unimproved condition, giving very little indication of the development which would bring it to its present high state of prosperity and progress. Wild game of various kinds was plentiful and it was not an unusual thing for him to see large herds of deer roaming over the forests where are now finely developed farms. He became familiar with the difficulties and hardships incident to frontier life and was early familiar with the arduous task of developing a new farm. He worked with his father until twenty-one years of age, when he started out to earn his own living by working by the month as a farm hand, being thus employed until 1834, when he rented a farm in his native county, operating it until the fall of 1836. After arriving in Calhoun county with his parents he and his brother John purchased of their father the tract of one hundred and sixty acres of land on section 11, Eckford township. Of this Augustus Lusk broke and improved fifty-six acres and in the summer of 1855 he built a house on his half of the quarter section. Some years later he purchased his brother's interest in the farm, which he improved, continuing the work of cultivation until he made it one of the best farms in this section of the country, splendidly equipped with good buildings and all modern accessories. As a practical farmer he was one of the factors that made Eckford township one of the prosperous farming communities of this portion of the state. In his work he was greatly aided by his devoted wife who always gave to him her encouragement and sympathy and who in the careful management of household expenses greatly assisted him in his financial affairs.

It was in June, 1851, that Mr. Lusk was united in marriage to Miss Mary J. Shaw, a daughter of William Shaw, a native of Glasgow, Scotland, with whom he long traveled life's journey. She was, however, his second wife. He had previously been married to Miss Ann Force, who died January 28, 1849, after a happy married life of nearly sixteen years. By that marriage four children were born, a son and three daughters, namely: Pruella, the wife of George Clinton, of Butte, Montana; Henry I.; Fannie

F., who became the wife of Judson Rundel, who died August 8, 1883; and Ellen A., who died in infancy. After losing his first wife, Mr. Lusk wedded Miss Mary J. Shaw. Her father was a weaver by trade and on coming to America settled at Rochester, New York, where he was married. He was drowned in the prime of life while rafting down the Genesee river. Mrs. Lusk, the elder of the two children of the family, was very young at the time of her father's death. Unto Augustus and Mary J. (Shaw) Lusk were born three children, a son and two daughters. Frederick S. died in Eckford township June 3, 1898. Florence A. is the widow of Robert Woodley, a farmer of Eckford township, who died December 10, 1899. His widow and two children survive him, namely: W. Augustus Woodley resides in Battle Creek, Michigan; Harold resides at home. Nellie May, the youngest child of Mr. Lusk, died January 2, 1889. She was the wife of William Mosher and at her death left a little daughter, Mae L.

Mr. Lusk was a very honorable man in all life's relations, true to his duty, to himself, his family and his country. He gave his political allegiance to the Democracy, casting his first presidential vote for Andrew Jackson in 1822. He filled a number of local offices with credit to himself and satisfaction to his constituents and was very deeply interested in what pertained to the welfare of his community or to the country at large. He and his wife were leading and influential members of the Baptist church at Marshall, in which he served as deacon for many years and she shared in the same kindly regard which was so long extended to him. Mr. Lusk was indeed well known in Calhoun county. Upright in thought and deed, he lived at peace with his fellow men

as a true Christian and one whose influence
was ever on the side of truth. Long a resident of Calhoun county when he passed
away on the 2d of February, 1894, his loss
was deeply felt, while one more name was
added to the list of the country's honored
dead.

WARREN SCOTT KESSLER.

This is essentially an age of production,
invention and manufacture and everywhere
throughout the country have sprung up factories which are turning out annually their
products to the markets of the world. In
no other era in the history of civilization has
man utilized to such an extent the elements
of which nature has supplied him and there
has been no more rapid advance or greater
improvement than along the line of the iron
industry. One of the leading enterprises of
this character is that conducted under the
name of the Malleable Iron Company of Albion, and of this company Mr. Kessler is
the president. His efforts, however, have
not been confined entirely to one line, many
other business interests having felt the stimulus of his energy and benefitted by his
sound judgment. He is regarded as most
reliable and trustworthy and his name has
become an honored one throughout southern
Michigan.

Mr. Kessler was born in Albion, New
York, November 20, 1845, a son of Andrew
J. and Anna (Slusser) Kessler, both of
whom are descended from Holland ancestors, who settled in Pennsylvania at an early
day. Phillip Kessler, the grandfather of our
subject, became one of the pioneer settlers
of western New York and served his country as a soldier in the War of 1812. An-

drew J. Kessler learned the blacksmith's
trade in early life, but afterward turned his
attention to farming. He was married in
Albion, New York, and in 1856 came to the
west, spending one year in Michigan, after
which he removed to Woodstock, Illinois,
where he followed his trade. Subsequently
he became a railroad contractor during the
construction of the early western roads, and
continued in that line of business up to the
time of his demise in 1874. His wife survived him for about ten years, passing away
in Sycamore, Illinois, in 1884.

Warren Scott Kessler completed his education at Todd's Academy, in Woodstock,
Illinois, and entered upon his business career in the capacity of a bookkeeper, while
later he engaged in the construction of railroads under contract through the northwest,
being thus employed on a number of the
new roads, including the Chicago, Burlington & Quincy, the Chicago & Northwestern,
the West Michigan and the Fort Scott &
Gulf, of Kansas. That business occupied
his time and attention until 1881, when he
became identified with the iron industry, in
Chicago, as a salesman for eastern mills.
This he continued for some time, dealing
with large firms connected with the trade.
In 1888, however, he removed to Albion,
where he established the Malleable Iron
business, which later was incorporated under the name of the Albion Malleable Iron
Company. Mr. Kessler became its first secretary and treasurer and in 1893 its president and general manager, and has since
acted in that capacity. The plant was at
first quite small, but after ten years the business demanded more commodious quarters,
and the company secured its present site and
erected the plant which stands to-day.
When the works are operated to their full

capacity employment is furnished to three hundred men. This is one of the largest concerns of the kind in Michigan and is splendidly equipped with modern improvements to facilitate the work. The business has become very extensive and profitable and its successful conduct is largely due to the supervision of Mr. Kessler. He is also the vice president of the Albion State bank, of which he was one of the incorporators, and served as a member of its board of directors. He is also interested in various other enterprises of the city, and owns valuable city and country real estate. In 1900, in connection with H. B. Parker, he built a fine brick block at the corner of Cass and Superior streets. It is two stories in height, ninety-two by one hundred and fifteen feet, is steam heated and finished throughout in oak. The postoffice and the store occupy the ground floor and the second floor is utilized by Murat lodge, F. & A. M., this being one of the finest lodge rooms in the state. The remainder of the building is used for office purposes and the structure is known as the Kessler & Parker block.

On the 15th of September, 1881, he wedded Mrs. E. A. Parker, of Chicago, who died May 20, 1896. He has been quite influential in political circles, has served as alderman of Albion and is now acting for the second term as a member of the board of public works. He was also for two terms chairman of the congressional committee. Socially he is identified with Murat lodge, No. 21, F. & A. M., to which he demitted from Oriental lodge, of Chicago. He was likewise connected with Chicago Chapter, R. A. M., of Chicago, and his identification with capitular Masonry is indicated by his membership in Albion Chapter. He belongs to Chevalier Bayard Commandery, of Chi-

cago, and to the Moslem Temple, of the Mystic Shrine, at Detroit. He became a charter member of the Leisure Hour Club and attends and supports the Presbyterian church. It is not difficult for one to determine the secret of his prosperity, for since he started out in life on his own account he has manifested strong purpose, close application and unfaltering diligence. He has made a study of business conditions and has become quick to recognize opportunity, which he has grasped at the right moment, not looking forward to any illusive hopes of the future. He has worked earnestly day by day, his efforts being characterized by the strictest commercial ethics, and as a result of his powers of concentration, his keen business sagacity and his unfaltering industry he stands to-day as a splendid representative of the industrial life and financial interests of Albion.

PETER MALLOW.

Peter Mallow, one of the enterprising farmers of Athens township, Calhoun county, was born on the Erie Canal between Albany and Utica, New York, April 24, 1840, his parents, Peter and Margaret (Peters) Mallow, being then enroute for a settlement in the middle west. The parents were both natives of France, having been born in the northeastern part of that country, from which they emigrated, in the fall of 1839. Their first winter in America was spent in New York City, when, upon the opening again of navigation, they sailed upon the Hudson river to Albany, thence across the state on the Erie Canal to Buffalo, there taking a boat on Lake Erie which landed them at Detroit, Michigan. From that city they journeyed to the southwestern part of Branch county, arriving in that locality with nothing more than stout hearts and energy, to give promise for the future. By tireless industry, perseverance and energy they accumulated a fortune valued at seventy-five thousand dollars. The death of both parents occurred in the locality where they had spent the greater part of their useful lives.

Our personal subject, Peter Mallow, was reared upon his father's farm, acquiring his education in the common schools of the county, while he also assisted in the home duties to which he had been trained. Upon attaining his majority he became independent in his labor, working as a farm hand until 1868, when he was united in marriage with Miss Louisa Eggleston. The young people then removed to Indiana, where they made their home for two years, returning at the expiration of that time to locate on section 24, Athens township, where he now owns a productive farm of one hundred and sixty acres, which he devotes to general farming and the raising of horses, sheep and cattle. He has remained in this locality for thirty-three years, devoting his energies to the successful cultivation of his land, making many improvements and clearing the timber, which has added much to the value of his property. He is a substantial and enterprising farmer and one of the men upon whom a neighborhood depends for that element which bespeaks the best in a community.

To Mr. Mallow and his first wife were born four children, namely: Maggie, who married Charles Simons; Frances; Peter, Jr., a resident of Athens; who married Miss Lettie Brown; and Ada, the widow of Bert Foster, one child, Lyle, having been born of the union. Mr. Mallow was later united in marriage with Miss Jane Wells, of which union were born three children, all of whom make their home with their parents: Banner, Lyndz and Bessie. In his political views Mr. Mallow is independent, giving the support of his voice and vote to the man best qualified for office.

ADOLPH JOHNSON.

Adolph Johnson, who is now general manager and designer of machinery manufactured by the Johnson Foundry and Machine Works, limited, is well known in industrial circles in Battle Creek, and as the founder and promoter of one of the great productive enterprises of this city he has contributed in material manner to its progress and commercial activity. By the concensus of public opinion he is numbered among those whose lives have proven an integral factor in the development of this place as a manufacturing and commercial center. He has wrought along the lines of important business enterprises and his keen discernment, perseverance and fund of unflagging industry have constituted the secret of a success which is well merited.

He was born in northern Sweden, November 17, 1866, and is a son of John and Christine (Sunberg) Jonasson. In the country of his nativity he spent his boyhood days, attending school until he was about fourteen or fifteen years of age, when he began learning the machinist's trade, at which he served a four years' apprenticeship. The arrangement was that he was to receive his

ADOLPH JOHNSON

board and three hundred dollars in compensation for his services during the four years' term. On the expiration of that period he worked in different cities as a journeyman and afterward began a business of his own at Sunsvall, Sweden, where he continued for about two and a half years. He afterward became superintendent in an establishment, but when a few months had passed he severed the ties which bound him to his native land in order that he might come to America and seek his fortune in the new world.

Ere leaving Sweden, however, Mr. Johnson was married, on the 10th of November, 1889, to Miss Emma Allen. Crossing the ocean he landed at Boston, Massachusetts, on the 25th of March, 1892, but did not tarry long in the east, coming at once to Battle Creek, Michigan, where his wife had relatives living, and here he was joined by Mrs. Johnson in September, of the same year. He secured employment in the machine department of the Duplex Printing Press Company, remaining there until 1894, when he removed to Michigan City, Indiana, where he was employed in the Allen Manufacturing Company as inspector of experimental and tool work. For about a year he remained with that firm and then removed to Jackson, Michigan, where he was identified with the Derby Manufacturing Company, being foreman at that place for a few months. Subsequently he was foreman for the Kirk Manufacturing Company, of Toledo, Ohio, until he returned to Battle Creek in the spring of 1900. Here he became a partner in the firm of Johnson & Zock, manufacturers of general machinery at No. 151 West Main street. They began operations on a small scale, but from the beginning the enterprise was attended with success and after a year Mr. Johnson
20

bought out his partner and enlarged the business, which he conducted under the name of the Johnson Machine Works. On the 4th of March, 1902, this was consolidated with the Battle Creek Foundry Company. This business has recently been organized and incorporated with a capital stock of four hundred thousand dollars, under the name of the Johnson Foundry and Machine Works, limited, of which Mr. Johnson is a director, large stockholder and general manager. In 1902 the present foundry was erected. The building covers an area of two hundred by sixty feet and one-half of the structure is two stories in height. The company manufactures special machinery, of which Mr. Johnson is the designer, the most important being that used by cereal food manufacturers and which has become widely known and is recognized by the leading firms as the most successful machinery of its class. The company also manufactures different lines of novelties designed by Mr. Johnson and gives employment to a large number of skilled workmen. The plant is equipped with the latest improved machinery in order to facilitate the business and to produce the best possible results in manufacture and the output is already large, while the trade is constantly growing. The inventive genius and practical knowledge of Mr. Johnson has been the foundation upon which this important productive industry has been built. He has given his personal attention to the supervision of all the details of the business, and added to his capability in the production of original designs, he has the keen preceptive power and managerial ability of an able financier.

Unto Mr. and Mrs. Johnson has been born one daughter, Elsie. They own their own home in Battle Creek and in addition to other city property Mr. Johnson is the owner of a good farm in Pennfield township. He gives his political support to any party, voting for the men whom he thinks best qualified for office. He belongs to the Independent order of Odd Fellows and to other fraternal organizations and has won the favorable regard of his fellow citizens in a marked degree. Viewed in a personal light he is a strong man of excellent judgment, fair in his views and highly honorable in his relations with his fellow men. The hope that led him to leave his native land in the days of his early manhood and seek a home in America has been more than realized. When he arrived in this country he had certain inherent qualities which formed a good basis for success, but he was unfamiliar with the language, the customs and the manners of the people. With ready adaptability, however, he familiarized himself with the ways of the new world and gained mastery over the English tongue. In his business life he showed ready adaptability, faithfulness and energy and his worth found recognition in promotions, while each advanced step gained him further opportunity for new development and the acquirement of a greater knowledge of business methods. He is now a prominent resident of Battle Creek and in a record of those who have been prominently identified with the development and progress of the city it is imperative that definite consideration be granted him, for he has not only become the promoter of an important industrial enterprise, but has so ordered his life as to gain and retain the confidence and esteem of his fellow men.

FRANK JOSEPH SHEDD.

A prosperous merchant of Burlington, Calhoun county, Frank Joseph Shedd was born in Madison township, Branch county, Michigan, October 16, 1864, a son of Joseph and Polly E. (Turner) Shedd. Both parents were natives of Genesee county, New York, where the father was engaged in farming, and after coming to Michigan in 1854 they settled first in Washtenaw county, removing to Branch county shortly before the birth of the subject. In the course of time they located in Burlington township, Calhoun county, where farming operations were continued on a farm in section 13. With the exception of five years passed in the township of Fredonia, this locality remained the home of the parents until five years previous to the death of the father, at which time they located in the village of Burlington. He died in 1894 at the age of seventy-two years, and is interred in the Burlington cemetery. Politically he adhered to the principles advocated in the platform of the Democratic party. Mrs. Shedd, who survives her husband at the age of seventy-six years and makes her home with her son, F. J., of this review, is the mother of the following children: Mary, who married Charles Tompson and resides in Madison, Branch county; Lucy, who married Nelson Osborne and resides at Battle Creek; Ruby, who married Raymond Rogers and also resides in Battle Creek; Harry E., who lives in Tekonsha township; and Frank Joseph.

Frank Joseph Shedd was reared to manhood in the southern part of Michigan, receiving his education in the Burlington school, which he attended until he was sixteen years old, after which he began work upon his father's farm, remaining so employed until 1888. He then sought and secured employment in a saw-mill, continuing in this occupation for two years. Having then acquired sufficient means to enable him to establish a mercantile business he at once located in Burlington, opening a general store, necessarily on a small scale. From this modest beginning has grown his present lucrative business, for the general demand, carrying a full line of all articles to be found in a general mercantile establishment.

In 1888 Mr. Shedd was united in marriage with Miss Carrie Strong, a native of Tekonsha township and a daughter of Oliver Strong, and to them have been born two children, Otto and Kittie. Like his father Mr. Shedd is Democratic in his political convictions and through the influence of this party he has often been called to serve the public interests. For eight years he served as township clerk, during three years of which time he also acted as postmaster of Burlington, receiving his appointment under the last administration of President Cleveland. In 1901 he was elected supervisor of the township and has in the past filled many of the village offices. In his fraternal relations he affiliates with the Masons, in the lodge at Burlington holding the office of master.

ANDREW THOMAS PRIOR.

The entire life of Andrew Thomas Prior has been spent in Calhoun county, as a farmer giving the strength of his manhood and intelligence to the agricultural supremacy of this section of the state. He is numbered among the native sons, his birth having occurred in Clarendon township, February 26, 1845. His father, John Prior, born in Elba, Genesee county, New York, January 13, 1817, was a pioneer of Michigan, as was also his grandfather, another John, the elder man having married Miss Barsheba Davis, the representative of a prominent Massachusetts family, on the 30th of September, 1807. The grandfather came to Michigan in 1839 and located at Cook's Prairie, where he purchased a quarter section of land upon which two log houses had been built, and in the course of time brought his land to a high state of cultivation. He died at the age of sixty-six years, while his wife lived to be ninety-six. Their son remained at home until he had attained his majority, when with five dollars as his available assets he came to Calhoun county, and in the midst of a wilderness country bent his energies to the accumulation of a competence. Against all the odds which were a part of a pioneer's life he was successful, living to see the land fully developed, roads traversing the farming lands, neighbors— three miles distant at the beginning of their residence in this section—in close proximity; markets for their produce, while in the early days they had been compelled to go to Albion to grind their grain, taking two days for the round trip, while flour was hauled from Albion to Adrian, a distance of fifty miles, with ox-teams. When he first located in this part of the state Mr. Prior hired horses to bring his household goods from Detroit, the half formed road leading through thick timber. An amusing incident in the life of

Mr. Prior was the purchase of a cow in Homer, having to borrow eight dollars to complete the bargain. While taking her home she attempted to run away, and with the energy of desperation he caught her tail and followed her through the forest for a distance of two miles, arriving at midnight at the home of N. G. Barker, a near neighbor, with whom he remained until morning. At the time of his death December 2, 1893, Mr. Prior owned one hundred and seventy acres of land, of which one hundred and thirty had been brought under a high state of cultivation. He had also put up modern and substantial buildings and had in every way brought his farm to rank with the best in the community. His wife, formerly Lucy L. Sweet, a Canadian, who was reared in New York, and to whom he was married March 6, 1838, died in April, 1894. She was the mother of the following children: Bathsheba, who married J. Knickerbocker, of Clarendon township; Andrew Thomas, of this review; Loretta, who married Doane Shedd, of Tekonsha; Philip; Benjamin; Mary and Herbert, the last four named now deceased. Mr. Prior became a prominent man in his community and as such discharged the duties of various township offices.

Until he was twenty-four years old Andrew Thomas Prior remained upon the paternal farm, engaged in the duties which fell to his lot as a farmer's son, during a part of the time attending the common school in the vicinity of his home. February 24, 1869, he was married to Miss Jennie Lacey, and she died February 23, 1880, the mother of three children, namely: Lida, born January 11, 1870, who married Harvey Doolittle and is now the mother of two

children; Burdette, born September 21, 1874, a druggist of Tekonsha, also owning seventy acres of land; and John, born July 1, 1877, and died March 6, 1883. The second marriage of our subject united him with Miss Cora Davis, of Marshall, the ceremony being performed September 5, 1883, and her death occurred July 20, 1885. March 9, 1887, Mr. Prior was again united in marriage, Miss Elvira Bushman becoming his wife. She died November 26, 1902, leaving two children, George H., born April 20, 1890, and Juliette, born April 1, 1893. September 8, 1875, Mr. Prior moved to this farm and with the exception of three years spent upon the old homestead has since made this his home. He owns eighty acres in this Tekonsha township, and one hundred and twenty acres in Clarendon township, and has made substantial and modern improvements upon both properties, a fine barn contributing to the convenience and general appearance of his home farm. He is engaged in general farming and is also interested to some extent in stock-raising. In January, 1897, in partnership with H. Horten, he went to the state of Alabama to solicit insurance, but Mr. Horten becoming ill with fever he was compelled to return north, which curtailed the financial success of the enterprise but did not deprive Mr. Prior from seeing much of the southern state. He has also traveled quite extensively in Michigan. Fraternally, Mr. Prior affiliates with the Masonic order, being a member of Washington lodge No. 6, F. and A. M., of Tekonsha. In politics he was once a Republican but upon mature thought has become independent in his views, preferring to reserve his right to cast his ballot for the man whom he thinks best suited for official position. He has always been frank and honest in his political views and has always expressed himself freely on the subject. Though never desirous of official recognition personally, he has nevertheless done all in his power to advance the best interests of the community and through his effective aid has added much to the general welfare of the township.

FRANK SAXTON LUDLOW.

Frank Saxton Ludlow is one of the prominent and respected citizens of Albion, and his home there is the center of a refined and cultured social circle. There are many elements in his life record that are worthy of presentation as examples deserving of emulation. He was a soldier of the Civil war. loyal and true to his country, and in days of peace he has been equally faithful to her welfare. His business career has been characterized by honorable and straightforward methods, and in all life's relations he has been actuated by high and worthy principles.

Mr. Ludlow was born in Tompkins county, New York, April 30, 1842, his parents being West H. and Ann Eliza (Saxton) Ludlow. The father was born upon a farm in the Empire state and for a time attended the district schools. In 1847 he came with his family to Michigan, settling in Parma township, Jackson county, where he purchased a partially developed farm of two hundred and fifteen acres. There he made his home until about three years prior to his death, when he removed to Whitehall, Michigan, but he afterward returned to the farm, which he had sold to his son, and upon

the old homestead he passed away in 1870. His wife survived him for about twenty years and was then laid to rest by his side in the Campbell Church cemetery, of Parma.

Frank S. Ludlow was only about five years of age at the time of is parents' removal to Michigan. He acquired his education in the district schools and was reared upon his father's farm, assisting in the work of field and meadow until after the outbreak of the Civil war, when, in March, 1862, at nineteen years of age, he enlisted for service with the Union army, joining Company K, of the Sixteenth Michigan Volunteers, at Springport, Michigan. as a private. He enlisted under Captain Cass for three years, or during the war, and the regiment was assigned to the Army of the Potomac.

With that command he took part in a number of important engagements, including the battles of Antietam, Gettysburg and the second battle of Bull Run. He had only served for a few months when he went to the regular artillery on detach duty, and was with the Fifth Army Corps. being with Companies B and D, the greater part of the time with the latter. When the command left Harrison's Landing Mr. Ludlow was assigned to the hospital corps, remaining there over night and then going with the ambulance corps the following day. When night came again he joined his company and was with the command continuously throughout his army service, except for the few hours he spent at Harrison's Landing. At Gettysburg he took an active part in the battle. being stationed on Little Round Top. After the close of hostilities and the surrender of Lee, in April, 1865, he received an honorable discharge on the 5th of May, 1865. when about five miles from Petersburg. He had gone through the entire war as a private, never faltering in the performance of any duty, however arduous, and thus he made for himself a most creditable and honorable military record.

On again coming to Michigan Mr. Ludlow resumed farming and later purchased his father's farm, continuing to make his home thereon until 1890. He was for many years an active, enterprising and energetic agriculturist, following advanced ideas of farming and causing his labors to return to him an excellent financial income. He resided upon the old homestead until 1890, when he removed to the village of Albion, having in that year erected a fine large brick residence at No. 1201 East Michigan avenue. It is supplied with all modern conveniences and is a most attractive and beautiful home. In it Mr. Ludlow has since lived a retired life, for his farm returns to him a good rental that supplies him with many comforts and luxuries. He still owns two hundred and fifteen acres of land in Jackson county—the farm his father purchased when he came to Michigan—and his wife is the owner of a farm of one hundred and seven acres, both pieces of property being supplied with good improvements.

On the 25th of March, 1875, was celebrated the marriage of Mr. Ludlow and Miss Mary E. Gassett, a native of Columbia, New York, and a daughter of Daniel P. and Charlotte Temple (Rawley) Gassett, who, in 1849, came to Michigan, locating in the village of Albion. Her father was a carpenter by trade and leaving his family in Albion he joined a party enroute for California, going to that state in order that he might benefit his health, which was in an impaired condition. Upon the Pacific coast he followed mining and was very successful in his operations there. After three years

spent in the far west he returned by way of the Isthmus of Panama, and after he came back purchased a farm in Jackson county, Michigan, of one hundred and twenty acres. He spent the greater part of his remaining days upon that farm, but was for two or three years a resident of the village of Albion. He died May 15, 1897, and is buried in Riverside cemetery, of Albion. His wife still survives him and yet makes her home in Albion. In the name of her daughter, Lottie L. Gassett, she gave money for the erection of the library building, in connection with Albion College, donating ten thousand dollars for this purpose. The building is known as the Lottie L. Gassett library. The daughter was a student in that college and was also a graduate of the Omaha Normal College, after which she engaged in teaching very successfully for many years in the west. She died, however, in 1899, and was interred in Riverside cemetery, and to her memory Mrs. Gassett erected the library, displaying a most commendable spirit in this work, for certainly the best use that can be made of money is to put it where it will benefit the living as well as honor the dead. It was so invested by the mother that it carries on the work of the daughter in which she was so deeply interested. Mrs. Gassett is now seventy-nine years of age and is splendidly preserved for a lady of her years, both mentally and physically. Her life has been fraught with many good deeds and kindly actions and she has gained a large circle of warm friends. Unto Mr. and Mrs. Ludlow has been born a daughter, Ruth A., who resides with her parents and is a teacher in the public schools of Albion. She is a graduate of the Albion high school, also of Albion College and has a Master's degree from the State University at Ann

Arbor, which was conferred upon her in 1900. She has always devoted her life to the teaching of English. Mrs. Ludlow was educated in Albion and prior to her marriage successfully engaged in teaching for six years in the district schools of Jackson county, Michigan. She is a member of the Presbyterian church and Mr. Ludlow is a liberal contributor to its support. She is well fitted to occupy a position of leadership in social circles, for she has a most charming manner, combined with strong mentality, executive ability and that trait which, for want of a better term, has often been called personal magetism. She is a devoted and loving wife and mother and her home is one of comfort. During the past eleven years she has been very prominent in club circles and she is also very interested in intellectual advancement. She completed the regular Chautauqua Course of Study and was president of the local circle for two years. She was also president of the Twentieth Century Club for a year and she is now a member of the Entre Nous Club, of which she was president for two years. She also belongs to the Hall in the Grove and was its president for three years. She is ever deeply interested in club work and her efforts in this particular field have been effective in promoting social and intellectual development in Albion.

Mr. Ludlow gives his political allegiance to the Republican party, and although he has never aspired to office he always keeps well informed on the questions and issues of the day. He belongs to Murat lodge, No. 21, F. & A. M., of Albion, of which he is a past master, and he also has membership relations with Hollingsworth post, G. A. R., of Albion. While in the army he was never wounded and for three years he never slept in a house. On more than one occasion his bed was little more than a mudhole, but so tired were the soldiers that they were glad to lie down and rest under any condition. In recognition of his services Mr. Ludlow now receives a pension. Both Mr. and Mrs. Ludlow have a wide and favorable acquaintance in Albion and Calhoun county and their beautiful home in the village is justly celebrated for its charming and gracious hospitality.

HARRY BLISS WILLIAMS.

The business interests of Tekonsha are well represented by this gentleman, whose enterprising spirit is in harmony with the progressiveness of the west. He is a dealer in groceries, provisions, boots and shoes in Tekonsha, and is one of the native sons of the village, his birth having occurred here on the 6th of May, 1871. His parents were Alvin and Mary (Bliss) Williams. Our subject was only six months old when his father died. In Tekonsha he was reared to manhood, acquiring a good education, which was completed by graduation from the high school, when he was nineteen years of age. He afterward attended Cleary's Business College at Ypsilanti, Michigan, and was there graduated in 1893. When fifteen years of age he started out upon an independent business career, and whatever success he has achieved has come to him as the result of his earnest efforts since that time. He was first employed as a salesman in the grocery store of H. N. Randall, in which he worked on Saturday and in the morning and evening of every day of the week. He afterward spent a year as shipping clerk in

Jackson, Michigan, and upon his return to Tekonsha was again in the employ of Mr. Randall for a time. From his father he inherited some village property, which he sold for seven hundred dollars, and with that capital embarked in the grocery business on his own account. For seven years he conducted his store and then engaged in clerking for a year, after which he entered into partnership with Henry Bartlett. He is now well known in the village, and has a well appointed store, carrying a carefully selected line of goods. He enjoys a liberal patronage, which has come to him in recognition of his reliable business methods and his earnest desire to please his patrons.

Mr. Williams was married in Girard township, Branch county, Michigan, September 29, 1896, to Miss Phoebe Shedd, a daughter of Samuel and Louisa (Eldred) Shedd. They have three children, Lelia, Alvin and Fern, all born in Tekonsha. The political support of Mr. Williams is given to the Republican party, and in 1902-3 he filled the office of village treasurer. In 1901 he was elected to the village council, in which he served for two years, and during that time was a member of the committee on streets, sidewalks and fires. It was during his incumbency that the greater part of the cement sidewalks of the town were laid. He has been a delegate to various conventions, county, congressional and state, and is untiring in his efforts to promote the growth and insure the success of his party. He is now president of the fire department of Tekonsha, and is a member of Avon tent, of the Knights of the Maccabees, in which he has served as finance keeper. Mr. Williams is yet a young man, but has exerted considerable influence in public and community affairs in his village, and his worth is widely recognized, for his business methods will always bear the closest investigation and his course in politics has ever been that of a loyal and progressive citizen.

WILLIAM H. FARRINGTON.

The name which introduces this review is one familiar to the residents of Battle Creek, and it is one which suggests to the honest man a feeling of confidence and security, while to the evil doer it betokens a power which is feared as the instrument through which he is most likely to meet with apprehension, and therefore pay the penalty for his crimes against the laws, which are the stable foundation of the peace and prosperity of his fellow beings. As chief of police Mr. Farrington has made a most honorable record and one which reflects credit upon his unfaltering allegiance to duty and the right.

William H. Farrington was born upon the farm near Pennville, Jay county, Indiana, on the 29th of December, 1855, a son of Jesse and Lydia (Lewis) Farrington. He spent his boyhood on the old homestead and acquired his education in the common schools. In 1865 he came with his parents to Calhoun county, living for a time in Harmonia, after which they removed to Battle Creek. Here at the age of eighteen years he entered the employ of the firm of Nichols & Shepard as a painter, continuing with that company for ten years. In 1884 he went to Washington territory in order to view the country, spending about a year in Washington, Oregon and California, but came to the conclusion that he preferred Michigan

WILLIAM H. FARRINGTON

as a place of residence and, returning to this state, settled upon a farm in Allegan county. There he carried on agricultural pursuits for about five years, during which time he bought and sold several pieces of property. In 1889 he returned to Battle Creek and took charge of the painting department for the Halladay & Lewis Company, contractors, with whom he remained for two years. In the spring of 1892 he became a member of the police force and acted as patrolman for five years. In 1897 he began working as a painter for the firm of Lewis & Sons, with which he was connected for one year and in the spring of 1898, when a change in the city administration occurred, he was appointed chief of police and has occupied this responsible position continuously since. On the 12th of May, 1903, he was re-appointed for another term of three years. During his incumbency he had made every effort possible to divorce the police department from politics, believing that incumbency should depend upon the qualifications of the man and not upon his political allegiance. Therefore, he has never based his appointments upon a man's support of any particular party and to-day Battle Creek has one of the most efficient police departments to be found in any city in Michigan. When he was chosen to the office of chief of police he had a little more than desk room in the corner of the treasurer's office, but in the same year the present commodious quarters were built and in every way since that time the police department has been improved and enlarged. In 1899 the patrol wagon was purchased, superseding the use of old wheelbarrows and express wagons. The number of policemen has been more than doubled in order to keep pace with the growth of the city. Separate apartments have been added to the jail

for the use of women and children, so that they need not be placed with depraved men. The equipments of the police service now are as complete and convenient as are to be found in any city of the state. In 1901 there were six hundred and forty-two arrests made and in 1902 eleven hundred and eighty-eight. Every effort has been put forth to suppress crime in any form, and the lawbreakers of the city are beginning to understand that they cannot with impunity abuse the privileges and rights the law accords to their fellow men. Mr. Farrington certainly deserves credit for what he has accomplished in the way of improving the department and in suppressing vice, and his course has the endorsement of all the best citizens of Battle Creek.

On the 17th of March, 1881, occurred the marriage of Mr. Farrington and Miss Minnie Camp, of Marshall. She was born on a farm near Marshall, a daughter of George and Catherine (Moore) Camp. Mr. and Mrs. Farrington were married, however, in Kalamazoo, and they now have one son, William Roy, who was born in Allegan county, Michigan, September 25, 1886, and is now a student in the high school, a member of the class of 1905. Mr. Farrington is a stockholder in several of the large manufacturing industries of the city. While in the employ of the firm of Nichols & Shepard he became a member of the volunteer fire department, and after a year or two joined the union hose team, the city allowing this team twenty-five dollars per year. From 1876 until 1884, he was connected with it and during that time the famous Potter House fire occurred, Mr. Farrington acting as pipeman on that occasion. In politics he is a Republican and his first presidential ballot was cast for Garfield in

1880. In 1878 he became a member of the Ancient Order of United Workmen and he also belongs to the Independent Order of Odd Fellows, to the Knights of Pythias, the Knights of the Golden Eagle, and Knights of the Maccabees. It is scarcely necessary to say that Mr. Farrington is a man endowed with the strongest individuality, intrepid bravery when in the face of most desperate situations, and a remarkable coolness and presence of mind under all circumstances. As a man among men he holds the confidence and esteem of those with whom he comes in contact in either a business or a social way.

THOMAS TINGAY.

Thomas Tingay, a well-known citizen of Marshall, was born in Chatteris, Cambridgeshire, England, April 1, 1835, one of a large family of children born to Robert and Frances (Lowe) Tingay. The father, born March 1, 1811, the son of Thomas Tingay, a butcher by occupation, was a well-to-do farmer in England, owning his own home, where his death occurred May 18, 1855, being buried in a cemetery in Chatteris. The mother was a daughter of John and Frances Lowe, also a farmer who owned his property. He was born 1780, and died at Chatteris in 1848. His wife was born April 6, 1780, and died in April, 1858. Mrs. Tingay died in London August 11, 1896. She had spent the last twenty years of her life there. She was born April 20, 1813.

Of the ten children, those besides Thomas Tingay, the personal subject of this review; are named in the order of birth as follows: Robert, born April 29, 1833, died July 16, 1890; Ann, born May 14, 1837, resides in England; Sarah, born March 1, 1840, makes her home in London, England; William, born July 30, 1842, died at the age of sixteen years; John born August 27, 1844, lives in Marshall, Michigan; Margaret, born September 7, 1846, also died at the age of sixteen; Lizzie, born January 12, 1850, is also a resident of London, England; George, born October 9, 1852, is a carpenter by occupation and lives at Warsall, England, near Birmingham. Staffordshire; Fannie, born January 21, 1856, resides in London. With mature years these members of a sturdy English family have developed those characteristics which distinguish the citizens of England, and have become helpful and prosperous citizens. Lizzie and Fannie Tingay are members of a family where the elder sister has held the position of housekeeper for thirty years. January 11, 1877, Mr. Tingay, of this review, started on a trip to England on the ship Brittaric. of the White Star line and after a voyage of nine days went to Chatteris where he visited his mother and met his sister Fannie, a young lady of twenty-one, whom he had never before seen. having left home before her birth.

He spent seven weeks in the land of his birth and returned home on the same ship which had carried him to England, his love and loyalty given to the country of his adoption.

Mr. Tingay left his home when only eighteen years old, sailing from England. May 24th, the Queen's birthday, and after a stormy passage of forty-two days arrived in New York City July 4. 1853, the date upon which he landed. He at once sought employment in the farming regions of the state, locating at Almon, New York, where he worked by the month, his remuneration being twelve dollars per month and his living. Ambitious to acquire an education he attended school during the winter months, at the same time earning his living by doing chores. After a year in that locality he went to Pennsylvania, where he worked three years on a farm at Ulysses, going then to Cleveland, Ohio, where he earned his livelihood for a year by cutting cord wood. On returning to Pennsylvania he worked in a lumber camp on Kettle creek, remaining so employed for six months, then going down the Susquehanna river on a lumber raft, finding his way back to Ulysses, where he worked on a farm for one summer. The following winter he went into the lumber camp at Young Woman's creek and worked until June of the next year, when he went to Cleveland again and was employed in the harvest fields until September. Until February he was once more occupied in a lumber camp, when he became ill, returned to Ulysses and was incapacitated for work for fourteen months. On his recovery he went back to Almon and was employed upon a farm until the fall of the year, when he went to Genesee, where he remained until the fall of 1864. December 6, 1864, mark his location in Marshall, since which time he has worked his way to a position of competence and general esteem. He first earned his livelihood by cutting cord wood, and the first summer after his marriage here he worked by the day until October 1, when he assumed charge of Colonel Dickie's farm of two hundred acres. After two years he went to Battle Creek and worked three months, and next conducted a farm at Bath Mills for one year. On returning to Marshall he engaged in teaming until the spring of 1885, when he removed to a farm owned by Charles T. Gorham, located three miles west of this city, remaining occupied as a farmer for thirteen years. In 1898 he again located in Marshall, his home now being at No. 533 North Linden street, which property he purchased thirty-three years ago, a fine, modern house and commodious and substantial buildings, now occupying the space destitute of improvement at the time of his purchase. On locating here five years ago Mr. Tingay engaged in the wood business and met with much success, now owning, besides the property mentioned thirteen acres of land. He is now retired from the active cares of life and is enjoying a season of rest, after many years of usefulness.

Mr. Tingay was married May 10, 1865, to Miss Emma Parr, who was born in Cambridgeshire, England, October 8, 1847, the daughter of William Parr, who brought his family to Marshall, where they now live. Mr. and Mrs. Tingay are the parents of five children, all of whom received a good education in the common schools of the county. The oldest son, William L., was born August 3, 1868, and is an engineer by occupation, his home being in Grand Ledge, this state. He married Miss Myrtle Case, and they have two children, Blanche, born September 24, 1895, and Marian, born November 12, 1896; the second son, Frank L., was born December 26, 1873, and now lives in Detroit; Mabel, the oldest daughter, was born July 3, 1874, and married Thomas Peggs, of Delrey, and they have one child, Alfred T., born August 25, 1903; Lizzie Belle was born August 19, 1881, and makes her home with her parents; Thomas, the youngest of the family, was born July 27, 1887, and is now employed in Greene's drug store, of this city.

Mr. Tingay is truly a self-made man in the best sense implied by the term. Empty-handed he set out in the world determined to overcome the obstacles which he fore-saw in his career, energy and ambition the only foundation upon which to build. Dur-in a long life of changing fortune one of his greatest trials has been ill-health, an obstacle which few would have surmounted in the manner which has characterized Mr. Tingay's efforts. In 1897 he was incapac-itated for a year. At one time in his career he did threshing with a flail for five cents per bushel in his efforts to earn a liveli-hood. Failing to secure the education he desired in early manhood, he has sought throughout the years to acquire a fund of information, by observation and reading, and thus has made himself a man of im-portance in his community. Though never desirous of official recognition he has yielded to the earnest solicitation of his friends and allowed his name to be brought before the public as that of a candidate for office, his name being on the Greenback ticket for alderman. His first presidential vote was cast for Fremont, and on one oc-casion he voted the Greenback ticket, though he is now a stanch Republican. He was elected to the office of treasurer of the school board in Marshall township, and served efficiently for two terms. Mr. and Mrs. Tingay have been members of the Presbyterian faith for forty years and he is now an elder in the First Presbyterian church of Marshall, having held member-ship here for the past twenty years. He is also an active member of the Sunday school.

· HERBERT WRIGHT CUSHMAN.

Herbert Wright Cushman, who is fill-ing the position of assistant cashier of the First State Bank of Tekonsha, was born in the city of Three Rivers in St. Joseph county, Michigan, February 10, 1873, his parents being Henry DePuy and Thirza A. (Wright) Cushman. The ancestral history of the family can be traced back through twelve generations to a very early epoch in the colonization of the new world. The first American ancestor was Robert Cushman who with John Carver as agents of the Pilgrims obtained from the King of England a patent permitting the Pilgrims to emigrate to America, where they might enjoy religious freedom. He did not cross the Atlantic in the Mayflower with the Pilgrims in 1620, but followed the next year in the ship Fortune, bringing with him his son Thomas, whom he placed in the family of Governor Bradford upon his re-turn to England the following year. He de-voted much of his life to the moral develop-ment of the people among whom he lived and he had the honor of preaching the first sermon in New England that was ever printed. His son, Elder Thomas Cushman, born in England in February, 1608, became a ruling elder of the church at Plymouth, Massachusetts, and served in that capac-ity for forty-three years. He married Miss Mary Allerton, a daughter of Isaac and Mary (Norris) Allerton, all of whom came to the new world in the Mayflower, her fa-ther having been one of the signers of the famous compact which was drawn upon board that vessel ere the Pilgrims landed at Plymouth Rock. He was assistant gov-ernor of the colony under Governor Brad-ford and his name has come down in his-tory as that of the first merchant of New

England. Mary Allerton Cushman, the wife of Elder Thomas Cushman, was the last survivor of the one hundred passengers who made the first settlement on the shores of New England. To Thomas Cushman and his wife were born eight children, Eleazer Cushman, being the seventh, was born February 20, 1656 or 1657. He married Elizabeth Combes and their son, John Cushman, who was born August 13, 1690, married Joanna Pratt. Of the children of this marriage Charles Cushman married Miss Mary Harvey and their son Isaac, who lived in Rutland, Vermont, died in 1783, leaving a son Ethiel, born in March, 1771, and married Anna Fenton. Joseph Fenton Cushman, son of Ethiel and Anna Cushman, married Rebecca Green and their son, Isaac Cushman, who was born September 27, 1821, married Maria H. DePuy. She was of the seventh generation of the descendants of Nicholas DePuy, who came from Holland to America, arriving at New Amsterdam, now New York City, in October, 1662. Isaac and Maria DePuy Cushman were the grandparents of Herbert Wright Cushman.

Their son, Henry DePuy Cushman, the father of our subject, was born August 16, 1846, and died February 11, 1900. His birth occurred at Spring Arbor, Jackson county, Michigan, where he acquired his early education, which was afterward supplemented by study in Albion College and in the pharmacy department of the University of Michigan, in which he was graduated. Entering upon his business career sas a druggist, he conducted a store at Albion for a time and afterward at Three Rivers and during his residence at the latter place he invented and manufactured the famous Cushman's menthol inhaler. In all

of his business dealings he was upright and honorable and his conformity to the strictest commercial ethics combined with his enterprise and capable business methods won him success in his commercial undertakings. His efforts also extended to many other fields of activity touching the general interests of society. He was a valued member of the Methodist church and for about twenty-eight years served as superintendent of the Sunday-school. Although he never sought or desired political preferment he was a stanch advocate of the Republican party and manifested a public-spirited interest in everything pertaining to the welfare of city, state and nation. He was prominent in Masonic circles and also affiliated with other fraternal organizations. A genial manner, deference for the opinions of others, his devotion to all measures for the welfare of his fellow men and his upright life made him a popular citizen well liked by all who knew him. His death occurred at his home at Three Rivers, Michigan, and his widow now resides at Minneapolis, Minnesota. She bore the maiden name of Thirza A. Wright and is a daughter of Josiah and Eliza A. (Smith) Wright. She was of the eighth generation of the descendants of Rev. Henry Smith, who emigrated from England in 1635 and in 1637 settled at Weathersfield, Connecticut, where he became the pastor of the first regularly organized church on the banks of the Connecticut river.

Herbert Wright Cushman, son of Henry DePuy and Thirza A. Cushman, was reared to manhood in Three Rivers, Michigan, and completed the high-school course there by graduation in 1890. He was one of the two of that class who successfully passed the teacher's examination and, that he was popular with his classmates is shown by the fact that he was chosen class president. In the fall of 1890 he entered Albion College and after a year spent in study there he entered the office of his father who was engaged in the manufacture of the Cushman menthol inhaler. For a year he remained in Three Rivers and then in 1892 returned to Albion to resume his studies, being graduated in the spring of 1895 with the degree of Bachelor of Science.

After the completion of his collegiate course Mr. Cushman went to Vincennes, Indiana, as manager of the Cushman Drug Company and continued at that place for about three years, when in the spring of 1898 he came to Tekonsha to accept a position with the Exchange Bank of Allen & Johnson, at this place, which upon being re-organized in 1902 was incorporated as the First State Bank and Mr. Cushman was given the position of assistant cashier. He has since been identified with the financial interests of the town and his business qualifications are such as to make him a capable officer in the institution.

At Albion, Michigan, on the 16th of October, 1895, was celebrated the marriage of Mr. Cushman and Miss Nettie B. Allen, a daughter of Sylvester B. and Cordelia M. (Robinson) Allen, who are mentioned at length in connection with the sketch of Frank E. Allen. . Mrs. Cushman was educated at Albion College and is a graduate of the Albion Conservatory of Music in 1893. They have two children, Dorothy M. and Robert Allen, both born in Albion, the former on the 19th of January, 1899, the latter April 16, 1902. Mr. Cushman is a stanch Republican, his first vote being cast for McKinley in 1898. In 1902 he was

elected one of the trustees of the village board which position he is now filling. He is thus actively associated with the administration of public affairs. He belongs to the Delta Tau Delta, a Greek letter fraternity, with which he became connected while in Albion College and is a member of the Presbyterian church, in which he is serving as a trustee. In 1903 he joined the Masonic order, becoming a member of Washington lodge, No. 7, F. and A. M., of Tekonsha. Of courteous manner, with deference for the opinion of others, possessed of good business ability and sound judgment he has already won for himself a creditable place in business circles and will undoubtedly have a successful future.

JOHN M. WILLISON.

John Melvin Willison, who is identified with farming in Pennfield township, Calhoun county, was born in Johnstown township, Barry county, Michigan, on the 21st of May, 1849, his parents being Elias B. and Nancy (Harkness) Willison. In the district schools Mr. Willison of this review began his preliminary education and later spent one. year as a student in the Richland Seminary, while for three years he was a student in Kalamazoo College. Thus he was well fitted for the responsible duties of life, and at the age of twenty-one years put aside his text-books and started out on his own account. For ten or twelve years he engaged in teaching school in both Barry and Kalamazoo counties and was a most capable teacher. At the end of that time he turned his attention to farming, in 1886, removing to the place upon which he now resides and which he had purchased in 1881. It comprises one hundred and sixty acres of land that is a valuable tract now under a high state of cultivation. In connection with his brother he also owns the old homestead in Barry county of two hundred and forty acres, which he aided in clearing and improving in his early youth. At one time he was engaged in the milling business at Climax, conducted a grist-mill there, hoping that his health might be benefited through a change of employment.

On the 30th of June, 1872, at Johnstown, Michigan, Mr. Willison was united in marriage to Miss Emily Iden, who was born in that place and is a daughter of Charles P. and Mary (Bristol) Iden. Her father was born in Newtown. Bucks county. Pennsylvania, in 1818, a son of Thomas and Rachel (Parry) Iden. His parents were members of the Society of Friends or Quakers and were of English lineage. Charles P. Iden received better educational facilities than were afforded many boys of the period and he owed this entirely to his own efforts. By acting as janitor he paid his tuition and in order to reach the schoolhouse it was necessary for him to walk four miles. During his early boyhood his parents removed to the western part of New York and afterward he came on foot to Battle Creek. His life was one of untiring industry and enterprise. He helped to build the mill race for the Augusta mills, and while thus employed made his home with the Stringham family. Soon after his arrival in Michigan he entered eighty acres of timber land from the government in the southern part of Johnstown township and about two years after took up his abode

upon that tract, making it his home for a long period. Pioneer conditions existed in this part of the state and the early settlers had to endure many hardships and trials incident to frontier life. They were cut off from the comforts and conveniences of the older east and had to perform many difficult and arduous tasks in reclaiming the wild land for purposes of civilization. Prices, too, for crops were very low and all produce had to be hauled to Jackson, Mr. Iden there receiving two dollars and a barrel of salt in compensation for a load of wheat. Charles P. Iden resided in Barry county until 1882, covering a period of more than forty years and aided in laying broad and deep the foundation for the present prosperity and progress of the county. As the years passed by he increased his landed possessions and became the owner of four hundred and sixty acres of land which he improved. His death occurred in 1890, when he was seventy-two years of age. his wife passed away some time before at the age of sixty-two years. Both were buried on the old family homestead. In the Iden family were eight children who are now living.

The home of Mr. and Mrs. Willison has been blessed with four children: Charles, who is a graduate of the Battle Creek high school, engaged in teaching for a year; Maurice, who is attending a commercial college in Battle Creek; Nina L.; and Catherine. In his political views Mr. Willison was a stanch Democrat and has been called to fill some local offices. In 1895 he was elected supervisor of Pennfield township, although he lives in a strong Republican district, there being about two Republicans to one Democrat in this locality. Mr. Willison, however, won the election by a two-thirds vote, a fact which shows that he is personally popular and that his fellow citizens entertain for him high regard and unqualified confidence. He has since been re-elected continuously and for one year was chairman of the board of supervisors. In 1901 he was a representative to the state board of equalization, and on a number of occasions has been a delegate to the county and state conventions of his party. Mr. Willison was also the vice president of the state association of supervisors and was at one time the nominee on the Democratic ticket for the office of senator for Kalamazoo and Calhoun counties, but because of the strong Republican majority in the district did not win the election, although he ran far ahead of his ticket. Mr. Willison has for some years been interested in, and for four years a director of the Calhoun County Mutual Insurance Company. He is a man of strong purpose, fearless in defense of his honest convictions and unfaltering in his allegiance to what he believes to be right. In business affairs he is energetic and progressive and in everything pertaining to the general good is found as a co-operant factor. Upon educational advancement and political life he has left the impress of his individuality and in Calhoun county he is also widely known as a leading agriculturist.

JOHN C. REYNOLDS, M. D.

With offices located in rooms 403-4 Post building, in Battle Creek, Dr. John C. Reynolds is enjoying a large patronage in his chosen profession, which indicates the confidence reposed in him by the public. Careful preparation and deep interest in the science of medicine have well equipped him for his chosen pursuit, and he has advanced to a foremost position in the ranks of the medical fraternity of Calhoun county. The Doctor was born near Port Hope, Canada, in the year 1857, first opening his eyes to the light of day on his father's farm. He is a son of Francis and Margaret (Kells) Reynolds, both of whom were natives of County Cavan, Ireland, but the mother was of English parentage. Both Mr. and Mrs. Reynolds were reared on the Emerald Isle, and were there married. Crossing the Atlantic to the new world in the twenties, they settled first in the Dominion of Canada, and when the Doctor was but four years of age they removed to Rochester, New York, where the father engaged in business as a stockdealer for three years. He then brought his family to Battle Creek, Michigan, settling in this city when it contained a population of only about four thousand.

Dr. Reynolds was a youth of seven summers when the family came to this state. He acquired his literary education in the schools of Battle Creek, continuing his studies until he reached the senior year of the high school, when he put aside his textbooks and entered the business world, accepting a clerkship with the firm of Galloup, Hollister & Reynolds. He remained with that company for three years, but his health failed, and in order to recuperate he went to Texas, where he remained for two years. Having then determined to enter professional life, he took up the study of medicine in this city, under the direction of Dr. A. S. Johnson. In 1880 he matriculated in the Pulte Medical College of Cincinnati, Ohio, where he was graduated with the class of

JOHN C. REYNOLDS, M. D.

1882. Dr. Reynolds began practice in Battle Creek, and soon secured a gratifying patronage, for he early demonstrated his ability to check disease and restore health. Through his alleviation of human suffering, he has become the loved family physician in many a household. In 1894 he pursued a post-graduate course in the Chicago Homeopathic Medical College, and has continually added to his knowledge of the medical science by reading, study and investigation until he is thoroughly in touch with modern methods of thought and of practice. While he is quick to adapt any new idea or line of work that will prove of benefit in his professional duties, he is never willing to discard old and tried methods for something whose worth is not clearly proven. Though he has always made the practice of medicine his chief interest, he has become connected with various manufacturing enterprises of Battle Creek in a financial way. He took stock in the Battle Creek Brewing Company, of which he is a director, and is also a stockholder in the Malt-Too Company, the Korn Krisp Company, and the Johnson Foundry and Machine Works, limited. He has likewise invested in real estate in Battle Creek, having some valuable property interests here. Thus his connection with business affairs has not only proven of benefit to himself, but also has been a benefit to the city by the promotion of industrial and commercial activity.

At Paw Paw, Michigan, on the 5th of August, 1885, Dr. Reynolds was united in marriage to Mrs. Lizzie H. Briggs, nee Hudson. She was born and reared at Paw Paw and was educated in the high school there. By her former marriage she had a daughter, Allene Briggs, who is the wife of Graham

Wells, of Battle Creek, Michigan. They have one daughter, Martha Elizabeth.

In his political views the Doctor is a Republican, following in the footsteps of his father in this direction. He cast his first presidential ballot for General Garfield, and has never faltered in his allegiance to the party since that time. He was elected alderman from the fifth ward in 1900, and served on the committee on public health and charity, of which he was chairman. He was likewise chairman of the fire department committee and belonged to the committee on parks and public buildings. It was Dr. Reynolds who introduced the bill to create Monument park, and during his term in office Monument Square was paved. In matters of citizenship he has always been progressive, and his co-operation has proved a valuable factor for the general improvement. Fraternally, he was raised in Battle Creek lodge, No. 12, F. & A. M., and demitted to Metcalf lodge, No. 419. He is also a member of Battle Creek chapter, No. 19, R. A. M., and Battle Creek commandery, No, 33, Knights Templar. He is also prominent in the Knights of Pythias fraternity and the Benevolent Protective Order of Elks. In the line of his profession he is connected with the State Medical Society, and the Calhoun County Medical Society. In manner he is free from all ostentation and display, but his intrinsic worth is recognized, and his friendship is most prized by those who know him best, showing that his character will bear the scrutiny of close acquaintance. He is a generous-spirited, broad-minded man, a true type of the American spirit, and an embodiment of that progress which in the last few years has drawn to this country the admiring gaze of the nations of the world.

21

FRANK W. COURT.

Frank W. Court, now the senior member of the firm of James Court & Son, at Marshall, Michigan, was born in Augusta, Kalamazoo county, on the 21st of July, 1863. He began his education in the schools of his native city and afterward continued his studies in Marshall. When a boy he began assisting his father, who had established business as a dealer in poultry, eggs and butter. He thus became familiar with the enterprise in its various departments and as he showed adaptability to the work and close application to his duties he was eventually admitted to a partnership and has for twenty years been actively identified with the firm. The business was established upon a safe yet progressive basis and has always been carried on in that manner. It is an enterprise that is of value to the community, furnishing a market to local producers, and at the same time it has proved a most profitable concern to the owners, large annual sales bringing a very gratifying income.

In 1887 F. W. Court was united in marriage to Miss Mary Lowe, of Marshall, Michigan, who was born at Chatteris, Cambridgeshire, England, and with her parents, John and Susannah (Briggs)) Lowe, came to Marshall in 1884. Their union has been blessed with three children: Frances M., George W., and Hazel J. Mr. and Mrs. Court are well known in the social circles of the city and the hospitality of the best homes of Marshall is cordially extended to them. Mr. Court is prominent in Masonic circles, in which he has attained a high degree. His membership is now with St. Albans lodge, F. & A. M., LaFayette Chapter, R. A. M., Council, R. & S. M., Marshall commandery, No. 17, Knights Templar, and he is a member of the Knights of Pythias at Marshall. In his life he exemplifies the beneficent spirit of the fraternity and is most true and loyal to its tenets and teachings. There have been no sensational chapters in his career, his course having been characterized by perseverance in business, close application and strong determination.

ABNER LOOMIS CARPENTER.

Though but recently an acquisition to the business life of Athens, Abner L. Carpenter has yet demonstrated his ability to lead in commercial activity. The name is well-known throughout this county, a complete history of the family being given on another page of this volume. Mr. Carpenter is a native of New York state, having been born in Naples, Ontario county, November 20, 1852, removing with his parents to Michigan when a mere lad. His parents remained in their first location in the state—Sherwood township, Branch county—for a short time, when they removed to Athens township, Calhoun county, where their son received his scholastic training in the district school in the vicinity of his home, while assisting with the home duties. He worked for his father until his marriage in 1874, when he rented a farm in Athens township, where he remained for ten years, his energy and industry resulting in sufficient means to enable him to purchase a farm of eighty acres. This was entirely new land, boasting no improvements nor upturned sod, located in the same township southeast of the village of Athens. With the energy and determination which had characterized his first independent venture in life, Mr. Carpenter set to work to reclaim the land and make of it one of the many desirable properties of the county. After ten years he sold out and purchased a hundred-acre farm located just west of the village, remaining upon this property until March 15, 1902. At that date he traded the farm for the grocery store, which is now absorbing his time and interests. He has successfully established himself in Athens, conducting his business according to conservative methods and giving to his large patronage a choice line of groceries.

Mr. Carpenter's wife was, in maidenhood, Miss Agnes Henry, a native of Marshall township, Calhoun county. Her parents were Hugh Gregg and Maria (Thrall) Henry, natives respectively of Naples, Ontario county, New York state, and Connecticut. In 1854 he removed with his family to Calhoun county, Michigan, purchasing a farm about three miles west of Marshall, where he engaged in agricultural pursuits until 1861. He then sold his property and located in Sherwood, Branch county, purchasing a hotel property, which he conducted for about six years. After disposing of this business he removed to Athens, where he made his home until his death. Both himself and wife are interred in the cemetery at Athens. They were the parents of the following children: James, William, Agnes and Inez, the wife of Calvin Lewis Wilson. All make their homes in Athens. To Mr. and Mrs. Carpenter were born six children, namely: Minnie, who married Albert Chichester and they now reside in this township, the parents of three children, Opal, Raymond and Marta; Ruth, the second daughter, died at the age of twenty-two years. She had graduated from the Athens high school when quite young, after which she taught for five years, making a name and place for herself among the progressive and up-to-date educators of the county. She was prominent in church and social circles as well as educational, being a member of the First Reformed church of Athens, a member of the choir and a teacher in the Sunday-school, and belonged to the auxiliary of the Knights of the Maccabees of this village, from all of these positions being greatly missed, not alone for the practical help she gave, but for the gentle and kindly nature, which won and retained for her a large circle of friends. She sleeps in the cemetery in Athens. Della, the third daughter, married Charles Bauer, and they are residents of this township, and the parents of two children, Earl and Leo; Lorane married Burton Martin, and they now reside in this township; and Orland and Jennie are still at home with their parents. In his political preferment Mr. Carpenter is an adherent of the Republican party through whose influence he has held for one year the position of county drain commissioner. Intelligently interested in all educational questions he has served and is serving as a member of the board of education. Fraternally, he is identified with the Knights of the Maccabees, being secretary of his lodge, while his wife serves in the same capacity for the auxiliary lodge of Athens. Personally, Mr. Carpenter is a highly respected and esteemed citizen, the many sterling qualities which have characterized his years of usefulness in the community, giving to him, to an exceptional degree, the confidence of his fellow townsmen. He has always been ready to support every movement which has for its end the welfare of the public, and uphold the

hands of those who were attempting reform and progression. He is justly entitled
to representation in this volume.

JAMES FINCH.

James Finch, a leading resident of Albion township and one of the oldest citizens of the county, was born in the town of
Greece, Monroe county, New York, his
parents being Asahel and Julia Ann (Wilcox) Finch. The Finch family is of Welch
lineage and was founded in America at a
very early day by Daniel Finch, who came
from Wales, and established his home in
Pennsylvania. He was killed in the Wyoming massacre of 1778, during the Revolutionary war. At that time, his son, Samuel Finch, the grandfather of our subject,
was taken prisoner, but while he was being
conveyed to Canada, he managed to make
his escape while the party was traveling
through the state of New York. His birth
occurred December 15, 1755, so that he
was then about twenty-two years of age.
He followed the occupation of farming in
the Empire state, becoming the owner of a
nice farm property in Monroe county. He
was quite successful in his business affairs,
accumulating a comfortable competence.
The last years of his life were spent in Law-
renceburg, Pennsylvania, where his death
occurred March 7, 1839, his remains being
interred there. At the time the Wyoming
Association erected a monument at the
place of the massacre, they sent a carriage
one hundred miles to bring Mr. Finch to
Wyoming, in order that he might locate
exactly the place where the massacre occurred. This he did, and his name appears

upon the monument among others who
were sufferers from that Indian uprising.
The names of three members of the Finch
family are inscribed on that memorial stone.
Samuel Finch married Polly King, who
was a member of the old King family of
Cayuga county, New York, and after the
death of her husband, she came to Michigan, where her last days were spent, and at
her death she was laid to rest in Homer
cemetery in Calhoun county.

Asahel Finch, the father of our subject,
was born near Painted Post, New York,
September 24, 1794, and acquired his education in the common schools. He afterward learned the brick-maker's trade and in
the spring of 1834, came to Calhoun
county, Michigan, beginning the manufacture of brick at Homer. This was the first
brick ever made in the county. In the fall
of that year he removed to the Forks, by
which name the present town of Albion was
then called, and built the first house west
of the river in that vicinity. At that time
the little hamlet contained but two log
houses on the other side of the river. There
for a number of years Asahel Finch and
his wife conducted a boarding house for
the men who were engaged in the construction of the mills, and digging the race-
way. Among the number of their board-
ers were Judge John Carroll, of New York,
Judge Bacon, of Monroe, Michigan, and
others who afterward became distinguished
and prominent citizens. Asahel Finch married Miss Julia Ann Wilcox, who was a
native of Connecticut and in her early girlhood days accompanied her parents to eastern New York, where she grew to womanhood and became the wife of Asahel Finch.
This worthy couple continued to reside in
Albion until 1860, and afterward took up

their abode at the home of their son James. Mr. Finch died August 23, 1864, and his wife, who was born December 19, 1802, passed away June 29, 1879, at which time she was laid to rest by the side of her husband in Riverside cemetery of Albion. They were both devout and earnest members of the Methodist church, Mrs. Finch especially taking an active part in its work. He gave his political allegiance to the Democratic party and in community affairs took an active and helpful interest, being numbered among the pioneer settlers, whose labors promoted the welfare and progress of the county at an early day. Unto Mr. and Mrs. Finch were born five children: Mariah Jane, the eldest, is the widow of William A. Warner and resides in Coldwater, Michigan; Harriet was the wife of Alonzo H. Colby, who went to California in 1849, and died there within a year, leaving to his widow the care of four children. Mrs. Colby afterward became the wife of Charles Diffenbaugh and is now again a widow. She makes her home in Texas with a daughter; Ariel died in 1849; Robert Y. is represented on another page of this work; James is the youngest of the family.

In his early boyhood days James Finch was brought by his parents to Michigan, where he was reared amid the wild scenes of frontier life, and his mind bears many pictures of pioneer experiences and conditions such as confronted the early settler of this region. He pursued his preliminary education in a log schoolhouse in Albion township and he afterward attended the Albion Seminary at an early day. The New Testament was used as a text-book in which the scholars learned to read. Throughout the period of his childhood

and youth, Mr. Finch remained under the parental roof and assisted largely in the development of the home farm and also worked under his father in a saw-mill in which Asahel Finch was head sawyer. He also learned the trade of a weaver in a mill that was operated in Albion. When his brother-in-law went to California in 1849, Mr. Finch took charge of the farm, being at that time twenty years of age. He operated the place for two years and then purchased a farm of two hundred and twenty-four acres in Sheridan township, on which a log cabin and a log stable had been built. His sister acted as housekeeper for him until the time of her marriage, and afterward his father and mother came to live with him.

It was in 1859 that Mr. Finch was united in mariage to Miss Jane Cornell, a sister of Ezra Cornell, the founder of Cornell University at Ithaca, New York. She was a daughter of Elijah and Eunice (Barnard) Cornell, who was born on the 18th of May, 1831, at De Ruyter, New York. Mr. and Mrs. Finch have become the parents of eight children: Robert F., born March 18, 1860, resides in South Dakota, where he is engaged in the agricultural implement business and is also a grain dealer. He married Miss Lizzie Billinghurst, a native of Sheridan township, and unto them was born one child, but the mother and child are now deceased. Robert F. Finch afterward married Avie Bird; Hattie and May Finch were twins, born March 7, 1862. The former became the wife of D. S. Howe, a resident of Albion and they have seven children: Ethel M., Julia Ward, Bessie, deceased; Helen, Ruth, James and Robert; Mary resides at home and is acting as her father's housekeeper;

James Cornell, born March 5, 1864, resides in Oklahoma City, and is commercial agent for the Missouri, Kansas & Texas Railroad Company. He married Miss Minnie Haynes, of Parsons, Kansas, and they have two children, Julia and Marvin H.; Frank Arthur, born January 29, 1866, resides in Evarts, South Dakota, being railroad agent for the Chicago, Milwaukee & St. Paul Railroad Company at that place. He is also a ranchman. He married Jennie Boudiette and they have two children, Gladys and Frank; Julia, born February 11, 1868, died at the age of four years; Edmund Roy, born October 27, 1873, spent one winter in northern Minnesota with a surveying party. He was a very promising young man, but an early death terminated his career, passing away on the 9th of May, 1903; Edgar Julian, born March 2, 1876, resides in Ipswich, South Dakota, where he is engaged in the hardware business and is also buying wheat for a large mill.

In 1866 Mr. Finch sold his farm in Sheridan township, and during that summer resided in the village of Albion, but in the fall of the same year purchased his present farm in Albion township, then comprising two hundred and forty acres of land. He has, however, sold one hundred and ten acres of the property. He has erected upon the place fine barns and a beautiful home, and has given his time and energy in undivided manner to the development of his land, until his farm to-day is one of the best improved in this part of the state. His home is an exceptionally fine one, and it stands in the midst of highly cultivated fields which yield to the owner a golden tribute for the care and labor he bestows upon them. In 1892 Mr. Finch was called upon to mourn the loss of his wife, who died on the 16th of October of that year. She was a member of the Methodist Episcopal church and a most estimable lady. To the same church the family belonged. Politically, Mr. Finch is a stanch Prohibitionist, prominent in the ranks of his party both locally and in the state organization. He was at one time a candidate for state senator on the Prohibition.ticket and was also a delegate to the Prohibition National Convention, held in Chicago in 1896. He believes firmly in temperance principles; regarding the issue as one of the most prominent before the people of the country to-day, realizing the trouble, sorrow and wrong that comes through the practice of intoxication, and feeling that every man is in a large measure his brother's keeper, Mr. Finch puts forth every effort to advance the cause of his party and to promote temperance principles among his fellow men. His efforts have accomplished much good in this direction. He is also a member of Murat lodge, F. and A. M., of Albion, and is a Royal Arch Mason. His life exemplifies the beneficent spirit of this craft which recognizes the fatherhood of God and the brotherhood of man.

HON. PERRY MAYO.

There are few residents of Marshall township whose connection with this portion of Calhoun county, antedates that of Mr. Mayo, and his mind retains many pictures of pioneer conditions such as existed in the early days of this portion of the state. In the years which have elapsed since his arrival he has exerted strong and beneficial influence in many lines that have promoted public progress and improvement. Few men of the state have done so much in advancing the agricultural interests of Michigan, and at the same time he has been alert and progressive in matters of citizenship, and has been widely recognized as a leader of the Republican party in the state.

Mr. Mayo was born in Hancock, Delaware county, New York, on the 14th of June, 1839, his parents being James and Sarah A. (Price) Mayo. The father was born August 12, 1810, in the city of Coventry, England, which had been the ancestral home of the family for several generations. The paternal grandfather was an officer in the English army and was killed at the battle of Waterloo prior to the birth of his son James. The latter was educated in Coventry and was brought by his mother to America, the family home being established at Stroudsburg, Monroe county, Pennsylvania, in 1828. There James Mayo learned the blacksmith's trade, at which he worked until his marriage. He was joined in wedlock to Miss Sarah A. Price, who was born there, a daughter of Eleazer Price, who was a soldier of the War of 1812, serving as captain of the Blue Mountain Rangers, an independent military company. He lived and died in Pennsylvania, at the little village called Priceburg, which was named in honor of the family. After his marriage Mr. Mayo removed to Hancock, New York, where he engaged in business on his own account, and later, about 1850, came to Michigan, settling in Convis township, where he engaged in blacksmithing and farming. He purchased a tract of new land, which was wild, improved it and thereon made his home. For a number of years he served as justice of the peace, his political allegiance

being given to the Whig party in early life, while later he joined the ranks of the new Republican party. He was quite successful in his business dealings, and that his labors were carefully directed by sound judgment, is indicated by the fact that he became the owner of a valuable tract of land of two hundred and eight acres. He died on the home farm in March, 1897, and his wife passed away in May, 1885. They were the parents of nine children who reached years of maturity, Perry Mayo being the eldest.

When a youth of eleven years Perry Mayo was brought by the family to Calhoun county. He completed his education by attending the common schools and also the Bellevue high school. He afterward engaged in teaching for a number of years, spending the summer months upon his father's farm. At the first call for seventy-five thousand men to aid in crushing out the rebellion in its incipiency, he enlisted in April, 1861, as a member of Company C, Second Michigan Infantry. This command went to Detroit and there enlisted for three years' service. They were the first three years' men of Calhoun county to leave the state. They went to Washington, D. C., took part in the first battle of Bull Run and were in all of the engagements under General McClellan in the peninsular campaign. Mr. Mayo was also with General Pope in the second battle of Bull Run, was with General Burnsides at Fredericksburg and served under General Sherman at Vicksburg. He participated in the siege of that city, his command re-enforcing the troops under General Grant. Mr. Mayo was also under General Sherman in the campaign, at the capture of Jackson, Mississippi; also in eastern Tennessee and at the siege of Knoxville. Returning to the Eastern army he was under General Grant in the battle of the Wilderness and Spottsylvania and was in the campaign against Richmond. He was wounded at Knoxville and again in the battle before Richmond, and on the 21st of July, 1864, he received an honorable discharge. Mr. Mayo thus participated in a number of hotly contested battles and was always found faithful to his duty, whether it led him into the thickest of the fight or stationed him on the lonely picket line.

When the war was over, he returned to his home and on the 19th of April, 1865, was united in marriage to Miss Mary A. Bryant, of Convis township, a daughter of James and Ann (Atmore) Bryant, who were also among the pioneer settlers of Michigan, having arrived in Calhoun county in 1836. Mrs. Bryant was born in Pennfield, but was reared upon a farm opposite the Mayo homestead, having been brought there when but two weeks old. Prior to his marriage Mr. Mayo purchased a farm of two hundred and thirty acres on section 6, Marshall township, on which he still resides. It was but partially improved when it came into his possession and he has added nearly all of the modern equipments. At the present time he has a number of excellent buildings, fine shade trees, an orchard and, in fact, all the accessories found upon a model farm. His land is very highly cultivated and in his general agricultural pursuits he has met with very gratifying success.

Mr. Mayo became one of the early prominent and influential members of the Grange and his wife also joined the organization. He was master of Battle Creek Grange for seven or eight years and was

its representative in the state Grange. In that body he was made overseer, state lecturer and general deputy, and for four years he was a member of the executive board. At the present writing he is assistant deputy lecturer of the Grange and has lectured on agricultural and educational subjects of general interest to the farmers. He has studied closely the needs of the farm, the possibilities of the soil under climatic influences, and the best methods for cultivating fields that they might bring the best possible return. Mr. Mayo has ever been a man of scholarly attainments and is an extensive reader, his reading embracing all topics. He is, moreover, a deep student and an earnest thinker, desirous of mental advancement and because of his lack of educational opportunities in his youth, he became one of the early students of the Chautauqua course and was graduated in 1888, having been a member of a reading circle that met at his own home for five or six years. This was conducted by his wife, who also took the course and was graduated at the same time with her husband. In the Grange Mrs. Mayo was also a most honored and influential worker. She acted as lecturer of the Battle Creek Grange for many years, was secretary of the county organization and was also deputy assistant lecturer for twenty years. As such her services were in constant demand as a speaker, and she was called from the Atlantic to the Pacific coast, addressing public gatherings at San Francisco, at the Ohio State Fair and various other places of prominence throughout the country. She was employed by the state boards of agriculture in Illinois, Indiana, Ohio and Michigan and was also one of the originators of the woman's branch of the work, and held the largest woman's meeting that ever convened in the state of Michigan in order to further her project. Mrs. Mayo was the originator of the idea for the establishment of a woman's department in connection with the State Agricultural College at Lansing, and obtained from the legislature the appropriation for the department and woman's dormatory. The Michigan State Grange has passed a resolution, asking the State Board of Agriculture to name the Woman's Building of the Agricultural College "Mayo Hall." Governor Luce also appointed her a member of the board of control of the Industrial Home for Girls at Adrian and she occupied that position for six years. Mrs. Mayo was a lady of superior mental culture and refinement. She was largely self-educated, yet her mind was broad, her ideas far-reaching and her views on many public questions of importance showed thorough investigation and knowledge of the subject. Although she served as a lecturer on the public platform from a sense of duty, she always regarded her home and her family as of the utmost importance in her life, and in matters of friendship she was also reliable. During her last five years, however, she gave up her public career in order to devote her time to the care of her daughter, Nellie, who was in an invalid condition as the result of an accident. At this time Mrs. Mayo gave her attention only to her writings. She received a very flattering offer from the publisher of the Ladies' Home Journal, who desired her to write twelve articles which were to fill one page of the monthly edition of the paper for a year. Her subject was to be "The Home Life on the Farm," but on account of her daughter's serious illness she had to decline the proposition.

Both Mr. and Mrs. Mayo held membership in the Methodist Episcopal church. She died April 21, 1903, leaving two children, the elder being Nelson S. He is a graduate of the Agricultural College of Michigan, also of the Chicago Veterinary College and is now professor of veterinary surgery in the Kansas State Agricultural College and is state veterinarian for Kansas. He has also been demonstrator of anatomy at Cornell University, New York; but resigned to accept the position of veterinarian at Connecticut Agricultural College, and was later offered the presidency of that college, but declined. He has recently published a valuable book, "The Care of Animals," that is having a very extended sale. It has been adopted by the state of New York as a textbook in the public schools. He married Miss Mary L. Carpenter, a sister of Judge Carpenter of the supreme court of Michigan, and they have three children, Marguerite, Dorothy and Robert. Nellie A., the younger child of Mr. Mayo, received a liberal education in the district schools and under private instruction, studying art and elocution. She is now at home and is editor of the home department of the "Michigan Patron," the official organ of the Grange. This department was established by Mrs. Mayo a year prior to her death.

Mr. Mayo was made a Mason at St. Albans lodge, No. 20, F. & A. M., at Marshall, but is affiliated with Battle Creek lodge, No. 12, and also belongs to C. Colegrove post, G. A. R., at Marshall. In politics he was for many years a stanch Republican,-was elected superintendent of schools under the old law, during which incumbency he served as examiner of the teachers of the township. He preferred, however, to devote his attention to private business interests, rather than to public offices. He was, nevertheless, in 1887, nominated and elected to the position of state senator at which time the district comprised Calhoun and Branch counties. Mr. Mayo assumed the duties of the office in January, 1888, and was chairman of the committee on Agricultural college, the Michigan Soldiers' Home, military affairs and a member of the committee on constitutional amendments and agriculture. He drafted the bill that prevented the sale of intoxicants to the inmates or employees of the Michigan Soldiers' Home and was instrumental in securing its passage. To him is also largely due the passage of the bill whereby one-half of the local license fund of Calhoun county is used for the support of the poor. In 1894 Mr. Mayo was nominated by the Free Silver party for the office of lieutenant governor and was the only candidate on the ticket that was endorsed by the Democracy. He made a strong canvass for the position, visiting both peninsulas, but it was a Republican year and he was not elected. He is a man of broad intelligence and genuine public spirit. Strong in his individuality, he never lacks the courage of his convictions, and the sterling integrity and honor of his character have gained for him the confidence and respect of men.

HON. FRANK E. PALMER, M. D.

Hon. Frank E. Palmer, who is now filling the position of chief executive of Albion and who for seventeen years has been a prominent practicing physician of that place, was born in Rochester township, Lorain county, Ohio, August 7, 1847, his parents being Gile E. and Phoebe Maria (Noble) Palmer. The father's birth occurred on the banks of the Hudson river in Columbia county, New York, September 26, 1807. The ancestry traces back to Sir Walter Palmer, who in the year 1620 came to America and afterward located at Stonington, Connecticut. The Noble family was also founded in America at an early epoch in the colonization of the new world. When twenty-three years of age Gile E. Palmer left the Empire state and removed to Penfield, Lorain county, Ohio, then to Prairie Depot, Wood county, Ohio, spending his remaining days there.

Dr. Palmer pursued his early education in the public schools of his native county and ere he finished his studies he entered the army, being at the time but sixteen years of age. He enlisted on the 19th of March, 1865, as a member of Company I, One Hundred and Ninety-seventh Ohio Infantry, and was discharged by reason of the general order on the 7th of August, 1865. He then became a student in Oberlin College at Oberlin, Ohio, and subsequently engaged in teaching, but while devoting his attention to that profession, concluded that he would make the practice of medicine his life work and entered upon preparation for the calling as a student in the office and under the direction of Dr. E. R. Sage, of Prairie Depot. Later he entered the drug store of Dr. G. W. Noble and while acting as a clerk in that establishment, also continued his medical studies. He was associated with Dr. Noble for a number of years and was a student in the Eclectic Medical College of Cincinnati. He next entered the Homeopathic Hospital College at Cleveland, Ohio, in which he was graduated in 1876 with the degree of Doctor of Medicine. He located for practice at Republic, Ohio, and while there became a member of the State Medical Society. His deep interest in his chosen calling, his close application to his work and his ability both natural and acquired, enabled him to readily win a very gratifying position as a representative of the medical fraternity in the place where he resided.

In 1882 Dr. Palmer was united in marriage to Miss F. Elizabeth Hamilton, who was born in Republic, Ohio, and had studied medicine in the same school in which her husband was a graduate. After their marriage they removed to Albion and did a general practice. Mrs. Palmer was one of the successful physicians of this city and had a large patronage. She enjoyed the esteem of the medical fraternity and of the residents of the city, and in the treatment of the cases entrusted to her care displayed marked skill and thorough understanding of the scientific principles of medicine and surgery. She was not only devoted to her profession but also took an active interest in public affairs and was a member of the school board for six years, acting as its president at the time of her death. This was an honor not often conferred upon a woman, but Mrs. Palmer was so well qualified for the discharge of the duties of that position that she received the strongest endorsement of all the best citizens of Albion. She was extremely public-spirited and progressive and yet she never allowed any outside interest to interfere with her professional duties, which claimed the greater part of her time. She passed away July 27, 1899. Both Dr. Frank E. Palmer and his wife were members of the State Homeopathic Medical Society and also of the County Medical Society.

At the time of the death of his wife, Dr. Palmer retired from active practice and directed his energies into other fields of business activity. He is now the president of the Albion Buggy Company, has been for a number of years a director of the Albion Malleable Iron Company and is a director and vice president of the Albion Commercial & Savings Bank. His business insight is clear and decided, his judgment rarely, if ever, at fault, and his counsel has therefore proven an important factor in the successful control of a number of the leading enterprises in his adopted town. In social circles he is prominent and is now a director of the Leisure Hour club, which has magnificently furnished club rooms. The membership is limited to one hundred and on its roll are the names of the leading business men of Albion. This is one of the finest clubs to be found in any town of its size in the country. Dr. Palmer is also a member of Murat lodge, F. & A. M., Albion chapter, R. A. M., Albion council, R. & S. M., and Marshall commandery, No. 19, K. T. He likewise belongs to Moslem temple of the Mystic Shrine at Detroit, and, because of his services in the Civil war, he is a member of E. W. Hollingsworth post, No. 210, of which he has been the commander. He has also been a representative of the local post in the state encampment. His first presidential ballot was cast for James A. Garfield. At that time he had not a home of his own and no place in the world that he could call home, but he had lived in Cuyahoga county, Ohio, long enough to vote and so he cast his ballot. He does not take an active part in political work at the present time, but formerly put forth effective efforts in behalf of Republican principles. In past years he served as a member of the city council, and entirely unsolicited on his part came the nomination for mayor. His fellow townsmen of all parties, however, urged his ac-

ceptance of the position, knowing his qualifications and his loyalty in all matters of citizenship. They realized that he would give
them a business administration and one
which would lead to practical and beneficial
results. Thus strongly urged by those who
desired his election he accepted the nomination and in the spring of 1903 was chosen
by popular ballot for the office. During his
administration the city paving has been carried forward to successful completion and
other progressive movements have been instituted. Progress and patriotism might
will be termed the keynote of his character,
for throughout his career he has labored for
the improvement of every line of business or
public interest with which he has been associated and at all times he has been actuated
by a fidelity to his country and her welfare.
During the past four winters Dr. Palmer has
spent his time largely in Florida and California, where he has various business interests. He stands as a representative of our
best type of American manhood and chiv-
alry and his genuine worth, broad mind and
public spirit have made him a director of
public thought and action.

RUSS A. WIEDERWAX.

Russ A. Wiederwax has long been a resident of Albion, where he is now engaged in
conducting a blacksmithing and carriage
shop and also in dealing in agricultural implements. He was born at LeRoy, Genesee
county, New York, January 16, 1853. His
paternal grandfather, John Wiederwax, came
from Holland to the new world about the
beginning of the nineteenth century and settled in the Mohawk valley. Walton Wieder-

wax, the father of our subject, was born in
the Empire state and was one of the early
residents of Genesee county, where he followed the trade of horseshoeing. He married Miss Ellen Bates, of LeRoy, New York,
and in 1855 came to Marshall, where he
opened a blacksmith shop and continued
business until his death. He died suddenly
in his shop May, 1883, and his wife passed
away on the 5th of May, 1882. Russ A.
Wiederwax was brought to Marshall when
a lad of only two summers. He entered the
public schools at the usual age and continued
his studies there until he had completed the
high school course, when he began learning
the trade of carriage ironing. He not only
mastered this business, but also learned
horseshoeing and other allied industries.
Subsequently he purchased a shop and conducted a successful business in Marshall until 1885, when he removed to Albion, purchasing property on East Cass street. Here
he has since conducted a general blacksmithing and carriage-making shop, his specialty being horseshoeing. He is also a
dealer in mowers, reapers and other agricultural implements and both branches of his
business are proving profitable. He likewise
has a pleasant home on Crandall street and
this is the visible evidence of his enterprise
and thrift. On the 8th of May, 1878, Mr.
Wiederwax was united in marriage to Miss
Jessie Carver, of Albion, a daughter of J. V.
Carver, and to them have been born six children: James, the first born, died in infancy,
and those living are Maude, the wife of Mor-
ell D. Shepard, of Albion, and has one son,
Russell; Robert W.; Mack; Jesse R.; Lawrence S. All have been given good educational privileges for Mr. Weiderwax real-
izes how essential is mental discipline as a
preparation for life's practical duties. In

politics a Democrat. he served as alderman from the fourth ward of Albion in 1901, and during his incumbency the fine Superior street bridge was constructed and the franchise bill for the electric railroad was passed. He has always favored progressive measures and in citizenship has proved loyal to the best interests of his community. Socially he is identified with the Odd Fellows, the Knights of the Maccabees, the Modern Woodmen of America, the Ancient Order of United Workmen and the American Federation of Labor. He was very active in the organization of the last named here and served as president for two terms. He is also a member of the State Association of Master Horseshoers and also the National Association of Master Horseshoers, being the only member of the latter residing in Albion. He is now one of the older residents in Calhoun county, having witnessed much of its growth and improvement, and he has an honorable and manly pride in the improvements and changes which have led to the substantial development of this section of the state.

JOHN FREDENBURG.

John Fredenburg, of Fredonia township, Calhoun county, was born in Columbia county, New York, October 12, 1820, a son of John B. and Bothia (Van Hagen) Fredenburg. John B. Fredenburg was a son of Benjamin; and his father a native of Germany, came to the United States prior to the Revolution, locating in Columbia councounty, New York, on the shores of the Hudson river in the Kinder Hook settlement. John B. Fredenburg became dissat-

isfied with his prospects in Columbia county, in which he had always made his home, and came as far west as Detroit, Michigan, in 1827, bringing with him his family. Not liking the west, they returned to New York state, locating on the old Holland Purchase tract in Orleans county, and there remained until 1836. April 1 of that year they once more journeyed west, traveling by ox-team from their home, two and one-half miles south of Albion to Buffalo, thence by boat to Detroit, and from there to Fredonia township, Calhoun county, locating at Lyon lake upon the farm purchased two years previous when on a trip here for that purpose. He at once erected a log house which was completed during the first days of June. To himself and wife were born the following children: Catherine, Henry, John, Benjamin, Ann, Jane, Eliza, Cornelia, and an infant, the only two living being John, of this review, and Benjamin, also a resident of Fredonia township. In his political convictions Mr. Fredenburg was a Democrat, and through the influence of this party was elected to various offices in the community, among them being that of township clerk and supervisor. In his younger days he had served in the War of 1812 as captain of a company in the Fifty-sixth New York Regiment. His death occurred in the fall of 1874, when over eighty-three years old, the mother having died in 1863, at the age of sixty-five years, and both are interred in the Lyon Lake cemetery.

John Fredenburg remained under the parental roof for many years after attaining his majority; from an early age, however, being self supporting. His education was acquired in the schools of the state of New York, after which he worked out by the month. After his marriage in 1853, he purchased a farm of one hundred and twenty acres, which had upon it only the most primitive improvements, in the shape of a log house and other buildings of corresponding quality. With the energy characteristic of the pioneer he gave himself heartily to the cultivation and improvement of his property, in time erecting his present fine house and barns, as well as bringing his land under cultivation, now engaged in general farming and stock-raising.

The wife of Mr. Fredenburg was, in maidenhood, Laura Kimball, a native of St. Lawrence county, New York. She received her education in Olivet College, after which she entered the schools of Calhoun county, teaching one of the first schools of Marshall. She also taught school in the district where she made her home for so many years. She was well-known and esteemed throughout the community and her death in 1885 was universally deplored. She is interred in Lyon Lake cemetery. She was the mother of the following children: Mary Eliza, who married John Seaver, of this township. They have two boys, Zurah and Roy; Charles, who lives in California and is married and has a daughter Bessie; Belle F., the wife of A. C. Pattison, whose sketch appears on another page of this work; and Stephen, who works his father's farm and makes his home with him. He married Rosa Beckett and they have three children: Clarence, Earl and Donald.

In his political convictions Mr. Fredenburg is a Democrat, and through the influence of this party served as township clerk in the early days, and was the first school inspector of the township. Both himself and wife were members of the Reformed church. Mr. Fredenburg is one of the oldest settlers of the township and is a man highly respected and esteemed for the many qualities which have made him of such service as a citizen of the community.

HENRY FOSS.

Among the enterprising agriculturists of Pennfield township was numbered Henry Foss, who was born in Mechlenberg, Germany, near Schwerin, his natal day being August 10, 1837. His parents were Joseph and Christiana Foss and under the parental roof Henry Foss spent his boyhood days. At the age of nineteen years he started for the new world, hoping that he might have better business opportunities in this country than could be obtained in the fatherland. He was ambitious and energetic and though he had no money he possessed strong resolution and courage. At the same time Miss Mary Hoff made the trip to America. They sailed from Hamburg and for ten weeks were upon the water. The voyage was a rough and tempestuous one, but at length they arrived safely in New York in February, 1857. Soon after landing they were married. They remained for a few days in the eastern metropolis because the snow was so deep that the trains could not leave the city. However, as soon as possible they proceeded on their way to Rochester, New York. When they arrived at Castle Garden they had no money and for nearly a week lived upon ship biscuit, which Mr. Foss had in his pocket. At length he met a friend in New York and of him borrowed enough money to go to Rochester. The fare for both was eight dollars and Mr. Foss secured nine dollars from his friend in order to have something left with which to buy food on arriving at his destination. When he reached Rochester he knew not where to go, but meeting a German he accompanied him to his home where he and his wife were given supper. This was the first regular meal they had had since landing in America. Mr. Foss at once began to search for employment and soon obtained work. From that time his progress was steady and continuous. He first followed farming, afterward was employed in a brick yard and, in fact, accepted any employment that would yield him an honest living. He was thus connected with various pursuits in the east, where he remained until 1861, when the hope of gaining a home of his own led him to come to Calhoun county, Michigan. Here he purchased a farm of two hundred acres in the central part of Bedford township, investing money which he had saved from his earnings. He possessed nothing that he had not himself gained through his own labor. The land which came into his possession was partly swampy, while other portions were hilly and upon much of it grew the native forest trees, but with characteristic energy he began to clear away the trees and to place the fields under cultivation. In course of time his labors were rewarded with good harvests and he erected substantial buildings and made other improvements, continuing his residence upon that farm for twenty-one years. He also became the owner of a second farm in Bedford township, containing seventy-five acres.

In 1882 Mr. Foss sold both of these farms and came to Pennfield township, purchasing there one hundred and sixty acres of land of Colonel Fonda's farm. He also bought sixty acres of the John Holcomb farm, so that his property comprised two hundred and twenty acres of the richest farming land in Pennfield township. There was no building upon the place when he took possession, but he soon erected a fine large residence, planted trees and shrubbery and made a beautiful home. The house is now surrounded with a well kept lawn and everything about the place indicates the cultured taste as well as the energy and enterprise of the former owner.

Unto Mr. and Mrs. Foss were born five children: John, who now resides in Emmett township, Calhoun county, wedded Emma Hagelschacht, by whom he has four children: Effie; Cora, who is the wife of Ila W. Allwardt and has one child; Lida and Clarence; Emma is the wife of John Hagelschacht and with their three children, Rosabelle, Jesse and Richard, reside in a pleasant home at the corner of Union and Maple streets in Battle Creek; Frank, who is living in Mitchell, South Dakota, married Rosa Pierce and they have three children, Henry, June and Perry; Enos, who lives upon the home farm, now engage in its operation. He wedded Eliza Case and they have three children, Viola, Hazel and Aldrich; Rosa, the next, is the wife of William Salisbury, of Battle Creek, and their children are Henry, Mabel and Howard. Mrs. Foss died November 25, 1892, when about fifty-five years of age and was laid to rest in Hicks cemetery, Pennfield township. She was long a devoted and faithful member of the German Lutheran church and to her family was a loving and tender wife and mother. Mr. Foss was also long a member of the German Lutheran church and was interested in whatever pertains to the intellectual and moral development as well as the material progress of his adopted county. There is much that is commendable in the life record of Mr. Foss and his history should serve as a source of inspiration to others who have to start out empty handed. He not only had no money when he came to this country, but he could not speak the English language and thus handicapped he started out in the new world. He worked hard by the day until he could gain a little capital and as he saved he formed the resolution to one day become the owner of a good farm. Ultimately he found opportunity to invest his savings to advantage, and became the owner of one of the valuable farm properties of Calhoun county, on which are good buildings; fences divide the place into fields of convenient size and the latest improvements are used in facilitating farm work. Mr. Foss cast his first presidential ballot for Abraham Lincoln but later in life became a Democrat, but would never accept office for himself. He never had occasion to regret his determination to establish his home in America, for here he not only gained a comfortable competence, but also won many warm and appreciative friends. His death occurred July 14, 1903. He was laid to rest by the side of his wife in Hicks cemetery in Pennfield township, Calhoun county, Michigan.

G. MORGAN HALL.

On the roll of business men in Battle Creek appears the name of G. Morgan Hall, a dealer in electrical supplies at No. 23 Mad-

ison street. A native son of Michigan, he was born in Ludington, October 21, 1880, his parents being Elias and Jennie (Shackelton) Hall. He was but four years of age when his parents removed to Reed City, and three years later they went to Grand Rapids, where the son attended the public schools and was graduated from the high school with the class of 1900. Soon afterward he entered the employ of the Citizen's Telephone Company, with which he remained for a year. During the months of vacation, while in school, he had worked for the Grand Rapids Electrical Company, and also did some contracting in that line on his own account among the factories of that city. He had thus acquired a good knowledge of the electrical business. In 1902 he entered the services of Westinghouse, Church, Kerr & Company of New York city and did the electrical wiring for them on the Grand Rapids, Grand Haven & Muskegon Railroad. In September, 1902, he came to Battle Creek and opened his present place of business, having since secured a good patronage so that the new enterprise is now proving profitable.

On the 10th of June, 1903, in Grand Rapids, Mr. Hall wedded Miss Ada Cliff, who was born in Kent county, Michigan, and is a graduate of the high school of Grand Rapids with the class of 1901. Mr. Hall holds membership relations with the Odd Fellows lodge, No. 29, of Battle Creek, also of the Supreme Tent of Maccabees, and is a member of the Baptist church. His political support is given to the Republican party. Though a young man, he possesses laudable ambition and strong determination, and these are qualities, which, when directed by sound judgment never fail to win success.

G. MORGAN HALL

FRANK E. ALLEN.

Frank E. Allen, cashier of the First State Bank at Tekonsha, is well known in financial circles and his business and executive force have made him one of the representative citizens of this part of the county. He was born May 12, 1867, in the village which is now his home, his parents being Sylvester B. and Cordelia Maria (Robinson) Allen. The earliest ancestry of the Allen family of whom there is authentic record was Judah Allen, who was born at Smithfield, Rhode Island, September 7, 1760. He died March 18, 1842, leaving a family of nine children and a large number of their descendants are now residing in Calhoun county. His fourth child, Erastus Allen, married Sinia Blakley Fegles and they became the parents of ten children, of whom Sylvester B. Allen was the eldest. He is represented on another page of this work. He married Cordelia M. Robinson, who was of the fourth generation and descended from Jeremiah Robinson, a seaman and whaler, who came to this country from Ireland in the eighteenth century. She is also descended in the eighth generation from Deacon John Moore, one of the early settlers of Dorchester, Massachusetts, who arrived there in 1630 and became a resident of Windsor, Connecticut, in 1640. In the tenth generation she is a descendant of Henry Wolcott, who arrived in Boston from England in 1630 and was a member of the upper house of the general assembly of Connecticut from 1643 until his death.

The boyhood days of Frank E. Allen were spent in Tekonsha and after completing the public-school course here he entered Olivet College in the fall of 1882. After a year's study in that institution he returned to Tekonsha and entered upon his business

22

career as a clerk in the private bank of Allen & Johnson, serving in that capacity until 1887.

In the meantime Mr. Allen was married on the 3d of June, 1885, in Coldwater, Michigan, to Miss Ida M. Blakeman, of Tekonsha, the wedding ceremony being performed by the Rev. D. F. Barnes. Mrs. Allen is a daughter of Henry Rockefeller and Amanda (Miller) Blakeman, and was born in Ontario county, New York. During her early girlhood she was brought to Michigan by her parents, who lived for a time in Hillsdale and then removed to Tekonsha. In 1887 Mr. Allen and his wife both entered Albion College. He was graduated from the commercial department in 1891, and the following year completed a course in the art department. gree of Bachelor of Arts. Mrs. Allen completed a course in the art department. They then returned to Tekonsha and Mr. Allen accepted the position of assistant cashier in the bank with which he had formerly been connected. He occupied that place until May 15, 1901, when upon the death of the cashier he was promoted to the higher position. This bank was established in 1877 by his father, Sylvester B. Allen, and John Johnson and is the only banking institution located in Tekonsha. In 1902 it was re-organized and incorporated as the First State Bank of Tekonsha, with Sylvester B. Allen as president, John Johnson as vice president, F. E. Allen as cashier and H. W. Cushman, assistant cashier. The board of directors at present is as follows: E. P. Keep, John Johnson, R. E. Waldo, B. G. Doolittle, F. E. Allen and H. W. Cushman. The institution is capitalized for thirty thousand dollars. Mr. Allen is a man of excellent business force and executive ability and his courteous treatment of the patrons of the bank together with his enterprising spirit has made him a popular official.

Unto Mr. and Mrs. Allen has been born one child, E. Mae, who was born in Tekonsha, March 4, 1886. She is now a student in Albion College, studying both music and literature. Mr. and Mrs. Allen belong to the Presbyterian church at Albion and both our subject and his wife are popular and influential young people of Tekonsha, having a very large circle of friends in the village and in other parts of the county.

FRANK J. DIBBLE.

For twenty years a teacher in the schools of Branch and Calhoun counties, Frank J. Dibble has occupied a prominent position in educational movements in this community. A native son of Michigan, he was born in Marengo, November 6, 1862, one of a family of six children. His parents, Wallace and Eliza M. (Silverthorn) Dibble, were born respectively in Ontario county, New York, February 3, 1834; and Hope, New Jersey, December 8, 1837. There were besides our subject the following children: Emma, born in 1854, married Silas L. Bayn and has five children; Wallace W., born in 1856 and died as an infant; Minnie A., born in 1849, who married Albert B. Church and has four children; Clara M., born in 1860, who married Peter V. Blashfield and has two children; and Jesse D., born in 1873, married Carrie Belle Gibson and has three children. The father came to Michigan in

1836 and became a farmer in Clarendon township, where he and his wife still make their home.

Frank J. Dibble remained in his father's home until he was twenty-two years old, combining with his home duties an attendance at the common schools, after which he set out in the world, dependent on his own resources. November 12, 1884, he was united in marriage with Miss Carrie M. Blashfield, a daughter of Alvin and Elizabeth (Marshall) Blashfield, the former born in Cortland county, New York, in 1818, and the latter in Madison county, same state, June 3, 1825. Mr. Blashfield died at the age of fifty-three years and his wife at the old home in Clarendon township, January, 1904. To Mr. and Mrs. Dibble have been born three children, only one of whom is now living, Calla C., the date of her birth being January 26, 1893. Mabel died at the age of four years and five months; Mellie L. died in infancy. In 1884 Mr. Dibble purchased a farm of fifty acres located on section 26, Clarendon township, where he has since made his home. In politics Mr. Dibble has been a Republican all his life and through the influence of his party has been elected at various times to fill important public offices, among them being that of school inspector, which he ably maintained for ten years; township treasurer for one term; township clerk for three years, to which position he was re-elected in 1899, and is now supervisor of Clarendon township. He is still engaged in teaching in the public schools of the county, a leading position being accorded him among the teachers of the community. Since he was sixteen years old Mr. Dibble has been an earnest believer in the Christian religion as taught by the Bible and though he has never allied himself with any church society he has still been active in the promotion of religious thought. For the past two years he has held the position of superintendent of the Methodist Episcopal Sunday school. Beyond the attendance of the common schools, his education has been due to his own efforts. He has applied himself assiduously to thoughtful reading and home study, acquiring a fund of information that is superior even to the college training, for it argues a practical contact with the questions which confront the young student. Earnest and indefatigable in his efforts he has met with the success which has characterized him among the citizens of Calhoun county.

META HOWARD, M. D.

Dr. Meta Howard, who is engaged in the practice of medicine and surgery at No. 111 West Porter street, Albion, was born in this city, a daughter of Henry and Adeline (Milliman) Howard. Her father was born in Norfolk, England, in 1828, and the mother's birth occurred in what was then the township of Sheridan, now a part of Albion, Michigan. When but eighteen months old Henry Howard was brought to America by his parents, Samuel and Mary Howard, who for a time lived in New York, where the grandfather of Dr. Howard died when his son was a lad of twelve years. The latter afterward came to Michigan with an older brother. He obtained a common-school education and throughout his active business career has carried on farming, being now the owner of about six hundred

acres of valuable land. He came to this state, however, a poor boy with but five cents in his pocket and he has made all that he now possesses in southern Michigan, following honorable business methods, his life being characterized by integrity and close application. He was married in Albion to Miss Adeline Milliman and they became the parents of five children. There was not a death in the family until the death of the maternal grandmother of Dr. Howard, who passed away in 1902, when almost eighty-nine years of age. The children are Mary, wife of Wallace Bayne, of Albion; Meta, of this review; Hibbard, who is engaged in the lumber business at Superior, Wisconsin; Stanton, who married Eva Ballard and has four children, is a farmer living in Albion; and Clara, the wife of Charles Burnett, of Albion, who has four children.

Dr. Meta Howard acquired a good liberal education and after completing the greater part of the high school course entered Albion College in the fall of 1876 and was graduated in 1884 with the degree of Bachelor of Arts. She afterward pursued a post-graduate course and in 1885 the degree of Master of Arts was conferred upon her. She entered upon the study of medicine under the direction of Dr. E. L. Parmeter and in the fall of 1885 matriculated in the Woman's Medical College of Chicago, in which she was graduated with the class of 1887. She was then house physician in the Missionary Training school for a few months and at the same time had charge of the woman's department of the dispensary. All this work was done preparatory to her work in Korea as a medical missionary. In September, 1887, she left Chicago for San Francisco, where she took passage on the steamer City of Pekin and was twenty-one days in crossing to Yokohama, where she remained a week engaged in sightseeing and shopping. She thence went to Kobe, where she spent a day and while there saw Mayor Harrison of Chicago, who was on his way around the world. She afterward proceeded to Nagasaki, where she spent a few days in sightseeing and thence proceeded to Fusan and on to Chemulpo and Seoul, Korea. She was the first lady physician there, and it was necessary that she learn the language of the people, which task occupied her attention for about six months. She, however, learned in six days to read the Korean language so that she could be understood by a native, as it is alphabetical and phonetic. She spent two years in Korea and established a hospital and dispensary at Seoul. She had from seventy-five to one hundred patients a day in the dispensary and from seven to eight in the hospital. Men physicians were not allowed to practice among the female patients, but Dr. Howard was permitted to treat both men and women and thus had a very extensive business. Owing to the climate, hard work and exposure, however, her health failed and in 1889 she returned to the United States. For several years she lectured in different parts of the country, visiting Nebraska, Pennsylvania, Ohio, Indiana, Illinois and Michigan. She made Albion her home, however, but did not begin the practice of medicine here until 1893, when she opened her office. Since that time she has been very successful and, in fact, the demands made upon her professional services are often greater that she can attend to. She belongs to the County Medical and State Medical Societies.

GEORGE SQUARES ROPER.

George Squares Roper, now deceased, was a citizen whose efforts promoted the material upbuilding and the social, moral and political status of his community, because his life was actuated by honorable and manly principles. He was born in Lincolnshire, England, October 13, 1849, the day of the first anniversary of his birth was spent on the Atlantic ocean, his parents, James and Sarah Roper, being at the time on a westward bound vessel that had left the English port for America. They landed at New York city and continued to reside in the Empire state until 1854, when they came to Calhoun county, Michigan, locating in Sheridan township, and, in 1855, he purchased a small farm in Clarence township. Thus it was that Mr. Roper, of this review, was reared to manhood in Calhoun county amid the wild scenes of frontier life. He attended the district schools of the county and as soon as old enough to follow the plow began work in his father's fields. He continued at home until about fourteen years of age, when he started out to earn his own living by working as a farm hand. Later he learned the blacksmith's trade in Albion and followed that pursuit for a number of years, working both in Albion and in Marshall. He also owned a shop in Clarence township. When he was nineteen years of age he went to the lumber camps at Saginaw, Michigan, and spent two years in that locality, working at his trade. In 1875 with the money that he had earned through his earnest and persistent labor Mr. Roper purchased forty acres of land in Clarence township and latter added to the property from time to time as his financial resources increased, until he became the owner of one hundred and thirty acres of rich and arable land. On this he resided until 1893, continuously cultivating his fields, adding new improvements and thus promoting the value of his property. This farm was sold in 1897 and he then purchased a farm in Sheridan township of one hundred and forty acres, which is now managed by his widow. In the fall of 1893 he took up his abode in Albion and purchased a home at No. 109 East Pine street. There he followed the carpenter's trade and also superintended his farm.

In 1873 Mr. Roper was united in marriage to Miss Emma Krenerick, who was born in Loudonville, Ohio. They resided for nearly two years at Rice Creek, and unto them have been born three children, but two died in infancy. The surviving daughter is Gertrude Louise, who is at home with her mother. Mr. Roper was a Democrat in his political affiliations and for two years he served as justice of the peace in Clarence township. On the 30th of July, 1903, when returning from his farm accompanied by his nephew, George W. Roper, the carriage was struck by a limited car of the Jackson & Battle Creek Traction Company at a grade crossing four miles west of Albion and both were killed. The remains of Mr. Roper were interred in Albion's beautiful cemetery—Riverside. He was a member of the Ancient Order of United Workmen, and commanded the good will and regard of his brethren of that fraternity. He was a man who took great pleasure in his home, where he was surrounded by the comforts of life and the love of a devoted wife and daughter, who mourn the loss of husband and father. His interest centered in his family

and he did everything in his power for their happiness and welfare. In matters of business he was straightforward and honorable and at all times he lived a life which won for him respect and confidence. His untimely death was the occasion of deep regret throughout the community in which he had lived from his early boyhood days.

CYRUS ROSEVELT MARTIN.

Cyrus Rosevelt Martin, now residing at No. 38 Massachusetts avenue, in Battle Creek, has been connected with railroad service in Michigan for many years and is also a representative of one of the important productive industries of this part of the state, while his investments in other paying enterprises show him to be a man of keen business discernment and resolute purpose, whose life has been measured by laudable effort and commendable ambition. He was born upon a farm in Jackson county, Michigan, on the 25th day of May, 1857, and is a son of Henry and Sarah (Coy) Martin. He was educated in the district schools of the township about four miles from Parma and upon the old homestead he resided during the first sixteen years of his life. At that time he started out in the world on his own account, first earning his living by working in a saw-mill at Manistee, Michigan. He was employed in operating the shingle saw for three years at the end of which time he severed his connection with the lumber business and became connected with railroad service.

It was in 1876 that Mr. Martin entered the employ of the Michigan Central Railroad Company in the capacity of a freight brakeman, being on the middle division of the main line, his run being from Jackson to Michigan City. He worked in that way for four years, after which he was promoted to the position of freight conductor ' and thus served for six years. At the end of that time he removed to Battle Creek and occupied a similar position with the Grand Trunk Railroad Company, which he held for four years. Subsequently he was made passenger conductor and has since acted in that capacity with the exception of a period of three years, during which time he held the office of road foreman, having charge of the entire system west of St. Clair river. At the present time he is in charge of the day train running east. For more than a quarter of a century he has been in the employ of the Michigan Central & Grand Trunk Railroad Companies and no higher testimonial of his capability could be given than the fact of his long retention in this service. In this connection he has won promotion because of his fidelity to duty, his obliging manner and his unfailing courtesy to the patrons of the line. His business ability, enterprising spirit and laudable desire to achieve success have been manifest in his investments in enterprises at home and abroad. He has made judicious use of his earnings as a railroad employee and is to-day reaping the reward of his labors along other lines of industrial activity. He is the vice chairman of the American Stone & Construction Company, of Battle Creek, which is manufacturing artificial stone, controlling the first concern of the kind in southern Michigan. Mr. Martin was one of the original promoters of the company, which was incorporated with a capital stock of five hundred thousand dollars. He was chosen a member of its first board of directors and appointed vice chairman at the organization of the company, which has erected a plant constructed entirely of its own product, using forty-eight thousand artificial stone blocks ten by thirty inches on the face. The building is sixty-five by one hundred and sixty-five feet with an additional structure for the engine room. The brick-making plant has a capacity of twenty-four thousand brick every ten hours and there has been installed the latest improved labor-saving machinery, including carriers and conveyors. The plant is conveniently located at the spur of the Grand Trunk Railroad, thus providing good shipping facilities. Mr. Martin was also one of the organizers of the New Mexico Oil & Development Company, which was incorporated in 1901, with a capital stock of three hundred thousand dollars. He was chosen president at the time of the formation of the company and is also one of its directors. This company has large landed interests, including eleven thousand acres in the oil regions of New Mexico, where wells are being developed. They have also struck water of great purity, this being the only good water supply within one hundred and twenty-five miles and its value in the arid region cannot be overestimated. Mr. Martin likewise has other investments and with a ready recognition of business opportunity and a comprehensive understanding of business situations he has won for himself an honorable position as a progressive yet safe investor.

It was in 1879 that Mr. Martin was united in marriage to Miss Abbie B. Hunt, of St. John, Michigan, and unto them has been born a son, George R., who married

Miss May Jones, of this city, where they make their home. He is now employed as a traveling representative of the Cero-Fruto Food Company.

Mr. Martin's study of the political issues and questions of the day has led him to give his support to no party, for he believes that he can best discharge his duties of citizenship by supporting the men whom he thinks most ably qualified for office regardless of party affiliations. He is quite prominent in fraternal circles, however, and is now a member of the Order of Railroad Conductors, serving for eight years as chief conductor of the local organization. He has also been a representative to the Grand Lodge for the past ten years and is now chairman of the grievance and appeal committee. He has labored earnestly and effectively in behalf of the best interests of the class of business men of which he is a representative. In 1892 he erected his beautiful home on Massachusetts avenue, in Battle Creek, and he also has a fine summer home at Gull Lake, on Franklin beach. Both he and his wife occupy an enviable position in cultured society circles and have many friends in Battle Creek. Biography is constantly asserting the fact that success comes not to the man who idly waits but to the faithful toiler, whose work is characterized by intelligence and force and who has the foresight and keenness of mental vision to know when and where and how to exert his energies. The life record of Mr. Martin is another exemplification of this truth. In view of the fact that he commenced his business career empty-handed, his success is the more remarkable and his history should prove an inspiration to many a young man on starting out, as he did a few years ago, with no capital save intelligence, integrity, determination and perseverance—which after all constitute the best capital and without which wealth, influence and position amount to nothing.

HENRY GOLDUP.

Henry Goldup, a prominent and respected farmer of Homer township, Calhoun county, Michigan, and one of the largest land owners in this part of the county, was born in East Kent, England, January 15, 1846, the years of his boyhood being spent in the land of his birth. When he was twenty-one years of age, having saved one hundred dollars from his wages the year previous for the purpose of emigration, he took passage on the City of Dublin, a vessel which used both steam and sail, but with only one smokestack, and after a voyage of twenty-one days, landed at New York city. He went at once toward the farming lands of the state, going up the Hudson river to Albany, locating then at Hoosic Corners, a little town about twenty-two miles from Albany, there engaging as a farm hand for two and a half years. With confidence as to the promises held out by the middle west Mr. Goldup came to Michigan, locating in Homer township, Calhoun county, where he has since made his home, winning the respect and confidence of all with whom he came in contact by his life of patient, persevering energy and untiring industry. He sought and found employment with Philo Gibbs, with whom he remained for three years engaged in farming, after which he entered the employ of C. C. Worthington. After two years spent with Mr. Worthington he was employed by John Powers, working his farm on shares for two years and then renting Truman Powers's farm for one year. With the proceeds of his industry and energy he purchased eighty acres of land on section 20 and erected a house and barn and made other improvements which added not ·a little to the value of his property. For seven years thereafter he also rented land of Mr. Boughton, at the close of which time he purchased eighty acres of the latter, and later made a purchase of forty acres located on section 19. In 1886 he removed to the Gibbs place on section 8, where he now makes his home, a few years ago having purchased a hundred and twenty acres across the road, on section 7, which he conducted m conjunction with the hundred and twenty acres which he had purchased before and the hundred and twenty acres which comprised the farm upon which he was living. A year ago he purchased the farm upon which he had made his home for so many years, in the meantime also renting the old Gibbs's homestead which he conducted for seven years. His energy and industry were limitless, though in 1903 he gave up the management of the later property on acount of agement of the latter property on account of an accident which befell his wife. To-day Mr. Goldup owns and operates four hundren and forty acres of land, comprised in four farms, each of which is well equipped with needful buildings, fine farm houses, barns, outbuildings, etc., all the result of his own unaided effort and thought.

Not a little, however, of the success which has come to Mr. Goldup has been added to by the same characteristics in his wife which have distinguished his own life.

She was in maidenhood Jane Ann Horner, a daughter of Henry Horner, a native of Ireland. She came to America in 1867, landing in New York city without friends and with only twelve shillings of English money in her possession. Not discouraged, however, by the prospect, she at once sought and found employment, and as a memento of the time when she stood face to face with the necessity for effort she still has in her possession ten of the original shillings with which she landed in America. Her union with Mr. Goldup occurred in 1868, and together they have made their struggle for a competence. Mr. Goldup's land is devoted to general farming and stock-raising. To Mr. and Mrs. Goldup were born sixteen children: Six died in infancy, and not named; Eliza, died at the age of seventeen; Thomas, married Nancy Linton and lives near his father's farm: James lives at home; Caroline died at the age of six weeks; Clara, married William Reichow. and is the mother of one child, Mark; Charles and Susan live at home: Florence is a teacher in the public schools of Homer; William lives at home and is still a student, and Bessie, also a student. all have attended the school at Homer. Mr. Goldup is a Democrat politically and though ever ready to lend his best efforts toward progression and reform, has never cared for official recognition. He is a member of the Presbyterian church at Homer.

JAMES P. HUGHES.

As an enterprising business man James P. Hughes has contributed much to the material upbuilding of the prosperity of

Marshall, of which city he has been a resident practically his entire life. He was born in Marengo township, Calhoun county, July 24, 1877, the oldest in a family of three children, the others being Jennie B. and Vivian Marguerite, whose parents, Paschal and Anna (Francisco) Hughes, are still living, making their home in this city. The geneology of this family is traced back to England, from which country Charles Hughes, the grandfather of James P. Hughes, our personal subject, emigrated in early childhood, being but eleven years old when he accompanied his parents to New York city. Being only in moderate circumstances his father bound him out at the age of fourteen to learn a trade; but not liking his situation the lad ran away one Sunday while the family were at church, his few belongings tied up in an old red handkerchief. His first employment was with a traveling circus, where he acted as teamster or baggage-man until they reached Mississippi; there the teams were sold and the circus paraphernalia was transferred to a flat-boat, enroute for New Orleans. At that time Mr. Hughes sought other employment but remained in the south, eventually marrying Margaret Scroggin, who had removed with her parents from Georgia, her native state. On account of the unsettled condition of the south in the years just previous to the war, Mr. Hughes removed with his family in 1860, to Lexington, Missouri, where they remained four years, losing all trace of his wife's family, who were naturally in sympathy with the southern cause. Mr. Hughes was inclined to be neutral in the struggle, but found it very unpleasant in the path of the warring sections, and therefore disposed of his property for sixteen hundred dollars, making a sacrifice in the sale for the sake of removal from the locality. He located in Battle Creek, this county, where he engaged in teaming as a means of livelihood, later purchasing property in Newton township, where he and his wife spent the remainder of their lives. Their last resting place is in Newton cemetery.

Paschal Hughes, the father of our subject, was born in Sunflower county, Mississippi, January 22, 1856, and removed with his parents to Missouri, where, as a child, he went over the field of Lexington three weeks after the battle was fought. He was but eight years old when he became a resident of Michigan and was reared to manhood in Newton township, receiving a common school education. Soon after his marriage in October, 1876, he purchased property in Marengo, where he remained two and a half years, when he sold out and bought a farm of two hundred and forty acres near Ceresco. Two years later he located in Marshall, having been appointed deputy sheriff, which position he filled in an efficient manner. Upon the expiration of his public services, he became a traveling salesman for the firm of Nichols & Shepard, handling threshing machines, not losing a day in a period of six years. His interests were then identified with Russell & Company, of Massillon, Ohio, remaining in that connection for one year, when for a like period he traveled for Reeves & Company, of Columbus, Ohio, and is now a resident of Marshall. In his political convictions Mr. Hughes is a Republican, following the example of his father, who, though a resident of the south and a slaveholder, still cast his ballot for the principles of the Republican platform, while several of his brothers, life-time residents of the north, were stanchly Democratic in their political affiliations. Fraternally, he is associated with the Ancient Order of United Workmen, holding membership in the lodge in Marshall.

James P. Hughes grew to manhood in this city, receiving his education in the common schools and high school. As a boy in years he began to earn money by peddling various articles in the streets, and at sixteen became a clerk in the postoffice here, acting as mailing clerk for two and a half years, his faithful discharge of duty, his punctuality and business ability winning for him the commendation of those under whom he worked. He was next associated with Prof. Andrew Chrystal in the manufacture of electrical appliances, remaining in this employ for seven years, carrying with him into the daily discharge of duty the same principles which had characterized his first efforts in the business world. That he is eminently fitted by nature to enjoy a position of importance in the commercial life of a community is a self-evident fact when viewed in the light of the success which he has already achieved. March 1, 1903, he became the partner of H. M. Holmes in the management of a clothing and gents' furnishing establishment under the firm name of Hughes & Holmes, located on West State street. Those who have witnessed the early efforts of Mr. Hughes appreciate the new position which he has taken up and look forward with confidence to a successful career for the young merchant.

The marriage of Mr. Hughes occurred May 1, 1900, Miss May Della Stone becoming his wife. She was born near Syracuse, New York, the daughter of William D. and Florence (Toll) Stone, who removed to Michigan when Mrs. Hughes was a child. The birth of one child has blessed this union, Martha, who was born January 25, 1902. Mr. Hughes is a prominent man in local politics, and has taken an active part in the promotion of Republican principles, of which he is a stanch adherent. In 1901 he received the nomination for the office of city school inspector, and though the Republicans were greatly in the minority at the election his popularity was attested to by the fact that he led his ticket. Fraternally he is recognized as a leading man, being identified with the Maccabees, of which he is the present commander; Modern Woodmen of America and Knights of Pythias, in the latter organization having filled several of the offices, being a past chancellor commander, the youngest member to have ever held the chair in the lodge at Marshall. Mr. Hughes is held in the highest esteem for the many qualities which distinguish him as a citizen of the community and he numbers many friends throughout the county.

HON. EDWARD P. KEEP.

Prominent among the energetic, sagacious and enterprising business men of Tekonsha is numbered Edward P. Keep, a dealer in lumber, coal, lime and cement. He is also a leader in community affairs, and his influence and efforts have ever been given for the substantial improvement and advancement of town and county, while his loyalty in citizenship is one of the salient features of his career. His native talent has led him out of humble circumstances into success through the opportunity that is the pride of our American life, nor is his success to be measured by material standards alone as he has developed that type of character which makes for higher ideals in business and in society as well.

Mr. Keep was born in Homer, Cortland county, New York, May 27, 1848. His paternal grandparents, Seth and Lois (Hitchcock) Keep, removed from Massachusetts to the Empire state, becoming early settlers of Homer. Their son, Timothy Keep, the father of our subject, was born in Homer, November 3, 1801, and there spent his entire life, following the occupation of farming throughout his business career. He married Miss Sylvia Backus, who died at the age of sixty-eight years, while his death occurred when he was seventy-seven years of age. In their family were six children who reached mature years; J. L., a resident farmer of Clarendon, Michigan; Caroline, wife of Charles Brown, of Homer; New York, by whom she has two children; Abigail, a resident of Homer; Dwight, who resides on the old homestead in New York, married Mary Kennedy, by whom he has four children; Edward P.; and Frank, who married Nancy Smith, died in Milan, Ohio, leaving two children.

The early training of Edward P. Keep was that of his father's farm and of the district schools near his boyhood's home. Later, however, he enjoyed the advantage of a two-years' course of study in an academy of Homer, New York, and when eighteen years of age he began teaching, which profession he followed in the state of his nativity until 1868, when he came to Calhoun county, Michigan. After teaching for one

winter in Fredonia township, he returned to the east in 1869, and it was not until 1875 that he made a permanent location in this county, but twenty-eight years have since come and gone, and while he has had a successful business career here, he has also contributed in substantial measure to the growth, development and advancement of the county. While still in the east he engaged in teaching and in farming and also became the owner of a half interest in a saw-mill. Upon his return to Michigan he established his present business in Tekonsha, where he has since dealt in lumber, coal, lime and cement. He had accumulated sixteen hundred dollars and with this capital he instituted his present enterprise, which with the passing years, has grown to very profitable proportions. He carries a large line of the various commodities mentioned and in addition to this he is interested to the extent of ten thousand dollars in a cement factory at Elk Rapids. He was one of the organizers of the company and served as a director for a number of years.

On he 2d of October, 1878, Mr. Keep was united in marriage to Miss Eva M. Allen, who was born on a farm in Tekonsha township, a daughter of Erastus and Sinia (Fegles) Allen. They now have a daughter, Lutie B., born in Tekonsha, September 16, 1886. She is a graduate of the high school of the class of 1902, and will complete the high school course in Coldwater, Michigan, in 1904.

Mr. Keep was reared in the faith of the Republican party and cast his first presidential vote for General Grant in 1872. In 1877 he was elected a trustee and for eight different terms he has filled that position and for four years was president of the board. He was also justice of the peace in 1877-8 and used his influence to settle cases through arbitration and without recourse to trial. In 1898 he was elected to represent his district in the State Legislature and was chairman of the committee on public lands. He also served on the committees on elections, state prisons and state public schools, and he introduced five bills, four of which became laws. When elected he had to overcome a very strong Democratic majority and in 1900 when again nominated, he ran one hundred and fifty votes ahead of his ticket. He is a Mason, having been raised in 1872 in Homer lodge, No. 352, F. & A. M., at Homer, New York. He afterward demitted to Washington lodge, at Tekonsha and is now serving for the ninth year as worthy master. He is a charter member of the Tekonsha lodge, A. O. U. W., was elected its first master and served for three years, also was representative to the Grand lodge. He belongs to the Michigan Association of Lumber Dealers, of which he was a director and vice president, and in 1900 he served as president. He has been a member of this since its organization. He was one of the organizers of the First State Bank of Tekonsha, and has been a member of its board of directors ever since, and at the present time is vice president of the bank. His strong and upright manhood, his reliability in business transactions, his loyalty to the tenets of the different societies with which he is connected, all make him a man whom to know is to respect and honor. Imbued with the progressive spirit of the west, he has advanced to a creditable position in social circles, and is none the less prominent in community affairs along fraternal and political lines.

REUBEN C. SIBLEY.

Reuben C. Sibley, now deceased, was identified with industrial interests of Albion as a contractor and builder, and as year after year he continued his connection with business affairs here, he became known as a man of sterling worth and upright principles. His death, therefore, was the occasion of sincere regret and he well deserves mention among those to whom the city acknowledges its indebtedness for active co-operation in affairs of moment to the community. He was born in Columbia county, New York, April 3, 1835, a son of William and Ruth (Vincent) Sibley. The father was a resident farmer of Columbia county and both he and his wife were representatives of old American families. Prior to 1850 he came to Marengo township, where he purchased new land and made a home. He afterward bought a farm in Clarence, which he also improved, and there he spent his remaining days, passing away in 1863. His wife survived him for some time and later lived with her son in Clarence. She was a member of the Methodist Episcopal church.

Reuben C. Sibley acquired his education in the schools of Columbia county, and living in a frontier district he early began the arduous task of assisting in the operation of the home farm. His school privileges, however, were largely augmented by his broad reading and he became a well informed man. At the age of fifteen years began earning his own living in Coldwater, Michigan, and he also sent a part of his earnings to his parents, continuing to assist them as long as they lived, and thus rendering them marked filial devotion. After a time he returned to Calhoun county and in Clarence township he enlisted for service in the Civil war in 1861, becoming a member of Company I, Sixth Michigan Artillery. He was with Farragut at New Orleans under the command of Benjamin F. Butler, and spent most of his time in the far south. On the expiration of his first term of three years he re-enlisted in the same company and regiment and continued with the army until the close of hostilities, four years having passed in military service ere he received his discharge, owing to the cessation of the war. He was never in the hospital for a single day, fortunately escaping wounds and illness. He proved a most brave and loyal soldier and belonged to that class to whom the country owes a debt of gratitude which can never be repaid.

After his return from the army Mr. Sibley continued to engage in carpentering and upon the death of his father, in connection with his brother, he purchased the old family homestead and cared for his mother until after her demise. Then disposing of his farming interests, he removed to Albion, where he was engaged in contracting and building in partnership with James Van Ness, under the firm name of Sibley & Van Ness. They did a large amount of work, building many of the fine residences of the city and the extent and volume of their patronage made them prosperous representatives of the industrial life of Albion. After his health failed, Mr. Sibley retired from active connection with the building interests.

On the 27th of December, 1866, occurred the marriage of Mr. Sibley and Miss Jane Adelaide Horton, of Clarence township, a daughter of John S. and Paulina (Carrier) Horton. The father was born in New Jersey and was a son of Edward Horton, a soldier of the Revolutionary war. Subsequently he removed to Cayuga county, New York, having a farm near Weedsport, where John S. Horton was reared to manhood. There he married Miss Carrier, a daughter of Amaziah Carrier, and began farming on his own account, having a tract of land near Weedsport. In 1833 he came with his family to Michigan and cast in his lot with the pioneer settlers of Calhoun county. Subsequently he took up his abode in Clarence township and it was upon that farm that Mrs. Sibley was born. Later he sold that property, however. He was quite prominent and influential in public affairs and filled the office of justice of the peace and other public positions. He likewise made conveyances and conducted law suits, although not an attorney. His death occurred in Lee township, April 10, 1881, and his wife passed away September 30, 1876. She was a member of the Presbyterian church and at one time Mr. Horton was a member of the Methodist Episcopal church and a lay preacher therein. Mrs. Sibley was born and reared in Calhoun county, spending her girlhood days under the parental roof. She now has a pleasant home at No. 714 North Clinton street.

Mr. Sibley gave his political allegiance to the Republican party, and while he never sought nor desired public office he was always deeply interested in whatever pertained to his county, its development and progress. He died September 1, 1892, leaving behind him the record of an honorable career. He was justly accorded a place among the prominent and representative citizens of Calhoun county, for he belonged to that class of men, whose enterprising spirit is used not alone for their own benefit.   He advanced the general good and promoted public prosperity, but he ably managed individual interests and all who knew him had the highest admiration for his good qualities of heart and mind.

FRANK GLEN POWERS, D. D. S.

Dr. Frank Glen Powers, engaged in the practice of dentistry in Marshall, was born on a farm in Climax township, Kalamazoo county, Michigan, December 17, 1869, his parents being James and Irene (Keyes) Powers. Until seventeen years of age he attended the district schools and spent his days in the usual manner of farmer lads, assisting in the work of the field through the summer months. In order to improve his education he then entered the Seventh Day Adventist College at Battle Creek, in which he completed a four years' course and was graduated at the age of twenty-one years. By his own labor he helped pay his way through college. He afterward engaged in teaching school for a year, but this was merely a preparatory step to other professional labor. Entering the office of Dr. W. W. Scott, of Vicksburg, Michigan, he pursued the study of dentistry under his direction and also became somewhat familiar with the practical work of the calling. Matriculating in the dental department of the University of Michigan, he was graduated in 1896, and soon afterward came to Marshall, where he opened his office and has since engaged in practice. In the seven years which have since gone he has become established in

his work as one of the leading members of the profession in the city, and in his practice he follows the most modern and improved methods, having his office splendidly equipped with all the latest dental appliances.

On the 11th of June, 1857, in Marshall, Dr. Powers was united in marriage to Miss Florence Maude Cooley, who was born in Parma, a daughter of Elizabeth Ann Cooley. She is a graduate of the high school of Parma, Michigan, and was successfully engaged in teaching prior to her marriage.   Three children grace this home: Carlton James, Donald S. and Roger Paul.

Dr. Powers was originally a Republican and voted first for Harrison. In 1892 by appointment he filled a vacancy on the board of aldermen and in 1893 he was the Democratic nominee for that position. He is a member of LaFayette lodge, F. & A. M., and has also taken the degrees of Capitular and Chivalric Masonry, belonging to the Chapter, and Marshall Commandery, No. 17, K. T. He also holds membership with the Maccabees, Odd Fellows and Knights of Pythias, and is popular in fraternal circles. The favorable judgment which his fellow townsmen passed upon him at the outset of his professional career has been in no degree set aside or modified, as his course has proven that the confidence reposed in him was well placed.

HON. ERASTUS H. HUSSEY.

Erastus H. Hussey, now an honored resident of Battle Creek, and one whose broad intelligence and culture makes him a desirable citizen of the community in which he lives, was a native of the Empire state. He was born January 19, 1827, a son of John and Prudence (Durfee) Hussey. His father was born in North Adams, Massachusetts, in 1796, and when very young was taken to New York by his parents, Sylvanus and Lydia (Lapham) Hussey, who were farmers, and settled in Cayuga county, where they carried on agricultural pursuits and reared their family. John Hussey married Prudence Durfee, who was born in Wayne county, New York, a daughter of Lemuel and Prudence Durfee. He then turned his attention to farming and continued to make his home in New York throughout his entire life.

In the common schools of New York, Erastus H. Hussey began his education, which he continued in an academy at Aurora, that state. From the time he was twenty years of age until his removal to the west, after his father's death, he had charge of his father's farm, being the owner during the latter years. His business ability was manifest in his capable management of the property, which returned a good income. While living in New York he was honored with election to the General Assembly as the representative of the southern district of Cayuga county, and for two years was a member of the House. From the time he attained his majority he was active in political circles there, as an advocate of Republican principles, and, though one of the younger members of the State Legislature, he took an active part in its work and aided in enacting the laws passed during that session. At the time of the Civil war his sympathies were strongly with the Union, but on account of physical disability he could not go to the front. He was, however, instrumental in sending two men in his place.

In 1865 Mr. Hussey first came to Michigan on a visit and in 1878 removed to Battle Creek. He has since resided in this county and has allied his interests with hers, laboring for the welfare and progress of the community, while promoting his individual affairs. He was married March 27, 1878, to Mrs. Susan Tabor Denman, nee Hussey, and that year he purchased a farm, having now two hundred and seventy-eight acres of fine farming land. He has, however, always lived with his wife's parents, to whom he has rendered the filial care and loving devotion of an own son. Mrs. Hussey's first husband was Henry V. Denman, a native of Newburg, New York, and they had one child, Frederick Henry, who died at the age of thirty-three years. He was cashier of a bank in Kansas, and he married Agnes Kate Strickland, by whom he had one daughter, Dicksie, the wife of Clifford Wheeler Mitchell, of Toledo, Ohio. She died July 16, 1903, at the age of twenty-three years. Mr. Denman was engaged in the conduct of a department store for a number of years, and later conducted a private banking business in Michigan. He died in 1875 and his remains were interred in the family lot in Oakhill cemetery.

Since purchasing his farm Mr. Hussey has been deeply interested in agricultural affairs and his enterprise, sound judgment, practical management and progressive ideas have made him successful in his work. He has a fine apiary and is thoroughly informed concerning bee culture. All branches of his business are proving profitable, for he is well versed in the best methods of producing crops and raising stock. Moreover, he readily comprehends a business situation and his judgment is rarely, if ever, at fault in determining the best method to pursue in the utilization of the means at hand. In Battle Creek and throughout the county he holds an enviable position in public regard and to-day one of the most respected and esteemed citizens of southern Michigan is Erastus H. Hussey, whose influence has ever been exerted for good citizenship and whose efforts have been far-reaching for public good. Mrs. Hussey was a member of the old Presbyterian church and both our subject and his wife were birthright members of the Society of Friends. He is now in good standing with that sect, and the noble principles it inculcates have been manifest in his career.

SAMUEL DICKIE, A. M. LL. D.

One of the most prominent educators of the state of Michigan, Dr. Samuel Dickie, president of Albion College, has also gained a national reputation in connection with his work in behalf of the Prohibition party. His effort has ever been directed along lines for the benefit of mankind and his utilization of his inherent talents has resulted in the promotion of intellectual and moral progress, and rendered him a natural leader of public thought and opinion.

Professor Dickie was born in Burford township, Ontario, Canada, June 6, 1851, a son of William and Jane (McNabb) Dickie, who were natives of Ayershire, Scotland, and when young people came to America. They were married in Canada and the father engaged in farming in Burford township,

Ontario, until 1858, when he removed to Lansing, Michigan, where he continued to follow agricultural pursuits. He gave his political allegiance to the Democracy and both he and his wife were members of the Presbyterian church. They spent their last days in the home of their son, Professor Dickie, the mother dying in 1889, and the father in 1890.

In the public schools of Lansing, Michigan, Dr. Dickie began his education, and in 1869 matriculated in Albion College, from which he was graduated with the class of 1872, winning the degree of Bachelor of Arts. He also gained the valedictorian honors. Through the four succeeding years he was superintendent of the high school at Hastings, Michigan, and in the meantime continued his studies and won the Master of Arts degree from his Alma Mater. In 1877 he returned to Albion College to accept the proffered chair of Mathematics, and has since been continuously connected with the institution, although not always as an educator. He resigned his chair in December, 1887, to accept the position of chairman of the Prohibition national committee. He served in that capacity for twelve years, during which time he visited every state and territory of the Union, speaking in every city containing more than twenty thousand inhabitants. Sixteen times has he visited the Pacific coast and is thoroughly acquainted with every part of the United States. He has had broad experience in connection with the executive work of the party, and as an orator won a national reputation. His scholarly attainments, the close and earnest study which he has given to the temperance question, his understanding of its political possibilities and above all his deep desire to arouse public sentiment to an appreciation of the

SAMUEL DICKIE

. moral side of the subject, all combined to make him a most forceful and convincing speaker.

Dr. Dickie resigned his position with the Prohibition national committee, to take effect December 31, 1899, and in connection with Hon. John G. Wooley, one of the foremost temperance workers and Prohibition leaders of the country, he purchased the "New Voice," a prohibition paper of large circulation in New York. They began its publication under the firm style of Dickie & Wooley, as joint editors and publishers, and removed the paper to Chicago. While continuing his residence in Albion, Dr. Dickie gave to the paper his thought along editorial lines, and also spent one day each week in Chicago assisting in the business management of this journalistic enterprise. The circulation was increased to over sixty thousand, and was the leading and most successful organ of the party. Dr. Dickie remained in connection with it for two years and then sold his interest to Mr. Wooley, who is now sole proprietor.

Since retiring from the field of journalism, Dr. Dickie has devoted his entire attention to the interests of Albion College, and in February, 1901, was elected its president, since which time he has been at the head of the institution in which his own education was acquired. During the five years just prior to his election to the presidency, he had the entire management of the endowment fund of the college, over two hundred and fifty thousand dollars, and so invested this that it now yields an excellent annual income. A new library building has recently been erected. It is a fine edifice, which with its furnishing cost fifteen thousand dollars. Perhaps Dr. Dickie's principal achievement with the financial interests of the school was

23

his effort to eradicate the indebtedness of ninety thousand dollars which had been accumulating for thirty years. He succeeded in providing for the discharge of this debt, and already one-half of the sum has been paid in. As president of Albion College, he has enlarged the scope of its work and has advanced its methods in accordance with educational ideas. From this institution he received the degree of Doctor of Law.

Professor Dickie is a man of excellent business ability and executive force. While progressing continuously along intellectual lines, his development has never been abnormal, but has been in harmony with the growth of a well rounded character, and his counsel in business affairs is wise, his judgment clear and correct, and his efforts helpful. He was one of the organizers and a member of the directorate of the Commercial & Savings Bank of Albion, and is a director of the Albion Buggy Company.

In 1872 Dr. Dickie was united in marriage to Miss Mary Brockway, of Albion, a daughter of William H. Brockway, one of the early and influential residents of the city. A leader in public affairs, he was a member of both branches of the State Legislature for a number of terms and aided in shaping the policy of the commonwealth. He also built the Lake Shore Railroad from Lansing to Jonesville and was an extensive contractor, building for himself nine stores which are still standing on the main street of Albion. He was likewise one of the early preachers of the Methodist Episcopal church in Michigan and thus contributed to the moral as well as the material development of the state and to its political progress. Mrs. Dickie was educated in Albion College and by her marriage, which was celebrated December 22, 1872, became the mother of four children:

Clarissa, wife of L. E. Stewart, of Battle Creek; Ada, the wife of Cornelius Hamblen, of Detroit; Mary, at home; and W. H. Brockway Dickie.

Professor and Mrs. Dickie are members of the Methodist Episcopal church and for a number of years he has been the president of its board of trustees. In 1896 he was nominated on the Prohibition ticket and elected mayor of Albion, and during his administration the first cement bridge of the city was built and other improvements undertaken. The breadth of his wisdom, his indomitable perseverance and his strong individuality have been manifest in every work that he has undertaken. His entire accomplishment represents the result of the utilization of his innate talents, and the directing of his efforts along lines where mature judgment and rare discrimination have led the way.

CHARLES ARTHUR STANDIFORD.

A fine representative of the younger generation of business men of Calhoun county is Charles Arthur Standiford, who was born in Sherwood township, Branch county, Michigan, November 8, 1866. His father, James Standiford, now a retired resident of Athens, was for many years identified with the agricultural interests of this section of Michigan, as well as occupying a substantial position in the business life of Calhoun county. He is the representative of an eastern family, having been born in Baltimore county, Maryland, January 28, 1818,

the son of Clement and Mary (Fitzpatrick) Standiford, both parents being natives of Maryland, the mother a descendant of Scotch ancestry. Mr. Standiford was reared upon the paternal farm and interspersed his home duties with an attendance at the common schools wherein he acquired a fair education. He was the eldest of the six sons born to his parents, and of the four who attained maturity he is the only one now living. He remained at home until he had attained his majority, when he began to work at the carpenter's trade, his instruction for the first three years being the greater part of his renumeration, as he received only about seventy-five cents per day. A few years before the Civil war he removed to Michigan, locating in Branch county, where he followed his trade for many years. While a resident of Maryland he had worked for some time as an undertaker, and after coming to Michigan carried on this occupation in conjunction with his trade, remaining located, however, upon his farm. In time his business increased to such proportions that he found it necessary to rent his farm and remove to Athens, where he conducted an undertaking and furniture establishment, meeting with success in the years that followed. With a faith in the possibilities of his adopted state he has invested his accumulated gains in real estate, owning two farms on section 4, Sherwood township, Branch county, one of eighty acres and the other of two hundred and six, while in Athens he had a brick block built on the lot adjoining the bank in 1885. He is a successful and esteemed citizen of this locality.

Mr. Standiford has been married three times, the first ceremony being performed in York county, Pennsylvania, August 18, 1839, uniting him with Miss Mary J. Bond, of which union there were born four children, namely: William, who is married and lives in Kalamazoo with his family of four children: Wesley, died in boyhood; Thomas, who died in Branch county, his wife surviving him; and Henry, who died at the age of four years. The mother died in Maryland. Mr. Standiford was married the second time in Jefferson county, Ohio, to Miss Hyantha C. Carter, of which union there was born one child, who died in infancy. By his union with Sarah C. Carter, a sister of his second wife, were born three children, of whom Milton is manager of the electric light plant in Athens; Charles Arthur is the personal subject of this review; and Maie married Daniel Peck, and has two children, Leslie and Sarah. Mrs. Standiford died in 1896. In his political affiliations Mr. Standiford is an adherent of the principles promulgated by the Democratic party, having cast his first presidential ballot in 1840, but has never cared to hold office. He is an active member of the Congregational church, in which he has served as trustee, treasurer and deacon, and fraternally is identified with Athens lodge, No. 220, F. & A. M., having acted as treasurer for twenty-five years. While in Baltimore he was also associated with the Independent Order of Odd Fellows, but dropped his membership after a number of years.

Charles Arthur Standiford, the personal subject of this review, was reared upon his father's farm in Branch county until he was eighteen years old, receiving a preliminary education in the district school, after which he attended the high schools of Union City and Athens. Upon the location of his par-

ents in Athens in 1884, he became a member of the firm known as James Standiford & Company, in the conducting of the undertaking and furniture establishment of his father, remaining connected with its interests until the disposal of the same in 1899, to F. O. Hutchins. In the last named year the Athens State and Savings Bank was organized with a capital of $15,000, establishing their business in the bank building of S. R. Culp & Son, having purchased the same. Mr. Standiford became a stockholder and cashier in the concern, which is rapidly assuming a place of commercial importance in Athens and the neighboring locality. They are now paying three per cent. on deposits and are constantly increasing their custom.

By his union in 1891 with Miss Jennie Ferris, Mr. Standiford allied himself with a prominent pioneer family of the state. The western settler of the family was Benjamin F. Ferris, who was born in New York state, the son of John and Mary (Mereyhew) Ferris, the death of the father occurring in his native state while his wife died in Calhoun county, Michigan, having come west to make her home with her children.

Benjamin F. Ferris was married to Miss Sabrah Stone, also a native of New York state, and with his father-in-law, of whom an extended mention is found elsewhere in this work, came in 1831. They located just south of what is now the village of Athens, where he lived for a number of years, later removing to Sherwood township, Branch county. In that location, in 1840, he built a hotel and conducted the same for many years, the house still standing as a reminder of the pioneer days of the state. Later in life he removed to Athens, where he lived in retirement. Both himself and wife are interred in the Sherwood cemetery. They were the parents of five children, namely: Asahel, the father of Mrs. Standiford; Byron, said to be the first white child born in Athens township; Albert; Norton, and Ellen, who died in infancy. The four last named were natives of Calhoun county. Asahel Ferris received a good education, attending the college at Albion when first established, and throughout his long life he constantly added to his store of knowledge by wide and varied reading, while following agricultural pursuits in Athens township. His death occurred December 21, 1900, at the age of seventy years, five months and twenty-one days, his wife having passed away February 21, 1897, both being interred in Sherwood cemetery. In his political affiliations he was a Democrat as was also his father, Benjamin F., the elder man having served as a member of the State Legislature when it was first held at Lansing. To himself and wife were born two children, Benjamin I., who died in youth, and Jennie, now Mrs. Standiford. Mr. Standiford has built a beautiful home in Athens where he lives with his wife and the one child born of their union, surrounded with the comforts of life, a choice library adding both pleasure and profit in the passing years. Interested in collecting mementoes of "ye olden tyme," they have in their home a clock one hundred years old, and also the first ballot-box used in Sherwood township. In politics Mr. Standiford is an adherent of the principles of the Democratic party, and through the influence of the same has been justice of the peace for twelve years, and is also a notary public. Fraternally he is a member of the Masonic order. Mr. Standiford, though young in years, has established a reputation for business sagacity and energy, and combined with other characteristics, inherited and acquired, gives promise of a successful career.

ALBERT LEROY DICKEY.

Albert LeRoy Dickey, of Albion township, Calhoun county, is numbered among the enterprising farmers of southern Michigan, and his efforts along agricultural lines have been productive of success in gratifying measures. He is a native son of this county, his birth having occurred in Fredonia township, June 8, 1842, his parents being Marsh and Susan (Smith) Dickey. The family is of Irish lineage, the ancestry being traced back to John Dickey and his wife Margaret, who came from Londonderry, New Hampshire, in 1729, and on their emigration they were accompanied by their two sons, Adam and Matthew Dickey.

Adam Dickey was born in Londonderry, Ireland, in 1722, and after arriving at years of maturity married Jane Straham. They became the parents of twelve children: Margaret, John, James, Adam, Benjamin, Sally, Eleanor, Isabel, Matthew, Joseph, Thomas and Jane. Of this family Benjamin Dickey became the grandfather of our subject. He was born at Ackworth, New Hampshire, September 13, 1775, and was united in marriage to Isabel Marsh, who was born in Londonderry, New Hampshire, July 25, 1777, and made her home with an uncle, Anderson Marsh, until the marriage of her sister, when she removed to Ackworth, New Hampshire, and there resided until she gave her hand in marriage to Mr. Dickey. She was descended from George Marsh, who came to America from England in 1635, landing at Charlestown, Massachusetts, on the 8th of June of that year. Benjamin Dickey and his wife continued to make their home in New Hampshire until 1823, when he removed to Holland, Vermont, there residing until 1837. In that year he established his home in Buffalo, New York, where he was engaged in dealing in brick. While living there his wife died of cholera and was buried in Buffalo. Benjamin Dickey passed away in Fredonia township, Calhoun county, Michigan, in August, 1849, and his remains were interred in Riverside cemetery. He had spent his last days with his children in this locality.

Marsh Dickey acquired but a limited education, for his services were needed by his father. He accompanied his parents on their removal to Vermont when fifteen years of age and continued to reside upon the old homestead until he attained his majority, when he started out in life for himself. Going to Brockport, New York, he was first employed as a farm hand there, and was later connected with the brick business. In the fall of 1831 he crossed the lake and after a stormy voyage of two weeks landed at Detroit, Michigan, whence he made his way to Prairie Round. He found the place with considerable difficulty. He and two other young men secured an Indian to act as guide, and followed the Indian trail for one hundred and fifty miles, covering the entire distance on foot. Mr. Dickey spent the succeeding winter with a cousin upon a farm in this locality and in the spring returned to Detroit and thence to Buffalo, walking the entire distance of one hundred and fifty miles from Prairie Round to Detroit in three days. From Buffalo he proceeded to Brockport, Monroe county, New York, and thence to Niagara county, remaining in the Empire state until 1840, during which time

he followed various business pursuits, principally, however, being engaged in farming and in the manufacture of brick.

In 1840, Mr. Dickey again came to Michigan, arriving in November of that year, accompanied by his family. He then located in Fredonia township, Calhoun county, purchased one hundred and twenty acres of land on section 13. Later he added to his farm by additional purchases, and improved and developed his land until the entire tract was under a high state of cultivation. He first erected a log cabin and lived in true pioneer style, but as his financial resources increased he erected a frame dwelling. In 1864, however, he sold that property and bought a farm on section 31, Sheridan township, and section 36, Marengo township, comprising two hundred and five acres. This was partially improved and he placed it all under cultivation. Year by year he continued his labors there, and his efforts for the development of his land resulted in making the property a valuable and productive one. He continued to reside in Sheridan township until the fall of 1883, when he purchased a home in the village of Albion, where he spent the remainder of his life, his death occurring in June, 1899, his remains being interred in Riverside cemetery.

On the 22d of October, 1834, Marsh Dickey was united in marriage to Miss Susan Smith, a daughter of Orin and Rhoda (Brainard) Smith, both of whom were natives of Connecticut. She was born July 24, 1813, in that state, and when a child accompanied her parents on their removal to western New York, where her girlhood days were passed and where she eventually gave her hand in marriage to Marsh Dickey. She became the mother of five children. Sylvester B. now makes his home at Kankakee, Illinois, and in Texas, spending much of his time at Houston in the latter state, where he has a nice plantation; George died in infancy; Albert L. is the third of the family; Francis died at the age of sixteen years while attending Albion College; Anderson George completes the family. The parents traveled life's journey in the bonds of wedlock for more than fifty-two years, and theirs was a most happy married relation, their mutual love and confidence increasing as the years passed by. They were very active in church work, being consistent Christian people, identified with the Methodist Episcopal denomination. For many years Mr. Dickey served as a trustee of his church. His character was above reproach, his life being honorable and upright and his wife, who displayed so many splendid traits, that, like her husband, she enjoyed the highest regard, confidence and good will of all with whom she was associated. They left behind them the memory of honorable lives and good deeds, and all who knew them felt the deepest regard when they were called from this life to the home beyond.

Albert LeRoy Dickey, whose name introduces this record, spent his early boyhood days in Fredonia township and accompanied his parents on their removal to Sheridan township. His early education was acquired in the district schools, and he afterward attended Albion College and also the Mayhew Business College at Albion. He lived with his parents until after his marriage, and always assisted his father in the operation of the home farm, early becoming familiar with the labors of field and meadow. In 1870 he and his brother, Anderson, purchased one hundred and fourteen acres of land on section 6, Albion township. This was improved, and to its cultivation they devoted their energies until the spring of 1874, when Albert L. Dickey sold his interest to

his brother and invested his money in one hundred and twenty acres of improved land in Marengo township. Upon that farm he and his family lived for seven years, and in the spring of 1881 he sold it and purchased a farm in Albion township, comprising one hundred and sixty acres on section 14. To that place he removed, continuing his residence for five years, when in the spring of 1886 he again sold and purchased his present farm. Within its boundaries are two hundred and twenty-seven acres of rich and arable land located on section 6, Albion township. Mr. Dickey, however, removed to the village of Albion, where he purchased a house and lot on Baptist Hill, which he occupied for two years. He then took up his abode upon his present farm in the spring of 1888, and erected an elegant home. He also built a fine large barn, and has made other substantial improvements, in fact, all modern equipments are found upon this place, including the latest improved machinery, and his fields are under a high state of cultivation, yielding to him annually good crops.

On the 14th of February, 1871, Mr. Dickey was united in marriage to Miss Louise M. Rogers, of Marengo township, who was born in 1851 and is a daughter of Isaac and Margaret (Travis) Rogers. Her father was a native of Greenwich, Washington county, New York, while her mother's birth occurred in Waterford, New York. She was a daughter of Lewis Chambers. Isaac Rogers came to Michigan in 1853, and settled in Marengo township, Calhoun county, his home being on section 16. He devoted his remaining days to agricultural pursuits, and both he and his wife died on the old homestead there, the remains both being interred in Oakridge cemetery at Marshall. Unto Mr.

and Mrs. Dickey have been born five children: George Marsh, who died in infancy; Nellie Augusta, who is a graduate of Albion College: Claude Rogers, who, after studying in Albion College and the University of Michigan went to Pittsburg, where he continued his studies as an electrician in the employ of the Westinghouse Company and now occupies a fine position in Los Angeles, California; Marsh Anderson, who is a graduate of the high school of Albion and has also been a college student; Pearl Louise, who is a graduate of the high school of Albion and is now attending the Ypsilanti State Normal school. The two youngest children are yet under the parental roof.

Mr. Dickey gives his political support to the Republican party, and as every true American citizen should do, keeps well informed on the questions and issues of the day, but he has never been an aspirant for public office. He and his wife belong to the Methodist Episcopal church of Albion, and he gives his aid and co-operation not only to the church, but also to other movements for the benefit of his fellow men and the progress of town and county. His entire life has been spent in this locality, and therefore his history is largely familiar to his fellow townsmen, who recognize the fact that his has been an honorable career worthy of their respect, confidence and regard.

ENOS SHORT.

The family of which Enos Short is a descendant, traces its ancestry back to Germany, the American progenitor settling in Pennsylvania, upon his immigration to the broader opportunities of the western world. The grandfather and father, named respectively Peter and Enos, were both farmers, and both understood the language of their forefathers. The younger man married Elizabeth Pote, a daughter of John and Elizabeth (Zimmerman) Pote, a family also identified with the agricultural interests of the country. The father died in New York state in 1854, the grandmother in 1861 and the mother in 1893, the interment of the latter being in McCosta county, Michigan. Of a family of nine children born to Mr. and Mrs. Short, six are now living, those besides Enos Short, the personal subject of this review, being as follows: John, of Big Rapids; Peter, of Sault Ste. Marie; James, of this vicinity; Perry, of Manstee, and Jefferson, also of this vicinity. The first three and a brother-in-law were also soldiers in the Union army.

Enos Short, Jr., was born in Ontario county, New York, in the town of Phelps, May 24, 1846. He was but eight years old when his father died, after which he came to Michigan to live with his paternal grandfather in the neighborhood of Fentonville, remaining for two years. On returning to New York he worked for a man by the name of Perry Huffman, after about two years finding employment with a peppermint grower, being paid five dollars and a half per month, and the following season, which was in 1861, working for a Mr. Clark for seven dollars and a half per month. At the breaking out of the Civil war, though only a lad of fifteen years, Mr. Short was so imbued with the spirit of patriotism that he enlisted, October 22, 1861, in Company F, Ninety-eighth Regiment, New York Infantry, under Captain Kreutzer, the regiment being commanded by Colonel Dutton. Through a service of three years, seven months and twenty-one days, this lad remained under the command of Captain Kreutzer, who afterward became colonel. The regiment went into camp at Lyons, New Yorfk, thence to Park Barracks, in New York city, Washington and Fortress Monroe, after which they participated in the Peninsular campaign, being first under fire at the battle of Seven Pines. At the engagement at White Oak Swamp they lost heavily in men captured, after which they retreated to Harrison's Landing, the Ninety-eighth regiment being then left on garrison duty at Yorktown until January 1, 1863. They then received orders to march to Newburn, North Carolina, and were members in the first expedition against Charleston, under the command of General Hunter. They remained in the neighborhood of Charleston on transports for three weeks, when they returned to Newburn and were there placed on guard duty for the remainder of the season, later being sent back to Pongo, Virginia, being engaged in guerilla fighting for the greater part of their time. January 1, 1864, Mr. Short re-enlisted for another three years, again becoming a member of Company F. The entire regiment was given a thirty day's furlough at that time, when they returned home, carrying with them their colors. On their return to active service they were quartered at Yorktown, under the command of General Grant, the first battle in which Mr. Short participated being Drury's Bluff. Following this was a charge on Fort Harrison, at which the division in which Mr. Short was a member was the support for the famous charge of colored soldiers. This was the most serious engagement in which he participated, his hip being broken by a shell. After a return to Fortress Monroe and later to Philadelphia, Mr. Short received his honorable discharge at the close of the war, in Elmira, New York, July 15, 1865, being mustered out of service. He was, without doubt, one of the youngest of those who served their country.

For the six years following his return to peaceful pursuits, Mr. Short was engaged as a farmer, working by the month in his effort to earn a livelihood. In the fall of 1873, he once more located in Michigan, settling in Convis township, where he worked on a farm, after which he went to Isle Royal, on Lake Superior, and found employment with the Marquette Copper Company for one season. He returned to this township and for a time thereafter was again employed upon a farm, after which he was occupied as a brakeman on the Michigan Central Railroad for a year and a half. He then learned the trade of a machinist in the shops of Jackson, spending two years in that locality when he went to Battle Creek and was employed for eight years. With the result of his industry and economy he was then enabled to purchase his present farm of one hundred and sixty-nine acres, located on section 12, Convis township, since which purchase he has rebuilt the house, erected new barns, and in many other ways has increased the value of his property. With the exception of four years, going in 1893 to Battle Creek, where he worked one year, and living three years in the city of Marshall, he has since made his home upon his farm.

August 25, 1875, Mr. Short was united in marriage with Miss Frances Hoxsie, the representative of a New York family of worth, her father, Ira Hoxsie, a blacksmith, having settled in Convis township in 1870. His wife was, in maidenhood, Eliza Price, the daughter of William Price, a lawyer and probate judge of Cayuga county, New York, and a valiant soldier in the War of 1812. Mr. Hoxsie died July 27, 1888, and his wife died at the home of Mr. Short December 1, 1896, the last resting place of each being in Austin cemetery, Convis township. These children survive, the two besides Mrs. Short being Viroqua and Burton.

Mr. Short is prominent in fraternal circles, being a member of the International Association of Machinists; of Olivet lodge. No. 167, F. & A. M., and Chapter of Bellevue, and both himself and wife are members of Olivet Chapter, No. 24, Eastern Star. He is also identified with Olivet Grange and the C. Colegrove post, Grand Army of the Republic, of Marshall. In his political convictions he adheres to the Republican party, and though never desirous of official recognition, still sharing the responsibility of public office, having served as justice of the peace from 1891 to 1895. As a citizen Mr. Short has proven himself public spirited and progressive, patriotic and loyal to the principles of our government, his personal success being the result of untiring energy and application. He is a valued member of the community, held in the highest esteem for the sterling traits of character which have brought about his success.

JOSEPH M. WARD.

No state in the Union can boast of a more heroic band of pioneers than Michigan and their privations, hardships and earnest labors have resulted in establishing one of the foremost commonwealths in America, the possibilities of which are even greater than those possessed by many of her sister states. The work of the pioneer, however, is nearly completed and every year sees more new graves filled by those who helped to build up this portion of the country, and soon the last of these sturdy pioneers will be laid away, but their memory will ever remain green among those who love them and appreciate their efforts. The names of few others have been more closely associated with the early history of Battle Creek and Michigan than that of Joseph M. Ward, and his valuable counsel and the activities of his useful manhood were of the greatest moment in the material advancement of this city and state.

Mr. Ward was born on the Holland Patent, of New York January 11, 1822. His father, John Ward, was a native of New England and served as a soldier in the War of 1812. Later he followed farming and tanning. He wedded Julia Kellogg, likewise a representative of an old New England family and in their home in the Empire state Joseph M. Ward, of this review, was reared. His preliminary mental training, obtained in the district schools, was supplemented by study at Hobart Hill in the academic institute of the Holland Patent. His business training was received under the direction of his father, whom he assisted in the fields and also in the tannery. It was not long after he attained his majority that he came to the west, which offered a limitless field for those who had the courage to face the difficulties and obstacles of pioneer life. On the 23d of May, 1845, he took up his abode in Battle Creek, which remained his place of residence until his demise. He was first engaged in the livery business with his brother, carrying on operations in that line for three years. His business activity, however, touched many fields of endeavor and he left the impress of his individuality upon the material development of the state to a great extent. In the fall of 1884 he joined Charles Mason in the establishment of a woolen goods manufactory and the enterprise prospered, becoming a business of much importance. Mr. Ward was connected therewith until the 1st of January, 1860, when he sold out. His next venture was in the grain and milling business and again prosperity attended his labors, he becoming one of the heavy operators of the state. He bought and sold grain on a very large scale and had a splendid mill at Battle Creek, and in addition to this owned elevators in various grain producing sections of Michigan along the Chicago & Grand Trunk Railroad. After a time he associated his son, Charles A. Ward, with him in business, and together they built the first grain elevator at Port Huron, it being for some time one of the largest in the state. Years went by and there was no abatement to the success which attended the efforts of Mr. Ward. It is true that all days were not equally bright, and that at times storm clouds threatened, but he possessed courage, resolution and unfaltering diligence, and this enabled him to advance until he had reached the goal of prosperity; and having obtained a handsome competence, he retired from active connection with business affairs in 1882. He retained his financial interest, however, in many enterprises, with which he had been long connected, and thus a splendid income was assured to him. Mr. Ward was very quick to recognize business opportunities and to utilize them, and while he won wealth for himself, his labors were largely of a character that advanced the general prosperity and growth of the community as well. He was interested in the City Bank of Battle Creek and was largely interested in and a director of the Battle Creek Machinery Company and its successor, the American Steam Pump Company, while of the Battle Creek Gas Light Company he became the first president. He was one of the heavy stockholders and a director of the Ward Lumber Company, which manufactured and dealt in hard wood lumber having an extensive trade and controlling a fine plant. The company also owned extensive timber lands in Mississippi county, Missouri, and the wise counsel of Mr. Ward, whose sound judgment and keen foresight have made him a valued factor in the control of its various interests, added largely to the commercial and industrial wealth of Battle Creek.

On the 1st of September, 1848, Mr. Ward was married to Miss Susan S. Mason, a daughter of Charles Mason, of this city. She died November 15, 1853, leaving one son, Charles A. Ward, formerly a banker and ex-collector of customs at Port Huron, now of Evanston, Illinois. On the 1st of June, 1858, he married Elizabeth A. Beckley, of Meriden, Connecticut, and unto them were born three children: Frank W., of Battle Creek, who succeeded his father in the milling and grain business; George, deceased, who resided in Detroit, where he became a prominent factor as a grain dealer and was the president of the Detroit board of trade, and William B., of Whiting, Missouri.

In matters of citizenship Joseph M. Ward was progressive and capable. He took an active and helpful part in everything which he believed would contribute to the substantial upbuilding of this city and was a charter member of the Battle Creek fire department. He was also one of the promotors and directors of the Peninsular Railway Company, now the Chicago & Grand Trunk Railroad. He indorsed the Democratic party, to which he always gave his support and earnest co-operation, but official honors had no attraction for him and he never served in public office save as alderman from the Fifth ward. His wife was a member of the Episcopal church and to its support he gave generously. He was a member of its building committee when the present house of worship was erected and assisted greatly in raising funds for its early completion. Mr. Ward was a prudent, far-sighted, sagacious business man and also possessed integrity and untiring industry, and these combined qualifications brought him a measure of success enjoyed by few. While he contributed generously of his means toward measures for the public welfare he also gave of his time, influence and counsel. He was a man of medium height, spare and active. He possessed regular features and a face that attracted his fellow men because of its strong purpose and character. He bore his years with grace and dignity and his was an honored old age. In manner he was ever kind and courteous and was an instructive and entertaining companion. His high position in business and social world was the direct recognition of his genuine worth. What he accomplished, well entitled him to a place among the leading men of the state. His demise, August 13, 1902, closed the life record of one who was honored in the community in which he lived

and who was universally respected by all. Expressions of regret were heard on every hand at the announcement of his death, for people throughout Battle Creek felt that they had sustained a personal bereavement and the city an irreparable loss. Few men have left an example more to be desired than he, and his progressiveness, business ability and the part he took in public affairs will long be felt in municipal business circles in Battle Creek; for without him that city could scarcely have hoped to attain to the position she now holds as one of the most important and progressive cities of Michigan.

SETH E. HISCOCK.

Upon the farm where he now makes his home Seth E. Hiscock was born November 30, 1841, a native of Leroy township, Calhoun county, Michigan. He was the son of an early settler of the state, Isaac Hiscock, born in New York state, probably in Monroe county, May 12, 1810. He came to Michigan in 1826, settling first in Washtenaw county, and in 1837 he located upon the farm now owned by his son, having purchased a hundred and twenty acres the year before. At that time there was no land but that heavily timbered, the nearest neighbor being a Mr. Willard, whose house was two miles away. Indians and wild animals were plentiful throughout the entire state. In the course of time he was financially able to add another hundred and twenty acres to the original number in the farm, after which he disposed of forty before his death, which occurred May 9, 1874. Mr. Hiscock was twice married, his first wife being, in maidenhood, Matilda Cook, and of this union was born one daughter, Mary, who married Nelson A. Norton, and is now the mother of two children. She lives in Alpine, Kent county, Michigan. His second wife was Sarah T. Lyon, who was born in New Jersey, a daughter of Mathias Lyon. She was married in her home in Ypsilanti, and survives her husband, now making her home in Kalamazoo, Michigan, at the age of eighty-eight years. She is the mother of the following children: S. E., of this review; Frank M., Phoebe E., who is the widow of L. C. Church; Jennie M., Rhoda R. and Hattie M.

S. E. Hiscock was reared to manhood upon the paternal farm, receiving his education in the district school in the vicinity of his home. His entire life was spent upon this farm and after receiving personal possession he purchased fifty acres more of land in the neighborhood. He was married November 20, 1867, to Miss Jane A. Gould, whose birth occurred January 8, 1846. She was a daughter of Fayette and Betsey Gould. Of this union were born the following children: Luell C., who died at the age of twenty-four, December 28, 1892; Edwin Dorr, born in November, 1869, married Mabel Bradstreet, a daughter of William Bradstreet, and they have three children, namely: Leonard C., Lee B. and Elon; Frederick, born in 1870, married Matie Ewer, daughter of Albert and Sarah A. Ewer, and they have two daughters, namely: Leora E. and Blanche L. In his political convictions Mr. Hiscock has been a Republican all his life, his first vote being cast for Lincoln for his

second term, and though in no sense desirous of official recognition, he has actively supported the principles of his party.

WILLIAM E. SLOWEY.

William E. Slowey, a tinware manufacturer and dealer in heating apparatus, in Albion, was born in Sag Harbor, Long Island, in December, 1848, his parents being Thomas and Bridget (Brennan) Slowey, both of whom were natives of Ireland, whence they came to the United States as young people. They were married in New York city, and Mr. Slowey's business there was the fitting up of ships for whaling expeditions. He came to Michigan in 1849 and located at Albion, where he engaged in farming, owning a tract of land in Concord township, Jackson county, not far from Albion. In 1852, however, he went to California by overland route and died there two weeks after his arrival. To his widow was thus left the care of their four children. She remained a resident of Michigan until her demise, spending some time in Albion.

William E. Slowey is indebted to the public school system of this state for the educational privileges he enjoyed. On putting aside his text-books he began learning the tinner's trade in Albion, being at that time but sixteen years of age. Subsequently he was employed as a journeyman, and progressing in his field of labor he was afterward made foreman in the shops of Sheldon & Fanning, occupying that responsible position for a quarter of a century. When they retired from business Mr. Slowey purchased their interests and continued in the trade on his own account. This was in 1892 and in the fourteen years which have since come and gone he has prospered. He makes a specialty in the manufacture of all kinds of tin and iron work, roofing and heating apparatus and has an extensive shop at No. 7 North Clinton street, where he furnishes employment to from five to seven skilled workmen. His practical knowledge of the business in all its departments enables him to superintend the labors of his men to the best advantage and his work is bringing to him a very desirable financial return. He is, indeed, the most extensive tinware manufacturer in this section and as his business has increased he has made judicious investments in realty in Albion.

Politically Mr. Slowey is a Democrat and has been a member of the county committee. In 1888 he was elected alderman from the Third ward and has filled that office for three terms. During his first term the city water works were established and during his last term the fine Superior street bridge was erected. He has always favored substantial improvements and progress, and his co-operation in measures for the general good have been effective and beneficial to the community. He belongs to the Catholic Mutual Benefit Association. Regarded as one of the strong men of the city, he well deserves his position in public regard, because he started out in life empty handed and not only provided for his own support, but also cared for his aunt and mother during their later years. He has utilized his time and opportunities to the best advantage and is now a leading representative of industrial interests in Albion.

CHARLES C. SWIFT.

There is an old German proverb that a man may have three possessions, the wealth that he acquires, the friends he wins and his own good deeds, but wealth often takes to itself wings and flies away. The friends may remain faithful to the grave, but there they turn and go to their own homes, but the good deeds accompany a man on his long journey and their memory remains to those left behind. There were in the life of Charles Cushing Swift many actions that indicated an upright manhood and strong probity of character. He closely adhered to upright principles and left to his family an untarnished name, while his example is indeed one well worthy to be followed.

A native of Dutchess county, New York, he was born December 25, 1825, a son of Samuel and Betsy M. (Woodworth) Swift. The Swift family was one of the oldest of New England and was of English lineage, while the Woodworth family was also established in America in early colonial days. Prior to the War of the Revolution the great-grandfather on the paternal side emigrated to New York, where for many years his descendents engaged in the tilling of the soil. His son, the grandfather of our subject, when a boy, often accompanied his father on whaling expeditions sailing from Cape Cod, and when about four score years of age greatly enjoyed recounting the thrilling experiences and narrow escapes which he had participated when on the water. When a boy of fifteen, unable to swim, he was once thrown into the sea, but was picked up before life was extinct. The maternal grand-

father of our subject was Abel Woodworth, an officer of the Revolutionary war
on board of a privateer. He took part in a
number of engagements, and for a time
was incarcerated on board a prison ship,
but survived the suffering there endured
and eventually died at an advanced age
in Austerlitz, New York.

The parents of Charles C. Swift were
born in Austerlitz, and in May, 1845, they
brought their family to Calhoun county,
Michigan, settling in Bedford township,
where the father died in 1848, and the
mother in 1854. Both were interred in
Oak Hill cemetery. Their children were
eight in number: Samuel, Elizabeth M.,
Nathaniel, Charles C., David S., Harriet
C. W., Kent and Abel W. Of this family
Elizabeth was an invalid for twenty-five
years and Charles C. Swift rendered her
every attention possible, doing all in his
power to make her life comfortable and
happy.

With his parents Charles C. Swift
came to Michigan and lived on the old
homestead farm, comprising two hundred
and seventy-five acres, which he aided in
clearing of the native growth of timber
and placing under cultivation. After his
father's death he continued to engage in
farming there and year after year tilled the
fields and harvested the crops until February, 1889, when he retired from active
business life and removed to Battle Creek,
purchasing a home at No. 117 Chestnut
street. The house had not been finished,
but he completed it, making it a beautiful
residence, in which he spent his remaining
days amid the comforts of life, his death
occurring January 1, 1891.

Mr. Swift was three times married.
He first wedded Caroline Cornell, whose

remains were interred in Oak Hill cemetery. There were no children by that
union. For his second wife he chose Mary
Wait and they had three children: Charles
E., of Chicago; Adah, deceased, and Mary
E., who resides with her stepmother and is
supervisor of drawing in the public schools.
The mother of these children was also laid
to rest in Oak Hill cemetery. After the
death of his second wife Mr. Swift married Miss Julia E. Read, a native of Vermont, who became a resident of Kalamazoo, Michigan, when twelve years of age.

In politics Mr. Swift was a Republican.
He served as treasurer of Bedford township and held other minor offices. He was
ever a most charitable man and was quick
to hold out a helping hand to the unfortu-
nate or distressed. He belonged to the
Congregational church, at Augusta, was
most liberal in its support and served as
one of its deacons, while his home was
ever open for the reception of its ministers.
He was a man of broad sympathy and deep
charity and looked with kindly feeling upon his fellow men. He was always slow
to condemn and ready to assist and in his
life he exemplified the true Christian spirit
of forbearance and brotherly love. His
widow and his daughter still reside in the
family home on Chestnut street and occupy
a leading position in the circles where true
worth and intelligence are received as
passports into good society.

ISAAC CLARK WILLIAMS.

A representative and honored citizen of
Pennfield township is Isaac Clark Williams,
who was born in Chidington county, Ver-

mont, July 9, 1832, and is a son of Isaac Clark and Sarah (Hodgeman) Williams, who were likewise natives of the Green Mountain state. The paternal grandparents were Isaac and Mary (LaFayette) Williams, the former a native of Wales and a member of the British army. Going to France he there met and married Miss Mary LaFayette, who was a relative of General LaFayette. The young couple were secretly married and when her parents discovered the fact they disinherited her. About that time the husband was ordered to America, where his wife soon afterward joined him. Not being in sympathy with the British cause in the Revolutionary war he deserted the English army and, being captured was condemned to die, but his brave wife returned to France and secured the means with which purchased his release. His sympathy was all with the colonists in their struggle to gain independence, but as he was in poor health he did not fight with the Continental army. However, he became an American citizen, locating in Vermont, where both he and his wife spent their remaining days. Unto Isaac C. and Sarah (Hodgeman) Williams were born the following children: Hubbard Burdick, Marvilla, the wife of Francis Madison; John Hoyt, Isaac Clark, Elibias, Sarah Ann, the wife of George Wilkes, Frederick Deuras, who is living in Emmett township, south of Battle Creek, and Wesley Clinton, who resides in Barry county, Michigan. When the subject of this review was a lad of thirteen years the parents came with their family to the west. They traveled by wagon to Burlington, Vermont, thence by steamer to Whitehall and by way of the Erie canal proceeded to Buffalo, where they took passage on a lake vessel bound for Detroit. The journey

was completed as it was begun—in a wagon—and the trip covered about three weeks. Reaching Calhoun county the father and his family settled upon a tract of eighty acres of land that had been given to Mrs. Williams by her husband's brother, Frederick D. Hodgeman. There were no improvements upon the place save a small log shanty. In this the family established their home, living in pioneer style in the early days. Many hardships and trials were to be endured, but they also had many pleasures, and the hospitality which existed among the early settlers was proverbial. The father and sons placed the land under cultivation and in course of time good harvests rewarded their labors. In 1861 the mother died and her remains were interred in the Hicks cemetery.

The educational privileges which were afforded Mr. Wililams, of this review, were extremely limited. He had the opportunity of attending school only through one winter. His services were needed upon the home farm and his early life was one of toil. At the time of the Civil war, however, he put aside all business and personal considerations in order that he might aid his country in her struggle to preserve the Union. He enlisted at Battle Creek in 1864, as a member of Company I, Merrill's Horse Cavalry and served until the close of hostilities, being with General Thomas in the Missouri campaign. For three months he was ill in a hospital. At the close of the war and honorably discharged, he returned to his home and resumed farming, which he has made his life work. To-day he owns forty-four acres of land, constituting a good farm.

On the 16th of September, 1854, Mr. Williams was united in marriage to Miss

Hannah Maria Webb, a sister of Thomas Webb, whose sketch is given elsewhere in this volume, in which connection is also a mention of the family history. Unto our subject and his wife have been born five children of whom four are yet living: Minnie Ann is now the wife of Harry E. Dunham, a resident of Battle Creek. She has two children, one, Cora D., by a former marriage. The other, Gladys, by second marriage, is the wife of Richard Bishop, of Battle Creek and they have three children: Isaac Bruce, Clarissa Lucile and Calispa Gertrude; Atta Emily, the second of the family, is at home. Rollin Isaac, who resides in Pennfield township, wedded May Huntington and has one child, Bertha Inez. Oralin Clark completes the family, and is at home.

Mr. Wililams is a member of Farragut post, No. 32, G. A. R., of Battle Creek, and in discharging his duties of citizenship he is as true and loyal to his country's welfare as he was when he followed the stars and stripes on southern battlefields. He is numbered among the pioneer settlers of the county, having for fifty-nine years made his home here.

LEWIS DANIEL BATT.

Lewis Daniel Batt is now living a retired life in Battle Creek. For many years his activity in the business world was continuous and far-reaching, and as the result of his close application to his work, his persistence of purpose and his honorable dealing he has won success and also an untarnished name in business circles. A native son of Calhoun county, he was born November 4,

1837, his parents being Samuel G. and Matilda (Mills) Batt. The father was born in Bennington, Vermont, November 30, 1803, and the mother's birth occurred in Clyde, New York, February 23, 1812. She was a daughter of Caleb Mills, who came to Calhoun county in 1836, and settled just across the road from the Batt farm. The paternal grandfather of our subject was a patriot of the Revolutionary war, but both he and his wife died before the birth of Lewis D. Batt. In the schools of Vermont, Samuel Batt was educated and later removed to Clyde, New York, where he was married and lived for several years. In 1836 he emigrated to Calhoun county and secured two hundred and forty acres of goverment land, of which he at once cleared one hundred and sixty acres. About forty years ago he purchased the Waldo mill which he operated for ten or twelve years and then sold to T. W. Tucker. About the same time he disposed of his farming property and retired from active business, merely giving his supervision to his real estate interests. He died September 26, 1875, and his wife passed away April 12, 1888. Thus the county lost two of its honored pioneer settlers, people who had come to the west at an early day and had been important factors in the primitive development of the county. In politics Mr. Batt was a stanch Republican and served as supervisor of his township for a number of years during the early part of the county's development. A man of prominence, he exerted a strong influence over public thought and feeling and the early policy of Calhoun county bears the impress of his individuality. When he came to Michigan his means were very limited. The journey was made by lake to Detroit, where he purchased a covered wagon and an ox team. In this

LEWIS D. BATT

primitive way the journey was concluded and he had to cut his way through the vast forests for miles in order to get to his claim. The family then lived in a covered wagon until a rude cabin could be erected. The first home had no floor and many of the hardships and trials of pioneer life were experienced by the members of the household. Both Mr. and Mrs. Batt were devoted adherents of the Methodist Episcopal church and their labors were felt in the moral progress as well as the substantial upbuilding of the community. In their family were five sons and five daughters and nine of the number are yet living: William, of Petoskey, Michigan, born December 7, 1835, was a soldier of the Civil war; Lewis D.; Luther M., born July 20, 1839; Louisa M., who was born July 29, 1840, and is the wife of Marcus Markham, of Coldwater, Michigan; Melinda, A., who was born October 28, 1842, and is the widow of John Ellis; Harriet E., who was born July 6, 1844, and became the wife of Alfred Swift, a prominent merchant, but both are deceased; Julia E., born February 4, 1847, and now the wife of John Weidley, of Brunson, Michigan; Cornelia H., who was born December 3, 1849, and is the wife of Theodore Markham of California; George N., who was born May 12, 1851, and is a farmer of Decatur, Michigan; and Charles H., who was born January 25, 1856, and is in the street car service in Detroit.

Lewis Daniel Batt began his education in the old log schoolhouse seated with slab benches, and never had the opportunity of attending school after he was sixteen years of age. Much of his time, in fact, prior to that period was spent in farm work. He lived on the old homestead and assisted his father in clearing and developing the land until twenty-three years of age. He was then married to Miss Rachel Burley, a native of New York and a daughter of Ira and Caroline Burley, who were among the earliest settlers and prominent citizens of Calhoun county. Mrs. Batt died three years after her marirage, leaving a son, Clarence M., who is now advertising manager of "The Star League" at Indianapolis, Indiana. He is married and has a daughter, Leola R. After losing his first wife Mr. Batt was married to Mrs. Melinda (Shedd) Davis, whose first husband had been killed in the army. They had one daughter, Georgia R., who died January 26, 1898. The mother died July 12, 1882. March 29, 1883, Mr. Batt married Harriet A. Ross, a native of Lancaster, New Hampshire, a daughter of John and Prudence (Clark) Ross, who came to Livingston county at an early day and later resided in Oakland county, Michigan.

After his first marriage Mr. Batt operated his father's farm for three years and then removed to the village of Tekonsha, where he was engaged in dealing in agricultural implements and also in contracting and building. In 1884 he came to Battle Creek where he conducted a lumber yard until 1895, and then retired from active business. He had prospered in his undertakings and as the years had passed he had added annually to his capital until he is now the possessor of a very handsome competence. He has built and sold twenty houses in this city and still owns three houses and twenty acres of city realty which he platted and placed on sale as Batt's Riverside Park. His own home is an elegant residence at No. 457 Lake avenue, supplied with all the comforts of life. Mrs. Batt is a charming woman and a most gracious hostess, having the happy faculty of making her guests feel at ease. Mr. Batt gives his political allegiance to the Republican party, but has never aspired to office. He deserves to be classed with the honored pioneer settlers of Calhoun county, for here his birth occurred two-thirds of a century ago. Throughout this period he has been an interested witness of the growth and substantial improvement of the county and in many ways has assisted in its development. His life record is known to many and is one which will bear the closest investigation, for he has guided his actions by rules of conduct that develop manhood.

HOLLIS BARTLETT SMITH.

In taking up the history of the representative men of Calhoun county mention should be made of Hollis Bartlett Smith, who is senior member of the firm of H. B. Smith & Son of the Indian Mill Stock Farm near the town of Marengo in Calhoun county, Michigan. His life record is an indication that success may be achieved by strong determination and energy. He started out upon his business career empty handed, but possessed strong purpose and firm determination and as the years have passed he has utilized his time and opportunity to the best advantage.

Mr. Smith was born in Sullivan county, New Hampshire, on the 9th of November, 1830, and is a son of William and Hannah (Gunnison) Smith, who are also natives of the old Granite state. The paternal grandfather, Reuben Smith, was born in Connecticut and served his country as a private in the War of 1812, taking part in the battle of Lake Champlain. Throughout the greater part of his business career he has carried on agricultural pursuits in New Hampshire.

William Smith was educated in the schools of his native state and continued to make his home within its borders until 1840, when he removed to Ontario county, New York, where he engaged in farming. There he died in 1844 at the comparatively early age of forty-two years, his remains being interred in the Bristol cemetery of Ontario county, New York. His wife passed away in Goshen, New Hampshire, in 1834, at the age of twenty-eight years and was buried in the Goshen cemetery. Both were adherents of Universalist faith and Mr. Smith was a Democrat in his political views. His business efforts were attended with a gratifying measure of success, he being regarded as one of the prosperous and enterprising agriculturists of his locality. In the family were three children: Ira W., now deceased; Hollis B.; and Elmira, who has also passed away.

Hollis B. Smith was a lad of twelve years when he accompanied his parents on their removal from New Hampshire to New York. He began his education in the schools of the former state and afterward continued his studies in Henrietta Academy in Monroe county, New York, remaining a student until about twenty years of age. Soon afterward he came to Calhoun county, Michigan, arriving in Marshall in 1850. He journeyed westward by rail to Buffalo and thence took passage on the steamer Mayflower for Detroit, whence he came across the country to Marshall. His brother had arrived here two years previous to this time, and when Hollis B. came they entered into a partnership relation under the firm name of Smith Brothers, who conducted the hotel known as the Marshall House, at Marshall. In 1854, however, Hollis Smith sold his interest in the business and became express messenger with the Michigan Central Railroad Company. Six months later he entered the office of that company in New York, being a clerk in the ticket office. For a year he was connected with the Chicago, Burlington & Quincy Railroad Company as general advance agent with headquarters in New York.˙ Following his marriage he purchased eighty acres of land in the northeastern part of Eckford township, Calhoun county, Michigan, and resided thereon for four years, after which he took up his abode in Marshall, where he was engaged in business for a year. On the expiration of that period he came to the Indian Mill Stock Farm, which comprises one hundred and fifty acres. This farm is pleasantly located a half mile east of the Marengo station. There is upon the farm a large two-story dwelling house. Mr. Smith has erected some new buildings and has improved old ones, and now has a valuable place well equipped for the purposes for which it is used. He is extensively engaged in the breeding of Mammoth Poland-China hogs and Shorthorn cattle and at the head of his herd of cattle is Peri Duke, No. 134923. He has sold some of the best hogs and cattle raised in this portion of the state and his business has been very profitable.

On the 19th of October, 1858, Mr. Smith was united in marriage to Miss Ruth D. Pattison, of Marengo township, Calhoun county, and unto them have been born two children: Gardner William, whose birth occurred January 24, 1861, and who was a student in the schools of Jackson, Michigan, and in a business college in which he was graduated. He was married March 31, 1885,

to Ida Houck, a native of Marengo township. They have two children, Wayne and Bernadine. He is now interested in the Indian ˙ Mill Stock Farm with his father. Gardner W. Smith, before his marriage, purchased eighty acres of land and is now engaged in general agricultural pursuits. He gives his political allegiance to the Democracy. Lulu M. Smith, the only daughter of our subject, died at the age of twenty-eight years and was buried in the Marengo cemetery.

Hollis B. Smith gives his political allegiance to the Democracy. For six years he was elected historian of the State Pioneer and Historical Society of Calhoun county and has been a member of the committee of the executive board for three years, while at this writing, in 1904, he is a member of the committee of historians. He has been master of the Marengo and Marshall Granges, and has been secretary and lecturer of the Calhoun County Grange. He is deeply interested in everything pertaining to public progress and improvement. His business interests have been so capably conducted that success has attended his labors and he well merits the prosperity that has come to him.

DAVID HENNING FRAZER.

David Henning Frazer is the general manager of the Battle Creek Gas Company and has charge of a business system which has added greatly to the benefit of the stockholders of the company, and at the same time has given excellent service to its patrons. He was born in Chicago, Illinois, March 14, 1877, a son of Sydney Lampman and Mary (Henning) Frazer, who are still residents of Chicago. In their family were three children: Julia, now the wife of Stephen J. Rathbun; David H.; and Sydney Lampman, who is the secretary of the Gas Company of Battle Creek and married Ola Snyder of this city.

David H. Frazer spent his boyhood days in Chicago and attended its public schools until about eighteen years of age. He then went to Springfield, Missouri, where he entered the employ of the Springfield Lighting Company as collector, spending about two years there. He afterward came to Battle Creek and in 1899 entered the service of the Battle Creek Gas Company as collector. Gradually he was advanced from one position to another, until made general manager. His maternal grandfather in connection with W. A. Foote of Jackson, Michigan, had purchased the gas plant in 1898 and built up the business. On the 1st of January, 1901, Mr. Henning died and Mrs. Frazer and other members of the family purchased his gas stock from his estate. Since becoming connected with the gas company the business has developed until the number of customers has been increased from six hundred to twenty-six hundred and where fifty stoves were annually sold now the number reaches over five hundred in a year. The entire plant has been rebuilt and in 1902 the offices were completed. The office building is a three-story structure well equipped for the purposes used, and the plant is supplied with modern machinery for the manufacture of a high grade of gas. The enterprise is of value to Battle Creek and the appreciation of the public is shown by the increased patronage.

David H. Frazer was married in Springfield, Missouri, December 1, 1898, to Miss Hattie Hubbell, who was born there, a daughter of L. W. and M. L. (Leach) Hubbell. They have two children: Ruth and David Henning, both born in this city. Mr. Frazer is a Republican in his political views. He was reared in the Episcopal faith and is now a member of St. Thomas's church, though a young man, he is occupying a responsible position in the business world, discharging his duties with accuracy and capability and has already attained success that many an older man might well envy.

JOHN B. PARKER.

During the pioneer epoch in the development of Michigan, the Parker family was established within the borders of the state and John B. Parker resided here from the age of three years until his death. Throughout his business career he carried on farming and his activity, energy and perseverance were the foundation upon which he builded his success. In all his dealings he was strictly honorable, never taking advantage of the necessities of his fellow men and he left behind him an untarnished name.

Born in Delaware county, New York, January 7, 1832, he was a son of Aaron and Roxanna (Backus) Parker, who were farming people of the Empire state and removed to Michigan in territorial days. They went first to Ann Arbor, but after a few days pushed on westward to Jackson, where they spent fifteen years, coming thence to Battle Creek township, Calhoun county, where the father purchased eighty acres of land and a mill privilege. There he operated a sawmill for two years and then sold for a good price. He also disposed of his land at a good advance and purchased eighty acres on section 33, Battle Creek township, where he lived until the death of his wife in 1851. His last days were spent in the home of his son John. He was a man of industrious habits, gifted with enterprise and his labors brought to him prosperity. He voted with the Republican party and both he and his wife were members of the South Battle Creek Baptist church and were buried in the church yard.

John B. Parker was little more than three years old when his parents came to Michigan and in the district schools he was educated, while on the home farm he was trained to the work of field and meadow. Throughout his business career he always carried on general farming and also engaged in the raising of Percheron horses. Whatever he undertook he carried forward to success and his farm indicated his careful supervision and progressive spirit, being always neat and attractive in appearance and improved with all modern accessories.

On the 25th of July, 1854, Mr. Parker wedded Miss Nancy Hyde, a daughter of Samuel and Polly Ann (Bates) Hyde, natives of Vermont and New York respectively. They removed to Michigan in 1836 and were pioneer settlers of Macomb county, while later they located upon the farm now owned by Mrs. Parker. There they built a log cabin and began life in Calhoun county in true pioneer style. They became the parents of seven children, but only two are now living: Samuel and Nancy. The parents were devoted and faithful members of the Methodist church and at death their remains were interred in Climax cemetery. Well do they deserve mention among the leading and respected early settlers of the state. Unto Mr. and Mrs. Parker were born the following named: Emmaretta, who died at the

age of sixteen years; Albert, who died in infancy; Adelbert, who resides with his mother; Ella, who died in infancy; John H., who died at the age of fourteen years; and Robert, who married Mabel E. Thompson and has three children: Nina, Nellie and Carrie.

Mr. Parker gave his political allegiance to the Republican party and in matters of citizenship was progressive, being interested in everything for the general good of the county. He belonged to the Methodist Episcopal church of West Leroy and his life was in consistent harmony with his Christian faith and profession. He was most devoted to his family and faithful in friendship and his loss was thus deeply regretted when he was called from this life.

IRWIN A. DOOLITTLE.

Irwin A. Doolittle, the present treasurer of Calhoun county, was born May 6, 1866, in Clarendon township, his parents being Augustus A. and Emma L. (Humeston) Doolittle. The father was born in Delhi, New York, July 16, 1830, and was a son of Benjamin Doolittle, who followed farming in that locality. The family is of English lineage and was established in America at the time the early pilgrims founded the colony of Plymouth, Massachusetts. About 1835 Benjamin Doolittle brought his family to Calhoun county, Michigan, and cast in his lot with its early settlers, securing a farm in Clarendon township. He aided in establishing the first school in the district in 1837 and continued to make his home upon the old farm until called to his final rest. As the years passed, he bore his full share in the work of early development and improvement, and his name should be enduringly inscribed upon the pages of pioneer history.

Augustus A. Doolittle received but limited educational privileges, attending only the primitive schools in a new district. His training at farm labor, however, was not meager, for he actively assisted in the arduous task of developing a new farm, remaining at home until after he had attained his majority, when he started out upon an independent business career. Locating on a farm which adjoined the old homestead, he there engaged in the tilling of the soil for some time, but subsequently purchased the old home property, thus becoming the owner of four hundred and fifty acres of rich land, lying partly in Tekonsha township. He was united in marriage to Miss Emma L. Humeston, who came from Ohio to Michigan with her parents, Mr. and Mrs. James W. Humeston, who settled on a farm adjoining the old Doolittle place The marriage was celebrated in 1864, and the young couple began their domestic life upon the farm, Mr. Doolittle devoting his attention to agricultural pursuits throughout his entire life. In politics he was a Republican and held some local offices, but whether in office or out of it he was always a loyal progressive citizen. He died September 21, 1900, and his widow is still living. Unto them were born six children: Irwin A., Laura L., now the wife of John Wetherbee; Bertha L., Dwight A., Ralph S. and Elsie E.

Mr. Doolittle acquired a preliminary education in the district schools, and afterward was graduated from the Tekonsha high school with the class of 1886. He then engaged in teaching for ten years through the winter months, while during the summer seasons his labors were devoted to agricultural pursuits. After his marriage he made his home in Tekonsha township, where he still owns a farm. It was on the 10th of April, 1889, that he was joined in wedlock to Miss Jennie H. Doyle, of Tekonsha township, a daughter of Peter J. Doyle. Unto this marriage have been born two children, Viola E. and Carl L., who are still living; Manly I, the first born, having died at the age of three years.

Mr. Doolittle has been a life-long Republican and has ever been deeply and actively interested in the success of his party. His fitness for public office has led to his selection for a number of positions of trust and responsibility. He was for four years school inspector and has put forth effective effort toward raising the standard of the schools. He was elected supervisor of his township in 1898 and occupied that position for four years. In 1902 he was elected county treasurer and has since acceptably filled that position. The nomination came to him unsolicited and was, therefore, a tribute to his personal worth and an indication of the confidence reposed in him. He regards public office as a public trust and his devotion to its duties and to the general welfare is one of his marked characteristics. He is a member of the Baptist church of Tekonsha, of which he served as a trustee for a number of years, and was also superintendent of the Sunday school. The work of the church received his earnest indorsement and active co-operation and his efforts have always been put forth along lines of progress and reform. Since elected to the office of county treasurer he has made his home in Marshall, but his acquaintance is by no means limited to this district, for he is widely known throughout the county and is everywhere respected for his genuine worth.

WILLIAM DE FOREST ADAMS.

The name which heads this review is one well known throughout Calhoun county as that of a man whose strong integrity, professional ability and association with a family of prominence, added much to the upbuilding influences of this section of the state. He was a native son of the state, having been born in Burlington, Calhoun county, June 25, 1839, the descendant of a well known eastern family, several of whose members had become pioneers of the middle west. His great-grandfather was Parminio Adams, of Connecticut, who died in Lysander, Onondaga county, New York, in 1806. He was the father of six sons, of whom Alexander, the grandfather of our subject, was born in Simsbury, Connecticut, in 1773, and in 1795 married Miss Sarah Wood. The year following his marriage he removed to Onondaga county New York, where he remained seven years. Of the three children born to himself and wife— Laura, Ansell and William—the birth of the latter accurred at Marcellus, Onondaga county, New York, in 1800. Ansell and William came west with ox teams, journeying through northern Ohio, Indiana and Illinois. Later they located in Calhoun county, becoming the owners of the land which forms the present site of Burlington, this

town being platted by the brothers, and the greater part of the property remaining in their hands for many years. William Adams was a skilled millwright, and with his brother built the first sawmill in this vicinity, which they conducted successfully for ten years. Of great business and executive ability, discriminating judgment and untiring industry, financial success attended the efforts of these two men, to whom Calhoun county owes the esteem which is ever the portion of a country's pioneers. September 5, 1834, William Adams was united in marriage with Miss Mehitabel Buckingham, of whose union were born the following children: Laura, born in 1835; Truman, in 1837; William DeForest, the subject of this review; and Sarah Angeline, born July 31, 1841.

William DeForest Adams was reared in his native county, receiving the benefit of the common schools of Coldwater, Branch county, after which he attended Albion College. In the latter institution he met Miss Sarah M. Setford, who afterward became his wife. She was the daughter of William and Emily Maria (Davis)) Setford, the latter being a native of London, England. William Setford was an emigrant to the gold fields of California. After his marriage Mr. Adams located in Burlington, where he remained a year and a half, when he removed to Marshall, for the purpose of studying law under the instruction of Sidney Thomas, a well known attorney of this city. Mr. Adams brought to his study of this profession an inherited talent, his uncle, Parley Wood, of Burlington, having been one of the most prominent lawyers in Calhoun county during his practice. With his natural ability Mr. Adams combined industry and perseverance and in due course of

time was admitted to a practice of his profession which placed him among the leading
lawyers of the county. He met with a success which justified his choice in the matter of a life work, carrying with him into
the discharge of his professional duties an
unimpeachable integrity, which gave to him
the entire confidence of all with whom he
came in contact.

In politics Mr. Adams was a Republican
and was always active in the promotion of
the principles which he endorsed. Though
never desirous of official recognition his especial fitness for public office often made him
the choice of the people at election time.
He made his influence felt in all avenues
wherein he was called to accept the responsibilities and duties, his professional, political and social life numbering him among the
citizens who bespeak the best in a community. Fraternally he was associated with
the Masons and the Ancient Order of
United Workmen. Mr. Adams's death occurred March 30, 1893. Of the three children born to Mr. Adams and his wife, Lena
B. makes her home with her mother in the
beautiful residence erected by Mr. Adams in
1870; Grace died at the age of two years;
and Frank De Forest, who was born in 1872,
is a resident of Duluth, Minnesota. Inheriting a talent for the profession in which his
father had become distinguished, he entered the University of Michigan at Ann
Arbor, graduating from the law department
in 1895, with both the degree of A. B. and
a law diploma, completing the course in the
two departments in four years. He had
previously graduated from the high school
in Marshall in 1891. He is now associate
lawyer in a large mining concern, receiving
for his services a handsome salary. Fraternally he is associated with the Benevolent

Protective Order of Elks and the Masonic
order. February 12, 1902, he was united
in marriage with Grace Gibson, of Cincinnati, Ohio. They have one son, Chester
DeForest.

JOHN TAIT.

John Tait, a contractor and builder living at No. 130 Champion street, in Battle
Creek, is a representative of the nation
whose sons have become famous throughout the world because of their deeds of
valor. The story of Scotch bravery has
been repeated in song and told by the nov-
elist and thus the attention of the world
has been attracted to Scotland. It was
in the town of Peebles, Scotland, that Mr.
Tait was born on the 26th of September,
1850, his parents being Peter and Christina (Fairley) Tait. On the home farm he
was reared and acquired a good education
in the parish school, which he attended
until thirteen years of age, when he began
working upon a farm. At the age of sixteen he commenced learning the carpenter's trade at Innerleithen, Scotland, and
during the first year of his apprenticeship
received twenty-five cents per day, while
in the second year of his apprenticeship he
received one dollar and seventy-five cents
per week, the third year two dollars and
the fourth year two dollars and twenty-five
cents. During the last two years he was
able to do a journeyman's work and he was
afterward employed in that way in Scotland for about ten years.

While in his native country Mr. Tait
wedded Jane H. Kay, of Fifeshire, Scotland, the wedding taking place June 18,

1875. She was a daughter of John and Margaret (Brown) Kay. In 1881 Mr. Tait came to America and the following year was joined by his family in New York city. There he did contracting and building as a stone cutter and mason and in August, 1892, he removed to Saginaw, Michigan, where he also did contract work. In 1899 he came to Battle Creek and superintended the erection of the sanitorium, after which he built the Masonic temple, at Athens, Calhoun county. He also built an addition to the Anhauser-Busch Bottling Works, in Battle Creek, and an addition to the Bismarck Hotel. He has taken contracts for the erection of several additions to the Malta-Vita factory, built the Korn Krisp factory and many other business structures here, and is now building the new Ward block. He is thoroughly reliable and his trustworthiness supplementing his ability has secured to him a large and growing patronage. His surplus earnings have been invested in various enterprises of the city, he being now a stockholder in the American Hull Bean Company, the Battle Creek Interior Finish Company, the Hygienic Food Company, the Coffeyette Company, the Battle Creek Refrigerator Company and the Battle Creek Dalomitic Brick Company.

Unto Mr. and Mrs. Tait have been born five children: Peter, born in Glasgow, Scotland, is a stone mason, of Battle Creek, and marired Mabel Stoddart, of Saginaw, by whom he has one child; Maggie B., born in Glasgow, is the wife of Fred Stuvenvaul, of Detroit, and has one son; Christina F., born at Innerleithen, Scotland, is the wife of Frank Swandeck, of Detroit; Harriet and Lizzie, born in New York city, are at home. On coming to

America Mr. Tait took out naturalization papers and since becoming an American citizen has been a stanch Republican. His business record is such as any man might be proud to possess, for starting out in life for himself at the early age of thirteen he has steadily progressed in the business world and to-day occupies an enviable position as a man of worth and enterprise, whose labors have been crowned with success.

WILLIAM W. INGRAM.

William W. Ingram, who is engaged in general agricultural and horticultural pursuits on section 24, Battle Creek township, Calhoun county, was born at Coldwater, Branch county, Michigan, April 28, 1863, a son of William W. and Susan L. (Stebbins) Ingram. The father was born in New York, April 1, 1814, and his father was a farmer near Plattsburg. In the spring of 1837 William Ingram, Sr., came to Michigan, traveling with two yoke of oxen across the country and reaching his destination after twenty-one days, about the 1st of April. He first came to Battle Creek, but soon went to Hastings, Barry county, where he settled upon a tract of timber land. He at once began the development and cultivation of a farm, which he continued to improve until 1862, when he removed to Coldwater, where he spent one year. He had three hundred and twenty acres in Barry county and upon his farm was a school house, church and cemetery. In the graveyard now lie buried the great-grandfather, grandfather and several uncles of our subject, in fact five generations are represented there. In 1863 the father came to Calhoun county and for two years lived in Leroy township, after which he removed to the farm upon which our subject now resides, in the southern part of Battle Creek township. Here he purchased one hundred and twenty acres, which he continued to cultivate and improve until his death, on the 4th of December, 1892. The mother of our subject was his third wife and they were married in the Empire state. They had three children: Ella, the wife of David L. Barker, of Argusville, North Dakota; William W., and Lillie, who became the wife of Lewis Fowles, and died six years ago. The mother passed away July 31, 1886, and was buried in Du Bois cemetery. Both parents were members of the Methodist Episcopal church and were worthy people. The father gave his political support to the Whig party until its dissolution and then joined the Republican party. He was a very successful farmer and aided all of his children in getting a good start in life.

In the district schools near his home William W. Ingram of this review was educated and he received ample training in farm work as he assisted his father in the labor of the fields. He has always lived upon the home farm and is now devoting his energies to its further improvement. His efforts are practical and progressive and he now annually harvests good crops and gathers much fruit, which finds a ready sale on the market and adds materially to his income. He has made a specialty of small fruit and is one of the largest producers of berries in this part of the county, usually having several acres under cultivation.

On the 23d of February, 1885, Mr. Ingram was united in marriage to Miss Frances Wray, a native of New York city, and they had one child, Frank W. The mother died in 1886. In 1887 Mr. Ingram married Miss Emma Chapel, of Battle Creek, and in 1900 he was again called upon to mourn the loss of his wife, who died in the month of August of that year. His political allegiance is given the Republican party and in 1903 he was elected justice of the peace of Battle Creek township, in which position he is now capably serving. He is a member of Ben Hur lodge of Battle Creek. He has sold a part of the original farm but still retains possession of eighty acres, and has a well developed property.

JOSEPH PACKER.

Among the residents of Battle Creek to whom has been vouchsafed retirement from labor in compensation for earnest toil, perseverance and unremitting diligence in former years is numbered Joseph Packer, who at one time was prominent in business circles in this city as a dealer in live stock, in grain and in groceries. He was born in the town of Wallingford, Rutland county, Vermont, on the 19th of October, 1829, and is a son of the Rev. Joseph and Maria (Wells) Packer. On the home farm in the Green Mountain state he was reared and to the public school system of that locality he is indebted for the educational privileges he enjoyed. He also attended an academy at Ludlow, Vermont. When eighteen years of age he began teaching, following the profession through one winter. Attracted by the business opportunities of the growing west he came to Battle Creek, Michigan, in 1849. On his trip here he was accompanied as far as Fort Ann, New York, by a younger brother. Thence he proceeded by cars to Schenectady, and by canal boat to Rochester, where lived his sister, Mrs. J. C. Stone. He arrived at her home about eleven o'clock at night and on ringing the door bell what was his surprise to see his father's head thrust from a second story window and hear his father's voice call out "Is that you, Joe?" It seems that his father had become uneasy after the boy had left him and fearing that he might not accomplish the trip in safety, he had himself started for Rochester and arrived there before his son. He then went on with him to Buffalo and saw him safely aboard the steamer. After landing at Detroit, Joseph Packer made his way by rail to Battle Creek, where he had an uncle, Edward Packer, who was then engaged in the drygoods business. Joseph Packer entered school here and attended until his health failed. He had always enjoyed good health prior to this time, but in the west he contracted chills and fever and could not rid himself of the disease until he returned to Vermont. Making the trip back to his old home he remained in the Green Mountain state until he had recuperated. He then worked in a tannery in Vermont and purchased hides for the business. Next he went to Boston and secured a clerkship in a wholesale clothing house, in which he was employed in 1851-2. In the winter of 1852 he went to Aurora, Ohio, and during his residence there his mother died. In the spring of 1853 he again came to Battle

Creek and in that summer entered the grocery business, in which he continued for about a year. He was meeting with good financial success, but his health again failed him and he decided to retire from that work. He contracted pneumonia and the Doctor pronounced his case hopeless but deciding that he would administer to his own needs he did so and recovered. Mr. Packer then turned his attention to the purchase and sale of live stock, hides and grain, following that business in Battle Creek until 1857, when he returned to Vermont. In the fall of 1860 while in his native state Mr. Packer was united in marriage to Miss Frances Henry. The only son of that marriage, Henry H. Packer, is now conducting a hotel in Hoosick, New York. In 1884, in Battle Creek, Mr. Packer was again married, his second union being with Mrs. Minerva Perquay. She was born in the town of Wells, Rutland county, Vermont, a daughter of Daniel and Laura (Downey) Shaw. She was but an infant when her parents left Wells and her first remembrance is of Lake George. She was then four years of age. The family resided in the vicinity of Lake George until she was a maiden of sixteen, when they removed to Glen Falls, New York, and she became a student in the Glen Falls academy. Subsequently she engaged in teaching for two years in Warren county, New York, following that profession there until her removal to Walworth county, Wisconsin, where she was married to Theodore C. Perquay and they returned to the Green Mountain state, where her husband carried on contracting and building. In 1869, however, they became residents of Battle Creek. Here Mr. Perquay took and executed the contract for schoolhouse No. 1. His first work was to build the Nichols & Shepard office and among others some of the fine residences of the city. His last work was the construction of the front of the Buckley block. He died in October, 1881, and on the 16th of March, 1884, Mrs. Perquay gave her hand in marriage to Mr. Packer. Although Mr. Packer has retired from the active control of business interests he has excellent investments in realty, and manufacturing enterprises, whereby he annually receives a good income. In an early day he gave his political support to the Free Soil party and stanchly advocated abolition principles. He did not have the opportunity to vote in 1852 because of his removal from the state, but in 1856 he supported John C. Fremont and in 1860 cast his ballot for Lincoln. He took a very active part in the campaign of that year, had the honor of driving Lincoln and Jack Chandler from Battle Creek to Hastings, returning the next day. He did not see Mr. Chandler again until about 1881, when they met in Akron, Ohio, when Mr. Chandler said that he remembered Mr. Packer and the drive alluded to. Of recent years Mr. Packer has given his support to the Prohibition party and is a stanch advocate of the cause of temperance. He was reared in the Baptist faith, and the Packer family is a noted Baptist family, as there have been ministers of that denomination in every generation for three hundred fifty years. Mr. Packer however, of late years has adopted much broader views along the line of "New Thought." For seventy-four years he has traveled life's journey and the rest which has come to him is certainly justly merited. He is a self-made man in the fullest sense of that oft misused term, his prosperity in life being due to his industry and integrity.

Fortune has certainly dealt kindly with him for he has reached an advanced age and is now surrounded with the comforts and many of the luxuries of a good quiet home.

JOHN C. BROWN, M. D.

From no professional man do we expect or exact so many of the cardinal virtues as from the physician. If the clergyman is austere we imagine that his mind is absorbed with the contemplation of things beyond our ken; if our lawyer is brusque and crabbed, it is the mark of genius; but in the physician we expect not only a superior mentality and comprehensive knowledge, but sympathy as wide as the universe. Dr. Brown in a large measure meets all of these requirements and is regarded by many as an ideal physician. Certainly, if patronage is any criterion of ability, he ranks high among the leading physicians and surgeons in Battle Creek, where he is now enjoying a large and lucrative practice.

The Doctor was born in the town of Owasco, Cayuga county, New York, July 1, 1853, and is a son of H. G. and Harriet L. (Von Blaricom) Brown. The mother died in the Empire state while her husband was serving his country as a member of the Union army during the Civil war and the father afterward married again. In 1868, when his son, the doctor, was a youth of fifteen years, H. G. Brown removed with his family to Indiana, settling upon a farm in Steuben county.

Dr. Brown there remained until 1872. His educational advantages were very limited up to that time. He had attended school for a year and a half, working for his board during that period. Subsequently he began teaching; and desirous to further perfect his own education, he attended the Normal School at Fremont, Indiana, where he was graduated with the degree of Master of Arts in 1874. He afterward taught for another year, being principal of the schools at Flint, Indiana, but he regarded this only as an initiatory step to other professional labor. Desiring to make the practice of medicine his life work he began study with Dr. H. D. Wood, of Angola, Indiana, as his preceptor. Later he entered the medical college at Fort Wayne, Indiana, in the fall of 1876, remaining a student there until 1878, when he opened an office and began practice in Flint, Indiana.

The doctor was married about that time in Flint, Indiana, on the 19th of October, 1878, the lady of his choice being Miss Dema E. Hall, who was born in Springfield township, LaGrange county, Indiana, a daughter of L. W. and Harriet L. (Simmons) Hall. The young couple resided at Flint until 1884, when he again entered the medical college at Fort Wayne, Indiana, and was there graduated with the degree of M. D. in the class of 1886. He then removed to Burlington, Calhoun county, Michigan, where he engaged in practice until October, 1893, when he came to Battle Creek. He had enjoyed a good patronage in the former place, but desiring a broader field of labor, he removed to this city where he soon secured a large practice, for the evidence which he gave of his skill and ability won for him the public confidence and therefore the support of many of the citizens of this locality. In 1894 Dr. Brown still further extended his professional knowledge by pursuing a post-graduate course in Rush Medical College of Chicago. He has also kept abreast with the advanced thought of the times concerning methods and medical practice by his membership in various societies for the dissemination of knowledge. He is a member of the Steuben County Medical Society of Indiana, of which he at one time served as president. He also belongs to the State Medical Society of Indiana and the Tri-State Medical Society, which embraces Indiana, Michigan and Ohio. He is likewise a member of the Calhoun County Medical Society and is its president, the Michigan State Medical Society and the American Medical Association.

Unto the Doctor and his wife have been born four children. Blaine, born on the 10th of March, 1880, at Turkey Creek, Steuben county, is a graduate of the high school of Union City, Michigan, and at one time was a successful teacher. He is now the secretary and one of the directors of the Flesh Food Company, of Battle Creek. Joe, born in Flint, Indiana, May 9, 1883, is a graduate of the high school of Burlington, Michigan, and is now at Ferris Institute of Big Rapids, Michigan, as a student. Hattie I., born April 9, 1892, in Burlington, and Rex, born November 15, 1898, in Burlington, are both at home.

Since age conferred upon Dr. Brown the right of franchise he has been a stanch Republican, keeping well informed on the issues of the day, but has never been an office seeker. He was made a Mason in Greenleaf lodge, No. 358, F. & A. M., at Algansee, Michigan, and afterward transferred his membership to the lodge in Union City, where he filled all of the chairs and also acted as representative to the Grand lodge, and is now a member of Battle

Creek lodge, No. 12, F. & A. M. He and
his wife are members of the Order of
Eastern Star, Bryant Chapter, of Battle
Creek, No. 153, and he is a past patron
of chapter 193 at Union City. He
also belongs to. Calhoun tent, No. 54,
K. O. T. M., at Battle Creek and was tent
physician for over twelve years at Burlington. He likewise has membership with the
Benevolent Protective Order of Elks at
Battle Creek and in these various organizations is both popular and prominent. His
chief attention, however, is given to his
professional duties which make strong demands upon his time. He is thoroughly
qualified for his chosen work and in the alleviation of human suffering his efforts have
proven of value in many a household.

WILLIAM HAUG.

William Haug, who for many years
was connected with farming interests in
Calhoun county, was born in Albany, New
York, February 26, 1832, a son of John
Christian and Catherine (Billings) Haug,
both natives of Germany. The mother was
a daughter of wealthy parents and when she
and her husband and their four children
sailed for America her father placed in her
hand an envelope with the instruction that
she was not to open it until they reached
New York. After a voyage of three months
they landed in the new world and when the
package was opened it was found to contain a considerable sum of money. The
money contained in the package was intrusted to a minister of the German Re-

formed church, who told them he would
take care of it for them. He invested it in
his own name and they were never able to
recover it, so they had to begin in America
as other poor people.

John Christian Haug lived about nine
years after they came to America. His
death occurred in Albany when William
Haug was about six months old. The
mother was left with eight children to support. When just a lad William Haug began to help earn a livelihood by taking a position as a bell boy at two dollars a month
in the home of a wealthy family.

The family first lived in Albany. The
mother afterward removed to Geneva, New
York, and in 1847 came to Calhoun county,
Michigan, with her sons, John, Michael and
William and her daughter Gertrude, now
Mrs. Adam Crosier. They settled on section 27, Bedford township, securing one
hundred and twenty acres of land and the
forty acres on which the home now stands
was improved. The old house still stands
in the rear of the present home and is probably the oldest frame structure in the
county. The mother lived to the advanced
age of ninety-seven years, dying in 1894,
and four of her children attended her
funeral but George, William and Michael
all died within three months of each other
in 1898. Caroline died in 1896.

William Haug was a youth of fifteen
years when he came with the family to Calhoun county and up to the time of his death
he resided continuously on the old homestead farm with the expection of a period of
three years when he was upon the road in
the employ of the American Express Company. This was from 1856 until the spring
of 1859, at which time he purchased the
home farm of his mother and began the

tilling of the soil on his own account. As the years passed he placed the land under a very high state of cultivation and made splendid improvements on the property, adding all modern equipments.

It was in 1859 that Mr. Haug wedded Miss Emma Fidelia Fellows, who was born in Barre Center, Orleans county, New York, a daughter of Asa and Lucy (Morse) Fellows, who were of English descent and came to Michigan in August, 1847, driving to Buffalo, thence proceeding by lake to Detroit. They settled on section 27, adjoining the Haug farm, securing one hundred and sixty acres of wooded land, of which only a small portion had been cleared. Mrs. Haug was the youngest of the three children, the others being Mrs. Lura A. Vedder, of Battle Creek, and Charles Newton, of Bedford township. The mother died in 1862 at the age of fifty-three years, and the father's death occurred in 1890, at the age of eighty-eight years, both being interred in Oak Hill cemetery. They were Presbyterians in religious faith. Unto Mr. and Mrs. Haug were born three children: Fred Stewart, who operates the home farm; Carrie Gertrude, at home, and Rose Christine, who died September 16, 1901.

Mr. Haug always voted with the Republican party but would never accept office as a reward for party allegiance. His time and attention were given to his farming interests and his chief delight was in providing a comfortable home for his family and promoting the happiness of his wife and children. He built a fine residence on his farm but was only permitted to enjoy it for three winters when death claimed him. Long a well known citizen and farmer of Calhoun county he enjoyed the friendship and good will of all with whom he came in contact and many friends shared the deep sorrow of the family when the husband and father was called away.

HON. PATRICK HART.

One of the prominent self-made men, enterprising merchants and well known political leaders of Battle Creek is Patrick Hart, who is engaged in dealing in cigars and tobacco at No. 6 State street. He was born in County Monaghan, Ireland, on the 25th of September, 1852, and is a son of Cornelius and Elizabeth (Carolin) Hart. When he was only three years old his parents came to America, making their way at once from the Atlantic coast to Michigan, where they established their home in Pennfield township, Calhoun county. The father had been a harness maker in his native country, but the style of harness there made were so different from those manufactured in the United States that he could not work at the trade without learning new methods and, feeling that he was too old to do this, he became a farmer. In 1861 he established his home in Battle Creek. Patrick Hart, the youngest in a family of six children, four of whom are still living, is the subject of this review. Susannah, who is the wife of Michael Marion, came to New York before the other members of the family emigrated to the new world, and was married in the eastern metropolis. She also became a resident of Calhoun county before the family was established here and died in February, 1902, at Battle Creek, leaving six children, of whom four are living. Margaret Hart came to America with her elder sister and in Marshall, Michigan, gave her hand to James Toole. She died in Pennfield, Calhoun county, leaving three children. Elizabeth, who came to the United States with her elder sisters, is the wife of Michael Reynolds, by whom she has six children, their home being at No. 69 Harvard street, Battle Creek. James Hart, who crossed the Atlantic with the family, married Catherine Cross and now lives at No. 202 Fountain street, east, Battle Creek. Fourteen children were born unto him and his wife of whom six are yet living. John, the youngest member of the family with the exception of our subject, is now in partnership with his brother Patrick.

It was in Battle Creek that Patrick Hart was reared to manhood, pursuing his education in the public schools until he had completed the grammar school course. He was sixteen years of age at the time of his father's death. When fifteen years of age he had begun to learn the cooper's trade and later worked as a journeyman until about 1878. His brother John had also become familiar with the same pursuit, and in 1878 they formed a business together on a small scale. Previous to this time, however, they had been proprietors of a grocery store, but in that venture lost nearly all that he had invested. In the coopering business, however, they prospered, securing a good patronage, which brought to them an excellent income and they continued in that business. He is now engaged in dealing in cigars, tobacco and newspapers at No. 6 State street and this enterprise has likewise become a profitable one to him.

After emigrating to the new world Mr. Hart took out naturalization papers and became an American citizen. In 1876 he cast his first presidential vote, supporting Hayes. During the '80s he was elected alderman of Battle Creek from the first ward and served as a member of the city council for four years, during which time he acted as chairman of the committee on side and cross walks and public health. He was largely instrumental in establishing the electric light system for the city, had a hard fight in securing the city water works; and in matters pertaining to the general welfare he was most active and influential, being always found on the side of reform, improvement and progress. The creditable record which he made as an alderman led to his selection for higher political honors, and in 1892 he was elected to represent his district in the State Legislature, where he served for one term. During that time he acted as a member of the committees on municipal corporation and the Kalamazoo asylum and he introduced several important bills, some of which were passed. He was reared in the Catholic faith and now holds membership in St. Phillip's church. He is widely and favorably known and is a popular resident of Battle Creek, having the good will and regard of people of all classes.

FREDERICK W. PEABODY.

Frederick W. Peabody, chief of the fire department of Albion and also interested in agricultural pursuits in Calhoun county, was born in Detroit, Michigan, June 9, 1862, and when only a year old was brought to this city, where later he entered the public school, continuing his studies until he had mastered the branches which constitute the high school curriculum. He afterward learned the

FREDERICK W. PEABODY

painter's trade, which he followed for a number of years, but since 1875 has been continually connected with Albion fire department, first with the old Alert Hose Company No. 1, when that was a volunteer company. First he served as torch boy and afterwards held all of the offices in his original company. His advancement has been continuous and he has made his way upward from assistant foreman, foreman and assistant chief to that of chief, having been appointed to the head of the department in 1887. He has since occupied that position continuously, with the exception of a period of four years, and in 1903 was re-appointed by Mayor Palmer. His service in this capacity, therefore, is greater than that of any other fireman in the county. When he first joined the department there was only an old hand engine, but the equipment has gradually increased and there is an excellent and modern engine, good hose wagon and a truck and ladder wagon. There is also a good brick building, which is used as the fire department house with an electric door opener and all modern devices. All of the improvements in the service have been made during the incumbency of Mr. Peabody as chief. He is a member of both the National and International Fire Chiefs' Associations and he has made the work of fighting fires a life study. In office he displays keen sagacity and in the face of danger is always cool and collected, thus being able to use his forces to the best possible advantage.

In Albion on the 4th of April, 1884, Mr. Peabody was united in marriage to Miss Nellie M. Robinson, and they have two children, Walter M. and Genevieve A. Mr. Peabody is the owner of a good farm in Homer township, but devotes his time to the interests of the fire department. In politics

25

he usually votes with the Democratic party, but is rather independent in his political views. Socially he is connected with the Knights of the Maccabees.

JULIUS A. GUITEAU.

The descendant of a French Huguenot family that escaped from France at the time of the religious persecution in that country, Julius A. Guiteau was born in Batavia, New York, in 1843.

His father, Orville, a native of the same locality, was a son of Martin Guiteau, and married Mahala Baker, whose birth occurred near Batavia, her father being Nathan Baker. Mr. Guiteau brought his family to Michigan about 1850, locating upon the farm which is now in the possession of our subject. The father's death occurred August 3, 1899, and that of his wife April 14, 1886. Besides our subject one daughter was born to them, Eliza, who married George Vanderburgh, and is now the mother of the following children: George, Clark, Frank and Warren.

In 1902 Julius A. Guiteau was united in marriage with Miss Priscilla Stevens, who was born in Vermont, the daughter of William H. Harmon. Her mother was formerly Lida Trescott, of Livingston county, New York, and she died in 1848, when Mrs. Guiteau was but five years old. The other children of this marriage were Marshall Edgar, Adelia Ann and Leamon M., all of whom are now deceased. The father died June 16, 1886, in Volcano, Amador county, California, to which state he had emigrated in 1853, where he engaged as miner farmer, deputy sheriff, and for six years filled the office of sheriff. Mr. Guiteau has been a Republican all his life, but having been actively engaged in farming upon the hundred and sixty acres which make up his property he has not had time or inclination to do more than cast his vote in the interests of good government.

GEORGE W. GREEN, A. M., M. D.

If success or fame could be purchased many a man now doomed to mediocrity for life would be before the public gaze commanding the honor and admiration of his fellow men. It is certainly a beneficial deprivation that it is otherwise—that distinction is won over the path of public usefulness. Merit alone gains prominence in the learned professions, and in no walk of life does advancement depend more surely and entirely upon individual accomplishment than in the practice of medicine. That Dr. Green is to-day one of the leading specialists of Michigan in the treatment of diseases of the eye, ear, nose and throat, is therefore proof of his excellent qualifications, his comprehensive knowledge and his adaptability in applying his medical lore to the alleviation of human suffering. He has practiced for fourteen years in Battle Creek, continually advancing in public regard and in success.

The doctor was born in Madison, Lake county, Ohio, on the 6th of March, 1837, a son of Jesse M. and Zilpha (Lovel) Green. The paternal grandfather, Joseph Green, was born in Sussex county, New Jersey, February 26, 1767, and thence removed to Pennsylvania. In August, 1779, when but twelve years of age, he enlisted for service in the Continental army in the Revolutionary war for three months, under Captain Brady, of Muncy, Lycoming county, Pennsylvania. Mr. Green performed garrison duty in Fort Brady, at Muncy, and was also employed at different times with scouting parties. He was probably the youngest soldier of the war to carry a musket, although other boys younger served as drummers and waiters for the line officers. In May, 1782, Joseph Green again enlisted, at Muncy, this time becoming a member of a company of rangers commanded by Captain Thomas Robinson in Colonel Hunter's regiment. To this company Ebenezer Green, Jr., the brother of the grandfather of the doctor, had belonged, but he was killed April 16, 1782, by the Indians. Joseph Green marched to Minegan's Fort, on the west branch of the Susquehanna river, where he remained for three months, with occasional service with scouting parties. With a part of his company he was then detailed to Fort Brady, where he was similarly employed for five months, when in December the company was disbanded, the Rangers understanding that hostilities had ceased. In June, 1788, Joseph Green removed to Chemung. New York, and in May, 1817, he settled at Madison, Ohio where he continued to reside until his death.

Jesse M. Green, the father of the doctor, was born in Chemung, New York, October 23, 1803, and with his parents moved to Lake county, Ohio. His educational privileges were those afforded by the schools of the day, but being of a studious nature he became a well read and broad-minded man. On attaining his majority he engaged in farming at Madison, Lake county, owning the old home farm which was purchased by his father in 1816. He was one of the leading and representative men of the locality and for many years was honored by his fellow townsmen with the highest office in the gift of the township. In 1827 he married Zilpha Lovel, who was born in Plainfield, Massachusetts, in August, 1809, a daughter of Ebenezer Lovel, who removed to Ohio in 1819. His wife had died during the infancy of her daughter. Mrs. Green, who was reared by her grandparents, Mr. and Mrs. Joseph Beals, until after her father's second marriage, when she returned to his home, accompanying him to Ohio. Joseph Beals was well known as the "mountain miller," was an active church worker and made his religion a part of his daily life, always doing unto others as he would have them do unto him. He was the subject of a book entitled "Mountain Miller," written by the Rev. Hallock. Unto the marriage of Jesse M. Green and Zilpha Lovel six children were born, the doctor being the fourth. The father died in 1875 and the mother passed away in 1881.

In the common schools Dr. Green began his education and in Madison Seminary prepared for college, after which he spent two years in the literary department at Oberlin College. Deciding to become a member of the medical profession, he became a student in the medical department of the University of Michigan in 1860 and was graduated with the degree of M. D., in March, 1862. For a year thereafter he engaged in the private practice of medicine, locating at Three Rivers, Michigan, after which he was appointed by Governor Blair, assistant surgeon of the Twenty-eighth Michigan Infantry. He was in the field service during his term and the first heavy engagement in

which he participated was at Nashville, Tennessee, in 1864. Later the regiment was transferred to North Carolina and was not discharged until June, 1866, having been retained to do garrison duty.

At the close of his military service Dr. Green resumed practice at Hudson, Michigan, where for ten years he was accorded a liberal patronage which made his work very successful from a financial standpoint and also indicated the trust reposed in him by the public. While there he became a member of the State Medical Society and the American Medical Association, and through the interchange of thought and experiences, which is the main feature of these organizations, he kept fully informed concerning the progress of the profession. About 1876 he removed to Chicago, where he became a member of the firm of Chapman & Green, manufacturing pharmacists. They did an extensive pharmaceutical business, employing ten traveling salesmen, and Dr. Green was connected with the enterprise for twelve years, at the end of which time he sold his interest. He then went to New York city, where he pursued a seven months' course in the New York Post Graduate College, giving especial attention to opthalmology and otology as well as to the study of diseases of the nose and throat. Returning then to the west, he located in Battle Creek in July, 1889, being the first specialist in his line in the city. His success from the beginning of his residence here has been uniform and rapid and is a merited tribute to his ability. He has gained a reputation of which he has every reason to be proud and is now accorded a gratifying practice, which speaks in incontrovertible terms of his excellent qualifications. While he is well versed in the general laws of medical practice, since coming to Battle Creek he has confined his attention entirely to his specialty.

On the 25th of June, 1862, Dr. Green was united in marriage to Miss Nancy E. Bugbee, of Niagara county, New York, a daughter of George L. Bugbee, a pioneer of that county. To the Doctor and his wife were born six children, five of whom are still living: Frank A., a graduate of the University of Michigan, and now a dentist of Geneva, Ohio; Walter J., who was graduated in the same school and is now practicing dentistry in Ashtabula, Ohio; Blanche, the wife of L. G. Nichols; Grace W., the wife of Claude Clark, treasurer of the "Toronto World," of Toronto, Canada; and George W., Jr., who married Winnifred Blackett and is a machinist of Battle Creek. Mrs. Green died July 18, 1902, in the faith of the Baptist church, of which she was long a consistent and faithful member.

The Doctor has also been a lifelong member of the Baptist church and is now president of the board of deacons. He has ever been active in the church work, has contributed liberally to its support and reared his children in that faith, all being members of the same denomination. The Doctor's beautiful home is located at No. 134 East Main street, where he has resided since coming to the city. He also owns the block at No. 10 West Main street. He has long been deeply interested in educational work and is now a trustee in Kalamazoo College, which institution conferred upon him the honorary degree of Master of Arts. In politics, while never an office seeker, he is an ardent Republican and since casting his first presidential vote for Abraham Lincoln he has voted for each presidential nominee of the party. He belongs to Farragut Post, G. A. R., and to the county, state and national medical societies. A man of scholarly attainments and strong intellectuality he looks upon the world from a broad standpoint, and while his professional duties have made heavy demands upon his time and attention, he has yet always found opportunity to co-operate in movements for educational, social and moral progress.

REUBEN H. COURT.

The Court family is too well known in southern Michigan for the subject of this review to need any special introduction to the readers of this volume. Reuben H. Court, now the junior member of the firm of James Court & Son, is a native resident of Marshall, where he was born on the 27th of June, 1877. His father, James Court, long a respected and prominent citizen of Calhoun county, is represented elsewhere in this volume. At the usual age Reuben H. Court entered school and therein continued his studies until he had completed the work of the high school of Marshall. He afterward attended the Battle Creek College and by broad learning was well qualified to meet the responsible duties of a business career. On putting aside his text-books he obtained a position in a wholesale commission house of New York city, where he gained many new and modern ideas concerning the handling of poultry. On the death of his brother, James Court, Jr., he was called home and entered the business at Marshall, which had been established by his father. The firm at that time was composed of his father and brother, F. W., and himself, and this relationship was maintained until the father's death in 1902, when F. W. and Reuben Court became partners, still continuing the old firm name. They are now conducting one of the most extensive, if not the largest, poultry, butter and egg business of the state. They have splendidly equipped plants at Marshall, Allegan and Bellevue, Michigan, and are also interested in a similar enterprise at Homer. The volume of their business is represented by a large figure and their annual trade has made their enterprise very profitable.

NICHOLAS HENRY HAMMOND.

Nicholas Henry Hammond was born in a small village on the banks of the river Moselle, in the Grand Duchy of Luxsemburg, Europe, on the 8th day of August, 1838, and is a son of John and Catherine (Thinus) Hammond. His father, in common with his fellow villagers, was a small land owner, tiller of the soil, and grape grower. Hearing much of America as the land of promise for the poor man, he decided to emigrate, and in April, 1847, left his native home accompanied by his wife and three children, two daughters and one son, the latter being the youngest and subject of this sketch. As usual, in those days, the trip across the Atlantic was made in a sailing ship, and in this case, occupied forty days' time in reaching New York.

The family arrived at its destination, Massillon, Stark county, Ohio, on July 4th,

1847, where the father had the usual experience of eking out a poor existence for several years among the close fisted "Pennsylvania Dutch" farmers, settled in that section. In the spring of 1850, the father decided to remove to Sandusky City, Ohio, where some weeks after arrival, he obtained employment, and from that time until the time of his death, May, 1852, he got along fairly well, being an industrious and sober man. After the death of the father, the family was thrown upon its own resources, and the subject of this sketch, though the youngest, did what he could in maintaining the family. Without going into small details, Mr. Hammond says his first employment for wages, of which he has any recollection, was when, at the age of eleven years, he worked in the harvest field for the munificent sum of twenty-five cents a day. Next followed two summers in a menial capacity in a saloon and restaurant, and then one summer as a cook on a sand and wood scow, plying between Sandusky Bay and the adjacent Lake Erie. It was in the fall of 1853, at the age of fifteen, that he secured a position as clerk in a grocery store where he remained four years. During this employment he attended the grammar school during the winter of 1854-5, working in the store before and after school hours. Being an apt scholar, he was advanced two grades during the three months' term, soon reaching the head of his class in most studies. He also, in 1856, took a course in an earlier day Business College, conducted by one Goldsmith, who soon after became identified with the Bryant, Stratton & Goldsmith College in Detroit. After leaving the grocery, his next employment was in a produce shipping business, and in the spring of 1859, he embarked in the grocery business for himself, but did not make it a success. The following year, among other employments, was that of a book agent.

When, after the bombardment of Fort Sumter, President Lincoln issued his call for 75,000 volunteers, our subject was one of those who responded, and on April 19th, enlisted in a fine company of young men recruited from town and country. At Camp Taylor, at Cleveland, where the company went, they were mustered into the United States service as Company E, Eighth Ohio Volunteer Infantry. Directly after, the regiment was sent to Camp Dennison, near Columbus, which at the time of its arrival in a rain storm, was a wheat-field, without shelter or protection of any kind. Though one of the first regiments at this camp, other regiments arrived and were sent to the front, this regiment remained in camp, without accoutrements until some weeks later a second call was made for three-year volunteers, and the regiment was re-organized for three years' service. Less than one-half of the company re-enlisted, and those mostly from the country. The others, whose military ardor, if not their patriotism, had been somewhat dampened by the experience they already had, were sent home on furlough, subject to call until their time expired, when they were mustered out of service. While the young men from the city did not at that time re-enlist, it is but proper to add, that, with very few exceptions, they entered the service again in different regiments and branches of service. Our subject was among the latter and preferring the discipline of the regular army, subsequently enlisted in that service. He was soon detailed on detached service with the rank of lower sergeant. After joining his company in the field, he

was soon promoted to first sergeant to fill a vacancy, which position he held while he remained in the service. His regiment participated in the final movement which culminated in Gen. Lee's surrender, though not coming in actual conflict with the enemy at the time.

After leaving the army, he engaged in general store business in Oakland county, Michigan, for some months, selling out his interest to a partner in the spring of 1866, when he went to Chicago, where for nearly eight years he was engaged in the tobacco and cigar business. Mr. Hammond was one of the victims of the great Chicago fire in 1871, which practically wiped out all he possessed. At the time of financial panic of 1873 it found him with big rent to pay and a shrinking business, and in March, 1874, he removed to his former home at Sandusky, Ohio, where for the next sixteen years, he carried on business. In the spring of 1879 he was engaged in the music and jewelry business in a small way, and having some spare room in his store, it was suggested that he put in a line of five and ten cent goods which at that time were a novelty. Mr. Hammond did so and from the start it was a success, and for eleven years it continued to grow and expand, adding department after department, until it occupied four floors, 33x125 feet in size, and employing from a dozen to forty or more people, according to the season, becoming one of the most noted and successful mercantile houses of the town. The close and unremitting attention and labors of this business proved a great strain, and Mr. Hammond, finding his health failing, deemed it prudent to retire. That the business was a success, it may be added, that his immediate successors are still carrying on the same business in the same location, though greatly enlarged, having added a wholesale department. Their premises now run through the entire block from street to street, a distance of three hundred feet.

After selling out early in January, 1890, Mr. Hammond found time hanging heavily on his hands, and the end of the same month found him in Battle Creek, where he bought out a similar business already established, but on a small scale, his object being mainly to furnish him occupation and pastime. In the spring of the following year he suffered with an attack of la grippe, which left him with a severe attack of sciatica, which later wholly incapacitated him from business; and the ailment continuing to certain extent, together with nervous prostration, again led Mr. Hammond to sell out, and since then he has practically retired from all business effort.

In 1893 Mr. Hammond had built the so-called "Hammond Block" on West Main street. This building has a frontage of 6 feet by 85 feet deep and is two stories and basement in height. To the rental and care of this building he gives the needed time and it provides him with a comfortable living. Mr. Hammond's education was not very extensive, and did not extend beyond the primary branches, except as already mentioned.

On the 11th day of January, 1868, at Brockville, Ontario, Mr. Hammond was united in marriage to Miss Julia Emily Martin, who was born at Phillipsburg, Ontario, July 23, 1841, of French extraction. They have two daughters. Florence, who was born in Chicago, December 5, 1873, was married to Charles W. Burnham in April, 1895, by whom she has one son, Charles Hammond Burnham, born May 15, 1896. The younger daughter, Nellie,

was born in Sandusky, Ohio, February 10, 1881, and she, as well as her sister, has received a good musical education, and are accomplished pianists and are among the leading vocalists of the city.

Mr. Hammond was a Republican before he was a voter, and cast his first presidential ballot for that nature's nobleman, Abraham Lincoln, and also for Grant in 1868. The early Republicanism had a moral issue—the slavery question—that being eliminated as a result of the fortunes of war, and Mr. Hammond becoming convinced that politics has become largely a struggle for the spoils of office is now an independent voter, casting his ballot for such men and measures as he deems right at the time. At one time Mr. Hammond was a member of the Masonic fraternity at Sandusky, but taking his demit with a view of joining at Chicago, where he then resided, other things intruded to prevent, and he now remains non-affiliated with any secret society or church whatever. Mr. Hammond, though of foreign birth, is a thorough American, without affectation or ostentation and with a sincerity which has no use for shame or hypocrisy, whether social, political, or religious.

In the summer of 1902 Mr. Hammond made a trip to Europe and then for the first time in fifty-five years, revisited the place of his birth, finding the houses just as they were in his childhood except that tile roofs had been substituted for straw. All that Mr. Hammond possesses has been honestly acquired by his own exertions and is the reward for industry, sobriety and frugality. Content with a modest competency, he is now enjoying the rest and satisfaction of a life well spent. He resides with his family in a pleasant home of his own on West Van Buren street.

AUSTIN W. ALVORD, A. M., M. D.

Dr. Austin White Alvord is a skilled physician and surgeon, occupying a prominent position as a member of the profession not only in Battle Creek but throughout the state. He comes of ancestry established in New England only a few years after the landing of the Pilgrims at Plymouth Rock. It was in 1635 that the first of the name in America crossed the Atlantic, locating near Gloucester, Massachusetts. Others of the family afterward removed to Granby, Massachusetts. Gad Alvord, the grandfather of the Doctor, married Phoebe White, a direct descendant of Peregrine White, the first white child born in the Plymouth colony. The grandfather was killed by accident when about forty-five years of age. Unto him and his wife were born eleven children, the tenth in order of birth being Alanson Alvord, the father of the Doctor. His birth occurred in Granby. Massachusetts, June 26, 1803. and he acquired a liberal education, largely through his own efforts. After spending two years in Yale College he entered the Union Theological Seminary of New York and on the completion of the course was graduated and ordained as a minister of the Congregational church. He then entered upon his ministerial labors at Chester, Massachusetts, in 1835, and through a number of years labored there, his efforts being a potent force in the moral development of the community. In 1847 he was one of seven home missionaries who went from Massachusetts to Illinois to inaugurate the work of the Congregational church in that state. He was present and assisted in the founding of the First Congregational church of Chicago, in 1851, and Dr. Alvord was also present on that oc-

casion. The new organization began its existence with thirteen members and to-day is one of the strongest churches in the city. Rev. Alvord became the pastor of the Congregational church at Downer's Grove, where he remained until he accepted a call to the pastorate of the church at York, Pennsylvania, in which place he continued his labors up to the time of his demise, in 1862. His influence was of no restricted order and there was not denied to him the harvest nor the aftermath of his labors. He was a man of scholarly attainments and untiring zeal, and became recognized as one of the strong representatives of the Congregational ministry. He married Miss Barrows, of Brimfield, Massachusetts, a lady of broad education and culture, who was chosen by Mary Lyons as one of her teachers when she founded her seminary for young ladies at Mount Holyoke. She traced her ancestry back to 1640, when a member of the Barrows family located in Salem, Massachusetts. Her grandfather was a soldier of the Revolutionary war and her father, Abner Barrows, was a farmer of Brimfield, Massachusetts. Unto Rev. and Mrs. Alvord were born four children, of whom the Doctor is the eldest. The mother died in 1849 and was buried at Concord, now Chapin, Illinois.

In his early youth Dr. Alvord acquired a good practical education in the common schools and afterward prepared for college at Chester, Vermont, and at Oberlin, Ohio. He entered Oberlin College, but during the junior year left that institution and entered the literary department of the University of Michigan, from which he now holds the degree of Master of Arts. On the completion of his literary course he engaged in teaching for a number of years, being superintendent of the schools at Owego, New York, at the time of the breaking out of the Civil war. Responding to the country's call for aid, he enlisted in Company H, One Hundred and Ninth New York Infantry and went to the front as captain, many of his former students going with him as members of the company. They went into camp at Binghamton, New York, and from there proceeded to Washington, where they were engaged in guarding the railroad for some time. Later they became a part of the Ninth Army Corps of the Army of the Potomac and participated in all of its campaigns up to the time of General Lee's surrender at Appomattox. Early in 1864 Dr. Alvord was promoted to chief quartermaster of the department of the South, on the staff of General Foster, with headquarters at Hilton Head and Beaufort, South Carolina. He acted as surgeon during the greater part of the closing year of the war. Though he had not graduated he had spent two years as a student in the medical department of the University of Michigan. By order of the secretary of war he was finally discharged for disability against his own wishes in October, 1864, for he was broken in health and his superior officers felt he could not stand the continued strain of his army duties.

Following his retirement from the army, Dr. Alvord completed his course in medicine and was graduated with the class of 1868 in the medical department of the University of Michigan, from which he therefore now holds two degrees. Establishing an office in Clinton, Michigan, he was there engaged in practice until 1882 when, in order to avoid the arduous duties of a large country practice he came to Battle Creek. Here he has since been recognized as a leading physician and surgeon of the city, and though he engages in general practice he has done a large amount of surgical work.

The Doctor is a member of the Calhoun County and State Medical Societies and of each has been the president. He was also a member of the first State Board of Registration in medicine that attended to the registration of medical practitioners in Michigan. He was chairman of the committee on colleges and standards and on examining different colleges he compelled all to come up to a high standard of requirements in order to be recognized in Michigan. In the Nichols Memorial Hospital of Battle Creek he has served as surgeon. For the sake of a respite from strenuous professional life the Doctor has interested himself in business.

In politics the Doctor is a stanch Republican but not an aspirant for office. Fraternally he is connected with A. T. Metcalf lodge, No. 419, F. & A. M.; is past high priest of Battle Creek Chapter, No. 19, R. A. M.; and past commander of Battle Creek Commandery, No. 33, K. T. He is a member of the Loyal Legion of Detroit and is past commander of Farragut Post. G. A. R. In 1861 Dr. Alvord was united in marriage to Miss Eliza Barnes, of Ann Arbor, who died leaving four children, of whom two are still living: Grace, now the wife of T. J. Kelleher, of Battle Creek; and Dr. William Roy Alvord, a practicing dentist of this city. In 1878 Dr. Alvord wedded Miss Fannie R. Little, of Grinnell, Iowa, who died in 1901, leaving two children, Louise and Max. His present wife, whom he married in July, 1902, was Mrs. Addie S. Anderson, of Midland, Michigan, the widow of Dr. Anderson. Their home, at No. 55 Fremont street, was erected in 1891. The Doctor is a member of the Presbyterian church and is a man of benevolent spirit and kindly nature. His charity and generosity have been often manifest in his professional services and yet entirely without ostentation or display. He stands to-day a leading representative of his profession in Michigan and receives that deference and respect which the world instinctively pays to the man whose success has been worthily achieved, who has acquired high reputation in his chosen calling by merit, and whose social prominence is not the less the result of an irreproachable life than of recognized natural gifts.

HON. MILES S. CURTIS.

While Hon. Miles S. Curtis is perhaps best known throughout the state in connection with his work in the Knights of Pythias fraternity, being grand keeper of records and seal, he is known and respected in Battle Creek because of an honorable business career and of unfaltering loyalty and effective efforts in behalf of the permanent welfare and substantial improvement of the city. One of his strongest personal characteristics is his executive ability, which has more than once been exercised for the general good of Battle Creek.

Mr. Curtis was born in Kingsville, Ashtabula county, Ohio, April 1, 1852. His father, Elijah Curtis, was born in New York state, March 3, 1817, and there attained his majority. When twenty-one years of age he removed to Ohio, settling in Ashtabula county, where he purchased land and developed a farm. While there residing his patriotic nature was aroused by the attempt of the south to overthrow the

Union, and in response to the president's first call for troops to serve for three months he joined the volunteer army. After the expiration of his first term, he re-enlisted for three years, as a member of the Twenty-ninth Ohio Infantry, with which he served until wounded, when he was honorably discharged on account of disability. Later he removed to Kansas, where he homesteaded a tract of land and also pre-empted land, situated in the central portion of the state. He had there a half section, which he cultivated and improved, making it a good property. He also invested in property interests near Battle Creek and in 1873 came to Calhoun county to reside, and made his home with his son, Miles, until his death in August, 1903. In early manhood he married Harriet St. John, whose death occurred when her son Miles was only six months old.

M. S. Curtis was educated in Grand River Institute, in Ashtabula county, Ohio, receiving liberal mental training. During the last year of the four years' course he held the position of instructor in penmanship in the school. In the fall of 1873, when twenty-one years of age, he came to Jonesville, Michigan, and soon afterward entered the law office of Witter J. Baxter, of that place, where he remained for one winter, but on account of the death of his aunt, with whom he was living, he gave up the study of law and in the fall of 1874 came to Calhoun county to take charge of his father's farm near Battle Creek. There he remained for four years.

On the 31st of October, 1878, Mr. Curtis was united in marriage to Miss Mary Nye, of this city, and for a year they resided in Battle Creek, after which Mr. Curtis purchased a farm of one hundred and fifteen acres in Pennfield township, adjoining the city limits. This came into his possession in 1879, and he resided thereon until 1895, engaged in general farming. In the meantime two sons had been added to the family—Lorell and Claude C. The former is now bookkeeper in the Merchant's Savings Bank and the latter was a clerk in the postoffice of Battle Creek for nearly three years, resigning to take a course in the University of Michigan.

In 1895 Mr. Curtis left his farm and removed to the city where he has since made his home, and with the public interests he has been identified in many ways. In business lines he is associated with its manufacturing interests. He was one of the founders and incorporators of the Battle Creek Iron Works Company, limited, and has been its treasurer since its organization. He is also interested in the Cero-Fruto Food Company and the Battle Creek Whip & Leather Company. In political circles he is also prominent and influential, being a recognized leader in the ranks of the Republican party, and yet he is in no way a politician in the commonly accepted sense of the term. He believes, however, that it is the duty as well as the privilege of every American to cast his ballot and thereby support the measures which he believes will best promote the welfare of county, state and nation. He has frequently been a delegate to county and state conventions and his opinions carry weight with party leaders. While residing in Pennfield township he was elected supervisor in 1890 and by re-election held the office for two terms. In 1894 he was nominated for representative from the western district of Calhoun county for the State Legislature and being elected served during the

session of 1895. He was the second member of the committee on the State University and was chairman of the state library committee. He was also very active in opposing the bill to reduce the liquor tax from five hundred to three hundred dollars, and his support of or opposition to any measure was given after careful deliberation. He attempted to inform himself thoroughly concerning the questions at issue, and his course gave uniform satisfaction, but at the close of his term he refused a nomination, having been elected to his present office as keeper of records and seals in the Grand lodge Knights of Pythias. Against his wishes he was made chairman of the Republican city committee of Battle Creek, in 1897, but when he found that he was the choice for the office he entered upon his duties with the same zeal and earnestness which he shows in anything he undertakes. In 1898 he was nominated and elected mayor and gave the city exceptionally good government. He started out with a business administration instead of a political one and during his term the city paid up an indebtedness of twelve thousand dollars which had been borrowed from the water fund. In other ways, too, through the co-operation of a strong council, he placed the city on a good financial basis. Since his retirement from the mayoralty he has refused other political honors with the exception of having been appointed police commissioner for three years on the constitution of the board under a revision of the charter.

Mr. Curtis is a member of Battle Creek Lodge, No. 12, F. & A. M.; Battle Creek Chapter, No. 19, R. A. M., the Royal Arcanum and is a charter member of the Benevolent Protective Order of Elks in Battle Creek. His leading fraternal connection, however, is with the Knights of Pythias. He was initiated in Battle Creek Lodge, No. 35, at its institution, June 27, 1879, and was at once chosen prelate. He afterward passed all the chairs, becoming chancellor commander. In 1880 he entered the Grand lodge, continued to attend each year and in 1885 was chosen grand outer guard. This was the only time he ever had an opponent for an office in the Grand lodge, until he had advanced to the grand chancellor's station. In 1892 he was appointed state deputy, in August of the same year was appointed supreme representative and in 1895 was elected grand keeper of records and seal, to which position he has since been unanimously reelected. A Pythian publication said of him:

"Were we to analyze his character and disposition we believe one of the strongest qualities to be observed would be that intense earnestness which has characterized so much of his life work. He does whatever he has to do with his whole heart and is never content with partial results. His well balanced mind and excellent judgment make him a safe guide. While possessed of the courage of his convictions he has the happy faculty of differing with one and yet not antagonizing his opponent. He is a fast friend and one to whom our brothers may link themselves with hooks of steel and be sure that betrayal is no part of his nature. He stands for all that is good and great in Pythianism and is the steadfast friend, sympathetic brother and prince of good fellows that a true Pythian always should be. Above all, Miles S. Curtis is a gentleman, not by artificial veneer and affectation, which form no part of a true

man's equipment, but because the Almighty turned him out from the crucible of creation, a gentleman by nature." With his family he occupies a pleasant home at 163 Calhoun street.

EARL G. WALLING.

Earl G. Walling, whose real estate operations and building interests connect him with the material improvement of Battle Creek, has lived in this city since 1890 and is one of Calhoun county's native sons, his birth having occurred in Tekonsha township on the 15th of October, 1860. His father, Sylvester G. Walling, was born near Auburn, New York, September 19, 1832, and was a son of Luther Walling, who in 1836 removed with his family to Calhoun county, Michigan, establishing his home here during an early epoch in the development of this portion of the state. He purchased land from the government, the deed being signed by Martin Van Buren and upon a farm which he there improved he made his home until his death. Sylvester G. Walling was reared there and afterward married Electa E. Graves, of Newton township, a daughter of James and Electa Graves and a niece of John Graves, a prominent criminal lawyer of New York. The young couple lived on the old home farm until 1868 and after residing in Burlington, Michigan, for eight years, Mr. Walling purchased the interests of the other heirs in the old Graves's homestead where he resided until he retired from active life, purchasing a home in Union City, Michigan. He was an extensive farmer and prosperous in his undertakings. His political support was given to the Democracy. He died August 3, 1901, and his wife passed away on the 14th of October, 1899.

Earl G. Walling, their only son, acquired his education in the district schools and in the high school of Union City, after which he engaged in teaching for one year. He then became associated with his father in farming interests, assuming the management of the home place, his father having become the possessor of the old Walling property which had been entered from the government. Subsequently this came into possession of Earl G. Walling and has never passed from the ownership of the family. No other farm in the township has been so long in the possession of a single family. Mr. Walling continued with his father until 1890, when he came to Battle Creek and here he has been engaged in carpentering and building, erecting residences which he afterward sells. He has carried on a general real estate and building business for himself for thirteen years and has prospered in this undertaking. He has also bought and sold property already improved and in his realty transactions has accumulated a very desirable competence. For the past six years he has been connected with the Nichols & Shepard Threshing Machine Company in the wood-working department.

On Christmas day of 1881 was celebrated the marriage of Earl G. Walling and Elizabeth Meserole, of Olivet, Eaton county, Michigan, a daughter of William and Julia (Woodmansee) Meserole. Her father came from the south and early settled in Eaton county, while the Woodmansees were of French origin. At the time of the Civil war Mr. Meserole joined Company K, Seventeenth Michigan Infantry and died of wounds and small-pox while in the army. His widow afterward married William Bolles, also now deceased, who was the first dry-goods merchant of Marshall, Michigan. At one time he owned eighty acres in what is now the heart of Chicago. He was a graduate of Harvard. For a number of years he conducted a trading post in northern Michigan prior to his coming to Marshall. She now makes her home upon a farm near Olivet. Mrs. Walling was reared and educated at Olivet, attending the college there and receiving splendid musical training. She has been a successful music teacher and is a lady of superior culture and innate refinement. She has back of her an ancestry honorable and distinguished and the antiquity of her family is indicated by the many beautiful and priceless heirlooms, which have descended to her from various generations. These include valuable and beautiful old mahogany and rosewood furniture, plates and dishes. She also has some lovely shawls of ancient weave and tortoise shell combs. Her musical talent as well as her social nature has made her a favorite in cultured society circles and the hospitality of the Walling household is greatly enjoyed by the many friends of our subject and his estimable wife.

While residing upon the farm Mr. Walling served as justice of the peace and in the city has taken an active part in political work, yet has never sought office as a reward for party fealty. He is a member of the Modern Woodmen of America and attends and supports the Independent Congregational church at Battle Creek. As a representative of one of the oldest families of the county he well deserves mention in this volume, and because of his own personal worth he is entitled to distinctive mention as a representative citizen.

MAXIMILIAN CHASE.

Maximilian Chase, now deceased, was perhaps better known to the people of Battle Creek as "Maxey" Chase. He was a resident of the city for about forty years. His birth occurred in Delaware county, New York, on the 18th of December, 1850, and there he spent his first twelve years, coming at that time with his parents to Michigan. He completed his education in the public schools of Battle Creek and, entering upon his business career, became a salesman in a jewelry store. He was afterward employed in a clothing establishment and later was connected with H. P. Larkin, for a number of years. On severing that connection he engaged in business on his own account as a wholesale and retail dealer in liquor and was also the agent of the Fidelity Brewing Company of Toledo. He was located at No. 30 East Main street, where he carried on a large business, also having warehouses elsewhere. For about fifteen years he was prominently identified with this line of commercial activity, devoting his entire energies and attention to the work.

It was on the 2d of March, 1875, that Mr. Chase was joined in wedlock to Miss Hattie Markham, of Eaton Rapids. Her father, Ebenezer Markham, was born in Connecticut and when a young man removed to Mansfield, Ohio, where he formed the acquaintance of Miss Sophia Smith, whose birth occurred in Pennsylvania. Their

marriage was soon after celebrated and they established their home in Mansfield, there they lived until Mr. Markham's death. The mother afterward removed to Eaton Rapids, Michigan, where she remained until her final rest. Unto Mr. and Mrs. Chase were born two children: Cora B. and Lelah May, both of whom, with their mother, reside at No. 29 South avenue, which has been the family residence for eleven years.

Mr. Chase was a member of the Knights of the Golden Eagles and in his political affiliations was a Democrat. Suffering from ill health for about a year, Mr. Chase was recommended to go to Denver in the hope that he might be benefited, and in that city he passed away May 20, 1903. He possessed a genial nature that had gained him many friends and thus his death was mourned by many outside of his immediate family.

EDWARD DAWSON DICKINSON.

Through many years of public service in the state of his adoption Edward D. Dickinson has come to be known and appreciated as an earnest and resourceful citizen, whose discharge of duties involved by his acceptance of office has been such as to warrant a continuation of the esteem and confidence of his fellow townsmen. He was born in North Chemung, Chemung county, N. Y., December 29, 1851, a son of Jesse and Belinda (Bacorn) Dickinson. The father was a farmer in New York but in 1866 he brought his family to Michigan, locating on a farm in Lenawee county, where they remained four years. They then removed to

Butler township. Branch county, where the death of the elder Mr. Dickinson occurred December 2. 1871.

Of the six children born to his parents Edward D. Dickinson is the second in order of birth and the eldest of the four who attained maturity, three of whom are now living. He was reared upon his father's farm in New York state until his sixteenth year, when he came with his parents to Michigan. His home duties were interspersed with an attendance at the district school in his immediate neighborhood, and later he was given the privilege of a course in a select school. At the age of nineteen years he became a teacher in the public schools, an occupation which proved profitable and pleasant for many years, teaching in all, forty terms. Teaching, however, was not the extent of Mr. Dickinson's efforts, for, besides, he acted as traveling collection agent for two years with headquarters in Pittsburg and Philadelphia. He then attended Fayette College, in Fulton county, Ohio, until compelled to take a much needed rest on account of his health. On returning to Michigan from the Ohio college he became the owner of an eighty-acre farm in Calhoun county, for which his father had bargained shortly before his death, not living, however, to complete the trade, and henceforth combined farming with his pedagogical labors. In 1903 he became a resident of Marshall, now making his home at No. 512 East State street.

The marriage of Mr. Dickinson occurred December 25. 1882. in Fairfield township, Lenawee county, and united him with Miss Lottie Sturtevant, who was born in that township. She was the daughter of J. Wesley and Adelaide (Failing) Sturtevant. who were among the early pioneer set-tlers of Royalton township, Fulton county, Ohio. After their marriage Mr. and Mrs. Dickinson both attended Fayette College for one year, her ambition keeping pace with his in the effort to become a helpmeet in the true sense of the word. Their union has been blessed with the birth of four children, of whom Ray, who has received a common school education, was born in Fairfield, Lenawee county, February 24. 1884; Edna was born in Clarendon; Roy, also born in Clarendon and died at the age of eight years; Lloyd was born in Clarendon, October 3. 1893. and Edward DeLyle. in Clarendon, November 3. 1901. In his religious affiliations, though reared a Baptist, Mr. Dickinson is a member of the Methodist Episcopal church, and has been liberal in his support of all church movements, his disinterested efforts serving to enroll his name among those whose hands have upheld the work of reform and progression. Since 1876 he has been active in the Sunday school, serving as superintendent until 1900, a period of faithfulness seldom surpassed. In his fraternal relations he is identified with the Masons. being a member of Butler lodge. No. 88. F. & A. M., and is also associated with the Maccabees, of Herrick-ville. Branch county.

In the matter of public services Mr. Dickinson has always taken an active part, his entire life a characterization of those qualities which inspire the confidence of all with whom he comes in contact. In his political convictions he is a birthright Republican, his first presidential vote having been cast for Hayes in 1876, and since then, though not a politician in the common acceptance of the term, he has still been active in promoting the principles which he endorses. While a resident of Clarendon he was elected township superintendent of schools, in which capacity he served acceptably from 1876 to 1879, his special fitness for educational work again calling him into the service of the community in 1885 as school inspector. This position was maintained until 1892, when he resigned to accept that of county drain commissioner, to which office he had been elected in the fall of 1891. That his discharge of duty has been in entire accordance with the needs and wishes of the people is indicated by the fact that he has since represented his party in this office, giving to his work the thought of a well-trained and practical mind, during his long period of service instituting many beneficial improvements and in every instance acting in a manner calculated to advance the interests of the general public. As an evidence of the esteem in which he is held by the citizens of Calhoun county Mr. Dickinson was re-elected in October, 1903, to his present office for another term of two years.

That Mr. Dickinson has met with success in the various lines which have formed his life work one has only to acknowledge results, evidences of which abound on every side; for, a man of strong personality and indomitable will, he has made his presence felt in every community which has claimed him for a resident. As a helpful, earnest and reliable citizen he deserves mention among those who have given material assistance in the upbuilding of this section of the state.

FRANK A. KULP.

Prominently identified with the legal profession, with corporate interests of Battle Creek and with political labors, Frank A. Kulp has become widely known not only in Battle Creek, but also throughout the state and has had marked influence on public thought and feeling through his clear and forcible presentation to the public of questions affecting the general good. He is now practicing law in Battle Creek, with a distinctively representative clientage, and is also serving as alderman of the city in which he has made his home for fourteen years.

Mr. Kulp was born in Philadelphia, Pennsylvania, August 10, 1873, a son of George B. and Anna R. (Longnecker) Kulp. The family came of German ancestry but through many generations had been established in the Keystone state. The father was born and reared in Philadelphia and on arriving at man's estate he entered the ministry of the Methodist Episcopal church, being a member of the Philadelphia conference for many years. He afterward transferred his relationship to the Michigan conference and is now pastor of Immanuel church, at Battle Creek, an independent body which he organized and which he has built up until it is now a leading congregation of the city. His wife is also living and they exert a strong influence in intellectual and moral development.

Frank A. Kulp, the eldest son in their family of five children, acquired his early education in the schools of his native city and was graduated on the completion of the high school course in Battle Creek, with the class of 1893. In the succeeding autumn he entered Albion College and in the fall of 1895 became a student in the law department of the University of Michigan, wherein he was graduated with the class of 1896, winning the degree of Bachelor of Law. Admitted to the bar on the 1st of

July, 1896, four days later he opened his office in this city and is now recognized as one of the rising young lawyers, receiving a good share of the public patronage. He is well versed in the principles of jurisprudence, displays marked devotion to his client's interests and great care in the preparation of his cases. He has also been active in promoting corporate interests in Battle Creek.

Perhaps Mr. Kulp is even more widely known through his connection with socialistic interests than through his business affairs. He is one of the most prominent socialists of the city if not the state, and the party was organized in his office, seven gentlemen being present on the occasion. This was the first organization of the Social Democratic party of the state. He has made a close study of the social conditions and problems of the country and through his labors the principles of the party have been brought before the public with the result that when a party ticket was placed in the field a large socialistic vote was polled. Mr. Kulp was elected in 1902 as alderman from the first ward—the first socialist ever elected in Michigan. He served on various important committees and took an active part in the city work, doing everything in his power to promote reform, improvement and permanent advancement. He was also the first man in the city to return his pass to the railroad company. In 1903 he was nominated for mayor and polled fifteen hundred and fifty-nine votes, while the previous year the vote of the party was only six hundred and forty-nine. He speaks throughout the state on the issues of his party, delivering addresses in the northern peninsula as well as in the southern part of the state and other places throughout the United States and Canada. He is a fluent

26

and forcible speaker, logical in argument, strong in his reasoning and convincing in his utterances.

Fraternally, Mr. Kulp is connected with Battle Creek Lodge, No. 29, I. O. O. F. On the 14th of March, 1897, he wedded Miss Irene Smith, of Battle Creek, and they have three children: Francis Bruce, Dorothy Irene, and Karl Marx, who died August 9, 1904. They have a beautiful and hospitable home on Battle Creek avenue, which was erected by Mr. Kulp.

HON. ARTHUR D. BANGHAM, M. D.

Aside from the important work which he has done for humanity in the line of his profession, Dr. Arthur D. Bangham is entitled to distinctive mention in this volume for other reasons. As state senator he has labored with patriotic zeal for the best interests of the commonwealth and has also been active in the promotion of some of the strongest fraternal organizations which have for their object the inculcation of principles which promote brotherly kindness, mutual helpfulness and which ameliorate many of the hard conditons of life. He is especially prominent and influential in community affairs and his senatorial service has also extended his labors to interests affecting the entire state.

Dr. Bangham is a native son of Calhoun county, his birth having occurred in Marengo township, November 8, 1859, his parents being Sandusky K. and Minerva E. (Hanchett) Bangham. The Bangham family is of German lineage. The father was born in York, Washtenaw county, Michigan, and was a son of John

Bangham. The grandfather was born in Newark, New Jersey, and when a young man removed to Somerset, Niagara county, New York, where he married a Miss Mead. After her death he married Mrs. Anna Emmons, who became the mother of Sandusky K. Bangham. John Bangham bought one hundred acres of the Holland purchase and engaged in farming in Niagara county. In his earlier manhood he had followed the tanner's trade and prior to his marriage, served his country as a soldier of the War of 1812. In November, 1834, he removed to Washtenaw county, Michigan, purchasing a slightly improved tract of land upon which he made his home and engaged in tanning until 1845, when he came to Calhoun county and secured a farm in Clarence township, making his home there until his death, carrying on general agricultural pursuits. His wife, surviving him for some time, died in 1876.

S. K. Bangham was reared upon his father's farm, largely passing his youth in this county. He acquired a good practical education and after his marriage to Miss Hanchett he located in Marengo township, where he owned a farm upon which his death occurred in August, 1866. His wife was a daughter of David and Mary Hanchett, who were pioneers of Marengo township, coming to this county from Cayuga county, New York. The wife died on the home farm about 1858 and Mr. Hanchett, surviving her some years, died in Marshall. Mrs. Minerva (Hanchett) Bangham survived her husband many years and never married again. Like him she was a faithful member of the Methodist Protestant church of Rice Creek, and her death occurred in February, 1903.

Supplementing his early educational privileges, received in the common schools, by a course in Albion College, Dr. Bangham afterward engaged in teaching school and subsequently entered the office of the late Dr. Smiley, of Marshall, Michigan, one of the leading physicians of his time in southern Michigan. A year later Dr. Bangham matriculated in the medical department of the University of Michigan, at Ann Arbor, and was graduated in 1882 as a member of the first class to complete a three-years' course, each year embracing nine months' study. The degree of doctor of medicine was conferred upon him and he then entered upon the active work of the profession. In the meantime he had received practical experience as one of the clinic assistants to Dr. Frothingham, professor of ophthalmology and otology.

Locating in Dexter, Washtenaw county, Michigan, Dr. Bangham there engaged in practice for a year, after which he disposed of his interests there and together with Hon. J. T. Honey and Edwin Bennett, of Dexter, took a trip through the west, visiting Washington, Oregon and California. They investigated the conditions of the west, looking for opportunity for favorable investment, and spent three months on the Pacific coast. On his return to Calhoun county Dr. Bangham, in the fall of 1883, purchased an interest in a drug store at Homer and also located for practice there, his professional connection with the town antedating that of any other physician of the locality. Later he became sole proprietor of the store, which he superintended in connection with the duties of a large private practice. He has kept fully abreast with the times in the progress that is continually being made by the medical fraternity and his reading and investigation have covered a wide range. In 1899 he took post-graduate work in the Chicago

Polyclinic. He is continually being called in for consultation, his professional brethren recognizing his ability, and the demands of a large private practice leave him little leisure. He belongs to the Calhoun County Medical Society, of which he was formerly the president, and is also a member of the State Medical Society.

Dr. Bangham possesses excellent business ability and keen foresight and in this connection has been the promoter of various interests of importance in trade circles. He was one of the organizers of the Battle Creek Food Company, that has a fine plant at Battle Creek, and is chairman of the board of managers of the corporation. He is also interested in the American Peat Fuel Company which has an actual investment of two hundred thousand dollars in a fireproof plant located at Capac. He is also chairman of its board of managers and has given much thought and time to the development of the enterprise in the past two years.

On the 26th of August, 1880, Dr. Bangham was married to Miss Estella Austin, of Marengo township, a daughter of Theodore N. Austin, one of the early residents of this county. She completed her education in the Marshall high school, and by her marriage she has become the mother of five children, but the first born, Austin S., died at the age of nine years. The others are Belle D., Harrison A., Flossie E. and Leila Ruth. The parents are members of the Methodist Episcopal church, of which the Doctor has been a trustee for many years, also church steward and superintendent of the Sunday-school. At the time of the erection of the new church parsonage at Homer, the finest in the conference, he was a member of the building committee. He has always been deeply interested in church work and the moral growth of the community, and his efforts in this direction have been effective and beneficial.

Dr. Bangham built for himself and family a fine home in Homer and its social functions are greatly enjoyed by their many friends. He was made a Mason in Humanity lodge, No. 29, F. & A. M., of Homer, is now its master and the representative to the Grand lodge. He also belongs to Homer Chapter, No. 130, R. A. M. and has been its high priest since its organization, covering more than twelve years. He has also been its representative in the Grand Chapter and at the present time is a member of its committee. He belongs to Albion Council, R. & S. M.; Marshall Commandery, No. 17, K. T., and was one of the organizers and is a member of Homer Chapter, No. 140, Order of Eastern Star, of which he was the first worthy patron, holding that position for six years. His wife is also a member of that chapter. The Doctor belongs to Homer lodge, No. 232, I. O. O. F., of which he is past grand; Homer lodge, No. 88, K. P., of which he is past chancellor; and was also one of the organizers of the Maccabee Tent and the Modern Woodmen Camp, at Homer. He is a past commander of the Maccabee Tent.

In political circles in southern Michigan Dr. Bangham is also active, prominent and influential, being one of the leading representatives of the Republican party. He was for a number of years village trustee and for two terms was village president, during which time the electric light plant was installed and the system of cement sidewalks was adopted—the village paying one-half of the expenses of laying these walks. He was president of the school board for one term and championed every progressive educational measure. In the active work of the party his aid has been marked. He was a member of the county executive committee for a number of years, including the period covering the McKinley campaigns. He belongs to the United States pension board of Marshall, and has been the president for a number of years, and in 1900 he was elected state senator from the ninth district, comprising Calhoun and Kalamazoo counties—one of the most populous and wealthy districts in the state. He received a plurality of nineteen hundred and six, the largest vote given any candidate on the ticket, and assumed the duties of the office January 1, 1901. He has been a member of the following committees: asylum for the insane at Newberry; education and public schools; reformatory at Ionia; state lands; state university; and saline interests. During that term he was actively interested in the passage of a number of important bills and was the father of a bill providing for the institution of a psychopathic ward at the University Hospital, which was passed, and when the ward is completed it will be the first of its kind under state supervision in the United States. The Doctor was reelected in 1902 by a good plurality and in 1903 he was made chairman of the committee on education and public schools and executive business, and also on the committees on apportionment, asylum for the insane at Traverse City, industrial school for boys; state lands; and state prison at Marquette. He was the father of an important bill amending the corporation laws, which passed both houses and is now on the statutes as the Bangham bill. He also introduced a bill, and secured its pass-

age, making it possible for each city and village to inspect their slaughter houses and meat supplies, which was received with favor by workers in behalf of improved sanitary conditions throughout the state. He also introduced another bill requiring undertakers to know something of embalming and the proper care of bodies for the purpose of protecting the public health and for the purpose of transportation. He was the father of the bill in 1901, and amended it in 1903, making this the first law governing undertakers of Michigan, placed on the statute books of the state. His interest in the welfare of the commonwealth is deep and sincere and his legislative course has shown marked familiarity with existing conditions and a close study of many methods of remedy where reform and improvement are needed. He takes an active part in the business which is transacted in the council chambers of the state and his course has ever been above suspicion. The good of the nation he places before partisanship and the welfare of his constituents before self-aggrandizement. He commands the respect of the members of the senate, but at home, in the county of his nativity, where he is best known, he inspires personal friendships of unusual strength, and all who know him have the highest admiration for his strong mentality, his professional skill, his loyalty in citizenship and his devotion to the public welfare.

During his term of service in the Senate he has probably secured the passage of as many good bills as any other member of that body.

The last of November, 1903, Dr. Bangham moved to another part of his senatorial district, Albion, that his children might have the educational advantages of Albion College. He has engaged in the active practice of medicine at Albion and vicinity.

HARLEY M. DUNLAP, M. D.

The tendency of the age is toward specialization. This is noticed in all walks of life and especially in the professions. To such a degree has investigation been carried on that the knowledge gained of one single science is too broad, complex and intricate for one man to thoroughly master in every detail. With a general knowledge of the underlying principles of the science, many men have continued their work along special lines and in their chosen department of labor have attained high proficiency and won marked success. This Mr. Dunlap has done and as an eye, ear, nose, throat and lung specialist he has a wide and enviable reputation.

The Doctor was born on a farm in Morrow county, Ohio, December 7, 1862, and is a son of William and Abbie M. (Dickerson) Dunlap. For some years he lived upon the old homestead and attended the country schools until he reached the age of fourteen, when he entered the Ohio Central College at Iberia, in Morrow county. He spent about four years as a student in that institution, and then, putting aside his text books, after having thoroughly prepared for his life work, he turned his attention to carpentering. In the fall of 1883, however, he came to the sanitarium at Battle Creek and began his medical studies with Dr. Kellogg as his preceptor. After studying here for a year he became a student in the medical department of the University of Michigan, in which he was graduated with the class of 1886. Returning to the sanitarium, he was then engaged in professional work in connection with that institution through the succeeding decade and in the fall of 1889, while still at the sanitarium he went to New York, where he pursued a post-graduate course of study and was graduated from the Post Graduate Medical College, in the winter of 1890. Once more he returned to the sanitarium in Battle Creek, where he remained until 1896. Since 1890 he has practiced as a specialist in the treatment of diseases of the eye, ear, nose, throat and lungs, and his marked capability in this direction has made his efforts of great value. Since 1896 he has been successfully engaged in private practice along the same lines. In 1892 he invented and patented a nebulizer, which is an aid to the treatment along his special lines. He then established a factory, having to furnish the capital for this enterprise and began the manufacture of his invention. Later he continued manufacturing under the name of the Globe Manufacturing Company, of which he is the sole proprietor. His nebulizer is being used in all parts of the world and is considered of great value by the medical fraternity. Each day he devotes the morning hours to work in the factory, while in the afternoon he practices his profession. In connection with the nebulizer he introduced a method of treatment known as the vapor massage for the treatment of the ear, nose, throat and lungs and this has come into almost universal use, having the endorsement of the medical fraternity throughout the world. The Globe Manufacturing Company is one of which little is heard locally, because of the fact that its output is used by the medical fraternity almost exclusively. The company manufactures a line of nebulizers, vaporizers, atomizers, air pumps, receivers, supplies, nebulizing fluids, hydraulic air compressors and other appliances used by specialists and physicians. The plant is complete within itself. Everything manufactured is turned out complete in the factory. The plant contains a wood-working department, a foundry, a nickle plating and polishing establishment, enameling room, paint room and everything necessary to the finishing of all of the products. The line is manufactured under the patents of Dr. Dunlap, who controls the factory. The goods are handled to an extent by jobbers, but the large majority of patrons are practitioners. The company has a considerable and growing trade on home treatment outfits, which are rapidly increasing in popularity. Special agencies at San Francisco, and Los Angeles, California; Portland, Oregon; Toronto, Ontario; and London, England; have been established, the output during the last year amounting to about fifty thousand dollars.

In 1885, in Battle Creek, Dr. Dunlap was united in marriage to Miss Rhoda S. Brigham, a resident of this city. She was born, however, in Ionia county, Michigan, her parents being Noble S. and Elsie (Howe) Brigham. They now have three children: Nenna B., William Elden and Ralph Emerson. The doctor was reared in the faith of the Disciple church, but when about eighteen years of age began investigating thoroughly the subject of religion, as did other members of the family and became a Seventh Day Adventist. In the line of his chosen work he has gained distinction as well as financial success. He has become a man of broad general informa-

tion, of liberal and progressive views and has made an untarnished record and unspotted reputation as a business man. In all places and under all circumstances he is loyal to truth, honor and the right, justly valuing his own self respect as infinitely more preferable than wealth, fame and position and yet, while maintaining an unblemished record he has at the same time won favor, distinction and a comfortable competence in his chosen field of labor.

ICHABOD W. TAYLOR.

Ichabod W. Taylor, a veteran of the Civil war and long a resident of Battle Creek, was born in Livingston county, New York, September 26, 1842. His parents were Demmon and Permelia A. (Barnum) Taylor. The father, a farmer by occupation, came to Michigan in 1854 and after spending two years at Ann Arbor removed to Battle Creek, going at once to Barry county, Maple Grove township, where he engaged in farming until the spring of 1857, when he moved into Castleton township and there his death occurred in 1860. His wife passed away at Middleville, Michigan, in 1871. Ichabod W. Taylor began his education in New York and completed it in the schools of Michigan. He then worked on a farm in Calhoun county and in Barry county, but after the Civil war began he put aside business considerations and enlisted on the 1st of May, 1862, at Hastings, Michigan, in Company D, Twenty-third Illinois Infantry, known as Mulligan's Irish Brigade. The regiment was sent to the front from Camp Douglas, Chicago, on the 1st of June, 1862. They were at Camp

Douglas and went to Wheeling, West Virginia, thence to Harper's Ferry and to New Creek. He participated in all the battles with his company, including the campaign in the Shenandoah valley. He was in the engagements at Fisher Hill and Winchester in 1863, the battle of Medley and of Cedar Creek, October 19, 1864. Soon after the brigade joined the army of the Potomac and was assigned to the Twenty-fourth corps. In the winter of 1864-5 they were encamped at Fort Harrison, seven miles down the James river from Richmond, and in the spring of 1865 made a trip around Petersburg toward Hatches Run, taking part in the fight from the time when the first gun was fired. They fought days and marched nights until Lee's surrender, on which occasion Mr. Taylor was present. Before the rebel commander gave up his arms, however, he charged their division three times in order to cut his way out, but could not do it. Mr. Taylor belonged to the division that made the charge upon Fort Gregg and at that time the rebels raised the black flag, meaning that they would not ask for nor give quarter. After the surrender the Twenty-third Illinois went to Richmond and as his time had expired Mr. Taylor was discharged there on the 5th of May, 1865, arriving home on the 18th of the same month. He had never had a furlough during all his long years' of service, but was ever found at his post of duty, faithful to the old flag.

For a time Mr. Taylor worked at brickmaking and in 1867 went to Middleville, Barry county, where he was employed in a sawmill. About that time, on the 30th of May, 1869, he wedded Wilma Cornelia Hungerford, of Middleville, a daughter of David and Catherine Hungerford, a cabinet maker. His wife died January 20, 1872, leaving a daughter, Katie, who was then

five months old and who is now the wife of Fred N. Jenne, a farmer, of Cortland, Kent county, Michigan. They have one son, Lewis, born January 17, 1897.

After the death of his wife Mr. Taylor removed to Grand Rapids, where he learned painting and paper hanging. He later became baggage master for the Grand Rapids & Indiana Railroad on the first train that ever ran into Petoskey. He was with that road until the spring of 1877, when he came to Battle Creek, where he has since worked at his trade as a painter and paper hanger.

On the 7th of October, 1877, Mr. Taylor was again married, his second union being with Mrs. Eliza A. Turner, of Battle Creek, a daughter of Seth Phillips, one of the pioneers of this city. In 1879 he bought a lot at the corner of Spring and Ravine streets and there built a home, having one of the attractive residences of that localtiy. Around his house is a very extensive and beautiful lawn. In politics he is a Republican and socially he is connected with Farragut Post, G. A. R., of which he has been commander and has frequently been its representative in the state encampments. His wife belongs to the Relief Corps. One of the honored boys in blue who still survives to tell of his experiences in the Civil war, Mr. Taylor well deserves representation in this volume and his life history will be gladly received by his many friends.

DR. HENRY SHARPSTEEN.

The above name is one that is familiar to the citizens of Marshall, Calhoun county, for it belongs to one of the oldest residents of the city, now actively engaged in the duties which have so long engrossed his attention as manufacturer and distributor of proprietary medicines. He was born in Livingston county, New York, December 6, 1827, a son of Samuel and Margaret (Slieght) Sharpsteen, natives respectively of Columbia and Duchess counties, New York, in which state they spent their entire lives and there passed to the higher life. Dr. Sharpsteen was reared in his New York home, receiving his preliminary education in the district school of the neighborhood, then attended the high school at Geneseo, after which he entered the Metcalf Brothers' drug store in Geneseo, New York, as a student in dentistry and physic. He remained three years, at the close of which time he was a licensed dentist and carried also a medical certificate, not caring, however, to practice this latter line except in consultation or in cases where assistance was imperative. In the spring of 1857 he went to Columbus, Wisconsin, where he accepted a position as clerk in a general store and deputy postmaster, remaining two years. February 15, 1859, he came to Marshall and engaged in the hardware business in partnership with Mr. Beers, the firm name being Beers & Sharpsteen. After two years Daniel Sharpsteen bought Mr. Beers's interest in the business, the firm then being known as D. & H. Sharpsteen. In 1864 our subject sold his interest to Mr. Parkhurst, but the latter failing to pay, Dr. Sharpsteen took back his interest, the business then being conducted under the firm name of Sharpsteen Brothers. This partnership was continued until the winter of 1868. In 1870 Dr. Sharpsteen engaged with H. A. Peterman and Hanley Johnson under the firm name of Dr. H. A. Peterman & Company, in the manufacture of patent medicines, the plant being located in a build-

ing owned by Dr. Sharpsteen. This firm was closed in April, 1873, when Dr. Sharpsteen continued in the business alone, doing principally a wholesale business. In 1890 he sold out one of the leading articles manufactured and at the present time devotes to the business only enough time to fill the orders which are sent in. One of the well-known manufacturers of the doctor's is the vegetable cure, the efficiency of which has been carefully tested, and on which he has a large sale for a remedy not advertised.

Mr. Sharpsteen has been twice married, the first ceremony uniting him, in 1858, with Miss Sarah Elizabeth Pulver, of Columbus, Wisconsin, to whom were born the following children: Ada, who married W. L. Higgins, of Cleveland, Ohio; and Verne, a lecturer and actor. Mrs. Sharpsteen died June 11, 1874, and is interred in Oakridge cemetery. The second marriage of Mr. Sharpsteen occurred December 8, 1875, and united him with Mrs. Lucia A. (Jillett) Sharpsteen, the widow of Alfred Sharpsteen, whom she had met and married in her native state of Vermont. They had then removed to Cayuga county, New York, and from there to Ontario county, where Mr. Sharpsteen died in 1873. He was a farmer by occupation. Mrs. Sharpsteen is a member of the Presbyterian church. Dr. Sharpsteen is a Republican, politically, and though never an aspirant for official recognition he has still given his support to all measures calculated to advance the general welfare of the community. Fraternally he is a member of St. Albans lodge, No. 20, F. & A. M., and has served as secretary of Lafayette chapter, R. A. M. Dr. Sharpsteen and his wife own considerable property in Marshall, a pleasant and comfortable home and also a store on State street. The doctor possesses, to an unusual degree, those qualities which have insured his success in the business world as well as making friends, whose esteem and confidence he enjoys to an unusual degree.

EDWARD B. KEET.

The study of biography yields in point of interest and profit to no other, for it is here that we learn how success has been achieved, the plans that have been followed and the methods that have been pursued. In the life record of Edward B. Keet are contained many valuable lessons, showing what can be accomplished by the young men of this free country, even though he has no capital with which to start out on life's journey. With a laudable ambition to achieve success Mr. Keet placed his dependence upon the substantial qualities of energy and close application and on this foundation he has reared the superstructure of prosperity, becoming one of the leading representatives of industrial interests of Battle Creek. He is now well known here as a capitalist and as the vice president of the Union Steam Pump Company.

Born in Waterloo, New York, July 17, 1849, Mr. Keet is a son of George and Maria (Beedle) Keet, the former born in Richmond, England, where he was reared and married. He there followed carpentering and joining. With his wife and four children he came to this country about 1841, locating in Waterloo, New York, where he continued business as a carpenter. He possessed superior mechanical skill, which combined with an excellent education and

good business capacity, made him a man of substantial means. He died at Waterloo when nearly eighty years of age and his wife passed away there in March, 1859. They had thirteen children, ten of whom reached years of maturity, Edward being the eighth. Their religious faith was that of the Episcopal church.

In his native place Edward B. Keet was educated, but his school privileges were limited and reading and observation in later eyars made him the well-informed man who here successfully established and controlled extensive business interests. When fourteen years of age he entered upon a four years' apprenticeship in the Silsby Steam Fire Engine Works at Seneca Falls, New York, receiving at first but twenty-five cents per day and in his fourth year a dollar per day. He had to board himself, though during the early part of his apprenticeship he lived with a sister. After learning his trade he came to Battle Creek, arriving June 6, 1867, and here he resumed his labor in the employ of Mr. LeFever, who had a small shop. Later, unable to secure work at his trade and willing to take any employment that would yield him an honest living, he became assistant to a mason, working on the brick block being built by William Andrus. In the fall of the same year, 1867, he began working for Nichols & Shepard and was in their employ as a machinist until 1881. In the meantime he had saved his earnings and made judicious investments in real estate. From 1881 until 1885 he was variously employed, being for seven months at Stillwater, Minnesota, and later with the Upton Thresher Company of Battle Creek. In January, 1885, he formed a partnership with Almon E. Preston, J. H. Gridley and

John Hyser under the name of the Union Manufacturing Company. They began business in what was known as the Smith & Adams blacksmith shop, Mr. Keet going to Chicago to purchase tools. They did good work as machinists and remained in that location until the growth of their business demanded larger quarters, when they removed to the Upton shops. Mr. Keet continued to do excellent work and also did the experimental work on the Duplex printing presses, remaining in the Upton shops until the shops of the Union Manufacturing Company were completed. They then began to manufacture steam pumps on a small scale and because of their good workmanship and the value of their product, their patronage readily increased and about a year later the company purchased the vacant property now occupied by the plant of the Union Steam Pump Company. This company was then organized with a capital stock of ten thousand dollars and Mr. Keet became a director and the vice president. The shop was built and equipped with modern machinery and from that time the business grew rapidly. The capital stock has since been increased a number of times and has now reached the figure of three hundred and fifty thousand dollars. Mr. Keet has remained vice president and one of the directors of the company and has been an active factor in its control. He always worked in the plant as a practical or consulting machinist until 1902, when he retired from the department. The plant now covers three acres and comprises five large buildings. Employment is furnished to about one hundred men, most of whom are skilled workmen and this does not include the clerical force or the traveling salesmen. A large product is shipped each year and this extensive industry is the outgrowth of the small concern established by Mr. Keet and his associates. He has likewise been interested in other business enterprises, has erected a large flat building and is one of the extensive stockholders in the Korn Krisp and the Tryabita Food Company.

The home life of Mr. Keet has been very pleasant. He was happily married to Miss Eleanor Bottomley, of Battle Creek, a daughter of John T. Bottomley, who still resides in this city, having come here from Philadelphia. Mr. and Mrs. Keet attend the Presbyterian church, of which she is a member. He is prominent in Masonic circles, belonging to Battle Creek Lodge, No. 12, F. & A. M., Battle Creek Chapter, No. 19, R. A. M. and Battle Creek Commandery, K. T. Since attaining the age of twenty-one years he has been an Odd Fellow and now belongs to Battle Creek Lodge, No. 29, I. O. O. F., of which he is a past grand and has represented his lodge in the Grand lodge. He is also past chief patriarch of the encampment and belongs to Calhoun Tent, No. 54, Knights of the Maccabees. Through his own exertions he has attained an honorable position and marked prestige among the representative men of the west, and with signal consistency it may be said that he is the architect of his own fortune and one whose success amply justifies the application of the somewhat hackneyed but most expressive title of a self-made man.

ZEBEDEE MACOMBER.

Zebedee Macomber, who is a retired farmer living in Battle Creek, was born in the township of Ripley, Huron county, Ohio, February 19, 1834, and is a son of

Egbert and Ann (Benedict) Macomber. His boyhood days were spent on the home farm and he assisted in the early spring planting and in gathering the crops in the late autumn. He lived with his parents until twenty-four years of age and in 1858 went to Cayuga county, New York, where he carried on farming. He remained there long enough to cast his presidential vote for Abraham Lincoln in 1860, and the following day he started for Michigan, locating at Canandaigua, Lenawee county, where he carried on agricultural pursuits for seven years. He then came to Calhoun county and purchased ninety acres of land on section 10, Emmett township, where he also spent seven years.

During that period he bought the first steam threshing machine ever used in this part of the state. It was a Columbus engine and a Nichols & Shepard separator, and in 1873 he had the old engine converted into a traction engine, which was also the first of that kind in Michigan. He continued threshing in connection with his general agricultural pursuits for a number of years. In 1875 he traded his property in Emmett township for land in Bedford township and purchased an additional tract there until he had two hundred acres on section 10. He made that farm his home for a quarter of a century and then removed to Battle Creek, where he has purchased a good residence on West Van Buren street. This he now occupies and is living a retired life in the enjoyment of the fruits of his former toil.

In 1858 Mr. Macomber was married to Miss Clara M. Wright, a native of New York, who died in 1879, and is interred in Oakhill cemetery at Battle Creek. They were the parents of eight children: Anna C., who is the wife of J. J. Halbert and resides in Bedford township; Carrie, who is the wife of Robert Crothers, of Detroit, Michigan; Lynn W., who is living in Battle Creek; Grant C., who is also a resident of this city; Walter G., who is the superintendent of a mine in California; Clarence H., a banker, who resides in Omer, Michigan; and two of the number who are deceased. Mr. Macomber gives his political allegiance to the Republican party.

LYNN W. MACOMBER.

Lynn Wilson Macomber is one of the enterprising and progressive young business men, possessed of laudable ambition to win success. He is now engaged in the sale and bottling of lithia water and in the establishment of this enterprise showed marked business capability. Born October 8, 1865, he is a son of Zebedee Macomber. During his boyhood he was brought to Calhoun county and pursued his early education in the district schools. To his father he gave the benefit of his services upon the home farm until twenty-two years of age and also assisted him in the operation of a steam thresher. He then entered the employ of the Advance Thresher Company of Battle Creek and as the result of his close application, fidelity and capability he was promoted until he became their traveling expert machinist. His connection with the company continued until 1898, when he resigned and purchased a small coal and ice business located at Goguac Lake. This he operated for three years and then organized the Consumers' Coal & Ice Company, becoming its treasurer. The company built an elevator to handle hard coal and the machinery of the plant was designed and placed in position by Mr. Macomber. It would unload two carloads of coal per hour —a capacity of fifty tons. In 1903 Mr. Macomber sold his interest in the Consumers' Coal & Ice Company to the Consolidated Ice Company so that he might devote his entire time and energy to the business of the Battle Creek Lithia Water Company, of which he is the sole owner. In 1898 he discovered a spring about eight miles west of the city whose waters are not excelled by any other in the United States. It was in the fall of 1902 before he could get possession of the land upon which the spring is located. Now he is pushing the business to its full extent and is giving to the residents of Battle Creek a water that is strictly pure, being filtered and put up in bottles for family use. They also manufacture from this natural mineral water, carbonated water of all kinds and lithia soft drinks. The plant is located at the corner of Jackson and River streets.

In 1900 Mr. Macomber was joined in wedlock to Miss Maude Decker, a native of Battle Creek and they have one son, Stuart Rhodes. Both Mr. and Mrs. Macomber hold membership in the Independent Congregational church. She is a leader in both musical and social circles of the city and is connected with various musical organizations here. Prior to her marriage she taught in the public schools of Battle Creek, of which she is a graduate. The family residence is at No. 19 Garrison avenue, and Mr. Macomber expects soon to erect a fine home at the corner of Orchard and Calhoun streets. In politics he is a Republican and fraternally is connected with Battle Creek lodge, No. 12, F. & A.

M., and the K. of P. He is also a stockholder in the Post Theater and is widely recognized as a most progressive, active and farsighted young business man whose career argues well for a prosperous future. He is well liked and popular, with a wide circle of friends, and well deserves mention in the history of the city in which almost his entire life has been passed.

HIRAM WILLARD BEALS.

Hiram Willard Beals, a well-known resident of Marshall, Calhoun county, Michigan, was born in Orson township, Allegany county, New York, July 12, 1827. He was one of six children, of whom he is the only one now living, the others being named in order of birth as follows: Roxanna, Lucinda, Maria, Mary Jane, Arnold. The parents, Comfort M. and Cynthia (Packard) Beals, were both natives of Springfield, Massachusetts. The father brought his family to Detroit, Michigan, June 6, 1836, shortly afterward locating in Eckford township, Calhoun county. He remained, however, in this location but a week, when he removed to Sandstone, Jackson county. After a residence of seven years in that locality he located in Parma township, Jackson county, five miles east of Albion, Calhoun county, and there continued in his trade of miller. His death occurred in that location and he is interred in Smithfield cemetery. His wife died in 1859. In his political convictions Mr. Beals was a Whig, giving his voice and vote in support of the principles he endorsed.

Hiram Willard Beals was but nine years old when the trip was made to the western state, but he well remembers the journey taken from Detroit with ox-teams, through a wilderness country, crossing streams by ford or ferry, and meeting with many Indians throughout the trip. He remained at home until the death of his father, after which he learned the trade of carpenter, which he has followed since, in his pursuit of a livelihood. When he first began to work he was paid $1.00 per day. December 19, 1855, he was united in marriage with Miss Mary Jane Scott, who was born in Connecticut, August 2, 1833. Her parents, Curtis and Sarah (Hurd) Scott, were both natives of New York state, where the father engaged in farming as an occupation, for a short time living in Connecticut. He died in 1876 at the age of seventy-three years, while the mother died in February, 1897, at the age of ninety years and one day. They were the parents of six children, those besides Mrs. Beals, the second in order of birth, being as follows: Cordelia, who lives in Harbor Springs, Michigan; Eliza Potter, who lives in Grinnell, Iowa; Reuben Elliott, who lives in Parma, Michigan; Harriet Ford, who lives in Mason, Michigan; and Frances Baker, who lives in Parma. On the day of his marriage Mr. Beals removed from Jackson county and located in Marshall, where he built his own residence, making his home for three years on Marshall avenue, where he removed to his present location. To Mr. and Mrs. Beals were born two children, of whom Claude W., born November 11th, 1861, was first married November 14, 1883, to Miss Stella Dutton, of Mendon, Michigan. She died, leaving one child, Carl C., born December 25, 1885. His second marriage was to Miss Ella Stanley. Their home is now in Lansing, Michigan, where he is employed

as a machinist. They are the parents of three children: Roy S., born December 16, 1892; Wayne, born June 10, 1896, and Paul Richard, born April 21, 1898. Sarah Hurd, the daughter, was born March 18, 1871, and married Fred Graves, a dentist of Battle Creek, where they now live. They have two children, Gladys, born November 14, 1891, and Kenneth, born February 15, 1896.

In politics Mr. Beals is and always has been a Republican. Though Mr. Beals received only a common school education he has kept himself well informed on the topics of the day by reading and observation. He has taken an active interest in the advancement of the general welfare and is esteemed by his fellow townsmen. He started life with nothing but a pair of willing hands and a firm determination to succeed and what he has to-day has been accumulated by his own hard labor and perseverance—a self-made man. He is still active in his chosen life's work.

Mrs. Beals is a member of the Presbyterian church of Marshall in which she has taken an active interest for many years.

GEORGE S. BARNES.

George S. Barnes, who is the editor and publisher of the Michigan Poultry Breeder's and Game Fancier's Journal at Battle Creek, is one of the worthy citizens of Calhoun county that the Empire state has sent to Michigan. He was born in the city of Rochester, New York, March 6, 1867, his parents being Wilsey G. and Madeline (Sackett) Barnes. When about three years of age he was brought by his parents to Battle Creek and here the mother died after their arrival. The father then returned to the east where the son, George S. Barnes, made his home with his uncle, Philander Barnes. He obtained his education in the public schools here and when sixteen years of age started out in life for himself by learning the type-setter's trade. For a year and a half he worked on the "Reed City Clarion" at Reed City, Michigan, after which he came to Battle Creek and was employed in various printing offices here. When about eighteen years of age he began the publication of the "Michigan Poultry Breeder," continuing the work of this paper at night, while in the daytime he worked in the office of other publications in order to provide for his own support and secure the money necessary to establish his business on a paying basis. After three years the business had become a paying one and he therefore severed his connection with other journals. The first paper was issued in January, 1885, and was sent out free in order that it might become known to the public and thereby win subscriptions. It was first an eight page paper, but it has since been increased in size, containing now twenty-four pages. It is sent to every state and territory in the Union and there is now an issue of several thousand copies made monthly. The name indicates the purpose of this journal and it has become a publication of marked value to those engaged in raising fine poultry. It treats of every subject bearing upon this work and Mr. Barnes himself has considerable practical knowledge of the business of raising fine poultry, for he makes a specialty of the breeding of single comb buff leghorns. Many times he has exhibited his chickens at the various poultry shows where he has won many prizes, gaining blue ribbons at Detroit,

Cleveland, Chicago, New York and other cities. As his business has grown in volume and importance and has become a large and profitable enterprise he has invested his income in real estate. He first purchased six acres on which is located his home and office, on Maple street. He also has property on Green street, on which is a four family flat building and also a house. Just outside the city limits he has a valuable farm of forty-three acres.

On the 6th of December, 1890, in Battle Creek, Mr. Barnes was united in marriage to Miss Fannie C. Webb, a sister of Mayor Fred H. Webb. She was born in this city and is a daughter of Caleb and Sarah (Green) Webb. In her girlhood days she learned type-setting in the office of the Journal and formerly assisted her husband in this business. They have one child, Madeline N., who was born on Green street in Battle Creek, September 6, 1890.

Mr. Barnes gives his political support to the men and measures of the Republican party, having affiliated with that organization since casting his first presidential vote for Harrison in 1888. He has served as alderman from the fourth ward for four years and was chairman of the committees on printing, the police department, and the side and cross walks, and he made strenuous efforts to divorce politics from the police department and his efforts proved of benefit in this direction. He also labored earnestly to establish a system of paving here and helped to carry the measure over the mayor's veto at the time when it was voted to lay the first pavement in Battle Creek. For five years he has been a member of the board of public works, having been the secretary of the board and at the present time is its president. Prominent among the energetic, far-seeing and successful business men of this section of Michigan Mr. Barnes is numbered. His life most happily illustrates what may be done by faithful and continued effort in carrying out an honest purpose. Integrity, activity and energy have been the crowning points of his success and it is along this line that he has gained for himself a creditable position among the men of affluence in Battle Creek.

THEODORE E. SANDS, M. D.

To a position of distinction and prominence Dr. Theodore E. Sands has attained in the practice of his profession in Battle Creek. He was born in the village of Shipping Port, Pennsylvania, June 5, 1862. His father, Elijah Sands, was captain on a river boat, running from Pittsburg to New Orleans. The son remained in his native town until about sixteen years of age and attended the public schools there. He then accompanied his parents, Elijah and Jennie (Jones) Sands, to Napoleon, Ohio, where the father engaged in the lumber business, while the son continued his studies in the high school there until he reached the age of eighteen. Later, he entered the law-office of Judge David Meekison with the intention of practicing law. He studied until he was ready to take the examination and was admitted to the bar as soon as he attained his majority. He entered upon practice at Napoleon, but did not find the profession congenial and he also possessed a strong desire to enter the medical fraternity, which was probably a potent force in causing him to leave the legal fraternity. In the fall of

1883 Dr. Sands became a student in the office of Dr. W. J. Fairfield, of Battle Creek, who was medical superintendent of the Health Home. He afterward pursued a course of lectures in the medical department of the University of Michigan and was graduated with the class of 1886. Returning to this city he became the successor of his former preceptor, Dr. Fairfield, and acted as superintendent of the Health Home during the remainder of its existence. It was superseded by the Nichols Hospital, with which Dr. Sands has since been connected as consulting and visiting physician and surgeon. He now has a large general private practice, making a specialty, however, of gynecology.

In 1890, in Battle Creek, occurred the marriage of Dr. Sands and Miss Hilah Miller, of this city, who was born in Rockwood, Michigan. She died January 26, 1904. In social circles they occupied an enviable position. Socially the Doctor is connected with Battle Creek lodge, No. 12, F. & A. M., and also with the Royal Arch Masons and Knights Templar. Dr. Sands was one of the original promoters and owners, and also the founder of Urbandale. He is interested in real estate and building throughout the city. His profession, however, has made the greatest claims upon his time and energies and he keeps in touch with the progress of the fraternity by his membership in the American Medical Association, the Calhoun County Medical Society, and the Battle Creek Academy of Medicine. He has prepared papers to be read before these societies and has also written for medical journals and these articles have shown thorough knowledge of the subjects treated. He has not only followed along lines where others have labored, but has carried his researches and investigations into new fields for the benefit of his fellow men, gaining experience that has been of value to the profession. The favorable judgment which the world passed upon him at the outset of his professional career has been in no degree set aside or modified, but on the contrary has been emphasized as the years have gone by, owing to his capability in the line of his chosen calling and his strict conformity to the ethics of professional life.

ENOS SMITH.

The early residents of Battle Creek who established the city along lines of progress leading to its present splendid development are fast passing away, but in coming years their history will be of interest to the people who reside here and that the record of their good deeds shall be perpetuated we compile this volume. Enos Smith was among the early residents, settling here in 1849. He was born in Genesee county, New York, February 21, 1821. He lost his father when young and went to live with a man in the neighborhood. He learned the wagon-maker's trade and followed this pursuit in the east until his removal to Otsego, Michigan, where he again secured employment in that line. At Jackson, Michigan, he wedded Harriet Holden, who died leaving him one son, Julian, now a resident of Jackson.

After his wife's death Mr. Smith returned to New York, where for a time he was employed as engineer on a railroad and on again coming to this state located in Battle Creek, in 1849. Here he conducted a wagon-making shop of his own

under the firm name of Smith & Gardiner, the firm owning the property at the corner of Monroe and State streets, where they conducted a wagon-making, blacksmith and painting business. They had a very complete shop and turned out a high grade of light and heavy vehicles and the firm name became a guarantee for good workmanship. Mr. Smith thus prospered in his undertakings and continued in business until after the close of the war, when he sold out to his partner. He then entered the employ of Nichols & Shepard, working on wheels and was with that establishment for fourteen years, when his health failing him, he retired from active labor.

On the 12th of March, 1851, Mr. Smith had been married, his second union being with Mary A. Phetteplace, who was born in Chenango county, New York, October 17, 1828, a daughter of Eseck and Submit (De Coston) Phetteplace. Her father was born in Rhode Island, October 23, 1800, and when a young man removed to New Berlin, New York, where in 1821 he wedded Miss De Coston, a daughter of Ebenezer De Coston, who was of French lineage and a man of superior education. Her paternal grandfather was Samuel Phetteplace, whose wife, Lydia Williams, was a descendant of Sir Roger Williams. Eseck Phetteplace was given a farm by his father, who was a wealthy man. Later, however, he sold that property and removed to Crawford county, Ohio, whence he afterward went to Michigan, settling in Coldwater in 1835. There he conducted a grist and sawmill. Subsequently he established his home at Pine Creek, Allegan county, where he conducted a mill for two years and later purchased a farm at Plainwell. While living thereon his wife died and he then went to Orangeville, where he engaged in the grocery business. His last years, however, were spent in honorable retirement from labor and he died at the home of his daughter in Plainwell, Michigan, October 22, 1892, respected and honored by all who knew him. Mrs. Smith was educated in the schools near her father's home and although he was a man of considerable means she witnessed many pioneer conditions because of the family home being established upon the frontier. Remaining at Plainwell until her marriage she has since lived in Battle Creek and her memory carries a picture of this city when it was but a village. Unto Mr. and Mrs. Smith were born four children, of whom D. L. died August 4, 1891, at the age of twenty-three years. The others are Ellis R., now a merchant of Battle Creek and the manager of the Post Theater; Mabelle E., at home; and Lynn, of Toledo, Ohio.

On coming to this city Mr. Smith purchased a home and always owned property here. He bought a large tract of land on North avenue and built the first home on McCamly street. He also built at No. 27 North avenue, where Mrs. Smith has now resided for nearly one-third of a century. At different times he owned considerable realty here and from his investments realized a good financial return. In politics he was a Democrat. He passed away May 2, 1896, and thus the county was called upon to mourn the loss of one who at a very early period in Battle Creek's development became a representative of her citizenship. His life was active and useful, his business dealings straightforward and in all relations he was honorable and upright. It is well when the closing years of a man's life may

be quietly and happily spent, free from the difficult task of adjusting himself to new business conditions, so radically changed from those of his early years of keen perception and ready adaptability. In such a way did Mr. Smith pass his last years and being called to his final rest, he left behind him a memory which is still enshrined in the hearts of his friends.

GEORGE B. GESNER, M. D.,C. M.,F.T. M. C.

The Gesner family is one, old in the history of military movements in Germany, where those of the name have flourished for many generations. The first American emigrant, D. H. Gesner, whose father served under Blucher at the battle of Waterloo, his sword being still in the possession of the family, became a pioneer settler in Canada. He was also a soldier, as was his son, John S. Gesner, a native of Clearville, Canada, and the father of George B. Gesner, the subject of this review, whose mother, Jennie Leitch, was of Scotch descent. The Canadian poet, Lampman, is a nephew of John S. Gesner.

In taking up the study of medicine Dr. Gesner has departed from the military careers which have distinguished his forefathers, but the success which he has met has justified him in his choice of a profession. He was born in Palmyra, Ontario, August 16, 1871, and after receiving his preliminary education, entered Ridgetown Collegiate Institute, from which he was graduated at the age of nineteen years. He had made his home with his parents until his nineteenth year when he became independent and sought his own way in the world.

27

After his graduation from the Ridgetown Collegiate Institute he entered the county training school at Chatham, Ontario, after a period of six months becoming a teacher there. He remained there for five years, receiving a good salary and splendid training, which proved a stepping-stone to his higher ambitions. He matriculated in Toronto University and in Trinity University, graduating from the latter institution in 1899, with the degrees of M. D. and C. M. He also became, by examination, in Trinity Medical College, Fellow of Trinity Medical College. Afterward he graduated from the Toronto General Hospital and the Victoria Children's Hospital. Dr. Gesner was always an enthusiastic student, and into his practice of medicine he has carried a fund of earnestness and ambition which has, without doubt, brought to him the success which does not always follow ability without these qualities. In September, 1899, the doctor opened his practice in Eckford, Michigan, where he remained for a little less than three years, removing then to his present location in Marshall. His practice here was opened in June, 1902, since which time it has become an extensive and renumerative one, embracing much territory and including many of the prominent families of this community, who are cognizant of the modern and practical methods of this young physician.

The marriage of Dr. Gesner occurred September 10, 1902, Miss Lettie May Decker, becoming his wife. They have a son, Paul Douglas, born October 16, 1903. Mrs. Gesner is a daughter of Rev. H. A. Decker, of St. Joseph, Michigan, the representative of an old German family. Dr. Gesner is a member of the First Presbyte-rian church of this city, and in his political convictions adheres to the principles of the Republican party. Fraternally, he is quite prominent, becoming identified with the Knights of the Maccabees, the Modern Woodmen, Knights of Pythias, and the Ancient Order of Gleaners. In the line of his profession he belongs to the Calhoun County Medical Association, State Medical Society and the American Medical Association. Dr. Gesner, though young, has made for himself a position of importance in his profession, and through his early accomplishment gives promise of a successful career.

JOHN JAMES HALBERT.

John James Halbert, one of the progressive farmers of Bedford township, was born in this township November 19, 1854. His father, William Stannard Halbert, was a native of LeRoy, Genesee county, New York, and a son of James and Alethe (Stannard) Halbert. The grandfather died when the son was still a small boy, and in 1846 the mother and her five children, Thomas, Jasper, William, James and Alice, came to Michigan, settling in Bedford township, Calhoun county, on the east road, where she lived some years. Mrs. Halbert eventually died in Battle Creek, and the family then separated.

Mr. Halbert's paternal uncle, Jasper Halbert, served in the Mexican war, and afterward went to California, where he married and spent most of his life. He brought his two daughters to Battle Creek to be educated, where they remained, and at which place their deaths occurred. He also died in Battle Creek, having returned about two years before his death.

William S. Halbert, the father of our subject, began farming in this county and followed that pursuit until his death, which occurred in 1867, when he was forty-two years of age. His wife survived him until June, 1898, passing away at the age of sixty-seven. She bore the maiden name of Louisa Armstrong and was a native of Tompkins county, New York, and a daughter of John and Mary (Davidson) Armstrong. Her parents were natives of the Empire state and in 1836 came to Calhoun county, when there was nothing but an Indian trail from Battle Creek to Bedford. They settled upon the bank of the stream near where the village of Bedford now stands and the father built a gristmill and saw-mill, which he conducted for several years. A part of this original farm is now in possession of our subject. At that early date there was an Indian village near the Armstrong home and the ladies of the family were very much afraid of the red men, who, however, never molested them. When they visited the pioneer cabin Mrs. Armstrong gave them everything they wanted to eat to keep on terms of friendship. In the family were several children, but only three reached years of maturity: Louisa, Alfred and Irwin. Our subject was only twelve years of age when Mrs. Armstrong, his grandmother, died, she having survived her husband many years. Unto William S. Halbert and his wife were born six children: John J., Jasper, Hector, Frank, Austin and Charles.

Of this number Austin died in infancy, Charles at the age of twelve and Hector at the age of forty-one.

In the district schools of the township John J. Halbert acquired his early education and later spent two terms as a student in Olivet College, Michigan. He has always resided in Bedford township with the exception of two years, which he spent working by the month in Ross township. He married Miss Anna Macomber, a daughter of Zebedee Macomber, whose sketch appears elsewhere in this work. Six children have been born to this union: Edith, Fred, Bernice, Merle, Carrie and Eldon.

Mr. Halbert now owns one hundred and forty acres of fine land and has erected there a very attractive residence. His farm is equipped with all modern improvements and accessories and is one of the model farms of the twentieth century. The fields are under a high state of cultivation and yield to the owner a good return for his care and labor. He is recognized as a progressive agriculturist and his life has ever been characterized by industry and thrift.

Jasper G. Halbert, a brother of our subject, is now residing in the village of Bedford. He was born on the old homestead December 31, 1856, and was educated in the district schools. Through the period of his boyhood and youth he largely assisted in the cultivation of the home farm. In 1891 he became connected with a grist-mill at Bedford, but prior to that time was associated with his brother, John J., in the ownership of the farm on section 15, Bedford township. He disposed of his interest in order to become identified with the milling business. He married Miss

Jennie Gifford, a native of this township, and they have two children: Keet and Helen. Jasper Halbert is a Republican in his political views and his wife is a member of the Congregational church.

Mr. J. J. Halbert is in possession of a letter written by Daniel M. Hutchinson to Mr. Halbert's maternal grandfather in 1838, and found by Mr. Halbert among waste paper on the floor of the old house over forty years afterward. It reflects the spirit of pioneer days, and is as follows:

KING'S FERRY, January 16, 1838.
Respected Friend, John Armstrong:—

Although it is some time since I have addressed a letter particularly to thee, yet I have written frequently to John Meachem and have directed my letters generally to him on account of his being often at the office, and because I have made him an agent to distribute the money I have transmitted and most of them which I have sent this summer contained money, nevertheless I intended them as common property and expected you to see or hear the contents, otherwise the neglect would be inexcusable. It is some time since I have heard from you, and I have been watching the office for more than a week expecting a letter from John; but no letter has arrived as yet to inform me what situation my accounts were in, whether the money I sent has discharged my debts or how much is yet behind. According to the statement J. Meacham made last summer of the amount of my debts, I have sent (including the orders I have paid) sufficient money to discharge them all, provided John has paid all over that I have sent, and provided also that none has miscarried, although it was not forward as soon as I could wish,

owing to the extreme difficulty at a short notice to procure money these hard times. How much has been expended since the mill was started or how far thee has been able to get thy wages by selling lumber I have not been informed, but feel in hopes to receive an account ere long how matters stand. It would have been a great gratification to me had I been able to go to Michigan this fall, and I suppose it would have been pleasing to you to have seen me, but sickness in my family and other circumstances have rendered it impossible, and when I shall get there I cannot now tell you, may be next summer. When I come again I am in hopes to see you in a snug little farm house by the mill with a state road running by it and houses going up all along the tract. Money has been so scarce it was discouraging last fall to think of making new improvements, but will be better soon, besides thee might work leisurely at a house, having the mill to assist, without expending a great deal of cash, and get it so as to be tenantable. Could you get a good road by the mill the people would settle on it, and you would sell lumber, sufficient to support you at any rate, besides you can raise some grain and grass. I hope you will not be discouraged because things have not turned as favorable as we expected. I mean because the people do not drag the lumber from the mill as fast as it is sawed. Nevertheless they will want it when they get in motion again, and I think that will be next spring. Last summer they were afraid if they came to Michigan they would starve. And that was not all. They could get no money to go on. The banks were calling in all their money and were letting none out. They have now got it in, and I guess the people will hardly take it out as fast as they would like to have them. We barter more than we used to, of course—don't need so much money. Instead of buying cloth of the merchant we get our wool manufactured on shares and sell the merchant cloth, and so in other things. It will require a little more patience, being thrown back one year by this pressure, in other words, it will take two years to accomplish what would have been done in one, but I do not believe your wife will be obliged to live alone in the woods much longer. Michigan will soon be settled and the Indians gone. I should like to have thee write to me as soon as thee has leisure. A half an hour spent each evening for a week would tell me a great deal. Any difficulties or troubles you may have I should be glad to hear of, that is, if it is possible I may assist you. If you enjoy good health it will be the greatest blessing. It has not been very healthy here this fall, owing, perhaps, to the large proportion of south wind we have had, but the number of deaths is not so great for the two months past as it was a month ago.

If you have as little snow in Michigan as we have in Cayuga the people will draw you but few logs this winter. The ground is entirely bare, and the weather, excepting some cold days, has been moderate, much more so than last winter was. All the summer was wet and cold. Business of all kinds has been dull for a year past and but little improvements making. It, however, begins to revive again. Produce keeps up to a pretty good price, but it is in consequence of the failure of crops, so the farmer gains nothing and the purchaser suffers loss. Wheat is worth twelve shillings,

corn eight, buckwheat four, oats two, pork six dollars per hundred, beef from four to six, etc. There appears to be a serious difficulty in Canada, and our people seem determined to have a hand in the job and I am fearful they will have a bloody time on the Niagara river before they get through. I do not expect it will affect you much in Calhoun except your sympathies from what you hear in the newspapers, which no doubt inform you of what is going on as well as we. I see my Calhoun paper copies the news. I have been pleased also to see advertised in that paper stocking-yarn, cloths and all kinds of wearing apparel, also all kinds of eatables and comfortables, so that if you get wherewith to buy them you need not suffer. I also see that a man in Marshall wants 50,000 feet of lumber, so it appears that article is not a complete drug everywhere.

I have not seen any of your relatives lately, but as far as I know they are in usual health. Tell Willard I should like to have him write me a letter stating what he is doing and what are his prospects, if he means to leave you or if he cannot stay comfortable in the old shanty and work at his trade. I intended to have seen his father-in-law before I wrote this letter, but time would not permit. I remain,

D. M. Hutchinson.

Excuse mistakes.

FRED HOPKINS HARRIS, M. D.

Dr. Fred Hopkins Harris, engaged in the practice of medicine and surgery in Marshall, is one of Michigan's native sons, his birth having occurred in Coldwater, December 6, 1875. His father, David Harris, was born on Cayuga lake, in Cayuga county, New York, August 20, 1836, and is a descendant of John Harris, who was burned at the stake in Harrisburg, Pennsylvania, in Revolutionary times. David Harris is a miller by trade and is now living retired in Coldwater, Michigan. He married Miss Marian Alden, who was born in Jonesville, Michigan, July 22, 1846, and is of the seventh generation in descent from John and Priscilla Alden, members of the Plymouth colony, whose romantic story is familiar to every student of American history. Her mother, Mrs. Mary A. Alden, nee Hopkins, is now a resident of Branch county, Michigan, and has attained the advanced age of eighty-six years: She was born in Tompkins county, New York, and is the oldest surviving member of the Hopkins family, who hold their annual reunions in northeastern Ohio.

Dr. Harris spent his boyhood and youth in his parents' home in Coldwater, Michigan, and is a graduate of the high school there, of the class of 1894. Not long after completing his literary course he began preparation for his profession and entering the medical department of the University of Michigan he was graduated in the class of 1898, numbering seventy members. He was elected class poet and prepared a poem for the graduation exercises. For a year following the close of his university course he practiced in his native city and was then appointed surgeon for the Elm River Copper Mining Company, at Elm River, Michigan. He served for one year and then came to Marshall, where he has now been in active practice for three years. He has built up a good business during that time, for he came

well qualified for the arduous duties of the profession, and his successful treatment of many difficult cases has won for him the public confidence and therefore the public support.

Dr. Harris holds membership in Marshall Camp, No. 2850, M. W. A., and he gives his political support to the Republican party. A lover of music, while pursuing his professional course he aided in organizing a band among the students of the University of Michigan, and continued one of its members as long as he was in the institution. He was reared in the Presbyterian faith and is now a member of the Episcopal church, in which he is serving as a member of the choir. In musical and social circles he is popular and his unfailing courtesy and deference to the opinions of others, combined with a genial, cordial manner, have gained him many friends.

ERNEST BURNHAM.

A citizen of unquestioned popularity and esteem, Ernest Burnham, school commissioner of Calhoun county, is upholding educational interests and advocating progressive public movements in Marshall and its vicinity. The family of which he is a member, came originally from the state of New York, where his father, Orsemus Burnham, was born November 13, 1829, while his parents were residents of the locality near Lockport, Niagara county. When eleven years old he removed to Michigan with his parents, Hiram Orsemus and Caroline (Robinson) Burnham, who located near Climax, Kalamazoo county. He married Margaret Smith, a native of Genesee county, New

York, whose parents had also early removed to the west, the ceremony being performed November 8, 1865. She died March 25, 1877, the mother of four children, those besides our personal subject being as follows: Smith, a professor of history in the State Normal School at Westchester, Pennsylvania, who married Ella L. Caster and has one child, Margaret; Philip S., a resident of Almosa, Colorado, where he is in the United States Mail service. He married Hannah Clough; and Fred, who died in infancy. Mr. Burnham was a Whig and upon the organization of the party he became a Republican. He is a helpful member of the Methodist Episcopal church.

The third in his father's family, Ernest Burnham, was born on a farm near the village of Climax, Kalamazoo county, Michigan, October 15, 1869. He early evinced a taste for study and was eager to acquire knowledge during his attendance at the district school in the neighborhood of his home, after which he attended the graded schools of Vicksburg for two winters, at the age of eighteen enrolling his name among the teachers of the county. After teaching for one year he became a student at the Battle Creek high school, from which he was graduated in 1891, a member of a class of fifteen of which he was chosen president. After his graduation he returned to his childhood home and taught school in district No. 5, where he had gained his first knowledge of books. Not content with less than a substantial foundation for the success which he hoped to possess in future years, he once more became a student, entering Albion College, from which institution he was graduated in 1896, being selected historian in a class of eighty-four. His Alma Mater conferred on him the degree of Master of Arts in 1902. While attending college he had

served as editor of the "Albion College Pleiad," and while in that capacity he had formed the acquaintance of V. J. Tefft, editor of the "Albion Recorder," and after the death of Mr. Tefft, he became editor of that paper for a period of three years.

Born and bred a Republican, he was always active in the promotion of the principles which he espoused. In 1896 the county went Democratic, and three years later Mr. Burnham was nominated on his party ticket to the office of school commissioner, and was elected by a plurality of three hundred and sixty-four votes. In 1901 he was re-elected to the same office, the plurality being two thousand and twenty-eight, and in April, 1903, he was again re-elected, with a plurality of twenty-two hundred and eight. His first two terms had been of only two years each, while his third election gave him four years under the new law. In October, 1903, the board of supervisors raised his salary to the maximum allowed by law.

June 22, 1899, Mr. Burnham married at Wilkesbarre, Pennsylvania, Miss Grace E. Armstrong, a native of Brooklyn, New York. She is the daughter of Rev. Edmund Valentine and Antoinette (Raymond) Armstrong, who removed to Michigan, afterward settling in Wilkesbarre. Mr. Burnham met his wife first at Albion College, from which institution she was graduated in the same class with him. In religion Mr. Burnham is a member of the Methodist Episcopal church, in which he officiates as trustee, and belongs to the Sigma Chi, a college fraternity. A man of much natural ability, culture and refinement, he has added to his native qualities by a thoroughly practical training, laboring with zeal and energy to fulfil his duties as a citizen of the community, as well as to acquire a personal success—a worthy and honorable ambition.

FRANK G. EVANS.

Frank G. Evans, the cashier of the newly organized Central National Bank, is one of the progressive business men of Battle Creek. Joining some of the leading business men and capitalists of the city in organizing this bank in 1903, he became its cashier and is a most valued factor in building up the business of this institution, which has already become extensive for an organization of such short duration.

Mr. Evans was born at Osage, Iowa, on the 22d of February, 1870, his parents being George and Lydia A. (Gould) Evans. His father removed from Rome, New York, to Iowa, when a young man, and with his brother settled at Waverly, where for a time, he was engaged in merchandising. He there married Lydia A. Gould, whose birth occurred in Vermont and who came with her adopted father, the Rev. John Gould, and his family to the west. He was a presiding elder of the Methodist Episcopal church and one of the leading ministers of the denomination in Iowa. Mrs. Evans's family name was Osgood, but being adopted in her early childhood, she took the name of her foster father. George Evans removed from Waverly to Osage, Iowa, where, as a business man, he became active and prominent in the commercial circles of that city, living there until his death which occurred about 1874.

It was in the schools of Osage that Frank G. Evans obtained his early education. He afterward removed to West Brookfield, Massachusetts, in 1884, his mother having passed away in the meantime, and there he again attended school, while later he became a student in the Worcester academy. In 1888 Mr. Evans removed to Battle Creek, Michigan, and

entered upon his business career as a clerk in the Boston Clothing store, where he remained for a short time. Subsequently he entered The National Bank of Battle Creek in a clerical position, continuing his connection with that institution until September, 1902, during which time he was promoted successively from one position to another, and at the time of his resignation was serving as teller, a capacity in which he had rendered good service to the bank for several years. While still connected with the institution he had become interested in different corporations of the city, and in 1901 became prominently identified with the Hern's Mail Wagon Company, limited.

In October, 1903, Mr. Evans assumed the duties which now largely claim his attention—those of cashier of the Central National Bank. This institution was organized with a capital stock of two hundred thousand dollars and a surplus of fifty thousand dollars and starts out under very favorable circumstances, having some of the strongest men of the city at its head and the largest capitalization of any bank in southern Michigan. It has commodious quarters at the corner of Jefferson and Main streets with the latest bank equipments for the convenience in the transaction of the business, and for safety in the care of the moneyed interests intrusted to the institution. There are large deposit vaults and all modern accessories of an up-to-date bank. Mr. Evans was chosen one of the directors, as well as cashier, and his previous experience in connection with banking, well qualifies him for the important duties which now devolve upon him.

Socially, Mr. Evans is connected with the Athelstan club and is one of its direc-

tors. It is a leading organization of Battle Creek and in its circles he is popular. He likewise is identified with the Knights of Pythias fraternity, and the Benevolent Protective Order of Elks. His political affiliation is with the Republican party, and he keeps well informed on the issues and questions of the day, but the honors and emoluments of office have no attraction for him. His views upon questions of public policy, however, are very apparent, and his influence may always be counted upon in behalf of good government and the advancement of the interests of the public. In all his varied relations in business affairs and in social life he has maintained a character and a standing that has impressed all with his sincere and manly purpose to do unto others as he would have others do unto him.

CHARLES COBURN RICE.

Charles Coburn Rice is classed among the diligent and progressive men of Battle Creek, where he is now residing. The Empire state has furnished to Michigan many of her worthy citizens and of this class Charles Coburn Rice is a representative. He was born in Clinton county, New York, September 2, 1850, a son of Horace and Betsey (Coburn) Rice, who removed to Michigan when their son was six years of age, settling on a farm in Berrien county, where he remained until a youth of seventeen. He then accompanied his parents to Kalkaska county, Michigan, where the father entered land from the government. With the aid of his sons he then cleared away the forest trees and a

good home was developed in the midst of the green woods, six miles from any other settlement. They had to cut their way through the forests and they experienced many of the difficulties and trials of pioneer life. Upon that farm the father spent his remaining days, passing away at the age of sixty-three years, while the mother reached the advanced age of eighty-five years. Although a frame residence replaced the pioneer log cabin many years ago, the latter structure is still standing and is yet covered by the original roof.

Charles Coburn Rice obtained a good common school education and when seventeen years of age began earning his own living by working as a farm hand by the month. On attaining his majority, he entered the employ of the Michigan Central Railroad, his first day's work being the spreading of gravel. The boss told him that he did not need more help, but on noting the young man's diligence the first day, employed him. After two months he was given a position as freight brakeman and when three years had passed in that way, he was made conductor on a freight train and continued with the road for six years. For some time he made his home in Jackson, Michigan, and in 1870 removed to Battle Creek, where he entered the employ of the Grand Trunk Railroad Company as a freight brakeman. When three months had passed he was made conductor and for nine years served in that capacity on freight trains, while for eight years he was a passenger conductor. In 1903 he purchased a farm of one hundred and ninety-seven acres bordering Goguac lake on the east side and the following year took up his abode on that place, making his home there until 1901. He then sold the property and removed to Battle Creek, where he engaged in business as a furniture dealer, upholsterer and mattress manufacturer, until selling out in September, 1903.

On the 27th of January, 1873, at Niles, Michigan, occurred the marriage of Charles C. Rice and Paulina Wyant, who was born in Ohio, a daughter of James and Phoebe Wyant. They have four children: Norine, born in Jackson, Michigan, engaged in teaching school for one term, after which she married Charles H. Bock, by whom she has two daughters, Margaret and Helen; Beatrice, born in Jackson, is the wife of William Greene, of Battle Creek; Bessie, born in this city, is now employed in the Phoenix Printing office, and Myra, also a native of Battle Creek, is at home. Mr. Rice gives his political allegiance to the Republican party and fraternally is connected with the Knights of the Maccabees. The family home is at No. 492 Lake avenue, and Mr. Rice now finds it possible to surround his wife and children with many of the comforts of life, for by strenuous toil in former years he has gained a comfortable competence.

EUGENE STEWART.

Eugene Stewart is the proprietor of the Stewart Laundry, of Battle Creek, which has become a very paying business. He was born in this city October 4, 1849, his parents being Leonard H. and Mary (McCamly) Stewart. The father was probably born in Rutland county, Vermont, and the mother in Orange county, New York. Her parents, Sands and Elizabeth

McCamly, were pioneers of Battle Creek and in honor of her father the street of Mc-Camly was named. He was one of the founders of the city and became owner of much real estate here. It was prior to his marriage that Leonard H. Stewart arrived in Battle Creek, where he was destined to become prominent in busines and public affairs. After teaching penmanship for several years and acting as salesman in various stores he took up the study of law, was admitted to the bar and through a long period was a successful practitioner. In public affairs he took an active and helpful part, served on the town board and was also postmaster of the city prior to the Civil war. His early political support was given to the Whig party, but on the organization of the Republican party he joined its ranks. His family numbered five children: Rose, the wife of Emery L. Graves, of Toledo, Ohio, by whom she has a son, William S.; Eugene, of this review; Louis, who married and died at Columbus, Ohio, leaving one child, Horace, a manufacturer, of Chicago, married Mattie Page and died in Chicago leaving a son, Roy; and Charles, who wedded Edna Winfield and lives in Battle Creek and is assisting in the laundry.

In his native city Eugene Stewart spent his boyhood days and attended the public schools. At fourteen years of age he began clerking and was thus employed until he attained his majority, when he determined to learn the machinist trade, which he followed until 1885. He was in the service of the Battle Creek Machinery Company, the predecessors of the American Steam Pump Company. In 1885 he established a laundry at No. 123 West Main street, beginning operations on a small scale. There he remained for ten years, when having outgrown his first quarters, he removed to 23 West Main street. In 1900 he built his present business block, which is a three-story brick structure, the first floor being used for laundry purposes, while the second floor is divided into offices and the third floor is the lodge room of the Knights of the Maccabees. Mr. Stewart first employed but three people and the success of his business and the extent of his patronage are indicated by the fact that he now furnishes employment to sixty people.

On the 2d of October, 1870, in Battle Creek, occurred the marriage of Eugene Stewart and Miss Elizabeth Dell, who was born near this city and is a daughter of Richard and Agnes (Lisk) Dell. Four children graced this marriage: Mary, at home; Mabel, who married Kuno Burbach, who died in April, 1902, in Phoenix, Arizona; Richard, who assists his father in business, and Agnes, at home. Mr. Stewart owns a pleasant residence at No. 63 Garrison avenue, which he erected in 1891. He is a Republican in his political views and cast his first vote for General Grant, while in Allegan county. About 1873 he became a member of the Ancient Order of United Workmen, in Battle Creek, and has served as financial secretary of the local lodge. He also has membership relations with the Knights of Pythias and the Elks. Starting out in life for himself at the early age of fourteen years and since dependent upon his own efforts for all that he has had and enjoyed, he certainly has made a record that is honorable and worthy of emulation. Realizing that success could be attained through persistent labor and close application, he resolved

that he would gain it along that line and his perseverance and diligence have indeed been the foundation upon which he has builded his prosperity.

ELI WILSON FLAGG.

This is a utilitarian age and labor is directed toward the development and use of natural resources and the direction of energy into channels that will produce material results. Mr. Flagg as an inventor has given to the world a number of useful and valuable devices and is to-day a leading factor in industrial circles in Battle Creek, occupying at the present time the position of superintendent of the separator department with the firm of Nichols & Shepard. He was born in Massena, in St. Lawrence county, New York, November 2, 1838, and when ten years of age accompanied his parents, Barzelo and Sarah (Wilson) Flagg, to Battle Creek. The father was a carpenter and followed that trade until his death, which occurred in 1852. Our subject was then but thirteen years of age and was the second in a family of eight children. Up to this time he had attended the public schools, but as his mother was left in limited circumstances and he was the oldest son, he had to become the main support of his widowed mother and the younger children. He began work as a farm hand and at one time made hay where the Nichols & Shepard shops now stand. At the age of fifteen he began work in the woolen mills and was thus employed for six years, receiving from twelve to sixteen dollars a month. His position, however, only continued through the summer season and in the winter he followed any pursuit that would yield him an honest living. In 1859 he entered the shops of Nichols & Shepard to learn the machinist's trade, receiving at first seventy-five cents per day, but his wages were soon advanced and in 1862 he was given two dollars per day. He continued with Nichols & Shepard until 1864, when he began working for Brown & Upton, manufacturers of threshers, with whom he continued until a few months prior to their removal to Port Huron, Michigan, in 1882. He was next connected with the Advance Thresher Company and had charge of their machinery department until 1886. While thus engaged he invented an improvement on the original vibrator. He took out patents on his inventions and sold them to Nichols & Shepard and since that time has made several other improvements in mechanical lines. In 1891 he took out a patent on a separating grate and check plate which separates the straw and grain at the cylinder. Nichols & Shepard began the manufacture of this improvement in 1900. It is called the Red River Special and the first one was sent to Iowa, where it did such good work that the company determined to manufacture the machine. In 1902 the patent was re-issued because of an improvement and still another gained a third patent in 1903.

On the 12th of November, 1863, Mr. Flagg was married to Elizabeth M. Jewell, a daughter of John M. and Naomi (Cooper) Jewell. They had two children: Ora May, now the wife of Fred Wells, of Battle Creek, by whom she has two children, Ruth and Dean; and John Jewell, who was educated in the high school of Battle Creek and in a commercial college and died in this city at the age of twenty-four years. The wife and mother passed away January 19, 1899, and

in Battle Creek, February 6, 1900, Mr. Flagg wedded Mrs. Marian (Dwinell) Edmonds, a daughter of Henry L. and Calista (Warren) Dwinell. Her father was born in Bennington, Vermont, and came to Battle Creek in 1831. His wife, a native of Holly, New York, removed with her parents to this city and was here married at the age of seventeen years. Mr. Dwinell owned and operated a farm near Wheatfield, Subsequently he removed to Eaton county where Mrs. Flagg, who was born in Battle Creek, was reared to womanhood. She attended school in Olivet and was first married during the Civil war, her husband losing his life in the army. She afterward became the wife of Mr. Edmonds and later gave her hand in marriage to Mr. Flagg.

Casting his first presidential vote for Stephen A. Douglas, Mr. Flagg was an earnest Democrat until 1896, when he became a Republican. In 1882 he was elected alderman from the first ward and was re-elected for three successive terms. He had been a member of the fire department from 1862 until 1882 and was active when in the council in having the department improved. During his second term he was made chairman of the fire department committee. He also served on the water works committee and did everything in his power to advance the welfare and promote the substantial improvement of the city. In 1903 he was appointed a member of the police commission. Fraternally he is an Odd Fellow, having joined Battle Creek lodge, No. 29, in 1867, since which time he has filled all of the chairs and was representative to the Grand lodge in Saginaw in 1876. He was then made deputy grand master and has largely furthered the work of the order. Of the encampment he is likewise a valued representative. In 1878 he became a member of Security lodge, No. 49, A. O. U. W., filled all of its offices and was a member of its Grand lodge in Detroit. Eli Wilson Flagg is well known in Battle Creek in business, political and fraternal circles and in all life's relations he has been found true to high principles, his probity of character winning him unqualified regard. His career has been one of usefulness to his fellow men along many lines of activity, and he deserves praise and honor for what he has accomplished, for starting out in life for himself at an early age with a family depending upon him for support, he faithfully met the obligations which devolved upon him, and, as the years have passed he has steadily worked his way upward until he now occupies a creditable position in financial circles and at the same time commands the respect of his fellow men.

WILLIAM E. HICKS.

Among the most energetic and progressive men of Battle Creek is William E. Hicks, and his reputation is well deserved, for in him are embraced the characteristics of an unbending integrity, unabating energy and industry that never flags. Through long years he has been engaged in the milling business as a member of the firm of Titus & Hicks and his acquaintance in business and social circles has been continually broadened, while his upright course has won for him the unqualified regard of his fellow men.

Mr. Hicks is a native of New York, his birth having occurred in Perry, Wyoming county, on the 21st of June, 1838. His parents were Ellery and Maribah (Wilcox) Hicks. In the fall of 1851 the parents accompanied by their six children came to Michigan, proceding by stage from Perry to Buffalo, thence by way of the lake to Detroit and across the country from the latter city by rail to Battle Creek. Our subject, however, did not complete the journey in this manner, but drove a team from Detroit to his destination. The father had been an iron manufacturer in New York, but in Michigan turned his attention to other pursuits. In 1852 he purchased a interest to the former proprietor, Mr. Buckley in connection with B. B. Hicks, his brother, but the latter afterward sold his interest to the former proprietor Mr. Buckley, who in 1853 was succeeded by Mr. Titus. This mill had been built in 1837 by the firm of Nobles & Whitcomb, who had sold it to Mr. Buckley and it had not been operated from the time of Mr. Buckley's purchase until Mr. Hicks became an owner. He was then active in its conduct until his death which occurred in 1860. His son, George B. Hicks, became a soldier of Company C, Twentieth Michigan Infantry. He went to the front as second lieutenant, but was afterward promoted to the rank of captain. At the time of his death, which occurred on the battlefield in a charge against the enemy, he had command of the Ninth Army Corps. He left one son, William E., who died in Indiana and who in turn left a daughter, Bessie. Charles Hicks, another brother of our subject, was a soldier of Company C, Twentieth Michigan Infantry, and served for four years in defense of the Union. He died in Los Angeles, California, after which his remains were brought back to Battle Creek for burial. He left two sons, Richard, who is in the office of the American Steam Pump Company; and Louis Ellery, who also lives in Battle Creek.

Reared under the parental roof, William E. Hicks obtained his education in the common schools and when sixteen years of age began working in his father's mill. Two years following the death of his father he became owner of the family's interest in the enterprise and has since continued in control. He is widely known as a most reliable and trustworthy business man and one whose success is well merited.

On the 19th of April, 1800, in this city, Mr. Hicks was united in marriage to Miss Theresa Loughead, who was born in Erie, New York, a daughter of James and Lavina Loughead, who came to Battle Creek in the same year in which Mr. Hicks's parents arrived. Her father was an officer on a vessel on Lake Erie during the War of 1812 and died in Erie, New York, before the removal of the family to the west. Unto Mr. and Mrs. Hicks have been born five children: Charles, who is a miller by trade; Jennie, the wife of M. H. Frink, of Easton, Pennsylvania, by whom she has three sons, Joseph M., Hicks M. and James E.; Fannie, at home; James, who is working in his father's mill; and Mary, the wife of Edward Dietrich, of Easton, Pennsylvania.

William E. Hicks has followed in the political footsteps of his father and given his support to the Republican party, but has never been desirous for political preferment. He was reared in the Methodist Episcopal church, but now belongs to the Episcopal church and is a member of Athelstan club, of which he was a director for six years. His life has been one of continuous activity, in which has been accorded due recognition of labor; and to-day, he is numbered among the substantial citizens of his county. His interests are thoroughly identified with those of the state and at all times he is ready to lend his aid and co-operation to any movement calculated to benefit this section of the country or advance its wonderful development.

WILLIAM SYKES WOODHEAD.

William Woodhead, now deceased, was a veteran of the Civil war. England was the land of his birth and his natal day, November 11, 1836. With his parents, Joshua and Ann (Sykes) Woodhead, he came to the United States from Leeds, England, about 1841, and the family located in the English settlement of Waterford, Wisconsin, where the father was engaged in the manufacture of woolen goods. The son obtained his education in Waterford and had to make his own way in the world from the age of thirteen, because of his father's death. Five years later he left Waterford and in 1854 went to Three Rivers, Michigan, where he secured employment in a paper mill, there learning the trade of a finisher.

It was while thus employed that Mr. Woodhead offered his services to the government, enlisting in Company G, Second Michigan Volunteer Infantry, with which he remained for three years. The regiment was assigned to the Army of the Potomac and he participated in many important engagements and was wounded on the 3d of May, 1864, in the battle of the Wilderness, within eighteen days of the expiration of his enlistment. He was then sent to the hospital and was afterward made hospital steward, which position he held for some time. He was then honorably discharged and returned home, but re-enlisted as a member of Company E, Eleventh Michigan Volunteer Infantry, with which he served for eleven months, or until the close of the war, holding the rank of first sergeant.

When the country no longer needed his aid Mr. Woodhead returned to Three Rivers, where he resided until 1880 and then removed to Jackson, having been appointed guard at the State Penitentiary there. He served for two years and afterward as keeper for three years, filling both positions acceptably. Because of his Republican affiliation he was not re-appointed during the Democratic administration and he then sought and obtained employment in a paper mill. In 1887 he came to Battle Creek and for seven years was in charge of the tool room in the Grand Trunk Railway shops.

Mr. Woodhead was very prominent in the Masonic fraternity, having been made a member of the order in Jackson. He demitted to Battle Creek lodge, F. & A. M., and was its master in 1893, while at the time of his demise he held the highest office with one exception in Battle Creek Chapter, R. A. M. He was also prominent in the Odd Fellows Society, serving as noble grand while in Three Rivers. He became a member of Pomeroy post, G. A. R., at Jackson, of which he served as chaplain and a recognition of the sterling worth of his character won him the respect of his brethren of the fraternity. He was a charter member of the Edward M. Prutsman post, G. A. R., at Three Rivers, and also a member of A. O. U. W.,

of Battle Creek. He was one of the best informed men in Masonry in the state.

Mr. Woodhead wedded Mrs. Mary L. Stamp, of Three Rivers. She was born December 16, 1841, at Utica, New York, a daughter of John J. and Mary (Burdick) Petrie. Her father was a mason by trade and lived and died in Utica. Her mother, born in Oneida county, New York, was a daughter of Clark Burdick. When Mrs. Woodhead was two years old she was taken to Alden, Erie county, New York, where she remained until a maiden of fourteen, when she accompanied her mother and the family to Three Rivers, Michigan. There she lived until her marriage to Samuel M. Stamp, who was a farmer's son. On the breaking out of the war he enlisted in Company E. Thirteenth Michigan Infantry and was killed at Bentonville, North Carolina. By his marriage three children were born, of whom two died in infancy. The other, Sarah, became the wife of Donald Macdonald, and died in Battle Creek April 21, 1901, leaving two sons, Robert S. and Alexander. Mrs. Woodhead remained at Three Rivers until her second marriage. She is a member of the Woman's Relief Corps, in Battle Creek, in which she is now filling office, and she likewise holds membership in the Order of the Eastern Star. She is a member of the Presbyterian church. Mr. Woodhead passed away July 18, 1894, and is interred at Waterford, Wisconsin. He left behind him an untarnished name, for in all of life's relations he was as true to duty and to the trust reposed in him as he was to his country in her hour of peril. Honorable and upright, he won the respect of those who knew him, and he well deserves mention in this volume.

WILLIAM H. FLAGG.

William H. Flagg, a retired machinist living at No. 91 Fountain street, west, in Battle Creek, was born in the township of Massena, St. Lawrence county, New York, October 24, 1840, a son of Barzelo and Sarah (Wilson) Flagg. His paternal grandfather, Elijah Flagg, was a soldier of the Revolutionary war and was one of the number who helped to survey the town of Massena Springs in St. Lawrence county. He afterward settled in that locality and there Barzelo Flagg was born and reared. The latter became a millwright and in the year 1850 started westward intending to go to Fond du Lac, Wisconsin. On account of illness in his family, however, he stopped at Battle Creek and, being pleased with this place, decided to remain. Three years later his death occurred in this city. In his family were seven children of whom William H. Flagg was the third in order of birth.

As the wife and children were left in limited financial circumstances it was necessary that William H. Flagg begin to earn his own living and he worked at what ever he could get to do. His educational privileges were meager. In the winter months he would hunt and trap in the woods and in the summer seasons he worked at the mason's trade. When the war came on there occurred a great change in his mode of living. He was one of the first to enlist at Battle Creek for three years' service and he went to the front as a private of Company C, Second Michigan Infantry. He participated in eighteen battles and many skirmishes, being at both engagements at Bull Run. In the second he was wounded in the left heel by a cannister shot, the same shot killing one man and taking the hand off from another.

His regiment covered the retreat at the first battle of Bull Run and was therefore in a very dangerous position. Mr. Flagg was also wounded at Blue Springs, being shot through both legs. He lay in a fence corner all night, receiving no care, but in the morning was picked up and taken to the field hospital. Again at Jackson, Mississippi, he was wounded in the skull. On many other occasions his clothing was pierced by bullets and he had a number of narrow escapes. It was on the 19th of April, 1861, that he enlisted for three months' service, but on the 19th of May was mustered in for three years and served the entire time. During the last sixteen months he was with Generals Burnside and Grant as United States topographical engineer.

After leaving the army Mr. Flagg learned the blacksmith's trade, working for a dollar per day and for eighteen years he served as foreman in the Upton blacksmith shop at Battle Creek. His capability is thus evidenced and his long continued service also indicates the confidence reposed in him by his employer. In official life he has been equally favored. He served as chief of police for one year and was street commissioner for three years and for five years was in the engine department of Nichols & Shepard.

On Christmas day of 1868 Mr. Flagg was married in Battle Creek to Mrs. Abbie R. Campbell (Burch), who was born in Cayuga county, New York, and after acquiring a good education, taught school for many years. After her marriage she carried on a dressmaking shop until they got a start. She has always been a very charitable woman and her benevolences have been many. She has been for several years the president of the Charitable Union of Battle Creek, which owns and controls the Nichols Memorial Hospital, and was one of its founders. Mrs. Flagg is also one of the board of managers of the Woman's League, chairman of the Woman's Relief Corps, and on committee on the Woman's Building of the Soldiers' Home, near Grand Rapids. Mr. and Mrs. Flagg have one daughter, Hattie, who was born in Battle Creek. She is a graduate of the high school here and is now the wife of George B. Willard.

In his political views Mr. Flagg has been an earnest Republican since voting for Grant in 1868. He attends the services and contributes to the support of the Independent Congregational church, of which his wife and daughter are members. He belongs to the Grand Army Post, and Mrs. Flagg is past department president of the Woman's Relief Corps of Michigan. Mr. Flagg also has membership relations with the Ancient Order of United Workmen. In 1883 he built a cottage on Lake Goguac at Willard Cove. This was the first summer cottage ever erected here, but now the cottages line the lake shore for nearly a mile. Both Mr. and Mrs. Flagg enjoy the warm friendship of a large circle of acquaintances and her charitable spirit and many kindly acts have endeared her to those with whom she has come in contact and his reliability in business and loyalty in citizenship have made him a worthy representative of Battle Creek.

NEWTON E. RETALLICK.

Connected with the insurance business, in Battle Creek, Newton Eldred Retallick is a well known and valued citizen of Calhoun county. He was born in Kalama-
28

zoo county, Michigan, June 3, 1857, a son of John Truscott and Hilinda (Newton) Retallick. On the home farm he was reared and received a common school education. When nineteen years of age he began teaching and through five winter terms followed that profession in the country schools of Kalamazoo and Calhoun counties. In the spring of 1881 he was elected township superintendent of schools and helped to elect the first county school superintendent, who that year was chosen by the township superintendents. Mr. Retallick served for a little less than a year, but visited every school in his township during that time. He resigned his position to become a brakeman on the Chicago & Grand Trunk Railroad.

In the meantime, on the 17th of October, 1878, at Climax, Mr. Retallick had wedded Miss Eunice Ann Eldred, daughter of John Alonzo and Polly J. (Peckham) Eldred. On becoming brakeman he removed to Battle Creek, where he has since made his home. After eighteen months he was promoted to the position of conductor on a freight train and when a year and eight months had passed, he left railroad work and became an accident and life insurance agent, following that pursuit for a year. He next engaged in the grocery business, and while conducting his store announced that he could no longer do a credit business, but would conduct his store upon a cash basis. His friends predicted disaster, but instead, success attended the enterprise under the new management and for three years he conducted his store in a profitable manner. Again he became connected with railroading, this time on the Battle Creek division of the Michigan Central, then called the Canada

& St. Louis Railroad. After ten months, however, he returned to the Grand Trunk, serving for six months as a brakeman, when he was again made conductor, acting in that capacity for twelve years. He made his last trip in April, 1902. He was in many wrecks, being in a head-end collision near Haskells, Indiana, and there he narrowly escaped with his life. In 1899 he was in a collision at South Bend, Indiana, the patent couplers pulling apart and the rear end of the train crushing into the forward section. He was on the steps of a coach in the rear section and they were running at the rate of fifty miles an hour when they struck. For two hours and a half Mr. Retallick lay unconscious and was reported killed, his wife arriving next day, expecting never again to see her husband alive. While still in the railroad service he began studying for insurance work and in April, 1902, once more entered that field of business. He is now representing the New York Life Insurance Company, with which he was connected seventeen years ago. He also represents the New England Mutual Life, of Boston, the National Life, which is the only one chartered by the United States government, The Continental Casualty, of Chicago, and the Aetna Accident Insurance Company, of Hartford. In the business he is now meeting with success.

Unto Mr. and Mrs. Retallick were born two children: Edith Blanche, who was born in Battle Creek, March 15, 1883, and is a graduate of the high school with the class of 1903, and Eldred Austin, born January 10, 1890. In 1889 Mr. Retallick with his wife and daughter took an extended trip through the west, visiting Chicago, Denver, Silver Plume, Leadville,

Salida, Manitou, Colorado Springs and Cannon City. At the latter place the excursion was met by a band and taken to the best hotel in the town where a fine banquet was served. They also visited Salt Lake City, Garfield Beach and Ogden, Utah; Spring Hill, Butte City, Dalton, Deer Lodge, Helena and Missoula, Montana, and Tacoma and Seattle, Washington, being in the last named city three days before the great fire. He also had a trip on Puget Sound, which he pronounces the best he ever took. The trip also included Olympia, Centralia and Portland, Oregon, and thence over the Mount Shasta route to Sacramento and San Francisco. By ocean steamer the party proceeded to Portland, Oregon, and afterward up the Columbia river, thence to Omaha, Nebraska, stopping at Tekamah that state. In Shenandoah, Iowa, they visited relatives and thence continued on their homeward way through Hastings and Hillsdale, arriving home after a journey of two months and five days, during which they had traveled eight thousand one hundred and fifty miles. In 1876 Mr. Retallick visited the Centennial, in Philadelphia; Niagara Falls and Canada, and in 1893 he, with his wife and daughter, attended the World's Fair Exposition, in Chicago. About seven years later he took his family to Niagara Falls and Canada. He believes in becoming acquainted with his own country and has seen many of its beauties and wonders. Since voting for Garfield in 1880 he has been a Republican. In 1903 he was elected alderman from the fifth ward and is now chairman of the water works and sewer committee and a member of the committees on bridges, public lighting, building inspection and permits. Mr. Retallick is a stanch advocate of law and its enforcement, and is active in the council in passing an ordinance regulating the closing of the saloons. He and his family are members of the First Methodist Episcopal church and at one time he served as a class leader and is now treasurer and trustee of the church. Socially, he is connected with the Independent Order of Odd Fellows and the Order of Railway Conductors, having filled nearly all of the chairs in the local division. In November, 1903, he was elected chief conductor of Division No. 6. In company with his wife he has attended the Grand Division, at Detroit, and also at Denver, though not as a delegate. In 1888 he erected a store building at No. 247 East Main street, a two-story brick structure, twenty-two by seventy feet, the first floor being occupied for business purposes, while the second floor is used as a residence. Mr. Retallick has led a busy life, his strenuous nature being utterly opposed to indolence and idleness, and through his perseverence and diligence and his careful management of business affairs he has won creditable success, being now one of the substantial citizens of Battle Creek.

CLAUDE COLE WARBURTON.

The business interests of Battle Creek find a worthy representative in Claude C. Warburton, who since 1892 has resided in this city and for three years has conducted a successful florist business here. He was born on the 28th of April, 1880, and is a native of Maple Grove, Barry county, Michigan, and a son of Joseph E. and Lettie (Cole) Warburton. The father was a native of Reading, Michigan, and a son of Joseph Warburton, Sr. By occupation the father became a farmer, following that pursuit at Maple Grove until 1892, when he came to Battle Creek. Having sold his farm in Barry county, he purchased property and built a home at No. 293 Emmett street. For a time he was engaged in the grocery business on Maple street and gained a large and gratifying patronage there. After several years, however, he sold it and has since been collector for the Rathburn Lumber Company, but in 1904 expects to join his son, Claude C., in a partnership in the florist business. He and his wife are well known members of the Methodist Episcopal church.

In the usual manner of farmer lads C. C. Warburton spent the days of his childhood and youth, and his education was acquired in the district schools until his removal to Battle Creek. On putting aside his text-books he became connected with the florist business in the employ of the firm of McCrea & Cole, under whose direction he gained practical and thorough knowledge of the work in all its departments. For four years he remained with that firm and added to the knowledge gained in his labors, through reading extensively, and improving every opportunity which would promote his efficiency in this line of activity. He has become thoroughly well posted on the subject of cultivating plants and flowers and he still continues his study, so that he has succeeded in gaining a foremost position in the ranks of the representatives of this vocation. In 1900 he purchased a lot on Emmett street, at the end of North Union street, adjoining his father's home, and there began business on his own account, starting with but one greenhouse. At first he did all the work himself. The following year, owing to his increasing trade, he found it necessary to enlarge his facilities by the building of an additional greenhouse and work room. That, however, soon proved inefficient, and in 1903 he added five thousand feet of glass, covering two large greenhouses. This makes his plant one of the most extensive in the city. He handles a general line of ornamental and flowering plants and cut flowers, making a specialty of carnations, of which he has now over three thousand plants. There is a local demand that requires the entire product of his greenhouses and the city business has proved profitable and gratifying. As his trade increases he also adds to his realty holdings, until he now owns and utilizes seven city lots, or more than one acre of land. From a small beginning he has steadily worked his way upward, and, making rapid advances in his business now stands among its foremost representatives as the result of his energy, ability and earnest desire to please his patrons.

Mr. Warburton was united in marriage to Miss Blanche R. Tuttle, of Battle Creek, on the 21st of January, 1903, a daughter of Mrs. John Tasker, of Assyria, Michigan. They have a son, born January 24, 1904. The young couple occupy a pleasant home at No. 165 North Union street and are accorded an enviable position in social circles.

WILLIAM J. SMITH.

Prominent among the young business men of Battle Creek is William J. Smith, who has been closely identified with the financial, commercial and industrial interests of this growing city of southern Michigan since 1890.

A native son of Michigan, he was born in Charleston township, Kalamazoo county, Michigan, on the 26th of October, 1865, and is a son of John A. and Katherine (Joyce) Smith. The father was born in Genesee county, New York, and came to Michigan in 1857, settling in Kalamazoo county, where he resided until 1866, when he removed to Leroy township, Calhoun county, where he was recognized as one of the leading farmers, and was several times called to public office. The family is of German ancestry and settled in New England at an early date in the colonization of this country. The mother was also a native of Genesee county, New York, and a daughter of John Joyce, a soldier of the War of 1812. The Joyce family was of Scotch-Irish origin and landed on the American soil at an early date. Both the father and mother held membership in the Methodist Episcopal church and took an active part in its work, also contributing generously to its support. Mr. Smith died March 29, 1891, but the mother still resides on the old homestead.

During his infancy William J. Smith was brought to Calhoun county and reared on the home farm, where he early became familiar with the duties which fall to the lot of the agriculturist. He attended the common schools of West Leroy until fifteen years of age and then entered the Battle Creek high school, where he spent two years. He was afterwards a student in Albion College for three years and subsequently took a course in the Detroit Business University, thus being well equipped for the responsibilities of a business career. When twenty-three years of age he established the Exchange Bank at Climax, Michigan, conducting it successfully for two years, when he sold out and went south, spending a few months there for the benefit of his health. In the fall of 1890 he opened the Farmers' & Mechanics' Bank of Smith, Cole & Company, a private banking institution of Battle Creek, of which he acted as cashier until the spring of 1898. In the meantime it had grown to be a very important financial institution of the city, carrying on an extensive business and enjoying a most unassailable reputation for reliability. The close confinement caused by his important banking duties, however, undermined Mr. Smith's health and he was obliged to put aside all active participation in business affairs for a time. The Farmers' & Mechanics' Bank was then consolidated with The National Bank of Battle Creek, and Mr. Smith has since been a member of its board of directors. This is the largest financial institution of the city, the deposits aggregating two million dollars. Mr. Smith is identified with many of the leading business enterprises of the city and is prominent as a director and in the management of these institutions.

On the 5th of November, 1890, Mr. Smith was united in marriage to Miss Mary Lovell, a daughter of Hon. L. W. Lovell, of Climax, and they have one son, Wendell Lovell Smith, born November 16, 1892. Mr. Smith has erected a beautiful home at No. 161 Maple street. His social relations connect him with the Benevolent Protective Order of Elks, the Knights of the Maccabees, the Modern Woodmen of America, the Athelstan club and the Sigma Chi, a college fraternity. He gave his political support to the Democracy until 1896, since which time he has voted with the Republican party. He has been active in support of the principles in which he believes and has been a delegate to state and other conventions of his party, but has no aspirations in the direction of office holding. By reason of his large success, his unblemished character, his just and liberal life and the universal esteem which he here enjoys, Mr. Smith might, without invidious distinction, be called one of the foremost citizens of Battle Creek.

ANDREW HELMER.

Andrew Helmer is numbered among the pioneer settlers of Calhoun county, having for almost sixty years made his home here. During this time he has seen remarkable changes, for the country has emerged from a wild and unimproved condition, and has been converted into fine farms, which surround thriving and enterprising towns and cities. All of the advantages and improvements known to the older east have been introduced here, and Calhoun county to-day ranks with the best counties in this great commonwealth. Andrew Helmer is practically living retired, his home being on section 4, Battle Creek township. He was born in the town of Cherry Valley, Otsego county, New York, on the 29th of June, 1827, a son of Philip and Sarah (Woodman) Helmer, both of whom were natives of the Empire state. Soon after the birth of their son Andrew they removed from Otsego county to Oneonta, where the father engaged in farming until 1844. He then made preparations to come to the west and by wagon went to Utica, New York, where he took passage on a canal boat on the Erie canal. Thus he proceeded to Buffalo, whence he embarked on a lake vessel for Detroit, and from the last named place he came by wagon to Battle Creek. There were seven people in the party in addition to Mr. and Mrs. Helmer, their two sons and a daughter. They started on the 20th of May and reached their destination on the 7th of June. Settling on the prairie they lived in a log cabin in true pioneer style. The mother, however, was not long permitted to enjoy the new home, for her death occurred in August, 1844, and in September of the same year the father, too, passed away, their remains being interred in the Young cemetery. In his political affiliations Mr. Helmer was a Democrat. He left to his family only eighty acres of land, and soon after the death of the parents the children separated. Andrew Helmer, who was then but seventeen years of age, began working by the month as a farm hand and was thus employed for seven years. At first he received a compensation of about eight dollars per month for his labor, but at the last he was being paid fourteen dollars per month. Saving his money he was at length enabled to purchase land on his own account, and in 1849 he became the owner of a tract of eighty acres on section 10, Battle Creek township. This was all covered with timber and he therefore had to clear away the trees before he could plow and plant. He improved forty acres of the tract, however, and then sold.

In 1854 Mr. Helmer sought a companion and helpmate for life's journey, being united in marriage, in that year, to Marcia L. Andrus, a sister of William Andrus, in connection with whose history on another page of this work is given a sketch of the family. Mrs. Helmer was born in Binghamton, New York, in 1834, and was brought to Michigan by her parents in September, 1835. The young couple began their domestic life in the township of Comstock, in Kalamazoo county, Michigan, and there Mr. Helmer engaged in the cultivation and improvement of a farm of one hundred and eighty acres for two years. He then sold out and returned to Calhoun county, establishing his home in Battle Creek township, where he purchased one hundred and sixty acres of land, located on the southeast quarter of section 9. Much of this was improved to some extent and he made many more improvements and resided therein until 1890, his time and energies being devoted to general farming, wherein he won desirable success. In 1890 he removed to the place where he now resides with his son. This farm is situated on section 4, Battle Creek township, and is devoted to general farming, fruit raising and gardening, a specialty being made of the cultivation of celery.

Unto Mr. and Mrs. Helmer have been born five children: Harriet, the eldest, became the wife of William Graham, who resides in Battle Creek township, but she died leaving a daughter, Iva, who makes her home with her maternal grandparents; Frank was the second of the family and died in childhood; William A., resides with his parents upon the home farm, owning one hundred and forty acres of well improved land in Battle Creek township; Nellie A., is the wife of Vannaten B. Huyler, a resident of Emmett township, and they have two children, Marcia and John; Mattie, the youngest, is the wife of Fred C. Stilson, a resident of Battle Creek, and they have one child, Donald R.

In his political views Mr. Helmer is a Democrat and for six terms served as supervisor, discharging his duties with marked promptness and fidelity. His election was certainly a compliment, because he lives in a strong Republican district, and yet has never been defeated when nominated as a candidate for any political position. He has the high regard and unqualified confidence of his fellow men and is known as a citizen who is deeply interested in public progress and improvement. Mr. Helmer has long since completed the psalmist's span of three score years and ten, being now seventy-six years of age. He is still, however, an active man, and as one of the leading agriculturists and honored pioneers of the county certainly deserves representation in this volume.

STEVEN S. HULBERT.

Steven S. Hulbert has devoted his attention to corporation and railroad law, and in the department of civil practice has gained a distinctively representative clientage. He makes his home in Battle Creek, where he is also financially interested in various manufacturing concerns that have been of marked value in the upbuilding of the city.

A native of New York, Steven S. Hulbert was born in Yonkers, December 8, 1853. His father, Victor M. Hulbert, was born in Massachusetts, educated in Rutgers College and in the Rutgers Theological Seminary, and was then ordained to the ministry of the Reformed church, after which he was called to the pastorate of various churches in the Empire state. He became one of the leading divines of that denomination and was a man of far-reaching influence. His Alma Mater conferred upon him the degree of Doctor of Divinity, and other

honors came to him in connection with his holy calling. He married Miss Jane A. Stilwell, who was descended from French Huguenot ancestors who came to America at a very early period in the colonization of this country.

Steven S. Hulbert acquired his early education in a military school at White Plains, New York, and after preparing for college entered the University of New York, wherein he completed his literary course. Thinking to make the practice of law his life work he began reading the text-books and commentaries with William A. Robertson as his perceptor. However, he spent most of his student days in the office and under the direction of Augustus Schoonmaker, of Kingston, New York, later attorney general of the Empire state and also interstate commerce commissioner under President Cleveland. Mr. Hulbert remained with him until 1876, when he was admitted to practice in the courts of New York, at Saratoga Springs. In November, 1880, he came to Battle Creek, where he located for practice, and soon formed a partnership with Floyd R. Mechem under the firm name of Hulbert & Mechem. This connection was continued for seven years, at the end of which time Mr. Mechem removed to Detroit, whence he afterward went to Ann Arbor, where he is now known as a strong law writer. Later, he formed a partnershp with his brother, George W. Mechem and the second firm of Hulbert & Mechem had a continuous existence until January, 1903, when by mutual consent it was dissolved, that each might practice along lines which he preferred and for which he deemed himself best fitted. Mr. Hulbert does no collection business, has no practice in the justice or criminal courts, and in fact, is solely a civil law practicioner. He is now attorney in charge of considerable territory in southern Michigan for the Michigan Central Railroad Company and his clientage embraces practically nothing save the legal interests of railroads, corporations and estates. His knowledge of civil law in its various branches is comprehensive and he keeps thoroughly in touch with its development and handles very important interests.

Mr. Hulbert is United States commissioner for his district. He has been connected with the establishment and conduct of various important business enterprises of value to the city as well as to the stockholders. He was one of the organizers and incorporators of the Battle Creek Electric Company, which was the first electric company here, and has been its secretary and one of its directors from the beginning, while at the present time he is also the treasurer. This is one of the large industrial concerns of the city, supplying not only light but power to many concerns. Mr. Hulbert was one of the prime movers in organizing The Power Company, limited, and was one of its first directors. He assisted in forming the Compensating Pipe Organ Company, limited, of which he is attorney, and he is also attorney for The National Bank of Battle Creek and chief counsel and attorney for the Battle Creek Sanitarium and other corporations.

On the 23d of December, 1879, was celebrated the marriage of Mr. Hulbert and Miss Ida Van Deusen, Kingston, New York, a representative of one of the old Holland families. They attend and support the Independent Congregational church and Mr. Hulbert has served as Sunday-school superintendent and as one of the trustees of the church. In politics he is a Republican but beyond performing his duty of citizenship by supporting men and measures by his ballot, he takes no active part in political affairs. Socially, he is connected with Athelstan club, of which he has been the president. He is a man of strong intellectuality and broad mental caliber, in whose nature there is nothing narrow nor self-centered. His companionship is select, rather than large, yet the many look up to him and respect him as well as do his more intimate associates. The favorable judgment which the world passed upon him in the early years of his residence here has never been set aside or in any degree modified, but on the contrary has been emphasized as time has gone by and his contemporaries at the bar unite in bearing testimony as to his high character and superior mind.

JULIUS PRATT KING.

Julius P. King, whose residence in Battle Creek covers thirty-five years, was born near Canastota, Madison county, New York, on the 29th of February, 1844, his parents being Elijah and Sabrina (Northup) King. The grandfather, Daniel King, was an old resident of Sangersfield, New York, and the father was there born and spent the days of his boyhood and youth. He was also married there and made the place his home until after the death of his wife. Later he removed to a farm near Canastota, on what was known as the old Mile Strip, where he continued to reside until he retired from business life. Later he came to Michigan. He married Sabrina, a daughter of Brazella Northup, and unto them were born nine children, eight of whom reached years of maturity. The mother died in 1851 and in 1862 the father came to Michigan, spending his remaining days at the home of his daughter, Mrs. Pierce, in Lee, Calhoun county, where he died in 1863.

To the public school system of his native county Julius P. King is indebted for the educational privileges he enjoyed in his youth. After his mother's death he lived at different places in the east and on the outbreak of the Civil war he enlisted in Company I, Fifteenth New York Engineers, in 1863. He had previously tried to enlist, but was not accepted on account of his youth. The second time he ran away and enlisted at Clockville, Madison county. The regiment went into camp at Elmira, New York, and from there proceeded to Fort Federal Hill and later to City Point, Virginia, and on around through Petersburg, being with the Army of the Potomac, at Appomattox, at the time of General Lee's surrender. Mr. King was at City Point when President Lincoln went there to see Grant. During his service he sustained an injury that caused him to remain in the hospital for some time and from which his arm has always suffered, never returning to its normal condition.

In September, 1865, Mr. King received an honorable discharge and then returned to New York, where he remained until his removal to Calhoun county in 1867. He first located between Marshall and Battle Creek and was employed at farm labor until he took up his abode in this city in 1877. For a time he was engaged in handling horses and for two years he conducted a store in Verona, meeting with success in that undertaking. Deciding to make his home in Battle Creek, he

has here served for many years as constable, being first elected in 1886 and chosen at each election since that time except during the period of four years in which he served as deputy sheriff and during a three years' illness, beginning in 1896. In that year he was unable to move himself, while for three years he was incapacitated for any work. In 1899, having partially recovered, he was again elected constable and has now served longer in that capacity than any other man in Battle Creek. He has always been an active Republican and a member of the city, central and executive committees. Political questions are to him matters of deep and vital interest, as they should be to every American citizen, and he loyally supports the principles in which he believes.

In 1872 Mr. King married Miss Antha S. Sprague, of Leroy township, Calhoun county, a daughter of Thomas Sprague, who came to this state in 1835, from New York. Mr. and Mrs. King have a pleasant home at No. 679 Maple street, where they have lived since 1886. They hold membership in the Methodist Episcopal church and he is a member of Farragut post, G. A. R. For twenty-three years he has been a member of Battle Creek lodge. No. 29, I. O. O. F., is a past grand of his lodge and has been representative to the Grand lodge. He is also a member of the encampment, in which he has passed all the chairs, while in the Uniformed Rank, of which he is a charter member, he has served as major general, and at the time he was taken ill he was serving as assistant inspector general of the state. He is thus prominent in Odd Fellow circles as well as in political life, and the judgment which the world passes upon him and his life record is a favorable one.

BENJAMIN FRANKLIN SANDERS.

An esteemed and honored resident of Burlington township, Calhoun county, Benjamin Franklin Sanders was born in Trumbull county, Ohio, May 9, 1835, the descendant of a Vermont family associated with the early history of the country. His father, John Sanders, was born in Orwell, Rutland county, Vermont, July 1, 1803, and being thrown upon his own resources at an early age was unable to attend school in the pursuit of an education. Ambitious to acquire knowledge he spent his evenings in study, after a hard day's labor in field or wood, a perseverance and industry which followed him in all his efforts in later life. In 1824 he came to Ohio, walking six hundred miles, and settled in Trumbull county, where he met and married Susan Davis, a granddaughter of Colonel Stark, who was a brother of John Stark. Mr. Sanders brought his family to Michigan in 1838, purchasing a farm on section 2, Burlington township, Calhoun county, where he remained until his death in 1872. He is interred in Burlington cemetery.

Benjamin F. Sanders remained with his father until he was twenty-two years old, a love of books inducing him to spend his evenings as did his father in years gone by, studying by the light of the open fire. When thirteen years old he began to learn the carpenter's trade, and upon beginning life for himself at twenty-two, worked at his trade in the summer time, while in the winter he worked in the lumber camps. After his marriage in 1861 with Miss Olive Norton he became interested in the real estate of the county, speculating in land for some time, finally purchasing the farm of a hundred acres, upon which he now makes his home. To himself and wife were born a son and daughter, the latter dying at the age of nine years. The son, Kennedy, who is married and lives in Kalamazoo, Michigan, travels for the Mutual Life Insurance Company. Mr. Sanders is independent in politics. He has been elected justice of the peace, being at present an incumbent of the office, which he has held for the past ten years. Many of the young people of the community were married by Mr. Sanders and he has also tried many cases, though he has always preferred that disputes should be settled out of court. In religion he is a member of the Freewill Baptist church, and has always aimed to carry his religion into his daily life, making its principles the foundation for all his actions. He has lived a just and helpful life, the position which he now holds in the esteem of his fellow citizens is the result of faithfulness to every duty which has become his as a resident of the community.

GEORGE CURRAN BENTLEY.

For more than sixty years George Curran Bentley has been a resident of Calhoun county, and has been actively identified with various enterprises of value in the commercial and industrial world. At the present writing he is an extensive farmer and stock-dealer, and in trade circles his name is honored because he has ever been found reliable and trustworthy.

Mr. Bentley was born in Marshall township, December 10, 1842, a son of George W. and Nancy Malama (Chapin) Bentley, who are represented on another page of this work. His birth occurred in one of the pioneer homes of this section of the state, a little log cabin which stood on the second farm that his father ever owned in Calhoun county. He accompanied his parents on their various removals, going from his birthplace to a farm near Ceresco and when ten years of age becoming a resident of Albion. After a few months spent in that city, however, his father removed to Mount Pleasant, Iowa, and three and a half years of his boyhood were passed in the Hawkeye state. On the expiration of that period the family home was established in Marshall, later in Emmett township and subsequently in Battle Creek township. Mr. Bentley, of this review, was reared in the usual manner of farmer boys and early gained practical experience concerning all departments of farm life. While living at Lake Goguac he was married October 2, 1866, in Marshall township, to Miss Sarah Knight, a daughter of Thomas and Ann (Wass) Knight. After returning to Marshall Mr. Bentley purchased the one hundred and sixty acre farm on which he was born. A year later, however, he sold this and he and his father purchased two hundred and forty acres of land, to which Mr. Bentley, of this review, has added from time to time until he now owns six hundred acres of valuable land. Upon that farm he and his family resided for a number of years, and his parents also lived there for twelve years, at the end of which time they returned to Marshall. Mr. Bentley, of this review, however, continued his residence on the old homestead until he took up his abode in Marshall. From this point he superintends his farming interests and is recognized as one of the most extensive agriculturists and stock dealers of his county. He makes a specialty of the breeding of Polled Angus cattle and has the largest as well as the finest herd in this section of the state with a number of registered animals at its head. He also owns the controlling interest in a ranch of two thousand acres located in Iosco county, Michigan, which is devoted to stockraising. In former years Mr. Bentley was quite actively identified with other business interests, especially along industrial lines. He was one of the founders of the Marshall Wagon & Windmill Company, which was incorporated January 1, 1894, with a capital stock of twenty-five thousand dollars. He became one of its first directors and in 1896 was elected its secretary and treasurer, holding the dual position until in connection with his son, Rupert A. Bentley, he purchased the interest of the other stockholders, father and son continuing the business alone until April 9, 1903, when they sold their interests and the plant. Mr. Bentley was likewise one of the organizers of the Marshall Creamery Company, which was formed in 1901, and of which he is still a director. This has become a paying investment.

Unto Mr. and Mrs. Bentley have been born five children: Benjamin Knight, who is married and lives on his father's farm, has three children—Truax, Benjamin and Marie; Jessie Rose is at home; Rupert Ashbel, who studied for some time at the Agricultural College, is now a plumber; Nancy Malana is the wife of Charles Lee Watson, of Telluride, Colorado; Murray Curran is a student in Marshall.

Mr. Bentley was reared in the Republican faith, his father having become a stalwart advocate of the party at its organization. In early manhood he shared his father's political opinions, but absence from home, while attending Eastman's Business

College prevented his voting at the first election. after he attained his majority. In 1868, however, he voted for Grant. He has served as town clerk in Marshall township for one year and has been a member of the county board of supervisors from the third ward of Marshall. He has frequently been a delegate to conventions of his party. His father was a Swedenborgian in religious faith. but Mr. Bentley attends the Episcopal church and contributes to its support. His interests center along lines which tend to promote the welfare. improvement and progress of his city and county. He has advanced various business activities of Marshall. taking a helpful part in many progressive movements and enterprising measures. and is a man of resourceful business abilty. of wide experience and marked energy. whose influence in commercial as well as agricultural circles has contributed to the general prosperity of his native county. His entire life having been passed in southern Michigan. he is widely known and his many good qualities have gained for him favorable regard.

HENRY KOONS BARRICK.

Henry Koons Barrick, a retired farmer, now living at No. 707 North Superior street. in Albion, was born upon a farm in Lyons. Wayne county. New York. March 30, 1815. His parents. John and Catherine (Koons) Barrick, were reared and married in Maryland. but soon after took up their abode in the Empire state. Three children had been born unto them in Maryland. the first in 1800. while the latter was about nine months of age at the time of the

removal to New York in 1804. Little is known concerning the ancestral history of the Barrick family, save that the grandfather was one of three brothers who settled near Fredericksburg, Maryland. His maternal grandfather, Henry Koons, was born in Alsace, and he and another young man were sent to move a family and their effects to the Rhine river that they might take refuge to America. On reaching their destination each young man began to banter the other about going to America with the family, until both finally decided to go, and sent their teams back home. Mr. Koons also settled in Frederick county, Maryland, where he was afterward married, his wife probably coming from Germany. In their family were fourteen children, who reached mature years. Mrs. Barrick being the youngest.

The subject of this review acquired a good common-school education. and he still has in his possession the book from which he solved his problems. After attaining the age of fifteen years. however. he had no further opportunity for attending school. but worked upon his father's farm, where he remained until twenty-four years of age. At that time he was married on the 3d of October, 1839, in the village of Phelps. Ontario county, New York. to Miss Lydia Westfall, who was born on a farm in Phelps township, Ontario county, in 1817, a daughter of George and Mary (Bennett) Westfall. The young couple began their domestic life on her father's farm and after a year removed to a farm of forty acres, in Wayne county. to which Mr. Barrick added until he had ninety-three acres.

In 1875 he sold that property for one hundred and forty dollars per acre, and the following year came to Michigan. residing in Hillsdale for about one year. He then purchased a farm of eighty acres southwest of Albion, adjoining the corporation limits, and took up his abode in the village, his attention, however, being given to the cultivation and improvement of his land.

Unto Mr. and Mrs. Barrick have been born five children: Mary, the eldest, is the widow of Charles Van Inwegen, and resides at Great Falls, Montana, with her three children; Henry was married at Devil's Lake, North Dakota, and has five children; Myron is married and has one child, and Jennie. Mrs. Van Inwegen also had two children that died in early life. The second child died in infancy unnamed; Catharine A. is living with her father; Sarah became the wife of Albert Braden, and died in Albion, leaving two children: Grace, who is the wife of Elmer Ball, of Albion township, and has three children, Lucile, Elton and Carleton; Edith, who died when twenty-three years of age; Helen is the wife of Harvey Geer, of Benton Harbor, Michigan, and has six children. Minnie; Mabel, the wife of Ross Anford; Alice, wife of Ira Hemingway, by whom she has a daughter, Helen Grace, wife of Morris Patton; Florence, who is engaged in teaching school, and Marion.

Mr. Barrick was reared in the faith of the Democratic party and cast his first vote on the second day after attaining his majority, at a township election. In the following fall he voted for Martin Van Buren and has since been a Democrat, but refused to support Horace Greeley. He and his wife are members of the Methodist Episcopal church, of which he is a trustee, and he was also for many years a class-leader. He took a very active part in the work of the Sunday school and all of his children are identified with the same church. He has now passed the eighty-ninth mile-stone on life's journey and his has been an honorable and upright career, in which he has commanded the respect of his fellow men.

WILLIAM RILEY PALMER.

A popular and prominent farmer of Newton township, Calhoun county, is William Riley Palmer, who has been identified with the agricultural interests of this section for many years. He was born in Burlington township, this county, January 1, 1853. His father, William Palmer, a native of Bedfordshire, England, born March 9, 1809, came to America in 1831, and locating near Poughkeepsie, New York, engaged in brick-making. After nine years in that location he removed to Burlington township, Calhoun county, Michigan, with the proceeds of his past industry purchasing a farm of forty acres, after which he engaged in farming as well as working at his old employment. From time to time as he was financially able, he made small purchases of land until he became the owner of one hundred and twenty acres, after 1863 devoting his entire time to the cultivation and improvement of his farm, abandoning his brick-making business on account of declining health. His death occurred March 9, 1874, his last resting place being Adscota cemetery, Burlington township. His wife who died April 1, 1871, and is also buried in Adscota cem-

-etery, was in maidenhood Hannah M. Merritt, a native of Ulster county, New York, where she married Mr. Palmer, with whom she came to Michigan. In his political professions Mr. Palmer was a stanch Democrat.

William R. Palmer was reared upon his father's farm in Burlington township, receiving his education in the Burlington school. He remained with his father until the death of the latter, when he engaged in farming on the old homestead for himself, continuing in that location for two years. He then sold that property and a year later purchased the farm which he now owns in Newton township, and upon which he has since been principally engaged in general farming. March 24, 1875, he was united in marriage with Miss Nettie Cameron, a native of Newton township, whose parents were born in New York state, of Scotch ancestry. The birth of one daughter has blessed this union, Lenna L., born April 3, 1876, and she is now the wife of Marshall Clemmer, of Battle Creek, by whom she has had one son. Politically, Mr. Palmer is a Republican, and through the influence of this party he was elected supervisor of Newton township, now serving his second term. He has also been active in the advancement of educational interests in the community, having served for nine years as a member of the school board. Fraternally, he is associated with the Knights of the Maccabees, and in his religious views he is liberal, not belonging to any church. He is a man of broad principles and helpful characteristics and during his long residence in Calhoun county has made his influence felt in the promotion of the welfare of the community.

STEPHEN MONROE, M. D.

Stephen Munroe, one of the pioneer physicians of Michigan, was born June 28, 1813, at Parma, New York, where his father, Stephen Munroe, had located when that section of the country was a forest into which civilization had hardly penetrated. The doctor's educational privileges were very limited for his mother died when he was but ten years old and at the age of thirteen he started out in life for himself, and from that time was dependent entirely upon his own resources. In 1843 he came to Michigan, settling at Jackson, where he built a furnace which he operated in company with his brother, James Munroe. While thus engaged he began reading medicine with one of the old physicians of Jackson, and later took his degree from the Bellevue Hospital Medical College at New York. Following this the doctor returned to Michigan and began the practice of medicine at Grand Haven, also engaging extensively in the lumber business, through which he succeeded in amassing a comfortable property. The medical practitioner of to-day has few of the hardships which confronted his brethren of half a century ago when there were no railroads, but when the duties of his profession called him long distances over a sparsely settled country, many cases of bravery and self-sacrifice were then shown by the physician, and Dr. Munroe was one of those who did his full share toward alleviating the sufferings of mankind. His was a most sympathetic, kindly, and generous nature, and he came to be the loved family physician in many homes.

In 1872 Dr. Munroe retired from the practice of medicine and removed to Albion, thereafter leading a retired life, but keenly interested in the progress of his country. So great was his interest in the forward march of the world, he often declared that he had lived fifty years too soon. He wanted to stay and watch the strides another quarter of a century would make. Naturaly modest and unassuming the doctor avoided prominence and never accepted office, but his genuine personal worth gained for him the friendship and respect of his fellow men as his professional skill had many times won their gratitude. He was always a liberal supporter of the churches of his own town and his aid was never withheld from any one in need of assistance. His life was characterized by a kindly spirit and good deeds.

In 1855 Dr. Munroe married Miss Orpha Cobb, of Stowe, Vermont. She lived only two years, after which the Doctor's home was presided over by his niece, Miss Sarah Munroe, who afterwards became Mrs. Howlett, and who remained with him until his death. The last few winters of the doctor's life were spent in southern California, where he owned a beautiful home, and where on December 28, 1890, he passed away. His remains were placed in the vault he had built in Albion, but his memory does not rest upon that monument of stone; it is enshrined in the hearts of those who knew him, and revered by his family to whom he was ever as a tender, loving father.

MRS. SARAH C. HOWLETT.

Mrs. Howlett was born at Parma, Monroe county, New York, and when seventeen years of age came to Michigan to live with her uncle, Dr. Stephen Munroe. Since the year 1872 she has been a resident of Albion, where she is well known and respected for her generosity and unassuming charities.

Mrs. Howlett was the first person in Albion to accept the Christian Science religion, the first services of that denomination being held in her home. In 1895 a church was organized, of which she has been the first reader for seven years, her life work being now in this field of labor.

JESSE MONROE HATCH.

Through earnest, honest labor, Jesse M. Hatch has won an enviable position at the bar of Marshall and southern Michigan, and although his privileges in youth were extremely limited and he received no assistance from influential friends and profited by no fortunate combination of circumstances, by the inherent force of his character, an unconquerable determination and most commendable ambition, he has won prominence and success in the arduous and difficult profession of the law.

Mr. Hatch was born on a farm in Lee township, this county, May 27, 1858, a son of James Warren and Juliette (Austin) Hatch. When the son was a lad of twelve years the father purchased a farm of one hundred and sixty acres about two and a half miles from Marshall in the township of Fredonia and soon afterward Jesse M. Hatch entered the public schools of Marshall and completed the high school course with the "Centennial class" of 1876. Subsequently he engaged in farm work through the summer months, while in the winter seasons he followed school teaching. His ambition, however, was not content with that restricted field of labor, and in 1877 he entered upon the study of law in the office of Willis I. Geer, with whom he boarded, and in return took care of Mr. Geer's horses and office. The elemental strength of his character was thus manifest and the evidence which he then gave of a strong, forceful nature, has since been shown throughout his entire career. Nothing daunted by difficulties and obstacles, he matriculated in the law department of the University of Michigan in the fall of 1878 and was graduated in 1880. During that time he boarded himself, doing his own cooking, thus keeping his expenses down to about one hundred dollars per year. After completing the course he continued his studies in the office of Judge Woodruff in order to familiarize himself with the practical workings of the courts and of law practice, as well as to add to his theoretical knowledge.

After a year he opened an office of his own over William Martin's store. Like all young lawyers with a reputation to make, and who have to compete with those already established in business, there were weeks of waiting, but his patronage gradually increased and is now extensive, connecting him with much important litigation. He remained in his first location until 1896, when he built the Hatch block and removed his office there. This is one of the good buildings of the city and brings to him a very desirable rental. The first fee which he won in the circuit court was only twenty-five dollars and this was divided with Joseph Noyes, also a young lawyer at that time, and now a practicing attorney and judge of Los Angeles, California. His first large fee was won in the Johnson will case, transferred from Kalamazoo to this circuit, for which he received one thousand dollars.

Mr. Hatch has twice been elected and served as prosecuting attorney, during which time he tried a number of important cases. He was the prosecutor in the case of Mary Sanderson, who was accused of poisoning her husband; in the case of Joseph Gregory, who had been arrested at least twenty times for burglary, but had never been convicted until Mr. Hatch was prosecuting attorney, when he was sentenced to ten years in the penitentiary; Sly brothers, charged with assault with intent to kill, one receiving fifteen, the other ten years; William Ryan, the most notorious burglar of this section, whose sentence was for seven years; and many others. In the preparation of all his cases he is very painstaking, carefully weighing all the evidence and presenting his points with clearness and in their proportionate value relations.

Mr. Hatch has held other offices, having for two terms been circuit commissioner. He is a Republican, supporting the party since casting his first presidential vote for James A. Garfield.

In Battle Creek, Michigan, October 9, 1885, Mr. Hatch was united in marriage to Miss Ella M. Willard, a daughter of Lovett J. and Lucy (Price) Willard. Her father was one of the organizers of the Advance Thresher Company. Unto Mr. and Mrs. Hatch have been born seven children: Jay Warren, Blaine Willard, Beatrice Augusta, Donald J., Louise, Hortense and Hazen.

In summing up the life work of Mr. Hatch it is a noticeable fact that his native talent has led him out of humble surroundings into success through the opportunity that is the pride of our American life. Nor is his success to be measured by material standards alone, for he has developed that type of character which makes for higher ideals in business and society and in his business relations and dealings he applies the high principles which govern his private life.

CHARLES ELLSWORTH KOLB.

Charles Ellsworth Kolb, residing at No. 31 Garrison avenue, in Battle Creek, is descended from a prominent family of ancient lineage in Germany. Remote generations numbered their representatives who were distinguished citizens and present generations have equal reason to be proud of the honor which is conferred upon the family name by those who now wear it. A cousin of our subject is a judge of the supreme court and others in Germany have attained positions of eminence and leadership. Charles E. Kolb is a descendant in direct line of Henry Kolb, who was born at Homberg, on the river Ohm, in the pricipality fo Upper Hessia. He was a hatter and married Eleanor Lauer, of Haarhausen, near Homberg. Their eldest son, John Frederic Kolb, was born at Homberg, December 6; 1767, and became a well known educator, being at the time of his death a preceptor at Gettenau, county of Vidda, in the principality of Upper Hessia. He also rendered his country military service, being at one time a trumpeter in the Horse-Guards Regiment. He married Anna Elizabeth Volz, who was born December 15, 1778, at Riechen, near Umstadt, in the province of Starkenburg.

29

She was the daughter of John Peter and Elizabeth (Storefelz) Volz, of Klein-Umstadt, near Riechen, and her father was at one time a town councilor. John Frederic Kolb died at Gettenau, August 7, 1832, and his wife departed this life there. January 9, 1831. They were the parents of six sons: Frederic William, grandfather of Charles E. Kolb; John Henry Lewis, born March 31, 1801; John Frederic, born December 1, 1802; Ernest Henry Christian Peter, who was born September 7, 1806, and died in Montgomery, North America, May 12, 1833; John George Philip, who was born February 21, 1810, and died September 5, 1827, when a student in the Schoolteacher's Seminary at Friedberg; and Lewis Henry Christian, born June 3, 1813.

Frederic William Kolb, the eldest son of John and Anna Elizabeth Kolb, was born October 16, 1798, at Bessungun, near Darmstadt, where his father was stationed in military service. He filled the office of chief controller which is equivalent to our state treasurership for a number of years, first serving at Hirschhorn, afterward at Mainz and later at Worms, where he died of consumption, April 17, 1837, when nearly thirty-nine years of age. He was twice married. On the 11th of February, 1825, in Darmstadt, he married Margaretha (Margaret) Louise Engeroff, who was born at Sprendlingen, county of Offenbach, in the province of Starkenburg, November 19, 1802, a daughter of Balthasar Benner and Eleanor Engeroff. She died June 20, 1835, and Frederic William Kolb afterward married Frederica Caroline Christiana Sickenius, the wedding taking place in the church at Zwingenberg, May 1, 1836, while on the 27th of May it was registered at the civil marriage office. She was born at

Zwingenberg in the county of Benheim, province of Starkenburg, February 5, 1799, a daughter of George Lewis and Wilhelmina Ernestine (Meyer) Sickenius. Her father was a paymaster in the army. Mrs. Kolb died in her native town April 14, 1839.

The seven children of Frederic William Kolb were all born of his first marriage, but his early death brought to his widow the care of his three youngest children, who were then hardly beyond infancy. Frederic William Albrecht Ludwig Dominicus Kolb, the third child, was born August 4, 1828, at Hammelsbach, Hesse-Darmstadt, and was given the Christian names of his sponsors, as was the custom in those days, but in this country he went by the name of William Albert Kolb. He was only about seven years of age at the time of his mother's death and a lad of nine when left an orphan. He was then reared by a lady who is still living in Germany and has attained the age of more than ninety years. His home was then in the little village of Zwingenberg, a few miles south of Darmstadt, where he lived until eighteen years of age and in the meantime acquired a good common school education. Although he had been left an estate he served a regular apprenticeship to the wagon-making trade and when he had completed his term he came to America, spending seventy-six days on the ocean voyage, which was made in 1846. After being employed for a time at his trade in Brooklyn, New York, he removed to Rochester, that state, where he spent about two years, when he came to Michigan and was employed as a journeyman in Lansing. He continued in the latter city from 1850 until 1852 and then came to Battle Creek, where

he entered the service of Elijah Clapp, and later formed a partnership for the purpose of manufacturing vehicles with his brother-in-law, Jeremiah Rall. After about a year spent in conducting this business Mr. Kolb entered the employ of Nichols & Shepard, with whom he continued for more than a quarter of a century or until he was about sixty-eight years of age.

Not long after his arrival in Battle Creek William Albert Kolb was married in this city, July 2, 1853, to Miss Sarah Euphemia Rall, who was born in Monroe county, New York, April 25, 1836, a daughter of John and Olive Jane (Young) Rall. Her father was the son of James Rall, who came to Michigan from New York during the pioneer epoch in the history of the former state and owned a farm between Battle Creek and Marshall. He was born in New Jersey in 1756 and died in 1859, at the very advanced age of one hundred and three years, but through some mistake the age of eighty-nine was engraven on his tombstone. He served his country as a soldier of the War of 1812. John Rall was a farmer and blacksmith, and on coming to the west located in Flint, Michigan. Mrs. Kolb was at that time about seventeen or eighteen years of age. She had previously formed the acquaintance of Mr. Kolb in Rochester, New York, and at the time of her marriage she was living with her brother in Pennfield township, Calhoun county. For about a year after their marriage Mr. and Mrs. William A. Kolb lived on Frelinghuysen avenue, Battle Creek, with Enos Smith, and then purchased a home at No. 76 Harvard street, where they remained many years. It was there their children, six in number, were born and reared. Augusta, the eldest, the widow of

Alanson Van Winkle, resides on Upton avenue, Battle Creek. Emma is the wife of Henry Wickham, living at No. 14 Chandler street; George Frederic is also living in Battle Creek. Charles E. is the next in order of birth. Mina L. is the wife of Dr. Arthur MacNeal, a practitioner of Berwyn, a suburb of Chicago, Illinois; and James Merrill married Etta Satterlee and lives at East Palermo, Oswego county, New York.

William A. Kolb, the father of this family, did not take out naturalization papers until 1862 and his son, Charles, now has these in his possession. After he became an American citizen he gave his political support to the Republican party, but was never an office seeker. He was reared in the Protestant faith but did not identify himself with any church. He became, however, a member of Battle Creek lodge, No. 12, F. & A. M. and after thirty-seven years connection with the fraternity, he was laid to rest with Masonic honors, passing away December 18, 1902. His widow still survives him.

Charles Ellsworth Kolb, their fourth child, was born at the family home at 76 Harvard street, Battle Creek, November 25, 1864, and spent his boyhood days in his native city attending the public schools until about seventeen years of age. He started out in life as a call boy with the Chicago Grand Trunk Railroad Company, his duty being to go to the homes of the engineers and call them to make their runs. He was afterward employed in the shops of Nichols & Shepard for a few months and then went to Toledo, Ohio, where for two years he worked in a general machine chop owned and conducted by Smith & Haldeman, doing machinist's

work at the lathe. While in the employ of that firm he learned stenography unaided by a teacher and obtained practice in reporting by taking down sermons or other public addresses. On the 25th of October, 1885, he entered upon the position of stenographer in the office of the Advance Thresher Company and while there he also studied bookkeeping. For about fourteen years he remained with that corporation as stenographer and bookkeeper at first, and afterward as traveling salesman and collector. He was then promoted to the position of manager of the collecting department for the United States and was also made general agent for Michigan and Ohio. Later he became credit manager, acting in that capacity until his health failed. He had started with the company at the modest salary of one dollar per day, but his worth found ready recognition and each promotion gave him greater opportunity for usefulness and for the acquirement of practical business knowledge. He resigned in April, 1899, but in the meantime had acquired an interest in the Peerless Portland Cement Company, of Union City, Michigan, and became its treasurer as well as a director. In 1898 he had become interested in a sawmill and in connection with his other duties he found he had to become the purchasing agent and would go to the woods and estimate and buy the timber. He took a million feet of lumber from the tree and sold it all as lumber in five months. At the same time he was performing important service with the Advance Thresher Company and as a director and the treasurer of the Peerless Portland Cement Company his duties and responsibilities became so great, however, that his health failed and he was obliged to retire from the electrical world of trade for a time. He went to Pennfield township and one mile north of Verona purchased one hundred and sixty acres of land, on which he erected a fine country home and also many other modern buildings. There he remained during his period of recuperation.

Later he again entered the business field, in which he had been such a forceful factor, so directing his labors that in each transition stage of his business career he has found new incentive for effort and great opportunity for accomplishment, his career being marked by steady and consecutive progress. In 1902 he became one of the organizers of the Advance Pump and Compressor Company, with a subscribed capital of one hundred and fifty thousand dollars. He built the plant, installed the machinery, prepared everything ready for the beginning of active operation, and since the organization has been one of the directors and was the first treasurer of the company.

In the meantime he had become financially interested in other enterprises and has been active in the management of most of them. In 1900 he bought stock in the H. B. Sherman Manufacturing Company and at its recapitalization he purchased a one-fifth interest and became a director and the vice president. In 1900 Mr. Kolb purchased stock in the Union Steam Pump Company and served as a director for one year, but later sold his interest. He was one of the original stockholders in the Citizens' Electric Light Company.

Mr. Kolb was married at Lacey, Barry county, Michigan, April 3, 1889, to Miss Olive S. Clark, who was born at Maple Grove, Barry county, a daughter of Norman E. and Elizabeth (Hill) Clark. Her father was born in the state of New York and her mother in England. Mrs. Kolb lived in Barry county until about fifteen years of age when she came to Battle Creek to attend school. She was graduated from the high school in 1882 and the following year began teaching in the district schools. Later she became a teacher in the public schools of Battle Creek and during that time became acquainted with Mr. Kolb. Five children have been born of their marriage: Mildred, Louise, Helen, Norman and Marian. Mr. and Mrs. Kolb have in their home a small mahogany table which was in possession of the Rall family in colonial times and which came to him through his mother. He also has a cut glass wine glass which his grandfather owned and which was received by him as an heirloom from his father. On one of the medallions is cut the name of Frederic William Kolb and on the others are views of places in Germany—a church, a bridge, a bedroom window and other scenes—six familiar scenes of his old home. His most cherished heirloom, however, is the old family Bible, which came to him through the terms of his grandfather's will, and the ownership of which carries with it the obligation to collect data to finish out the family record begun by its original owner.

In January, 1903, Mr. Kolb became a member of Battle Creek lodge, No. 12, F. & A. M., but otherwise has no fraternal relations. From early boyhood his attention has been largely claimed by busy duties. Although he started out amid humble surroundings he has achieved success through the avenue of opportunity which is the pride of our American life. He has wrought along lines of modern business enterprise and has accomplished his object because of well laid plans, carefully executed, of business obligations promptly met, and of honorable purpose and laudable endeavor.

JAMES M. FRENCH.

Well known in agricultural, business and political circles James M. French has been a dominant factor in the general advancement of Calhoun county. He was born in Broome county, New York, December 29, 1837, the fourth in a family of eight children born to his parents, Thomas A. and Polly S. (Temple) French, both of whom were natives of Massachusetts, born respectively in 1808 and Steptember 9, 1809. Of the four sons and four daughters, those besides our subject were as follows: Nancy, who died when she was twelve years old; Mary Ann, who died when twenty-one years old; Rebecca J., deceased, who married James S. Hudson and became the mother of four sons and four daughters; Martin D., who married Belle Cole in 1863; Dallas A., who married Ida Loomis; Nancy A., who married William Cowles, of Burlington township; and Sidney, who died at the age of nine years. Both parents had become residents of New York state in childhood, their home remaining there for some years after marriage, when the father brought his family to Michigan. He settled upon a farm three miles northwest of the village of Burlington, where his death occurred in 1848. The cares and responsibilities of the family thus devolved upon the mother, by the courage with which she took up the burdens and her efficiency in conducting the affairs of the farm proving herself a woman of exceptional character. She successfully maintained her home, keeping her children with her until they were of sufficient age to meet the responsibilities of life. Her death occurred March 1, 1896.

James M. French was but six years of age when he removed with his parents to this state and county, where the greater part of his life has since been spent. Until he was twenty-one he remained at home, working for his mother. In 1860 he decided to emigrate to California, taking with him his wife, formerly Miss Catharine C. Osborne, of Calhoun county, Michigan, and their one child, on the overland trip. After five years in the west he returned to Michigan with his family, purchasing the old homestead, where he made his home for a brief time, when he sold out and locating in Burlington, became the owner of a hotel. This he conducted successfully for some time, when he traded it for a farm upon which he lived for two years. Returning to Burlington he engaged in the mercantile business, continuing in the same until 1873, when this interest was traded for a farm in Tekonsha township. In the same year he disposed of this property and again located in Burlington, engaging as a stock dealer. He was appointed deputy sheriff, serving from 1872 to 1882, in which service he made many arrests, traveling throughout Indiana, Illinois and Ohio in search of criminals. He had charge of the jury which convicted of murder a man named Hardy, the oldest prisoner now in Jackson penitentiary. His political recognition did not terminate with his office of deputy sheriff, for he also represented the people's interests efficiently as township treasurer for one term. A man of recognized ability, and careful, conservative business methods he was chosen by the people as a trustee of the village and also acted as president.

To Mr. and Mrs. French were born the following children: William C., who married Elizabeth Gall, of Detroit, in which city they now reside; Eddie, the second child, died at the age of three months; Celia A., who married Charles F. Rickett, of Marshall; Frank M., who married Margaret McPherson, of Eckford, Michigan, their home now being in Marshall; Schuyler C., who married Winnie Miller, of Marshall, in which city they now reside; and Lois E., who married George E. Killborne, of Sherwood, Branch county, their home now being in Sherwood township. Mr. French is a Master Mason and a member of the Ancient Order of United Workmen. On his farm of one hundred and forty acres, having purchased a hundred acres in 1882 and added the remainder at a later date, he is engaged in a successful agricultural line, still giving of a broad and earnest character to the upbuilding of public interests.

HENRY R. RANDALL.

Prominent among the agriculturists of Eckford township is numbered Henry R. Randall, who has found in the business conditions of the new world the opportunities which he sought for advancement. Realizing that there is no excellence without labor, and not afraid of hard work, he came to America with the hope of bettering his financial condition and has through unremitting energy steadily advanced toward the goal of prosperity. He was born in Kent, England, his parents being John and Sarah (Longhurst) Randall, of the parish of Hoo. He continued under the parental roof until fourteen years of age, when desiring to earn his own living he ran away from home and secured employment on a farm where he remained for three years. During the succeeding two years he worked elsewhere as a farm hand and then became a wagoner, being thus employed for three years.

Mr. Randall was married at the age of twenty-three years, in 1847, to Miss Matilda Elizabeth Tadman, a native of Kent, England, and after his marriage he continued to work as a wagoner until May 3, 1855, when he took passage on a westward bound sailing vessel that left the port of London for New York. The voyage covered six weeks and the ship encountered some very severe storms. He was accompanied by his wife and two children and on the 15th of June, 1855, he landed in the American metropolis. At once, however, he came to the Mississippi valley and established his home in Eckford township, where his wife's people were living. For three years he worked by the day and month as a farm hand and then for four years operated a farm for a gentleman who lived in Marshall. He afterward engaged in farming on shares for two years and on the 15th of March, 1864, he took up his abode upon his present farm, it having been his home continuously since, covering a period of four decades. He purchased this property then comprising a tract of eighty acres, but he afterward extended its boundary and now a valuable tract of land of one hundred and forty-two acres yields to him a golden tribute for the care and labor he bestows upon it. Only about fifteen acres of the land was cleared at the time he made the purchase, but he prepared the remainder for the plow, placed it under cultivation and has continued his farm labors with excellent success, becoming one of the prosperous agriculturists and stockraisers of his community. He is a typical representative of the Anglo-Saxon race, possessing many of the dominant traits of the people whose rule is becoming so universal.

In 1893 Mr. Randall was called upon to mourn the loss of his wife who died on the 29th of September of that year. She was born June 27, 1826, and thus passed away at the advanced age of sixty-six years. They had become the parents of six children, of whom five are now living. Matilda married Henry Aurand and with their five children—Effie, Pearl, Ethel, Fay and Nina—they make their home in Tekonsha township. Edward is represented on another page of this volume. James, who resides in Girard, Branch county, this state, married Miss Mary Hindbauch, and they have five children, John, Floyd, William, Hattie and Chauncey. Mary, the fourth member of the family, makes her home with her father. John married Miss Clara Stimetz, by whom he has two children, Edward and Hazel, and they make their home in East Litchfield, Hillsdale county, Michigan. Mr. Randall also has five great-grandchildren.

In his political views Henry R. Randall is independent, supporting the men whom he thinks best qualified for office regardless of party affiliation. While in his native country he held membership with the Church of England, and he now attends the Episcopal church at Marshall. One of the dominant characteristics of this land is the opportunity it affords to all men for advancement and the winning of success, and the life record of Henry R. Randall is another proof of the advantage that may be gained in a country unhampered by caste or class. He has steadily made progress along substantial lines and is now one of the representative and well-to-do farmers of Eckford township.

EDWARD THOMAS RANDALL.

Edward Thomas Randall, who is now engaged in farming in Eckford township, where he owns an excellent farm of one hundred and twenty acres, which has been acquired entirely through his own labor, industry and careful management, was born in Kent, England, on the 3d of May, 1853, and is a son of Henry R. and Matilda Elizabeth (Tadman) Randall. In his early boyhood he accompanied his parents to America, pursued a public-school education in this country and at the age of eighteen years started out in life on his own account. He has since been dependent entirely upon his own resources and everything he possesses he has earned through his own labor, and therefore deserves great credit for what he has achieved.

In the year 1877 Mr. Randall sought and won a companion and helpmate for life's journey, being united in marriage to Miss Amanda Decker, a daughter of Simon Decker. They have one daughter, Carrie Elizabeth, who is a graduate of the Albion high school with the class of 1899. Mr. and Mrs. Randall began their domestic life upon a rented farm and he continued to thus carry on agricultural pursuits until 1891, when, with the capital he had saved he purchased eighty acres of land in Eckford township. Taking up his abode upon his own farm he has since devoted his energies with untiring persistency to its cultivation and improvement and he has since extended its boundaries by the additional purchase of forty acres. He is engaged in general farming and stock-raising, making a specialty of the raising of horses and hogs and his wife is interested in the raising of poultry. Good grades of live stock are kept upon the farm and everything about the place indicates the careful supervision of a progressive owner who, in his methods of work, is practical and enterprising.

Both Mr. and Mrs. Randall are members of the Methodist Episcopal church at East Eckford, are deeply interested in its work and co-operate in many of the church activities. He is serving as one of the church stewards and has also been superintendent of the Sunday-school. The cause of education finds in him a warm friend and for nine years he did effective service in behalf of the schools as one of the directors. His political allegiance is given to the Republican party and he served as assessor at Wilderville and also in the district in which he now lives. He is well liked in his community because of his progressive ideas relative to everything pertaining to the county's welfare, also because of his honorable business methods and the possession of the many sterling traits of character which win friendships.

SILAS DECKER.

A farmer of Eckford township, Calhoun county, Michigan, Silas Decker was born in Union county, Pennsylvania, February 15, 1852, one of a family of four children born to his parents, two of whom died in infancy, the other who survived being Amanda, who became the wife of E. T. Randall. The parents, Simon and Mary Ann (Reitz) Decker, were both natives of Union county, the birth of the former occurring June 6, 1825. He was the son of Peter Decker, also of Pennsylvania, whose father was a German emigrant. Peter Decker was a farmer who spent his entire life in Pennsylvania and there his death occurred. He trained his son Simon to the duties of a farmer and the latter after renting property in Pennsylvania for some time, drove to Seneca county, Ohio, there renting land for six years, coming in 1862 to Michigan, traveling in the same manner to his western destination. The first three years were spent in Branch county where he purchased a farm of one hundred and eight acres and improved and cultivated the same, coming, in 1865, to Calhoun county, settling upon a farm of eighty acres of improved land. The death of the mother occurred March 26, 1889, and she is buried in West Eckford cemetery. Both Mr. and Mrs. Decker were members of the Reformed Dutch church. Mr. Decker is a man thoroughly educated in the language of his forefathers, speaking, reading and writing German fluently. He started in life with only his own ambition as a promise for the future, and before he ceased from active labor was numbered among the successful farmers of the community. In his political preferment he was a Democrat. His death occurred November 3, 1903, at the home of his son.

Silas Decker received his education in the district schools of Ohio and Michigan, at the age of nine years removing with his parents to the latter state, his duty on the journey being to drive the cows. With no incentive beyond his own ambition he fitted himself for teaching by home study, after which he taught in Calhoun county for eleven winters. Until 1884 he lived with his parents when he went on to a farm of ninety-two and three-fourths acres of improved land, since which time he has erected all the buildings which now add value to the property. He has also added forty acres to the original number, devoting the land to general farming and stockraising and at the same time conducting his father's farm.

The marriage of Mr. Decker occurred March 26, 1879, and united him with Miss Emma Bender, who was born in Ceresco, Calhoun county, a daughter of William and Susan (Lehr) Bender, the former of whom is now deceased. They were both natives of Northampton county, Pennsylvania, and came to Calhoun county in 1862. settling in Marengo township, where he engaged in farming. His death occurred in 1881. To Mr. and Mrs. Decker have been born two children namely: Lewis Jefferson and Susan Emily. The former received his education in the district school and Marshall high school, after which he became a student in a commercial college of Detroit. He married, December 9, 1903, Miss Irene Fish, of Marengo township, Calhoun county; while the latter was educated in the district school. Both are members of the paternal home. Mr. Decker and his wife are both members of the Methodist Episcopal church. Politically, Mr. Decker is independent, reserving the right to cast his ballot for the man best qualified for the position. Though always active in public support and endorsement of public measures Mr. Decker has never allowed his name to come up for official recognition. As a

citizen much interested in educational work he has served as county superintendent of schools. Mr. Decker is appreciated for the many qualities which have distinguished his life in its every day affairs—a broad minded, public spirited man in every way and one upon whom a community may safely rely for its substantial element.

PETER CROSBY.

The world passed favorable judgment upon the life history of Peter Crosby, for there were many elements in his character that commanded for him universal confidence and esteem. The place which he occupied in the regard of those with whom he came in contact was a tribute to that genuine worth and true nobleness of character which are everywhere recognized and honored. His business methods were above question and over all his trade transactions there fell no shadow of wrong or suspicion of evil. He was always fair and just and his prosperity came as a natural consequence of industry and application, his success bearing testimony to his rare judgment in business affairs.

Peter Crosby was born near Bath, Steuben county, New York, April 10, 1823, a son of Anthony and Ruby (Potter) Crosby. His parents died when he was quite young and he was thrown upon his own resources at the early age of ten or twelve years. It was a serious task for the boy to face the world dependent upon his own labor for a living, but the elemental strength of his character was brought out and developed and, making the most of his opportunities, he gained the good will and confidence of all with whom he was associated. He managed to obtain a good common-school education by working on a farm for his board during the winter months and attending the district schools. When eighteen years of age, in company with his brother, Randall Crosby, he came to Battle Creek, arriving here in 1841. He purchased what is now known as the Vail Fuller place, a farm of one hundred and forty acres. As he had no money he had to go in debt for this property, but with characteristic energy and strong resolution he began to clear the land, cutting away the timber and making the fields ready for cultivation. Soon crops were planted and in due course of time rich harvests were garnered. As he found opportunity he erected good buildings upon his place. The money for this work was obtained by working for others and whenever he could secure a few hours for himself he devoted these to the care and cultivation of his own property. Thus, year by year, he added to his capital and applied what he earned to pay off the indebtedness upon his place. He also erected a good home, in which he lived until 1865.

On the 4th of July, 1851, Mr. Crosby was united in marriage to Miss Mary J. Webster, a daughter of William and Malinda (Jones) Webster, both natives of the Empire state, the latter born in Fredonia. Prior to their marriage, however, both became residents of Ohio, living near Findlay. In that locality Mr. Webster followed his trade of carpentering and joining and it was during the family residence there that Mrs. Crosby was born. About 1840 Mr. Webster brought his family to Michigan, settling at what is now Charlotte. There he purchased a farm upon which a part of the present site of Charlotte is built. He also had another farm about three miles away, but desired to live near the town in order that his children might have good educational privileges. In his youth he had learned to set type and he assisted in setting the type on the first paper ever published in Charlotte, a journal edited in behalf of the Whig party. Mr. Webster was not long permitted to enjoy his new home, however, for he was accidentally killed by the falling of a tree on the 1st of April, 1843. His widow afterward sold a part of the property and removed to Branch county, Michigan, where Mrs. Crosby spent her girlhood days. She was to her family a devoted mother and she lived to see her daughter happily married and to find with her in her declining days a pleasant home. She passed away at the residence of Mrs. Crosby, March 6, 1883.

Unto Mr. and Mrs. Crosby were born three children, Julius E., the eldest, is now residing in Emmett township. The second son is Will A. Crosby, a practicing attorney of this city. The daughter, Belle A., is the wife of Judge Joel C. Hopkins, who is now serving on the circuit bench of this district.

After leaving his farm and removing to Battle Creek Mr. Crosby became the owner of a number of farms, judiciously investing his money in real estate, in fact, he was one of the extensive land owners in this vicinity, having several valuable tracts. In his purchases and sales of land he realized good returns, for he was a man of excellent business judgment and quick to recognize a good opportunity for investment. In Battle Creek he purchased a pleasant home at No. 400 Lake avenue, in which he lived throughout his remaining days and in which Mrs. Crosby still makes her home. In 1894 he suffered from a paralytic stroke and for six years thereafter was an invalid. His death occurred January 15, 1901, and his loss was deeply deplored throughout the entire community. He had begun life an orphan boy with no capital, but he was industrious and determined. He realized, too, the power of honesty, as well as energy in the affairs of life and throughout his entire business career there was no word of censure uttered against the methods which he employed to gain a living. In fact his example is well worthy of emulation. While not a member of any church he was very liberal in his contributions to religious bodies. When the Salvation Army was organized here he built the Mission or what is now known as the Crosby block on Jefferson street, south, giving to the army the use of the building, rent free for five years. He also gave the land on which the Baptist chapel on Lake avenue was built. He had great sympathy for the frailties of his fellow men and broad charity. He was always anxious and willing to help and encourage those who were making an effort to follow an upright course. There was certainly more Christianity manifested in his career than is often shown by those who utter loud professions. His social, kindly nature endeared him to many friends, and though he has passed away his memory is yet cherished by many with whom he came in contact. He left his impress for good upon the county in which he settled in pioneer times and his name should be inscribed high on the roll of honored pioneers.

JULIUS E. CROSBY.

Julius E. Crosby, who is engaged in general farming and stockraising, was born in Battle Creek township, February 28, 1853, and now makes his home in Emmett township. He is a son of Peter and Mary Jane (Webster) Crosby. He began his education in the district schools near his boyhood's home and at the age of ten years accompanied his parents on their removal to Battle Creek, where he completed his literary education, attending school No. 1 until eighteen years of age. He next became a student in Bell's Commercial College of Battle Creek and on leaving that institution engaged in farming for a short time. Subsequently he went to northern Michigan, where he was engaged in the lumber business as a tallier and shipper, spending ten years in that portion of the state. On the expiration of that period he returned to Battle Creek and settled upon the farm which he now owns, comprising two hundred and seventy-eight acres of rich and arable land in Emmett township. He has remodeled the buildings and has developed an excellent property, constituting one of the best farms of the neighborhood.

In 1875 Julius Edward Crosby was united in marriage to Miss Ida M. Lang, of Greenville, Michigan, and they now have one child, Hazel Belle. They hold membership in the First Methodist Episcopal church at Battle Creek and are interested in its success and welfare. Mr. Crosby gives his political allegiance to the Republican party and at one time was treasurer of the village of Leroy, Osceola county, Michigan, for two terms. He was also justice of the peace during the years 1893 to 1897. In 1896 he was elected supervisor of Emmett township on the Republican ticket, serving one term, and in 1902 was elected and again in 1903 and is now the incumbent of that position, discharging his duties with promptness, fidelity and strict impartiality.

JOHN F. COOL.

John F. Cool, now deceased, was born in Warren county, New York, in 1816, and died in Calhoun county, Michigan, in 1863. He is yet remembered by many of the early citizens of this county, for he was a worthy resident, living a life of industry and integrity. His boyhood days were spent in the east and there he was married in 1845 to Miss Sarah Snover, who was born in New Jersey and was a daughter of Samuel and Deliah (Brugler) Snover. About the year 1854, Mr. Cool came to Michigan with his wife and four children, desiring to improve his financial condition by taking advantage of the business opportunities in the new and growing west. He located on section 12, Albion township, Calhoun county, where he purchased two hundred and four acres of raw and unimproved land. A brick house was in process of erection on the place, but otherwise there were no improvements. Mr. Cool at once began to develop his farm and completed the house, carrying on the work of cultivation for many years with excellent success. In course of time his fields yielded to him rich harvests and as the result of his untiring labor and energy he transformed his wild land into one of the best farms in this part of the state. He continued to make his home thereon until his demise, and erected one of the finest residences in this part of the county. After his death, his sons added good substantial barns and outbuildings, and all modern equipments.

Unto Mr. and Mrs. Cool were born seven children. Samuel S., the eldest, is a crockery salesman, residing in Huron, South Dakota. He wedded Miss Elizabeth Miller, of Albion, Michigan, a daughter of George Miller, and they have three children, John, George and Catherine; DeWitt Wilson, the second son, died at the age of seven years; Crittenden Clinton, a farmer of Albion township, where he has a valuable tract of land and a fine home, married Miss Lydia Ackley, and they have one child, Leventia; John Austin died at the age of two years; Leonard D., who is also a landowner of Albion township, married Miss Georgia Kanoff, and they have three children, Ada, Edith and Charlotte; Warren Jay, who resides on the home farm and has a fine residence of his own just across the driveway from his mother's home, married Miss Kate Warner; Leventia is the wife of Charles Welch and they have a daughter, Mildred Iona, who is a student in the public schools of Albion. Mrs. Welch and her daughter reside with her mother.

Mrs. Cool is a very pleasant lady, kindly and hospitable, and she has the happy faculty of making her guests always feel at home, so that the Cool farm is a favorite resort of her many friends. She is a member of the Presbyterian church to which Mr. Cool also belonged, his life being in consistent harmony with its principles. He was a very successful man in his business affairs, and his course was ever characterized by untiring labor and perseverance, coupled with unfaltering honesty. He, therefore, won the esteem of all who knew him and when he was laid to rest in Riverside cemetery at Albion, where a beautiful stone marks his grave, his many friends throughout the community felt the deepest regret. He left to his family, however, the record of an honorable life and an untarnished name.

JOHN H. MASTON.

As a prominent and influential citizen of Homer, Calhoun county, Michigan, John H. Maston is numbered among the representative men of his community. He was born in Ontario county, New York, June 14, 1836, and is a son of John D. and Diadama Maston, who removed to Michigan in 1847 and located at Grass Lake, Jackson county, where they made their home for thirty-two years. In 1879 they removed to Homer, Calhoun county, where the death of each occurred, and they are both interred in Hickory Grove cemetery, Grass Lake. They were the parents of ten children, of whom seven were sons, two serving in the Civil war, namely: Mortimer, of Company C, First Michigan Engineers, and Manson G., a boy scarcely sixteen years old, who went out in the Seventeenth Michigan, and was taken prisoner at Knoxville, Tennessee, and placed on Belle Island, where his death occurred.

John H. Maston was reared in the paternal home at Grass Lake, receiving his education in the academy of that name. On leaving his studies he taught for one year, after which he entered the employ of the Michigan Central Railroad, in 1856, beginning as a clerk and two years later becoming the head of the department of freight accountants, which position he maintained for ten years. He then resigned to accept the position of division superintendent on the south division of the Louisville, New Albany & Chicago Railroad, remaining, however, but a short time before he became identified with the company that opened up the block coal mines in Clay, Indiana, this company shipping the first block coal ever sent from that locality to Chicago. In 1873, during the great financial panic, this company met with such losses that it was compelled to cease business operations, but was afterward reorganized by a number of its old stockholders. Mr. Maston, at that time, was worth twenty thousand dollars, but was only able to realize about seven thousand, with which he went to Mt. Pulaski, Illinois, where he engaged in the grain business, becoming the owner of a large elevator and conducting an extensive business. He remained so employed until 1878, when he again entered the employ of the Michigan Central Railroad as general car agent with headquarters at Detroit, continuing until 1891, when he resigned and removed to Homer, his present location, his only business interests at the present time being the management of a valuable farm of one hundred and seventy acres, a large part of which is located in the corporation and is devoted to general farming.

The marriage of Mr. Matson, which occurred in 1885, united him with Miss Charlotte Churchill. She was a daughter of Henry and Lydia Churchill, who came to Michigan about 1840, the father becoming an extensive land owner, and also engaging extensively in sheep-raising. He was one of the prominent and influential men of the times. Mr. Maston, in his political preferment, is a Silver Democrat, and in the interests of this party he has held various offices in the community, being a member of the village council of Homer from 1892 to 1896, inclusive, the last three years of that time acting as president of the village. Religiously, both himself and wife are members of the Episcopal church, in which Mr. Maston has officiated for a number of years as senior warden. Mr. Maston has made a success of his life, when viewed either in the light of financial or moral worth, for his fortune has been built upon strong moral principles and unswerving integrity, and it is for these qualities that he is honored among his fellow townsmen.

JAMES O. VAN ZANDT.

James O. Van Zandt, one of Marshall's enterprising young men who is capably filling the position of superintendent of Oakridge cemetery, was born April 24, 1868, in the city which is still his home, his parents being Bornt and Emily (Wagner) Van Zandt. The father was born in New York and in his boyhood days accompanied his mother to Marshall, Michigan, where she continued to make her home until her death, her remains now resting in Oakridge cemetery. Bornt Van Zandt married Emily Wagner, who was born in Michigan, and was a daughter of James and Sarah (Peck) Wagner. Her father was a native of Canada and in that country was left an orphan when seven years of age. He afterward went to the state of New York, where he was married and in 1832 came to Calhoun county, Michigan, settling six miles northeast of Marshall in Marengo township, where he spent his remaining days. He took up two hundred acres of land from the government, which he placed under cultivation and was accounted one of the enterprising and progressive farmers of his locality. Both he and his wife died on the old family homestead and lie buried in Johnston cemetery of Marengo township. The mother of our

subject died August 23, 1901, and her remains were interred in Oakridge cemetery at Marshall. Mr. B. Van Zandt served his country as a soldier of the Civil war, enlisting in a Michigan regiment, with which he did active and effective aid for the cause of the Union. He is a member of Colegrove Post, G. A. R., of Marshall, and was a valued and enterprising citizen of his locality.

James O. Van Zandt is the youngest of four children and is a native son of Marshall, who has risen from a humble position in the business world through hard and conscientious labor. As a lad he attended school in his native town and entered upon his business career as an employee in the Bullard factory, becoming connected with the woodworking department, where he was employed until March, 1898, when he accepted the position of superintendent of Oakridge, the beautiful cemetery at Marshall. Under his careful supervision and management this has become one of the most lovely cities of the dead to be found in the state of Michigan. The cemetery comprises fifty-six acres and the first burial was made therein on the 26th of June, 1839. Mr. Van Zandt is continually studying to improve the appearance of the cemetery and he spares no labor in this direction. He employs six men all of the time in keeping it in good condition and he certainly deserves much credit for what he has accomplished in this direction.

On February 13th, 1889, occurred the marriage of James O. Van Zandt and Miss Ella Boyer, of Auburn, New York. They have three sons: Earl, Lynn and Clay. Mr. Van Zandt is a member of the Masonic lodge at Marshall in which he is now serving as senior warden, also a Knight Templar. He also belongs to the Knights of Pythias fraternity and is one of the charter members of the Modern Wooden of America Camp, of which he is now venerable consul. He belongs to the American Association of Cemetery Superintendents and in his political affiliation is a Democrat. His life has been one of untiring activity and his persistent energy and labors have been the means of bringing to him merited success.

GEORGE DOOLITTLE.

The elements of success are not hard to seek. There is no secret path by which one must reach the goal of prosperity, for the road is open to all; and it depends upon persistency of purpose, persevering effort and strong determination whether the individual shall accomplish the task that he sets out to perform. Mr. Doolittle, in an active business career, has made for himself a place among the substantial citizens of Calhoun county and is now living in Albion township, where he has valuable and desirable farming interests. He was born in Delhi, Delaware county, New York, on the 28th of May, 1828, and is, therefore, about seventy-five years of age. His parents were Benjamin and Betsey (Stuart) Doolittle, the latter a daughter of James Stuart, who was a captain of the Revolutionary war, serving with a New York regiment. Benjamin Doolittle was born in Connecticut and in the year 1836 he brought his family to Calhoun county, Michigan, driving from his home in New York to Buffalo, thence proceeding by boat to Detroit and from the latter city driving across the country to Calhoun county. He settled first in Clarendon township. On going from Homer the wagon became stuck in the mud and he had to hitch a yoke of cattle to his team in order to draw them out. They were at that time within two miles of their destination. In June, 1836, Mr. Doolittle purchased one hundred and sixty acres of land from a man who had just located in this locality. It was an oak opening, no improvements having been made and he hired the man of whom he had made the purchase to clear twenty acres of the land and put up a log house. Upon that farm Mr. Doolittle resided until his death and placed it under a good state of cultivation. He was a man of marked activity and energy in business affairs, and as his financial resources increased he made judicious investments of his capital until he was the owner of nearly four hundred acres of fine farm land, some of which was in a swampy condition when it came into his possession, but which through his efforts was transformed into a productive tract. In politics he was an old line Whig, and in matters of citizenship he took a deep interest, co-operating in many movements for the early development and progress of his county. He held membership in the Episcopal church, while his wife belonged to the Methodist church. This worthy couple were the parents of eight children, of whom three are yet living: Phoebe, who is the widow of Daniel Spencer, resides in Albion; George, of this review; and Anthony, who is living in Clarendon township. The father died in 1871 at the age of seventy-nine years, and the mother passed away in 1885 at the age of eighty-three years, the remains of both being interred in Clarendon cemetery.

George Doolittle spent the first eight years of his life in the state of his nativity and then accompanied his parents on their removal to Michigan. After arriving here he continued his education in a log school house and later attended a select school at Homer, conducted by a Mr. Wescott. At the age of nineteen years he began teaching and followed that profession through seven winter terms, while in the summer he worked at farming. After teaching for a time he purchased a small tract of land of sixty-five acres. This was undeveloped, but it formed the nucleus of his present farming possessions which are now quite valuable and extensive. In 1856, when he was twenty-seven years of age, Mr. Doolittle was united in marriage to Miss Catherine E. Benham, who was born in Roxbury, Delaware county, New York, and was a daughter of Norman and Helena (Crispell) Benham. Her father was a native of Connecticut, and was a schoolteacher by profession, but died when his daughter was only six years old. He had come to Michigan in 1837, and settled in the southeastern corner of Albion township, where he purchased seventy acres of unbroken land. Not long afterward he was called to his final rest and left to the care of his widow nine children, the eldest of whom was twenty-one years of age. Only two are now living, the sister of Mrs. Doolittle being Mrs. Louisa McAllister, of Homer township. The father had died when little more than forty years of age, but the mother survived for many years and passed away in 1875 at the age of seventy-five years. Their remains were interred in the South Albion cemetery.

Ere his marriage Mr. Doolittle had purchased other property, aside from that of which he first became owner and had one hundred acres. On this he erected a frame house before his marriage so that he had a comfortable home in which to receive his bride. There he lived until the spring of 1863, when he sold his property and purchased eighty acres of land on section 24, Albion township. On this he erected buildings and carried on the work of progress and improvement in an effective way. Later he added to his property a tract of forty acres, and upon this farm he resided continuously until the fall of 1882, when he purchased a place on East Michigan avenue in Albion. He then rented his farm and maintained his residence in the village until 1893. A short time previously he had purchased one hundred and five acres of his present farm and in 1893 took up his abode thereon. Here he has since made his home, his place being located on section 11, Albion township. He has one hundred and fifteen acres on the old homestead and altogether owns six hundred and ninety-one acres, so that he has become one of the leading landowners of this portion of the state. Most of the farm is highly cultivated, and the well tilled fields yield golden harvests which annually add materially to the income of Mr. Doolittle. Most of his land is now rented, and in addition to his farm property he also owns city property.

Unto our subject and his wife have been born three children: Ella D., who is the wife of Louis Haight and resides on West Division street, in Albion. She has two children, George and Milo; Harriet D. is the wife of Ira Travis, a resident of Salt Lake City; Alice is the wife of William Howard, of Tekonsha, and they have one daughter, Catherine. All of the children have attended the high school and college of Albion and the two youngest are graduates of these institutions.

In his political support Mr. Doolittle is a Republican, having hearty sympathy with the principles of the party. For eight years he has served as justice of the peace, and for thirty-five years he has been notary public. When a young man, it was his ambition to study law, and in 1872 he secured a set of law books. He became quite familiar with the contents of these volumes and gave his legal advice freely to all who came to him for assistance in this direction. He has accumulated an extensive law library and has handled a number of cases in the circuit court. He has made general farming his life work, however, and it has been along this line that he has achieved success. Throughout the period of his residence in Clarendon he served as school inspector. He belongs to the Farmers' Alliance and in early life he became a member of the Methodist Episcopal church.

Mr. Doolittle's connection with Calhoun county dates from a very early period in its development. When he came to the west Indians were numerous in this section of the state, and they were great beggars, securing all from the white men that they could obtain in the line of food and supplies. There was much wild game in this part of the state. He has killed many deer in the early evening hours, and thus venison was no uncommon dish upon the board. Great changes have occurred since that time, and Mr. Doolittle has borne an active and helpful part in the transformation that has been wrought. He has taken great pride in what has been accomplished in the county along lines of improvement and upbuilding and through his farming operations he has added materially in reclaiming the wild region for the purposes of civilization. Many an acre he has placed

30

under the plow, and his farming operations have added materially to the agricultural wealth of this section of the state. He has now passed the seventy-fifth milestone on life's journey, and in the evening of his life he is enjoying the fruits of former toil, conscious of the fact that all he possesses has been earned through his own untiring industry and unflagging perseverance. Such a record should serve to inspire and encourage others, as it shows what can be accomplished by persistency of purpose and honorable labor.

HARVEY M. GRAHAM.

In pioneer times Harvey Marion Graham became a resident of Michigan and after many years connection with agricultural pursuits is now living retired in Athens, in a beautiful home which is the visible evidence of his life of thrift and enterprise. He was born in Washington county, Indiana, November 21, 1824, and his parents, Hugh and Rachel (Ross) Graham, were natives of Virginia. The mother died July 14, 1838. In 1834 an aunt who resided in Kentucky, took Mr. Graham with her to her home in Hardinsburg and there he attended school. After completing his education he began clerking in the store of his uncle, who was a tobacco merchant and wealthy slave holder. In 1837 he returned to Washington county, Indiana, where he remained until 1840. He then walked to Delphi, Indiana, where he worked for nearly two years at the tailor's trade, and was afterward employed in a general merchandise store by one man until 1849. In that year he started across the plains for

California, attracted by the discovery of gold upon the Pacific slope. He traveled with a party of more than one hundred people, reaching his destination after two hundred and thirty-two days spent upon the way. For about three years he remained in the mining regions and then by way of the isthmus returned to his home. He had also been interested in a store in California and had charge of the hauling of goods from Stockton to the store, remaining as its manager while the other partners worked in the mine. Because of failing health he returned to Indiana and after crossing the isthmus proceeded to New Orleans and up the Mississipp river, thence crossing the country to Evansville. He then continued his journey on the Wabash river to Terre Haute and by canal to Delphi. In the last named place he engaged in buying and selling horses and upon one of his trips came to Michigan.

Being pleased with the state and its prospects, Mr. Graham located in Athens township, Calhoun county, where he purchased a tract of wild land of one hundred and fifty-four acres, paying a sum of two hundred dollars in cash and incurring an indebtedness of eighteen hundred dollars for the remainder. Not a furrow had been turned or an improvement made, and Mr. Graham had never farmed a day in his life. It will thus be seen that he had a great undertaking before him, but with firm determination he set to work to clear and cultivate his land, which he continued to operate for nine years, meeting with good success. He then sold the property and purchased one hundred and sixty-five acres on the Battle Creek road, four miles northeast of the village of Athens, where he resided continuously until 1893, when he traded his farm for village property. He has since lived in Athens one of its respected and honored citizens. On the 22nd of January, 1903, his home was destroyed and nearly all of its contents were burned. A hotel which he owned in the village was also destroyed by fire in 1890, after which he erected a fine brick hotel now known as the Graham Hotel. He has likewise added to the improvements of the village through the erection of five houses here.

Mr. Graham was united in marriage to Miss Mary Ann Hanson, a daughter of John B. and Isabella Hanson, who were natives of Onondaga county, New York, and removed to Calhoun county, Michigan, in 1844, settling in Leroy township. Subsequently they located in Athens township, where they spent their remaining days. Three children have been born unto Mr. and Mrs. Graham: Earl Lee, who died in childhood; Claude D., of Branch county, Michigan, who married Minnie Young and has two sons, Lee Abraham and Hugh Marion; and Millie Ross, the widow of Jay P. Lee, late of Lansing, Michigan, where he was a practicing attorney for a number of years, makes her home with her parents. She pursued her education in the colleges in Union City and Ann Arbor. Mr. Graham is a Republican in his political views, has held a number of minor offices and for many years has served as justice of the peace. In his business life he was active and diligent, and displayed keen judgment in the management of his affairs. As the result of his capability he is now possessed of a handsome competence that enables him to enjoy life without further labor. His friends are many and he is known as a popular and worthy resident of Athens.

GEORGE A. ROWLAND.

George A. Rowland is a self-made man, who owes his prosperity entirely to his own afforts. For many years he was engaged in business as a tanner and currier, but is now living retired at No. 702 North Superior street in Albion, where he erected a fine brick residence in 1891. He was born in Michigan, January 26, 1835, a son of Charles and Charlotte (Wilcox) Rowland. When our subject was but two years of age his parents removed to Ypsilanti, Michigan, and later took up their abode on a farm near Monroe, Michigan. About 1840 they settled at Tecumseh, where the father worked in a tannery. Later he removed to Clinton, where in a partnership he built a tannery and to its operation devoted his energies. He became quite well-to-do, gaining a comfortable competence. After the destruction of his tannery by fire he went to work upon a farm, being there employed for about a year. On the expiration of that period he and his brother built a tannery in Tecumseh, which they conducted for a time and later sold. They then returned to Clinton, where, in connection with Edwin R. Smith, Mr. Rowland built another tannery. There he spent his remaining days. In his family were six children. Charles C., the eldest, has for thirty years been an engineer in the woolen mills at Clinton, Michigan. He married Malissa Burton and had two children. Grace E., who died in early womanhood, and Wirt C., who is an architect of Detroit. George A. is the second son of the family. Jane Elizabeth became the wife of Albert Burton, both died and are now survived by two daughters. Mrs. Hattie Johnson, of Clinton, and Kate, the wife of Dr. E. M. Conklin. Mary is the wife of Frank D. Lancaster, of Clinton, Michigan, and had a daughter, Mrs. Jennie Burroughs, who died at the age of thirty-one years. William Albert, a resident of Caro, Tuscola county, Michigan, married Esther Lazelier, and their children are Frank, Helen, Charles, Mabel, Blanche and Alta. Helen, the oldest, died at the age of nine years.

George A. Rowland accompanied his parents on their various removals and entering the common schools of his native state, obtained his education. When fourteen years of age he began clerking in a grocery store, but a year served to prove to him that this labor was not congenial. He then began an apprenticeship at the tanner's trade under his father, for whom he continued until twenty years of age. His father paid him forty-eight dollars the first year, ninety-six dollars the second year and after that a dollar per day. Later he worked for an uncle at Tecumseh and then spent a year in Adrian, Michigan, after which he returned to Clinton and was with his father until twenty-eight years of age. In 1864 he came to Albion and accepted the position of manager of the finishing shops of the tannery owned by George M. Cady. He was in these shops for nine and a half years, when on account of impaired health, he resigned his position and removed to Clinton, where he engaged in the livery business in partnership with his brother-in-law, F. D. Lancaster. He spent two and a half years in that way and upon the recovery of his health he returned to Albion, where he accepted a position as salesman in a grocery store. He was thus employed for fourteen or fifteen years, on the expiration of which period he retired from active business life.

Mr. Rowland was married on the 1st of November, 1860, in Clinton, Michigan, to

Miss Eliza H. Felton, who was born on a farm, a mile and a half from Clinton, her parents being Benjamin Keyes and Julia Ann. (St. John) Felton. Mr. and Mrs. Rowland became the parents of two children: Ezra, born in Clinton, died in infancy; Lua Helen, born in Clinton, April 8, 1864, is now the wife of Isaac Nelson Miller, a dealer in hay and grain at Albion, and they have three children, Charles Rowland, Rowland James, and Clara Marie.

On attaining his majority Mr. Rowland gave his political support to the Democratic party and voted for Buchanan. He was elected alderman from the first ward of Albion for two terms, but removed to Clinton ere the expiration of his term. He was reared in the faith of the Presbyterian church, but after his wife became a member of the Episcopal church he attended its services. The business interests of Mr. Rowland have made him widely acquainted in southern Michigan and his upright career has gained for him the respect of all with whom he has come in contact.

SEYMOUR C. ESLOW.

The name which heads this review is one well-known to the pioneer residents of Calhoun county, the first one of the family to settle in Michigan being Isaiah Eslow. He was engaged in the lumber business in the east but emigrated to the west in 1835, coming across the lake to Detroit and thence by wagons into Homer township, Calhoun county, where he took up eighty acres of land, located on section 10. Thereafter he knew no other home but this which was then covered with a dense growth of tim-

ber, the balance of his life being spent in the cultivation and improvement of his property. With the help of his son, Thomas E., who was born in New York state and came west with his parents at the age of eight years, he succeeded in clearing the greater part of the land and making it productive. His death occurred in this locality and he is interred in the old cemetery in Homer. Thomas E. Eslow grew to manhood upon his father's farm, receiving his education in the primitive schools of this county. After the management of the farm passed into his hands, he replaced the old log house which had sheltered the family for so many years with a new frame structure and added in other ways to the improvement of the property, and by industry and energy was enabled to add one hundred acres to the farm left him by his father. He married Mary Delia Champion, also a native of eastern New York, and she is still living in the village of Homer, while her husband died November 4th, 1900, at the age of seventy-three years, and is also buried in the Fisher cemetery. He was a Democrat politically and held various offices in the township, never shirking a public duty. Both himself and wife were members of the Methodist Episcopal church and both were active in religious work, he acting as steward of the church for many years. They were the parents of two children, namely: Eddy L., who died at the age of sixteen years, and Seymour C., the personal subject of this review.

Seymour C. Eslow was born in Homer township, Calhoun county, Michigan, July 4, 1868, and was reared on the farm upon which the boyhood of his father was spent, and like him also attending the district schools of the township, which were, however, greatly improved as time passed. His additional privileges consisted of a course at the Homer high school, after wihch he entered Albion College, where he attended for four years. Upon leaving that institution he secured the school in his home district and taught there the following year, after which he engaged in farming, renting the old home farm. Upon the death of his father he assumed charge of the home farm, which he has since capably managed. In addition to his farming interests he has always been a man of note in his home township, as a Democrat taking an active part in the political life of the community. In 1897 he was elected to the office of county surveyor, serving one year, and in 1902 he was elected supervisor of Homer township, the only Democrat on the ticket elected to office that year, a fact which speaks eloquently of the esteem which is accorded Mr. Eslow.

The marriage of Mr. Eslow united him with Miss Anna L. Dickey, a daughter of William Henry and Lucinda (Barton) Dickey, natives respectively of Manchester and Marshall, Michigan. Mrs. Dickey being a daughter of William S. and Louisa (Olds) Barton. In religious affiliations both Mr. and Mrs. Eslow are members of the Methodist Episcopal church of Homer.

ALBERT S. PATTISON.

The Pattison family is one known and revered in Calhoun county, for as pioneers of the state the elder members left the impress of strong personality, of earnest and forceful character upon the development of the community which named them as citizens. The first of the name to settle in the west was Sunderland G. Pattison, the father of our personal subject. He was born in Farmington township, Ontario county, New York, September 30, 1811, and at the age of fifteen years commenced running a line boat on the Erie canal between Buffalo and Albany, continuing in this occupation for four years. After his marriage in 1831 he engaged in the grocery and milling business, but was induced, after a couple of years, to try his fortunes in the state of Michigan through the reports of such multifold opportunities. In 1834 he settled in Marengo township, Calhoun county, purchasing from the government the farm upon which his grandson, Arthur L. Pattison, now lives. When he first located in Marengo he put teams on the road between Marshall and Detroit and engaged in the transportation of goods until the completion of the Michigan Central Railroad to Jackson. He was also interested in the cattle business in that early day, chiefly providing the settlers with provisions and supplies. His wife was formerly Maria Smith, a native of the same locality in New York, and of this union were born six children, one of whom died in infancy. The others, named in order of birth, are as follows: Albert S., born in Palmyra, New York, April 6, 1833; Ruth D., born October 18, 1835, and was married to H. B. Smith, October 19, 1858 (see sketch on another page of this work); Elizabeth G., born February 20, 1838, and married Isaac D. Comstock July 25, 1857; Ada M., born April 18, 1843, and married Frank L. Gunnison; and Georgiana, born June 5, 1840, married May 21, 1867, Robert McPherson, and died March 19, 1869. In his political affiliations Mr. Pattison was a Democrat, having cast his first ballot for Andrew Jackson. The death of Mr. Pattison and his wife occurred upon the farm where they had made their home so many years, the date of his demise being August 19, 1882, and that of hers in the fall of 1877. Mrs. Pattison had been an invalid several years prior to her death. Mr. Pattison was of Quaker parentage and inherited many of those qualities which are ascribed to the teachings of that religious body. It may be truly said of him that he was a representative man of Marengo township, one most closely identified with its public interests from a very early date. As to the value of the property which he cultivated and improved a slight idea can be gained from the fact that in 1851 he was presented with a solid silver cup at the county fair, this inscription upon it: "Calhoun County Agricultural Society, October 2, 1851. Presented to S. G. Pattison as a premium for the best farm."

Albert S. Pattison, our personal subject, was brought to Michigan when only a year old, and thus his entire life was practically spent within the borders of our state. He was reared in a home of plenty but was early trained in the practical duties which insure one's success in life's ventures, and at the age of twenty-one years he set forth on his own resources. By means of personal labor, business ability and good management, he accumulated a large amount of property, owning a large farm adjoining the paternal home before that passed into his possession by the death of his father. This farm, which was once accorded the first premium for value, is at once the pride not only of its owners, but of the town, county and state, for it is without doubt one of the finest in Michigan. Mr. Pattison, in addition to a gift of $2,500 to each of his children when they started out into the world for them-

selves, owned four hundred and five acres of land at the time of his death, having brought the same to a high state of cultivation and development. He had not only beautified his immediate surroundings with a growth of maple trees, but for three quarters of a mile on both sides of the road he had set out trees. In 1896 he retired from the active duties of farm life, removing to Albion, where his death occurred December 12, 1902.

On the 26th day of April, 1854, Mr. Pattison was united in marriage with Miss Helen S. Hopkins, of Homer, a woman of rare personal worth whose life beside that of Mr. Pattison's was full of helpfulness. To them were born six children, of whom four are now living, namely: Albert C.; Arthur L.; Anna, who married Louis K. Cook; and Georgia, who married George S. Avery. The deceased were William Hobart, died February 6, 1881, at the age of twenty-one years; Mary E., died February 20, 1868, at one year of age. The death of Mrs. Pattison occurred October 20, 1881. The second marriage of Mr. Pattison occurred April 16, 1890, and united him with Miss Emma Albertson, of Eckford. His home, beautiful in all its appointments, had ever been the center of social gatherings and continued to be so up to the time of his death.

In political affairs Mr. Patison was always deeply interested, and devoted much thought and study to the subject of county and municipal government. Though admirably qualified for public office, and so recognized by his fellow citizens, he steadfastly refused all official positions, caring nothing for the emoluments of such. He was a Democrat and stanch in his convictions. Mr. Pattison was not only a progressive farmer and an enterprising citizen, but he contributed much to the material advancement of agricultural progress. His was a strong, earnest and forceful manhood, living a broadminded, charitable and kindly life which will long bear a remembrance in the lives and hearts of those who knew him in the strength of his sturdy manhood.

ALBERT CLAIR PATTISON.

Albert Clair Pattison, a young and honored citizen of Marengo township, Calhoun county, Michigan, was born in Eckford township, same county, on section 2, August 26, 1857, a son of Albert S. and Helen S. (Hopkins) Pattison. (See sketch in this volume.) Mr. Pattison was reared and educated in his native county, attending the district school in the vicinity of his home, after which he entered the Marshall high school, in which he remained a student for two years. Of practical business ability, enterprise and ambition he early sought an opening in commercial affairs, his first venture of the kind being the sale of agricultural implements in Albion. In the fall of 1883 he engaged in a general merchandise store in the village of Marengo, succeeding H. M. Evans, where he remained until 1886, during which time he acted as postmaster under the presidential administrations of Arthur and Cleveland. Since that time he has resided upon the farm of eighty acres which his father gave to him in 1879, in 1887 erecting a fine residence, barn and various other improvements, which have added no little to the value of the property .

December 24, 1887, Mr. Pattison was united in marriage with Miss Belle Fredenburg, of Fredonia township, Calhoun county, and a daughter of John and Laura (Kimball) Fredenburg. Mr. Pattison is now engaged in general farming, but still finds time to give attention to the political affairs of the community, being elected in 1899 township clerk, which office he still holds. He is a strong Silver Democrat in his political affiliations and is active in the support of the principles of his party.

ARTHUR LEE PATTISON.

A careful and conservative farmer, Arthur Lee Pattison is following out the methods of his father upon the old homestead, where he has been located since February, 1896. He was born in Marengo township, Calhoun county, Michigan, June 2, 1869, a son of Albert S. and Helen S. (Hopkins) Pattison, for more complete details concerning whose life refer to the personal sketch of the father, which occurs in this work. Mr. Pattison was reared and educated in his native county, attending the district school in the vicinity of his home, the high school of Kalamazoo for one year, and the Michigan Agricultural College, of Lansing. Shortly after completing his studies he went south, locating in Chattanooga, Tennessee, where he was engaged in the dry goods business for a period of three years, after which he removed to Pittsburg, Pennsylvania, and was employed as a clerk in a dry goods establishment of that city. In February, 1896, he returned to Marengo township, and assumed charge of his father's farm of four hundred and five acres, his parents then locating in Albion, retired from the active cares which had so long formed a large part of their lives. The farm is devoted to general farming and stock raising, while conservative modern methods are employed in the work and everything brought to the highest standard of excellence.

The marriage of Mr. Pattison occurred in Chattanooga, Tennessee, and united him with Miss Grace L. Carpenter, the birth of one child having blessed this union, Arthur Lee, Jr., born September, 1897. In his political preferment Mr. Pattison is a Democrat.

EDWIN RUTHVEN MILLS.

The oldest business man on State street, Marshall, at the present time, and one who, in the past, has given much toward the successful development of the resources of this section of the state, is Edwin Ruthven Mills, whose birth occurred in Cattaraugus county, New York, October 20, 1824. Mr. Mills is the representative of an old and prominent family on American soil, the first emigrant being a lad of seventeen years, who came from England about 1620, his earnest desire to settle in this country having led to his signing away his time for seven years, during which he acted as bond servant. The family afterward became influential in the New England states, a granduncle of our personal subject, acting as a Minute man at Dorchester Heights. He afterward located in Needham (now Randolph), Massachusetts, while our subject's grandfather settled in Maine. He remained in that location until about 1808, when he removed to New

York state. His occupation was that of a farmer throughout his entire life. He was a major of militia, and was active during the War of 1812, at that time disposing of his landed property and placing the money received in a bank, which afterward failed and ruined the family fortunes. Lewis Mills, the father of Mr. Mills, and a man also very prominent in the pioneer history of Michigan, was born in Livermore, Maine, then the province of Massachusetts, May 5, 1803. He was five years old at the time of the family's removal from Maine to New York, and it was there that he was reared to manhood, in the religious faith of the Presbyterians. He married Eliza Turner, of Norfolk, Connecticut, who was born April 12, 1805, died November 8, 1891, and is interred in Ionia, Michigan. To them were born seven sons and four daughters, all but two daughters and one son now surviving. The father was a blacksmith by occupation, but was a man of wide reading and strong intellectual attainments, and with the desire to educate his children he removed to Oberlin, Ohio. While there the famous Rev. Finney, of that city, induced him to become a minister in the Congregational faith, and after the determination became fixed in his mind he lost no opportunity to make it a realization. The following three years were spent in study and work at his trade, for three hours a day performing the duties of a blacksmith, after which he gave himself up to study, which later events proved him eminently fitted, by nature, to pursue. In 1842 he came to Michigan, locating in Coldwater, where he became pastor of the Presbyterian church. In the useful years that followed Mr. Mills founded a number of churches, and also served as pastor of churches in Clarendon and Eckford townships, this county, and later was pastor of churches at Saginaw, Farmington, Howell and Ionia. April 19, 1872, his death occurred in Ionia, where he had preached the gospel for a number of years, and where he is now sleeping his last sleep. He was a man of much natural eloquence and earnestness of speech, and one whose success cannot be measured in words. Though long since passed away he is not forgotten among those with whom his life work lay.

Edwin R. Mills remained at home with his parents until he was seventeen years old, and after receiving a common school education, attended the preparatory department of Oberlin College. He then went to Stafford, Genesee county, New York, where he spent three years learning the trade of harness maker, after which he came to Coldwater, Michigan, where his father was then engaged in preaching. September 13, 1844, he secured a position in a shop in Marshall, while a part of his time was passed in Union City, in the same employment. In 1849 he purchased a shop which was located just across the street from his present business. In 1851 he put up a building at No. 210 East State street, his present location, and has remained here ever since, though the year following witnessed the destruction of his property by fire. He has since that time erected the substantial brick building which now serves him for a harness shop and store. During the earlier years he did quite an extensive manufacturing business.

June 5, 1851, Mr. Mills was united in marriage with Miss Caroline A. Lockwood, a native of New York, and of this union was born one son, Edwin Lockwood, his natal day being January 17, 1853. After receiving a commercial education at Ann Arbor, he became interested in the lumber business, and was acting as overseer at the time of his death, which occurred in 1880, through the sinking of the steamer Alpena, on Lake Michigan. By caring for two of her sisters who had typhoid fever, Mrs. Mills contracted the disease and died March 1, 1853, four of eight children in her father's family dying about the same time. On the 2d day of October, 1856, Mr. Mills was married to Miss Mary Anna Benedict, the daughter of a farmer of Elmira, New York, meeting her while she was on a visit in Marshall. Three children were born to them, two of whom died in infancy, the one son living being Frederick Henry, born August 28, 1857. He married Clara Hall, of Bridgeport, Connecticut, and is now a successful broker in Boston, Massachusetts, having been in the business there for sixteen years. They have two children, Walter Hall and Marshall Benedict. Mr. Mills is a Republican in his political convictions, his first vote having been cast for Burney, Abolitionist, having since voted every ticket put up by his party. He was present when the Republican party was organized, at Jackson, in 1854, and though always casting his vote and giving his influence toward better government has never cared personally for official recognition. Religiously he has been a member of the Presbyterian church for over sixty years and formerly a teacher in the Sunday school. Mr. Mills has indeed been the architect of his own fortunes, for he started out in the world entirely dependent on his own resources, and from the foot of the ladder has attained a position of competence, and won the respect·and esteem of his fellow citizens for the sturdy qualities which have distinguished his life among them.

DAN W. CONNERS.

The business interests of Albion are well represented.by Dan W. Conners, a leading plumber and general contractor, whose activity, unflagging industry and close application have resulted in making him one of the progressive and influential citizens of his adopted county. He was born in Dayton, Ohio, May 20, 1865. His parents, Dennis and Nancy (Cain) Connors, were natives of Ireland, and when young people came to the United States, establishing their home in Dayton, Ohio, where they were married. During their residence there they witnessed the growth and improvement of that city in a large measure. In his earlier years Mr. Connors engaged in business as a stock-driver and through the exercise of energy and enterprise he came to be one of the well-to-do and prominent residents of Dayton. He was also a leading factor in community affairs, served as alderman of the city and was city assessor for a number of years. He died in Grand Rapids in 1894, and his wife, surviving him a few years, passed away in 1900.

Dan W. Connors entered the public schools at the usual age and when he had pursued his studies until sixteen years of age, he put aside his text-books, and in 1881 entered upon an apprenticeship to learn the plumber's trade. When his term of service had expired he removed to Piqua, Ohio, where he was employed for a time, and then went to Grand Rapids, Michigan. Subse-quently he traveled through the northwest and afterward returned to Grand Rapids, opening a plumbing establishment on East Bridge street. A few years later he closed what had been a successful business career there and removed to Albion in 1896. Here he was employed for a time by Mr. Porr, and when he had become acquainted with the people of the city he bought out his employer and has now the largest plumbing business and, in fact, the only exclusive plumbing establishment in Albion. He keeps all modern plumbing supplies and up-to-date appliances and in different seasons of the year employs from five to thirty men. He is likewise engaged in general contract work, taking contracts for paving and other public constructive work. Recently he has completed a large paving contract on Superior street. In this branch of his business he is a member of the firm of Dean & Connors. They also take contracts for sewer work and to-day rank first among the contractors of the city. Mr. Connors is a wide-awake and enterprising business man and has extended his efforts to other fields of activity, being interested in some of the corporations of this part of the state and likewise in realty, owning considerable property.

Mr. Connors was married on the 3d of July, 1898, to Mrs. Ida Martin, of Grand Rapids, a daughter of Chancey Nellis, one of the early residents of that city. By her former marriage she had a daughter, Bertha, who is now the wife of Cleveland Watson Mr. and Mrs. Connors have a pleasant home at No. 211 West Cass street, which he purchased soon after his arrival in Albion. He exercised his right of franchise in support of the men and measures of the Democracy and was elected alderman for the first ward in 1903, but resigned on account of his city contracts. He had not sought the office and, in fact, it was given to him without his consent. Socially, he is connected with Albion lodge, I. O. O. F., Albion lodge, No. 57, K. P., Albion lodge, No. 36, A. O. U. W., and Battle Creek lodge, D. O. K. K. He is a member of the Albion fire department, being foreman of the hose company which position he has held for the past four years. His energies have largely been directed with singleness of purpose and to business channels, with the result that his close application and enterprise have enabled him to meet competition, to overcome all obstacles and steadily advance to a foremost position as a representative business man in his adopted city.

HENRY STETSON THOMAS.

Henry Stetson Thomas, well and favorably known throughout Calhoun county as a successful farmer of Athens township, was born in Columbus, Ohio, February 11, 1842, the son of Stetson and Betsey (Kinney) Thomas, natives respectively of Vermont and New York states. He remained under the paternal roof until he had attained his twentieth year, when he enlisted in July, 1862, as a member of Company C, Seventeenth Michigan Volunteer Infantry, the regiment under the command of Colonel Withington, and the company under Captain Andrews. They were first stationed at Camp Detroit after which they were sent to Washington and Fort Baker. The first engagement in which Mr. Thomas participated was South Mountain, after which battle the regiment was constantly engaged, in the year that followed, losing many men by

bayonet charges, as well as in general engagements. In the battle of Antietam Mr. Thomas was wounded, losing a finger on the left hand, and in March of the following year he was honorably discharged for disability.

Returning to St. Joseph county, he located upon his father's farm, where he remained for one year. Deciding then to try a residence in the western states he went to California, starting from New York City in November, and twenty-three days later arriving in San Francisco, having gone by way of the Isthmus of Panama. After a residence of five years he returned east by the same route, paying twenty-five dollars for his passage, while his first trip had cost him one hundred and twenty-five. He remained in Michigan upon the old farm in St. Joseph county for one year, when he again returned to California, where he traveled up and down the coast for a year. He then located in Kansas, where he was successfully engaged in stockraising for a like period, after which he returned to Michigan and has since made this his home, with the exception of three years spent as stock overseer on Franklin Parish's farm, in Louisiana. Upon locating in Michigan he purchased part of his present farm of seventy acres, in the succeeding years increasing the number to three hundred and forty, in addition to which he owns seventeen hundred acres in Newaygo county, Michigan.

In December, 1871, Mr. Thomas was united in marriage with Miss Sarah Kellogg, whose birth occurred upon the farm where she and her husband now live. She was a daughter of George Kellogg, a native of Ohio. Of this union were born one daughter, Mytrie, who died in infancy; two sons, Emerson, born May 7, 1872, is now a student in the University of Wisconsin in electrical engineering; and Stewart K., born May 5, 1876, is a graduate of the high school of Athens in the class of 1903, and is completing a further course in the business college of Battle Creek. A Republican all his life, Mr. Thomas's first vote was cast for President Lincoln, and religiously he is a member of the Unitarian faith. With a mind eager for information, Mr. Thomas has enjoyed his extensive traveling and has used every opportunity to add to his knowledge.

HON. HENRY A. CLUTE.

A valiant soldier of the Civil war, a legislator who stood manfully by his principles in the face of opposition, and a successful business man, who in his career has triumphed over difficulties and obstacles which would have discouraged many a man of less resolute spirit, the entire life history of Hon. Henry A. Clute is such as to commend him to the respect, confidence and admiration of his fellow men. He was born in Wayne county, near Newark, New York, March 24, 1840, his parents being Henry L. and Alazan (Rhodes) Clute. The mother was a representative of an old Connecticut family. Henry Clute, the grandfather of our subject, was descended from one of the early Dutch families of the Empire state, three brothers of the name settling in Easopus Meadows soon after the founding of New York city. Henry L. Clute, the father, resided at Johnstown, New York, his native city, until thirty years of age and was there married. He engaged in tanning and also in the manufacture of gloves and about 1835 removed

to Wayne county, New York, where he again engaged in the manufacture of gloves and mittens and in the tanning business, remaining there until 1842. At that time he traveled through the western country in order to buy deer skins. At Windsor, Michigan he changed the money which he had brought from the east into "wild cat" currency and then, not being able to secure the number of skins that he had expected, he invested in eight acres of land in Convis township, at what is still known as Clute's Corners.

Soon afterward Mr. Clute returned to New York and in 1844 brought his family to Michigan, journeying by canal to Buffalo, thence by way of the lake to Detroit, and on across the country with teams. He settled upon his land, at once began to clear and develop it, and as time passed he also added to his property until he was the owner of four hundred acres. He continued his farming operations there until his death, which occurred in 1855, when he was fifty-one years of age. His widow long survived him and was residing upon a part of the old home farm at the time of her death, which occurred when she was eighty-eight years of age. In the family were six children, four sons and two daughters, our subject being the second son.

Henry A. Clute was but four years of age when brought by his parents to Michigan. His educational advantages were only those afforded by the common schools, but his training at farm labor and kindred work was not meager. In the winter that he was nine years of age he drew seventy cords of wood to Marshall with a yoke of oxen, receiving a dollar per cord for the wood when it was delivered. Many duties and tasks devolved upon him in his early boyhood. For a brief period he attended Olivet College, but after his father's death, being the eldest son at home, it was necessary that he remain there and take charge of the farm. This he did, accomplishing the task in a most worthy manner, although the burden was a heavy one for young shoulders. His father left to him eighty acres of land and he was to receive an additional forty acres upon the death of his mother. In 1857, the mother renting the farm, the family removed to Corunna, Shiawasse county, Michigan, and as he had opportunity, he attended the Union school for several years. He was ambitious to secure an education and embraced every privilege accorded him in order to extend his knowledge

In 1861 the family returned to the farm and Mr. Clute, of this review, took possession of his own land, in addition to managing the old homestead. Not long after the Civil war was inaugurated. It was his great desire to go to the front to aid in the preservation of the Union and on the 30th of August, 1862, he enlisted in Company H, of Merrill's Horse, an organization then in the field. He preferred to go to the front at once as a private, rather than wait for the formation of a new regiment, in which he might have secured official rank. He joined his command at Mexico, Missouri, having experienced considerable difficulty in getting transportation and finding it necessary to go by way of Louisville and St. Louis. The regiment was engaged in scouting duty all through Missouri and in 1863 went to Little Rock, but Mr. Clute was left at the general hospital at Ironton on account of his eyesight. Later he was granted a furlough and was

home for forty days under treatment. Upon his return to St. Louis he was put on detached service in the department headquarters and while there had his eyes treated at his own expense by good specialists. He was there until Price made his last raid in Missouri, when he obtained a leave of absence from the department and, joining his regiment, chased Price across the state, marching twice across the state, one thousand miles, in fifty days. Later, when the regiment was ordered to Chattanooga, Mr. Clute asked to be returned to his command and was with the regiment until the close of the war, taking part in the movements under General Thomas. In June, 1865, he was honorably discharged, after almost three years of faithful military service.

Returning to the north, Mr. Clute resumed farming operations as manager of the old homestead place, as well as of his own land. He worked earnestly and indefatigably, and as time progressed and his financial resources increased, he was enabled to add to his property until he owned three hundred and eighty-seven acres in the home place and one hundred and sixty acres in Kansas, which he also improved. As a companion and helpmate for life's journey he chose Miss Florence Crossman, whom he married in 1867. She was born at Marengo, Michigan, a daughter of Luther Crossman, who was one of the pioneers of Calhoun county, arriving in 1832. He settled in Marengo township, and being a carpenter and joiner, he built the first frame barn in the county. In this part of the state he lived until called to his final rest. Mrs. Clute died September 10, 1888, leaving eight living children: Charles H., Schuyler L., Homer A. and

George C., who are farmers; Grace, the wife of Frederick Wilber, of Ypsilanti, Michigan, and Henry L., who is a graduate of the electrical department of the Michigan University, and is now with the Westinghouse Company, of Pittsburg; Sidney M. and Florence J., in Ypsilanti, Michigan, at school.

Mr. Clute continued upon his farm in this county until 1882, when he went to Kansas and purchased and improved a farm, upon which he lived for three years. He was also engaged in dealing in stock, and conducted a lumber yard at Waverly, that state. He is called the father of that town, having instituted a number of important business enterprises there, and in his business operations was a very successful man. He afterward returned to his farm in Calhoun county and continued its cultivation until his sons were old enough to take charge, when, in 1892, he took up his abode in Marshall, where he now resides. He had improved over a half section of land, had erected fine buildings, and, indeed, had developed a farm property of which he has every reason to be proud.

For his second wife Mr. Clute chose Mrs. Jeanette Crossman, a daughter of Caleb Hanchett, who was also a pioneer settler of this county. She had, by her first marriage, one daughter, Mabel, who was educated in music in Oberlin, Ohio, and in Chicago.

Mr. Clute has been quite active in politics. He was formerly a supporter of the Republican party, and as such was elected supervisor in 1874, in a strong Democratic township. He was absent the following year, but in 1876 was re-elected. In 1878 he went to Texas on account of his health, and while there the Greenback party was formed and he became one of its supporters. He was elected to the office of supervisor on the Greenback ticket on his return over both the Republican and Democratic tickets, and while in Kansas he was a justice of the peace. After his return to this county in 1885 he did not again engage actively in political work until 1896, when he was nominated on the Union-Silver ticket for representative to the State Legislature and was elected by a majority of five hundred. While a member of the minority party in the house, he never wavered in his allegiance to his principles. Since that time he has been retired, but his interest in county, state and nation has never abated, and his co-operation may always be counted upon for the public good.

For many years Mr. Clute has been connected with the Grand Army of the Republic, his membership being now with C. Colegrove post, of which he was the commander in 1903. He also filled that position about three years ago, and during that time was chairman of the building committee and also chairman of the committee to solicit funds for the erection of the fine Grand Army Memorial Hall, which was completed in 1902. It is supplied with reading rooms, a Grand Army hall and library, and in the basement there is a dining room capable of seating one hundred and thirty people at a time. Mr. Clute has attended national encampments at various places, including the one of 1903, at San Francisco, and while on that trip he traveled almost eight thousand miles. Honored and respected by all, there are many bright pages in the history of Mr. Clute, recording most commendable deeds. Deprived in youth of many of the privileges which boys enjoy, he developed a strong and self-reliant character that has enabled him to work his way steadily upward in his business career. His military service and political record are alike commendable and thus he well deserves mention among the representative men of his adopted county, men whose lives are a credit and honor to the people who have honored them.

PHINEAS I. SIMONS.

A prominent place in the regard of his fellow citizens is given to Phineas I. Simons, a native son of this county, his birth having occurred in Athens township, November 16, 1844, and since attaining manhood his interests have been principally identified with those of the locality in which he now makes his home. He is the son of Rodney Simons, who lives just over the line in Branch county. While still a mere lad he was taken by his parents to Branch county and there reared to manhood's estate, receiving his education in the primitive schools of the state, his first attendance being in an old log house, after which he became a student in what was then known as the "brick school." He remained at home until 1865, while assisting his father on the home farm, also making small ventures for himself. Having attained his majority, he started out to make his own way in the world, his only capital, the energy and industry which had formed a large part of his early training. Reared to a knowledge of farming, he naturally turned his attention to that branch of industry, giving his time to the farmers of the neighborhood for a monthly remuneration, continuing so employed for the period of two years. He then rented a farm which he managed for

himself for the ensuing two years, when in 1869 he made his first purchase of land, becoming the owner of sixty acres of timber land in Athens township, on section 13. He began at once to clear the land, which he held for about eighteen months, when he traded it for a saw-mill, located about three-quarters of a mile east of the village. After operating the mill for two years, he traded it for a saw and shingle mill in the village, being then in partnership with C. C. Wilson. This mill property was burned in 1873, but was immediately rebuilt by its enterprising owners, and in the spring of the following year Mr. Simons purchased his partner's interest and continued alone in the operation of the mill until the spring of 1894. He then disposed of his interests and erected the elevator, which occupies a space of ground near the station of the Michigan Central Railroad, and has since conducted this latter enterprise with increasing profits, while he also does custom grinding. In addition to his interests in Athens he also owns a well-improved farm of two hundred and forty acres located in this township, a tenant at present occupying and farming the land.

On November 6, 1872, Mr. Simons married Estell J. Ferris, of St. Joseph county. She died October 19, 1876. He took for his second wife Marcia Barron, a daughter of W. M. Watkins, of St. Joseph county. She died September 17, 1888, in Athens township, and for his third wife he married Elnora Streeter, of Union City, a daughter of Chauncey Buell, an early settler, and during his life a prominent farmer of that locality.

Mr. Simons has always been a public-spirited and enterprising citizen, and as such has been active in promoting the general welfare of the community. A Democrat in politics, he has been supported by that party in various offices of the community, upon the incorporation of Athens being elected a trustee, which position he maintained until 1903. He has also given efficient service as a member of the school board. In fraternal circles he is identified with the Masonic order, being a member of the lodge at Athens, where he now occupies the chair of senior warden. He has passed the chapter and council, and is also a member of the Eastern Star. Faithful in the discharge of duty and stanch in his support of all measures which have for their end the promotion of public interests, Mr. Simons is regarded as a valued citizen, and one who has fully performed his share in the material advancement of agricultural and industrial interests of the county.

ADOLPHUS C. WATERMAN.

Adolphus C. Waterman, a retired farmer and miller, living in Athens, was born four miles west of Penn Yan, in Yates county, New York, July 14, 1829, a son of John B. and Betsy (Gleason) Waterman, the former a native of Rhode Island, and the latter of onnecticut. They, however, lived in the same neighborhood, their homes being merely separated by the boundary line between the two states. They were probably married in Connecticut, and for some years afterward lived in Rhode Island, where three of their children were born. The father was a mechanic and millwright. He removed from New England to Yates county, New York, and in 1837 went to Jackson Prairie, in Steuben county, Indiana, whence in 1839 he came to Calhoun county, Michigan, and for a few years rented land of Asahel Stone, an old acquaintance. Later he purchased

eighty acres of wild land two miles north of the present site of Athens. His death occurred in 1847. In the family were eight children: Louise, who died in Yates county, New York; Benoni, who died in Denver, Colorado, leaving a wife and three children who still live in that state; Lucy Ann, who was the wife of William Hanson and died at her home in Lockport, Illinois, leaving two children; John, who died in Lockport, Illinois, and left one child; Henry, who made his home in Calhoun county and at his death left three chidren born of his first marriage and five of the second marriage; Betsy, wife of Elisha Wallace, of Battle Creek, by whom she has three children; Adolphus C.; and George, who died in Indiana, at the age of three years.

In 1848 Adolphus C. Waterman went to Lockport, Illinois, where he began working with his brother, who was a mechanic and had taken the contract to build six sets of gates for six locks in the canal. The father had intended to go to that place to superintend the work, but his death intervened and Mr. Waterman, of this review, and his brother had, therefore, the superintendency of the business. Adolphus Waterman assisted in building two of the gates on the Illinois and Michigan Canal and continued at Lockport until 1850, when he and his two brothers, John and Benoni Waterman, started for California overland. They crossed the Missouri river on the 2d of May and arrived at Georgetown, California, on the 10th of July, traveling but sixty-eight days. Their supply of food became exhausted ere reaching their destination, however, and they had to live on half rations for a time. Mr. Waterman went to the mines, three miles above Downeyville, at a place called Gold Bluff. Early the following spring his brother John returned to the east, and in the fall of 1851, Adolphus and Benoni Waterman came again to Michigan, bringing back with them about ten thousand dollars, which showed that they had been successful in their operations in the far west.

Adolphus Waterman invested in about two hundred acres of land on both sides of the main street in Athens and erected a building upon the site of his present home, thus becoming the owner of the first house in the town. Here he has resided continuously since. He was married on the 10th of March, 1852, to Miss Sarah C. Gurnsey, who was born at Gorham, Ontario county, New York, a daughter of Jonathan and Betsey (Blakeslee) Gurnsey. Her father came to Michigan in 1847, and purchased land in Branch county, but subsequently sold out and purchased the farm upon which our subject now resides. In 1848 the family arrived, numbering the father, mother and Mrs. Waterman, having journeyed by rail to Buffalo, and thence by steamer to Detroit, where the brothers drove teams across the country. A part of the house in which Mr. Waterman now resides was built when her father purchased the land, and both Mr. Gurnsey and Mr. Waterman have added to this residence, making it a commodious and modern home, where three children have been born unto our subject and his wife: Arthur G., who was born in Leroy township, December 15, 1854, and having graduated in the University of Michigan, is now a prominent attorney of Chicago; John Benoni, who was born in the house where his parents are now living, March 2, 1865, and having graduated from the Kalamazoo Business College, is now auditor for the Nichols & Shepard Company at Battle Creek; and

31

Grace, who was born December 28, 1871, and is a graduate of the Battle Creek Business College.

Mr. Waterman was reared in the Democratic faith and voted for Pierce. He became a reader of the New York Tribune when Horace Greeley was its editor and attempted to endorse Republican principles, but found that they were at variance with his ideas of government. He, however, voted for Greeley in 1872, and since that time has not considered himself bound by any party ties. After his marriage he gave his attention to farming for some time. In 1863 he dug a race three quarters of a mile long, from Notaway creek, and forming partnership with James Halbert, they erected a mill for custom grinding. Two years later Mr. Halbert sold his interest and subsequently Mr. Waterman became sole próprietor. He then changed it to a merchant mill and engaged in the manufacture of flour by burr stone process. This mill is still standing and is now operated as a roller process plant. Mr. Waterman continued in the milling business until in the nineties. In 1901 he began studying the subject of cement building blocks and in May, 1902, filed an application for a patent, which was granted July 21, 1903. While that was pending, he began investigating and experimenting along the line of railroad ties and has taken out an application for a patent upon his invention in that direction. As early as the seventies he began working to secure the building of a railroad through Athens. Failing to secure three different roads, he was finally successful in securing the extension of the Michigan Central line through the village. He was its first vice president and had charge of the first survey.

Mr. Waterman platted the village and has put forth effective efforts for its upbuilding, promotion and substantial improvement. His life has been one of activity and he has been prominent and influential in community affairs.

NICHOLAS SCHOTT.

Nicholas Schott, the owner and manager of a two-hundred-acre farm in Leroy township, Calhoun county, Michigan, was born in Bavaria, Germany, February 5, 1832. He was one of eleven children born to his parents, Peter, a farmer, of Bavaria, and Maria (Neis), also a native of that province. Of the five sons and six daughters, but three are now living, those making their home in America, namely: Margaret Voght, of Mayville, Michigan, the mother of three sons and three daughters; Charles, who married Miss Charlotte Skinner. They are the parents of six sons and have also adopted a girl; and Nicholas, our subject.

Mr. Schott came to America in 1846 and located near Buffalo, New York, engaging as a farmer, that being the work to which he had early been trained. At twenty-six years of age he came to Michigan and engaged in farming in Kalamazoo county, where he remained until August 8, 1862, when he enlisted in Company F, Nineteenth Michigan Infantry, being first located at Camp Dennison. In September his regiment was sent to Kentucky, in the following spring participating in the battle at Thompson's Station, where a brigade of eleven hundred men killed a large number of Confederates. In the midst of the battle Mr. Schott found himself surrounded by Confederates and was forced to surrender, after which he was marched to Libby Prison, where for forty days he experienced the horrors of incarceration in a southern prison. At the time of his capture he weighed one hundred and eighty pounds and when finally exchanged was unable to walk alone, his health had become so impaired. Shortly after his exchange he was sent to Columbus, Ohio, from which city he walked to his home. When again able, he rejoined the army and went to Nashville, in the spring of '64 joining the forces of Sherman. May 2, of that year, the troops moved toward Atlanta, at the beginning of the campaign, which continued for four months, marching from Atlanta to the sea. While in Savannah Mr. Schott was the victim of the ague, for the period of two weeks being in the hospital. While in the south he visited the plantation of the Confederate general, Hardee. Upon leaving Georgia the troops started north through the Carolinas, being actively engaged at Goldsboro, Bentonville and Averysboro, coming safely through a fierce engagement at the latter place, acting then as sergeant, having received his promotion to that office, after which they marched on to Richmond and Washington, being mustered out of service in the latter city. Mr. Schott received the remuneration for his years of service in Detroit and soon after purchased a farm of eighty acres and engaged at once in the peaceful pursuits of farm life. After clearing his farm and bringing it to a state of cultivation he sold the same and invested in a hundred acres of the property which he now owns, later adding another hundred acres in the same locality. In matters of public interest Mr. Schott has always proven himself a useful citizen, giving his services readily in an official capacity. He has been especially faithful in the discharge of duty, for twenty-seven years acting as school assessor, and as drainage commissioner for a number of years.

The marriage of Mr. Schott occurred in 1865 and united with him Miss Betsy Wolcott, whose death occurred February 7, 1872. She was a member of the Congregational church, of West Leroy. To them were born two children, namely: George, of Montana, in which state he was a surveyor for twelve years and is now a teacher in the Agricultural College, of Montana, which is located at Bozeman, and Albert James, who was born January 17, 1872, and died March 3, 1897. A young man, who was a leader among his acquaintances, as well as in church affairs, being a member of the Congregational church. His funeral was one of the largest ever held in this neighborhood. Mr. Schott's second marriage was to Catherine T'Eneycke, a native of the Empire state. To them were born two children, Barbara, who married Rollo Hawkins and resides with our subject, and Sarah Emogene, who died October 29, 1901. Mrs. Schott's death occurred November 27, 1902, and she is laid to rest in the family lot in the Congregational cemetery, of West Leroy.

It took thirty-four days for Mr. Schott to cross the ocean from London to New York in a sailing vessel. He started out in life without any capital except willing hands and a firm determination to succeed and his life record shows that he has met with success. He is a member of the Congregational church, although of late years he has not attended on account of his hearing. At the close of the war he took part in the Grand Review

in Washington, D. C. He draws a pension from the government for his services during the time of her peril. Mr. Schott is spending the evening of life retired from the active duties of a successful career and an honorable and upright life.

HARLAN K. WHITNEY.

One of the primary laws of nature is that concerning effort and result. It holds in every walk of life, in every class of society and is the fundamental principle of accomplishment. No advancement is secured without persistent and earnest effort on the part of someone, and no success is worthy to be called such when the effort is not put forth upon the part of the individual who enjoys the fruit of the labor. In the career of Harlan K. Whitney it a noticeable fact that the place to which he has attained in the business world has come as the direct and merited reward of his labor. He stands today as one of the foremost representatives of surveying and civil engineering in Michigan, nor is his reputation in the line of his profession confined by the boundaries of this state.

Mr. Whitney is a native son of Battle Creek, born on the 6th of December, 1864, a son of H. A. Whitney, who is represented elsewhere in this work. His public school course was completed by graduation from the high school with the class of 1883. He afterward spent two years as a member of the engineering force of this city in 1891-2 and during that period gave close and assiduous attention to the mastery of civil engineering and surveying. In the spring of 1893, he started upon an independent business career in partnership with John Elsmere under the firm style of Elsmere & Whitney, surveyors and civil engineers. This partnership, however, continued only one season, being dissolved during the winter of 1893-4. Mr. Whitney, however, continued the business and soon secured a large and constantly increasing patronage. In 1895 he entered the engineering department of the University of Michigan at Ann Arbor and spent one year there in order to perfect himself in his chosen pursuit. He gave especial attention to surveying and civil engineering and since that time has continued in the active practice of his profession at Battle Creek, having advanced step by step and finding in each forward movement broader scope for further and more effective effort. He has secured a large patronage extending to various parts of this state, nor has his business been confined to Michigan, his work having called him as far south as Alabama. His labors there were in connection with surveys for a cement factory proposition. He is now known as the leading civil engineer conducting a private business in Battle Creek.

Mr. Whitney filled the position of city engineer for the city of Albion for two years, during which time the first triple-arch concrete and steel bridge ever constructed in the United States was built in Albion under his supervision, and during the same period he conducted the general city work. He also gave his attention to his local business in Battle Creek, and later planned and laid out a modern system of sewerage for a part of the city of Albion, including the business section. His plans were adopted by the city and a portion of the sewers constructed under his immediate supervision. He was also deputy county surveyor for two years during which time he did all of the county work

in that line. He laid and supervised the building of three miles of railroad for the Cement Company at Union City, Michigan, and has carried forward his work along progressive lines that has made his a successful business career. He has given special attention to city platting and has platted and laid out many prominent additions to Battle Creek, including Morgan Park. He has platted in the neighborhood of one thousand acres of land. He also laid out the grounds and walks for the Phelps Sanatorium, the finest piece of landscape gardening in this part of the state. He has also done considerable work in artistic platting and added to his comprehensive knowledge of the great scientific principles which underlie his profession, he has intimate acquaintance with the practical part of his work and possesses the enterprise and keen discernment which are essential factors in the successful financial conduct of any business interest. He early became interested in the Advance Pump and Compressor Company at Battle Creek and has also made investment in other industrial concerns of this city.

In the line of his profession Mr. Whitney is connected with the Michigan Engineering Society. In politics he is a Prohibitionist, which allegiance indicates his views on the temperance question and his loyalty to his belief. A member of the Presbyterian church, he is now serving as one of its elders and also as clerk of the session, and has been an active worker in the Sunday school for twenty years. In the work of the Young Men's Christian Association he is deeply interested and helped to organize the present association in Battle Creek, becoming one of the first directors and also its first recording secretary. He has ever continued in this line of Christian activity and his efforts have been effective and beneficial. In his business he has attained more than the success that can be measured by material standards for he has always labored for high ideal and ethical relations between man and his fellow men in all trade transactions, and his own career exemplifies the power of absolute honesty as well as of energy in business life.

OTIS A. LEONARD.

Otis A. Leonard, who is well known in insurance circles and as secretary of the Homestead Loan and Building Association, of Albion, was born at Linden, Genesee county, Michigan, June 17, 1868, his parents being Allen and Lovina (Hyatt) Leonard. Both were natives of New York and with their respective parents removed to Genesee county, Michigan, where their marriage was celebrated. The paternal grandfather, Samuel Leonard, was a pioneer land owner of Livingston county, and there lived for many years. His last days, however, were spent in Linden. The maternal grandfather of our subject likewise lived on a farm in that locality, and Allen Leonard devoted his time and energies to agricultural pursuits, becoming an extensive farmer; the profitable return from his business enabling him to spend his last years in retirement from labor. He died in 1880, at the age of fifty-nine years and is still survived by his wife.

After attending the public schools in his home town, Otis A. Leonard became a student in Albion College and after completing a preparatory course entered upon the regular college work, being graduated in that institution with the class of 1891, the degree of Bachelor of Arts being conferred upon him. He then located in Albion, where he was first employed as a salesman in a grocery store and later in a clothing store. When he saw a favorable opening in the insurance field he bought out an old established insurance office and has since been engaged in the insurance and loan business, representing twenty-seven of the old time companies and also handling loans and investments. His business interests have been largely along lines leading to the substantial improvement and development of his community. He was one of the early members of the Homestead and Loan Association and for ten years has been its secretary. This has a large membership and is a successful local company. Such an institution is always of value to a community, enabling many to secure homes through that agency, who otherwise could not afford to build. Mr. Leonard is also interested in other enterprises of the city and is a wide-awake, alert and enterprising man, belonging to that class upon whose efforts rests the business development and substantial progress of the city.

In his political views he is a Republican. Mr. Leonard has taken an active and interested part in promoting the successes of the organization, has been a member of the Republican central committee of the county and is now the secretary of the Lincoln Republican club. In 1893 he was elected supervisor for the second ward of Albion, and since that time has been continued in the office by re-election. He has served on a number of the important committees, was chairman of the board for one year and for two years has been chairman of the claims committee. Fraternally, he is connected with Murat lodge, No. 14, F. & A. M.; Albion Chapter, No. 32, R. A. M., and Albion lodge No. 57, K. P.

Mr. Leonard was married, at Albion, October 26, 1893, to Miss Elizabeth I. Fisk, a daughter of Dr. L. R. Fisk, at that time president of Albion College.

MYRON HENRY NICHOLS.

A forceful exponent of the law, Myron Henry Nichols, for many years prominent in the courts of Calhoun county, Michigan, has made for himself a record enviable indeed from a legal standpoint. Mr. Nichols is a native of the county wherein so much of his professional life has been spent, his birth having occurred in Clarendon township October 12, 1857. His parents, John Wesley and Suzama (Clark) Nichols, both natives of New York state, meeting and marrying after their removal to Michigan, were well-known pioneers of this state, the greater part of their lives being passed in Branch and Calhoun counties. After their marriage, in Branch county, they removed to a farm in Clarendon township, this county, where they made their home for many years, the death of the mother occurring in that locality. Shortly before his death Mr. Nichols located in Homer. Both parents are buried in Clarendon cemetery. Both were of the South Baptist church denomination, both having been faithful and prominent members of the same for many years. Mr. Nichols was a Republican politically and a patriot in his country's cause, enlisting as a soldier in the Civil war, a member of

Company B, Eleventh Michigan Volunteers, serving as a private until his honorable discharge on account of illness. He was a member of the Grand Army of the Republic of Homer, and was held in high esteem by all who knew him.

Our personal subject, Myron H. Nichols, was reared in his native county, receiving his preliminary education in the district school in the vicinity of his home. Later he attended school at Jackson for the period of six months, after which he taught for a period of six years and then attended the Northern Indiana Normal School, at Valparaiso, for one term, and then taught one term of winter school. At the close of that time he again went to Valparaiso, taking a two-years' law course, graduating from the institution in 1888, in a class of ninety students. He immediately located in Homer and entered the law firm of Mains & Mains, with whom he remained for three years. He then opened an office of his own, successfully conducting a general practice, which has grown to remunerative proportions, as his evident ability and legal knowledge has come to be more widely recognized in the passing years. He does a general practice in the justice, circuit and supreme courts, and also bankruptcy courts.

In 1894 Mr. Nichols was united in marriage with Miss Elizabeth Linton, and to them have been born four children, named in order of birth as follows: J. Howard, Haskel L., Homer C. and Nympha Dora. Mrs. Nichols is a member of the Presbyterian church. Mr. Nichols is a Republican in his political convictions, and as such has neglected no opportunity to advance the principles which he indorses. In the interests of the party he has served in the various village offices, being president of the village of Homer for one term, village attorney for five years, justice of the peace one term and director of the school district. While attorney for the village he conducted several suits which attracted universal attention, having a great influence upon points of law throughout the state. In addition to his legal interests Mr. Nichols also deals in real estate. In fraternal relations Mr. Nichols is a member of the Knights of Pythias, of Homer, and a charter member of the Modern Woodmen of America, belonging to Homer camp, No. 3055, of which he acted as clerk for a number of years, and holds the office at the present time. Mr. Nichols is a progressive and public spirited citizen, and he has ever been ready to lend his aid in the direction of material advancement for the city, county or state.

MONFORT D. WEEKS.

Among the more prominent members of the bar, and the leading business men of Albion, Monfort D. Weeks is numbered. His life history is without startling incident, but is that of a man, who, realizing that the world has a duty for every man, has resolutely set to work to accomplish the task entrusted to him, and in his faithful performance of each labor has found new incentive and encouragement for further and broader effort. As an attorney, and as the guardian of various private trusts, he has ever been found most loyal to the interests given into his care, and has gained the favorable regard of the public at large.

Mr. Weeks was born in Flowerfield, St. Joseph county, Michigan, February 14, 1849. His father, Lorenzo D. Weeks, was born in Monroe county, New York, December 19, 1819. His father was a Methodist circuit rider and was an intimate friend of Lorenzo Dow, in whose honor he named his son. Rev. Weeks died during the early boyhood of his son and the mother afterward married a Mr. Straw and removed to western Michigan, where Lorenzo Dow Weeks was reared to manhood and learned the carpenter's trade, in connection with which he followed the occupation of farming. He married Miss Betsey Ann Monfort, of Monroe county, and after spending about two years in Michigan, they returned to New York, where Mr. Weeks continued to engage in farming and carpentering. He also lived for a time in Delaware, where he engaged in fruitgrowing soon after the Civil war, following that pursuit until his death. His widow spent her last days in Albion. She was a daughter of David C. Monfort, of Sibleyville, New York, a farmer by occupation. During the War of 1812 he served as a musician. His father, Peter Monfort, was born in New Jersey and at an early day went with his son to western New York and afterward became a pioneer of Monroe county, settling there when the site of Rochester was little more than a swamp, there being but one or two little log huts in the place. Peter Monfort was a son of Abram Monfort and a grandson of Peter Monfort, Sr., a prominent resident of New Jersey, where he owned a large body of land on the Raritan river. He was of Holland birth.

Monfort D. Weeks began his education in the public schools of Monroe county, New York, and continued his studies in a seminary at Delaware, while in 1869 he matriculated in Cornell University in which he pursued a scientific course. His father died in the early spring of 1873 and he then had to leave college in order to settle up the estate and care for his mother. For a number of terms he engaged in teaching school in Delaware, and in the summer of 1876 came to Albion, Michigan, where he entered the office of A. M. Culver and began the study of law. On passing the required examination he was admitted to the bar in September, 1878, and at once located for practice in Albion. He was not long in securing a clientage of profitable proportions, for he soon demonstrated his ability to cope with intricate problems of jurisprudence. He has made a specialty of probate work and corporation practice and has practiced largely in the circuit and supreme courts.

Mr. Weeks has also figured prominently in public affairs. He served his county for three terms, from 1881 until 1883, and from 1893 until 1897, as circuit court commissioner, and has been city attorney. now holding the office for the eighth term, since the city was organized in 1885. He acted in this capacity for two terms under Democratic administration, although he has always been known as a stanch Republican and an active worker in the party. As owner and as administrator and a guardian he has had charge of considerable property, and to him has been entrusted the settlement of a number of estates. For some years he has been a director of the First National Bank and was one of the incorporators of the Commercial and Savings Bank, while of the Cook Manufacturing Company and of the American Harness Company he is a director. He is local attorney for the Gale Manufacturing Company and also the C. Prouty Company.

In 1882 Mr. Weeks married Miss Louisa B. Foster, of Albion, a daughter of Ira and Lydia Foster, and they have a son, Harold B., who is a graduate of the Albion high school and is now a student in the Michigan Agricultural College. The family home is on Austin avenue and Mr. and Mrs. Weeks are active and influential members of the First Baptist church, in which he is serving as a trustee and deacon, while for many years he was superintendent of the Sunday school. Socially, he is connected with the Knights of Pythias fraternity. His interests are broad, and while his attention has been chiefly given to his profession, in which he has attained enviable local rank, he has at the same time been accounted one of the promoters of the intellectual, social and moral progress of the community.

RANSOM C. POOLE.

Ransom C. Poole, an honored veteran of the Civil war, now living in Emmett township, Calhoun county, was born in the town of Stafford, Genesee county, New York, February 24, 1842, a son of David and Maria (Chapman) Poole, both natives of Connecticut. The father was born August 8, 1798, and the mother's birth occurred May 25, 1798. The year 1854 witnessed their arrival in Michigan, where the father secured one hundred and twenty acres of land, of which forty acres had not then been broken. He at once began to develop and improve the property and made his home thereon until his death, which occurred August 24, 1859. His wife survived him until August 24, 1876.

Ransom C. Poole began his education in the schools of New York and continued it in the district schools of Michigan and in School No. 1, of Battle Creek. Farm work in its various departments early became familiar to him and he remained on the old home place until 1867, when he removed to Pennfield township and purchased a farm of eighty-three acres, which he sold in 1879. In 1881 he became the owner of his present property, comprising one hundred and thirty-three acres, in Emmett township. He has a fine home here and richly cultivated fields and annually his crops return to him a very desirable income. For many years he has been actively engaged in general farming and the prosperity which has come to him is the result of his energy, diligence and capable management as an agriculturist.

In 1865 Mr. Poole was married to Miss Evaline M. Stiles, a daughter of Zebediah and Cynthia (Clark) Stiles, who were natives of New York and at a very early epoch in the development of Michigan came to Calhoun county. They cast their lot amid the pioneer settlers and secured eighty acres of wild land which the father developed into a good farm. He died while on a visit in the east and his wife died on the old home farm here. His birth occurred in St. Lawrence county, New York, and the remains of both were interred in Oak Hill cemetery. Mrs. Ransom C. Poole died October 13, 1903, and is buried in Oak Hill cemetery.

At the breaking out of the Civil war in 1861 Mr. Poole enlisted in the first company that left Battle Creek—Company C, Michigan Second Volunteer Infantry, under Captain Byington. He participated in the battle of Bull Run and many engagements including the siege of Vicksburg, being present at the surrender. On the 4th of June, 1864, he was mustered out of the service. He was ill a number of times

during his army life and has never yet fully recovered from the effects of his military service. In his political views he is an earnest Republican, but has never sought office as a reward for party fealty, ever preferring to give his time and attention to his business affairs in which he has been quite successful, so that he now owns a valuable farm and is accounted one of the substantial citizens and agriculturists of his community.

JOHN CONRAD KUECHLE.

A successful baker of Marshall, Michigan, living at 224 South Hamilton street, is John Conrad Kuechle, who was born in Bridgewater, Washtenaw county, Michigan, December 2, 1851. His parents, Philip and Marie (Rein) Kuechle, were both natives of Wurttemburg, Germany, the birth of the father occurring there June 25, 1814. He was a butcher in his native land but not finding the opportunity there that he desired in his life work, he emigrated to the land of greater promise, America, in 1846, locating in Bridgewater, Michigan. The following year he was married and November 25, 1855, he came to Marshall where he remained until his death, March 28, 1903. From 1859 to 1866 he conducted a meat market, in the last named year disposing of his interests in this line. In his political convictions Mr. Kuechle was a Republican until the formation of the Greenback party, when he became a Democrat and remained one until his death. Through the influence of his party he served in the city council as alderman from the fourth ward. He was a member of the German Lutheran church and was one of the organizers of the church of that denomination in Marshall, for many years being active in various official positions. To himself and wife were born six children, those besides our subject being as follows: Kate, born in August, 1849, married Carl Weber, a baker by occupation, and they have one son, Carl C., who clerks for Mr. Kuechle; Philip, born October 19, 1850, married Minnie Hartel, and they have one child, Arthur. They live in Fort Wayne, Indiana, where he is engaged in the meat business; George J., born March 29, 1854, a butcher in Marshall, who married Lizzie Hartkorn, and they have two children, John and Marjorie; Anna Marie, born July 6, 1856, married William S. Forler, of Warsaw, Indiana, there engaged in the hotel business. They have five children, namely: George, Mabel, Edmund, Marie and Conrad.

When he was fourteen years old John Conrad Kuechle found employment away from home, beginning with a blacksmith, for whom he worked two and a half years. He then learned the trade of a baker, working for John L. Evans, with whom he remained for a number of years, after which he was variously employed until about thirteen years ago, when he bought the business for himself, which he has since conducted and has met with gratifying success. In 1894 he purchased a lot and erected his present handsome residence. His marriage, February 16, 1886, united him with Miss Elizabeth Rebecca House, who was born in St. Thomas, Canada, September 6, 1867. Her father, John Franklin House, was one of six sons and daughters born to his parents, all natives of Canada, and all of whom are now living ex-

cept Mr. House, whose death occurred in North Branch, Michigan, January 14, 1878, and is buried in that locality. He was a farmer, and came to Marshall thirty-nine years ago, where his wife, formerly Mary L. McNamer, now makes her home. Two children were born to them. Mrs. Kuechle being the only one now living, her brother, Frank, having died in 1883, and is buried in Marshall. Religiously Mr. Kuechle is a member of the German Lutheran church, and fraternally affiliates with the Knights of Pythias, the Maccabees and German Workmen's Benevolent Association. Politically he has been a Democrat all his life, his first vote having been cast for Horace Greeley, and through the influence of his party he has served as city treasurer for two terms, 1888 and 1889, and as alderman for two years, from the fourth ward, in which he has voted all his life. Mr. Kuechle speaks fluently the native tongue of his father, having great admiration for the Fatherland. In 1902 he made a trip to Germany on the ship Kronprintz Wilhelm, which broke all previous records, crossing from New York city to Bremen in five days and nine hours. He spent eight weeks in Germany and two in Switzerland, traveling in all the principal cities of both countries, stopping in Cassel, Leipsic, Carlsbad, Berlin, Stuttgart, Munich, Strassburg, Mannheim, Frankfort, Zurich and Lusanne; climbed the Jungfrau and other famous peaks and stopped for a time at Cologne. He brought back many souvenirs of his trip and one incident abroad which was especially enjoyable was a Fourth of July celebration at Stuttgart. He found the hotels of Germany better than those of our country, and German people, as a rule, modern in their methods of business; the condition of the two countries being very similar with the exception that opportunities for advancement are far greater in the land of his father's adoption. It is his intention to make the trip again in a few years and again enjoy the beautiful scenery, which was even grander than he had expected. Mr. Kuechle has also done some traveling in his own country, having attended the World's Columbian Exposition in 1893, and seen much of the country of the eastern states.

ANDREW J. VAN WORMER.

Andrew J. Van Wormer has been a resident of Calhoun county since 1836, and his honorable life entitles him to representation among the leading and influential men of the county, who in the past or at the present time have aided in molding public policy and in promoting the material, social, and intellectual and moral welfare of this part of the state. His home is now in Albion. He was born in Allegany county, New York, January 15, 1831. His father, Jeremiah Van Wormer, was of Holland lineage, the family being established in the Mohawk valley at a very early day. William Wattles, the maternal grandfather, was one of the heroes of the Revolutionary war, serving with the rank of captain. He made his home in the Mohawk valley. Jeremiah Van Wormer was born in that locality near the ancestral home and was there married to Miss Eunice Wattles, who resided near Sempronius. Later he removed to Allegany county, New York, where he engaged in farming and subsequently he resided in

Cohocton, Steuben county, New York, in 1836, when he started for the west, driving across the country with two teams to Jackson county, Michigan. He settled in Concord township, five miles from Albion, when that was a new and undeveloped country. He purchased land from the government and made a home, instituting many improvements, and afterward adding to his place until it comprised one hundred and twenty acres. He served his country as a soldier of the War of 1812 and his political allegiance was given to the Democracy. Both he and his wife were early members of the Methodist Protestant church in Jackson county and their home was always open for the entertainment of the ministers who visited this region in pioneer times. Mr. Van Wormer passed away December 5, 1851, and his wife died in 1876, when almost ninety years of age. In their family were ten children, but only two are living: Lois, the wife of A. J. Thompson, of the village of Concord, Michigan; and Andrew J., of this review. The record of those who have passed away is as follows: Mrs. Electa Parmeter died in Concord township, Jackson county, Michigan. Aaron entered the Union army in a Missouri regiment at the time of the Civil war, but served only three months, after which he was discharged on account of physical disability. He was a graduate of Geneva (now Hobart) College, of New York, was a man of marked capability and scholarly attainments and for six years served as circuit judge of Phelps county, Missouri. He died in Raleigh, that state, leaving several children, of whom Andrew, named in honor of Mr. Van Wormer, of this review, is a prominent attorney of New York city. Mrs. Salina Parmeter died at the age of eighty-four years in

Spring Arbor, Michigan. Mrs. Fannie Vinecore died at the age of ninety years in Nebraska. William died at Concord, Michigan. Jerry W., who enlisted in 1861 in the First Michigan Cavalry, served in defense of the Union throughout the Civil war and afterward died at Spring Arbor, Michigan. Mrs. Angeline Turner passed away in Jackson. Michigan. Lawrence died in Concord, this state.

In taking up the personal history of Andrew J. Van Wormer we find that in his early boyhood days he attended the common schools and worked upon the old homestead farm, early becoming familiar with the arduous task of developing new land. He was but five years of age when brought to Michigan by his parents and with the family he experienced many of the hardships and trials incident to pioneer life. His father died when the son was twenty-one years of age and at that time Andrew J. Van Wormer took charge of the old homestead and eventually bought out the interest of the other heirs. His mother always made her home with him. At length he became possessed of the entire farm and added to it until he now has one hundred and eighty-four acres of very rich and arable land. He was a successful general farmer and also dealt in high graded stock, making a specialty of the raising of horses. He raised the horse that was afterward known as "Little Randall" and which sold for twelve thousand dollars. He also owned other good animals and his farming and stock-raising interests proved very profitable.

As a companion and helpmate for life's journey Mr. Van Wormer chose Miss Emily M. Gregory, a daughter of Noah and Lucinda (Hackett) Gregory. Her father was born in Connecticut and when a young man removed to Batavia, New York, where he was married. Later he resided in St. Catherines. Canada, where he followed the mason's trade. Mrs. Van Wormer was born during the residence of the family in St. Catherines. Canada, and the marriage occurred on the 13th of February, 1853, in Albion. Six children graced this union, of whom four are living: Eleanor, the wife of Grove Carpenter, of Concord, by whom she has two children—Lelie, wife of Charles Rainville. of Joliet. Illinois, and Harold; Flora G. is the wife of Fred Holmes, of Joliet, Illinois; Ernest Levi, who resides upon the home farm and is engaged in business as a painter and decorator, married Miss Lura Weitzell and they have three sons, Clarence, Andrew and Robert; Lillian Belle is the wife of Caleb Antram, an attorney of Joliet. Illinois, and they have two sons. Robert and Fred.

Mr. and Mrs. Van Wormer resided upon the old home farm until the spring of 1894, when, having acquired a competence, he retired from active labor and has since enjoyed a well earned rest. He built a fine home at No. 316 Irwin avenue in Albion and there he is now living. His political allegiance was given to the Democracy in early life, but afterward he became a Prohibitionist and has been a stanch supporter of the party for many years. For forty years he has held membership in the Methodist Protestant church and was active in organizing a Methodist class in Concord. When the church building was erected it stood upon part of his land. He had taken an active part in drawing up the plans and circulating the subscription paper and was chairman of the building committee. To him is due the greatest credit for the erection of the Van Wormer church and well did he deserve to have it named in his honor. He has always held official positions in the church and for many years was a local minister, having been ordained over twenty years ago. His membership is yet with the organization which he was instrumental in founding. After all that may be said of a man the world judges him not so much by the success that he has achieved, but by the character that he has developed. It is the only thing that makes his memory honored and his name cherished after he has passed away. Throughout a busy and useful career Mr. Van Wormer has always guided his actions by honorable principles and the teachings of Christianity and his career commands the highest respect and confidence. The work of the church has been materially promoted through his efforts and influence and although he has achieved success in his business life he will leave to his family what is much more precious than money—the priceless heritage of an untarnished name.

HOLLAND J. ROWE.

Among the representative farmers of Calhoun county, Holland J. Rowe occupies a prominent place, his well cultivated farm of one hundred and sixty acres in Athens township adding greatly to the value of property in the community. He was born in Onondaga county, New York, July 30, 1829, a son of Libies and Harriet (Barber) Rowe, both of whom were natives of Vermont. Soon after their marriage the parents had removed to the western part of New York, from which location they moved to Monroe, Michigan, where they lived for some years and then settled in Sherwood township, Branch county, Michigan, in 1838, there purchasing a farm upon which they lived for many years. The father died at the age of seventy-three years and both parents are interred in Sherwood cemetery. As pioneers in both western New York and Michigan they had given their best efforts toward the settlement and upbuilding of the communities wherein they had made their home. To Mr. and Mrs. Rowe were born eight children, those besides Holland J., the fifth in order of birth, being as follows: Two who died in childhood; Elizabeth Ann, who became the wife of N. A. Billings, and is now deceased; Nathan, who was crippled, also deceased; L. E., a resident of Toledo, Ohio; Mary Jane, who died at the age of three years; and Mason, also deceased. By his second wife Mr. Rowe had one son, Myron, who now lives in Iowa, and four children who died in infancy.

When only two years of age Holland J. Rowe was taken by his parents to Monroe county, Michigan, seven years later becoming with them a resident of Branch county, where he continued to make his home until attaining his majority. He received a limited education in the common schools of both counties, the greater part of his time being spent in assisting with the daily work on his father's farm, clearing and cultivating his land. In 1850 he set out in the world to make his own way, the first year being employed at ten dollars per month by an uncle who lived in Toledo. He then returned to this section of the country in 1858, purchasing a farm of eighty acres, nearly all of which was timber land, paying eight hundred dollars, which he had saved from his earnings for nine years. With the energy and industry characteristic of the pioneer he gave himself up to the improvement and cultivation of his land, in time doubling the number of acres. He is now engaged in general farming and stockraising, in the latter industry making a specialty of Durham cattle, having the best bred stock in this part of the country. All the improvements have been of his own efforts, having erected a fine large house and barn, and various other outbuildings.

In 1860 Mr. Rowe was united in marriage with Miss Harriet Palmer, who was born in Newton township, Calhoun county, Michigan. She was a daughter of John and Elizabeth (Acker) Palmer, natives respectively of Northampton, England, and Somerset, Niagara county, New York, her father having come to America in 1828 at the age of nineteen years. He became a gardener, locating near Poughkeepsie, and later near Albany. Afterwards he engaged in farming, coming in 1830 to Michigan, where he took up land in Newton township. It was in that locality that he met and married his wife, by whom he has had six children, those besides Mrs. Rowe, the eldest, being as follows: Celesta, who is the widow of Elmer Rowe, an uncle of our subject, who lived in Union City; George, who also resides in Union City; Charles, who resides in Bronson; Mary Jane, who died in childhood; and Wilfred, who died at the age of eleven years. Both parents are buried in Union City, the father passing away in 1893. To Mr. Rowe and his wife were born two children, of whom Mary Jane married Edward Wisner, of Toledo, and is the mother of two children, namely: Harriet Rowena and Clara Elizabeth; and Nathan L. married Rose Lockwood and resides in Toledo. In his political convic-

tions Mr. Rowe does not hold fast to the principles of any one party, but reserves the right to cast his ballot for the man whom he considers best qualified to discharge the duties of office. He has not himself cared for official recognition, but has in every way given his efforts toward the advancement and development of the community and has upheld good government by voice and vote. He is recognized as a man of sterling worth and appreciated for the many good qualities which have made him of such use as a citizen.

JOHN THOMAS LANE.

The name which heads this review is one that belongs to a family numbered among the early settlers of Calhoun county. The genealogy of the family is traced to English scenes, the parents, James and Sarah (Finch) Lane, being natives respectively of near Pershore, Worcestershire, and Forest River, Sussex county, England. The family came to America in 1835, the voyage consuming six weeks and three days, and immediately after landing in New York city they came direct to Michigan, where the father located on the farm which is now the home of his son. He remained in Marshall, then a little town of only a few houses, for about six weeks, putting up on his seventy-five acre farm on section 27 a little shanty 10x12 feet in size, which gave shelter to this pioneer family until the following spring. Mr. Lane then built a log house which remained their home until 1851, in the meantime clearing the farm and by industry, energy and perseverance bringing the land to a high state of cultivation and improvement. His efforts were not without their reward and in the last named year he was enabled to erect a large frame house, which for twenty-seven years thereafter was known as a first-class hostelry of this community. Success attended the efforts of the elder Mr. Lane and in time he became the owner of much property, having over three hundred and fifty acres of land. The last ten years of his life were spent in retirement, after many years of usefulness as a citizen, as a farmer advancing the agricultural interests of the community, and as a Democrat in politics lending his best efforts toward the promotion of the principles which he endorsed. Though not an office seeker he never shirked his responsibility as a citizen, discharging with efficiency the duties of various township offices. In his religious convictions he affiliated with the Seventh Day Adventists, though he had been reared in the Church of England. To Mr. and Mrs. Lane were born the following children, who have emulated the example of their father and early achieved a success in life: John Thomas, the personal subject of this review, who was born in London, England, October 20, 1834; Charles J., a practicing physician of Marshall; Caroline, who married Harvey Potter and lives in Convis township; Edward F., who also lives in Convis township; and William A., also a physician, who is now serving as probate judge.

When twenty years of age John T. Lane was given his time by his father, after which he worked on neighboring farms, his remuneration being fourteen dollars per month and board. The practical training which he had received along the lines of industry and economy became now a factor in his life, and evidence of the fact being that at the end of the season he had spent but two dollars of the money paid him for his work. In a short time he was able to purchase forty acres of land in Convis township, following the example of his pioneer father by erecting a log house which was to be his home while he cleared and improved his property. After a period of four years he traded this farm for one comprising seventy-nine acres, upon which he remained for nine years, when he removed to the old homestead, since 1869 making this his home. He is now engaged in farming, his practical and progressive methods having brought him the success for which he has labored.

On December 27, 1855, Mr. Lane was united in marriage with Miss Maria T. Alton, who was born near Portage, Allegany county, New York, March 21, 1834. She was ten years old when she was brought to Hancock county, Illinois, by her parents, Elliot and Hannah (Wheelock) Alton, and she there grew to womanhood, receiving an excellent education in the schools of the county. She was the eleventh in a family of thirteen children, and a year after the death of her mother in 1851, near Nauvoo, she began teaching in Lake county, Indiana, her mother having also followed that occupation before her marriage. Later she came to Calhoun county, Michigan, to live with her sister, Mrs. Hannah Brown, and taught here until her marriage. To Mr. and Mrs. Lane were born the following children: Francis, who died in infancy; Charles S., an auctioneer and farmer in Convis township, and by his marriage with Epha D. Winans has two daughters, Nerna B. and Edna; Fannie B., who married Clayton Cox, a miller and millwright of Minot, North Dakota, and now has five children, namely: Charles C., Harry Elwood, Gilbert H., Leota and Ercell. In religious affairs of the community both Mr. and Mrs. Lane have always taken the deepest interest. Both are members of the Seventh Day Adventist church, in the organization of the congregation in Convis township Mr. Lane acting in conjunction with Solomon Sellers, was a member of the building committee and is now a trustee. Mrs. Lane is a thorough Bible student, was formerly active in Sunday school work, serving as teacher and superintendent for many years. In his political convictions Mr. Lane was reared a Democrat, his first presidential ballot being cast for Buchanan. Later he adhered to the principles of the Greenback party but is now a Populist. During the many years which Mr. Lane has passed in this community his many sterling qualities have won for him the esteem and confidence of his fellow citizens. On the old homestead, section 27, Convis township, was organized the first caucus and the first town meeting were held.

REV. DEMPSTER D. MARTIN, B. D.

Rev. Dempster D. Martin, B. D., is one of the notable representatives of the Methodist Episcopal clergy in Michigan, and in the fall of 1903 was appointed to the position of presiding elder of the Albion district, comprising five counties. He now makes his home in Albion, Michigan, and by virtue of his office has jurisdiction over eighty-six churches. He was born in Martinsville, Wayne county, Michigan, April 1, 1862, and is a son of Winslow P. and Alida (Disbrow) Martin. The father was born in North Adams, Massachusetts, and was a direct descendant of Christopher Martin and his wife, who were among the arrivals on the Mayflower and whose names appear on the monument which has been erected to the memory of the Mayflower passengers at Plymouth Rock. Daniel Martin, the great-grandfather of our subject, was a contractor and builder and assisted by his son Joe, then fourteen years of age, built the first cotton mill in America, this being located in Providence, Rhode Island. Joel Martin, the grandfather, settled near Lowell, Massachusetts, but later on in life came as a pioneer settler to Michigan, making his home in Wayne county. The settlement was named Martinsville in honor of the family and for a number of years Joel Martin was a prominent and influential resident of that community. In the east he had followed merchandising, but practically lived in retirement after his removal to the west.

Winslow P. Martin acquired his preliminary education in North Adams, Massachusetts, and afterward continued his studies in Lockport, New York. When a young man he came to Michigan, where he owned a large farm located in Wayne county. He also had farm property in Hillsdale county and afterward removed to that place with his family. He was, however, a life-long and honored minister of the Wesleyan Methodist church and established many churches of that denomination in southern Michigan. To-day the influence of his labors and efforts are still felt as a potent factor for good and Michigan acknowledges her indebtedness for his labor in behalf of her moral progress. In 1885 he removed to South Dakota, where he was engaged in active church work and also organized many new congregations. His death occurred in Northville, South Dakota, in the year 1888. His wife was born in the Catskill mountains in New York, a daughter of Elias Disbrow, who was a witness of America's development through almost the entire nineteenth century, his birth occurring in 1802, while his death occurred during the closing days of the year 1900. Mrs. Martin, who still survives her husband, is now residing with a daughter in Fremont, Nebraska.

Rev. Dempster D. Martin, who is the fifth in order of birth, in a family of eight children, acquired his education in the public schools of Wayne and Hillsdale counties and at intervals worked upon his father's farm. In Hillsdale College he was graduated with the class of 1891, on which occasion the degree of Bachelor of Divinity was conferred upon him. He had begun the full literary course and had also combined with it theological work as a preparation for the ministry. On leaving college he became a minister of the Wesleyan Methodist church, with which his father had long been associated. He served for a short time as pastor of the churches at Pittsford, Brighton, Allegan and Coldwater, but desiring to broaden his capacity for good he gave up his pastorate at Coldwater and entered Hillsdale College, where he pursued a complete course and at the same time continued his pastoral labors. In 1890, on resigning his pastorate at Coldwater, he joined the ministry of the Methodist Episcopal church and later in the same year united with the Michigan Conference

32

of that denomination. His first pastorate following that step was at Sherwood and during his year's stay the membership of the church was nearly trebled and a handsome house of worship was purchased from the Unitarian Association and turned over to the Methodist Society entirely free of debt. Rev. Martin next went to Reading and while there built a new church edifice and parsonage and through his efforts the membership of the church was almost doubled. For four years he continued as pastor there and was then appointed to the church at St. Johns, Michigan, where during a four-years' pastorate a beautiful new church and parsonage were erected, valued at thirty thousand dollars. They were also entirely clear from debt. In 1898 Rev. Martin was appointed to the pastorate of the First Methodist Episcopal church of Battle Creek. This is one of the largest churches of the conference, having a membership of about six hundred at the present time, although when he took charge of it the membership was but four hundred. More than one-half of the present members were admitted into the church under his ministry, a large number of them being received on confession of faith. During the same period the old parsonage on Bennett street was sold and a commodious new residence at the corner of East Fountain street and South avenue was purchased. Several improvements were also made upon the house of worship, but as it still remains inadequate to the growing needs of the society, plans have been perfected for the erection of a new church edifice on the old site. The work of the church in its various departments was thoroughly organized and Rev. Martin remained as pastor there until appointed presiding elder in the fall of

1903. During the greater part of his connection with conference work Rev. Martin
has been a member of the examining committee, examining young ministers who are
applicants for admission into the church
and as this is the largest conference in
Methodism his position is therefore a responsible one.

On the 23d of April, 1884, Rev. Martin was united in marriage to Miss Ora
Van Horn, of Howell, Michigan, a daughter of Morris B. Van Horn, a farmer and
capitalist. Unto them have been born two
children, Ethel A. and James Morris, the
latter now in business college.

Rev. Martin also keeps in touch with
the business world and the time which he
has for his own use, aside from its ministerial duties he devotes to business interests, being now connected with a number
of corporations in Battle Creek. The
church, however, is always his first interest
and his influence in behalf of Christianity
is of no restricted order. He has labored
earnestly and zealously in behalf of his
church, his work being an integral factor
in the growth and development of Methodism in southern Michigan and long after
he shall have passed to his reward the seeds
of truth and righteousness which he
planted will bear fruit. He is well qualified
for his work, for he is a man of scholarly
attainments and in the pulpit is a speaker
of force, his utterances being logical and
convincing. At this point it would be almost tautological to enter into any series
of statements as showing Rev. Martin to be
a man of broad intelligence and genuine
public spirit, for these have been shadowed
forth between the lines of this review.
Strong in his individuality, he never lacks
the courage of his convictions, but as dom-

inating elements in his individuality he possesses lively human sympathy and an abiding charity, which, as taken in connection
with the sterling integrity and honor of his
character, have naturally gained for him
the respect and confidence of men.

JAMES I. MAIN.

Success comes not to the man who idly
waits but to the earnest toiler, whose efforts are directed by discriminating judgment, and it is in this way that Mr. Main
has become one of the prosperous residents
of Tekonsha, where he is now engaged in
dealing in drugs, groceries, wall paper,
paints and oils. He is one of Calhoun
county's native sons, his birth having occurred on a farm in Clarendon township,
on the 17th of September, 1844. His parents were John and Lucyett (Hitchcock)
Main. His paternal great-grandparents
were born in Scotland. The grandfather
was James Main, and the father of our subject was born in Saratoga county, New
York, October 10, 1810. After acquiring
his education in the public schools he engaged in teaching in both New York and
Michigan. He was married in Bergen,
New York, to Miss Lucyett Hitchcock, who
was born in 1812 at Marshall, Oneida
county, New York. The father had come
to Michigan in 1835, and entered land from
the government and in June, 1837, he was
married in the Empire state, after which
he returned with his bride to Michigan,
making his home upon his farm until 1869.
He then established his home in Tekonsha,

where he died in 1880, while his wife passed away in 1900 at the age of eighty-seven years.

Under the parental roof James I. Main spent his boyhood days, and after attending the district schools he entered Olivet College at the age of twenty-two years and therein pursued his studies for four terms. Subsequently he engaged in teaching school for four winters and during the summer months assisted in the work of the home farm.

On the 28th of October, 1869, in Byron, Genesee county, New York, where he had been engaged in teaching in 1868, Mr. Main was united in marriage to Miss Anna E., a daughter of John and Mary A. (Smith) Warboys, and with his bride returned to Calhoun county, where for two years he engaged in operating his father's farm, comprising one hundred and sixty acres. Mrs. Main was born in Cumberland, Oxfordshire, England, and was but six years old when her parents came to America, settling in New York. In the family were thirteen children, all of whom reached years of maturity and all but one married, while twelve are still living. Our subject prospered in his agricultural work and in April, 1872, he removed to the village of Tekonsha, where he joined his brother, Harlan A. Main, in the conduct of a drug store. His brother, who was also postmaster at that time, died eleven months later and Mr. Main of this review continued the business alone, and was also appointed postmaster by telegraph until he could be duly appointed. He served in the office for two years and at the same time carried on his mercantile interests. After his brother's death the frame building in which the store had been conducted was removed to make place for a brick block, which was erected

in 1875. Mr. Main continued in the new building for several years and in 1883 enlarged his stock by adding a line of groceries. In 1885 he built his present building and is now conducting a profitable trade. He has studied closely the demands of the public, and his earnest desire to please his patrons combined with straightforward dealing, has made him one of the popular merchants of the town.

Unto Mr. and Mrs. Main have been born five children, but the eldest, Nellie B., died at the age of two years. Harlan A., a graduate of the schools of Tekonsha township, spent one year in study at Alma, Michigan, and then pursued a course in pharmacy at Ada, Ohio, after which he became a registered pharmacist, but his business career was terminated in death at the early age of twenty-five years. Fred W., born in Tekonsha township, March 9, 1876, is now engaged in business as a dealer in agricultural implements in the village of Tekonsha, and has been treasurer of both the village and township. Dell E. is the wife of Frank D. Schafer, of Tekonsha. Bessie completes the family.

Mr. Main exercised his right of franchise in support of the men and measures of the Republican party until recently, but is now independent in politics, and his fellow townsmen, recognizing his worth and ability, have called him to public office. He served on the village council and was a member of the first election board, being appointed by the governor. He continued to act in that capacity for several years and has also been a school director for nine years, the cause of education finding in him a warm friend. An active and loyal member of the Presbyterian church, he is now one of the ruling elders and has been clerk of the sessions for twenty-two years. He belongs to the Ancient Order of United Workmen and has filled the office of recorder for five years, while for seven years he has been financier in the local lodge. In 1872 he erected his pleasant home at the corner of Church and North street and here he has resided continuously since. In his business career he has never been known to take advantage of the necessities of his fellow men; and his co-operation has always been counted upon in matters of citizenship relating to the public welfare.

SAMUEL A. HOWES.

Samuel A. Howes, well known in business, political and social circles in Battle Creek, where he has made his home since his boyhood days, was born in Camden, New Jersey, January 20, 1867, and is a son of George E. Howes, who is represented on another page of this volume. The son obtained his early education in the public schools of Philadelphia, Pennsylvania, and in 1877, when ten years of age, came with his parents to Battle Creek, continuing his studies until he had completed the high school course. He afterward spent two years as a student in the Seventh Day Adventist College of this city, subsequent to which time he entered upon his business career in the office of the Union School Furniture Company, under I. L. Stone. There he received his preliminary business training, remaining with the company for six years and finding in each advancement which came to him in recognition of his ability and fidelity, the opportunity for further progress and for the acquirement of broader knowledge concerning the business world and its methods.

Following the severance of his connection with the Union School Furniture Company, Samuel A. Howes was admitted to a partnership in the business of the firm of Howes & Bush, of which his father is the senior member. This firm owns and controls a cold storage plant for the storage of fruit, and Samuel A. Howes still retains his connection therewith. He was instrumental in incorporating the Consumers' Ice & Coal Company, became its secretary and is still the secretary of its successor, the Consumers' Coal Company, controlling an extensive trade as wholesale dealers in coal. At the time of the amalgamation of the two ice companies of the city, incorporated under the name of the Consolidated Ice Company, Mr. Howes was chosen vice president and still fills that position.

He has not only been a factor in those enterprises which contribute to commercial activity, but has also been identified with interests that have promoted the substantial improvement and upbuilding of Battle Creek, and in this connection was one of the incorporators of Foster Park, one of its finest additions. Associated with several leading business men he laid out and placed upon the market fifty-four acres, divided into city lots. This constitutes one of the most desirable residence portions of the city, being attractively located near Goguac lake.

Mr. Howes's interest in community affairs has also been manifest in co-operation in political and social activity and in endorsement of various measures which have had for their object the upbuilding of Battle Creek. His political allegiance is given the Republican party and in its local ranks he is an active worker. In 1898 he was his party's nominee for county clerk but was not elected. In the same year, however, he received an appointment from President McKinley to a position in the ordnance division of the war department and spent one year in Washington, D. C., after which he returned to Battle Creek, to resume active connection with his business and other interests here. He is a charter member of the Elks lodge, of which he was secretary for two years and belongs to both the subordinate lodge and uniformed rank of the Knights of Pythias fraternity. He is a member of the Athelstan club, the leading social organization of Battle Creek, and for a number of years prior to his sojourn in Washington was its secretary. He also belongs to the Battle Creek Gun Club, in which he has held different offices, being now field captain.

On the 20th of May, 1886, Mr. Howes was married to Miss Mary G. Crooker, of Battle Creek, a daughter of H. D. Crooker, one of the older business men of the city. They have five children: Althea, Raymond, Margaret, Harrison and Alfred. Their beautiful home, at No. 17 Elm street, was erected by Mr. Howes in the summer of 1903.

STEPHEN HUXLEY.

A prominent and influential position is accorded Stephen Huxley among the successful farmers of Athens township, Calhoun county; his connection with the agricultural interests of the community having added to their value in various lines. He was born in Summit county, Ohio, near Akron, March 6, 1834, a son of William and Electa Huxley, and at the age of thirteen years, by the death of his father, he was compelled to become self supporting. He was a strong and capable lad, and was undaunted by the responsibility which became his at so early an age, going first to Wisconsin, near Whitewater, where he remained for a time, and returning later to Ohio. By persevering effort he was financially able at the age of twenty-one to purchase eighty acres of land, adding, in time, to the original purchase until he now has one hundred and sixty acres. This consisted principally of timber land, which he has cleared and improved, now devoting his energies to general farming and stockraising, his success entirely the result of his own efforts.

On February 5th, 1860, he was united in marriage with Miss Sarah Hart, whose parents, William F. and Susanna (Ferry) Hart, were natives respectively of Stillwater, Saratoga county, New York, and Almond, Allegany county, same state. After their marriage in the latter location they removed to Ohio, settling near Upper Sandusky, for eight years making that their home. They then removed to Calhoun county, Michigan, in 1844, purchasing a farm where they lived for two years. Upon disposing of this property they came to Athens, locating upon a farm of eighty acres in the northern part of Athens township. In 1873 Mr. Hart retired from the active cares of life, locating at Athens, where his death occurred in 1883, at the age of seventy years, while that of his wife occurred six years later, at the age of seventy-three years. For many years they had been identified religiously with the Methodist Episcopal congregation. They are both interred in North Athens ceme-

.tery. To them were born five children, of whom Mrs. Huxley is the eldest; Margaret Ann died in Ohio; Reuben Hart is in Leroy; Lucy E. died at the age of four months; Silas Ferry died in 1883 at the age of twenty-nine years. Mr. Huxley has a good war record; he was an Abolitionist as well as a Republican, answering the call for love of country and principle. He enlisted in Company A, commanded by Capt. David Oaks, Jr., serving three years, during which he participated in many engagements; the principal ones in which he was active being Gallatin, Tennessee; Fort Riley, Stone River, Elk River, Davis Cross Roads, Chickamauga, Missionary Ridge, Gravesville, Buzzard's Roost, New Hope Church, Kenesaw, Rough Station, Peach Tree and Siege of Atlanta. During this time the regiment lost two hundred and eighty-six men, Mr. Huxley being in the field hospital at Chattanooga, and also at Nashville, being incapacitated for two months. He was honorably discharged at Sturgis, September 3, 1864.

To Mr. and Mrs. Huxley have been born five children, namely: Jennie, who married George Morehead, of Athens; William, who married Miss Mary Hosey, and resides at Athens; Irwin and Irvin, twins, the former of whom married Lettie Sherman, and now lives in Athens, while the latter married Mary A. Addison, and now lives in Leonidas; and Anna, who married Virgil Robinson and resides in Moscow, Michigan. She is the mother of one daughter, Lenora May. Mr. Huxley is a member of Frank Mason post, No. 244, of Athens, and politically supports the principles of the Republican party, though personally he has never cared for official recognition. Mr. Huxley is a self made man in the best

sense implied by the term, whatever of native ability and integrity he possessed being added to by earnest practical living. which has brought its own reward in the character which has made of him a citizen upon whom the honor of a community may safely rest. By the success which he has achieved and the manner of his effort he has won the entire respect and esteem of his fellow townsmen.

ROBERT Y. FINCH.

Robert Y. Finch is filling the position of justice of the peace in Albion, and with one exception, his residence in the city covers a longer period than that of any other person living here. He was born in St. Catherines, Ontario, Canada, March 26, 1827, a son of Asahel and Julia A. (Wilcox) Finch. The father's birth occurred in Goshen, Orange county, New York, about 1794. Tradition says that the ancestors of the family came from Wales at an early day. Henry Finch, the great-grandfather of our subject, removed to Wyoming, Pennsylvania, and was living there at the time of the massacre by the Indians during the Revolutionary war, and he lost his life at the hands of the red men. His son, Samuel Finch, the grandfather of our subject, managed to escape and made his way to Washington's army, in which he inlisted, serving throughout the War of the Revolution. His death occurred in Tioga county, Pennsylvania, about 1839. His son, Asahel Finch, was reared in Monroe county, New York, and there married Miss Julia A. Wilcox, who was born in Berlin, Albany county, New York, but removed to Monroe county in her girlhood days. Mr. Finch continued to reside in Monroe county until 1834, when he came to Albion, Michigan, and in September of that year he was poined by his family. Here his death occurred when he was seventy years of age and his wife passed away at the age of seventy-six.

Robert Y. Finch received only the educational privileges that were afforded in a new country. He was reared amid the wild scenes of pioneer life and in his youth worked at various kinds of employment that would yield him an honest living. At the age of eighteen he apprenticed himself to learn the molder's trade and followed that pursuit for a number of years. On the 1st of March, 1849, he started from Albion with an ox-team for California in company with about twenty-six men. They journeyed by way of Council Bluffs, the North Platte and Salt Lake City, arriving at Placerville, California, on the 22d of September. The magnitude of the undertaking can be imagined when it is remembered that this was the first year in which the overland trip was made to the gold fields of the far west. Only one of the party, in addition to Mr. Finch, is now living. On reaching California Mr. Finch made his way to the mines and later engaged in teaming, while subsequently he turned his attention to merchandising near Sonora in southern California. He remained on the Pacific coast for about fifteen months and prospered in his work there. He then returned to Michigan on a visit to his parents, traveling by way of the Panama route and New York and arriving at his home in January, 1851. It was his intention to again go to California, but finding that his parents were in poor health he was obliged to remain. In connection with his brother, he then purchased a farm

in Sheridan township, Calhoun county, and carried on agricultural pursuits. He placed his land, comprising two hundred and twenty-four acres, under a high state of cultivation and made excellent improvements upon his farm, transforming it into one of the fertile properties of the township. In 1865 he sold out and returned to the city, where, during the most of the intervening time, he has been engaged in the foundry business. He has also, to some extent, operated in real estate.

Mr. Finch was married to Miss Celia Spencer, of Strongville, Ohio, and died in 1900. They had three children: Ella Lois, who died in 1876; Julia B., wife of Frank G. Bothwell, of Albion; and Harry S., who is living at Texarkana, Arkansas. In 1902 Mr. Finch was again married, his second union being with Mrs. Mary E. Shipman, a daughter of Rufus Burr, one of the pioneers of Sheridan township, in which place Mrs. Finch was born and spent her early years. They have a pleasant home at No. 218 West Porter street and they attend the services of the Methodist church, contributing to its support. He has been a member of Murat lodge, No. 14, of Albion, for forty-three years and has held different offices in the organization. He is also connected with Albion Chapter, R. A. M. His political allegiance has been given to the Democracy since casting his first presidential ballot for General Cass, but he has never been an aspirant for office. Some local positions have been given him by his fellow townsmen who recognized his worth and ability and he was a trustee of Albion during its villagehood and has also been a member of the city council. For two terms he was city treasurer, having been elected in 1897 and again in 1898. In 1902 he was chosen justice of the peace and his time is now largely occupied with the trial of cases, in which he renders decisions that are strictly fair and impartial, so that his course has won him high commendation.

CHARLES B. ROE, Sr.

An honorable retirement from labor and a period in which to rest and enjoy life is the fitting reward of an active and useful business career and this has been vouchsafed to Charles B. Roe, who, since 1881, has lived in Battle Creek. He was born near Weedsport, New York, November 14, 1842. His father, Stephen Roe, was a native of Essex county, New York, where he was reared, and in Cummington, Massachusetts, he wedded Clarissa Godfrey. He then located near Weedsport, as a shoemaker, and died there in 1845, leaving a widow and nine children. Mrs. Roe later became the wife of Hiram O'Bryan, of Scotch ancestry. In 1851 they removed to Medina county, Ohio, and in 1857 settled in Windsor township, Eaton county, Michigan, where both died.

Charles B. Roe was about thirteen years of age when his mother and stepfather removed to Michigan and as he had a good position in Ohio he was left behind. He soon gave up his work, however, and went to Sandusky where he met Stephen A. Rogers, who, taking a liking to the boy, adopted him and gave him an education. He had previously studied to a limited extent in East Liverpool, Ohio, and continued his studies in Sandusky with the intention of entering Oberlin College in 1861, but the Civil war came on and he enlisted as Charles B. Roe in response to the first call for seventy-five thousand men, becoming a member of Company E, Eighth Ohio Infantry, with which he went to camp at Dennison. They built that camp and at the expiration of six weeks Mr. Roe re-enlisted for three years in Company E, of the Eighth Ohio, under the name of Charles B. Rogers, as he did not care to have his folks know of his enlistment. He was sent to Wheeling, thence to Grafton and afterward participated in the battle of Phillipi and many skirmishes. He was in the first battle at Winchester and at Fort Republic, and being captured was afterward sent home on parole. At once, however, he re-enlisted, joining Company D, Tenth Ohio Cavalry, with which he was sent to Nashville, Tennessee. He took part in the battle of Stone River, went with Sherman on his celebrated march from Atlanta to the sea coast and did hard scouting in that campaign. He also proceeded on the march through the Carolinas and on to Washington, where he participated in the grand review. The government pays Mr. Roe a pension for his services during the time of its peril.

Following the close of the war Mr. Roe came to Michigan to visit his parents, and locating in Windsor township, turned his attention to farming. He was afterward variously employed up to the time of his marriage, which occurred on the 8th of December, 1877, Miss Katherine Beecher Cook, of Marshall, Calhoun county, becoming his wife. Her parents were Hon. Asa B. and Jerusha P. (Beach) Cook, both of whom were born in Jay, Essex county, New York, where they were married. Mr. Cook was a merchant and in the fall of 1832 located in Marshall, Michigan, then a little hamlet of log cabins. Prospering in his mercantile affairs he also extended his field

CHARLES B. ROE, Sr.

MISS VEDA THERRESSA ROE

of labors and operated two mills. At the time of his death he was president of the First National Bank. In early life a Whig, he was one of those who organized the Republican party under the old oak tree at Jackson, Michigan. Among his schoolmates were James G. Blaine and Governor John G. Bagley, of Michigan, and his second sister, Susan F., became the wife of Rev. Daniel Filmore, a prominent Methodist minister of Boston and a brother of President Filmore. Mr. Cook served as a legislator and later was sent to Congress, being in the house when James G. Blaine was its speaker. He was frequently a delegate to the Republican national conventions from the time of the organization of the party until his death and aided in nominating President Hayes. One of the distinguished citizens of Michigan, he honored the state which honored him by public preferment and his name is enduringly inscribed on the pages of its history. He died in Marshall, March 4, 1878. His wife had passed away August 18, 1867. She was a member of the Methodist Episcopal church and he contributed liberally to its support and was chairman of its board of trustees. Their daughter, Mrs. Roe, attended the public schools until the time of her mother's death, when at the age of fourteen years she became a student in the Ripley Female College at Poultney, Vermont, in which she was graduated. She attained great proficiency in music and afterward engaged in teaching at Marshall.

At the time of their marriage Mr. and Mrs. Roe located in Marshall township, where he was engaged in farming until coming to Battle Creek in 1881. Here Mr. Roe worked at carpentering for a time and later became chrysographer for the Duplex Print-

ing Press Company, labeling all of their presses in gold. For the past fifteen years, however, he has lived retired. He is a valued member of Farragut post, No. 32, G. A. R., and his wife belongs to the Woman's Relief Corps, of which she has been organist. They are devoted members of the First Presbyterian church. Unto them have been born six children, three of whom are living: Charles B., born in Battle Creek, January 25, 1880, is a machinist in the Advance Thresher Company, and married Fannie C. Hick, daughter of Charles Augustine and Emily Amelia (Lunt) Hick; Veda Therressa is the second; General Alger Russell, named after General Alger, born May 24, 1892, completes the family.

VEDA THERRESSA ROE.

Veda Therressa Roe, who is widely known as the child pianist of Battle Creek, was born in this city, October 10, 1890, and attended the public schools. Very early she displayed marked musical talent and began her musical studies before she was seven years of age. She soon became known as a musical prodigy here and began playing in public at the age of eight years, in the Opera House. She has since been on the program at many entertainments, always playing before appreciative audiences and receiving many encores. She has had as her instructors the best musicians of this city, Prof. W. S. Columbus, Prof. Edwin Barnes and Mrs. Margaret Duffy Werstein, and is now a registered music teacher and has had some scholars, but her parents prefer that she should wait until she is older before engaging actively in such work. Her talent and skill, however, are extraordinary. Her touch and technic seem perfect and she plays with feeling and expression. Competent critics have often been heard to praise her very highly and she certainly has a brilliant future before her.

JOHN JAMES HURLEY.

John J. Hurley, who for many years was connected with agricultural pursuits, but is now living a retired life in Albion, was born in Staffordshire, England, July 27, 1852. His mother died when he was very young and when he was nine years of age he accompanied his father and his stepmother on their emigration to the new world. They came across the Atlantic to Canada and settled first in Toronto, where they remained for three months. They then continued their journey, going to the copper regions of Lake Superior, where they remained a short time, then came to Jackson county, Michigan, and for a short time lived upon a farm about four miles west of the city of Jackson. The father had followed mining in England and after coming to this country he worked in the mines near Jackson and later operated the mines near Sanstone and Spring Arbor, Michigan. He is now deceased and his remains are interred in the cemetery of Jackson, Michigan.

Mr. Hurley, of this review, began his education in the public schools of his native land and afterward attended the district schools of Jackson county. In his youth he also became familiar with farm work and assisted his father upon the home farm until twenty-five years of age except one

year spent in Albion and Lansing when he was twenty, after which he spent two years at mining. On the expiration of that period he went to South Dakota, where he worked with a surveying party and there remained for two years. During that time he purchased two claims each of one hundred and sixty acres, comprising land which he had helped survey. He then spent a winter at Albion and Jackson after which he returned to South Dakota, where he remained until 1885, devoting his attention to agricultural pursuits. He made a specialty of the production of flax and continued in business there until 1885, when he sold out and returned to Albion, purchasing a farm in Sheridan township. Of this he afterward sold sixteen acres to the Jackson & Battle Creek Traction Company, and upon it their carshops are now located. At that time Mr. Hurley removed to the village of Albion, where he is now living retired, although he still has extensive property interests, which return to him a good rental. In 1900 he built the large Hurley block, which extends from the river to the Michigan Central tracks, and he likewise has a large brick livery barn.

In 1885 Mr. Hurley was married to Miss Metta E. Green, a daughter of Elijah and Emily (Burr) Green, both of whom are now deceased. Her father was the son of Hezekiah and Lucy (Vaughn) Green, who was born April 13, 1841, and is a descendant of General Nathaniel Green, of Revolutionary fame. His boyhood days were spent upon his father's farm and his elementary education was acquired in the district schools. His academic instruction was received in Bridgewater, Oneida county, New York, and later he learned the trades of a carpenter, joiner and millwright. On the 7th of October, 1833, he was united in marriage to Miss Harriet Potter, and in September, 1836, he started for Michigan, intending to select a location. He entered land in Eaton county and then returned for his family in the following February, but in March his wife died and he then came back alone to this state. Locating in Albion he worked at his trades and built the first overshot water wheel used in Sheridan township. Soon afterward he entered into partnership with Zina Stowell to construct a saw-mill on the great branch of the Kalamazoo river. It occupied the site of the present Hurley block of Albion, in fact, was torn down by Mr. Hurley in order to make room for the proposed improvement. On the 1st of May, 1842, Mr. Green was again married, his second union being with Mrs. L. Shipman, a widow. Unto them were born six children, of whom two died in childhood, while those that reached mature years are Clermont, Denio V., Ella J. and Metta E.

After his second marriage Mr. Green removed to a farm upon which he and his wife passed a peaceful, quiet and happy life, enjoying the comforts of the home which he had provided. He was regarded as one of the leading agriculturists and strong business men of his locality, was strictly honorable in all his dealing, farsighted in his management and unfaltering in energy. He died in 1887 and his wife passed away in 1888, their remains being interred in Riverside cemetery at Albion. They spent the last few years of their lives in the city.

Unto Mr. and Mrs. Hurley have been born two children, Amber Hazel and Ethel Lyle. Mr. Hurley is an Episcopalian in religious faith and a Democrat in his political belief, but has never aspired to office, preferring to do his duty to his county, state and nation as a private citizen. He is well and prominently known in business circles of Albion, and is classed among the representative citizens. He owes his success entirely to his own efforts. Starting out in life empty-handed he has depended entirely upon his own resources for what he has achieved, and that he is now one of the substantial citizens of the city is indicative of an industrious and well managed business career.

GEORGE W. BENTLEY.

In a history of those whose life activity has contributed to the material improvement and substantial upbuilding of Calhoun county, mention should be made of George W. Bentley, who for many years was actively connected with agricultural pursuits. He located in this portion of the state in pioneer times and remained one of its honored and respected residents up to the time of his demise. His birth occurred in the village of Driffell, Yorkshire, England, on the 24th of February, 1809, and in his boyhood days he came to America with his parents, John and Ann Gentley, county, New York, where the father purchased land and developed a farm. It was upon the old homestead there that George W. Bentley was reared, and practical training in the work of the home farm made him familiar with all departments of agricultural life.

Mr. Bentley was twice married. Ere leaving the Empire state he was married and his first wife died there. In 1834 he came to Michigan with Nathan Benedict, with whom he worked at the carpenter's trade in Marshall. Here he met and married Miss Nancy M. Chapin, the wedding taking place in Fredonia township. She was born in Oneida county, New York, a daughter of Ashbel and Tirza (Sanderson) Chapin. Her mother was born in Massachusetts and in early life was taken to the Empire state by her parents. Mrs. Bentley accompanied her parents on their removal to Michigan in 1835. Mr. and Mrs. Bentley became the parents of two children: John, who died in infancy and George Curran Bentley, who is represented elsewhere in this work.

For many years George W. Bentley was actively identified with farming interests in Calhoun county. He first owned one hundred and twenty acres of land in Convis township and later purchased one hundred and sixty acres on section 16, Marshall township, where he carried on general farming. A number of years afterward he became the owner of three hundred and seventy acres near Ceresco, and about 1852 he removed to Albion. After a few months, however, in the fall of 1852 he went with his family to Mount Pleastnt, Iowa, where he dealt largely in land and also established and conducted a bank, but after three and a half years spent beyond the Mississippi he returned to Michigan, locating in Marshall. A few months passed and he then purchased two hundred and ninety acres of land in Emmett township, where he carried on general agricultural pursuits for six years. The next farm which he owned was situated in Battle Creek township and comprised one hundred and sixty acres adjoining the city limits. Part of this is now lying within the corporation boundaries, having been included in an addition to the city. For three years Mr. Bentley remained upon that farm and then returned to Marshall, but subsequently purchased a farm of six hundred acres three and a half miles west of Marshall, conducting one of the largest farms of his day in this portion of the state. There he was actively engaged in agricultural pursuits in 1872, when he retired from farm life and took up his abode in Marshall. He became one of the charter members of the City National Bank and was one of its directors and its president during the existence of that institution. The bank did a successful business until 1891, when it was closed on account of the defalcation of the assistant cashier who entailed the bank in losses to the amount of one hundred and thirteen thousand dollars. Mr. Bentley remained a resident of Marshall until the death of his wife in 1885, then took up his abode with his son, George Curran, with whom he remained until his own demise on the 1st of March, 1901.

In politics Mr. Bentley was an Abolitionist when it required great personal courage to defend one's views upon that question. When the Republican party was formed to prevent the further extension of slavery he joined its ranks and was in Jackson in 1854, when the party was organized "Under the Oaks," now famous because of this event, which has had so important a part in shaping the history of the nation. He was also present as a delegate to the convention which named Mr. Bingham for governor of Michigan. He never sought the prominence that came through political preferment, although he was an active worker in the ranks of his party. He served, however, as supervisor of both Emmett and Battle Creek townships, but he preferred to give his aid to his party and his country as a private citizen rather than one who wielded the power of office. His religious faith was that of the New Jerusalem church, to which both he and his wife belonged, it being a representative of the Swedenborgian denomination. For almost six decades he continued a resident of Calhoun county, watching its development from early pioneer conditions as it emerged to take its place among the strong and dominant counties of the state, rich in its agricultural, industrial and commercial resources. The activity of his business career resulted in the acquirement of a handsome competence and his business methods were characterized by all that was honorable in his dealing with his fellowmen. He made for himself a record which causes his name to be respected and his memory cherished in the years which have come and gone since he has departed this life.

WILLIAM JAMES HARTUNG.

William James Hartung, who was classed with the successful farmers and honored citizens of Calhoun county, was born in Belvidere, New Jersey, on the 21st of September, 1845, and was a son of William Hartung. When eighteen years of age he came to Michigan, settling first in Oakland, while later he took up his abode in Albion township, Calhoun county, where he remained with his parents up to the time of his marriage, which occurred on the 23d of December, 1869. He wedded Miss Elizabeth Houck, who was a daughter of Philip and Hannah (Kearn) Houck. Both were natives of Pennsylvania, born in the eastern part of that state, and in early life came to Michigan with their respective parents. Philip Houck became a leading, influential and esteemed farmer of Concord township, Jackson county, Michigan, where he took up land from the government. This was a wild and unimproved tract when it came into his possession, but he at once began to clear it and upon the place he erected a log cabin, which in later years gave way before a good frame residence. He prospered in his undertaking, his efforts as an agriculturist bringing to him a fair measure of success. As his financial resources increased he added to his property, from time to time, until he became the owner of four hundred acres, which he retained in his possession up to the time of his death. He was born in 1816 and passed away in 1888, having thus reached the seventy-second mile-stone on life's journey. His wife died when Mrs. Hartung was only eight months of age, and she was laid to rest in the Fisher cemetery in Calhoun county, and the father was buried at Albion. Mr. Houck was a Republican in his political affiliations, and both he and his wife were earnest, consistent Christian people, who held membership in the Methodist Episcopal church. They commanded the confidence, good will and friendship of all who knew them and their loss in the community was deeply mourned. They had one son, John A., who now resides in Albion township. After his marriage, Mr. Hartung located upon his father-in-law's farm, where he continued until after the death of Mr. Houck, when he took up his abode on the farm which is now the home of his widow. There he secured one hundred and twelve acres of land just outside the corporation limits of Albion. His time and energies were devoted to agricultural pursuits and he placed his fields under a high state of cultivation and made good improvements upon his place. He was greatly respected by all who knew him, and although he lived a quiet and unassuming life, his genuine worth of character gained for him the respect and friendly regard of all with whom he was associated. ·

Unto Mr. and Mrs. Hartung were born two children: Willoughby Philip, who is a graduate of Albion College, married Miss Carrie Snyder and resides in Albion township, Calhoun county; Clarence Roy, who is a graduate of the Albion high school, and spent two years and a half as a student in the Albion College, is now assisting his mother in the operation of the home farm. Mr. Hartung held membership in the Methodist Episcopal church of Albion, to which his wife still belongs. He was also a member of the Tribe of Ben Hur at Albion. and he gave his political allegiance to the Republican party. Upon that ticket he was elected alderman and filled the position for four years, serving in that office at the time of his death, which occurred on the 9th of February, 1900. The entire period of his manhood was passed in this county and, his active business career was such as gained for him an enviable reputation. He was ever honorable and straightforward in his business dealings, faithful in friendship, and devoted to his family, and his memory is therefore cherished by all with whom he had come in contact.

FRANK ALLEN.

Frank Allen, who has long been connected with the railroad service, and has steadily worked his way upward until he is now filling the important and responsible position of train master, and also chief train dispatcher with the Detroit, Toledo and Milwaukee Railroad, was born at Lenawee Junction, Michigan, on the 2nd of May, 1866. His paternal grandfather was Loren Allen. His great grandfather became one of the pioneers of Michigan, making his way to Lenawee county, where he entered land from the government and made his home. Daniel Allen, the father of our subject, was born in Toronto, Canada, and spent his early life in Lenawee county, where he was engaged in farming and was also interested in threshing. He there married Miss Hannah Pennington, who was born in Macon, Lenawee county, and was a daughter of Joseph Pennington, a pioneer farmer of this state. Both Mr. and Mrs. Allen are still living, making their home in Ridgeway, Michigan, and Mrs. Allen is a consistent member of the Methodist Episcopal church. At the time of the Civil war Mr. Allen offered his services to the government and went to Detroit, but was never ordered to the front.

Not long after the birth of our subject, the family removed to Ridgeway, Lenawee county, where Frank Allen acquired a good practical education in the public schools. He worked upon the home farm, and in 1883 secured a position in the office of the Michigan & Ohio Railroad Company at Britton, Michigan. He had previously studied telegraphy and he desired to learn railroad work. In February, 1884, he did his first relief work; acting as agent and operator. He continued on relief duty until October, 1884, when he was appointed agent at Jerome, there remaining until May 20, 1885, at which time he was appointed agent at Ceresco. He continued there only until the 25th of June, when he was transferred to Richland, a larger station. He was then but nineteen years of age and his appointment showed the marked confidence which the company had in his ability. On the 14th of September, 1886, he was made agent at Tecumseh, Michigan, and on the 3d of January, 1889, he was appointed night train dispatcher at Toledo, Ohio. On the 17th of March, 1891, he was made second trick train dispatcher in the same office, where he remained until May, 30, 1895. He was next appointed chief train dispatcher and superintendent of telegraph, with office in Toledo, where he continued until the 1st of August, 1897, when the Detroit & Lima Northern Railroad purchased the land and took charge, and the offices were removed to Tecumseh, Michigan, where Mr. Allen occupied a similar position until December 1, 1897. His next promotion made him train master and he served thus until October, 1898, when he was appointed chief clerk to the freight agent of Toledo, Ohio, and on the 5th of March, 1899, he became chief train dispatcher and superintendent of telegraph, with headquarters at Marshall, the division of the railroad. Until the 1st of February, 1902, he discharged the duties of that position, and was then made train master and chief train dispatcher, in which capacity he is now serving in a most capable manner. He has been with the road continuously through all of its changes and by his ability has steadily worked his way upward to one of the highest positions within the gift of the company. He belongs to the Train Dispatchers' Association of America.

Mr. Allen was married on the 2d of July, 1895, to Miss Minnie R. Ransom, of Ridgeway, Michigan, a daughter of William B. Ransom, one of the early residents and farmers of Lenawee county. They have two children: Harry D. and Edith M. and they lost their first born, Blanche, who died in infancy. Mr. and Mrs. Allen are members of the Methodist Episcopal church and he belongs to the Royal Arcanum.

HON. ERASTUS HUSSEY.

Honored and respected by all, there was no man in Michigan who held a more enviable position in the regard of acquaintances and friends that did Hon. Erastus Hussey. The reasons for this are not far to seek as he was ever actuated by the highest priciples, by moral courage and unfaltering adherence to what he believed to be right. His strong mentality well fitted him for leadership and he left a marked impress upon public thought and action. He figured largely in connection with the great events which changed the history of the nation in the middle of the nineteenth century, served his state in its legislative assembly and became one of the founders of the Republican party.

Erastus Hussey was born in Scipio, now Ledyard township, Cayuga county, New York, December 5, 1800. His ancestry can be traced far back in English history. Christoper Hussey, the first of the name to come to America, left his native land on account of religious persecution and settled on Nantucket Island. The family characteristics are sociability, benevolence and generosity, combined with a strong love of freedom and equality. The men are large, with strongly marked features and traits are so decided as to be easily recognized. Erastus Hussey spent his boyhood and early manhood on a farm on the east shore of Cayuga lake, in New York, and his educational privileges were limited to those afforded by the common schools of that time. After he was fourteen years of age he attended school only through the winter months for his labors were needed on the home farm, but he had access to a good library and eagerly availed himself of the opportunity for reading in his leisure moments. As he approached manhood he prepared for teaching and later followed that profession through the winter seasons, while in the summer months he followed farming, many years being thus passed. He was ambitious to become a lawyer, but circumstances decided otherwise and he continued in agricultural life. On attaining his majority he visited Erie county, New York, intending to locate there, but not being pleased with the country, continued his journey through Ohio and Indiana to Michigan, where he determined to locate. He had no capital but he had been able by his industry and economy to save the sum of two hundred and fifty dollars with which he started for this state, intending to purchase land. He started on foot for Buffalo, walking forty-five miles the first day, and reaching the port he took passage on the Superior, the only steam craft on the lake, and on the 25th of September, 1824, landed at Detroit. After exploring the country for a time he finally decided to enter one hundred and sixty acres of land, and on the 9th of October returned to Detroit where he made claim to the tract he had chosen. He was the first purchaser to occupy a claim in what is now Plymouth township, Wayne county. The following day he took passage for Erie, Pennsylvania,

and thence walked ninety miles to Collins, where, again among friends, he taught school for four months, after which he returned to his home. In 1826 he again came to Michigan and made some improvements, returning in the late autumn to the Empire state.

On the 21st of February, 1827, Mr. Hussey was married to Sarah Eddy Bowen, a daughter of Benjamin and Lucretia Bowen, of Cayuga county, New York. She was born in Worcester, Massachusetts, January 24, 1808, and was of the eighth generation from Welsh ancestors. The young couple started for their home in the western wilderness, where they arrived on the 27th of July and at first occupied a dilapidated cabin having but one window. Mr. Hussey's capital then consisted of but forty-seven dollars and his land. Soon both he and his wife became ill, but their lives were saved through the timely ministrations of Dr. Webb, the pioneer physician, and also a well known friend. A log cabin being built upon their farm, they moved into it on the 1st of January, 1828, and there on the 27th of the month was born their only child, Susan Tabor, now the wife of E. H. Hussey, whose sketch appears elswhere in this volume.

That spring Mr. Hussey entered upon his public career, being elected road commissioner, in which capacity he served for nine years. In the meantime he continued his farm work and built a beautiful home. Frequently he supplemented his capital by money earned in teaching through the winter. In 1836 because of failing health, he sold his farm for two thousand dollars, which he invested in land farther north and then once more on account of his health he went to the east, accompanied by his, wife and daughter. They traveled through Ohio, Pennsylvania, New York and the New England states to the Atlantic coast in their own carriage, and through the succeeding winter Mr. Hussey again engaged in teaching, but when spring came he returned to Michigan, which in the meantime had been admitted to the Union. He was desirous of aiding in shaping the policy of the new commonwealth and through many years was a most active factor in public life. assisting materially in molding public affairs, ever prompted by conscientious and patriotic zeal.

Locating in Battle Creek in September, 1838, he joined Platt Gilbert in the manufacture of boots and shoes, in which he had previously had some experience, and they also conducted a grocery store, but after a year Mr. Hussey sold out. In 1839 he became proprietor of a dry-goods store, which he conducted for several years. and in 1843 admitted to a partnership Henry B. Denman who afterward married his daughter. In 1847 this firm was dissolved by mutual consent, and Mr. Hussey closed out the business. During that year he built two-fifths of the Union block, the first brick structure in the city. All public matters relating to the general welfare elicited his support and what he believed to be for the public good received his most earnest endorsement. He was among the first to advocate the establishment of a union school, supported by a general tax, making education free to all. He met fierce and bitter opposition but persevered and to-day the present admirable school system of Battle Creek is the direct result of his labors. He was chosen one of the trustees of the new

33

school and served as a director for three years. About 1847, the "Michigan Liberty Press" was established as the organ of the Liberty party in the state and Mr. Hussey became the manager of its editorial department, while later he took entire charge of the paper, the motto of which was "Eternal enmity to all kinds of oppression." Mr. Hussey was a strong Whig and cast his first presidential vote for John Quincy Adams. Becoming an opponent of slavery, his advocacy of universal liberty soon brought him prominently before the people. He held the office of town clerk for three terms. Previous to this time the town had always been regarded as a Democratic stronghold. Continuing an active advocate of anti-slavery, his home became a station on the famous underground railroad, and his wife and daughter ably assisted him in caring for negroes who sought shelter. On one single night they harbored forty refugees. In 1840 Mr. Hussey was a stanch supporter of Harrison as he believed the Whigs would take measures to curtail the slave power, but President Tyler dispelled this illusion and he then joined the Liberty party, becoming one of its organizers. About this time the postmaster of Battle Creek refused to deliver his paper through the mails and Mr. Hussey then went upon the road to carry his message of liberty by personally addressing the people. During his absence his wife filled the editorial chair, and in 1849 the newspaper office and all its fixtures were burned. He then started the paper at Marshall, but after a few issues it was discontinued. In debate and upon the public platform his voice continued to be heard in support of the principles in which he so strongly believed.

In 1849 Mr. Hussey was elected to the House of Representatives, being one of five members of the Freesoil party in that body. In 1852 he was nominated for lieutenant governor and although defeated for that office was re-elected the same year as county clerk by the Coalition party. In February, 1854, he presided over the state convention of the Freesoil party at Jackson and was there appointed a member of a committee to call a meeting at Kalamazoo to consider the propriety of holding a convention of all liberal men opposed to slavery. At Jackson it was decided to hold a meeting in Marshall, in July, 1854, and there Mr. Hussey was made a member of the committee to draft and present a platform. It was adopted without a dissenting vote, and became the platform of the new Republican party, thus to Michigan belongs the honor of organizing and naming the party. Mr. Hussey being one of the leading movers. In the fall of that year he was elected to the State Senate, was chairman of its finance committee and a member of the joint committee to perfect what became known as the prohibitory liquor bill, the passage of which awoke widespread interest. He also introduced the personal liberty bill, which, without conflicting with the United States law, protected Michigan from kidnappers and secured the rights of fugitive slaves. Notwithstanding strong opposition it passed the senate and the house and was regarded as the most important measure of the session. When the Republican party placed its first presidential candidate, Fremont, in the field he became an earnest worker for him.

There were times when Mr. Hussey enjoyed rest from the turmoil and strife of political life. In 1855 he built and fitted up a beautiful home on North Washington avenue, calling it Oak Lawn, and there many happy days were passed. In 1859 when the village became a city he was elected one of its first aldermen, and was actively connected with municipal affairs for many years. In 1860 he was a delegate to the Chicago convention which nominated Abraham Lincoln. In 1867 he was elected mayor of the city and his administration was practical, progressive and beneficial. After his retirement from the office, he lived a more quiet life, spending much of his time in travel. He had seen the great principle of liberty for which he had labored so faithfully, adopted, and was content to take a less active part in public affairs, although his interest in the welfare of the country never abated.

Both Mr. and Mrs. Hussey were deeply interested in all matters pertaining to the intellectual and moral progress of Battle Creek. They encouraged the spreading of useful knowledge in the pioneer town and succeeded in establishing a library for the scattered settlers. In 1864 she joined heartily in the movement for the founding of a Ladies' Library Association and her efforts, in conjunction with others, were successful. Both were members of the Society of Friends and were most earnest Christian people. Mr. Hussey passed away January 21, 1889, and his wife on the 22d of March, 1899. The world is the better for their having lived. Who can measure their influence or gauge the good which they wrought! Their memory remains as a blessed benediction to those who knew them and to all who live after them will the fruits of their labor be apparent.

EL DORADO GREENFIELD.

El Dorado Greenfield, proprietor of the Athens mills, is an active and leading representative of industrial interests in Athens, Michigan. He was born in El Dorado county, California, December 5, 1853, a son of Daniel and Catherine Greenfield. His paternal grandparents were Jeremiah and Mary (Waldron) Greenfield, natives of New York, whence they removed to Indiana at an early epoch in its development, living in La Grange county throughout their remaining days. The family is of German descent. The parents of our subject were natives of New York and they made the overland trip to California, being six months upon the way. When they started, their little son George was but six months old, and the subject of this review was the first white child born in El Dorado county, California. In 1855, by way of the Panama route, they returned to New York, and thence went to La Grange county, Indiana, in order that they might care for the aged parents of Mr. Greenfield. In his farming operations the father of our subject was very successful and he also accumulated a comfortable competence in the midst of the west. He died January 17, 1861, and his wife passed away in 1883.

Of their three children El Dorado Greenfield was the second in order of birth. In the district schools he was educated, and in 1865 removed with his mother to Sturgis, Michigan, thence to Athens and in 1871 the family went to Battle Creek. He continued his studies both in Athens and Battle Creek and in the years 1873-4 was on a steamboat on Lake Michigan, serving as fireman and then as engineer. On leaving that service he returned to Springfield, Indiana, where

he engaged in farming until January, 1882, when he again took up his abode in Athens. Here he embarked in the hardware and grocery business, conducting his store until January 22, 1883, when a disastrous fire swept away all that he had. The succeeding year he erected the store now occupied by A. H. Harrison and in that building he conducted business until 1892, when he sold out. In 1895 he purchased a lumber yard which he operated until 1899, when he exchanged this for the Athens Flouring Mill, of which he is now the proprietor. The mill is operated by both steam and water power, and manufactures flour not only for the home trade, but also for the foreign markets, shipping quite extensively to other places. He likewise manufactures feed and is conducting a profitable business.

On the 10th of December, 1884, Mr. Greenfield was united in marriage to Miss Ada J. Bisbee, who was born at Grafton, Ohio, June 22, 1857, a daughter of Henry L. and Amantha. T. Bisbee. Mr. Bisbee was a native of Vermont, as was also his wife. He came to Michigan in 1865 and located in Sherwood township, Branch county, where he engaged in farming for many years. He moved to Athens a few years prior to his death, which occurred April 12, 1890. Unto Mr. and Mrs. Greenfield has been born a son, George Henry. They attend the Congregational church and Mrs. Greenfield is a member of the Ladies' Aid Society. In politics he is a Republican and has served as trustee of the village, but prefers to assist in public measures as a private citizen rather than as an official. In matters pertaining to the welfare of Athens, however, he is progressive and public-spirited and his efforts have thus been effective and helpful. He is a

Royal Arch Mason and is now master of the Third Veil in Athens lodge. Since coming to Athens he has purchased the S. S. Ware place, located near the mill, and has improved it, making it a pretty home. He also owns land, and his wife has a fine farm south of the village, constituting the old Bisbee homestead. Mr. Greenfield likewise has property in the south and as his financial resources have increased has made judicious investments in realty. Both he and his wife are widely known and occupy an enviable position in social circles in Athens, where their own home is celebrated for its gracious and charming hospitality.

HON. ALVAH D. ELDRED.

The name which heads this review is one known and honored throughout Calhoun county, Michigan, for it was in this locality that most of the life of Hon. Alvah David Eldred was passed. He was born in Ontario county, New York, February 29, 1832, a son of Robert and Amelia Eldred. He received his education in his native state, where he remained until 1852, at that time leaving home and coming as far west as Detroit, Michigan. From that city he went north to McComb county, where he learned the trade of carpenter and joiner, remaining there in the prosecution of his work for some time. While there he met and married Miss Helen Bartlett, January 9, 1855, a daughter of John and Elmira (Knapp) Bartlett, and a year later the young people removed to Calhoun county, with modest means, able only to acquire an acre of land. This was located upon the line between Cal-

houn and Branch counties and here they remained for many years. Mr. Eldred was a man of untiring industry, energy and perseverance and by good management as well as constant work at his trade he became the owner of seventy-two acres of well developed farm land. Much of this was timber land, and to the efforts of Mr. Eldred is due its present value; he often returned home after a hard day's work at his trade, and would then burn brush by moonlight. Until 1880 this farm remained the home of Mr. Eldred and his family, when he purchased property in the village of Tekonsha, whither he removed, leasing his farm until 1900, when he sold it. He took a great pride in his village home and spent much time in beautifying the surroundings, setting out various kinds of trees, shrubbery, flowers, etc.

In his political convictions Mr. Eldred was a stanch Republican, and for many years was prominent in the political movements of the community. For fourteen years he served as highway commissioner of Tekonsha township, was president of the village of Tekonsha for two terms and justice of the peace for a great many years, holding that office at the time of his death. For four years, from 1885 to 1889, he represented the second Calhoun district in the State Legislature, and as a man of prominence and ability was often called upon to act as administrator and executor for many estates. He was a man of unquestioned integrity, and purity of life, an honored citizen who enjoyed the esteem of all who knew him, while his friends were unnumbered. He was always upright in business and whenever called upon for public office gave to it his most profound thought, considering it of the utmost importance to be faithful in the discharge of duty involved by his acceptance of official authority. He was also prominent in business affairs of the village. One important position occupied by him being that of a director of the Tekonsha bank.

Mr. Eldred became a Mason, August 4, 1854, and was an active member in the organization until his death. On St. John's day, in 1875. he was presented by the lodge with a handsome and valuable watch as a token of regard, and upon the completion of twenty-five years as worshipful master, in 1882, he was also presented with an appropriate jewel. From 1878 to 1879 he served as deputy grand master; in 1880 he was grand junior deacon of the Grand lodge, of Michigan; in 1881 he became senior deacon; and in 1882-83 was junior grand warden.

Mr. Eldred and his wife adopted and reared two children, of whom Benjamin married Miss Clara Acker and now resides at Jackson; and Minnie married Henry Dean, an undertaker of Tekonsha, and they have two children, Alvah D. and Ben Hur. Mr. Eldred, though departed this life, has left behind him a record of a well spent life and one that may well serve as an example for the younger generation to emulate.

THOMAS JOSEPH SHIPP.

Among the prominent farmers of Eckford township, Calhoun county, Thomas Joseph Shipp is deserving of mention as an active and enterprising citizen and one who has lost no opportunity to advance the general welfare of the community. He is a native of Marshall, Calhoun county, Michigan, the date of his birth being April 17, 1845.

His father, Joseph Shipp, was a native of England, born May 28, 1816, in Chipping Sodbury, Gloucestershire, a son of William, a baker and miller by occupation. Joseph Shipp remained at home with his parents until 1832, when he came to the United States, locating first in Chautauqua county, New York, where he found employment near Silver Creek for the period of ten months. In 1833 he went to Toronto, Canada, the following year coming to Marshall, Michigan, where he engaged in buying and selling stock, subsequently entering the bakery business in partnership with Edward Bostwick. This occupation was continued for one year, and in 1841 Mr. Shipp revisited his home in England, while there marrying, March 13, 1842, Miss Elizabeth Saunders. She was the sixth child of Thomas and Ann (Smith) Saunders. both natives of England, her father being a superintendent of a large estate there until he came to America in 1832. During the summer he worked in the woolen mills of Pittsfield, Massachusetts, and in the fall moved to Chautauqua county, New York, where he negotiated for some land. The proceedings, however, were abruptly terminated by the death of Mr. Saunders, who was drowned while crossing Silver lake in a canoe, after which event his family returned to England.

After his marriage in England Joseph Shipp brought his bride to America in June, 1842, making the voyage in a sailing vessel. After landing at New York city they journeyed up the Hudson river to Albany, thence to Buffalo on the Erie canal, across the lake to Detroit, by wagon to Jackson and from there to Marshall by stage. Mr. Shipp leased a saw-mill at Ceresco which he operated one year, after which he turned his attention to farming, in the fall of 1843 purchasing a quarter section in Emmett township, building a log cabin into which he moved his family and set about the task of clearing up the land. After two years he removed from the location, having put eighty acres under cultivation, locating in Marshall where ·he spent one year, after which he again located upon the farm and remained ten years. He then sold the property and once more removed to Marshall, opening a meat market which he conducted until 1861, at that date again returning to his agricultural pursuits. He purchased at that time three hundred and twenty acres in Eckford township on sections 20 and 29, a part of this land being under cultivation. With the energy and ambition characteristic of his entire life he at once set about the improvement of this new home, erecting a substantial and commodious house, a basement barn and various outhouses about 1870, the balance of his years being spent in that location. He is interred in the West Eckford cemetery, his death having occurred August 26, 1887, the last sixteen years of his life being those of trial for he was unable to work on account of ill health. He was, however, a man of Christian faith,—a member of the Baptist church and an active worker in the denomination,—and bore his affliction with patience and fortitude. Politically, he was a strong Republican and was always responsive to the duties of citizenship. For one year he served on the board of supervisors and as township treasurer. He was a man of solid worth and sound, practical ability, and stood high in the esteem of his fellow citizens. His wife survives him and still makes her home upon the old farm.

The early days of Thomas Joseph Shipp were passed in the home of his parents with whom he remained until the spring of 1881, receiving his education principally in the schools of Marshall. In the last named year his father divided his farm, giving him a quarter section, upon which there was a debt which our subject has since paid off. About ninety acres of this land at that time was tillable, and in the same year Mr. Shipp erected a dwelling house, and three years later put up a large barn, sufficient for the accommodation of his stock and farming implements. The farm is now devoted to general farming and stock-raising.

November 22, 1871, Mr. Shipp was united in marriage with Miss Frances S. Skinner, a native of England and daughter of John and Mary Ann (Rogers) Skinner, who came to America when she was but four years old. Their first year was spent in the state of New York, after which they came west and located in Eckford township, Calhoun county, Michigan, where the father was numbered among the prosperous farmers of this section. To Mr. and Mrs. Shipp were born three children: Frank J., the eldest, after receiving a preliminary education in the district school, attended the Marshall high school one year, when he entered Albion College, from which he was graduated in 1896. He then located in Gaylord, Michigan, where he has risen to prominence in pedagogical lines, holding the position of superintendent of schools there for a number of years. He married Miss Vieva Parmater, of Gaylord, and they now have two children, Eleanor Beatrice and Elizabeth. William Samuel, the second son, also attended Albion College and the University of Michigan, at Ann Arbor, Michigan, graduating from the medical department in 1903, with the degree of M. D. He is at present located in the hospital of the university. The only daughter, Elizabeth Mary, is now at home, being called from her studies at Kalamazoo College by the death of her mother, cheerfully taking up the burdens which the elder woman laid down. Mrs. Shipp died April 22, 1901, at the age of fifty-two years, her last resting place being West Eckford cemetery. She was a woman of fine character, strong, earnest Christian,—a member of the Methodist Episcopal church,—well beloved by all who knew her.

Mr. Shipp is also an active member of the Methodist Episcopal church, and has always been active in his support of all religious work. For several years he has served in the capacity of trustee for the church. Fraternally, he is a member of the Knights of the Maccabees, of Eckford, and is also identified with the Ancient Order of United Workmen, of Marshall. As a Republican in politics he has always given his best efforts toward the support of the principles he endorses. His faithfulness in every public duty has commended itself to his fellow townsmen, who in 1885 elected him supervisor of the township, which office he acceptably filled for sixteen years, in 1890 acting as chairman of the board. Mr. Shipp is endowed with energy, enterprise and good business capacity and as one of the foremost citizens of the township he has done no little in shaping the course of public events in the past score of years.

HENRY WILLIS.

So long as there are dwellers in the broad state of Michigan, so long should Henry Willis be honored, for he was one of the pioneer settlers of Battle Creek, whose unselfish and conscientious efforts in its behalf were far-reaching and beneficial. He belonged to that class, limited in numbers, but prodigious in strength, who were the leaders in spirit, thought and action in the formative period of the state's history. He was even enough ahead of his day and generation that the fullest appreciation was not accorded him by his contemporaries. He looked beyond the exingencies of the moment to the possibilities of the future, and with wonderful foresight recognized what might be done for the furtherance of the best interests and permanent improvement of the state. Men of broad mental caliber, generous spirit and with capabilities for leadership, however, found in him a kindred spirit and he engaged in high measure the friendship and regard of the really prominent citizens of Battle Creek.

Mr. Willis was born in Baltimore, Maryland, in 1800, a son of Thomas and Elizabeth Willis, who were natives of England. Both died during the early boyhood of their son Henry, and as they had no relatives in this country the children of the family were then bound out, mostly among people of the Society of Friends. Henry Willis was taken to Lancaster county, Pennsylvania, where he was reared by a family of Friends, spending the greater part of his youth upon a farm. He afterward learned shoemaking, and in Chester county he was united in marriage to Miss Hannah Marsh, a daughter of James and Lydia (Moore) Marsh, who were also members of the Society of Friends. For a short time thereafter Mr. Willis remained in Chester county and then went to Philadelphia, where for a time he conducted a shoe store. He next removed to a locality near Columbia, Pennsylvania, where he engaged in brick manufacturing on the Susquehanna river, and subsequently lived in Enterprise, Lancaster county, Pennsylvania, and it was there that his wife died in 1834. He had three children by that marriage: Isaac and Lydia, of Battle Creek, and Milton, of San Francisco, California. The eldest child, George, and the youngest, William, departed this life prior to the father's death. After the death of his first wife he married Phoebe Mott, and their children were Henry M. and Edward.

While in Enterprise, Pennsylvania, Mr. Willis entered railroad work, being appointed by the governor as superintendent of the Portage Railroad, over the Alleghany mountains, from Philedelphia to Pittsburg, which position he held one term. He was next employed to build what is now the Michigan Central Railroad, from Detroit to Ypsilanti. After his second marriage, however, he resigned his position in connection with the state and came to Battle Creek, purchasing a tract of land extending from Main to Hall streets and over which the Grand Trunk Railroad is now built. There he engaged in the nursery business, and many of the bearing apple trees seen in the orchards of this locality have grown from stock purchased in his nursery. He was very successful in that enterprise and conducted the business for a number of years. He next turned his attention to the manufacture of pottery, having found clay that was suitable. Later he managed a tract of land at St. Mary's lake owned by the Baldwin Locomotive Manufacturers, of Philadelphia, and thereon built a saw-mill. He also established a

large water-cure institution there, but after a few months it was destroyed by fire. He likewise engaged in the manufacture of brick on that place, and as his land was largely covered with timber, he devoted a part of his time to clearing this away and otherwise improving the property. After selling out there, he took up his abode near Battle Creek, on what is now North avenue. He had fine springs upon this place and from his experience concerning water supplies, which he had gained during his railroad work, he thought that these springs were sufficient to supply the city with water. He was urged by many people to establish water-works and he completed the reservoir and laid some pipes. He had spent much money in that way when the city decided to get water from Goguac lake, and therefore his labor was fruitless. Many now see that it was a mistake that his plans were not adopted, for, as he predicted, Goguac lake has become a pleasure resort and many feel that the water may be contaminated.

Mr. Willis was perhaps some decades ahead of his generation in his ideas in regard to water and sanitation, but time has proven the correctness of his views. He was also very active in trying to locate the road from Battle Creek to Hastings. The people of the latter place were anxious for the railroad and he told them that if the people of Battle Creek did not take up the matter, Jackson would. Mr. Willis was so sanguine that Battle Creek would help that he had the road surveyed at his own expense, but again he was doomed to disappointment, as the people of this city allowed the city to slip from their grasp and it was built to Jackson. When it was too late many regretted their negligence and lack of foresight in this matter, and wished they had followed Mr. Willis's advice.

Mr. Willis was very much interested in having a ship canal built from Lake Michigan to the Detroit river, and had the route surveyed, but he was not able to effect legislation necessary for the construction of the canal. He was much interested in railroad work, and became acquainted with officials of the Grand Trunk Railroad Company, Sir Henry Tyler being the president. That gentleman invited Mr. Willis to return with him to London in 1884, and the latter, who was then eighty-four years of age, accepted the invitation and had a very enjoyable trip. In October, of the same year, the citizens of Battle Creek held a meeting, asking for the extension of the Grand Trunk to this place, and having awakened to a recognition of Mr. Willis's worth and capability in this regard, asked him to return to London to attend the railroad meeting, and lay the matter before the board. Therefore, he went again to England, but the proposition made by the people of Battle Creek was not accepeted by the company. Not long after he again reached this city, his health began to fail, and while he wrote much upon subjects of general interest, he was unable to take an active part in public affairs. He died in December, 1886, and his wife passed away in 1890.

Mr. Willis was a member of the Friends' Society in the early days when it held meetings here. It would be to intrench on the province of history to recount the many things which he did in behalf of the city, in which he so long made his home. Suffice it to say that many lines of progress and improvement received his substantial aid and active assistance. His strong traits of character were of the highest order. None questioned the honesty or loyalty of his purpose and his integrity was ever one of his salient traits. Those who knew him well cherished his friendship as something sacred, and yet revere his memory.

BENJAMIN F. TAYLOR.

Now retired from the active cares of life, Benjamin Franklin Taylor is making his home in Athens, Michigan, enjoying the fruits of his years of industry. He was born in Jackson county, Michigan, August 20, 1841, the third in a family of seven children born to his parents, George and Mary (Moon) Taylor, natives respectively of Orange county, New Jersey, and Herkimer county, New York.

George Taylor was the son of Elihu and Elizabeth (Bennett) Taylor, also natives of New Jersey, who located in Orange county, New York, when their son was about ten years old. In 1834 they removed to Jackson county, Michigan, where Mr. Taylor purchased a farm, located just across the road from that of his son, who had settled in that location two years previously. The remainder of their lives was spent in this location, the mother dying in 1851, and the father in 1864. George Taylor was reared to manhood in New York state, receiving his education in the schools thereof, after which he became interested in agricultural pursuits. In 1832 he decided to emigrate to the middle west, locating then in Jackson county, Michigan, where he purchased a farm, in connection with the interests of the latter, at one time, conducting a boarding house for several years.

He also dealt largely in real estate, owning at one time twelve hundred and forty acres of land in Jackson county, his efforts accomplishing much in the way of advancement for the county. Several years after his settlement in the state he met and married Miss Mary Moon, who had removed to Michigan in the early '30's, with her parents. They made their home in Jackson county until 1860, when they removed to Athens township, purchasing a farm of three hundred and twenty acres, located a half mile east of the village of Athens. This property he farmed for five years, after which he engaged in the sawmill and foundry business, in Athens, also conducting several other industries in connection with this interest. His death occurred May 7th, 1889, and that of his wife in January, 1881, and they are both interred in the cemetery at North Sherwood. Both himself and his wife were active in the moral support of the community, being among the first members of the Congregational church, in Jackson county, after their removal to Calhoun county becoming identified with the church of the same denomination here, where they were active and influential members. He married for his second wife Mrs. Eliza Best, who survived him about one year. In political affiliations he was once a Jackson Democrat, but later in life indorsed the principles of the old line Whigs. Of the seven children born to them six attained maturity, those besides Benjamin F., of this review, are named in order of birth as follows: Sarah, who died July 24, 1903, and is interred in the cemetery at Sherwood; Harriet, the fourth child, who married Edgar Doty, late of Los Angeles, California; Ella, who married C. D. Johnson, of Athens; George, who resides at Spokane Falls, Washington, and Elizabeth, a resident of Manton, Michigan.

Benjamin F. Taylor received a common school education in Jackson county, where he remained until he was nineteen years old. His first duty in manhood was a response to the call of his country by enlisting October 10, 1861, in Company H, First Michigan Engineers, in which he served as a private until his honorable discharge October 30, 1864. While in the service he saw much hardship and danger, serving in the department of Cumberland and Tennessee, the Kentucky campaign in 1862, under General Buell, and in the famous campaign which led up to the capture of Atlanta, he was busy repairing roads and bridges, the guns of the company stacked near while they worked, for the advance of the army. After his discharge at Atlanta, Georgia, Mr. Taylor returned to Michigan, coming to Athens, his former home. He afterwards purchased one hundred and thirty-three acres of the farm owned by his father and at once engaged in general farming, an occupation which he found pleasant and profitable throughout the active years of his life. In 1902 he removed to the village of Athens, surrendering the cares of the farm to his oldest daughter.

January 1, 1865. Mr. Taylor was united in marriage with Miss Adelia I. Gardner, a native of Canada, and to them were born five children, namely: George, who resides at home; Minnie, who married Riley Walker, by whom she had two children, Jennie and Dewey, whose home is upon their father's farm; William E., who married Miss Grace Williams and resides in Council Bluffs, Iowa; Myrtle May, who is stenographer for the Advance Thresher Company, at Battle Creek, and Edwin A., who resides at Grand Island, Nebraska. Mrs. Taylor died January 26, 1892, and is interred in the cemetery at Athens. Mr. Taylor was afterward united in marriage with Mrs. Ella F. Foote. Both himself and wife are members of the Athens Congregational church, in which he officiates as trustee, a position he has held for fifteen years. Since his identification with church interests he has held various offices, serving as treasurer for some time. Fraternally he is a member of the Masonic lodge, at Athens, and in memory of his years of service in the cause of his country he belongs to the Frank Mason post, G. A. R., having served as post commander, and for the past two years has acted as adjutant. He is a Republican in politics and has always given his influence for the advancement of his party. He is an esteemed and highly respected citizen, his many years of usefulness having done much for the moral, social and agricultural life of the community with which he has identified his interests.

NORMAN B. SHERMAN, M. D.

The ability of Dr. Norman B. Sherman as a medical practicioner and surgeon is widely acknowledged in Marshall in the liberal patronage which is accorded him. He has been engaged in practice here for eight years and has won for himself the favorable regard of the public. His birth occurred in Cortland, New York, April 24, 1836, his parents being Jirah and Jane (Chapman) Sherman. The father was born in Philadelphia and the mother was of German birth.

After their marriage they removed from Philadelphia to New York and Rev. Jirah Sherman became a member of the New York Methodist Episcopal conference. For many years he devoted his life to the ministry of that denomination and was located at various places in New York. His last years were spent in retirement in Cortland, New York, where he died in 1862, his wife surviving him for about three years.

Dr. Sherman is indebted to the public school system of the Empire state for the early privileges he enjoyed. He afterward attended an academy at Cortland, New York, and then engaged in teaching for a time, while subsequently he took up the study of medicine preparatory to making its practice his life work. His early reading was accomplished in the office and under the direction of Drs. Goodyear and Garlick. He afterward pursued a regular course in the Albany Medical College and was graduated in 1861. He then located for practice in his home town and was unusually successful in the beginning of his professional career. He remained a resident of that place for a long period and the duties of his profession made almost constant demands upon his time, so widely was his native and acquired talent acknowledged. He became a member of the Cortland County Medical Society and also of the New York State Medical Society. In 1895, however, he sold his practice in the Empire state and came to Marshall, Michigan, where he entered upon his professional work and now has has a large city practice.

Dr. Sherman was united in marriage to Miss Alvina Hunter, who at her death left two children, William, now deceased, and Dora, the wife of Burr Lott, of Michigan. For his second wife Dr. Sherman chose Jennie Moe, of Lansing, Michigan, a daughter of Charles Moe, one of the leading residents of that city, in which place she was born and educated. The Doctor and his wife now reside at No. 115 Kalamazoo avenue. While residing in the Empire state he was an active member of the Independent Order of Odd Fellows, but is not now affiliated with that organization. In politics he is a Republican, and while living in Cortland held the position of health officer for a number of years. He was also alderman of the city for a long period and did effective service as a member of the school board. Anything that tends to bring to man the key to that complex mystery which we call life, elicits his earnest attention and ofttimes receives his hearty endorsement. He is quick to adopt any new methods which he believes will prove of value in his medical or surgical practice, and at the same time he never discards an old and time tried remedy or method in order to take up with any idea of whose practical value he is not assured. He has done much to alleviate human suffering in this county during the eight years of his residence here, and has won popular as well as professional regard in Marshall and the surrounding district.

CHARLES W. LEWIS.

Charles W. Lewis, who follows farming on section 35, Eckford township, is the owner of eighty-four acres of land in that locality and also eighty acres on section 26. He was born in Stafford, Genesee county, New York, September 13, 1856. His paternal grandparents were Richard and Mary Lewis, who died in Stafford, New York. John Lewis, the father of our

subject, was born in Lancastershire, England, and in 1844 came to America, where he was united in marriage to Miss Livilla Gleason, a daughter of Fortunatus and Joanna (Farwell) Gleason. Her father was born in New Hampshire and her mother in Vermont, and they were probably married in the Green Mountain state, removing to Genesee county, New York. Mrs. Gleason died in the Empire state and after a few months her husband went to Burlington, Michigan, to live with a son. He survived, however, for only a brief period, and his remains were laid to rest in the Burlington cemetery. Mr. and Mrs. John Lewis began their domestic life in the Empire state and there the former died when his son Charles was but four years of age. In 1865 Mrs. Lewis came to Michigan and settled upon the farm where our subject is now living, there spending her remaining days. She had but two children, the elder being Myrta, who became the wife of William S. Harris, and died on the old homestead farm May 23, 1896.

Charles W. Lewis was a youth of nine summers when his mother came to Michigan. Prior to that time he had received practically no educational privileges, but after arriving in this state he enjoyed the benefit of instruction in the common school and also in the graded schools of Homer, following which he pursued a business course in the business college at Hillsdale, Michigan, where he was graduated when twenty-one years of age. He had intended to enter a bank, and indeed had a position open for him, but deciding that he preferred agricultural life he returned to the old homestead.

Mr. Lewis was married in Homer, Michigan, November 15, 1877, to Miss

Addie Wait, a daughter of Nelson and Orpha (Sylvester) Wait. She was born in Eckford township, Calhoun county, and her father was a native of Vermontville, Vermont, where he was reared to manhood, his parents being Greene and Lydia (Moon) Wait. The mother of Mrs. Lewis was born in Monroe county, New York, and it was there that her parents were married. The maternal grandparents of Mrs. Lewis were Seth and Laura (Burton) Sylvester, both of whom were born in the east. The former died in Eckford township and the latter at Litchfield, Michigan. About 1840 the parents of Mrs. Lewis came to Michigan, settling in Eckford township, removing to Newton township, and later returning to the former place. There Mr. Wait died, while his wife passed away in Jonesville, Michigan. In their family were five children: Laura, who is the widow of Chauncey Markham, of Washington, Indiana, and has four children; Martha, who became the wife of Jeremiah Foster and died in Pulaski township, Jackson county, Michigan, leaving three children; Luther A., who married Bethuel Martin and lives in Jonesville; Stephen, of Lansing, Michigan, married Fannie Osborn and has three children.

After his marriage Mr. Lewis located on his mother's farm and this he rented and operated on shares for several years. Eight years later he purchased the eighty-acre tract of land on section 26, Eckford township that he now owns. He made that his home until after the death of his mother and sister, when he inherited the old homestead, upon which he has lived for eight years. He has remodeled the buildings and now has a fine place, well improved in all particulars. Unto him and his wife has been born one son, Arthur, whose birth occurred in Eckford township March 28, 1889, and who is now a member of the Homer high school of the class of 1905.

Mr. Lewis cast his first presidential vote for Garfield in 1880, and has taken an active interest in political affairs. He has been a delegate to the county conventions and was elected a member of the board of reviews in 1886, and since that time has served for four additional terms, although not consecutively. In 1894 he was appointed census enumerator, and he was elected and served for two terms as township treasurer. In 1901 he was elected supervisor for Eckford township and while a member of the county board served on the committee on official claims during the first year. In the second year he was appointed a member of the same committee, and was chairman of a committee on drainage. In 1902 he was appointed a member of the building committee, consisting of two persons, to supervise repairs on the county buildings, and in 1903 he was elected chairman of the county board, being the incumbent at the present writing. He has long been a member of the Republican county committee and puts forth every effort in his power to promote the success of his party, while as an officer he is most loyal and true to the best interests of the entire community, placing the general good before partisanship and the public welfare before personal aggrandizement. Mr. Lewis is a member of the Free Baptist church, of which he has been a trustee. He belongs to Homer camp, No. 3055, Modern Woodmen of America, is also connected with the Modern Maccabees, at Eckford, and has filled the position of com-

mander for about eight or nine years. He
has also been representative to the Great
camp, at Detroit, at Saginaw and at Marquette. As a public officer he has made a
creditable record and as a farmer he has
shown himself most enterprising and progressive.

MILTON OSBORN, M. D.

The name of Dr. Milton Osborn is enduringly inscribed on the pages of Calhoun
county's history, for he located in the county
about 1849, and continued one of its honored and valued residents until his death.
His life was devoted to labors wherein
wealth and influence availeth little or
naught. the measure of success depending
upon mentality, ability—both natural and
acquired—and the broad culture of the individual. Possessing all the requisite qualities of the able physician, Dr. Osborn advanced to a position prominent among the
representatives of the medical fraternity in
Calhoun county.

A native of New York, he was born in
Batavia, January 18, 1821, a son of Richard
and Lydia (Bristol) Osborn. His people
were pioneer settlers of western New York,
removing to Batavia when that entire district was almost an unbroken wilderness.
When a youth of thirteen years, Dr. Osborn
came to Michigan with Mr. and Mrs. Hanes,
the latter being his eldest sister. He was
educated in Adrian, Michigan, and determining to make the practice of medicine his
life work, he pursued his reading under the
direction of a physician of this state until
he entered the Western Reserve Medical
College, at Cleveland, Ohio, in which he was
graduated in the class of 1849. He imme-

diately afterward came to Calhoun county,
locating for practice at Rice Creek, six miles
north of Albion. He had been graduated in
the same class with Dr. O'Donohue and Dr.
Bristol, who later became practitioners in
Albion. Dr. Osborn remained at Rice Creek
for six years and obtained a good country
practice. In 1855, however, he removed to
Albion in order to have a broader field of labor, and entered into partnership with his
former classmate, Dr. O'Donohue, this relation continuing until the outbreak of the
Civil war, when Dr. O'Donohue went to
the front as a surgeon. Dr. Osborn continued in charge of the practice here and secured a large patronage, being long considered one of the leading and capable physicians of this part of the state. He gave
years of thought and painstaking preparation to his profession and was thoroughly
qualified for its practice. Nature endowed
him with the qualities necessary for success
as a practitioner for he was sympathetic, patient and thoughtful and in the hour of ex-
tremity cool and courageous. Though his
professional cares engross much of his attention, he has always found time to keep
posted upon the practical details of the improvements of the science and availed himself of every development in remedial agencies. He was a member of the County Medical Society and enjoyed the highest esteem of his professional brethren who recognized his close fidelity to the ethics of the
profession as well as his ability in his chosen
calling.

On the 1st of June, 1863, Dr. Osborn
was married to Miss Clara Van Wyck, of
Marshall, a daughter of Cornelius and
Christina (White) Van Wyck. Her father,
who was born in Dutchess county, New
York, and was of Holland lineage, went as

a young man to Cayuga county, New York, where he was married in 1837. Immediately afterward he started with his bride for Michigan, locating at Marshall, where he was engaged in farming. During his active life he lived in Marshall and Adrian, Michigan, and for some years prior to their death Mr. and Mrs. Van Wyck made their home with Mrs. Osborn. The former died in May, 1902, the latter in 1887. They were consistent Christian people, holding membership in the Methodist Episcopal church. Mrs. Osborn spent her early life in Marshall, pursuing her education in the city schools and was married in Adrian, to which place her parents had in the meantime removed. Six children graced this union, of whom four are living. Thirza is the wife of George C. Ballentine, of Clarendon township. Charles D. is married and is connected with the Big Four Railroad office at Cincinnati, Ohio. Jay M. is now studying dentistry in the University of Glasgow in Scotland. He is a graduate of the dental department of the University of Michigan, but having a position in Kimberly, South Africa, is now pursuing an advanced course in order to win a British degree. He intends to locate at Kimberly, South Africa, as a dental assistant there. Emma A. is now a teacher in Portland, Michigan, and is a graduate of Albion College. Both Dr. and Mrs. Osborn were members of St. James's Episcopal church and he served as warden and vestryman for many years. His political allegiance was given to the Democracy and though never an aspirant for office, he was at one time nominated for the legislature, but the district being strongly Republican, he was defeated. Socially he was identified with the Masonic fraternity and attained the Knight Templar degree in the commandery in Jack-

son, Michigan. He died March 14, 1884, and his death was the occasion of sincere and wide felt regret. He had qualified himself thoroughly for his profession, realizing the great responsibility which devolves upon the physician. Moreover, he possessed a sympathetic, kindly nature that prompted him to put forth every effort in his power to aid his fellow men. All of his strong traits of character were such as commended him to the confidence and good will of the public and he enjoyed the warmest regard of all with whom he was associated.

JOHN MARTINSON.

John Martinson, a successful farmer of Tekonsha township, Calhoun county, was born in Lincolnshire, England, December 15, 1846, his parents coming to America when he was about four years old. After a journey of five weeks they landed in New York city, whence they journeyed to Clyde, Wayne county, New York, making that their home until 1866, when the located in Tekonsha township, Michigan. Both father and mother, the latter formerly Elizabeth Douse, also of English birth, are buried in the Tekonsha cemetery. In the family were three other sons besides John Martinson, namely: George, Charles and William H. and one sister, Harriet, now Mrs. James Umstead, of Marshall. All are located in America.

Until he was twenty-one John Martinson remained at home with his parents, after which he worked out for one year at nineteen dollars per month. He then began farming for himself on a farm belonging to John B. Bliss, located north of Tekonsha, remaining in that location for three years. October 23, 1872, he was united in marriage with Miss Julia E. Granger. She was the daughter of S. S. Granger, who was born in Sweden, New York, July 3, 1820, and died October 8, 1893, and Sophronia (Howard) Granger, born the same place September 5, 1818, and died in January, 1896. Of the four children born to Mr. and Mrs. Granger, George married Adella Wood and they have one child; Julia is the wife of John Martinson, of this review; Ithamar R. married Alice Nicholas, and Sylvester S. married Nellie Bliss. To Mr. and Mrs. Martinson were born the following children: John S., born August 3, 1873; William Burdette, died at eighteen months of age; and Don G., born November 13, 1884. On December 24, 1902, John S. married Miss Bessie L. Pritchard, and is now engaged in farming, as is also his brother. In his political convictions Mr. Martinson adheres to the principles advocated in the platform of the Democratic party, though he was originally a Republican, casting his first vote for Grant. He has voted the Democratic ticket since Cleveland's administration. Personally he has never sought nor cared for official recognition.

ALBERT GURDON PALMER.

A successful career has been that of Albert Gurdon Palmer, now located in Marengo township, Calhoun county, upon a farm of one hundred and thirty acres of valuable land, well developed and improved, with handsome and modern build-ings and all equippments for remunerative work. He was born in Morrisville, Madison county, New York, October 21, 1835, a son of Gurdon and Henrietta (Brown) Palmer, who lived and died in that locality. Mr. Palmer received his education in the district schools and also attended the Cazenovia Seminary, remaining at home until he was twenty-two years old, when he came west, locating in Rockford, Illinois. He remained a year in that location, after which he went to Wisconsin for the period of a year, then returned to his native state and spent the summer. In 1859 he came to Michigan, working by the month for five years in Calhoun county, after which he rented a farm for two years. He then went to Iowa, purchasing a farm of eighty acres in the vicinity of Independence, but leasing the farm while he was employed in making brick, which was to be used in the insane asylum at Independence. After four years in this employment he traded his farm of eighty acres for one of one hundred and thirty acres, his present property, and has since made this his home, keeping in splendid condition the new house and barn which had just been erected on the property. He is now engaged in general farming and stock raising.

The marriage of Mr. Palmer occurred March 20, 1872, and united him with Miss Ann E. Johnson, a native of New York state. She came to Michigan when only five years old, with her parents, Oliver Cromwell and Mary Ann (Chandler) Johnson, both of whom were natives of Onondaga county, New York. The father rented land and engaged in farming in this vicinity until his death, both himself and wife being buried in the Johnson cemetery. Mr. Palmer is a Democrat in his political convictions, and is an enterprising and public spirited citizen, always ready to lend his aid toward movements which have for their end the welfare of the community.

DANIEL M. McAULIFF.

It is a fact well attested by experience that the business men who are practical and enterprising make the most capable public officers and far exceed those in efficiency who make politics a business. Mr. McAuliff is now serving as city treasurer of Albion and is also a prominent dealer there in agricultural implements and carriage robes. He was born in Albion April 11, 1875, a son of Patrick and Mary (Wrenn) McAuliff. The father was born in Ireland and soon after his marriage came with his bride to the new world, spending his remaining days in Calhoun county. The son was here reared and educated, continuing his studies until he had mastered the work of the high school, in which he was graduated with the class of 1891. In that year he entered the hardware store of A. P. Gardner as a clerk and bookkeeper, and was with that gentleman as long as he continued in business, having for some time the management of the establishment. When Mr. Gardner sold out Mr. McAuliff remained with his successor until 1897, when he accepted a position as manager with E. C. Lester in the implement business and in 1899 bought out his employer. This is one of the old established enterprises of Albion. Mr. McAuliff now handles all kinds of agricultural implements, carriages, harness, carriage robes and seeds. He em-

34

ploys a number of salesmen and is conducting a very successful enterprise, his trade extending over three counties.

On the 2d of September, 1899, Mr. McAuliff was united in marriage to Miss Catherine Walch, of Albion, and they have two children, Joseph W. and Richard D. They hold membership in St. John's Catholic church, of which Mr. McAuliff is now treasurer, and their home is a pleasant residence on Walnut street. He is an active member and one of the directors of the Leisure Hour Club. In politics he is a Democrat and although he has never sought or desired political preferment he was in 1902 elected city treasurer. He filled the position so acceptably that in the succeeding year he was nominated by acclamation and received the largest majority ever given any candidate in the city. No higher testimonial of his efficiency and personal popularity could be given. He is now prominent in both business and public circles and has attained to his present enviable position through ability and energy. Having always lived in this city, his life history is familiar to his fellow townsmen and the fact that those who have known him from boyhood are numbered among his stanchest friends, is an indication that his has been a most honorable career.

JOHN M. BRIGHAM.

John Morrison Brigham, by reason of his highly artistic work, won recognition in a short time in Battle Creek, in photographic circles, and now after five-years' residence in the city is regarded as the leading representative of the profession. He was born at Gunn Plains, Allegan county, Michigan, February 17, 1863, a son of Stillman and Mary (Chapin) Brigham. The father was born at Shutesbury, Massachusetts, and with his parents, Mr. and Mrs. Curtis Brigham, removed from Massachusetts to Michigan, living for a short time at Yorkville. They then removed to what was then known as Gunmarsh, Allegan county, where Curtis L. Brigham spent his remaining days. He was a shoemaker by trade and followed that pursuit in connection with farming. He was also one of the first preachers to locate in Allegan county, and was active in proclaiming the gospel among the pioneer settlers. It was in that locality that the father of our subject was reared, and the occupation which he followed in his youth was the one which yielded him a living when he started out in life on his own account. Later, however, he abandoned farming and is now living in Plainwell, Michigan, where for some years he has conducted a photograph gallery. He married Miss Mary Chapin, of Battle Creek, a daughter of Dr. J. B. Chapin, one of the early physicians of this city, and for many years a capable practitioner here. He died in 1893. Both Mr. and Mrs. Brigham are members of the Baptist church.

In the common schools of Plainwell John M. Brigham began his education, and later attended the Indiana Normal College, at Valparaiso, Indiana. He afterward took up the study of photography at Plainwell, beginning when eighteen years of age. He owned his first gallery there and it is still in operation. For six years he attended the National Photographic conventions, which are practically a high school of in-

struction in this line. After he began competing, placing his own work on exhibition there, he won four medals and two diplomas for posing, chemical effect and lighting combined.

After having attained a high degree of perfection in his chosen calling, he located at Battle Creek in October, 1898, opening a fine studio at "Point Place." Almost immediately he gained recognition for his artistic work, and his business has therefore gradually increased until the volume of his patronage and the class of his productions give him rank as the leading representative of his art in southern Michigan. He has a splendidly equipped studio and with the advancement which is continually being made in this line he keeps in touch and, in fact, is in a large degree, a leader in pleasing innovations.

Mr. Brigham was united in marriage to Miss Ida M. Potter, of Mankato, Minnesota, and they are members of the Baptist church, of this city, while in social circles, where true worth and intelligence are received as the passports into good society, they occupy an enviable position.

RIAL ALLEN CARPENTER.

An honored and respected resident of Athens, Calhoun county, Rial Allen Carpenter is enjoying a season of rest after many years of activity as one of the most successful farmers of the community. He was born in Naples, Ontario county, New York, October 28, 1844, the son of Calvin L. Carpenter, whose sketch appears upon another page of this work. Mr. Carpenter accompanied his father to Michigan in 1853, celebrating his ninth birthday while en route. On their arrival in Michigan, the family settled in Sherwood township, Branch county, and there he attended the common schools, later becoming a student in Athens township, Calhoun county, whither his father removed. He remained at home until March, 1865, when he enlisted in Company A, Twelfth Michigan Infantry, and was stationed at Camden, Arkansas, until his honorable discharge in 1866. He then returned to Michigan and began life for himself, working on farms in the neighborhood of his home by the day and month until 1870. In March of that year he was married, after which he rented a farm for one year, when he purchased forty acres of land located in Athens township, northwest of the village of Athens, where he made his home for five years. He then sold this property and purchased a farm located one mile southeast of the village, in the same township. This property he continued to cultivate and improve for some years, but on account of impaired health, he removed in 1880 to Athens and engaged in the hardware and grocery business, being located upon the site now occupied by Daniel's jewelry store. After three years he returned to his farm and once more engaged in agricultural pursuits. In 1896 he again located in the village, having previously purchased a pleasant home, and has since lived in retirement. His farm, which is now rented, consists of one hundred and eighty acres of highly developed farming land, its value much enhanced by modern and up-to-date equipments, as well as handsome and commodious buildings. The barn-yard is entirely under cover, while the barn, which is the largest in this part of the country, has the following dimensions: on the north side,

108 feet long by 24 feet high; on the west side, 100 feet long by 20 feet high; and on the south side 64 feet long, the storage capacity being three hundred tons. Mr. Carpenter devoted the land to general farming and dairying, and was also largely interested in poultry raising, considerable of his time being given to this latter industry, in which he met with gratifying success.

Mr. Carpenter married Melvina E. Doty, who was born in Bristol, Ontario county, New York, February 12, 1846. Her father, Chester Doty, was born in East Bloomfield, Ontario county, New York, January 11, 1816, the son of Chester and Cynthia (Reed) Doty, natives respectively of Massachusetts and East Bloomfield, his birth having occurred September 10, 1784, and that of his wife June 3, 1784. He married Rosinda Pierce in New York state, where he remained as a farmer until 1846, when he removed to Sherwood township, Branch county, Michigan. Ten years later he located in Athens township, Calhoun county, residing on his farm just south of the village of Athens, where his death occurred May 3, 1895. He is interred in Sherwood cemetery. His widow is living in the village of Athens at the advanced age of eighty-seven years. They became the parents of six children, namely: Ralph John, who was born June 23, 1837, and is a resident of Battle Creek; Edgar, who was born June 10, 1840, resides in Los Angeles, California; Oscar, who was born May 19, 1843, and died January 14, 1881; Melvina, the wife of Mr. Carpenter; Eliza, who was born August 4, 1853, in Sherwood, Michigan, married George Greenfield, of Athens, her mother being a member of her home; and Julia I., who was born February 6, 1858, and died January 13, 1897. The first four named were natives of Bristol, Ontario county, New York. Chester Doty was a man of prominence in all communities with which he identified his interests, while a resident of New York serving as a captain of militia, and in Sherwood township, in the interests of the Republican party, he acted as township treasurer for three years. To Mr. and Mrs. Carpenter was born one daughter, Lina Estelle. In October, 1896, she married John J. Snyder, who conducted Mr. Carpenter's farm for five years, but is now engaged in the hardware business in Athens. They are the parents of four children, namely: Carroll C., Mary Ruth, Merna and Neil Allen. Mrs. Snyder was given every advantage in the matter of education, having graduated from the Athens high school.

Mr. Carpenter is justly numbered among the promoters of the best interests of the community in which he has made his home for so many years. Always actively interested in the welfare of the public he has faithfully served as street commissioner for the greater part of the time since the village was incorporated, having been elected to the position through the influence of the Republican party, of which he is a stanch adherent. He was one of the organizers and promoters of the American Cement Post Company, of Athens, and for one year acted as general manager, thus assisting materially in the development of industrial resources. Fraternally, he is a member of the Masonic lodge of Athens, while both himself and wife belong to the Eastern Star. They are also members of the Protective Legion, of which he is now serving his second term as president. He is likewise identified with the Frank Mason post, Grand Army of the Republic, and is a past commander. Every po-sition which Mr. Carpenter has been called upon to fill has felt the influence of his personality, his strength of purpose and business ability, all duties being capably and faithfully performed. His own ability and integrity, as well as his connection with a family of prominence, have numbered him among the representative citizens of the community.

CALVIN LOOMIS CARPENTER.

The Carpenter family, first represented in Michigan by Calvin Loomis Carpenter, until his death March 18, 1886, a successful farmer and honored resident of Calhoun county, came originally from England, his grandfather having settled in Connecticut at an early day. He became a soldier in the Revolutionary war and met his death October 17. 1777, at the battle of Bemis Heights. He left a widow and two children. a son and daughter. The son, Robert by name, was born in 1775, and after the death of his father. he was taken into the home of a man named Loomis, who reared him to manhood, giving him the advantage of a good education as well as a practical training along other lines. He subsequently married Phoebe McNair, who was born in Connecticut in 1781, the descendant of Scotch ancestry, and whose death occurred in 1868. To them were born the following children: Abner, born December 21, 1799; Sally, born September 25, 1801, and died April 28, 1888; Benjamin C., born July 25, 1804; Nathaniel, born September 14, 1806; Calvin L., the personal subject of this review, born in Middlesex, New York, August 2, 1808; Betsey, born September 14, 1810, and died September 12, 1892; Robert O., born October 21, 1812, and died in August 1871; Margaret, born September 17, 1814; Nancy, born November 13, 1816, and died in 1895; Rowena, born July 10, 1819, and died December 29, 1893; William, born April 6, 1821, and died September 7, 1897; Phoebe, born April 9, 1823, and died October 23, 1877; and Christiana, born May 11, 1826.

Calvin L. Carpenter was married in 1831 to Eleanor D. Pierce, the oldest daughter of Henry L. Pierce, of Bristol, New York, and to them were born the following children: Armida A., born October 12, 1832, and died January 8, 1870; Calvin L., born March 1, 1833, and died July 19, 1884; Henry L., born August 6, 1834; William Q., born January 7, 1836; Ellen M., born January 6, 1838, and died January 25, 1895; Robert, born April 29, 1839; Melissa L., born June 24, 1842; Phoebe J., born August 25, 1843; Rial A., born October 28, 1844; Alva A., born August 22, 1846; Thomas J., born December 25, 1848; Oliver J., died February 2, 1852; Abner L., born November 20, 1852; and Rowena L., born September 12, 1854, and died January 27, 1859. Mrs. Carpenter died November 7, 1870, at the age of fifty-seven years and twenty-five days. Mr. Carpenter came to Michigan in 1853, accompanied by his family with the exception of one daughter, who had married in Allegany county, New York, and settled in Sherwood township, Branch county. He remained in that location until 1859, when with his family he removed to Athens township, Calhoun county, where he purchased forty acres of timber land, built a log house and with the help of his sons, brought the land to a state of cultivation. At the breaking out of the Civil war, two sons, Loomis and Robert, responded to the first call, and

before peace was declared two other sons, Rial and Henry, also volunteered. The sons who first enlisted were both wounded, but all returned safe to their home at the close of the war. After the death of his first wife Mr. Carpenter was united in marriage with Mrs. Betsey Wilder. Mr. Carpenter was a man of push and energy, and throughout his long life in this section of the state retained the respect and esteem of all with whom he came in contact. A notable event in the lives of all who bear the name of Carpenter is a family reunion which is held every year, the first one being observed in 1893.

MONTFORD BALCOM MURRAY.

Montford Balcom Murray, secretary and treasurer of the Albion Malleable Iron Company, with which he has been connected since its organization, was born in Reading, Hillsdale county, Michigan, November 7, 1862, his parents being William H. and Marietta (Balcom) Murray. The father was a native of the Empire state and was brought to Michigan by his parents when only a year and a half old. His boyhood days were spent in this state, and after putting aside his text-books he acquired a practical knowledge of the carpenter's trade and later engaged in contracting and building in Hillsdale county. Subsequently he retired to a farm, where he is now living. He was married in Reading, Michigan, to Miss Marietta Balcom, a daughter of Abner Balcom, who came to Michigan from Ontario county, New York, her death occurring in 1879. Mr. Murray was in former years quite prominent in public af-

fairs, was earnest and active in his support
of the Republican party and at different
times acceptably filled public office.

Montford B. Murray pursued his education in the schools of Reading and entered upon his business career as a telegraph operator in the employ of the Lake
Shore & Michigan Southern Railroad
Company. Subsequently he went to Ypsilanti, where he remained for two years as
chief clerk and telegraph operator, and a
similar period was spent at Banker's, Hillsdale county. He was station agent at Albion for one year, coming to this city in
1887. It was during that year, however,
that the Albion Malleable Iron Company
was organized and incorporated and when
the business was put in active operation
Mr. Murray accepted a position as bookkeeper. Not long afterward he purchased
stock in the enterprise and was elected a
director, since which time he has served
continuously on the board. He was for a
short time vice president of the company,
but resigned that position when in August,
1893, he was made secretary and treasurer.

Mr. Murray is also one of the incorporators and directors of the T. C. Prouty
Company, manufacturers, of Albion, and
has investments in other interests.

On the 8th of November, 1883, was
celebrated the marriage of Mr. Murray
and Miss Frances Horne, of Charlotte,
Michigan. They have four children: Effie, Ethel, William H. and Sarah. Mr.
and Mrs. Murray hold membership in the
Presbyterian church, in which he is serving as elder and trustee. Both he and his
wife have been very active in church work
and their efforts have been very effective
and far-reaching. He is also a member of
the Leisure Hour club and was one of its
incorporators, while with Albion lodge,

K. of P., he is also identified. His study
of the political issues of the day has led
him to give his support to the Republican
party and while he keeps well informed on
the issues of the day that divide the country into great political organizations, he
has never sought or desired office. The development of his native talents and latent
powers, the improvement of opportunity
which comes to all and his strong purpose
and straightforward dealing have been the
salient features in a career which is as commendable as it is successful.

LOUIS C. MILLER.

Unlike many American families, the
Millers, well-known in Calhoun county,
Michigan, where those of the name have
long been identified with the development
of resources, have carefully preserved their
ancestral records, being able to authentic-
ally trace the genealogy back to the first
settler on American soil. The great-great-
grandfather of our subject, Louis C. Miller,
came to America from Ireland about the
time of the Revolutionary war, participating in this struggle in the interests of the
British crown and meeting death before its
close. He had brought his family with him
and after the war, about 1804, they located
in New York state. His son, Daniel Miller, born December 25, 1772, probably in
the state of New Jersey, married Mahita-
ble Horton, the representative of a family
that had settled on Long Island about
1640, members of which served in the Continental army. December 30, 1799, was
born David Horton Miller, through the
family from whom the name Horton came,

tracing the relationship to Peter Hallock, who crossed in the Mayflower. He married Polly Carrier, and in 1837 they came to Michigan with a family of a son and daughter and located in Sheridan township, Calhoun county, when the land was nothing but a wilderness. For many years he was engaged as a farmer and surveyor, and was also one of the pioneer ministers of the Methodist Protestant church, and was active in the formation of the church at Rice Creek. His son, Charles A., born in Cayuga county, New York, July 1, 1828, married Ellen Barker, a native of Le-Roy. New York, her natal day being October 19, 1831. She also was the representative of a distinguished eastern family, the first of the name having settled in Connecticut, where they allied themselves with the Platt family, who have long been prominent in the public life of that state, and are to-day identified with its interests. The original Barker log house was still standing a few years ago. Simon Lewis Barker, our subject's maternal grandfather, was born August 4, 1806, the son of Ezra, who was born October 11, 1780. His mother was Lucy Platt, born August 1, 1782, the daughter of John Platt, born November 18, 1746, and his wife, formerly Lucy Webb, was born February 17, 1746. Charles A. Miller became a man of much prominence in the community wherein he made his home for so many years. In youth he attended Olivet College, and though he did not graduate he acquired a wide information, which helped him immeasurably in later years. He was a member of the Methodist Protestant church, and was always active in religious work. In political life he was a Republican, and through the influence of his party was called upon

to serve in public capacity, holding the position of supervisor. In the matter of occupation he was a farmer and was also interested in stock raising, making a specialty of sheep, the fine breeds which he had on his farm being exhibited at various county and state fairs. To himself and wife were born the following children: Myra A., born July 17, 1852, married Marcus J. Wells, and they have seven children, namely: Ruth M., born February 16, 1880; Howard, born February 24, 1882, now deceased; Earnest, born April 22, 1884; Frank E., born August 26, 1887; Morris M., born November 3, 1885; Clara C., born July 29, 1889, also deceased, and William P., deceased, born September 3, 1891. David Howard, the second, February 15, 1855, died March 7, 1862; Louis C., is the subject of this review; Charles O., whose sketch also appears in this work; Nellie, born December 23, 1861, lives in Chicago; Mary E., born December 28, 1864, is a lawyer located in Chicago, and Carrie I., born May 18, 1867, married James E. Ott, of Marengo township, Calhoun county, and they have one son. Orville, born February 8, 1891. All the members of this family became graduates of the Marshall high school, while Mary graduated from the normal school at Ypsilanti.

Upon his completion of the high school course Louis C. Miller attended the law department of the Univeristy of Michigan, until his graduation in 1882, with the degree of L. L. B., immediately after which he began the practice of law, in Marshall. He has since made his home and has risen to a position of prominence. Early in his professional career he served as county clerk, during the years 1887 and 1888, having been appointed to fill a vacancy by Judge

Frank A. Hooker, and also circuit court commissioner for one term, and is now completing his third term as alderman from the first ward, of Marshall, being chairman of the ordinance commtitee, holding his political offices through the influence of the Republican party, the principles of which he strongly indorses. He wrote the franchise granting the electric railroad the right to pass through the city, also it is worthy of mention that the first sewers were put in and first paving done during his incumbency. November 10, 1887, he was united in marriage with Miss Mary E. Potter, a daughter of Homer and Phoebe (Tilton) Potter, the first of this family to settle in America being a pioneer on the Mayflower. To Mr. and Mrs. Miller have been born five children, namely: Carrie L., born January 20, 1889; Louis P., born June 12, 1891; Bertha A., born November 6, 1894; Phoebe E., born June 2, 1897, and Charles Albert, born August 11, 1901. Carrie is now a student in the Marshall high school. Mr. Miller is a man of much ability, a strong and earnest personality, qualities which have won for him the esteem and confidence of all with whom he has come in contact. He is still a young man, and though he has won a success there is still a career of exceptional promise before him. His standing is perhaps best shown by the fact that at present he is writing the head notes for the supreme court feports of the state.

SAMUEL BOSSERD.

A successful farmer of Marengo township and one who has been actively identified with the development of the community is to be named in the person of Samuel Bosserd, now acting as supervisor of this township. He was born in North Hampton county, Pennsylvania, January 31, 1857, a son of Jacob and Catharine (Ackerman) Bosserd, both of whom were natives of the same county, the father being a son of John Bosserd, who was born in Bucks county, and removed to North Hampton at an early date. Jacob Bosserd came to Marengo township in 1865, locating with his family on the Territorial road, on section 27, becoming the owner of a farm of one hundred and twenty acres. His death occurred in this location in 1886 at the age of seventy-one years, his wife having died two years earlier at the age of sixty-four, and both are interred in the cemetery on the Territorial road, in Marengo township. He was a blacksmith by trade but had devoted his time principally to agricultural pursuits. In politics he was a Whig in his young days and became a Republican in later life, though never desirous of official recognition personally. He was a member of the Evangelical Methodist church and was always active in religious work. Of the seven children born to them David resides in Burlington township, this county; Mary married George W. Crawford, of Missouri; John, William and Isaac are deceased; Samuel is the personal subject of this review; and Joseph F. resides in Marengo township.

In the district schools of Marengo township Samuel Bosserd received his education, attending school in the winter and working with his father during the summer months. He remained in the paternal home until the death of the father, at that time having charge of the farm. In 1887 he purchased a farm of one hundred and fifty-five acres located on section 11 and upon this property he has since made his home, meeting with success in his efforts, his time being devoted to general farming and stockraising. He was united in marriage November 13, 1878, with Miss Alma J. Griffin, who was born February 1, 1857, a native of Marengo township, and a daughter of Jarvis and Minerva (Campbell) Griffin. Her father came to Calhoun county from Canada in 1885, locating in the village of Marengo, where he opened a shop and worked at his trade of blacksmith. He was married in the village In 1865 he enlisted in Company B, Ninth Michigan Infantry as a private and died in hospital at Chattanooga, his last resting place the National Cemetery. Mrs. Bosserd has one brother, Addison J., a resident of Detroit. To Mr. and Mrs. Bosserd have been born five children, namely: Elmer Joseph; Clarence A.; Laura A.; Ruth A.; and George S. In his political convictions Mr. Bosserd is a Democrat and through the influence of this party he has been elected to various official positions in the community, acting as treasurer for two years, commissioner for a like period, and in 1902 was elected supervisor, serving for two terms. Mr. Bosserd is a man of much ability and enterprise and much of the development of resources in Marengo township is the result of his disinterested efforts.

GEORGE McCORMICK.

George McCormick is a representative of one of the oldest pioneer families in Calhoun county, and is himself a native son of the county, but it is not these facts alone that entitle him to mention in this volume, but because of his activity in agricultural circles, his honor in business life, his loyalty in citizenship and his devotion to all that pertains to the welfare and progress of his town, township and county. He was born in Sheridan township on the 7th of October, 1846, and is a son of George and Julia (Neale) McCormick. His paternal grandfather was Alexander McCormick, who was of Irish birth. In the year 1836 George McCormick, Sr., came to Michigan, settling in Sheridan township, where he purchased a tract of land and built thereon a home. Pioneer conditions existed everywhere in the county, much of the land was still unclaimed and uncultivated, and the settlements were widely scattered. It remained to such brave pioneer people as the members of the McCormick and Neale families to reclaim this region for the purposes of civilization, and lay the foundation for its present prosperity and progress. Mr. McCormick with characteristic energy began the development of his land and the cultivation of his farm, continuing its improvement up to the time of his death, which occurred in 1854, when he was yet in the prime of life. It was after his arrival in Michigan that he married Miss Julia Neale, a daughter of Seeley and Pollie (Stewart) Neale. Her father was born in Connecticut and was a son of Noah Neale, who was a native of Massachusetts. Seeley Neale lived for seven years in Erie county, Pennsylvania, and thence took his family across the lake to Detroit, Michigan, in 1823. While lviing there he made a trip to Washtenaw county, this state, to look up a good location, and while on the trip he was lost for seven days in the woods. At length he was found by some Frenchmen and brought back to Detroit, when life was almost extinct from exposure and lack of food. Undeterred, however, by this experience from living upon the frontier as a pioneer settler, he came to Calhoun county in 1831, locating in Marengo township, where he entered a farm of six hundred and forty acres, becoming one of the first settlers of the county. He was one of the commissioners of the territorial road and he served his country as a private soldier in the War of 1812. His father was the first person buried at Marengo. Seeley Neale and his wife lie buried in the Territorial cemetery, in Marengo township. He gave the land for cemetery purposes, and it is meet that his earthly remains should have a resting place there. His daughter, Mrs. McCormick, who was born in the Empire state, is still living, and now resides with her son George at the advanced age of eighty-seven years. She has lived a true consistent Christian life and is a member of the Methodist Episcopal church.

George McCormick, whose name introduces this record, spent his boyhood days on the old family homestead. He acquired a common school education and also pursued his studies for one year in Albion College. His father died when the son was seven years of age and he continued to remain on the old home farm, assisting in its cultivation and development until twenty years of age. He then started out in life for himself and purchased eighty acres of land, upon which he lived for seven years, when he traded his original property for the quarter section upon which he now resides. Subsequently he added to this one hundred and ten acres, so that he now has a valuable and extensive farm of two hundred and seventy acres, on which he has erected substantial buildings and made excellent modern improvements. Some of the land had

never been broken when it came into his possession, but his unfaltering energy and unflagging purpose wrought a wonderful transformation in the appearance of the farm, and made it a very productive tract, so that annually the sale of his crops brings to him a very substantial financial return. In addition to general farming he is extensively engaged in the raising of Merino sheep, of which he has large flocks, and makes extensive sales each year.

In 1882 occurred the marriage of Mr. McCormick and Miss Emma J. Ostrom, a native of Orleans county, New York, and a daughter of Leonard L. and Polly (Jackson) Ostrom. Both parents were natives of the Empire state and in 1869 they removed to Calhoun county, Michigan, settling in Sheridan township. He spent his remaining days in this locality and lies buried in Albion cemetery, passing away in 1872, while the mother is now living at Albion. They were the parents of two children: Emma J. and Helen, the latter the wife of William Eldredge. Mrs. McCormick is a most estimable lady, and has proved an able assistant and helpmate to her husband on life's journey, as well as a most congenial companion. Unto them have been born three children: Mabel, who is a graduate of the high school at Albion, and spent a year and a half as a student in the Agricultural College, in Lansing, Michigan, is now the wife of H. Earl Young, of Huntington, Indiana; Bessie is a graduate of the Albion high school, and Ida, who is now a student in the high school at Albion. The last two daughters are still with their parents, and theirs is an ideal home. It is noted for its gracious and pleasing hospitality, which is greatly enjoyed by many friends; for Mr. McCormick, his wife and daughters are all held in high esteem throughout the entire community. He has served as justice of the peace for thirteen years, his term being consecutive, save for the intermission of one year. His social relations connect him with Murat lodge, F. & A. M., of Albion, and Albion Chapter, R. A. M. He is also a member of the Ancient Order of United Workmen and is a Democrat in his political affiliations. In all his business affairs he is straightforward and honorable, and his life has been characterized by industry, capable management, perseverence and fair treatment of his fellow men. Both he and his wife are held in high regard by all who appreciate genuine personal worth.

THOMAS HARTLEY.

The success which had come to Thomas Hartley was entirely the result of his own efforts, the reward of a concentrated energy and ambition, and as the architect of his own fortunes he builded wisely and well. He was one of three sons and four daughters born to his father, Charles Hartley, his birth occurring in Berks county, Pennsylvania, May 27, 1828, of which state his father was also a native, the latter being born April 2, 1807, and dying at the home of his son, June 6, 1854. The elder man emigrated to Michigan when the land was a wilderness, and deer and wild turkeys were plentiful. Thomas Hartley remained at home until he was twenty years of age, his duties being those of a farmer from his earliest recollection. On account of a large

family and straitened circumstances he was unable to gain an education, being compelled to seek his own living at a very early age. Upon entering life for himself his first work was cutting cord wood at ten dollars per month, and afterward he was employed on a farm to swing the cradle at the same wages, being able to cut four or five acres of grain per day. He continued to work by the month until he was twenty-four years old, his first purchase of land consisting of forty-six acres, still a part of the old homestead, the number being increased until he owned two hundred and sixty-six acres, besides a hundred and twenty-six acres which he had given to his children. Mr. Hartley lived in the house which his father had built, but had remodeled and improved the building, making a fine and imposing exterior, as well as putting up other buildings, among which are three barns, which have added greatly to the value of the property. Two fine springs which never freeze over, but run the year round, are upon the farm, which has also undergone the improvement of careful draining.

With but one hundred dollars Mr. Hartley took upon himself the responsibilities of matrimony, marrying Miss Ann Bennett, January 23, 1851. She was born March 23, 1834, a daughter of Ezra and Sara Ann (Osborn) Bennett, natives respectively of Pennsylvania and New York, the mother dying when Mrs. Hartley was but seven years old. Of this union were born the following children: John, born April 27, 1852; Roselma, born April 17, 1856; Charles E., born July 27, 1858; William, born December 25, 1859, and died January 23, 1860; Sophronia, born February 15, 1862; Albert, born April 6, 1864; Harry E., born September 25, 1865; Frank A., born April 15,

1867; and Thomas, born October 14, 1871. Having been deprived of educational advantages himself, Mr. Hartley realized his loss and endeavored to provide for his children along these lines. Harry and Albert both graduated from the normal school at Valparaiso, Indiana, while Thomas graduated from the Homer high school. The two sons first named are grain dealers, the former in Goodland, Indiana, and the latter at Wadena, same state, while Thomas is a hardware merchant in Goodland. Charles and Frank live on farms in the vicinity of the old home. John was married to Louisa Lewis, September 9, 1871, and they have four children, namely: Elmer, who is married and has one child: Ray, Mabel and Edith. Roselma married Herbert Doolittle, February 18, 1874, and they have had five children, namely Lee, Mattie, Arah, Nellie and Anna. After the death of the mother, April 26, 1894, the youngest child, Anna, was adopted by Harry E. Hartley. Charles E. married Louise Moss, August 4, 1881, and they have four children, namely: Lilly, John, Clarence and Lyle. Sophronia married Albert J. Ogden, October 25, 1883, and they have one child, Ellsworth. Albert married Mary Blackstone, October 16, 1889, and they have two children, namely: Florence and Charles. Harry E. married Lilly Wood, November 12, 1889. Frank A. married Augusta Moss, May 30, 1886, and they have four children, namely: Ross, Edna, Belle and Frank. Thomas married Mary Kirby, June 30, 1896, and they have one child, Kirby. Mr. Hartley had twenty-two grandchildren and one great-granddaughter. In religion he was a member of the Presbyterian church of Homer, in which city he made his home for four years, returning, however, to the farm ten years ago. A Republican all his life, he never sought official recognition, but gave his best efforts toward the promotion of good government in township, county and state. He was a man of many good qualities, fond of his home and his family; and in his long residence in this community became known as a citizen of worth and ability, and as such was given a high place in the esteem of his fellow citizens. He was a broadminded, enterprising man and made his influence felt for the betterment of the community which so long numbered him as one of its representative citizens.

Mr. Hartley passed away at his home in Clarendon township after a sickness of slight duration, his death occurring Sunday, February 28, 1904, his wife and all of his children being present at his bedside. His funeral was from his home, March 2d, his six sons acting as his pall bearers, tenderly laid him to rest in Clarendon cemetery.

CHARLES O. MILLER.

Charles O. Miller, the youngest son of his father's family, was born November 20, 1859, and after receiving a good common and high school education he became a student in the law department of the University of Michigan, at Ann Arbor, from which he was graduated in 1883. With his brother, Louis C., whose sketch precedes this, he became interested in the practice of law in Marshall. The firm is known as Miller & Miller, and has one of the most extensive clientages of any law firm in the city. He is a stanch supporter of the Republican party and served as deputy county clerk for thirteen years, being appointed in 1887.

He also served as justice of the peace for seven years and four months and city attorney for one year. Though young in years he has accomplished much for the advancement of his profession and has attained an enviable position among men of legal science in Marshall and the community.

On Thanksgiving Day, November 29, 1888, Mr. Miller was united in marriage with Miss Inez Leversee, daughter of Jacob and Marina (Avery) Leversee, of Calhoun county, and of this union has been born three children, namely: Carl L., born October 4, 1889; Helen B., born October 27, 1893, and Mildred M., born August 27, 1895.

Both Mr. and Mrs. Miller are members of the Baptist church, in which Mr. Miller has taken a very active part. He has served as treasurer of the church, superintendent of the Sunday school and at present is a deacon, which position he has held for many years, having held the office longer than any other present member, with one exception, and is also clerk of the church at the present time.

ESTUS H. COLLER, D. D. S.

Dentistry is almost unique among the professions, in that there are three essential qualifications to success in that calling. It demands not only a comprehensive knowledge of the science, but also good business and financial ability, and mechanical skill. As Dr. Coller is possessed of these requirements, he is rapidly working his way upward to a prominent position in the ranks of the dental fraternity at Battle Creek.

One of Michigan's native sons, his birth occurred in Fulton, Kalamazoo county, May 10, 1867. He is a son of Eli and Miranda (Smith) Coller. The father was born in New York in 1834 and was one of the early graduates of the medical department of the University of Michigan, at Ann Arbor, completing the course there before he had attained his majority. Since that time he practiced in Michigan for the past fifteen years in Battle Creek, where he died, December 13, 1903. He married Miss Miranda Smith, of Lenawee county, Michigan, and unto them were born three children, who reached years of maturity, the subject of this review being the youngest.

Dr. Estus H. Coller obtained his preliminary education in the public schools, and afterward attended a select school, conducted by Professor M. B. Rork, who was a noted educator in this part of the state in that day. On the completion of his literary course, he engaged in teaching school for some time and then, having made choice of the dental profession as a life work, he began preparing for practice in 1890, by becoming a student in the dental department of the University of Michigan, where he spent three years. When he had mastered that branch of learning, he was graduated in 1894, with the degree of Doctor of Dental Surgery. At once he returned to Battle Creek, where he opened an office and has since practiced. Professional advancement is proverbially slow, but character and ability will come to the front anywhere and in recognition of his skill Dr. Coller is now accorded a liberal pat-

ronage, which comes from the best class
of people. He is a member of the State
Dental Society, and is continually reading
and studying that he might keep in touch
with the advancement that is being made
by the dental fraternity. Since the erection of the Post building his office has been
located therein, and he has a pleasant and
well equipped suite of rooms.

Prior to attending the university, Dr.
Coller was united in marriage on the 28th
of September, 1891, to Miss Grace I. Hanson, of Battle Creek, a daughter of John
B. Hanson, who was a resident of Athens,
but later became connected with the Advance Thresher Company, of this city,
which was his business relation at the time
of his demise. Unto the Doctor and his
wife have been born three sons: Ross H.,
John H. and Frederick Lee. The Doctor
is a Republican in politics, and with firm
faith in the principles of the party, always
supports its men and measures, but he has
never been a seeker after political honors
or emoluments. He holds membership
with the Knights of Pythias fraternity, with
the Ancient Order of the United Workmen and with Athelstan club, the last
named being the leading social organization of this city.

IRVING D. EVERTS.

Irving D. Everts, a representative of one
of the pioneer families of Michigan, and a
well known resident of Albion, was born
near Dansville, Ingham county, Michigan,
on December 23, 1852. His father, Wil-

liam B. Everts, was a native of Onondaga
county, New York, and there spent his childhood and youth. After attaining man's estate he was married there to Susan C. Coch-
ran and during the early forties came to
Michigan, purchasing a farm in Ingham
county, which he improved and cultivated
for many years. During the Civil war he
enlisted and for three years served as a
member of Company B, Seventh Michigan
Volunteer Infantry, going to the front in
the early part of 1861. He served for a
number of months and then came home on a
furlough, but ere the expiration of his leave
of absence he died in November, 1861. He
left a widow and five children, of whom
three were born of his first marriage. His
political support was given to the Democracy, but he was never an aspirant for public office. The mother of our subject continued to reside in Ingham county and on
leaving the farm took up her abode in the
village of Dansville, where death occurred
on the 25th of June, 1896.

Irving D. Everts was educated in the
schools of his native town, and there learned
the trade of a carriage blacksmith, which he
followed in Dansville until nearly twenty-
five years of age. He then removed to Mason, Michigan, and afterward went to Charlotte and then to Dallas, Texas. In all these
places he continued in the same business,
working at his trade in various parts of the
country, until his return to this state. He
took up his abode in Albion on the 20th of
December, 1890, and was engaged in the
manufacture of buggies for six years. Since
that time he has been connected with the
Gale Manufacturing Company. In July,
1897, he was made foreman of their steel
department, which is the oldest and most
important department of their plant. In this

position he has under his direction forty men, and he is a most capable foreman, his services proving of value to the company which he represents.

On the 7th of June, 1884, Mr. Everts was united in marriage to Miss Florence F. Fisher, the wedding being celebrated at Waxahachie, Texas. Her parents were Samuel and Fannie M. (Fuller) Fisher, the former born in Pennsylvania and the latter in New York. Mrs. Fisher was a daughter of William Fuller, who came to Eaton county, Michigan, at an early day accompanied by his family. Mr. Fisher afterward came with his parents, settling two miles from Charlotte, in Eaton county, the family home being established in the midst of a heavy timber country. Adam Fisher, the grandfather, began at once to clear and develop the property and there he carried on farming until his death. Samuel Fisher was an agriculturist and also a veterinary surgeon, living in the vicinity of Charlotte. It was in that locality that he married Miss Fuller and there he made his home until 1875, when he removed to Texas, where he engaged in farming and also in the practice of veterinary surgery near Waxahachie, where he still makes his home. The mother of Mrs. Everts passed away when the daughter was but fourteen months old, leaving two children. Mr. Fisher afterward married Catherine Kippingler, who died leaving six children and his present wife was Mrs. Lois Bassett, nee Bray. Mrs. Everts was born in Charlotte, Michigan, in 1856, and was there reared and educated, accompanying her father to Texas and remaining with him until the time of her·marriage. She has become the mother of three children, but only one is now living, Muriel F. By a former marriage Mr. Everts had two children, Burton I. and Edith L.

The family home is at No. 115 West Pine street, in Albion, and the family all attend the Baptist church, of which Mrs. Everts and her daughter are members. Mr. Everts gives his political allegiance to the Republican party and for four years he served as alderman in Mason, Michigan. In Albion he has for two years been a member of the city council, representing the first ward, and he was chairman of the committee on streets and bridges during the construction of the Cass street bridge. The following year he was appointed a member of the board of public works, and in that capacity took a very active and helpful part in promoting public improvement. Socially he is identified with Albion lodge, No. 70, K. P., and with the uniform rank, and he also belongs to the Dramatic Order of the Knights of Korassan.

ASAPH A. HOLCOMBE.

No history in Calhoun county would be complete without reference to Asaph Augustus Holcombe, who for many years was engaged in merchandising in Athens, where he now makes his home, and who is a representative of one of the most active and prominent pioneer families of this portion of the state. He was born in Naples township, Ontario county, New York, April 19, 1827, a son of Alfred and Ann S. (Stone) Holcombe. The paternal grandfather, Rodrick Holcombe, a native of Connecticut, married a Miss Winthrop, whose father, also a native of Connecticut, was a very wealthy man and spent his fortune for the cause of liberty at the time of the Revolution.

Alfred Holcombe was born in Windsor, Connecticut, in 1800, and wedded Miss Stone, whose birth occurred in Ontario county, New York. Her parents were Asahel and Ann Rebecca (Gurnsey) Stone, the former born in the Nutmeg state. The latter was a daughter of Southmayd Gurnsey, a soldier of the Revolution, who was present at the time of the capture of Major Andre. After the war he removed from Connecticut, his native state, to Yates county, New York, and in 1840 came to Calhoun county, living a retired life with his daughter, his wife having previously died. Asahel Stone, the maternal grandfather of Mr. Holcombe, was born on a farm, and although he attended school for only four weeks, he became a great reader and a well informed man. In business he was active and energetic and at different times was connected with merchandising, milling and other pursuits. He also served as a representative in the New York state legislature, and in early life read law and became quite proficient at the bar, practicing in New York and in Michigan. In 1836 he came with his family to Calhoun county, entered land from the government and at the time of his death was the owner of one thousand acres in Athens township. An active political worker, he was a stanch Democrat and served as supervisor and in minor offices in Athens township. He had three children: Mrs. Anna S. Holcombe Sabrah, wife of Benjamin F. Ferris, and Laura, wife of Norton P. Hobart, who at one time was a member of the state legislature. Mr. Stone died about 1845, and his wife in 1860. In pioneer times he was a man of great influence and very popular.

Alfred Holcombe, the father of our subject, lived in Connecticut until nineteen years of age, when he went to western New York and engaged in trading with the Indians in Naples. In 1828 he made a trip to Mackinaw, Michigan, where he sold clothing to the soldiers, and while there learned of this county. In 1829, with two companies he started in search of the St. Joe valley and although he did not find it he gained knowledge of Battle Creek and vicinity. He then returned to New York and in 1831 came to Calhoun county, where he secured government land and planted thereon a crop. He then returned for his family and bringing them to Michigan spent his remaining days as an agriculturist of Calhoun county. His death occurred in 1877 and his wife died in 1898, when about ninety years of age. In politics he was a Democrat and held some township offices. Of the five children of the family four are now living: Asaph; Laura, the deceased wife of William Boughton; Matilda, of Athens; Mary, the wife of Watson Garton, of Evansville, Indiana; and Fredus, who is living with his sister in Athens.

Asaph A. Holcombe was brought by his parents to Calhoun county when about four years of age, pursued his education in a log schoolhouse, and between the ages of twenty-one and thirty-five years engaged in farming. He then opened a dry-goods and general store in Athens, or rather upon the site of the town, for there was nothing but a hamlet there at that time. For thirty years he continued in merchandising, enlarging his stock to keep pace with the growth of the town, and enjoying a large patronage, which rendered his business profitable. When three decades had passed he retired from commercial life and has since been engaged in farming, supervising the cultivation of his farm of sixty acres. In Athens he has erected a commodious and handsome residence, in which he and his wife are now living.

In 1858 Mr. Holcombe wedded Miss Laura A. Hobart, who was born near Penn Yan, Yates county, New York, a daughter of Baxter and Esther (Clarke) Hobart, the former a native of Massachusetts and the latter of New York. Mr. Hobart was a colonel in the War of 1812 and was at Buffalo the day following the burning of the city by the British. His father, William Hobart, was a chaplain in the Revolutionary war. Unto Mr. and Mrs. Holcombe were born four children, but one died in early life. The others are: William H., of Los Angeles, California, who married Ida Vail, of Battle Creek, and has a daughter, Donna; Nettie, wife of George Miller, of Athens, by whom she has two sons, Karl and Lyle; and Leo, who is in the First National Bank at Union City, Michigan.

A supporter of the Democracy, Mr. Holcombe was elected on its ticket to the office of alderman but has never been an office seeker. A large tree which stands by the Congregational church near his home was the one under which his grandfathers Stone and Holcombe and B. F. Ferris ate their first dinner in the spring of 1831, and the Indians, noting their shining tinware, thought it was silver, and ran up to see it. Both Mr. and Mrs. Holcombe are representatives of prominent pioneer families of the county who have been active factors in the development and upbuilding of this part of the state. In Athens our subject and his wife have many friends, and theirs is a most hospitable home. Their many excellent traits of character have gained for them high regard and they deserve to have their names inscribed on the pages of their county's history.

35

HON. LOTE C. ROBINSON.

Hon. L. C. Robinson, who follows farming on section 20, Eckford township, and is now representing his district in the State Legislature, was born in Battle Creek township, Calhoun county, November 15, 1857. His paternal grandparents were Chauncey and Anna (Lewis) Robinson. His father, Solon E. Robinson, was born in Clarendon, Orleans county, New York, August 17, 1820, and was reared to manhood in the Empire state. He came to Michigan in 1840 and located in Tekonsha township, Calhoun county, where he purchased land and began the development of a farm. In that locality he met and married Miss Mary Jane Granger, who was born in Sweden, Monroe county, New York, a daughter of Ithamar and Cornelia (Westfall) Granger. Her father had come to Michigan with the family in 1841. Mr. and Mrs. Robinson had been born in adjoining townships in New York and had seen each other, but had never spoken until they became acquainted in Michigan. When their son, Lote C., was ten years of age they removed to a farm on section 20, Eckford township, which has since been the family home. They became the parents of five children: James C., who married Ella Hopkins and is a resident of Olympia, Washington; Frank F., of Chicago, who married Caroline Frasier, and has two children; Edwin D., of South Haven, Michigan, who married Stella Bickford and has three children; Chauncey C., who married Helen Van Pelt, and died at Rifle, Colorado, leaving three daughters; and Lote C., of this review. The father gave his political allegiance to the Republican party and took an active interest in its growth and success. He held various offices in Tekonsha township, including the position of supervisor, and in 1873 he was elected to represent his district in the State Legislature. A prominent member of the Baptist church, he served as one of its deacons for a number of years and died in that faith on the old home farm February 22, 1899, his remains being interred in West Eckford cemetery.

In his boyhood Lote C. Robinson acquired a fair common school education and on attaining his majority began earning his living as manager of the old home farm, having become familiar with the work of field and meadow under his father's direction. He was married December 15, 1880, in Eckford township, to Miss Fannie Chapman Overy, who was born in Sheridan township, Calhoun county, a daughter of Thomas and Fannie (Chapman) Overy. Her parents were born and reared at Hawkhurst, England, and ere their marriage came to America. Their wedding was celebrated in Rochester, New York, and in 1855 they removed to Michigan. Mr. Overy was killed on the railroad in Marengo township, Calhoun county, in 1863, and his widow afterward became the wife of John Skinner, by whom she had one child. By her first marriage she had seven children, Mrs. Robinson being the third in order of birth. Mrs. Skinner died in Eckford in December, 1901, and her remains were interred in West Eckford cemetery, while the father of Mrs. Robinson was laid to rest in Marengo. Unto our subject and his wife has been born a son, Solon Thomas Overy Robinson.

Since casting his first presidential ballot for General Garfield in 1880 Mr. Robinson has been a stalwart Republican. In 1889 he was elected clerk of Eckford township for a term of two years and in 1896 was chosen treasurer and also occupied that posi-

tion for two years. He has been chairman of the Republican county committee for four years and has been a delegate to various conventions of his party, including the state conventions in which Governor Pingree and Governor Bliss were nominated. In 1902 he was elected to the Legislature and is now serving on the committees on towns and counties, on labor and on the Industrial School for Girls at Adrian. Socially he is connected with the Knights of Pythias lodge at Marshall, the Maccabees tent at Eckford, the Modern Woodmen camp at Homer and the Elks lodge at Battle Creek. He enjoys the high esteem of the brethren of these fraternities and is equally prominent and honored in political circles, for he is fearless in defense of his own convictions and unfaltering in his allegiance to what he believes to be right. As a member of the general assembly he is making an excellent record as a legislator, giving to each question which comes up for settlement his earnest consideration and supporting those measures which he believes will contribute to the welfare and upbuilding of the commonwealth. His public and private career are alike above reproach and suspicion and the name of Lote C. Robinson is an honored one in Calhoun county.

BYRON G. DOOLITTLE.

Byron G. Doolittle, of the A. H. Randall Milling Company of Tekonsha, was born on a farm in Clarendon township, Calhoun county, Michigan, March 28, 1868. His great-grandparents in the paternal line were Benjamin and Hannah Doolittle, who had a family of six sons and six daughters. They removed to Delaware county, New York, and there spent their last days. Their son, William Doolittle, grandfather of our subject, was born in Litchfield, Connecticut, May 26, 1775, and when a boy accompanied his parents to the Empire state, where he married Polly Ann Hubbell, who was born in Delhi, Delaware county, New York, February 24, 1806, the wedding taking place February 12, 1824. William Doolittle engaged in farming in Delaware county, New York, until 1835, when he removed to Monroe county, Michigan, where he spent two years. He then secured a claim of timber land in Clarendon township, Calhoun county, on which he built a log cabin and then began to clear and cultivate his fields, living there for a number of years. He and his family experienced all the hardships of frontier life, and they had made the journey westward in the primitive manner of the times. Leaving New York on the 17th of September, 1835, they traveled by wagon and were six weeks in reaching their destination. Mr. Doolittle continued farming until his death, which occurred July 1, 1854, and his widow died in Tekonsha, May 14, 1886. He was a charter member of the Baptist church of Tekonsha, to which his wife also belonged, and he served as a deacon and took a very active part in the church work. His political allegiance was given the Republican party. In their family were six sons and six daughters: John Smith and Isaac Hubbell, twins, were born December 3, 1824, and the former married Adelia Humeston in February, 1846, and is living in Tekonsha; Frederick Benjamin, born December 24, 1825, was married October

4, 1851, to Anona Cumber, of Delhi, Iowa, where they are now living; Henrietta, born April 1, 1827, became the wife of Squire Newberry July 9, 1863; Nathan, born June 28, 1828, died November 18, 1829; James Augustus, who was born March 31, 1830, was married January 1, 1856, to Nancy P. Wells, and died December 2, 1893; Nancy Arminta, born February 4, 1832, died July 9, 1888, in Tekonsha; Sarah Reynolds, born September 17, 1833, was married November 4, 1857, to Henry Perrine, and is now a widow living in Tekonsha; Monroe D., born in Monroe county, Michigan, January 24, 1836, was married February 22, 1871, to Flora Hartson, of Tekonsha; Mary Elizabeth born in Clarendon township, Calhoun county, October 16, 1838, died July 28, 1839; Eunice Adelia, born September 11, 1840, died September 7, 1851; and Emeline H., born July 29, 1842, was married March 16, 1864, to O. D. Smith and died in Joliet, Illinois, April 19, 1903.

Isaac H. Doolittle, father of our subject, was born in New York, December 23, 1824, and was ten years of age when his parents came to Michigan. He was therefore reared amid the wild scenes of frontier life and assisted in the arduous task of developing a new farm. In 1856 he married Rhoda Benham, and throughout his active business career he carried on agricultural pursuits.

Their son, Byron G. Doolittle, spent his boyhood days in the usual manner of most lads of the period, working in the fields and meadows when his time and attention were not occupied with the duties of the schoolroom. After attending the district schools he entered Albion College at the age of seventeen and remained a student there for four years, thus becoming well qualified to take up important duties in connection with a business career. He afterward spent two years in Iowa, where he was employed as clerk in a bank from 1889 to 1891, and upon his return to Michigan in the latter year, he engaged in the boot and shoe business in Tekonsha, one of the firm of Simonson & Doolittle, which he followed until 1893, after which time he conducted the business alone. In that undertaking he prospered, but sold his store in 1902 to good advantage. He was then out of business for a brief period, and in April, 1903, purchased the interest of Mrs A. H. Randall in the A. H. Randall Milling Company of Tekonsha, and is now active in the management and control of this growing industry.

Mr. Doolittle is a valued member of Washington lodge, No. 7, F. and A. M., and since he joined the organization in 1895 has been its secretary. He has taken a very active interest in local politics and since casting his first presidential vote for Harrison in 1892 has been a stanch Republican. The following year he was elected clerk of Tekonsha township and also clerk of the village, and in the former position he served until 1903 and is still holding the latter office. In the year 1903 he was elected a member of the board of supervisors from Tekonsha township, and as an official he has exercised his prerogatives for the advancement of many measures promoting the material interest and substantial improvement of town and county. He is a worthy representative of an honored pioneer family and his personal qualities also entitle him to mention in this volume.

GEORGE CLINTON HAFFORD, M. D.

As a representative of the medical fraternity, possessing skill and ability and showing marked devotion to his chosen calling, Dr. Hafford has become widely and favorably known. He is now practicing in Albion and the liberal patronage accorded him is an indication of the trust reposed in him by the public. He was born in Pierrepont Manor, Jefferson county, New York, July 10, 1862, his parents being Jacob T. and Lydia (Matteson) Hafford. The family is of English lineage, the first of the name in America coming from the "Merrie Isle" on the ship Planter. The family home was thus established in Massachusetts in 1635, but at a more remote period the ancestors of Dr. Hafford were residents of Wales. His grandfather was Jacob Hafford, of New York. The father, also a native of the Empire state, was a well educated man always interested in intellectual progress. For many years he followed carpentering and building and resided at various places. During the time of the gold excitement in California he visited the Pacific coast. He was married to Miss Lydia Matteson, of Ontario, and spent his later life as a farmer near Milan, Michigan until four years prior to his death, when he became a member of the household of Dr. Hafford. Here he passed away on the 4th of October, 1902. His widow survived him until March 15, 1904, when her death occurred at the advanced age of seventy-six years. She was laid to rest at Niles, Michigan.

Dr. Hafford, having pursued his early education in the common schools in the vicinity of Milan entered the printing office of the "Monroe Democrat" at Monroe,

Michigan, when but thirteen years of age. He continued there for two years, when suffering from lead poisoning, he was forced to abandon his work. In the meantime he had continued to read and study and thus became qualified for teaching. Successfully passing the required examination, he spent one term as a teacher and then entered the office of Dr. Pyle of Milan, Michigan, who directed his reading for a year, at the end of which time he entered the medical department of the University of Michigan at Ann Arbor. He matriculated in the fall of 1883, pursued a full course of three years and was graduated with the degree of Doctor of Medicine in 1887. Subsequently he entered the office of Professor Frothingham, and in the succeeding spring went to the upper peninsula, locating at Manistique. There he engaged in the general practice of medicine and surgery until 1895, securing a very extensive patronage. He was there at the time the "Soo" Railroad was built and his practice extended many miles over that road. In 1895, when the panic in lumber caused great financial depression, he left the company with which he had been associated and became surgeon for the Bay De Noquet Company at Nahma, Delta county, acting in that capacity for three and a half years. Desiring, however, to engage in the private practice of medicine in a larger field and also wishing to provide better educational privileges for his children he returned to Albion, Michigan, where he has since been located. While in Nahma he had pursued a course in the Post Graduate school in New York, spending the summer of 1893 in that institution. He afterward pursued special work in Chicago in order to become thoroughly equipped for the practice of surgery and the treatment of diseases of women. In May, 1897, he located at

Albion and as the successor of Dr. H. D. Thomason, whose estate he purchased, he has since been recognized as one of the best general practitioners of this part of the state, and his skill in surgery has made his services in constant demand in that direction. In the summer of 1903, he did special work at the University of Michigan, and his knowledge of the science of medicine has been continually broadened by reading and thorough investigation. He was formerly president of the Calhoun County Medical Society and is now the first vice president of the State Medical Society. He has also held other important positions in connection with that organization, including that of chairman of the surgery section. He is a member of the Northern Tri-State Medical Society, the American Medical Association and an honorary member of different county medical societies in Michigan. That he commands the respect and confidence of his brethren of the profession is indicated by the official honors bestowed upon him in the organizations with which he is identified.

On the day of his graduation in the State University—June 30, 1887—Dr. Hafford was united in marriage to Miss Cora E. Ulsaver, of Saline, Michigan, a daughter of Stephen Ulsaver. The children born unto them are five in number: Alpheus Tisdale, Clinton S., Doris, Cora and Clarence E. Dr. Hafford and his wife hold membership in the Presbyterian church and he was made a Mason at Lakeside lodge, No. 371, F. and A. M., of Manistique, Michigan, but has since demitted to Murat lodge, No. 14, of Albion. He likewise holds membership in the chapter and council and is heartily in sympathy with the work of the order and its purpose. He belongs to both the subordinate lodge and the uniform rank of the Knights of Pythias and is now major surgeon of the First Battalion of the Third Regiment of the Michigan Brigade, comprising the four companies of Battle Creek, Charlotte, Mason and Albion. He likewise belongs to the Independent Order of Odd Fellows, to the Modern Woodmen camp and to the Knights of the Maccabees lodge and socially he is identified with the Leisure Hours club. In politics a Democrat, he was elected alderman in 1901, from the fourth ward, to fill a vacancy and was re-elected in 1902. He has been chairman of the finance committee and to him is given the honor of doing more than any other one man to establish city paving, the paving being laid in 1903. He was likewise very active in securing the passage of the ordinances granting the street lighting and electric railway franchise. He has also served as health officer under Democratic administrations and while at Manistique was a member and secretary of the pension board.

Dr. Hafford is a man of most progressive spirit as is manifested by his continual advance in his profession, his endorsement of public measures for the general good and his hearty co-operation in many movements for the welfare of this city. In his profession he has attained an enviable place. Accurate in the diagnosis of a case, using his remedial agencies to the best advantage and never encroaching in the slightest degree beyond the strictest ethics of his profession he has won for himself a reputation which is most creditable and honorable.

EDSON TREDWELL.

Edson Tredwell, a resident of Burlington, Calhoun county, was born in Pennfield township, Monroe county, New York, January 6th, 1842, the representative of a family of English ancestry, the first emigrant to America having been Edward Tredwell, who settled in Connecticut about 1736. His son, Samuel, became the father of a son called Edward, whose son was in turn named Benjamin. The son of Benjamin, David Tredwell, married Phoebe Lion, their son being called Burr, who married Sarah Armstrong and their son, David S., married Anna B. Gage, whose children are numbered among the present generation of the Tredwell family. David S. Tredwell was a shoemaker by trade, and coming to Michigan in 1847, settled on section 24, Newton township. The following year he located on section 36, where he purchased a farm of one hundred and forty acres, upon which he remained until his death.

Edson Tredwell was reared upon his father's farm, interspersing his home duties with an attendance at the common school in the vicinity, acquiring a practical education, as well as a beneficial training along agricultural lines. On August 11th, 1862, he enlisted in Company I, Twentieth Regiment Michigan Infantry, entering at once upon an active career in the field. He served under the command of Captain Charles C. Dodge, while the regiment was commanded by Colonel Adolphus W. Williams, and through courage in action was made corporal of his company, June 8th, 1864, having command of the company, being the only officer with the company for a short time. He participated in the following engagements: Fredericksburg, Virginia, December 12th and 13th, 1862; Horseshoe Bend, Kentucky, May 10th, 1863; siege of Vicksburg, from June 22nd to July 4th, 1863; Jackson, Mississippi, July 11th to 18th, 1863; Blue Spring, Tennessee, October 10th, 1863; London, Tennessee, November 10th, 1863; Lenoir Station, November 15th, 1863; siege of Knoxville, from November 17th to December 5th, during which time he was engaged at Fort Sanders, November 26th; Thurlyford, December. 15th, 1863; Strawberry Plain, January 22nd, 1864; Chuckey Bend, March 14th, 1864; Battle of the Wilderness, May 5th, 6th and 7th, 1864; York River, May 9th, 1864; Spottsylvania, May 10th, 11th and 12th, 1864; North Anna, May 24th and 25th, 1864; Bethesda Church, June 2nd and 3rd, 1864; Cold Harbor, June 7th, 1864, and the siege of Petersburg beginning June 18th, 1864. He was wounded twice through his period of service, the first time at the siege of Knoxville by the bursting of a shell November 9th, 1863, and the second time at Petersburg receiving a gunshot wound in his right arm. He received an honorable discharge May 29th, 1865.

Mr. Tredwell was married January 1st, 1866, to Miss Mary Wolven, to which union there were born the following children: William Franklin, born October 9th, 1866, and married Carrie Smith, of Chicago, where they now reside; Sarah E., born July 10th, 1868, married C. W. Bond, of Mecosta county, Michigan; Ida S., born May 20th, 1870, married Andrew C. Stone, and died in 1887; David W., born April 9th, 1872, is now a resident of Battle Creek; Oscar B., born May 20th, 1874, died September 9th, 1878; Annette, born December 27th, 1876, and married Daniel Greenman, their home being in Marshall township; Thomas J., born December 7th, 1879, makes his home in Calhoun county; Charles E., born May 12th, 1881, is now a resident of Burlington; Gilbert B., born April 20th,

1885, also lives in Burlington; Beulah, born April 7th, 1888, makes her home with her parents; and Mildred S., born February 21st, 1891, is also at home. In his political preferment Mr. Tredwell is a Democrat, having cast his first presidential ballot for George B. McClellan, and in religion is an Universalist. Until it disbanded he was a member of the Edmond post, No. 191, G. A. R. Mr. Tredwell has served his country, state and county in an acceptable manner as soldier and citizen, giving his best efforts toward the maintenance of right and principle.

DAVID MATHER.

More than thirty years have passed since David Mather became a resident of Calhoun county and during this time he has been closely identified with its agricultural and commercial interests as an active business man. A long line of distinguished names are found in his ancestral history, the line being traced back to Richard Mather, a noted divine who came from England to Boston, Massachusetts, in 1635. There he continued his ministerial work until his death. His father was Thomas Mather, of Lowton, Lancashire, England. The parents of our subject were Enos and Tamar (Houghton) Mather, both of whom died in New York.

David Mather was born in the town of Royalton, Niagara county, New York, January 26, 1838, and there he was reared on the home farm and acquired a good education. Later he engaged in farming through the summer months, while in the winter season he followed the profession of teaching in the Empire state until 1872, when he came to Calhoun county, settling in Leroy township. Purchasing a farm, he continued its cultivation for twelve years when he turned his attention to merchandising and grain dealing. He built a store and stocked it with a general line of merchandise, but found that the indoor life was detrimental to his health and after six years sold out. He then became proprietor of a lumber yard in the same place, East Leroy, in which business he continued for six years, when he removed to Athens. About four years ago he established his lumber yard here and has since dealt in coal in addition to lumber, lime, cement and all kinds of building supplies. His honorable business methods and enterprise have gained for him a large patronage and he is now a leading representative of trade interests in the town.

In 1866, in the Empire state, was celebrated the marriage of Mr. Mather and Miss Henrietta Miller, and they now have two sons. Charles M., the elder, now engaged in the lumber business in Milan, Michigan, married Miss Lottie Weed and they have a daughter, Edna. Frank H., the younger son, is associated with his father in business. The parents and both sons are members of the Methodist Episcopal church, and Mr. Mather has served as trustee and class leader. The cause of education finds in him a warm friend, and as president of the school board he is doing effective service in the interests of education and intellectual development in Athens. He is also a member of the village council and for two years he filled the position of township clerk of Leroy. He is deeply interested in the cause of the Republican party, yet has never been an active

politician in the sense of office seeking, his political honors coming to him from his fellow citizens as their recognition of his capability and devotion to the general good. In addition to his home and business interests in Athens he owns one hundred and nineteen acres of land in Leroy township, which he rents, and his property is the visible evidence of an active career characterized by energy and probity.

FRANK W. CULVER.

Frank W. Culver, superintendent of the water works of Albion, Michigan, was born at Mosherville, Hillsdale county, Michigan, October 2, 1871, a son of Henry J. and Mary D. (Riggs) Culver. His paternal grandfather resided in the vicinity of Lyons, New York, whence he removed to Hillsdale county, Michigan, establishing his home there among the pioneer settlers. He purchased and improved government land and continued to engage in general farming with success until his death. Joseph Riggs, the maternal grandfather, also came from Lyons, New York, where he had been proprietor of a drug store. On arriving in Michigan he purchased an extensive farm and was a prominent and successful agriculturist. For many years he served as justice of the peace and in all matters of citizenship was progressive and loyal. The great-grandfathers of our subject were soldiers of the War of 1812.

Henry J. Culver was born in the Empire state and in his childhood days was brought to the west, where he was reared to manhood. He afterward married Miss Riggs, who was born at Lyons, New York, near the birthplace of her husband, and she, too, was brought to Michigan in her girlhood days. After their marriage the young couple took up their abode upon a ranch, Mr. Culver owning a large tract of land in Illinois, on which he engaged in the raising of sheep, for that part of the state was largely an unsettled district. He followed that pursuit for about three years and then removed to Detroit, Michigan, where he was variously employed for a number of years. He acted as state agent for the Singer Sewing Machine Company and was a most capable representative of that business. When the agency was removed elsewhere, he embarked in business for himself in Detroit, as a flour and feed merchant and was thus engaged until his death, conducting two stores, one at No. 341 Woodard avenue and the other at No. 342 Michigan avenue. His death occurred in 1881 and his widow is now living in Lansing, Michigan. In politics Mr. Culver was a Republican, but was never an aspirant for office, preferring that his energies should be given to his business affairs. He attended and supported the Baptist church.

Frank W. Culver began his education in the city schools of Detroit and after his father's death attended the high school at Hillsdale, Michigan, and later continued his studies in Albion College. After leaving school he found employment as a clerk with Fred L. Crane, with whom he continued for four years. He was afterward with the Computing Scale Company at Dayton, Ohio, as traveling salesman, his territory being mostly in Kentucky, although he traveled through Michigan and other places. He was very successful as a salesman and continued with the company for eighteen months, when he left the road in order to

engage in business for himself at Lexington, Kentucky, as a wholesale dealer in produce, including both fruits and vegetables. There he built up a large business and continued in that place for two years. On the expiration of that period he sold out because his partner desired to close up the business on account of a death in his family.

Mr. Culver then returned to Michigan, establishing his home in Albion, where he entered mercantile circles as a grocer. A year later he sold his business to his brother, Fred J. Culver, and was afterward variously engaged for some time. For three years he was connected with E. A. Robinson. In the meantime he had been quite active and influential in local political circles in the Democratic party and he served on the ward and Democratic county committees. He is still acting in the latter capacity. His worth to the party, and his value as a citizen, well qualified him for political positions, and in 1900 he was elected city clerk for Albion. Twice he has been re-elected to office, filling it with credit to himself and satisfaction to the public during a term of three years. In September, 1900, he was appointed superintendent of the city water works and has since acted in that capacity, during which time the mains have been extended five miles, while a new eight-inch artesian well has been brought to flow six hundred gallons per minute. The amount of water used has largely increased and the waste has greatly diminished. The plant is equipped with a Hughes steam pump and condensers. As superintendent Mr. Culver looks after every detail of the work in his department and has shown himself well worthy of the trust reposed in him.

On the 8th of February, 1893, Mr. Culver was united in marriage to Miss

Blanche Carver, of Albion, a daughter of J. V. Carver. They have six children: Lillard W., Clair N., Gladys, Dorothy M., Hildreth B. and Francis F. The parents attend and support the Methodist Episcopal church, Mrs. Culver being one of its members. Mr. Culver belongs to Albion lodge, No. 60, I. O. O. F., is commander of Supreme tent. No. 18, Knights of the Maccabees and also belongs to the Michigan Tent of Modern Maccabees, while of the Supreme lodge he is deputy state commander. A genial manner and cordial disposition have made him popular in both business and fraternal circles and in Albion Mr. Culver is very widely and favorably known.

JACOB ESCHER.

In an analyzation of the character and life work of Jacob Escher, one of the leading residents of Albion, we note many of the characteristics which have marked the German nation for many centuries—the strong purpose, the reliability and the energy which has made them valued factors in any part of the world to which they have gone. Civilization is largely due to the Teutonic race, for the sons of Germany have continually gone beyond the borders of the Fatherland, carrying with them the learning and progress of their own country, together with the perseverance and reliability of the individual.

Mr. Escher was born in Wurttemburg, Germany, February 26, 1838, his parents being Jacob and Elizabeth (Whitley) Escher. The father was a weaver and about 1850 came to America with his family, locating in Philadelphia, where he spent his remaining days. His widow afterward came to Albion and died in this city.

Jacob Escher began his education in the schools of his native country, and when a youth of twelve years accompanied his parents on the long voyage across the Atlantic. They took passage on a sailing vessel, which after thirty-eight days reached the harbor of Philadelphia. In that city he continued his studies but after putting aside his text books he learned the trade of gardening as an apprentice, serving with one of the three or four florists then in Philadelphia. When he had devoted three or four years to the mastery of the business of a florist and nurseryman he entered the employ of J. V. Merrick, with whom he remained for a number of years. Mr. Merrick was the gentleman who built the great Ironsides. Mr. Escher had charge of his garden and the laying out of his grounds and his marked ability in the line of his chosen calling won him the highest commendation of his employer. While in Philadelphia Mr. Escher was married on the 25th of February, 1862, to Miss Mary Jane Kennedy, who was born near Glasgow, Scotland, and belonged to a family connected with one of the early and prominent families of that country. Her parents, John and Ann (Jameson) Kennedy, lived and died in Scotland and Mrs. Escher came with an aunt to Philadelphia. In the spring of 1863 Mr. Escher and his bride came to Albion and here established the first greenhouse of the place. He also raised the first vegetables to be placed on the city market. The people at that time did not know what it was to buy vegetables, but he soon succeeded in establishing a good business.

He also raised the first celery in Michigan, beginning in this work long before Kalamazoo became famous for this product. After he succeeded in introducing this to the city market he cultivated from forty to sixty thousand plants. He also raised strawberries, bringing the plant from Philadelphia with him. As they were a novelty in the district he received twenty-five cents per box for the berries He also raised raspberries before they were generally introduced into this part of the state and he was the first to purchase marsh land which hitherto had been considered worthless. He paid two dollars per acre for the tract. which he realized would have to be drained and in other ways improved. But he knew how to develop it and has made it one of the best fruit farms of this entire section. His friends all thought him foolish to attempt to make the land of any value, but time has shown the wisdom of his course. For many years he conducted a large market garden, covering twenty-four acres, and he also did an extensive business as a florist, cultivating various flowers that were raised for sale in this part of the state. He likewise planted an early vineyard, which he conducted for a number of years and in which he raised the first Niagara grapes produced in Michigan, which he sold at a good profit. It was always his plan to be the pioneer in the production of any fruits or flowers in his locality and because of his introduction of various kinds he met with excellent success. For a number of years he employed several men, his business exceeding that of any other horticulturist and florist of the community. He now owns twenty-seven acres of land within the city limits and upon this has erected a fine home, in which he has since resided. He likewise has other

city realty and is to-day regarded as one of the substantial and successful men of Albion.

Unto Mr. and Mrs. Escher have been born ten children, eight of whom are yet living: Frederick Kennedy, of South Dakota; Pauline, the wife of Creighton D. Lane, of Albion; Albert, of Hammond, Indiana; Clara; Emily; Jennie, wife of Ernest W. Lumm, of Battle Creek; William, of Albion; and Mabel. All have been afforded good educational advantages. Mr. Escher is a Presbyterian and Mrs. Escher is a member of the Episcopal church. He is connected with the Ancient Order of United Workmen. In politics he is rather independent and while a strong temperance man he has stood by the Prohibition party, yet when other parties have placed candidates in the field, whom he has regarded better equipped for office he has never hesitated to give to them his support. He believes that the best results will be brought about by moral suasion, and his entire life has been characterized by honorable dealings, by upright purpose, and by lofty principles. He certainly deserves much credit for what he has accomplished. As the years have advanced he has won prosperity and his life record should prove to others that success may be gained through persistent effort and laudable ambition guided by common sense and honorable methods.

MILES TOWNSEND.

Miles Townsend, one of the native sons of Michigan, has for many years been closely connected with agricultural interests in Calhoun county; and although he is not engaged at the present time in the active work of the farm, he still gives personal supervision to the operation of his land, and his sound judgment and capability are most important elements in the success which has attended his business career. He resides in Marshall, while his birth occurred near Ypsilanti, Michigan, on the 9th of July, 1841. His parents were Lewis and Maria V. (Trumble) Townsend. The father was born in Monroe county, New York, October 19, 1817, and was a son of Ezra Townsend, an early settler of that county. The mother was born in the same locality November 16, 1820. Ezra Townsend came with his family to Michigan at an early day, settling in Washtenaw county, among its pioneer residents. He entered land from the government and continued to make his home there until his death. In the same locality Lewis Townsend purchased his first farm, which he had to clear and improve, not a furrow having been turned when he took possession of the place. He there resided until the fall of 1851, when he sold that property and purchased a large farm in Marengo township, Calhoun county, placing this tract under a high state of cultivation. He continued to make it his home until about 1868, when he once more sold and took up his abode upon another farm of two hundred acres, which he owned in the same township, residing there until his removal to Marshall. He was very thorough in his work, enterprising and progressive in his methods, and the results which attended him were those which the world terms successful. During the two years following the close of the Civil war his farming operations coupled with the sheep industry netted him eighteen thousand dollars. He became quite an ex-

tensive landowner for that day, having about six hundred acres. When he had acquired an independent competence he removed to Marshall, and remained a resident of the town until his death on the 25th of August, 1894. His wife had passed away February 6, 1885. They attended the Christian church for many years, but after the death of his wife Mr. Townsend became a member of the Presbyterian church. His political allegiance was given first to the Whig party and afterward to the Republican party, and for twelve years he served as supervisor of Marengo township. In the family were six children, five of whom reached years of maturity, namely: Viletta T., now the wife of M. E. Barhite, of Kalamazoo, Michigan; Miles; Jerome B. and Myron, now deceased; Owen L., of Marshall; and Evelyn T., who died in 1844.

Miles Townsend received only limited school advantages and it has ever been a matter of deep regret to him that he could not have enjoyed better privileges in that direction. He attended the common schools of Marengo township and also spent one year in Olivet College, but on the expiration of that period was taken ill with measles and a relapse left him nearly blind for three years. He has, however, been an extensive reader and has thus supplemented his school privileges by broad and comprehensive knowledge gained from books. In his reading he has given special attention to agricultural subjects, acquiring valuable information concerning the best methods of operating his land and enhancing its productiveness. In his early boyhood days he was trained to the work of the farm, becoming familiar with the labor of field and meadow and putting into practical use the knowledge that was imparted to him concerning agricultural life. He remained at home until twenty-two years of age and in the spring of 1863 began farming for himself. His father gave him a team and a few of the necessary agricultural implements and he began operating land on shares, thus continuing his farming operations for seven years. With the money that he thus acquired through his industry and labor, he purchased a small farm in 1870. The following year he sold this property and bought one hundred and eleven acres of land near Battle Creek, where he carried on general farming. In 1878 he again sold and this time invested his money in one hundred acres of land in Marengo township, which he equipped with modern improvements, transforming it into one of the model farms of the county. There he resided continuously until 1895, when he removed to the city of Marshall, where he has practically lived retired, although giving his attention and supervision to his various farming interests. In 1897 he erected a beautiful home on a large plat of ground, which he owned at the corner of Kalamazoo avenue and Prospect street. The house was built according to plans which were made by Mr. Townsend and is considered by all who have seen it a model of beauty, indicating that the designer possessed a high degree of artistic taste. He is at the present time one of the largest landowners in the county, his holdings aggregating eight hundred acres in this locality, in addition to valuable real estate in Kansas. After going to Battle Creek Mr. Townsend received some assistance from his father and from time to time was aided in this manner, but he had made a thorough success of farming prior to receiving his inheritance, having demonstrated his ability to successfully control important agricultural interests. He had acquired property through his own labor and in its conduct manifested marked energy and strong determination. Difficulties and obstacles, such as come to all men in a business career, had to him served but as a stimulus for effort and activity, and as he prospered he made judicious investment, his labors being guided by sound and reliable judgment.

Soon after starting out upon his business career Mr. Townsend was married on the 1st of January, 1866, to Miss Hattie Newton, a daughter of Tyler and Sarah (Kellum) Newton, of Marengo township, who died on the 4th of April, 1898. On the 5th of September, 1899, Mr. Townsend was again married, his second union being with Miss Gertrude Gilman, a daughter of John and Malvina (Henry) Gilman. Both are active members of the Christian church in which Mr. Townsend now holds several official positions. He is deeply interested in religious work, taking a helpful part in the various activities of the church since he united therewith. In his political views Mr. Townsend has ever been a Republican, active in support of the party and its principles and while living in Marengo township he was elected supervisor and occupied the position for three years or until his removal to another part of the county. In 1899 he was honored by election to the office of mayor and after serving for one year declined a re-nomination. His administration, however, was regarded as most beneficial to the city, for during that year the fine stone and cement bridge over the Kalamazoo river was built and the sewer system was instituted. He followed faithfully progressive measures that were of a practical nature, ever having in view the interests of the citizens and city and as chief executive of Marshall he was fearless in enforcing the laws and ordinances of the city. A public-spirited man, zealously advocating political, intellectual and moral advancement. He has contributed liberally to the support of Defiance College at Defiance, Ohio, and has served as a member of its advisory board. Benevolent and kindly in spirit he has ever given generously of his means to those less fortunate than himself and in this way has done much to ameliorate the hard conditions of life for others. His career has been guided by upright manly principles and in Michigan where his entire life has been passed he is known as a most reliable business man.

LOUIS M. BROWN.

Louis M. Brown, who is acting as superintendent of all construction work outside of the factories of the Postum Cereal Company, Limited, of Battle Creek, is a native son of that city, born October 8, 1876. His parents are Braeton J. and Katherine (Abbott) Brown.

He began attending public school at the age of five and pursued his studies until sixteen years of age. At the age of ten he began selling cut flowers on the streets and with his mother carried on this business for seven years, having exclusive sale at the Kellogg Sanitarium. This was the first of a flower boy in Battle Creek.

During summer vacations his time was spent in working at different places, never taking more than two weeks for pleasure. As well as selling flowers he worked mornings and evenings for W. H. Eldred, confectioner. During the summer vacations of 1890-1 he worked for the Western Union Telegraph Company as messenger and wore the first messenger uniform in Battle Creek. Through the careful guidance of a good mother, the cut-flower business was made to help earn the home where his parents now live. In 1896 he worked his way through Krugs's Business College by doing the janitor work.

March, 1897, he went with the Postum Cereal Company as billing clerk. From this he worked himself up through the different departments and in the year 1898 took charge of the building of dwelling houses in the Cliff addition on a part of the company's interests. He spent about a year on the road and was the first salesman to start Grape Nuts, beginning with Grand Rapids, Michigan. He traveled through Ohio, Indiana, Illinois, Michigan and parts of Pennsylvania and Iowa. In September, 1898, he took charge of the tearing down of the old buildings where the Post Tavern and Post Building now stand and had full charge of these buildings until their completion, during this time he also superintended the putting in of the foundations of the Battle Creek Paper Company and the Postum power plant, having as high as 350 men under him at one time.

Mr. Brown was married at Grand Ledge, Michigan, January 23, 1902, to Miss Martha A. Taber, a daughter of Frank A. and Esther (Jarvis) Taber. Mr. and Mrs. Brown are members of the Independent Congregational church and he is connected with the Masonic, Benevolent Protective Order of Elks, Knights of Pythias and Knights of the Maccabees fraternities.

In 1902 he became assistant manager for the Battle Creek Paper Company, Limited, but failing health and the need of some one to look after the buildings in the Post addition caused him to change his position. He drew the plans and superintended the construction of about 170 homes built for the working people on the easy payment plan. He drew the plans and superintended the building of the Marjorie block, the C. L. Post storage building, the Flat building, the company's booth at the St. Louis World's Fair and had full charge of the Grandin advertising agency building.

In 1899 he aided his brother, Bernard Brown, to get a start in the electrical business in Battle Creek. Energy, determination and indefatigable labor have been the foundation upon which he has built success.

In his political affiliations he is independent, supporting the men whom he regards as the best qualified for office. He has ever been accounted one of the energetic, wide-awake young business men of his native city and his course has awakened admiration and regard.

SAMUEL R. CULP.

Samuel R. Culp, now deceased, was for many years an integral factor in the business development and the upbuilding of Athens. His name was an honored one on commercial paper and he was widely esteemed because of his integrity and thorough trustworthiness in all business transactions. A native of Ohio, he was born in Gilford township, Medina county, April 10, 1830, his birthplace being his father's farm, whereon he was also reared, early becoming familiar with the labors incident to the cultivation of the fields. He remained in Medina county until twenty-eight years of age, and in his youth attended the district and select schools of the neighborhood. Seven years after attaining his majority he came to Michigan, first settling in Kalamazoo county, when he took up a claim of timber land and engaged in the operation of a sawmill. As he cleared his land he converted it into productive fields and continued its cultivation for ten years, at the expiration of which period he removed to Athens.

Mr. Culp became identified with the business interests of this place as a general merchant, forming a partnership with Mr. Hitchcock, with whom he was connected for a decade. Before withdrawing from commercial pursuits in 1882, he founded a private bank, admitting his son, J. F. Culp, to a partnership, and for a time the store and bank were carried on simultaneously. Under the name of S. R. Culp & Son's Bank, Mr. Culp was a factor in financial circles in Athens until his death, which occurred on the 31st of October, 1893, when he was sixty-three years of age. The bank had secured a good patronage and had been one of the strong financial institutions of this part of the county. Mr. Culp had also been a factor in the material improvement of the town, through the erection of a block of brick stores and also a brick bank building. His deep interest in Athens and her welfare led him to give active co-operation to many measures for the general good, and he was always regarded as a most enterprising and valued citizen. Mr. Culp voted with the Democracy and was supervisor of his township while living in Kalamazoo county during the Civil war. Later he served as supervisor in Athens township. He became a member of the Masonic lodge in Athens, and the Royal Arch chapter in Union City, Michigan, and his life was in harmony with the high principles which form the basis of the craft. He took a deep interest in the intellectual development of the community and as a member of the school board labored effectively to promote educational advancement. His was a well rounded character and the qualities of his manhood made him a popular citizen.

In 1850 Mr. Culp wedded Miss Hannah Overholt, who was born in Pennsylvania, and was taken by her parents to Ohio when eighteen months old. By her marriage she became the mother of four children, but three died in early life and she is now living with her son, Jerome Franklin, and his family, in Athens. He was born in Montville, Ohio, August 21, 1851, and when a boy accompanied his parents to Kalamazoo county, Michigan, where he attended the district schools. Following the removal to Athens in 1866, he attended the high school here, and also spent two years in Hillsdale College, later pursuing a course in civil engineering in Ann Arbor, between 1874 and 1876. Returning to Athens on the completion of his collegiate work, he went into his father's store and in 1882 was admitted to a partnership in his father's business. In that year the private bank was established and was conducted conjointly by them until the father's death, after which J. F. Culp was alone in the

bank until April 15, 1899, when he sold out to the Athens State & Savings Bank. He is, however, still a director in the institution. In the great fire in Athens the firm's property was destroyed but they immediately rebuilt. In 1896 Mr. Culp became interested in a drug store, of which he soon afterward became sole proprietor and he now carries a stock valued at three thousand dollars.

On the 20th of July, 1876, Mr. Culp was united in marriage to Mary J. Goodrich, of Ann Arbor, and they have three children: Marie D., the wife of Frank Gampher, of Elkhart, Indiana. She has a son, Deurand Newman, by a former marriage; Margaret and Harold G., at home. A prominent Mason, he belongs to the lodge at Athens, the chapter at Union City, the commandery at Battle Creek and the mystic shrine at Grand Rapids, and is also a member of the Odd Fellows lodge in Athens. On the Democratic ticket he was elected to the village council the year following its incorporation. From his boyhood days he has made his home in Athens and his cordial manner, genial disposition and deference for the opinions of others have rendered him a popular citizen, whose friends are numerous.

THOMAS WEBB.

Thomas Webb, who is engaged in general farming in Pennfield township, was born in Sidford, Oxfordshire, England, December 3, 1840, and is a son of Joshua and Betty (Hitchman) Webb. The father was also a native of Sidford, his birth occurring in December, 1800, while his wife was born in Hooknorton, Oxfordshire, in April, 1802. In 1853, accompanied by their six children and an adopted daughter, they sailed for America, and after a voyage of six weeks landed at New York, on the 2d of June, coming thence to Battle Creek, Calhoun county, by way of rail to Buffalo, then on Lake Erie to Detroit and then by rail. On reaching Battle Creek the father rented a house and for a short time worked by the day. He was a cooper by trade and followed that business while in England, but after coming to this country he worked at it only in doing little odd jobs. He had but a small amount of money at the time of his arrival but, anxious to secure a home for his family, in the summer of 1853 he purchased a small tract of land on section 10, Pennfield township, and when he moved to the place he had but twenty-five cents left. This was nearly all wild and the only improvement on the place was an old log cabin without a roof or floor. They put in chips for a floor, the family residing therein for some time. Mr. Webb devoted his energies to the cultivation of his land and the improvement of his farm. He died in the cabin home in 1870 at the age of seventy years, and his wife, surviving him for about eight years, passed away at the age of seventy-six. Both were interred in what is known as the Hicks cemetery. They were Episcopalians in religious faith and in England took a prominent and active part in the work of the church, but after coming to this country, feeling strange in the new land, they lived quite retired. All that Mr. Webb possessed was acquired through his own efforts. When a young man he had worked at farm labor and afterward followed the cooper's trade and to some extent he worked at the butcher's trade. He also supplemented his

36

income to some extent by serving as janitor of a church in England for twelve years. That position there was termed clerk, which was there pronounced "clark," of the church, and it included the cleaning, sweeping, dusting and opening of the church for services, and the winding of the clock in addition to the reading of the responses at the weddings and baptisms. His industry was one of his marked characteristics and was manifest after he came to the new world in the care and operation of his farm. His political support was given to the Republican party. Unto him and his wife were born six children: Mary, who became the wife of George Green, who came to America with the family, but had no acquaintance with the family till on the boat, and both are now deceased; Caleb, who married a sister of Mr. Green, and they, too, have passed away; Joshua, who resides in Pennfield township; Jonathan, who resides in Union City, Michigan; Maria, who is the wife of I. C. Williams, a resident of Pennfield township; and Thomas, of this review. Rebecca, an adopted daughter, now deceased, became the wife of S. A. Boothe, who resides in Greenville, Michigan.

Thomas Webb attended school in England until he was ten years of age, at which time he went to work. It was a very early age for a boy to commence earning his own living, but he proved himself faithful to the task assigned him. After coming to America with his parents, he remained with them until his majority, attending school in Pennfield three months, and working on the home farm, also assisting neighboring farmers. In August, 1868, he was joined in wedlock to Miss Mary J. Morehouse, who was born near Hastings, Barry county, Michigan, a daughter of Nicholas Morehouse. By this marriage were born two sons: Albert, who resides at home; and Calvin E., who makes his home in Battle Creek. The latter married Rosina Smith and has one child, Altha E. In 1880 Mr. Webb was again married, his second union being with Mrs. Mary Ette Stewart, nee Mead, a daughter of Enoch and Hannah (Cole) Mead. Mrs. Webb's father was a native of Dutchess county, New York, and her mother was born in Montgomery county, New York. Mrs. Webb was born in Bedford township, Calhoun county, Michigan. The Cole family was one of the first established in New York and is of Holland lineage. The parents of Mrs. Webb came to Michigan about sixty-one years ago and took up their abode near the center of Bedford township, Calhoun county, where Mr. Mead bought a tract of land from a man who had entered it and began to develop a farm. His was the only frame house in the township at that time. He continued the cultivation of his land for some time, but afterward sold it and purchased a farm two miles from it, and later sold that and bought in Pennfield adjoining the one on which our subject now lives, and upon which he spent his remaining days. He died July 9, 1883, at the age of seventy-seven years and his wife passed away on the 6th of November, 1881, at the age of seventy-five years, both being interred in Hicks cemetery. They were the parents of six children: Emeline, who became the wife of Eli Stilson, both of whom are now deceased; Marvin, who resides in Pueblo, Colorado; Harvey, who was a member of the Union army during the Civil war and was killed in the second battle of Bull Run, and left one son, Alson Mead; Warren, who died in the army of camp fever, and left one child, now Mrs. Florence Smith, of Battle Creek; Elmina, the wife of

Alfred Carpenter, of Battle Creek; and Mary Ette, the wife of our subject. By her first marriage Mrs. Webb had two children: Floyd R., now a resident of Montana, married Lelia Cole, who has five children, Gladys, Howard, Bessie, Lillian and Josephine. Lena A., who is the wife of George G. Wilber, of Battle Creek. Mr. and Mrs. Webb now have an adopted daughter, M. Elva, who yet resides with them.

Before his first marriage, Mr. Webb purchased the farm adjoining that on which his parents lived and after his marriage he and his wife boarded with his brother until he could get a home built. As soon as possible, however, they moved into their own house, living there after his second marriage and until they came to their present home in 1886. Mr. Webb first purchased a tract of land of ninety acres and later another of thirty, which is the old family homestead and which he still owns. He thus had one hundred and twenty acres. He next bought seventy-eight acres where he now lives, making one hundred and ninety-eight acres of rich and valuable land, and is regarded as one of the leading farmers of the community. Upon his place he has good improvements and his fields are well cultivated and his stock is of good grades.

In his political views Mr. Webb is a Republican and is a loyal and devoted member of the Methodist Episcopal church. He has filled all of the offices of the church, but in recent years, because of his failing hearing, he has largely withdrawn from active church work. The first re-union ever held by the Webb family was in the present year, 1903, at the home of Joshua Webb in Pennfield township at which sixty-five were present. The next re-union is to be held at the home of our subject. Thomas Webb has spent almost his entire life in this county, as he was only a young boy of thirteen at the time of his parents' emigration to the new world, and his connection with this locality therefore covers fifty years, during which time he has witnessed remarkable changes, wrought by time and man. Pioneer conditions have long since given way before the advancement of civilization and he feels a just pride in what has been accomplished by the county as it has advanced along all lines of general progress and improvement until it to-day ranks among the leading counties of this great commonwealth.

The historical sketch of the family, which follows, was prepared and read by Mrs. Mary Ette Webb, wife of Thomas Webb, at the first reunion of the Webb family, which was held in 1903, at the home of Joshua Webb, in Pennfield township, Calhoun county, Michigan.

Joshua Webb, Sr., was born in Sidford, Oxfordshire, England. When about twenty-five years of age he was married to Miss Betty Hitchman, whose birthplace was Hooknorton, Oxfordshire. In early life his occupation was that of a farm laborer, but he later learned the trade of coopering, which he thenceforth followed while he lived in England. He also did the work of neighborhood butcher, and for twelve years was janitor, or clerk, as it is there called, of the Episcopal church. In that country this work includes cemetery work; cleaning, sweeping, dusting and opening the church; winding the clock, acting as reponsor at weddings, baptismals, etc. There were born to Mr. and Mrs. Webb six children, who grew to manhood and womanhood, and they adopted one daughter.

In the year 1853, in the month of April, a little company of eleven, consisting of Joshua Webb, Sr., his wife and children and the eldest son's wife and her brother, George Green, set sail for the new world. After six weeks on the water they arrived in the city of New York. They traveled by rail to Battle Creek, arrived at midnight and stayed in the depot until morning, when they found themselves in a small town. They did not experience much difficulty in securing a house. They also soon found work, being only a few hours without employment. Soon after their arrival the eldest daughter, Mary, married George Green. During the summer Mr. Webb purchased the farm of Ed. Packer, of Pennfield township, and moved upon it with his family. There he and his good wife lived the remainder of their days. The farm is now in the possession of the youngest son, Thomas. Mr. Webb died October 20, 1870, aged seventy years. His wife survived him eight years and one day, dying at the age of seventy-six years. The only members of the family now remaining are Jonathan, Joshua, Jr., Maria and Thomas. Caleb and his wife Sarah; Mary and her husband, George, and Rebecca have crossed the dark river to meet father and mother in the great beyond, from whence no traveler ever returns.

This little band of pioneers who began life in the then wild township of Pennfield now numbers as their descendants nearly one hundred children, grandchildren, great-grandchildren and great-great-grandchildren. During the time the family has lived in the county it has seen the forests of Pennfield township pass away, and in their places are rich farms, fine fruit orchards, fields of waving grain, broad meadows and lovely flowers. Ox-teams and carts have given place to horses and carriages, bicycles, automobiles and steam cars to carry them over the fine roads that have taken the places of rough ruts and corduroys. They have seen the introduction of electric cars, wire and wireless telegraphy, telephones, graphophones and talking machines of many kinds. In their time the art of photography has risen from the daguerreotype, ambrotype, leathertype and tintype to the incomparable modern photograph. Upon the farm have come the sulky plough, spring harrow and other improved machinery to take the place of the old-time tools. The mowing machine has displaced the scythe, and we have the reaper and binder instead of the sickle. The steam threshing machine has crowded out the flail. The public school system has been marvelously improved and extended. The small town of Battle Creek, the Webbs have seen grow to a large and busy city, noted for its many factories; and many of the family are employed there in the various establishments, while others are in business for themselves. And over all reigns as mayor the Hon. Fred H. Webb—"the first Webb born in America."

JOSHUA WEBB.

Joshua Webb is the owner of a fine farm of one hundred and eighty-five acres in Pennfield township, where he is actively engaged in general agricultural pursuits. He was born in Oxfordshire, England, July 3, 1834, and his parents, Joshua and Betty (Hitchman) were also natives of that locality. The grandfather, Richard Webb, was a miller and lived and died in Oxfordshire. After his marriage, the father of our subject learned the cooper's trade, which he followed for some time and was also a butcher. For twelve years he served as clerk of the Episcopal church, his duties in-

cluding the reading of the responses, the winding of the clock, the sweeping, the tolling of the bell and the digging of the graves. In 1853 he sailed from Liverpool and after forty days on the Atlantic, landed in New York city. The following evening he proceeded up the Hudson river to Albany, thence by the Erie Canal to Buffalo and by the lake to Detroit, completing the journey over the Michigan Central Railroad to Battle Creek, where he arrived on the 8th of June. On the 18th of July he purchased eighty acres of wild land and built a log cabin, without a floor. In this the family lived, in true pioneer style, until a more comfortable home could be built. The father continued to operate the farm until his death, which occurred October 20, 1870, when he was about seventy years of age, his birth having occurred December 13, 1800. His wife, who was born in 1802, survived him eight years and one day. In religious faith they were Episcopalians and the father was a stanch Abolitionist and later a Republican. They were the parents of six children: Mary, the wife of George Green, who came with the Webb family from England; Caleb, deceased; Jonathan, of Union City, Michigan; Joshua; Anna Maria, wife of I. C. Williams, and Thomas.

Joshua Webb received limited educational privileges in his native land. When about six years old he attended a "Dame school" for a short time and later was a student in another school in which he studied reading, writing, arithmetic and spelling. After working for a few years he once more attended school. He learned to write on the back of an almanac. He worked for nine years by the day in England; again by the day and month in America, at first receiving but an English shilling per day. Here he was employed by Mr. Packer, and in this way paid for the lumber used in building the house upon the old homestead farm. The first winter he also cut cord wood from what is now the Post addition to Battle Creek. He and his brother, Jonathan, would work together to support the family and when they had no other employment would clear the home farm. In the spring of 1854 they purchased their first cow. In 1855 they received a gold dollar which they gave to their mother, who kept it until her death and it is now a cherished possession of Mrs. Joshua Webb. Three of the family, Jonathan, Joshua and Thomas, worked together until they had a good farm of two hundred and thirty-seven acres.

On the 8th of April, 1863, Joshua Webb married Sarah E. Brown, a native of Sullivan county, New York, a daughter of Jesse and Deborah (Montanye) Brown. The father died when she was about six years old, and in 1857 the mother came to Battle Creek with her family. Unto Mr. and Mrs. Webb have been born four children, Isaac L., proprietor of a grocery store in Battle Creek, married Allie Smith and has a daughter, Helen; Cora is the wife of Charles E. Abell, of South Haven, Michigan, and has two children, Vera and Frank Carlos; Frank L. is a painter of South Haven and married Stella Hall; Jessie M. is at home.

After his marriage Mr. Webb lived for two and a half years near the Hicks cemetery and acted as its sexton. He then removed to his present farm in April, 1865, and that year planted his apple orchard. The following year he built his present home and has since continued the work of development and improvement until he now has a model farm. He planted the seed of some black walnut trees and to-day has a splendid walnut grove as a result. His farm is well improved and valuable and he is a successful farmer and self-made man who started out in life in very limited financial circumstances and has steadily worked his way upward to the plane of affluence.

ROBERT J. KELLEY.

An attorney of Battle Creek, making a specialty of corporation law, a valiant soldier of the Civil war and a legislator whose efforts were of signal advantage to the state. He was born in Monroe, this state, September 3, 1843, a son of John and Mary N. (Henderson) Kelley. The father was a native of County Down, Ireland, and as a young man came to the United States in 1814, settling in New Hampshire. He was connected with factory work in Dover and while residing there he met and married Miss Mary N. Henderson, a native of the old Granite state. About 1838 he removed to Monroe, Michigan, and soon after turned his attention to farming, which he continued to follow until his demise in 1868. His wife survived him until 1871, and at her death left eight children. In 1861, at the time of the outbreak of the Civil war, four sons and six daughters of the family were living and the sons all entered the army, three of them becoming members of the Eighteenth Regiment of Michigan Volunteers, while Robert J. joined the Fifth Michigan Cavalry. Thomas Kelley, the eldest son, gave his life in defense of the Union, his death occurring near Lexington, Kentucky.

Robert J. Kelley was reared upon the homestead farm in Monroe county, Michigan, and supplemented his early educational privileges by a high school course in the city of Monroe. He was in 1861 a student in the Ypsilanti Seminary, of which Professor Joseph Esterbook was the principal. On the 2d of September of the following year, he espoused the cause of his country, enlisting in Company K, Fifth Michigan Calvary, which was assigned to the Army of the Potomac. He served with that command until the close of the war and the Fifth Michigan with the First, Sixth and Seventh Regiments of the same state constituted General Custer's brigade, which won distinction and again and again received favorable comment from the war department as well as from the press. Mr. Kelley participated in many important battles. including those of Gettysburg, Brandy Station, Cold Harbor, Travillion Station, the action in front of Petersburg and Dinwiddie Courthouse. The Fifth Michigan was on the extreme left of the army at the time of General Lee's surrender at Appomatox. Mr. Kelley also participated in the grand review at Washington, after which the regiment was ordered to Fort Leavenworth, Kansas, and thence returned home, being mustered out at Detroit, Michigan, on the 3d of July, 1865, at which time he held the rank of sergeant major.

Following his military experience, Mr. Kelley completed his academic course at Ypsilanti, Michigan, and then entered the law department of the University of Michigan at Ann Arbor, being graduated in March, 1868, after which he was admitted to the bar. He located in Alpena, Michigan, in 1869, and not only became recognized as an able, conscientious and successful lawyer, but also became a recognized leader in political circles in which connection he aided in molding the policy of the Republican party of his district. His capability and loyalty in citizen-

ship led to his selection for the office of state legislator from the Alpena district in 1877 and while a member of the house he was instrumental in securing the passage of the bill for the first state gravel road ever constructed in Michigan. He also secured the legislation for the organization of township into districts, whereby all public schools in a township were controlled by a central board of trustees.

Mr. Kelley continued in active practice at Alpena, until 1888, when he was elected judge of the Twenty-sixth circuit and served for two full terms, retiring from the office on the 31st of December, 1899. That circuit included Alpena, Presque Isle, Otsego and Montmorency counties, and he was elected upon the Republican ticket. In May, 1900, he removed to Battle Creek, where he is now engaged in the practice of law, being the local advisor of a number of the leading corporate interests of Battle Creek. In addition to his law practice he has become interested financially in various manufacturing concerns of Battle Creek.

Judge Kelley was for many years very active in political circles in the state, his opinions carrying weight in councils of the Republican party. He also attended the national convention and in 1884 was a delegate to the convention which nominated James G. Blaine. In recent years the demands of an increasing law practice have left him little time or opportunity for active political work. Socially, he is connected with Alpena lodge, No. 199, F. & A. M., of which he is a past master. He is also past high priest of Thunder Bay chapter, R. A. M., and now belongs to Battle Creek chapter, to Battle Creek commandery, No. 33, Knight Templars, and to the Detroit consistory, and the Moslem Temple of the Mystic

Shrine at Detroit. He holds membership relations with Farragut post, G. A. R., of Battle Creek, and is its commander at this writing, in 1904. He also belongs to the Ancient Order of United Workmen, the Knights of the Maccabees of the World, and the Benevolent Protective Order of Elks.

Judge Kelley was married in August, 1872, to Miss Marion Rutherford, of Alpena, Michigan, a daughter of Adam Rutherford, who was a well known resident of that city. They have one daughter, Mary C., now the wife of Willard A. Cokley, of New York. Mrs. Kelley is a member of the Episcopal Church and the Judge is one of its supporters. The bent of Judge Kelley's active mind makes him take a lively pleasure in the study of the science of government. Although he has held but few political offices and while upon the bench carefully lifted the judicial ermine above the mire of parties, he has been a more active and efficient politician than many who have devoted their undivided time to public affairs and who have obtained far greater official distinction than ever fell to him. He has kept abreast with the best thinking men of the age and his continually developing mental powers have shown their strength in the discussion of questions affecting the welfare of the state and nation as well as in the handling of important legal interests.

LEROY ERNEST ELDRED.

LeRoy Ernest Eldred, the official stenographer of the thirty-seventh judicial circuit, was appointed to this position by Judge Herbert E. Winsor on the 10th of April, 1901, at which time the circuit was formed. He

is splendidly qualified to discharge the duties of this position and his course has given excellent satisfaction to all concerned. A native of New York, he was born in Elmira, Chemung county, on the 21st of October, 1871, his parents being Daniel L. and Lottie (Parkhill) Eldred. The father was born in Vermont and subsequently removed to New York, becoming one of the first official court reporters of the Empire state. This was in the early days when stenography was first used and before the invention of the typewriter. He acted as an official reporter of Penn Yan and in other circuits in New York. While living in the east he was married to Miss Lottie Parkhill, of Amsterdam, New York, and they made their residence in Elmira until their removal to Battle Creek. Mr. Eldred is now officially connected with the Battle Creek Sanitarium.

LeRoy Ernest Eldred acquired his early education in the public schools of his native city, is a graduate of the Elmira academy, and subsequently he was graduated from the high school of Battle Creek with the class of 1891. He then went south and was engaged in business at Palm Beach, Florida, for a few years. He established a plantation for the production of pine apples and other small fruits and still owns that property. While still a school boy he had mastered stenography, using the Graham system, and after his return to Battle Creek he was for some time private secretary to Dr. J. H. Kellogg, of the Battle Creek Sanitarium. While filling that position he received the appointment to his present office.

Mr. Eldred was married while at Palm Beach, Florida, to Miss Satie M. Wilson, of that place, a daughter of W. W. Wilson, a prominent farmer of Eaton county, Michigan. They now have two children, Gertrude Arline and Loren Bert. Both Mr. and Mrs. Eldred hold membership in the Episcopal church of Marshall, where they have resided during the past two years. Already they have gained the friendship of many of the leading residents of the city and the hospitality of their own home has been greatly enjoyed by those who know them. Mr. Eldred belongs to the National Shorthand Reporters' Association and is connected ·with several fraternal societies, including the Knights of Pythias lodge and the Knights of the Maccabees. He has held various offices in these organizations, was one of the early members of the Uniformed Rank in the Knights of Pythias organization and is now its colonel. He is also representative to the Supreme division and is affiliated with the Great camp. His manner is pleasant. genial and courteous and his personal characteristics have made him a popular resident of Marshall.

GEORGE ENCKE.

George Encke, one of the leading farmers of Calhoun county, thoroughly conversant with the best methods of operating the fields, and now residing in Albion, was born in Williamsburg, Pennsylvania, December 27, 1852. His father, Edmund H. Encke, was a native of Pennsylvania, and was of German lineage. By trade he was a millwright. He married Miss Marietta Green, who was born in Noulton township, New Jersey, just across the river from Pennsylvania. After their marriage they resided at Williamsburg, Pennsylvania. for a number of years and subsequently Mr. Encke purchased and operated a mill at Hope, New Jersey. He after-

ward became owner of the Swazy mills, two miles from Hope, and there he lived until his removal to Michigan in 1865. Here he purchased a farm two miles south of Albion and continued its cultivation and improvement up to the time of his death.

George Encke began his education in the public schools of New Jersey and continued his studies in the common schools of Michigan. He received training at farm labor and continued to assist his father in the operation of the old homestead until his marriage, which occurred in 1876, the lady of his choice being Miss Della Bidwell, of Albion. She was a daughter of Wellington Bidwell, one of the first settlers of Calhoun county, and a dry goods merchant at Albion at the time of his daughter's marriage. Mr. Encke acted as salesman in his father-in-law's store until he started upon the road with a wagon supplied with a good line of dry goods. He thus became connected with merchandising and found this a paying venture. following the same for about six years.

In the meantime Mr. Encke had been called upon to mourn the loss of his first wife. who died after a brief married life of only two and a half years, leaving one child, Laverne. who is now in Illinois. For his second wife Mr. Encke chose Miss Anna Orr, of Pulaski, Michigan, a daughter of Adam Orr, a well known farmer. who came from Vermont by way of New York state to the west. He was a cousin of Hon. Zachary Chandler, of Michigan. Mrs. Encke died five years after her marriage. For his third wife Mr. Encke was married to Miss Mabel Frost, of Albion, a daughter of George Frost, and a native of Blissfield, Michigan. The year after the death of his second wife Mr. Encke retired from his farm and took up his abode in Albion, where he now has a beautiful home at the corner of Irwin avenue and Adam street. There he has a large lot, on which is a commodious residence, a barn and fine improvements. In fact this is one of Albion's notable homes. After his removal to this city Mr. Encke conducted a grocery store for several years and prospered in this undertaking, in which he continued until 1899. when he sold out. He then purchased a farm in Sheridan township, Calhoun county, and is now giving his attention to the cultivation of strawberries, fruits, melons and grapes. He also has a good apiary and has handled bees for thirty-five years. In fact he has come to be the leading apiarist in eastern Calhoun county and has given to the subject much study and consideration. His honey product last year will amount to more than three thousand pounds, and as it is always of excellent quality he commands the highest market price. He is now one of the representative and well-to-do citizens of Albion and his present prominent position is due to his own business ability and strong purpose.

GEORGE W. MARKHAM.

George W. Markham, a respected citizen of Eckford township, Calhoun county, and one of the large land holders of the locality, was born in Livington county, New York, December 6, 1850, a son of Guy and Clarissa (Chamberlin) Markham. Both parents were the representatives of old and distinguished New England families, on the paternal side descended from Joseph Markham, whose father and three brothers served valiantly in the Revolutionary war, the former being in the battle of Monmouth under the command of General Washington. All four were commissioned officers and participated in many of the principal engagements of the war. One event of note in the life of the elder man was in connection with Arnold's escape to the British lines. Mr. Markham at the time standing in his tent door as the general made his escape. Joseph Markham also served in the War of 1812 as a private. After the close of the Revolutionary war he took up a westward march, locating in Livingston county, in western New York, with but twenty shillings in money as his capital upon which to build his future competence. His first night in the west was spent in the limbs of a tree, which he climbed to escape the wolves which were attracted by the fire he had built. He lived to be ninety-four years old, the remainder of his life being passed among the scenes of western New York. Mrs. Markham was a daughter of Charles and Katharine (Howell) Chamberlin, and a descendant of the Chamberlin family, whose genealogy has been carefully preserved since the first settlements of Massachusetts, with whose history their fortunes have been closely identified. Guy Markham, the father of our personal subject, was a man of untiring energy and industry and succeeded in acquiring considerable property in his New York home, but animated with much the same spirit which had started his father toward the west, he brought his wife and one child to Michigan in 1860, locating in Eckford township, Calhoun county, where he purchased a farm of three hundred acres, on section 8. This location remained his home throughout the balance of his life, which ended in 1897. His widow still survives him and lives with her son, George W. Mr. Markham was a Democrat in his political convictions and was always active in the promotion of the principles which he indorsed. Both himself and wife were esteemed and respected throughout the community, the old phrase "good neighbors" applying in its broadest sense to the life they lived.

George W. Markham attained considerable education in his native county, receiving his education in the district school in the vicinity of his home. He was ten years old when he accompanied his parents to Michigan, as the only child remaining with them throughout their entire lives. He was married December 31, 1878, to Miss Ida Webster, who was a representative of a New York family, though her birth occurred in Chicago. Illinois, and of this union was born one child, Ethel Markham. Mr. Markham now owns three hundred and thirty-one acres of fine farm land, which is devoted to general farming and stock-raising. Inheriting from a long line of ancestors those qualities which make for the betterment of character, Mr. Markham has added by years of training a high principle and splendid integrity, which has made his influence in the community a power for good and right living. He enjoys the esteem and confidence of his fellow men and the personal satisfaction which results from a conscientious effort to order one's life according to high principle.

CHARLES L. TRAVIS.

A career of exceptional interest and one that has been associated with the material advancement of various sections in the states of the middle west, is that of Charles L. Travis, now numbered among the progressive farmers of Calhoun county. A native son of this state, he was born five miles east of Marshall, in Marengo township. July 15, 1849. in a little log house which was the home of his parents, Leonard W. and Deborah (Turner) Travis. The father was born in Scattucook, New York, March 7, 1809, and while still a lad learned the trade of a carpenter. a remarkable talent assisting him in the mastery of this work, a tool chest of splendid workmanship made by him at the age of nineteen years, being now in the possession of his son, Charles L. Travis. When a young man he located in Colon, Michigan, in 1836 coming to Detroit on foot, meeting on this trip the young lady. who, on October 15, 1837, became his wife. Afterward he homesteaded a half of three hundred and twenty acres and purchased the remainder, his home continuing in that location for a period of two years. when he sold the land and went back to his native state. He remained in New York for four years, when he once more located in Michigan, his finances amounting only to the worth of an eighty-acre tract of land comprised in his first western farm. This he purchased and made his home for two years, after which he became the owner of one hundred and sixty acres in Marengo township, Calhoun county, principally timbered land, which he disposed of in 1863, sixteen years after his purchase. He then purchased a farm of one hundred and sixty acres in Marshall township, where he made his home until his death, January 5, 1887. During his residence in Michigan he had contributed no little to the agricultural development of the state, becoming the owner of many farms, which he improved and cultivated. He also became a power in the moral life of the various communities with which he identified his interests as a member of the Methodist church giving his best efforts toward the support of his religious convictions. In Lee Center there still exists a material evidence of his labors in a Sunday school, which he organized many years ago. Wherever he lived "There he builded an alter," and the fire was kept burning. One of his last acts of benevolence was to remember the widows and orphans of the Michigan conference. Besides Charles L. Travis he was the father of four children, the eldest of whom was Ashley, born January 6, 1840, and died May 2, 1863, of typhoid fever, while engaged as bookkeeper on the steamer Woodruff. He was a graduate of a commercial college of Detroit. Jacob, the second in order of birth, was born March 7, 1844, and on attaining manhood married and now has a family of six children. Since 1870 he has made his home in Kansas and owns a farm in Oklahoma. The fourth son was Frank Travis, who was born April 13, 1854, and died June 6, 1903. He was a man of exceptionly brilliant mind, of large ambitions, and of forceful, earnest characteristics, and the impress of his personality was felt upon all communities which recognized him as a member. He was a graduate of Albion College and a teacher in the public schools, in time marrying Ella Randolph and removing to South Dakota, where he discharged the duties of various public offices in an able and efficient manner. The youngest of the family was George, who was born June 7, 1858, and died February 4, 1899, his death the direct result of over-study in his efforts to prepare for the ministry.

Charles L. Travis, the personal subject of this review, remained upon the paternal farm in Michigan until he was twenty-two

years old, when he went to Kansas and rented one hundred and sixty acres of land and engaged in farming for himself. After eighteen months he returned to Michigan to help rebuild the family home, which had recently burned. In the fall of the same year Mr. Travis married and settled upon his present farm, where he remained nine years, at the end of which period he went to Ree Heights, South Dakota, and located a cattle ranch south of that town. For the following six years he was prominent as one of the largest ranchmen in the county, his splendid management resulting in large returns for his efforts. For a short time he was owner of a farm north of Pierre, when he became foreman of the street car line in that city, which position he maintained for one year. He then became interested in the real estate business, traveling for the Western Loan and Trust Company for several years, during which time he amasssed a considerable fortune, but through a decline in the value of property and speculations eventually lost the greater part of it. Following upon his withdrawal from real estate interests he farmed for eighteen months near Sioux City, and for three years near Joplin, Missouri, when he located in the latter city and established a retail oil business. He met with the success which follows close application and ability, but after three years sold out and returned to Michigan on a visit, remaining, however, to care for his brother Frank, who was then ill. Upon the death of the latter Mr. Travis became the owner of his present farm.

Mr. Travis has been twice married, the first ceremony being performed November 27, 1873, uniting him with Miss Eulala E. Patterson, who died in 1887. She became the mother of three children, of whom Ella was born September 2, 1874; Leslie was born July 23, 1876, and Bertha, who is still at home, was born July 22, 1885. Leslie graduated from a commercial college and attended Pierre University, and is now a city mail carrier, which position he has held for eight years. He married Miss Grace Turk, of Joplin, Missouri, and they have one child, Harry, who was born February 26, 1901. The second marriage of Mr. Travis occurred May 19, 1889, Miss Elizabeth Higgins becoming his wife. She is a representative of one of the stalwart families of the middle west, her parents being Peter, who was born November 15, 1842, at Chatsworth, Illinois, and Phoebe (Flesher) Higgins, their home being in Sioux City, Iowa. Mrs. Higgins was the daughter of Stephen Flesher, who was one of a family of seven brothers who served in the Civil war, and all of whom had sons in the same service, the youngest being only fourteen years of age. Every member of the family, with the exception of one grandson, survived the struggle, though they passed through many hardships and dangers, one being held in Libby prison for some time. The thrifty traits which distinguish the Pennsylvania Germans—the maternal grandfather having emigrated from the Fatherland— is particularly noticeable in this family. There are eight children, of whom Mrs. Travis is the eldest, having been born in Gilman, Illinois, September 14, 1868, and the others, all but one of whom are living and own their own homes in Sioux City, are as follows: John, Ellen, Ada, William, Robert, May, deceased, and Charles. To Mr. and Mrs. Travis were born the following children: Kyle, born August 26, 1891; Paul, born December 24, 1893, and Ruth, born February 2, 1896.

Second to none other has been the interest of Mr. Travis in the political affairs of the communities where he has lived. Always a stanch Democrat he has spared no time nor effort to advance the principles of that party, and his influence has been of much moment on different occasions. During the senatorial deadlock in South Dakota Mr. Travis appeared before the caucus and proposed the name of Rev. Mr. Kyle, a Congregational minister, who was then a members of the legislature, but who had not been mentioned as a candidate for the senate. The suggestion took the caucus by storm and his man was successfully elected to the United States senate. The eldest son of Mr. Travis's second marriage was named for the senator. Though always active in political affairs, Mr. Travis has never cared for official recognition, preferring not to hold office. However, during his residence in Pierre he served as alderman, and in the convention at Redfield received a flattering vote for governor, which he turned over to Loucks. During one memorable campaign he made thirty-one political speeches and never spoke in a precinct that he did not carry, an evidence of not only his rhetorical ability, but also of the personal character of the man. A man of deeds rather than words he has successfully established his position as that of a citizen whose influence has always been lent toward the advancement of all worthy enterprises, whose best efforts have been given for the maintenance of principle and right.

WALTER MARION HOVEY.

A very popular and esteemed citizen of Marshall, Calhoun county, is Walter Marion Hovey, veterinary surgeon and keeper of the county farm of Calhoun county, which is located in Marengo township, two miles northeast of the city of Marshall. He was born in Madison county, New York, in 1860, a son of Charles J. and Mary Elizabeth Hovey, who now reside at Cooperville, Ottawa county, Michigan. When a lad of six years Mr. Hovey came with his parents to Ottawa county, Michigan, growing to manhood in the paternal home and receiving his education in the school in the vicinity of his home. Later he attended the International College of Veterinary Surgery, from which institution he was graduated in 1896, with his degree. He then opened an office in Cooperville, Michigan, in partnership with an older brother, in which connection he remained until 1899, when he removed to his present location in Marshall. He has succeeded in establishing a large patronage throughout the community, for he has come to be known as a successful man in his business. In addition to his other property he has a large farmer's shed in the city with a capacity of one hundred horses, all under cover. In April, 1903, he was employed to conduct the county farm.

In 1888 Dr. Hovey was united in marriage with Miss Carrie Morey, of Marshall, and they have one child, Lewis. In his political convictions Dr. Hovey is an adherent of the principles advocated in the platform of the Republican party.

FRANK A. FRANCISCO.

A successful stockman of Calhoun county is Frank A. Francisco, who was born in Newton township, upon the farm which he now occupies, April 14, 1857. His parents were Francis and Froretta (Lewis) Fran-

cisco, both of whom were natives of Ontario county, New York, the father coming to Michigan in his boyhood days, where he found employment in the farming regions of the state. With the frugal and thrifty habits inculcated in the lives of the natives of the east, he acquired sufficient means to purchase a farm in 1852, where he remained until his death, October 10, 1894, his last resting place being Newton cemetery. Frank A. Francisco was reared to manhood in this location, and while receiving a practical training along agricultural lines, attending the Newton township district school. Later he attended the schools of Ceresco for two years, after which he entered Olivet College. His school days were ended rather abruptly through serious trouble with his eyes, when he entered upon the life work to which he had early been trained. With his farming interests he at first began to deal in stock, buying, selling and shipping, and with the substantial results of this effort eventually establishing a stock farm, where he now keeps the best grade of stock that the country affords.

Rebecca D. Bly, a native of Genesee, New York, became the wife of Mr. Francisco, December 11, 1878, and of this union were born three children, one of whom died in infancy, while Jessie May and Harold B. are both members of their parents' home. In his political affiliations Mr. Francisco adheres to the principles advocated in the platform of the Republican party, and fraternally is associated with the Knights of the Maccabees. He is a much esteemed and valued citizen, his energy, perseverance and industry having numbered him among the financially strong men of the county, while his personal characteristics are such as to win for him the respect and confidence of the entire community.

FRANK PULLMAN.

Frank Pullman, who follows farming on section 31, Fredonia township, and is the efficient supervisor of this township, was born in Burlington township, Calhoun county, June 17, 1858, a son of Arza and Jane (Hathaway) Pullman. The father was born in Schoharie county, New York, in 1818, and was a son of Darius and Lucinda (Betts) Pullman. He was reared and educated in the county of his nativity and was there married to Jane Hathaway, also a native of that county and a daughter of Josiah and Betsey (Foster) Hathaway. Coming to Michigan in 1857, Mr. and Mrs. Arza Pullman located on a farm in Burlington township, where he became the owner of one hundred and fifteen acres of land, continuing its cultivation until his death. He was a Republican in politics and a member of the Congregational church. He died November 1, 1888, and his wife on the 4th of January, 1874. In their family were nine children and all older than our subject were born in New York, while he and the younger members of the household are natives of Michigan. Albert and Adelbert, twins, are married and reside in Burlington township. Lucinda married Carey Stark, of Albion, by whom she had one child, and after the death of her first husband she married Reuben Page, of Albion. Willard, who is married and has one child, lives in New York. Charles is living in Mason county, Michigan. Emmett, of Mason county, is married and has three children. Frank is the seventh of the family. Mary is the wife of William Cleveland, of Albion, and has two children. Winifield G. resides in Fredonia township.

Frank Pullman, having acquired a good education in the common schools, started out in life for himself at the age of nineteen years, working at various pursuits that would yield him an honest living. He was married in Fredonia township, November 16, 1888, to Miss Mary Caroline Mohr Hardt, who was born in Washtenaw county, Michigan, a daughter of Christian and Caroline (Mohr) Hardt. They had one child, Lola Caroline. The wife and mother died June 24, 1896, and was laid to rest in the Lutheran cemetery.

In his political affiliations Mr. Pullman is a Democrat and his first presidential vote was cast for Grover Cleveland in 1884. He has taken some interest in politics, yet he is not an office seeker. In 1902, however, he was solicited to become a candidate for township supervisor and was elected, while in 1903 he was again nominated and elected, receiving an increasing majority on the second occasion. He attends the Lutheran church, contributing to its support and he is a member of the Knights of the Maccabees, Burlington lodge, F. & A. M., and the Eastern Star Chapter, at Burlington. Throughout his business career he has carried on agricultural pursuits and in the control of his property shows business dispatch, enterprise and capable management.

SYLVESTER B. ALLEN.

Too often is it found that the successful business man concentrates his entire effort upon his industrial or commercial activities to the exclusion of other interests, which tend to develop strong and honorable manhood. This was never the case with Sylvester B. Allen, for while he attained most enviable success he at the same time found opportunity to promote the general welfare, to aid the needy and to assist in the work of the church. His nature was kindly and generous, and justice and the more gracious attribute of mercy tempered his opinions of those with whom he came in contact. So honorable and upright was his career that he won the unqualified regard of all with whom he was associated, and when he passed away the community in which he lived felt that it had sustained an almost irreparable loss.

Mr. Allen was born in Java, New York, January 16, 1837, a son of Erastus and Sinia B. (Feagles) Allen. His father was a teacher in early life and afterward became a farmer. In 1843 he started for Michigan with his family, traveling across the country with team and wagon. He settled in Girard, Branch county, and after living there for a number of years, removed to what became known as the home farm, in Tekonsha township, Calhoun county. This property is still owned by his descendants. He was a strong Presbyterian in religious faith and when the church was built at Tekonsha he gave all of his wheat crop one year to assist in the raising of the funds, even having to buy flour after that for use in his own family. He was known as one of the strong and earnest men of his neighborhood, being well educated and with an evenly balanced mind and kindly disposition. He died on the old homestead. His wife passed away at the home of a daughter in Tekonsha. In their family were ten children, six of whom reached mature years, while four are now living, namely: Mrs. L. M. Batt and Mrs. E. P. Keep, both of Tekonsha; Mrs. S. A. Wilder, of Albion, and Mrs. Sarah Allen, of Iola, Kansas.

In the district schools Sylvester B. Allen began his education, which was con-

tinued in a select school. He enjoyed more than ordinary educational privileges and in later life he continually broadened his mind by reading and observation. He was trained to farm work and remained with his father on the old homestead until twenty-five years of age, having charge of the farm from the time when he was old enough to assume the responsibilities, owing to his father's continued ill health. He was very successful in his work and his brothers and sisters afterward acknowledged their indebtedness to him for his capability in controlling the home place and the active assistance which he rendered them in various ways. In addition to the cultivation of the fields he engaged in stock buying and also dealt in wheat, and in every department of his work prospered, because he conducted his affairs with keen discrimination, unfaltering industry and close application.

On the 26th of June, 1862, Mr. Allen was united in marriage to Miss Cordelia M. Robinson, of Clarendon township, a daughter of Andrew J. Robinson, who was one of the early residents of the county. Her father was for many years connected with railroad work and later engaged in agricultural pursuits. After his marriage Mr. Allen purchased a tract of land adjoining Tekonsha and established his home in the village. There he continued his farming operations throughout his entire life, and his widow yet owns that property, comprising about two hundred and fifty acres of rich land. Forty acres of the home place has been platted as an addition to the village of Tekonsha, and all of the railroad buildings are located on that part of the original tract. For a number of years during his residence in the village Mr. Allen was extensively interested in the buying and selling of grain and stock. Whatever he undertook he carried forward to completion, for every step in his business career was carefully made and his sound judgment enabled him to readily comprehend intricate business situations. He was also engaged in the brokerage business and again he met with prosperity. In connection with John Johnson, under the firm style of Allen & Johnson, he established the Exchange Bank, of Tekonsha, which was thus continued until 1902, when it was incorporated under the name of the First State Bank of Tekonsha, Mr. Allen becoming its president. In the meantime, however, in the year 1887, Mr. Allen removed with his family to Albion. He had over twenty-four years resided at the old home in Tekonsha, but desiring to afford his children better educational privileges, took up his abode in Albion and soon became a prominent factor in its business circles. He was the founder of the Commercial and Savings bank at that place and associated with him strong business men in the enterprise. He accepted the vice presidency of the institution, and with the other stockholders established one of the finest banking houses in this section of the state. He was likewise actively interested in the Albion Malleable Iron Company and the Albion Buggy Company, and at the time the electric light plant was installed he became one of the directors of that enterprise. Various other business interests claimed his attention and co-operation and he advanced to a place prominent among the most prosperous, capable and far-sighted business men of the county.

Unto Mr. and Mrs. Allen were born three children: Frank Erastus, who is now cashier of the First State Bank of Tekonsha, also owns a farm of three hundred acres in that locality and is engaged in buying and raising stock. He married Miss Ida M. Blakeman and they have a daughter, Eva May. Nettie B. is the wife of Herbert B. Cushman, who is assistant cashier of the First State Bank of Tekonsha. They have two children: Dorothy Madalene and Robert Allen Cushman. Alta May, the youngest, is the wife of E. R. Loud, an attorney of Albion. She was for five years a teacher of languages in the college at Albion, and like the other members of the family was a graduate of Albion College. She also completed a course of study in a conservatory.

Mr. Allen remodeled the residence at No. 504 East Erie street, in Albion, transforming it into a beautiful home, which is still occupied by his widow. He was a Democrat of strong political views, and while he never faltered in his allegiance to the principles of the party in which he believed, he would never accept office. He might, had he so desired, attained to high political honors, and his upright character would have made him an official whose course would have been above reproach. He preferred, however, to do his duty as a citizen in a private capacity, and he rendered substantial aid to many movements that had for their object the general good. He belonged to the Masonic lodge at Tekonsha and later demitted to Murat lodge, F. & A. M., at Albion. For thirty-four years he was a member of the Presbyterian church and throughout that period was true to his professions. He made little boast of his religion, but in his life exemplified the true spirit of Christianity. He was sympathetic and tender, his heart being quickly touched by a tale of woe or distress. He was glad to give his counsel and advice to those who sought it, and he always advised others as he would himself. In speaking of his business career his pastor said: "He was preeminently a business man, one of the men who, conducting their own affairs successfully, are able to assist others to success. His clear insight into a business proposition was most remarkable in his best days. He has taught us the possibility of accumulating a fortune along the lines of strict integrity, and I believe that I am correct in saying that every man, desiring to succeed by honest methods, found a friend in S. B. Allen. The one who has had the most intimate and longest business relations with him testifies that he was all to him that a brother could be. We are often tempted to speak lightly, even sneeringly, of business success, but I tell you that when it is accomplished by no loss in character or surrender of the moral sense there are few greater honors." Viewed from any standpoint his life may be termed a success. He not only attained wealth, but he was rich in the friendship and regard of his fellow men. He passed away October 11th, 1903, and when the news of his death spread throughout Albion it was felt that one of the worthy citizens had been called hence, and in Tekonsha, where he had so long resided, his demise was as deeply and sincerely mourned.

SANDS McCAMLY.

As one of the well remembered and highly respected founders of Battle Creek, the name of Sands McCamly stands prominent. He was born in Orange county, New York, October 16, 1793, his parents being David and Phoebe (Sands) McCamly, Jr.,

37

who emigrated from Ireland to Orange county, New York, where the family were prominent as agriculturists.

About 1830 Sands McCamly came to Michigan, and liking the location of the site of the present city of Battle Creek, he purchased a half interest in the tract of a Mr. Sackett, who had previously entered it from the government. He had prior to this married Eliza Coleman, who was born November 5, 1805, in Orange county, New York, and married November 8, 1823.

In the spring of 1832 Mr. McCamly brought his family here and later bought the entire original tract and undertook its development, selling a part to Jonathan Hart, Abraham and Isaac Merritt, who were pioneers, and to other actual settlers. His influential position is indicated by the fact that he was the first postmaster of Battle Creek.

Mr. and Mrs. McCamly were widely known for their charity and kindliness, and their name is still cherished in this vicinity, although they passed away many years ago, Mr. McCamly having died in 1864, and his wife in 1859.

SETH LEWIS.

Seth Lewis, deceased, of Marshall, Calhoun county, Michigan, was the founder and for many years the editor of the Marshall Statesman, one of the oldest papers in southern Michigan. He was born in Wells, Ruthland county, Vermont, February 11, 1814, a son of Dr. Reuben and Deborah (Potter) Lewis. When he was three years old his father moved to Strykersville, Genesee county, New York, where he attended the public schools until he was fifteen years of age. Compelled then to depend upon his own resources, he left home and found employment upon a neighboring farm, where he worked through the summer months, continuing to attend school during the winter seasons until he was seventeen. He was then employed as a printer's apprentice on the Wyoming County Sentinel, published at Warsaw, New York, remaining almost constantly in that office until 1839, and becoming a practical printer in all departments. Early in the last named year he came to Michigan with the intention of making the west his permanent home. Not realizing his expectations, however, he returned east, where he remained but a few weeks, when he once more came to Michigan, being then induced by his cousin, John Potter, of Marengo, to settle permanently in this county after visiting various places in the state. In August of the same year he purchased what was left of the plant of the Marshall Republican, and September 12, 1839, issued the first number of the Western Statesman, which name was changed at the beginning of the fourth year to the Marshall Statesman. Until 1866 Mr. Lewis continued the publication of this paper, when he sold out (nominally); six years later, however, again assuming its management. After the period of about a year he again transferred his interests, and again in 1877 repurchased the plant. Thereafter, until his death, he remained the editor of this paper, stanchly supporting through its columns the best in civic affairs.

In politics Mr. Lewis was a Whig of the anti-slavery type, as long as that party was in existence. He favored the calling of the convention in 1854 which resulted in the disorganization of that party, and was present "under the oaks" at Jackson, at the birth of the Republican party, counciling and aiding in the movement, and from that time until his death was a strong advocate of the principles of Republicanism, making his influence felt throughout the state. He published a partisan paper and made politics his study. He seemed at times possessed of prophetic wisdom, so certainly did he foretell the result of elections before they took place.

With all qualifications fhat go to make the success of a public officer, Mr. Lewis was often called upon to serve in an official capacity, being elected in 1855 as village recorder of Marshall, which position he held for one year. May 21, 1861, he was appointed by Lincoln postmaster of Marshall, remaining in the capacity until October 16, 1866, when he was removed by Andrew Johnson for the reason that he would not advocate a policy contrary to his principles. During the two sessions of the State Legislature in 1869 and 1871 he served as postmaster of that body, and was superintendent of the poor of Calhoun county from 1855 to 1861. For several consecutive years he acted as secretary of the Calhoun County Agricultural Society. Fraternally, Mr. Lewis was prominent in the community. He became a member of Peninsular lodge, No. 5, I. O. O. F., after its organization, after which for some time he served as secretary and later held all the chairs; for many years prior to his death he was identified with the Grand lodge, and was also a member of Marshall Encampment No. 2. He was a charter member of and held various official positions in Marshall Division Sons of Temperance, No. 18, which was organized in May, 1847. After that lodge ceased to hold regular meetings he was one of the petitioners for a charter for the Independent Order of Good Templars, and one of the first officers of the lodge, which was organized here in January, 1853, and subsequently served as chief templar. He was one of the principal movers in the reorganization of the lodge of the Sons of Temperance, known as Marshall Division, No. 7, in 1859. and remained an active and influential member during its existence. In the matter of religious faith he had been a faithful and consistent member of the Presbyterian church, having identified himself with this doctrine at twenty years of age. He was one of the organizers of the church of that denomination in Marshall and was a member of the choir at the time of dedication of the first church building. In civic society and in the church he was a worthy member, and in his domestic relations was kind and indulgent as a husband and father; as a companion agreeable, and obliging as a friend. His death occurred October 8, 1879, and he is buried in Oakridge cemetery, Marshall.

The marriage of Mr. Lewis January 5. 1842, united him with Miss Celina Church, the ceremony being performed in Marengo township, Calhoun county. Mrs. Lewis was born November 20, 1822, at West Rush, Monroe county, New York, the fifth child and third daughter of Robert and Elizabeth (Ennis) Church, who located in Marengo township on the farm which is still held in the family. The paternal ancestry is traced back to Sergeant Richard Church (brother of Col. Benjamin Church, "the Indian fighter"), who came to America in 1630. with Governor Winthrop, and afterward married Elizabeth Warren, who came with her father, Richard Warren, in the Mayflower. To Mr. Lewis and his wife were born three children: William Rutledge, Eber Church, who died at the age of one year, and Edwin Seth.

The birth of Will R. Lewis occurred July 23, 1847, in Marshall, and in this city he attended school until February 2, 1862, when he entered his father's printing office, serving three and a half years as an apprentice. For four months of this time he had charge of the office during his father's service as postmaster. During the winter of '65 and '66 he attended Eastman's Business College at Poughkeepsie, New York. Upon his return to Marshall he was appointed assistant postmaster by his father, but when the latter was removed from office he also lost his position; in 1867, however, he again became assistant under Postmaster Samuel S. Lacey. In 1869 he resigned to become a partner in the Marshall Statesman with F. H. Burgess, and when his father purchased the paper he remained in the office. September 10, 1873, he was appointed assistant postmaster and continued as such until April 1. 1884, when he became postmaster. holding the office until September 15, 1885. when he was retired by the Cleveland administration. He had charge of the Statesman from December 4, 1879, to July 5, 1893, when the property was disposed of by the family. He was married October 26, 1869, to Miss Helen A. Reed, and of this union have been born four children, namely: Arthur R., Charles W. A., Isabella M., and William L. Mrs. Lewis was born at Grand Haven, Michigan, a daughter of Grosvenor Reed, one of the early settlers and the first prosecuting attorney of Ottawa county, this state. Mrs. Lewis is a charter member of Mary Marshall Chapter, D. A. R., of Marshall, and is descended from Colonial and Mayflower ancestors.

Whatever of virtue is possessed by the present generation of the name of Lewis has been transmitted from a sturdy line of ancestory; connected both by paternal and maternal lines with American history since 1627 and 1630, on the former date George Lewis coming from East Greenwich, England, to Plymouth, Massachusetts, and on the latter date Sergeant Richard Church came from England with Governor Winthrop's fleet. George Lewis afterward joined Rev. Mr. Lathrop's colony in founding Barnstable, Massachusetts, in 1639. The following are the names in the paternal line of ancestry: George, Edward, John, Gershom, Nathaniel, Reuben, Seth and Will R. On the maternal side the names are as follows: Richard, Caleb, Isaac, Caleb, Joshua, Caleb and Robert, the last named being the father of Mrs. Seth Lewis. The family is one that is well known and honored for its long identification with public affairs in the state of Michigan.

HON. BENJAMIN F. GRAVES.

Hon. Benjamin Franklin Graves, formerly a judge of the supreme court, was born at Gates, near Rochester, New York. His boyhood was spent in the common schools and working on a farm. He was fond of study and took much pleasure in reading, but his means for gratifying this taste were very limited. During early childhood he was quite delicate, but as no other life opened to him, he was obliged to engage in manual labor. In the winter of 1837 he was attacked by a dangerous illness, and was sick many weeks. During his convalescence he learned from his physician that he could not continue physical labor without great risk to his life, and he at once decided to study law. He was not ignorant of his great

lack of physical culture and mental discipline, nor unmindful of the severity and duration of the task before him. He saw clearly how much he had to accomplish without pecuniary help or the aid of influential friends. In the spring of 1837 with the assistance of an uncle-in-law, he obtained a place in the law office of Curtis & Thomas, of Albion, New York. They were gentlemen of character and learning and at once gave him all possible help and encouragement. He remained with them until fall, and at that time was enabled to change his situation for another in which he could make small earnings. He accordingly entered the office of Mortimer F. Delano, at Rochester. Mr. Delano then held the office of Surrogate in connection with Addison Gardner, who was judge and vice-chancellor of the great western circuit of the state. In the course of a few months Judge Gardner resigned, and formed a law partnership with Mr. Delano. Mr. Graves became a student with the firm and with some intermission continued until his own admission to the bar; this took place at Rochester in October, 1841. The supreme court was then composed of Messrs. Nelson, Cowen and Bronson. Mr. Graves gratefully remembers the kindness he received from his preceptors and their families, especially the cordiality and encouragement of Judge Gardner, in whose family he resided many months. In the winter succeeding his admission to the bar, Mr. Graves was invited by Mr. Elwood, who was then clerk of the state senate, to accept the position of journalizing clerk for that season. He accordingly went to Albany, and acted until the legislature adjourned. As he did not find an agreeable opening for practice in New York, Mr. Graves turned his attention toward Michigan. After some inquiry he was led by representations of friends toward Battle Creek, then a small hamlet, but containing the germ of a prosperous and thrifty town. Reaching the place in the spring of 1843, he immediately commenced practice, which he continued until 1857, a period of fourteen years. In the meantime he was appointed master in chancery and was three times elected magistrate. His business was never extensive. His taste led him to prefer judicial service, and to evade indiscriminate practice. The legislature of 1857 provided for an independent supreme court, to supersede, from the beginning of 1858, the old supreme court, composed of the circuit judges whose terms expired in 1857. The new supreme court was to consist of four judges, to be elected at the time of the election of the circuit judges, but by a vote of the people at large. The full term was fixed at eight years, and the first term was ordered to begin January 1, 1858. Judge Graves was elected circuit judge of the fifth judicial circuit, which at that time, comprised the counties of Eaton, Calhoun, Kalamazoo, Allegan and Van Buren. In the next session of the legislature, Allegan was taken off and united with other counties to form the ninth circuit. Until that time there had been but six circuits. Hon. Abner Pratt resigned his position as judge of the circuit in June, 1857, and Judge Graves was immediately appointed to fill the vacancy. He was, accordingly, judge of the old supreme court during the rest of its existence. When his term as circuit judge expired, he was re-elected, receiving, quite generally, the votes of both parties. His labors were heavy; he was required to hold sixteen circuits a year, eight of which were held in the populous counties of Calhoun and Kalamazoo. He was exceedingly strict and firm in matters of prac-

tice, and the bar soon learned to understand his methods and act accordingly. In the winter of 1866, from overwork in badly ventilated rooms, he was threatened with an attack of paralysis. He was compelled to allow suspensions of service, and to discontinue for most part, night sessions. Finally, becoming convinced that entire rest was necessary, he sent in his resignation to take effect July 1, 1866.

He then made a journey to the east with his family. After returning in the fall, he engaged in counsel business, and acted occasionally as referee. He had sold his homestead and purchased a small farm which he proceeded to improve. He was then elected justice of the supreme court, his term to begin January 1, 1868. At the expiration of that term he was re-elected by the unanimous vote of both parties.

He was originally a member of the Democratic party, but early became dissatisfied with its course in regard to matters of slavery. He favored the position taken by Van Buren and Adams in 1848, believing that it would help to check all sentiments opposed to the rights and duty of congress to forbid slavery in the western territories. Mr. Graves voted for Mr. Van Buren and was steadfast in the views which actuated that vote, but he was reluctant to sever fully his early party connections until the repeal of the Missouri Compromise, and the efforts made to enforce the entrance of slavery into Kansas. That act decided him. He voted for Fremont against Buchanan, and has since continued with the Republican party.

Judge Graves has a large library of all the leading law publications. He is pleasant and social in manner and highly esteemed. He now makes his home in Detroit, Michigan.

LEONIDAS DWIGHT DIBBLE.

Leonidas Dwight Dibble, deceased, was one of the most public spirited citizens of Battle Creek. While, as one of the most brilliant attorneys-at-law and counselors of the state, he never forgot that bond of common interest which should unite the people of every community, and was always ready and willing to aid in every enterprise for the public good.

Mr. Dibble was born in Moravia, Cayuga county, New York, January 13, 1834. He was a son of Orsamus and Ann Maria (Scranton) Dibble. He obtained his education in the common school and prepared for college in the academy at Moravia, and in 1841 (September), he entered Geneva college (now Hobart) at Geneva, New York, and was graduated in August, 1845. He stood first in mathematics and third in general average at commencement and was given third honor—that of delivering the Latin salutatory oration. After graduation he was appointed tutor in Greek and Latin, in his Alma Mater, which chairs he held two years. Subsequently he was tendered the professorship of mathematics. He always had a taste for reading and studying, and had a remarkably retentive memory.

While yet in college he began to read law in the office of Whiting, Smith & Whiting, at Geneva, and was admitted to the bar by the supreme court of New York in August, 1847. In the spring of 1848 he formed a partnership with Isaac A. Gates, of Homer, New York, and this firm continued until the spring of 1850, enjoying a large practice in the supreme court. In 1850 Mr. Dibble had a violent attack of the then prevailing gold fever, and, disposing of his property and interest in the law business he journeyed to the Golden state, where he spent a year in the mines, returning with sufficient gold dust to well pay him for his trip. It was in June, 1851, upon his return from California, that he entered into partnership with Hon. Benjamin F. Graves, which partnership continued until 1857, when Mr. Graves was elected circuit judge. Mr. Dibble had purchased a farm and moved upon it because of failing health, but he continued the practice of his profession for a few years after Judge Graves's election. Later he took as a partner Henry H. Brown and soon after they admitted a young man by the name of Charles E. Thomas to do the light work and attend to the practice in the justice courts. Mr. Dibble had a very large practice in the courts of Michigan and also in the federal courts.

August, 1873, he became a member of the Peninsular Railroad and became its first president and its counsel. It was through his untiring energy and business ability that the road was built and through his honesty and manliness that he lost thousands of dollars by refusing to sell out when he might have done so, but was afraid others would suffer should he do so. He was well known and recognized as one of the best and most honorable attorneys and counselors in the state of Michigan. Mr. Dibble was captain of light artillery, Michigan State Troops, for four or five years previous to the breaking out of the Civil war. When war was declared he raised Company C, Second Regiment, Michigan Infantry, in less than twenty-four hours, and later, with his money and time, and by addressing public meetings assisted in enlisting several hundred men for other Michigan regiments. He, however, could not go to the front as he was not accepted by the government on account of a rupture. In 1859 he was appointed chairman of the committee to draft the city charter for Battle Creek. In 1852 he was elected township clerk and was ex-officio school inspector. He was a charter member, and the first high priest of the Royal Arch Chapter of Free and Accepted Masons of Battle Creek, and was one of its most influential and valued men.

Mr. Dibble was the leader in organizing the Peninsular Railway Company, now the Grand Trunk, and was its president from 1865 until 1870, during that time he raised the means, built and equipped the road from Lansing, Michigan, to Valparaiso, Indiana, a distance of one hundred and sixty-six miles, at which time it was consolidated into the Chicago and Lake Huron Railroad. On the morning of September 14, 1865, he drove the first spike in the construction of the road and shoveled the first shovelful of earth. The spike was a gold-plated one, and in the presence of hundreds of people it was driven at a point just east of the offices of Nichols & Shepard Thresher Company. In his political affiliations he was a Democrat, but would never accept office. His church home was the Episcopal.

On December 29, 1847, he was united in holy bonds of matrimony to Miss Phoebe Antoinette Chatterton, a daughter of Jacob and Mary Chatterton, of Gaines, Orleans county, New York, and unto them were born three children; Frank Dwight, now of Grand Rapids; Mary Leonora, who married Greenville Macard, and resides in Battle Creek; and Caroline Loomis Burch, who resides at 157 West Fountain street, Battle Creek.

Mr. Dibble's death occurred October 21, 1901, and thus Battle Creek and the state of Michigan lost one of its most loyal citi-zens. His integrity won the confidence and respect of all and his social qualities were such, when he was enjoying health, that he was a general favorite. Always kind and courteous, a willing friend to the deserving, he possessed in an eminent degree the qualities of a leader, and in his profession attained a deserved prominence. A man of less ability could not have accomplished what he did in railroad construction. His clear intellect, logical mind and strong personal magnetism were the key-notes of his success before juries and enabled him to sway assemblies in a wonderful manner. He was laid to rest in Oakhill cemetery in Battle Creek beside his wife.

SAMUEL M. REED.

Samuel M. Reed, who is agent for various life and fire insurance companies in Albion, is also recognized as one whose interests in municipal affairs is deep and sincere and at the present writing he is serving as an active and helpful member of the board of education. He was born near Ypsilanti, Michigan, on the 12th of July, 1859, and is a son of David Page and Anna F. (Marks) Reed. The father was born in Ontario county, New York, and was a son of Samuel Reed, one of the pioneers of the western portions of the Empire state. Later he removed with his family to Michigan and settled in Washtenaw county, which was then a frontier district, so that his son, David Page, early became familiar with the hardships and difficulties incident to the establishment of a new home in a region where civilization had but recently been planted. He aided in clearing a farm and cultivating the fields and continued his residence in Washtenaw county until 1865. In the meantime he had begun business for himself and carried it on with such success that he was well known as an extensive farmer. At length he sold his property there and removed to Olivet for the purpose of giving his children better educational advantages. In politics he was a stanch Republican and while living in Olivet he held the office of councilman. He married Miss Anna F. Marks and both held membership in the Congressional church, of which Mr. Reed was a very active member, serving for many years as a deacon. He made his home in Olivet until about the time of his death which occurred in Albion on the 25th of February, 1893. His wife survived him until March 11, 1896.

Samuel M. Reed acquired his early education in the public schools of Olivet and then entered upon a classical course in Olivet College, where he spent two and a half years. His entrance into the business world was as a clerk in market houses. He was employed in this way at Charlotte and at Battle Creek and in 1882 he came to Albion, where for a number of years he continued clerking. He then turned his attention to general merchandising, which he carried on for eight years, when he sold his business and has since been conducting an insurance office, handling both life and fire insurance. He represents the Metropolitan Company both in Albion and in Marshall and has been particularly successful as a representative of the life insurance business. However, he also represents a number of the old line fire insurance companies and writes a large amount of business annually.

On the 3d of October, 1883, Mr. Reed was united in marriage to Miss Florence A.

Reed, of Albion, and they became the parents of three children: Minnie E., Edward R. and Bessie L. The parents belong to the Presbyterian church and Mr. Reed has held nearly all of the church offices and has been very active in Sunday school work, formerly serving as superintendent. He belongs to Albion lodge, No. 57, K. of P., of which he is a past chancellor, while for three terms he represented the local lodge in the Grand lodge. He is also a member of the Modern Woodmen camp at Albion and is now its clerk. His political views accord with the principles of the Republican party and he has been very active as a champion of its interests. He has served during many years on the ward and city committees and for five years was chairman of the Republican committee of Albion, during which time McKinley and Hobart were elected. For some time he was also a member of the county executive committee. In 1890 he was chosen alderman from the third ward of Albion and was re-elected and filled the position until he resigned on account of the pressure of private business interests. In 1902 he was appointed one of the special assessors to make out special assessments against the city of Albion. In 1899 he was elected a member of the school board and during two years of a three years' term he was secretary of the board and active as a champion of many measures for the introduction of broader and more advanced methods in education. In September, 1903, he was again elected to the office for a three-years' term, and is now chairman of the committee on buildings and grounds. His interest in municipal affairs is deep and abiding and has taken material form in active co-operation along lines that have brought about splendid improvement and progress.

HENRY A. TILLOTSON.

Among the earliest pioneers of Calhoun county was numbered Henry A. Tillotson, who arrived in Marshall in 1835. Many of the now thriving towns and cities of the county had not yet sprung into existence and the work of progress and improvement seemed scarcely begun. The most far-sighted could not have dreamed of the wonderful development which was soon to work a great transformation, but such men as Mr. Tillotson and his neighbors resolutely set to work to replace primitive conditions by the equipments that indicate an advanced civilization.

Mr. Tillotson was born at Genoa, Cayuga county, New York, March 13, 1825, his parents being Zenos and Samantha (Phelps) Tillotson. The father was born July 24, 1802, and on the 16th of October, 1823, he wedded Miss Phelps, whose birth occurred in Cayuga county, New York, in January, 1802. He was a farmer by occupation, and in 1834, leaving the Empire state, he located on a tract of land near Marshall, Michigan. The following year he brought his family to Calhoun county and here made his home for a long period. From the government he secured a quarter section, on which is now built the eastern part of Marshall and the remainder of the tract lies in Marengo township. He was a member of the board of village trustees at an early day, and after the incorporation of the city he served as alderman for a number of years. He was also postmaster under James K. Polk for four years and his loyalty to the public good was above question. His death occurred September 9, 1876, and his wife passed away March 16, 1889. She was one of the first members of the Episcopal church of Marshall, and her husband and children also attended its services.

Henry A. Tillotson, coming to Calhoun county when ten years of age, pursued his studies to some extent in the public schools and afterward he and his brother attended the Clinton Seminary, in Clinton, Oneida county, New York. When he had completed his education there he returned to his home. His father was at that time running the stage from Jackson to St. Joseph, Michigan, and Mr. Tillotson, of this review, went to the former place to take charge of the business there. The next spring he removed to St. Joseph and was in charge of the business at that point until he was transferred to an office in connection with the operation of the line of steamers running between St. Joseph and Chicago. When the railroad was completed to Marshall, Michigan, he had charge of the first train running into the city. He was serving as conductor under the old state administration and continued to act in that capacity until the line of the road was extended to Niles. He also had charge of the postoffice at Marshall for four years, his father having been appointed to the position of postmaster. Later, Mr. Tillotson turned his attention to merchandising, which he conducted for two years, when he sold out and accepted a position as conductor on the Michigan Central Railroad. He ran the first night train between Detroit and Chicago. In the winter following the construction of the line to Chicago the company placed him in charge of the ticket office at Detroit, where he remained until 1855. He was then one of the pioneer railroad men of the state, and in 1854 was presented with a solid gold watch chain, on which was a beautiful charm appropriately inscribed, given to him by the conductors of the Michigan Central Railroad. On retiring from the office at Detroit he returned to Marshall and took up his abode on his farm of one hundred and seventy acres, of which one hundred and ten acres were within the city limits. He there carried on farming and gave special attention to the raising of full blooded stock. He was the first to introduce the registered shorthorns and he did much to improve the general grade of stock raised through this part of the country. At one time he owned an animal that sold for three thousand dollars. Mr. Tillotson continued in that business until 1867, when on account of ill health he retired and since that time has had few business enterprises.

Mr. Tillotson served as justice of the peace from 1885 until 1902, and was also supervisor, alderman and city marshall. His political allegiance has long been given to the Democracy. Socially he is connected with St. Albans lodge, No. 20, F. & A. M., of which he was master for seven years. He likewise belongs to Lafayette chapter, No. 5, R. A. M., of which he was high priest for more than twenty years, and he has been thrice illustrious master of Hiram council, R. & S. M., for three years. He is also a member of Marshall commandery, No. 17, K. T., and he belonged to both the subordinate lodge and encampment of the Odd Fellows society. He acted as noble grand and as chief patriarch in the respective organizations, but he demitted from the Odd Fellows fraternity on account of giving most of his time and attention to the Masonic work.

Mr. Tillotson was united in marriage to Miss Cornelia R. Ketchum, a daughter of Sidney Ketchum, the founder of the city of Marshall, the wedding being celebrated September 19, 1845. Mrs. Tillotson was born January 3, 1828, at Peru, New York, and was brought by her parents to Marshall in 1831. She was a student in school here, continued her studies in the Ladies' Seminary at Canandaigua, New York, and completed her course in Albion, Michigan. Unto Mr. and Mrs. Tillotson were born six children, three of whom lived to mature years and only two now survive. Of these Edward J. died in Omaha, Nebraska; Mary M. is now the wife of A. W. Saxe, of Buffalo, New York; and Frank M. is a resident of Marshall, Michigan.

Mr. and Mrs. Tillotson held membership in the Episcopal church, of Marshall, of which he was a vestryman. Mrs. Tillotson died January 28, 1902, and Mr. Tillotson is now making his home with his son in Buffalo, New York. He was very prominent and influential in Calhoun county at an early day and his labors in behalf of the public welfare made his efforts very valuable to the community.

HARRY BEEBE PARKER.

Every legitimate business enterprise adds to the commercial prosperity of town or city and a community is judged by the character and extent of its trade interests, for this is a utilitarian age. The leading citizens, therefore, are the men who are in control of important and extensive business affairs, and it is one of the most promising signs of the times that the young men are working their way to a foremost position as leaders in industrial and commercial circles. Among the representatives of this class is H. B. Parker, now the vice president and assistant general manager of the Malleable Iron Company, of Albion, Michigan. He is yet a young man, his birth having occurred in Chicago, Illinois, August 21, 1871, his parents being E. A. and Almira L. (Beebe) Parker. His paternal grandfather was a minister of the Congregational church at Galesburg, Illinois. The father was general ticket and passenger agent of the Chicago & Northwestern Railroad Company for some time, and afterward for the Chicago, Burlington & Quincy Railroad, being connected with the latter organization at the time of his death, which occurred in 1875. His wife was a daughter of Calvin T. Beebe, one of the early and pioneer settlers of Jackson, Michigan, who died at the age of eighty-five years. Following the demise of her first husband Mrs. Parker became the wife of W. S. Kessler. She died on the 20th of March, 1896.

Mr. Parker acquired his education in the city schools of Chicago and was pursuing the high school course when in January, 1889, he left school and came to Albion with Mr. and Mrs. Kessler. It was at that time that the Malleable Iron Company was organized and Mr. Parker became connected therewith. He began work in the factory and steadily advanced, becoming familiar with every part of the business in all of its particular workings, becoming a director and vice president in 1892, acting in that capacity continuously since. In 1899 he was made assistant general manager and in that capacity takes an active part in the carrying on of the business. The Malleable Iron Company at Albion ranks as the second largest of the kind in the state. The plant is located adjacent to the Michigan Central Railroad tracks and covers seven acres. More than two hundred and fifty men are employed, and thus the business is a valu-

able one to the city, furnishing the means of maintenance to many families. Mr. Parker has also been interested in real estate and in connection with Mr. Kessler, in 1900, erected the fine new postoffice block. He is also secretary and treasurer of the Marion Oil & Gas Company, with wells at Findlay, Ohio. The oil lands of this company are excellent producers, and that business is proving profitable as are also other interests with which he is financially connected.

On the 28th of November, 1895, Mr. Parker was united in marriage to Miss Theo Gardner, a daughter of Hon. Washington Gardner. They attend the Methodist Episcopal church, of which Mrs. Parker is a member, and to the support of which Mr. Parker generously contributes. He belongs to Murat lodge, No. 14, F. & A. M., Albion chapter, R. A. M., and Marshall commandery, K. T. His political support is given to the Republican party, but he is not active as a worker in its ranks. Already in the business world he has attained an enviable position and he owes his advancement entirely to his capability, earnest application, strong purpose and laudable ambition.

HON. WALTER W. WOOLNOUGH.

Full of years and full of honors, Walter Waters Woolnough, political editor of the Daily Moon, the pioneer newspaper man of Battle Creek and the oldest editor in Michigan, died February 2, 1904, at his home, 163 North avenue, at the ripe old age of eighty-three years.

Walter W. Woolnough was born in the county of Suffolk, England, in July, 1821. In 1833 he emigrated with his parents to this country, and settled in Rochester, New York, where he acquired a knowledge of the art of printing in the office of the Rochester Republican. In 1843, at the close of his apprenticeship, he sought the west as his, field of labor, and became foreman in the office of the Ashtabula. (Ohio) Sentinel, the official organ of the late Joshua R. Giddings. The Sentinel was at that time a vigorous anti-slavery Whig paper, and while engaged in its publication the subject of this sketch imbibed those ideas on the rights of man which controlled his political action in the future.

In 1845 Mr. Woolnough removed to Battle Creek, and printed the Western Citizen, the first paper ever published in this city. The following year, the publication of the Citizen having ceased, he issued the Michigan Tribune, which was one of the most zealous anti-slavery Whig journals published in the west. The paper failed in 1848 for want of patronage, it being too advanced for its clientage.

In 1852 he became the editor and publisher of the Battle Creek Journal, continuing the same until 1863, when he disposed of the establishment to Mr. Charles E. Griffith. From that time until 1871 he was not engaged in the profession; but in February of that year he renewed his connection with journalism, and became editor and publisher of the Michigan Tribune (a newspaper commenced in August, 1870). The Tribune was regarded, under his management, as a paper of very decided opinions, emphatically expressed, with respect to civil service reform, and reconciliation between the two sections of the union, which had been estranged by the rebellion. In that terrible contest between two opposing forces in civilization—Freedom and Slavery—Mr. Wool-

nough labored diligently and gave freely of his means to sustain the government, and rejoiced when the bloody strife ended, and the cause of humanity triumphed.

In 1878 he disposed of his interest in the Michigan Tribune to his partner, W. H. Bodine, who a little later sold to Barnes & Buckley. Mr. Woolnough invested in Kansas farming lands, with the intention of moving to that state, but abandoned that project. In 1883 he took the position of political editor of the Moon, which post he retained to the day of his death.

Mr. Woolnough began his political career as a Whig, taking his stand in the memorable campaign of 1840, though then too young to be a voter. Very soon after that time the power and purposes of the slavery propaganda began to be developed, and he allied himself with the anti-slavery wing of the Whig party. He refused to aid in the election of General Taylor, because of the circumstances connected with his nomination and also because of the belief that the southern slaveholders had chosen him as their agent to extend and strengthen the "peculiar institution."

In 1854, when a majority of the Whig members of congress from the south, and some from the north, voted for the repeal of the Missouri Compromise, opening the territories of Kansas and Nebraska to slavery, he became convinced of the necessity for a new political organization, and advocated in the Battle Creek Journal and elsewhere, the dissolution of the Whig party and the formation of the Republican party, as the only effective means of resisting the encroachments of the slave power.

He took an active part in that memorable meeting "Under the Oaks" at Jackson from which dates the birth of the Republican party. He labored hard in the campaign of that year and helped win the first Republican success in the Union when the Michigan Republicans wrested a victory from the hands of the old Democracy, united with a portion of the rapidly dissolving Whig party. From that time until 1872, Mr. Woolnough heartily supported the measures and policy of the new party, entering largely into the councils, and serving four years as a member of its state central committee.

In 1872 his belief in the paramount importance of reconciliation between the north and the south, and his confidence in the integrity of Horace Greeley, commanded his support of that gentleman for the presidency; and in 1876, in continuation of efforts in that behalf, he labored through the Michigan Tribune and on the platform for the election of Samuel J. Tilden. In the spring of that year he was invited by William Cullen Bryant, Carl Schurtz and others to be one of a conference to meet at the Fifth Avenue Hotel, New York city, to deliberate with respect to the action to be taken in the then approaching presidential campaign, to best promote civil service reform, and restore a more fraternal feeling between the north and the south. He did not attend, but responded to the invitation with a personal letter, in which he expressed his warm sympathy with the object of the conference.

Since 1872 Mr. Woolnough has been found in the independent political ranks, but no plea of "regularity" could induce him to work for a policy he did not believe sound and right in its ranks any more than it could years before when he deserted the Whig party and helped found its successor.

In matters of a local character, Mr. Woolnough has taken an active interest; his labors to promote the moral and material growth of Battle Creek have been earnest. As a writer, he was ready and pointed, seldom indulging in rhetorical flourish; as a speaker, he always commanded the attention of his audience, and impressed them with much of the earnestness and zeal which he brought to every subject he discussed.

He received many evidences of the appreciation of his fellow citizens. In 1858 he was elected a member of the legislature, and took ground in that body in favor of a higher standard of education by public tax; in support of a state registry law, etc.; was alderman from the third ward four years, justice of the peace, and served nine years as a member of the board of education. In 1864, by request of the governor of the state, he went to City Point, Virginia, in company with two physicians, to assist in taking care of wounded Michigan soldiers, remaining there his allotted time.

Mr. Woolnough was married in August, 1843, to Miss Emeline D. Manley, of Ashtabula, Ohio. Four children (daughters) were born unto them, two of whom survive. They are Mrs. Frank W. Clapp and Mrs. Emeline W. Egery, both of this city. Mrs. Woolnough died March 10, 1899.

From the Battle Creek "Moon," we quote: "A slight stroke of paralysis was the immediate cause of death, though he had been so feeble all winter that the end was not unexpected. Yet it comes as a great shock to his hundreds of friends for there were few who realized that the body of their old friend had become so weak. It was a general wearing out, gradual and slow but nevertheless sure, that took him away. His appointed time had come and he passed peacefully on to meet his Maker.

A slight chill Monday morning was the first indication of the end. Even then there was no apprehension among those closest to him. He grew gradually worse, however, and a doctor was summoned. But he was beyond the aid of earthly physicians and sank quietly away until the end came at 1:30 o'clock, Tuesday morning. His two daughters, Mrs. Frank W. Clapp and Mrs. Emeline W. Egery, with Mr. Clapp, were at his bedside when the last call came and "Finis" was written at the close of a long and useful life.

Though his body had been failing for months, his mental powers were as steady and his memory as sure as when he wrote his first "leader" two generations or more ago. He kept as close watch of the events of the day throughout the world as he ever did, and his views on questions of public moment were always of interest for they were always formed on a full knowledge of the question. His mind was active and clear even to the day of his death.

It was a pleasure to converse with him for his memory of bygone policies and politicians was as clear cut and as accurate as if he were talking of men and matters of yesterday. He had enjoyed a personal acquaintance with many of the men who made the history of this country two generations back and his reminiscences were a source of never failing interest to his friends of the latter days. Zachariah Chandler and Austin Blair, two of Michigan's greatest men during the war time period, were personal friends of Mr. Woolnough and have made his home their headquarters when, during political campaigns or at other times, they happened to be at Battle Creek. Many other well known men were his intimates.

Yet, with it all, he did not live in a "dark and musty past." His interests were always up to date and he kept up with the policies of the times though he could not always agree with them. His knowledge of the everyday doings of the world was intimate, for he was a great reader and kept himself well posted on current events. He liked the society of younger people and was always pleased when some of them called on him. There is more than one young man to-day who regrets that he postponed a call on the old gentleman until it was too late.

For over twenty years, since 1883, he has been connected with the Daily Moon as political and editorial writer, and the force of his mind can be seen when it is known that as late as Saturday he prepared his usual column of editorial matter, writing much of it with his own hand and preparing the balance of it from his list of exchanges. He has never missed a day in years of having his matter promptly on hand. Though his bodily infirmities have not permitted him to be at the office of the paper for several months, his mind has been with it all the while, and it has been ever in his thoughts. His daily duties for its welfare have always been performed with punctuality and scrupulous exactness.

He was of the old-style editor, now almost extinct, who walked up to a case when an editorial utterance was in his mind and put the thought in type, ready for the press, without the intervention of pen or paper. For years that was his custom with this paper, until failing health prevented, and his matter flowed from his brain to the composing stick without ever being hung on the "copy hook." For the last three or four years he has been too feeble to do much at the case, however, and the introduction of the more modern machine methods did away with the necessity therefor.

Fifty years ago this month he bought the lot at 163 North avenue, where he had lived all these years, and two years later he put up the house he occupied for so long."

HON. JONATHAN HART.

Jonathan Hart, now deceased, was one of the honored pioneer settlers of Calhoun county, arriving here in 1835 when the district was largely unimproved. In fact, it was considered a far western region and the greater part of the land was still in its primitive condition. The forests stood in their primeval strength, the streams were unbridged and the land was uncultivated. Mr. Hart joined the early settlers and laid the foundation for the present prosperity and progress of the county, and well does his name deserve to be inscribed upon the pages of the history of this portion of Michigan.

He was born at White Creek, Washington county, New York, and there spent the days of his childhood and youth. He married Miss Mary Merritt, a sister of Isaac and Joseph Merritt, also pioneer settlers of Calhoun county. With his wife and two children he came to Battle Creek in 1835. The present populous and enterprising city was then a mere crossroads village and it was supposed that Verona was destined to become the leading town of the county. He purchased a large tract of land, a part of which is now covered with one of the best residence portions of Battle Creek, and in addition to the cultivation and improvement of his farm, he was engaged in merchandising, being one of the first general merchants of the place. In his business affairs he was active and energetic and his labor returned to him very creditable success. He afterward disposed of his mercantile interests and built and operated what was known as the Hart mill, the first large flouring mill of the city. When the mill was destroyed by fire he at once rebuilt it and continued its operation until his death.

A few years after arriving in Calhoun county Mr. Hart was called upon to mourn the loss of his first wife, who died leaving two children, Cynthia, who became the wife of David Cady, a son of General Cady; and Thomas Hart, who died in Battle Creek. Mr. Hart afterward wedded Mary Tabor, of Washington county, New York, a daughter of Lewis Tabor.

In public affairs Mr. Hart took quite a deep and active interest, and he left the impress of his individuality upon the thought and feeling. At one time he represented his district in the State Legislature. He was reared in the faith of the Society of Friends, and throughout his life strictly adhered to that belief. He was largely instrumental in the erection of the first meeting house of that religious sect in Battle Creek. His death occurred in 1859, and his wife, surviving him for about twenty years, passed away in 1879. He was an honored pioneer, a respected citizen and a successful business man, who aided in laying broad and deep the foundation for the present prosperity of Battle Creek.

Miss Elma Gifford, who was a member of the Hart family through many years, was born in Saratoga county, New York, a daughter of Jonathan and Cynthia (Tabor) Gifford. Her mother died when she was but a child and she was then reared by her aunt, Mrs. Hart, and has always resided in Battle Creek, living with Mrs. Hart until the latter's death. Miss Gifford has always been a member of the Episcopal church and has been very active in the work of the church and Sunday school. For seventeen years she was a teacher in the public schools of Battle Creek, being connected with school No. 2. She passed through all of its grades and at one time had charge of that school. Few

teachers of the city have been so long connected with the educational interests of Battle Creek as has Miss Gifford, and none have
given more general satisfaction.

JAMES DEVINNA LA BAR.

James Devinna LaBar is one of the
revered patriarchs of Battle Creek, having
attained his ninety-seventh year. He was
born in the third presidential administration in America and his mind, therefore, retains an intimate knowledge of many of the
great and important events which have occurred in this country, and which are to the
vast majority a matter of history and not of
recollection. He was formerly engaged in
business as a practical and ornamental
painter but is now living a retired life at
his home at No. 139 Maple street, in Battle Creek. He was born in Ithaca, New
York, October 9, 1807, and is a son of
Charles and Margaret (Bloom) LaBar.
His father was a tailor by trade, but purchased and conducted a farm about four
miles from Ithaca. It was in that locality
that James D. LaBar was reared, acquiring
a fair common school education. When
sixteen years of age he went to Northumberland county, Pennsylvania, where he began working as a painter and in 1835 came
to Michigan, locating at Bellevue, Eaton
county, among the pioneer residents of this
state. In 1844 he arrived in Battle Creek
where he continued work at his trade. Some
time afterward he purchased eighty acres
of land with the money which was inherited
from his father, and owned that property
until becoming tired of paying taxes
thereon, he sold it. The now prosperous

and thriving city of Battle Creek was at the
time of his arrival here but a small village,
and he purchased the lot on Maple street
when the land there was used as an oat field.
The lots were worth one hundred and forty
dollars, but he paid ten dollars extra in order
to make his purchase on the installment plan.
On this site he built a little cabin, which
was occupied by him for several years and
then sold it, after which he erected his present home. Throughout these years he continued an active factor in business life and at
one time established a furniture store, but
did not find that a profitable enterprise.
Subsequently he opened a billiard room and
in its conduct realized a good competence.

On the 6th of April, 1850, Mr. LaBar
was united in marriage in Battle Creek to
Miss Ludencia Cole, who was born in the
township of Fredonia, Calhoun county,
Michigan. They became the parents of one
son, Volney Cole, who lived to be about
thirteen years of age.

Mr. LaBar has always given his political
allegiance to the Democratic party, believing
firmly in its principles and yet never seeking
office as a reward for his party loyalty. His
first presidential vote was cast for Andrew
Jackson, the seventh president of the
United States, and since that time he has
never faltered in his allegiance to the candidates of his party. He was reared in the
faith of the Dutch Reformed church, but
later became a member of the Episcopal
church and at one time served as a vestryman. He has also been a member of the
Independent Order of Odd Fellows, and of
the Masonic fraternity. He attained the
Royal Arch degree in the latter and has
served as secretary of his lodge. It is given
to few to travel to such length upon life's
journey as has Mr. LaBar, who is now in his

ninety-seventh year. He has, therefore, been a witness of wonderful changes in this country and has ever manifested a deep and appreciative interest in the world's progress and especially in the advancement made in the United States.

INDEX.

INDEX.

CPSIA information can be obtained
at www.ICGtesting.com
Printed in the USA
BVHW04*1722060818
523683BV00018B/1383/P